A HISTORY OF BYZANTINE MUSIC AND HYMNOGRAPHY

MS. LINCOLN COLLEGE D. 35, FOL. 6, LATE XIIIth CENTURY

A HISTORY OF BYZANTINE MUSIC AND HYMNOGRAPHY

BY

EGON WELLESZ

FELLOW OF LINCOLN COLLEGE
OXFORD

SECOND EDITION
REVISED AND ENLARGED

OXFORD
AT THE CLARENDON PRESS
1961

Oxford University Press, Amen House, London E.C.4
GLASGOW NEW YORK TORONTO MELBOURNE WELLINGTON
BOMBAY CALCUTTA MADRAS KARACHI KUALA LUMPUR
CAPE TOWN IBADAN NAIROBI ACCRA

FIRST EDITION 1949
SECOND EDITION, REVISED
AND ENLARGED 1961
PRINTED IN GREAT BRITAIN

PREFACE TO THE SECOND EDITION

STUDIES in Byzantine music have made remarkable progress since the publication of the first edition of this book in 1949. The field of research has been widened by the inclusion of melismatic chant and other forms of liturgical chant which we had hitherto not attempted to decipher. On the other hand, the number of scholars working on Byzantine music has increased and there are more musicologists interested in Byzantine music as an important branch of Christian Chant in general.

For these reasons it was not sufficient to reprint this book; considerable enlargement and revision have proved necessary. The sections which needed most expansion were those on 'Byzantine Liturgy' (pp. 130–45), on the 'Poetical Forms' I (pp. 191–7), and 'Byzantine Musical Notation' (pp. 246–60, 271–84, 305–8). A new section on 'Melismatic Chant and Psalmody', a new field in our studies, had to be added (pp. 329–48, Appendix pp. 401–15). It was, furthermore, necessary to bring the 'Introduction' up to date (pp. 20–28). Minor additions were put together in an appended section under the title 'Excursuses', to which reference is made in the text by an asterisk *.

As mentioned in the preface of the first edition Byzantine musical manuscripts have neither a standardized system of accents, nor of punctuation. They have, however, dots, carefully placed at the end of the lines of the poems. When examples are taken from manuscripts, the transcription follows the original as closely as possible.

Inconsistencies between Greek and Latin forms of names and terms could not be avoided. Some authors, for example, whose articles are quoted, prefer the Latin form *Hirmologium*, others the Greek spelling *Heirmologion* or *Hirmologion*.

I am deeply grateful to the late Professor A. M. Friend, Jr., of Princeton University, who invited me to go in the Summer semester 1954 as a Visiting Scholar to the Dumbarton Oaks Research Library and Collection (Harvard University), in Washington, and to take part in the 'Symposium on Byzantine Liturgy and Music'. This stay and another one in the Winter semester 1956–7 enabled me to pursue my work in the Dumbarton Oaks Library, which specializes in Byzantine studies. My thanks are due to John Thacher, Director of the Dumbarton Oaks Research Library and Collection, to Professor Sirarpie Der Nersessian, and to Professor

E. Kitzinger, Director of Studies, who supported my work in every conceivable way. Miss Patricia Kean, Fellow of Lady Margaret Hall, Oxford, has again been very kind in helping me to prepare the manuscript for the press.

The last word of gratitude is due to my dear friends and colleagues, Professor Carsten Höeg and Professor H. J. W. Tillyard, with whom I have had the privilege of co-operating for more than a quarter of a century on the *Monumenta Musicae Byzantinae*.

E. J. W.

Oxford
May 1958

Note on the Frontispiece

THE plate given as frontispiece is taken from the Typikon, the Rule for the Convent of Our Lady of Good Hope (*τῆς ὑπεραγίας θεοτόκου τῆς Βεβαίας Ἐλπίδος*) at Constantinople. The Typikon was bought by George Wheeler, a Fellow of Lincoln College, at Athens during his journey to the East in 1675–6 and given to the College together with other manuscripts. The first part of the Typikon[1] was composed by Theodora, the daughter of the Sebastokrator Constantine Comnenus Palaeologus, and niece of the Emperor Michael VIII Palaeologus (1259–82), the first Emperor of the Palaeologian dynasty.

Theodora and her husband, the Great Stratopedarches John Comnenus Doukas Synadenos, were the founders of the Convent of Our Lady of Good Hope, and Theodora, under the name of Theodoule, became the first abbess. The second part of the Typikon was written by her youngest daughter, the nun Eudokia, who enlarged the monastery. The last pages were added by later members of the family in 1397, 1398, and 1402.

On folios one to nine we find a unique series of miniatures, representing the family of the founders, on the tenth the Blessed Virgin of Good Hope, on the eleventh Theodora-Theodoule as Abbess and on the last the Abbess together with the nuns. The plate here reproduced represents the Protosebastos Constantine Comnenus Raoul Palaeologus, a son-in-law of the foundress and his wife Euphrosyne Doukas Palaeologina, one of the daughters of the foundress. The miniature is an extremely fine example of Byzantine craftsmanship of the period in which Byzantine music had reached its zenith.

[1] The text of the Rule, followed by the history of the foundation of the Convent, is given by H. Delehaye in his study 'Deux Typica byzantins de l'époque des Paléologues', in *Mémoires, Deuxième Série*, tome xiii, of the Académie Royale de Belgique (1921), pp. 18–105 and 141–72.

FROM THE PREFACE TO THE FIRST EDITION

THE idea of this book goes back to a course of lectures which I delivered thirty years ago in the University of Vienna. At that time studies in Byzantine music were only beginning and very few melodies had been transcribed. The subject, however, seemed to me so absorbing that I decided to continue my investigations and to study the whole complex of Eastern Christian music in order to get the right approach to its most important branch, the music, in ceremonies and liturgy, of the Byzantine Empire. In the introductory chapter the reader will find a detailed report of these studies and their connexion with those of other scholars.

There is a great difference between the scheme of this book as it was originally planned and its present form. A great deal of what I had to say was worked out in books and articles published since 1917, to which reference is made in the bibliography. The most important decision was to deal with the origins of Christian music in a separate work, in which it was shown that both Byzantine and Western Chant ultimately derived from a common source, the music of the Synagogue, and that a close relationship existed between a number of Western melodies and the parallel Eastern versions. This relationship between East and West, well known to liturgiologists, had to be made clear to students of the history of music by an analysis of the melodies of Latin hymns with Greek prototypes. I must therefore refer readers interested in these problems to this book, *Eastern Elements in Western Chant*, published in 1947 as the first volume of the American Series of the *Monumenta Musicae Byzantinae*.

This separate treatment of the origins made it possible to write a history of the development of Byzantine music and hymnography, and it is hoped that this may be of service not only to musicologists but also to students of Eastern theology and Byzantine civilization. I also found it necessary to outline the background, Greek and Hebrew, from which Byzantine hymnography developed. I came to the conclusion that while both words and music were of Oriental origin they were judged by Patristic and Byzantine writers in the light of Platonic and Neoplatonic thought, and that as hymnography developed the spirit of the Greek language transformed the expression of the melodies, so that this originally foreign material was naturalized by a continuous process of assimilation.

For a long time the student of hymnography was discouraged from an investigation of Byzantine poetry, partly by the bulk of the material to be found in the service books, partly by the quality of much of it, verbose and lacking in inspiration in comparison with classical Greek poetry. It is true that in the great mass of Byzantine liturgical poetry a large proportion is artistically worthless, but it is also true that much inspired poetry can be found if the whole material is investigated. It is well known that the same is true of Latin hymns, and, further, if a comparison is made, it will be found that many Byzantine hymns equal, when they do not surpass, the best Latin poems in imaginative power and technical achievement. It is from these hymns, appreciated for what they are without reference to the standards of classical poetry, that Byzantine hymnology must be approached.

It is impossible, however, to consider the texts apart from the music. The fusion of words and music is complete: the texts cannot be judged apart from the melodies nor the melodies apart from the words to which they were sung. The Eastern melodies show less variety in construction and detail than their Western parallels, the Gregorian melodies. But once we are accustomed to the fact that they are built up on a certain number of formulas which are characteristic of the mode of the hymn we can see how ingeniously the musicians shaped and varied the patterns transmitted to them from one generation to the next, embellishing them slightly, until in the period of the Maïstores, or Melurgi, the ornamentation became more florid and the music of greater importance than the words. This new development, which is a purely musical one, has been dealt with in a number of detailed studies, above all in J.-B. Rebours's *Traité de psaltique*. I have therefore restricted the present history to the period in which hymnography was productive from the point of view of both text and music. I hope one day to be able to supplement it by a study of the Melurgi.

Mr. K. Sisam, Secretary to the Delegates of the University Press, first suggested, in 1941, that I should write a book for the Clarendon Press which would sum up the results of my studies, and I wish to express my gratitude for the support and encouragement that he and the Delegates have given me. I started the work as soon as the manuscript of my *Eastern Elements in Western Chant* was complete, and finished it in August 1946. That it took me so long to write a book on a subject with which I had been acquainted since the early days of my studies may be explained by the fact that I have not relied in any section on reproducing quotations of sources at second hand, but have always gone back to the original texts. This procedure proved exacting but often led to unexpected and valuable results. This was particularly the case in the chapters which dealt with Greek musical theory, the pagan background, the alchemical treatises, and music in ceremonies.

Since the ground covered by these sections was not part of my former studies, I discussed many of them with my friends, and asked them to read parts of the manuscript before I gave it to the printer. I was fortunate in having the advice of P. Kahle on Hebrew and Syriac poetry, of Rudolf Pfeiffer and Mrs. Isobel Henderson on Greek musical theory, of P. Maas and G. Zuntz on Byzantine poetry. I have also to thank the Rev. A. A. Farrer, who revised the translations of the hymns. . . .

A word must be said about the Greek quotations given in the footnotes, and about the text, accentuation, and punctuation of Greek hymns. There are few critical editions of Byzantine ecclesiastical writers. Most of the quotations therefore had to be taken from editions which are far from faultless. An attempt to trace the texts back to the manuscripts would have made it impossible to carry out the main purpose of the book. The text of Ps.-Dionysius the Areopagite in Migne's *Patrologia Graeca* is, as everybody knows, in a very corrupt state; the text of Nicolas Mesarites in Heisenberg's edition has an unusual accentuation. But since the present book is not intended for philological purposes, no attempt has been made to standardize the texts. This would, in any case, have been to create an artificial uniformity in texts spread over many centuries.

The texts of hymns in musical manuscripts have no accents, and the division into lines and half-lines is indicated by a dot above the line. The dot means a half-clause, full-clause, or short pause in the melody, and does not punctuate the sense. The printed service books of the Greek Church keep the dot, but add a quite arbitrary punctuation by commas and full stops, and so do the various modern editions. Here too no attempt at standardization has been made. In the manuscripts *iota subscriptum* is used rarely and irregularly. It has usually been supplied, in conformity with the modern method of printing classical Greek.

Byzantine accentuation was not the same as that of classical Greek; the system of pitch had been abandoned, and a stress accent substituted. The music proves that, as far as poetry is concerned, the line contains only three or four main accents. The best method, therefore, of printing it would be to mark only these, with acutes, as P. Maas proposed. This question, however, is fully discussed in the chapter on words and music.

The present book was not merely written in Oxford. It owes its shape and outline to the spirit of Oxford. I have already mentioned some of my friends who were always ready to help when the subject matter took me beyond the range of my own studies. Miss Patricia Kean helped me to prepare the manuscript for the press and read the proofs. She also compiled the Index, as she did for my *Eastern Elements in Western Chant*. I wish to express to her my gratitude for her support.

The book could never have been written without the help which I received from the University and the haven which Lincoln College gave me by electing me a Fellow in 1939. I therefore wish to dedicate it to the Rector and Fellows as an expression of my gratitude and friendship, and I have chosen as frontispiece a miniature from a manuscript in the possession of Lincoln College, now deposited in the Bodleian Library. . . .

E. J. W.

Lincoln College
Oxford 1948

CONTENTS

PLATES

Frontispiece

At end

ABBREVIATIONS

NOTE. *The following abbreviations are used in the bibliography and in the footnotes to the text:*

Abh.B.A. Abhandlungen der bayrischen Akademie der Wissenschaften, philos.-philol. Classe.
A.B.S. Annual of the British School at Athens.
A.M. Acta Musicologica.
B. Byzantion.
B.Z. Byzantinische Zeitschrift.
C.A.H. The Cambridge Ancient History.
C.M.H. The Cambridge Medieval History.
C.S.H.B. Corpus Scriptorum Historiae Byzantinorum.
D.A.C.L. Dictionnaire d'Archéologie chrétienne et de Liturgie.
E.O. Échos d'Orient.
J.H.S. The Journal of Hellenic Studies.
J.L. Jahrbuch für Liturgiewissenschaft.
J.R.S. The Journal of Roman Studies.
J.T.S. The Journal of Theological Studies.
L. Laudate: Quarterly Review of the Benedictines of Nashdom.
O.C. Oriens Christianus.
M.M.B. Monumenta Musicae Byzantinae.
P.G. J. P. Migne, Patrologiae cursus completus, series Graeca.
P.L. J. P. Migne, Patrologiae cursus completus, series Latina.
Rass.G. Rassegna Gregoriana.
R.É.G. Revue des études grecques.
R.G. Revue Grégorienne.
R.O.C. Revue de l'Orient chrétien.
Sb.B.A. Sitzungsberichte der bayrischen Akademie der Wissenschaften, philos.-philol. und histor. Classe.
S.I.M. Sammelbände der Internationalen Musikwissenschaft.
T.S.G. Tribune de Saint Gervais.
Z.M.W. Zeitschrift für Musikwissenschaft.

INTRODUCTION

A SURVEY OF STUDIES IN BYZANTINE MUSIC AND HYMNOGRAPHY

I. BYZANTINE MUSIC

THE term 'Byzantine music' has been applied by modern scholars to Eastern ecclesiastical chant, sung in Greek, and to the melodies of a certain group of ceremonial poems in honour of the Emperor, the Imperial family, and high dignitaries of the Orthodox Church. The restriction of the term to these two groups of chants is not quite accurate, for it excludes secular music, to which Christian authors and Byzantine historiographers frequently refer. No trace, however, of this secular music has come down to us, and the only knowledge we have of it is derived from the Fathers of the Church and the Byzantine chroniclers who contrast the evil influence of theatrical music with the purifying spirit of sacred music. Remnants of Byzantine popular songs may still live in Greek popular music of the present day, but no attempt has yet been made to analyse the melodic structure of these songs and to separate the different layers by stylistic analysis, a procedure which would enable us to compare the corpus of secular melodies with ecclesiastical, and to determine whether any relationship can be observed between them. We must, therefore, use the term 'Byzantine music' here in the same restricted sense as our predecessors; but we shall try to add some information from literary sources so as to give a more complete account of the position which both ecclesiastical and secular music occupied in the Eastern Empire.

There are three groups of sources on which our knowledge of the subject is based:

(1) Manuscripts, containing (*a*) collections of ecclesiastical hymns, chants from the Ordinary of the Liturgy, and other liturgical melodies; (*b*) acclamations and *Polychronia*, sung by alternating choirs in honour of the Emperor, the Empress, and high dignitaries of the State and of the Church.

(2) Treatises on musical theory and notation.

(3) Descriptions of secular and ecclesiastical ceremonies and feasts accompanied by hymns, chants, and instrumental music.

As in all other studies connected with the history of medieval music, any progress is dependent on two factors: (1) the existence of a sufficiently large number of manuscripts containing musical notations from different successive periods to cover most of the ground under consideration; (2) the possibility of drawing conclusions as to the deciphering of the earlier stages of notation by comparison with the final stage, the reading of which offers no difficulties.

We shall have to prove explicitly later on that both these considerations impose further restrictions on the scope of our inquiries. Many of the early musical manuscripts have perished, probably because they were illuminated and were for that reason destroyed during the Iconoclastic controversy. But many manuscripts containing hymns with superposed musical signs have been preserved from the 'Second Golden Age' of Byzantine art, from the ninth to the beginning of the thirteenth century, and even more from the third period between the conquest of Constantinople by the Crusaders in 1204 and the end of the Empire in 1453.

From the beginning of Byzantine studies in the West these manuscripts aroused the interest of students investigating the liturgy of the Eastern Church. The list of scholarly works begins as early as the middle of the seventeenth century with two publications, from both of which valuable information can even now be obtained about the part played by music in the service of the Greek Church: Leo Allatius's *De libris ecclesiasticis Graecorum dissertationes duae* (Paris, 1646), and J. Goar's *Εὐχολόγιον sive Rituale Graecorum* (Paris, 1647), a commentary on the 'Great Euchologium'. A. Kircher, on the other hand, a very unreliable compiler, dealt only superficially with Byzantine music in his *Musurgia universalis sive ars magna consoni et dissoni*, vol. i. 7, pp. 72–9 (Rome, 1650).

II. EARLY WORK ON BYZANTINE MUSIC AND HYMNOGRAPHY

The first scholar to draw attention to the musical signs was Montfaucon, the originator of Greek palaeography. He gives a list of them in his *Palaeographia Graeca* (Paris, 1708), pp. 231 sqq., without trying to transcribe them into Western musical notation. An attempt to do this seems to have been made some seventy years later by M. Gerbert, Abbot of St. Blasien, who dealt extensively with the music of the Eastern Church in the second volume of his study *De cantu et musica sacra, a prima ecclesiae aetate ad praesens tempus* (St. Blasien, 1774). Gerbert even claimed in this work to have succeeded in transcribing some of the melodies; but as he gave no examples of his accomplishments his assertion cannot be proved. Another treatise of this period, based on Late Byzantine musical theorists, can be found in the *Geschichte des transalpinen Daciens* (Vienna, 1781–3), vol. ii, pp. 430–547, by F. J. Sulzer, an assessor in the Austrian army. One would not expect to find a learned dissertation on music in a book of this kind, yet Sulzer's work must be considered a careful attempt to solve the problem of the last phase of Byzantine notation.

Whilst Sulzer's study remained almost unnoticed, another attempt, made some years later, met with greater success. This was an essay 'De l'état de l'art de musique en Égypte' by G. A. Villoteau, published together with other studies on Oriental music in the fourth volume of the *Description de l'Égypte* (Paris, 1799). Villoteau's work was the first comprehensive study on Greek ecclesiastical music and of its notation and theory. It was written by a musician of wide knowledge, and retained a prominent place in musical literature up to the middle of the nineteenth century. Villoteau's essay is the last of the first group of studies on Byzantine music. Further progress, especially in collecting information about the earlier phases of Greek ecclesiastical music, could not be made at that time, since the difficulty of deciphering the musical signs seemed insurmountable. This fact also explains, in part, the disinclination of students, writing on the history of music, to carry out investigations into a remote subject which, like all branches of Byzantine art during the greater part of the nineteenth century, lay outside the general interests of the period, and seemed therefore doomed to failure.

A new impulse was needed to revive the study of Byzantine Chant. It came from the investigations into Byzantine hymnography of Cardinal Pitra, particularly from the publication of his *Hymnographie de l'église grecque* (Rome, 1867), in which he expounded his discovery that the hymns of the Greek Church were composed in strophes of equal metre. The discovery was made by chance. During a stay in St. Petersburg in 1859 Pitra was studying a manuscript which contained a hymn to the Blessed Virgin. His curiosity was roused by red dots, which not only divided the different sections, but also marked off phrases of varying length. These red dots were to be found at the same intervals in every strophe, and always followed the same number of syllables. After further investigations a second more splendid copy of the same hymn was found with golden dots at the exact places where the plain copy had red dots. The importance of the discovery was obvious. 'Le pélerin était en possession du système syllabique des hymnographes.'[1] After examining more than 200 manuscripts Pitra was able to state that Byzantine hymns were composed in metres, no longer based on quantity, as was the case in classical poetry, but on the principle of the stress accent.

Pitra's discovery marked the beginning of systematic research into Byzantine hymnography; nearly every study written before its publication is to-day only of historic interest.[2] This fact becomes evident when we consider that only four years before the publication of Pitra's *Hymnographie* a great authority on the Eastern liturgy, J. M. Neale, wrote in the preface to his translations of Byzantine hymns: 'But in attempting a Greek Kanon, from the fact of its being in prose—(metrical Hymns, as the reader will learn, are unknown)—, one is all at sea. What measure shall we employ? Why this more than that? Might we attempt the rhythmical prose of the original, and design it to be chanted?'[3]

Once Pitra's discovery became known, it seemed strange that the metrical structure of the hymns could have remained so long obscure. Goar, at least, had a clear idea of the structure of the hymns when he wrote in the Commentary of his *Euchologium* (1647), p. 434:

Libros notis musicis exaratos inter cantandum rarissime conspiciunt vel etiam habent Graeci: communesque ideo et verbis et cantu memoriae tenaciter infigunt hymnos, ad quorum normam alios pari syllabarum

[1] *Hymnographie*, p. 11.

[2] Pitra's claim to have been the first to discover the metrical structure of Byzantine hymns has been challenged by W. Meyer (Speyer) in a paper 'Pitra, Mone und die byzantinische Strophik' in *Sb. B.A.* (1896), pp. 49–66, in which he proved that F. J. Mone had come to the same conclusions as Pitra, fourteen years earlier. W. Meyer quotes a passage from the first volume of Mone's *Lateinische Hymnen des Mittelalters* (1853), p. xi, from which it appears that Mone, in fact, discovered the rhythmical structure both of Eastern and Western hymns independently and some years before Pitra. But we do not agree with Meyer's assumption that Pitra knew Mone's book and was unconsciously influenced by it when he made his discovery.

[3] J. M. Neale, *Hymns of the Eastern Church* (London, 1863), p. xiii. Hatherley made no change in the sumptuously printed fourth edition of 1882, by which time the rhythmical theory was already a well-established fact.

numero constantes cantando inflectunt, quorum ideo primordia canticis aliis inscribunt, ut ad eorum regulam sequentes indicent esse decantandos. Hi vocantur *Εἱρμοί* sive tractus, ut qui sequentes modulos ad suam musicam inflexionem trahant.

This account covers the whole ground of Pitra's discovery; and on some points it goes even farther. In a review of Pitra's book, which assumed the size of an independent work,[1] H. M. Stevenson tried to answer the question. As he explains, it is obvious from passages in both Eastern and Western commentaries that the hymns were thought to be written in a kind of 'cadenced prose'. Such a rhythmical scheme was not considered as a sufficient basis for a poetical form, since no traces could be found either of classical metres or of the popular Byzantine *Stichos politikos*, with the exception of three Kanons of St. John Damascene for Epiphany, Easter, and Pentecost, composed in iambic verses. It was the general view of ecclesiastical writers that these chants were called hymns only because they were sung to melodies, the repetition of which made it necessary to divide the whole hymn into sections, i.e. strophes. Apart from this arrangement, made necessary by the repetition of the melody, they were regarded as prose compositions. This is made clear by a passage in a commentary by Theodorus Prodromos, dating from the twelfth century, on hymns of Kosmas of Jerusalem and John Damascene. He speaks of the Kanons of Kosmas as written in prose (δίχα μέτρου). The same view is put forward five centuries later by a Western scholar, S. Wangnereck, commenting on the Odes of the *Menaia*.[2]

III. J.-B. PITRA AND W. CHRIST

Before Byzantinists had time to realize the implications of Pitra's discovery, another work on the same subject was published. This was the *Anthologia Graeca carminum Christianorum*, edited by W. Christ and M. Paranikas (Leipzig, 1871), up to the present the most comprehensive collection of Greek ecclesiastical poetry from Early Christian times to the great period of Byzantine

[1] H. M. Stevenson, 'L'Hymnographie de l'église grecque', *Revue des questions historiques* (Paris, 1876), pp. 482–543. See also H. M. Stevenson–J.-B. Pitra, *Theodori Prodromi commentarios in carmina sacra melodorum Cosmae Hieros. et Ioannis Damasc.*, etc. (Rome, 1888).

[2] 'Non proinde ambigam Menaeorum innumeras odas . . . in suis omnibus strophis ex mera omnino prosa constare: *Pietas Mariana*, praef. 2. This view is repeated in H. Maracci's *Mariale S. Josephi hymnographi* (Rome, 1661), p. 401. Gretser, *De Cruce*, ii, p. 283 (1600–5), goes even farther, by assuming 'lex potissimum videtur hymnographi voluntas.'

hymnography. The collaboration of a student brought up in the tradition of the Orthodox Church with a Western scholar who had specialized in classical prosody proved fortunate. From Paranikas, W. Christ learned the melodies of the Greek Church. When he tried to sing them himself, he became aware of the coincidence of the musical and verbal phrases.[1] Thus he made the same discovery as Pitra, that of the isosyllabic structure of the phrases of each strophe of the Odes. But he went a step farther and attributed to the verbal accent in the line of a Byzantine hymn the function of the metrical accent in classical poetry. The basic principle of the hypothesis is correct, and here Christ ought to have stopped, but, influenced by his studies in classical prosody, he attempted to explain the rhythm of Byzantine hymns by an elaborate system of metrical feet, as though he were dealing with classical poetry.[2] This view was erroneous on the score of both text and music, because the poetry was no longer based on quantity, and, before it came under the influence of the Turks, the measured rhythm of Neo-Greek melodies was unknown to Byzantine music. It is difficult to reconcile this theory with his other conjecture that the abandonment of quantitative accentuation might be due to the influence of Hebrew poetry, particularly the Psalms.[3] Indeed, it seems that Christ, influenced by Pitra, was approaching a solution of the metrical rules of Byzantine hymns, but was led astray by the modern rhythmical version of the melodies. We are confirmed in this opinion when we read the chapters on the music and the musical notation. The music that Christ and Paranikas describe there is Neo-Greek music after the reform of Chrysanthus in 1821.[4]

While Christ's anthology succeeded in raising the interest of classical scholars in the art of hymn-writing, another collection of hymns published only a few years later by J.-B. Pitra brought liturgiologists into this new field of research. Pitra's anthology, published as the first volume of his *Analecta Sacra spicilegio Solesmensi parata* (Paris, 1876), contains works of only twenty-five hymn-writers besides a number of anonymous poems, but the most famous of them, particularly Romanus, are represented by a great number of their poems. It is, in fact, one of Pitra's great

[1] *Anthol. Gr.*, praef., p. v.

[2] Ibid., pp. lxxiii sqq.

[3] Ibid., p. lxxix.

[4] Chrysanthus of Madytos, *Εἰσαγωγὴ εἰς τὸ θεωρητικὸν καὶ πρακτικὸν τῆς ἐκκλησιαστικῆς μουσικῆς* (Constantinople, 1821).

achievements that he assigned to Romanus the most prominent place in the collection, and drew the attention of Western scholars to the poet, whom on the day of his feast (1 October) the Eastern Church praises as 'the first origin of the beautiful chants', 'the father' of hymnographers, the composer of 'angelic hymnody'.[1] After the example of Pitra research into Greek hymnography had as its main object for some considerable time the reconstruction of the texts and metre of the Kontakia of Romanus.

IV. LATER STUDIES IN BYZANTINE HYMNOGRAPHY

The discovery of the poetical structure was only one, though perhaps the most important, of Pitra's contributions to the study of Byzantine hymnography. Having succeeded in reconstructing the metrical scheme, indicated in the manuscripts by the dots at the end of cola and periods, he turned his attention to the origin of the genre, approaching the problem as a liturgiologist, who saw the hymns as part of the service and as subordinated to its requirements. Though he came to no definite conclusions, his various remarks in the *Hymnographie* and the *Analecta* gave valuable hints to his successors, above all, his suggestion that it was in the hymnography of the Syrian and the other Eastern Churches, and even in the Jewish hymns, canticles, and psalms that the origins of Byzantine hymn-writing might be found.[2]

Pitra's hypothesis was confirmed by J. W. Bickell in his *Regulae metrices Biblicae* (Innsbruck, 1879), p. 3: 'rectam viam odas Graecorum ecclesiasticas metris constare et a madraschis Syrorum derivatas esse probabat, has ipsas e sacra Hebraeorum poesi ortum habere coniectavit'; but it was W. Meyer (Speyer) who first carried out detailed research into Syriac hymnography. He showed that the hymns of Ephraem must be regarded as models for Greek Kontakia, the early form of Byzantine poetry. 'It was from Semitic Christians'—this is the main point of his essay—'who were nearer to the source of Christianity than the Greeks and Romans, that rhythmical poetry came to Greek and Latin Christians.'[3] Meyer's views at first met with some opposition. G. M. Dreves, the learned editor of the *Analecta Hymnica*, attacked them particularly strongly in a review in the *Göttingische*

[1] Cf. *Anal. Sacra*, i, p. xxvi.

[2] Cf. *Hymnographie*, pp. 33–4.

[3] 'Anfang und Ursprung der lateinischen u. griechischen rhythmischen Dichtung', *Abh. B.A.* xvii. 2 (Munich, 1884), p. 108.

gelehrte Anzeigen (1886). But soon opinion changed. H. Grimme in his *Der Strophenbau in den Gedichten Ephraems des Syrers* (Freiburg i. B, 1893) supported W. Meyer's theory by comparative studies in Syriac and Byzantine metrics. After this the connexion between Syriac and Byzantine ecclesiastical poetry was no longer disputed. Studies in Byzantine hymnography were rescued from their isolated position and linked up with work on Semitic poetry.

Pitra's other suggestion, that Jewish hymnography should be investigated, was followed up by D. H. Müller in his stimulating book *Die Propheten in ihrer ursprünglichen Form* (Vienna, 1896). Though some parts of the book are now out of date, its leading ideas have proved to be right. D. H. Müller showed that the speeches of the Prophets were composed in a definite poetical form, consisting of strophes and antistrophes which could be of either equal or unequal length.[1] The unit of the strophe is the sentence, covering one or two lines. The combination of two or more sentences of similar but not identical character is effected by the poetical means of *parallelismus membrorum*, e.g. Amos ix. 3:

> Though they dig into hell, thence shall mine hand take them;
> though they climb up to heaven, thence will I bring them down.

Strophe and antistrophe are related by the *responsio*, a similar poetical device which connects a group of sentences of either similar or contrasting character, e.g. Amos i:

3. Thus saith the Lord; for three transgressions of Damascus, and for four, I will not turn away the punishment thereof; because they have threshed Gilead with threshing instruments of iron.	6. Thus saith the Lord; for three transgressions of Gaza, and for four, I will not turn away the punishment thereof; because they carried away captive the whole captivity to deliver them up to Edom.

It was shown by Müller that the poetical structure of the speeches of the Prophets, fundamentally strophic in form and using the *responsio*, could be traced back to Babylonian texts, thus confirming another hypothesis of Pitra.[2]

[1] Cf. D. H. Müller, *Die Propheten*, pp. 190–1.

[2] 'Il importerait enfin de se rendre compte de l'hymnographie biblique, des chants de l'antique

Müller's theory is the basis of two essays by Th. Wehofer: 'Untersuchungen zur altchristlichen Epistolographie'[1] and 'Untersuchungen zum Lied des Romanos auf die Wiederkunft des Herrn'.[2] Though little known, Wehofer's studies in Early Christian and Byzantine literature are among the best on the subject, and we shall have to refer to them when dealing with the origin of Byzantine hymnography. He succeeded in demonstrating the dependence of Romanus on Ephraem, not only in style and literary form, but also in doctrine.[3] These detailed inquiries, however, were made possible by previous research into the texts of some of the Kontakia of Romanus by K. Krumbacher.

In his 'History of Byzantine Literature', first published in 1890, K. Krumbacher gave an excellent survey of ecclesiastical poetry, which was enlarged in the second edition of the work in 1897.[4] Though less extensive than E. Bouvy's[5] treatment of the subject, it can still be regarded as the best introduction to the works of the leading hymn-writers. This historical outline was followed by a series of studies on Early Byzantine poetry, most of them dealing with the reconstruction of the texts and the metrical structure of the Kontakia of Romanus.[6] Here, for the first time, the principles of textual criticism applied to the editing of Greek and Latin classical texts were applied to the works of Byzantine hymnographers. In the preface to *Studien zu Romanos*[7] Krumbacher points out the difficulties he encountered in preparing texts which could be considered philologically correct. Arbitrary omissions and alterations by scribes make a satisfactory edition of these hymns a much more difficult task than the editing

Israël, auquel nos premiers [= Early Christian] mélodes auront fait plus d'un emprunt. N'est-ce point de là que viennent, non seulement les acrostiches, les stances alphabétiques, les refrains, les alternances, les parallélismes, mais tous les secrets de cette prosodie syllabique, dont nous avons parlé? ... Et avant les cantiques du Pentateuque, n'y avait-il pas déjà des psaumes et des hymnes?' J.-B. Pitra, *Hymnographie*, p. 34.

1 *Sitzungsber. d. kais. Akad. d. Wiss. in Wien, phil.-hist. Kl.*, cxliii (Vienna, 1901), 230.

2 Ibid. cliv, part 5 (Vienna, 1907), edited after W.'s death by A. Ehrhard and P. Maas, p. 195.

3 Cf. *Unters. z. Lied. d. Romanos*, ch. 3, pp. 20 sqq.: 'Die geistige Abhängigkeit des Romanos von Aphrem dem Syrer'.

4 Karl Krumbacher, 'Geschichte d. byz. Litteratur von Justinian bis zum Ende des oström. Reiches (527–1453)', Munich, 1897, published in the *Handbuch d. klass. Altertumswiss.* ix. 1.

5 E. Bouvy, *Poètes et Mélodes. Études sur les origines du rythme tonique dans l'hymnographie de l'église grecque* (Nîmes, 1886). A biographical list of Byzantine hymn-writers is given in G. I. Papadopoulos, *Συμβολαὶ εἰς τὴν ἱστορίαν τῆς παρ' ἡμῖν ἐκκλ. μουσικῆς* (Athens, 1890).

6 The main essays of Krumbacher are: 'Kasia', *Sb. B.A.* (Munich, 1897); 'Studien zu Romanos' (ibid. 1898); 'Umarbeitungen bei Romanos' (ibid. 1899); 'Romanos und Kyriakos' (ibid. 1901); 'Die Akrostichis in der griechischen Kirchenpoesie' (ibid. 1904); 'Miszellen zu Romanos', *Abh. B.A.* (Munich, 1907).

7 pp. 69–72.

of a classical text. This wearisome preparatory work was so great that it was impossible for Krumbacher to finish the complete edition of the Kontakia of Romanus, on which he was working at the end of his life. The task has been completed by P. Maas.[1] In the meantime selections from the Kontakia of Romanus were published by Italian scholars in two critical editions: eight hymns by G. Cammelli[2] in 1928, and ten hymns by E. Mioni[3] in 1937.

While these studies were proceeding, progress was also made in the investigation of the Semitic origin of Early Byzantine poetry. In an essay, *Das Kontakion*, P. Maas[4] put forward fresh evidence for the relationship of the Kontakion with the main forms of Syriac poetry, viz. Memrâ, Mâdrâshâ, and Sôgithâ. The question was further investigated by C. Émereau in his thesis *Saint Éphrem le Syrien* (Paris, 1919), and in numerous articles by A. Baumstark, a summary of which is given in his *Liturgie comparée* (Amay, 1939). Through these investigations the relationship of the hymns of Ephraem and Romanus, for a long time the subject of controversy, has been finally established.

The dependence of Romanus on Syriac poetry, however, is only a detail, though an important one, in the problem of the development of Byzantine homiletic poetry from Syrian sources. New light has recently been thrown on the problem by the discovery, by C. Bonner, of the *Homily on the Passion* of Melito, Bishop of Sardis.[5] The publication of this document, which dates from the second half of the second century, made it clear that the origins of the poetical homily, Greek and Syrian, can be traced back to the early days of Christian literature. Its use of hymnodic passages derived from the Psalms and the Wisdom books of the Septuagint,[6] and of other passages which seem to belong to a Christian redaction of a Jewish hymn,[7] suggests that Melito's homily must be considered as a link in a chain of poetical homilies leading back to Jewish homiletics. This fact completely changes our attitude to the question of the Syrian origin of the Kontakion.

[1] P. Maas's MS. of the Kontakia of Romanus is at Athens and was to be published by the Greek Academy.

[2] *Romano il Melode. Inni*, a cura di G. Cammelli, Testi Cristiani, vol. ii (Florence, 1928).

[3] E. Mioni, *Romano il Melode. Saggio critico e dieci Inni inediti* (Turin, 1937). From the bibliography at the end of Mioni's book the number of recent studies on Romanus can be seen.

[4] *B.Z.* xix (1910), 285–306.

[5] *Studies and Documents*, edited by Kirsopp Lake and Silva Lake, vol. xii (N.Y. and Lond., 1940).

[6] Ibid., p. 23.

[7] Ibid., p. 25.

It is easy to understand that at an early stage in investigations into the problem scholars were only attracted by the hymns of Ephraem and Romanus because they were the most conspicuous products of both Syriac and Greek ecclesiastical poetry. For us, however, now that the immediate problem of their relationship has been solved, it is more important to prove that an uninterrupted liturgical tradition existed from the days of the Synagogue to the Byzantine melodies of the mid-seventh century, according to which the reading of the Scriptures was followed by the recitation or chanting of a poetical homily.[1]

We shall also have to explain the reason for the abandonment of this usage, leading virtually to the end of the Kontakion, and to the rise of a new genre, the Kanon, differing from the Kontakion both musically and poetically.

V. LATER STUDIES IN BYZANTINE MUSIC

We have now to return to the study of Byzantine music, and to give a survey of its development after the publication of Villoteau's book of which we spoke earlier in this chapter. Investigations into the music did not seem to have any prospect of success at the beginning of the nineteenth century, as it was recognized that the problem of Byzantine notation had first to be solved before any attempt could be made to approach the music itself. At that time the study of music palaeography, one of the most important branches of studies in the history of music, was only in its beginning. The problem of the Plainchant notations, more important for Western scholars, had not yet been tackled, as the signification of the musical signs, the neumes, could not be defined. However, a certain similarity in all the notations in liturgical manuscripts, both Eastern and Western, was soon observed. In his *Résumé philosophique de l'histoire de la musique* (Paris, 1835) F. J. Fétis[2] pointed out the similarity between Byzantine, Armenian, and Ethiopian notations, and deduced from it the Oriental origin of the neumes, which he thought had come to Rome in a roundabout way through the northern regions of Europe. The Oriental hypothesis was

[1] Cf. my article: 'Melito's Homily on the Passion. An Investigation into the Sources of Byzantine Hymnography', *J.T.S.* xliv (1943), 41–52, and P. Kahle: 'Was Melito's Homily on the Passion originally written in Syriac?', ibid., pp. 52–6.

[2] Life in *Biographie universelle des musiciens*, i. 505 sqq.

opposed by R. Kiesewetter,[1] who maintained that the neumes originated in Rome. Kiesewetter's arguments made Fétis retract his former views. In the fourth volume of his *Histoire générale de la musique* (Paris, 1877) we find a new theory developed, viz. that the neumes were of Germanic origin, as the oldest documents gave neumes of 'Lombardic' character.[2] A third theory, increasing still more the already existing confusion, was put forward by Th. Nisard,[3] who considered the neumes to be a kind of tachygraphy already used by the Romans. While these hypotheses were being discussed, E. de Coussemaker, a famous scholar in the field of medieval music, had already shown the way which finally led to the deciphering of Western neumes. He found out that the main types of neumes derived from the accents: acute, grave, and circumflex.[4] Thus the often complicated forms of the later stages of notation could be traced back to their simple, primitive forms.

Coussemaker's hypothesis on the origin of the neumes was generally accepted[5] as the solution of the problem, and gave rise to detailed investigations into the musical notation of Western ecclesiastical manuscripts. In this particular field of studies Benedictine monks of the abbey of Solesmes in France played an important part from the middle of the nineteenth century. The aim of the School of Solesmes was the restoration of the Gregorian melodies to their original form, as the study of the old antiphonaries and graduals had shown that the versions in the official liturgical books, based on the *Editio Medicaea*, did not conform to those preserved in medieval manuscripts. Dom André Mocquereau (1849–1930), founder and editor of the *Paléographie*

[1] R. Kiesewetter, *Über die Musik d. neueren Griechen, nebst einer Abhandlung über die Entdeckung des Herrn Fétis an der Tonschrift d. heutigen Griechen* (Leipzig, 1838), p. 17.

[2] The same fantastic hypothesis occurs again in O. Fleischer, *Die germanischen Neumen als Schlüssel zum altchristlichen und gregorianischen Gesang* (Frankfort, 1923). Cf. P. Wagner's review of Fleischer's book in *Z.M.W.* v (1922–3), 560–8.

[3] Th. Nisard, 'Études sur les anciennes notations musicales de l'Europe', *Revue Archéolog.* 1849–50. The 'stenographic' theory reappeared recently in K. A. Psachos's *'Η Παρασημαντικὴ τῆς Βυζαντινῆς μουσικῆς* (Athens, 1917), to which we will have to refer later on. For a short time the theory caused some confusion, for it found adherents among people who believed that the present state of Neo-Greek melodies was identical with that of the melodies preserved in medieval MSS.

[4] *Histoire de l'Harmonie au moyen âge*, 1852, p. 154.

[5] 'C'est là une vérité, croyons-nous, définitivement acquise à la science, bien que ceux qui ont le plus victorieusement soutenu cette thèse, comme Coussemaker par exemple, n'en aient pas toujours tiré toutes les conséquences, et qu'ils aient même, par la manière dont ils ont ensuite interprété les neumes, paru en avoir oublié la véritable origine.' Dom Pothier, *Mélodies grégoriennes*, 1880, p. 31.

musicale,[1] demonstrated this in numerous articles on the development of neumatic notation and on the rhythm of Plainchant.

It is well known that the main goal of the School of Solesmes was achieved in 1903 when Pius X in his Motu proprio *Inter pastoralis officii* ordered the restoration of the Gregorian melodies according to the principles expounded by Dom Mocquereau and his collaborators. The effect of this important decision was an increased effort to support the new *Editio Vaticana* of Plainchant by investigations into the development of Western neumes, and these studies gave a new impulse to investigations into the Eastern ecclesiastical notations, particularly into the notations of Byzantine liturgical manuscripts.

J.-B. Thibaut, a French student of Early Christian liturgy, had already published two studies on Byzantine notation in the *Review of the Russian Archaeological Institute.*[2] Both he and J.-B. Rebours had edited several treatises on Byzantine musical theory,[3] but were unable to decipher the notation. O. Fleischer was able to achieve an almost complete reconstruction of the melodic line of melodies transmitted in Late Byzantine notation. In his book, *Die spätgriechische Tonschrift* (Berlin, 1904), Fleischer published in facsimile an elementary treatise, a kind of grammar of music, together with a critical edition of the Greek text, a translation, and a commentary. He was apparently unaware that V. Gardthausen had already investigated a *Papadike* in his essay 'Zur Notenschrift der griechischen Kirche' in his *Beiträge zur griechischen Palaeographie,* vi (1880),[4] where a list of seventy-seven musical signs is given. Gardthausen, however, did not attempt to explain the musical significance of the signs, as in his view there was no satisfactory solution to the problem.

The manuscript Fleischer chose for his study originally belonged to the Basilian monastery of San Salvatore near Messina, from which it was brought to the University Library of

[1] *Paléographie Musicale: Les principaux Mss. de chant grégorien, ambrosien, mozarabe, gallican, publiés en fac-similés phototypiques*, sous la direction de Dom André Mocquereau (Tournai, 1889–). In addition to this monumental series, the School of Solesmes has published, since 1910, a series of *Monographies Grégoriennes.* Cf. also *Revue Grégorienne, Études de chant sacré et de liturgie*, published since 1911.

[2] 'La Notation de Saint Jean Damascène ou Hagiopolite', *Izvestija russk. archeol. Inst.* iii (Constantinople, 1898), 138 sqq.; 'La Notation de Koukouzéles', ibid. vi (1900), 360–90.

[3] J.-B. Thibaut, 'Traités de musique byzantine', *R.O.C.* (1901), vi. 596 sqq.; J.-B. Rebours, 'Quelques Mss. de musique byzantine', ibid. 1904–5.

[4] *Sitzber. d. sächs. Ak. d. Wiss.* 1880.

Messina together with other musical manuscripts written in Byzantine musical notation. The treatise which Fleischer edited was intended for the use of the priests; hence the name *Papadike*, by which it is known among Byzantine and Greek ecclesiastical scholars. The *Papadike* has been transmitted in numerous copies, some of them more comprehensive than others. Fleischer believed that the *Papadike* of Messina contained the oldest and best version; but now that other texts of the treatise have been examined this view can no longer be maintained.[1] The importance of the *Papadike*, however, as the best source of information about the Late Byzantine, or Kukuzelean, notation is unquestionable, since no other treatise contains so many tables clearly showing the interval-value of the various musical signs. But the *Papadike* must be used in conjunction with the other treatises which deal more extensively with the rhythmical significance of Byzantine musical signs.

Fleischer's efforts to develop the method by which the melodic framework of the Byzantine melodies could be transcribed into our modern staff notation, mark the first step towards a solution of the problem of Byzantine musical notation. It was soon recognized that the principles, which proved to be valid for deciphering the last phase of Byzantine neumes, from the fifteenth to the eighteenth century, could also be applied to that of the middle period of notation, from the twelfth to the fifteenth century. Only a year after the publication of Fleischer's book, Dom H. Gaisser of the Collegium Graecum in Rome published his essay 'Les Heirmoi de Pâques' in *Oriens Christianus* in 1905, without knowing Fleischer's work. Dom Gaisser's article on the *Heirmoi*, the model-strophes of the Easter Hymn, is the first detailed study of Byzantine hymnography by a scholar equally capable of approaching the problems of the music and of the poetry. He also made a skilful transcription of the melodic structure of the chants, but did not succeed in finding a solution to the modal and rhythmical problems.

A contribution to Byzantine musical palaeography was made

[1] Cf. my study 'Die Rhythmik der byzantinischen Neumen', *Z.M.W.* ii (1919–20), 629 sqq. Here the *Papadike* of Cod. graec. Petropolit. 711, reproduced by J.-B. Thibaut in the appendix to his *Monuments de la notation ekphonétique et hagiopolite de l'église grecque* (1913), was chosen as the basis for my investigations. Since then I have examined more MSS. containing the *Papadike*, without having been obliged to change my view. It will, however, be necessary to collate all versions of the *Papadike*, as is planned by the editors of the *Monumenta Musicae Byzantinae*, in order to establish which MS. contains the most reliable and complete text of the treatise.

by A. Gastoué in the introduction to his *Catalogue des manuscrits de musique byzantine*, published by the Société internationale de musique (Paris, 1907). He pointed out, as Dom Gaisser had done, the close relationship of the different stages of Byzantine neumes, from the eleventh century to the modern Chrysantine notation. A table containing the musical notation of the Troparion *Βηθλεέμ, ἑτοιμάζου*, from seven manuscripts demonstrates the correctness of his theory.[1]

Hugo Riemann's *Die byzantinische Notenschrift im 10. bis 15. Jahrhundert* (Leipzig, 1909) marked a definite step backwards in the progress hitherto achieved. Riemann lacked an adequate training in Byzantine palaeography,[2] and was hampered by his preconceived ideas on rhythm, which made him adapt all melodies to a four-bar system. With the discussion caused by Riemann's book the decisive phase of investigations into Byzantine musical notation began. It was opened by an article on the hymns of the nun Kasia, in which H. J. W. Tillyard[3] refuted Riemann's theories of the interpretation of both the intervals and keys. But the problem of rhythm, indeed the crucial problem, still remained unsolved.

VI. THE DECIPHERING OF THE MUSIC

It was at this point that my own investigations started, the first results of which had taken shape in two essays, published in *Oriens Christianus*, 'Die Kirchenmusik im byzantinischen Reich' (1916), and 'Die Entzifferung der byzantinischen Notation' (1918). In studying the treatises on Byzantine musical theory I succeeded in finding the clue to the deciphering of Byzantine musical notation.

From the theoretical treatises, particularly from the *Papadike*, we learn that the interval-signs of the middle period of Byzantine notation are divided into two groups, viz. Somata (*σώματα*) and

[1] pp. 43–5; Gastoué's transcription into modern staff notation on pp. 46–7 is not satisfactory.

[2] It is sufficient to give one example of Riemann's incompetence as a palaeographer. The Byzantine modes 1–4 are indicated in the MSS. by the Greek letters *α′*, *β′*, *γ′*, *δ′*, since the Greek and, following them, the Byzantine mathematicians used letters, and not ciphers. Riemann, being ignorant of this fact, tried to find out what the letters meant. As they did not have the usual shape, and the third letter, *γ*, was written either Γ̈, or simply rendered by the two apostrophes ", he interpreted *α′* as standing for *φρύγιος*, *β′* for *λύδιος*, *γ′* for *μιξολύδιος*, and *δ′* for *δώριος*. Consequently melodies of the first mode (*α′*) are transcribed by Riemann in the second, those of the second (*β′*) in the third, those of the third (*γ′*) in the fourth, and those of the fourth (*δ′*) in the first.

[3] H. J. W. Tillyard, 'A Musical Study of the Hymns of Casia', *B.Z.* xx (1911), 420–85.

Pneumata (πνεύματα). The Somata (bodies) can only move by steps upwards and downwards. The Pneumata (spirits) can leap over two, three, and four intervals. In addition there are some signs which are neither Somata nor Pneumata, such as the Aporrhoë (ἀπορροή), a sign standing for a gliding movement of two consecutive descending seconds, and the Ison (ἶσον), indicating the repetition of a tone at the same pitch. The latter sign is neither Soma nor Pneuma, for it stands neither for a movement by steps nor by leaps.

The system of Byzantine notation shows a certain economy in the use of interval-signs. The composer had only three signs at his disposal for indicating the melodic movement of a second, a third, or a fifth upwards, and three others for the same movement downwards. He had to use a combination of two or three signs when he wanted to indicate a fourth, a sixth, or an octave. This was done by superimposing a Pneuma or—where the interval of an octave was wanted—two Pneumata on a Soma. There is, however, another combination of Somata and Pneumata to be found in manuscripts of Byzantine music which the singer had to interpret in a different way. We learn from the *Papadike* that if a Pneuma is preceded by a Soma, the intervals should not be added as is the case when the signs are written one above the other. The significance of a Soma followed by a Pneuma is that it is only the interval represented by the Pneuma that is taken into account, while, according to the theorists, the Soma is made 'voiceless' (ἄφωνον). The *Papadike* is not very clear about the significance of the transformation of the Soma from its original use as a Second into an additional sign. None of the scholars who tried to decipher Byzantine musical manuscripts was able to give a satisfactory explanation of what the term 'voiceless' meant. Gaisser, Gastoué, and Fleischer did not pay any attention to the remarkable fact that the Byzantine system of musical notation contained no less than six signs for the ascending second, while only one can be found for the Ison, and for the third and fifth upwards and downwards. Riemann did not overlook the fact, but, influenced by his rhythmical theories, he failed to see the essential point. But it seemed to me that the clue to the problem of Byzantine musical notation was to be found in just these two facts: that there were six different signs for the ascending second, and that these Somata lost their interval-value in a certain combination with Pneumata. I shall try to give a short account of the main points of my discovery.[1]

A collection of treatises on Byzantine musical theory published by J.-B. Thibaut and J.-B. Rebours provides detailed information about the six signs which are used to indicate the interval of an ascending second. These signs do not only indicate the melodic direction, but also the manner in which it should be executed. Five of these signs combine with the interval-value a particular dynamic or rhythmical nuance; one sign, the Oligon, stands for the movement of the melody a second upwards without any particular nuance. For writing down other intervals, e.g. a third or fifth, the Byzantine composer had at his disposal, in each case, a single neutral sign, i.e. a sign without any dynamic or rhythmical nuance. If he wanted to give this melodic step a particular nuance, as implied by one of the five signs for the second, he set this sign before the Pneuma indicating a third or fifth. In this combination of the two signs the Soma lost its interval-value, it became 'voiceless', but it retained its dynamic or rhythmical significance, which it lent to the neutral sign. If the composer wanted a fourth or sixth to be sung, he set one of the Pneumata indicating a third or a fifth above a Soma. In this grouping the Soma maintained its interval-value (third + second = fourth; fifth + second = sixth), and the combination was executed according to the nuance contained in the Soma. Thus the Middle Byzantine notation provided a most ingenious system which endeavoured to transmit a great variety of rhythmical and dynamic nuances, using only a very limited number of signs. Instead of using six different neumes for each interval to indicate the most frequently occurring nuances, the Byzantine musician needed only six signs for the ascending second. By combining these signs with those for other intervals he was able to indicate precisely, both rhythmically and dynamically, how each step of a melody was to be performed. Only a few more dynamic signs were required to complete the number of nuances, and, at a later stage of notation, a large number of red auxiliary signs were superposed to regulate the execution of the florid style of the so-called Koukouzelian period. These complementary red signs,

[1] Cf. E. Wellesz, 'Zur Entzifferung der byz. Notenschrift', *O.C.*, N.S. vii (1918), 98–118, 'Die Rhythmik der byz. Neumen', *Z.M.W.* ii (1919–20), 617–38, and iii (1920–1), 321–36, and 'Über Rhythmus u. Vortrag der byz. Melodien', *B.Z.* xxxiii. 33–66.

the 'Great Signs' (μεγάλα σημάδια), were obviously introduced to facilitate the phrasing of the now very extended cantilenas.

I came to the conclusion that other scholars who had approached the problem of Byzantine notation had seen in these complementary signs the essential rhythmical indications, and were too ready to assume that the neumes indicated the steps of the cantilenas. It was clear, however, from the study of manuscripts of the earliest phase of Byzantine notation that even as early as the tenth century the neumes were used to direct the singers how to execute the nuances of the melody. Bearing this in mind it is possible to reach a better understanding of Byzantine musical notation and of its ingenious development from scanty indications for the singer, in its first phase, to an elaborate system at its acme.

The views developed here were confirmed by H. J. W. Tillyard's studies on the same subject, which came into my hands in 1922. A Greek scholar, Tillyard had started his investigations under the guidance of Dom H. Gaisser. Very soon, however, his careful palaeographical studies made him oppose the views held by Gaisser and Riemann, and he came to virtually the conclusions outlined above.[1] A difficult problem, to which Riemann[2] had first drawn attention, still remained to be solved: the significance of the signatures (μαρτυρίαι), indicating the starting-note of the melody, and the mode (ἦχος) in which it had to be sung. This problem, particularly perplexing in the case of the second mode, was solved through the minute investigations of Tillyard, published in his study, 'Signatures and Cadences of the Byzantine Modes'.[3]

Once the problem of Byzantine neumes had been solved, the transcription of Byzantine hymns from manuscripts of the twelfth and thirteenth centuries could be carried out more extensively. The close collaboration between Tillyard and myself, beginning in 1927, led to the foundation in 1931 of the *Monumenta Musicae Byzantinae* after a conference at Copenhagen, to which C. Höeg had invited us in the name of the Rask-Oersted Foundation. It was decided at the conference to use a uniform method for the transcriptions of Byzantine melodies and to introduce, with slight

[1] Cf. H. J. W. Tillyard, 'Rhythm in Byzantine Music', *A.B.S.*, no. xxi (1916), 125–47, and 'The Problem of Byzantine Neumes', *J.H.S.* xli (1921), 29–49.

[2] 'Die *Μαρτυρίαι* d. byz. liturg. Notation', *Sb. B.A.* 1882.

[3] *A.B.S.*, no. xxvi (1925), 78–87.

modifications, the rhythmical signs already used in my transcriptions.[1] The Royal Danish Academy agreed to the plans for the study and publication of Byzantine music put forward at the conference, and decided to publish the *Monumenta Musicae Byzantinae* under the patronage of the Union Académique Internationale. In order to gather the material for our studies and publications, C. Höeg was sent to Greece and the Near East to take photographs of the most important manuscripts. After a few years of preparatory work a facsimile-edition of the *Sticherarion*, Codex theol. gr. 181 Vindob., was published jointly by the editors as the first volume of the main series of the *Monumenta Musicae Byzantinae* (*M.M.B.*) in 1935. In the same year the first and second volumes of the *Subsidia*, Tillyard's *Handbook of the Middle Byzantine Musical Notation*, and Höeg's *La Notation Ekphonétique*, were published. The series of the *Transcripta* was begun with *Die Hymnen des Sticherarium für September* (Wellesz) in 1936, and *The Hymns of the Sticherarium for November* (Tillyard) in 1938. A second volume of the *Facsimilia*, the *Hirmologium Athoum*, Codex 470 of the Iberon Monastery of Mount Athos, was also published in 1938. Plans for further publications were discussed at a conference of the Union Académique Internationale in London in May of that year, and at a meeting of the editors in Oxford in May 1939. The outbreak of the war interrupted the contact of Tillyard and myself with Höeg, who has nevertheless published in 1941, Part I of Tillyard's *The Hymns of the Octoechus*.

Thanks to the initiative of Mr. Th. Whittemore, Director of the Byzantine Institute, Boston, and the support given by the American Council of Learned Societies and the British Academy, an American Series of the *Monumenta Musicae Byzantinae* was started in 1941 which undertook to publish my *Eastern Elements in Western Chant* and H. J. W. Tillyard's transcription of *Twenty Canons from the Trinity MS., Cambridge*. In October 1945, after the end of the war, C. Höeg came to England again, and at a meeting of the editors in Oxford, plans for the future were discussed, especially the edition of the transcriptions from the *Hirmologium Athoum* which had been transcribed by my former pupils and collaborators Dr. Aglaia Ayoutanti, Dr. Maria Stöhr,

[1] See my report of the conference in *Z.M.W.* xiv (1931–2), 61, and Tillyard's 'Conference on Byzantine Music' at the beginning of his study 'The Morning Hymns of the Emperor Leo', Part 2, *A.B.S.*, no. xxxi, pp. 115–16.

and myself. The publication of the 1,724 hymns in this manuscript is now in progress; it began with the edition of the Hirmi in the first Mode by C. Höeg, who gave a detailed introduction to the study of the Hirmologion and comparative notational tables from various manuscripts to the transcriptions of the first Canons of the first authentic and first plagal modes.

Our method of transcription has been adopted by other students who are working on Byzantine music, e.g. by O. Tiby in his book *La musica bizantina* (1938) and O. Strunk in his article on 'The Tonal System of Byzantine Music' in *The Musical Quarterly*, 1942, pp. 190 sqq. Dom Lorenzo Tardo's transcriptions in his *L'Antica melurgia bizantina* (1938) vary rhythmically from those of the *Monumenta Musicae Byzantinae*, but the sub-title of Tardo's book—*nell' interpretazione della Scuola Monastica di Grottaferrata*—justifies his method of transcription, as he is reproducing the local tradition of singing in the Basilian monastery.

In practice, however, hardly any difference in the execution of the melodies can be noticed, as one can find out for oneself by listening to records made at Grottaferrata under the supervision of Dom Tardo and those made under my own supervision for the *History of Music in Sound*, vol. ii (H.M.V.).

This similarity in outlook, as far as the most important problems are concerned, led finally to a close co-operation between the editors of the *Monumenta* and the scholars at the Badia Greca of Grottaferrata. It was officially confirmed in 1950 by the co-optation of the Very Rev. Archimandrite Isidoro Croce to the Editorial Board. At that time already, Dom Bartolomeo di Salvo had joined Dom Tardo in working on the early phases of the musical notation and has since produced a number of valuable studies.[1]

The general acceptance of our method of transcribing facilitated the spread of studies in Byzantine music. The growing interest in Byzantine Chant became evident at the Bicentennial

[1] B. di Salvo, 'La notazione paleobizantina e la sua trascrizione'; 'La tradizione orale dei canti liturgici delle colonie Italo-Albanesi di Sicilia comparata con quella dei codici antichi bizantini', *Atti del Congresso Internazionale di Musica sacra*, Rome, 1950; 'La notazione paleobizantina e la sua trascrizione', *Bollettino della Badia di Grottaferrata*, N.S. iv (1950), 114–30 and v (1951), 92–110, 220–35; 'Qualche appunto sulla chironomia nella musica bizantina', *Orientalia Christiana Periodica*, vol. xxiii (1957).

of Princeton University in 1946, and at the first Congress of Sacred Music in Rome in 1950, where the present writer was in charge of a section on Eastern Chant. The same interest was noticeable at the second Congress in Vienna in 1954 and the third in Paris in 1957. We may ascribe the changed attitude towards our studies partly to the growing appreciation of Byzantine Chant with which wide circles became acquainted through records and radio, partly to the recognition of the importance of the knowledge of Eastern Chant for the development of Western Chant, particularly of those bilingual melodies in Western Graduals and Antiphonaries of the Beneventan and Ravennatic rites, which are remnants, one could say 'incrustations', of the early layer of chants in the repertory of melodies which are now considered to be the *chant 'vieux romain'*, the Roman Chant before the reshaping of the melodies in the Carolingian era.[1]

Thus the investigation into the bilingual melody *Ote to Stavro—O quando in cruce* of the Beneventan rite, which I had analysed in my *Eastern Elements in Western Chant* (1947) and compared with the version of the Greek Troparion as it was sung in Constantinople, on Mount Athos and in Grottaferrata, was of far greater importance to studies in early Western Chant than I would have dared to expect.

In his two studies on 'Les Chants en langue grecque dans les liturgies latines' in *Sacris Erudiri*, vols. i (1948) and iv (1952), Dom Louis Brou gives a list of forty-five bilingual chants; but these are only the melodies of which the texts have come down to us in both Latin and Greek; they do not include those melodies which are obviously of Greek origin but have come down to us only in the Latin version.

On p. 168 of the *Eastern Elements* Charlemagne's active interest in the Chant of the Eastern Church is mentioned and the passage from *De gestis Beati Caroli Magni*[2] quoted, in which it is

[1] Cf. B. Stäblein, 'Zur Frühgeschichte d. römischen Chorals', *Atti del Congresso Intern. di Musica Sacra*, Rome, 1950, pp. 271–6; Dom J. Hourlier et Dom M. Huglo, 'Un important témoin du chant vieux-romain: le Graduel de Sainte Cécile du Transtévère', *Revue Grégorienne*, xxxi (1952), 26–37; Dom M. Huglo, 'Le Chant "vieux-romain". Liste des manuscrits et témoins indirects', *Sacris Erudiri*, vi (1954), 96–124; H. Hucke, 'Die Einführung des gregorianischen Gesanges im Frankenreich', *Römische Quartalschrift*, xlix (1954), 172–87; 'Gregorianischer Gesang in altrömischer und fränkischer Überlieferung', *Archiv für Musikwissenschaft*, xii (1955), 74–87; E. Wellesz, 'Recent Studies in Western Chant', *The Musical Quarterly*, xli (1955), 177–90

[2] In *Monumenta Germaniae Historica, Scriptores*, ii. 751, 757, reprinted in Migne's *P.L.* P. Wagner, in his *Einführung in die gregorianischen Melodien'*, vol. i (Leipzig, 1911), dismisses the report as a 'fairy-tale'.

reported that Charlemagne ordered the translation into Latin of some Greek hymns to which he had listened in concealment, when members of a Byzantine legation sang chants of their Church during their stay at the Franconian court. In an article 'Sur quelques tropaires grecs traduits en latin' in *Annales Musicologiques*, vol. ii (1954) the late J. Handschin went further into the matter.

In another edition of the *Gesta* he found a more detailed description of the chants the Byzantines sang; these were the Antiphons of the Morning Offices on the Octave of Epiphany *Veterem hominem cum sequentibus.*[1] With the help of Dom B. di Salvo and O. Strunk he was now able to show that the Greek chants which were sung were closely related to the group of Latin chants which have survived in several Antiphonals, e.g. that of Worcester, *Paléographie Musicale,* vol. xii, pl. 58 sq.

The essential fact for us lies not so much in the investigation as to which of the Western manuscripts contain the best version for comparison, but in the confirmation of the correctness of the assumption which I held from the beginning, i.e. that Byzantine music was diatonic before the Empire came under the overwhelming influence of Arabic, and, even more, of Turkish music. Byzantine music cannot have sounded strange to Western ears. Would Charlemagne have told his clergy to translate the Greek texts into Latin, would he have ordered them to include a set of Greek antiphons in the Latin Service if the melodies had, on account of their intervals, sounded different from the liturgical Chant he was used to? Certainly not. Byzantine Chant must have been as diatonic as that of the Latin Church.

The few details mentioned above are sufficient to show the important role which chant in Greek played in the creation and development of Latin Chant, i.e. both, in the early days of Christianity, when it was introduced from the Syro-Palestinean Church and, at a later date, when some chants were taken over from the Eastern Church.[2] Musicologists like A. Gastoué, W. Frere, and, above all, P. Wagner, who were liturgiologists as well,

[1] G. Meyer von Knonau, 'Monachus Sangallensis (Notkerus Balbulus) De Carolo Magno', *Mitteilungen zur vaterländischen Geschichte. Herausgeg. vom Histor. Verein des Kantons St. Gallen*, xxxvi (1920), 38. This text is a reprint from Jaffé's edition in *Bibliotheca rerum Germanicarum*, tom. iv, pp. 631–700. The full text has been used by Dom Pothier in his study on the same subject in *Revue du chant grégorien*, x. 81–3.

[2] Cf. E. Wellesz, 'Gregory the Great's Letter on the Alleluia', *Annales Musicologiques*, tome ii (Paris, 1954), pp. 7–26.

were convinced of the existence of this influence but were not in possession of the material which would have proved their theory. It was only after a great number of Byzantine melodies had been transcribed that it was possible to confirm what until then had to be regarded as a hypothesis, though a very suggestive one.

VII. THE PRESENT STATE OF STUDIES IN BYZANTINE CHANT

Down to about 1950 the transcriptions of the editors of the *M.M.B.* were taken from the Hirmologion and Sticherarion, the first containing melodies in a more or less syllabic style, the second one melodies partly in a slightly ornamented style. The deciphering of the musical notation of the thirteenth and fourteenth centuries did not offer any difficulties in principle as long as one had a clear, carefully written manuscript to transcribe, since the riddle of the notation had been solved thirty years ago. The difficulties consisted in mistakes of the scribes, illegible musical signs, and other faults which could be eliminated by comparison with other manuscripts of the same monastic tradition. The task of transcribing the melodies from the two collections and the work on the earlier phases of the notation was so substantial that the editors had not been able to direct their attention to the chants in the melismatic style.

At the Congress in Rome P. A. Laïly presented us with his Doctorate thesis on a manuscript in the Vatican library, Cod. Borgia gr. 19.[1] Here some of the richly ornamented melodies are transcribed and commented upon by Laïly. Looking back we may say that he came very near to a satisfactory solution.

At the same time C. Höeg and I visited the Badia di Grottaferrata near Rome where the famous Codex Ashburnham. 64 from the Laurenziana in Florence was on loan, and was shown to us by the kindness of the Very Rev. Archimandrite and Dom Bartolomeo di Salvo. Codex Ashburnham. 64 is a Psaltikon, a book for the soloist. It contains in the main a collection of Kontakia, but also liturgical chants proper, all in the melismatic style of the thirteenth century, that means in a very florid style, though not yet in the rather superficial *coloratura* style of the fourteenth and fifteenth centuries.

[1] P. A. Laïly, *Analyse du Codex de musique grecque No. 19*, *Bibliothèque Vaticane* (*Fonds Borgia*), Jerusalem, 1949.

Codex Ashburnham. 64 is of particular value to the student of Byzantine Chant because it contains in a very legible notation and script all the twenty-four stanzas of the 'Akathistos' hymn, the most famous Kontakion of the Greek Orthodox Church. It was arranged that Höeg should prepare a facsimile edition of Codex Ashburnham. 64 and the present writer a transcription of the 'Akathistos'.

We shall have to deal with the ambiguities of the notation in a chapter on the melismatic chant which is added to this edition. Here, however, it may be said that I worked for three years on the deciphering of the notation, because the scribe had obviously copied it from a manuscript in which the intervals were not fixed and the sign of a descending third could mean either third or a fourth, and so on. The work on the transcription of the 'Akathistos' confirmed the view which I expressed repeatedly, that Byzantine musical notation was merely an *aide-mémoire* to the singer, not only in the earlier stages of musical notation when the range of intervals was not fixed, but also in the notation of the thirteenth century, the so-called 'Middle Byzantine' notation, with theoretically fixed intervals. The singer who used the hymnbook knew the melodies by heart. He therefore rarely corrected mistakes of the scribe, resulting from carelessly copying an old manuscript and leaving some ambiguous intervals written in the old way. The notation, indicating the approximate interval, was enough help to sing the right notes. It would be wrong to decide on notational grounds alone what to do in a case where no clear decision can immediately be taken, we must find out what interval the old scribe wanted to write down. That procedure made it necessary to compare the melodic lines of all the twenty-four stanzas to see what the scribe wrote in the corresponding stanzas, all of which varied at least slightly from the model stanza, and to find out that solution which fitted best the palaeographical evidence and the run of the melody in the other stanzas. Now that this work is done,[1] the transcription of other Kontakia from thirteenth-century manuscripts offers no difficulties provided that the intonation-signs are correct; glancing over the pages of the facsimile edition we find certain traditional clauses and formulae, the recurrence of a certain number of ornaments which ap-

[1] E. Wellesz, *The Akathistos Hymn*, *M.M.B. Transcripta*, vol. ix (1957); C. Höeg, *Contacarium Ashburnhamense*, *M.M.B. Facsimilia*, vol. iv (1956).

pear to be characteristic of the genre, not only of a single Kontakion, or Doxology, or Alleluia.

The transcription of the melodies and the investigation into the early stages of Byzantine musical notation has prepared the ground for the work which must now be done: the study of the technique of Byzantine musical composition, its characteristic features, and its place in the entirety of Christian Chant. This is a task to which everyone who has worked in this field has paid attention, but which must be even further developed. It becomes increasingly important as we see more and more that the study of Byzantine Chant cannot be restricted to the treasury of melodies sung in the churches of the Empire, but that our studies must include its ramifications towards the Latin West, and also towards the Slavonic North and East.

A beginning has been made in both directions. We have already mentioned the Eastern elements in the West and their influence upon a re-appraisal of plain chant. Investigation into the Old Slavonic notation has confirmed what Russian musicologists[1] stated at the beginning of our century, i.e. that Byzantine Kanons, Kontakia, and Stichera were taken over by the Slavonic neighbours in the North, most probably the *Bulgars*, and transmitted to the Russians in Old Slavonic, a translation in which the stresses of the text correspond admirably to the high points of the melodic line.[2]

It would surpass the scope of the present book to discuss the problems of Old Slavonic notation and melody construction in relation to those of Byzantine music. We must leave such a discussion to scholars who have specialized in these subjects. The question of notation has recently been dealt with by Madame Palikarova Verdeil in her Doctorate thesis, *La Musique byzantine*

[1] The literature is given in O. Riesemann, 'Die Notationen des Alt-russischen Kirchengesanges', *Publikationen d. Int. Mus. Ges.*, Beihefte 2. Folge (1909).

[2] Prof. Roman Jakobson, Harvard University, spent several days in Jan. 1957 at the Dumbarton Oaks library in Washington and compared with me the setting of the words to the music; R. Jakobson from the point of view of Old Slavonic metrics, I from that of Greek accentuation. We both worked on the transcriptions made from the Chilandar fragments as a Harvard doctorate thesis, *The Byzantine Elements in Early Slavonic Chant* (1956), by M. Velimirović. The close relationship between Old Slavonic and Byzantine Chant can be studied from E. Koschmieder's 'Die ältesten Novgoroder Hirmologien-Fragmente', *Abhandl. d. Bayr. Akad. d. Wiss.*, *Philosoph.-hist. Kl.*, *N.F.* xxxv (1952), xxxvii (1955), who prints on the left the Old Slavonic Hirmologia and the Byzantine Cod. Coislin 220, and on the right parallels from a Russian seventeenth-century MS. in Krjuki notation.

chez les Bulgares et les Russes,[1] and the problems of melody construction have been expounded in a very comprehensive study by M. Velimirović.[2] There is, however, one point to be mentioned which seems to me of paramount importance, i.e. the imperative need of connecting our studies with those of Comparative Liturgiology.

On various occasions I pointed out that it was indispensable to place Byzantine hymnography in its liturgical environment. This became even more urgent when our studies were extended to the various forms of melismatic chant. The first opportunity of demonstrating the importance of bringing the chant into close relation with its liturgical function offered itself at the 'Symposium on Byzantine Liturgy and Music' at the Dumbarton Oaks Research Library and Collection in Washington in 1954, at which I read two papers on the subject: a general survey of 'Byzantine Music and its place in the Liturgy' and a special one on 'The Akathistos Hymn';[3] Oliver Strunk read a paper on 'The Byzantine Office in Hagia Sophia' in which he examined the 'Chanted Office of the Great Church' and the differences between monastic and non-monastic practice.[4] In the same way C. Höeg's *Tableau analytique* in the preface to the facsimile edition of the *Contacarium Ashburnhamense*[5] gives a clear and succinct guide to the liturgical function of the hymn, its connexion with the feast of a Saint or an Apostle.

The days have gone by when the text of a hymn was considered without bearing in mind that it was sung, not read; and when, on the other hand, artificial rhythmical schemes were introduced, without taking notice of the rhythmical signs with which Byzantine musical notation abounds. There is general agreement, at least among musicologists, that words and music are inseparably linked together and that the text should not be altered to bring it into conformity with that of other manuscripts on purely philological grounds. In my study of the text of the *Akathistos*[6] I ventured to say that the so-called south Italian manuscript tradition did not originate in the Basilean monasteries of Sicily and

1 *M.M.B. Subsidia*, vol. iii (1953).

2 Cf. note 2 above.

3 Cf. E. Wellesz, 'The Akathistos, A Study in Byzantine Hymnography', *Dumbarton Oaks Papers*, ix and x (1955/6), 141–74.

4 Cf. O. Strunk, 'The Byzantine Office at Hagia Sophia', ibid., pp. 175–202.

5 *M.M.B. Facsimilia*, vol. iv.

6 Cf. *M.M.B. Transcripta*, vol. ix, p. xxxv.

Calabria, but can be traced back to the St. Catherine's monastery on Mount Sinai and originated on Syro-Palestinean soil.[1]

As far as we can see at present the differences in text and melody can be reduced to two main groups of manuscripts: to those deriving from the monastic centre of Jerusalem and to those in use in the northern sphere of the Empire, representing the rite of the episcopal churches, above all that of Hagia Sophia, the Imperial Church of Constantinople; but as in Western liturgy the data which we gather from the manuscripts do not show a clear division. The struggle between the monasteries and the episcopal churches went on for many centuries, in the course of which both rites acquired elements from the opposite camp. It will be a most rewarding task to follow up the trend of thought developed by A. Baumstark in his two outstanding essays,[2] when the bulk of Byzantine Chant is available in print and to compare the result with that gained from parallel studies in Western Chant.

This brings us to the end of our survey. It can be seen from it that the hard work of generations of scholars was finally crowned with success. The main hindrances to a precise and reliable interpretation of the signs of the Byzantine musical notation from the end of the twelfth century have definitely been removed. At the same time great progress has been achieved in clarifying the character of the early phases of Byzantine musical notation. Work recently done in the field of our studies rests on a secure basis and need no longer be set out in this survey; it will be referred to at the appropriate place in this book and registered in the Bibliography.

Here I should like to emphasize once more that the study of the music of the Eastern Church is of far-reaching importance for the history of music in general. A great wealth of hitherto unknown music is being made accessible since the work of transcription of Byzantine neumes into modern staff notation has

[1] I am glad to say that Professor E. A. Lowe, to whom I told my line of thought in 1956, fully approved of my theory and presented me with his recently published study on 'An unknown Latin Psalter on Mount Sinai', *Scriptorium*, ix (1955), 177–99, in which he comes to the same conclusions. From a number of Kontakaria which were written on Mount Sinai it becomes evident that features of decoration and colour which were always regarded as typical of south Italian MSS. are actually characteristic of Sinaitic MSS. The same can be said about textual variants, with which we shall have to deal more extensively at the proper place.

[2] 'Das Typikon der Patmos-Handschrift 266 und die Altkonstantinopolitanische Gottesdienstordnung', *Jahrbuch für Liturgiewissenschaft*, vi (1923), 98–111; 'Denkmäler der Entstehungsgeschichte des byzantinischen Ritus', *O.C.*, Ser. III, vol. ii (1927), pp. 1–32.

begun. But the solution of the problem of Byzantine notation has had an even more important result: now that Byzantine music can be examined together with the Chant of the Latin Church it will be possible not only to investigate the common kernel which goes back to the days of Early Christianity, but also to investigate in both Eastern and Western Chant the origins of European ecclesiastical music.

CHAPTER I
THE ORIGINS OF BYZANTINE MUSIC

I. THE ORIENTAL HYPOTHESIS

IN A.D. 324 Constantine the Great, as part of his plan for the transformation of the pagan Roman Empire,[1] began to rebuild and fortify the small Greek town of Byzantium, with the intention of making it the capital of the Empire in the East. On 11 May 330 he attended its solemn inauguration and endowed it with the rights and privileges of Rome. From that time forward 'Byzantium' disappeared and the town took the name of New Rome (*Νέα Ῥώμη*) or Constantinople. In the few cases where the old word Byzantium or Byzantis does occur, the use is deliberately archaic.

The inhabitants of the Empire were called Romans (*Ῥωμαῖοι*), for, with Julian the Apostate's championship of Hellenism, the name 'Hellenes' (*Ἕλληνες*) and the conception of Hellenism fell into disrepute. It was not until the fourteenth century that a new classical movement began and we find 'Byzantium' used once again for Constantinople and 'Hellenes' for Romans, and then chiefly by Western writers who saw in Byzantine literature a continuation of Greek classical tradition. These pioneers of Byzantine scholarship, basing their argument principally on the fact that, although it had lost its old vigour, the language remained the same, succeeded in convincing the rest of the learned world that Byzantine civilization was nothing more nor less than the continuation of that of ancient Greece. Thus, from a linguistic point of view, Byzantine civilization came to be regarded as a coda to the ancient and the Hellenistic world.

In opposition to this theory the Oriental hypothesis has recently been put forward, emphasizing the influence of Semitic and even Iranian civilization on the Hellenized countries of the Near East which formed the most important part of the Byzantine Empire.[2]

After the penetration of the East by Alexander the Great, a

[1] Cf. S. Runciman, *Byzantine Civilization*[2] (London, 1936), p. 14.

[2] Cf. J. Strzygowski, *Orient oder Rom* (1901), *Kleinasien* (1903), *Altai-Iran und Völkerwanderung* (1917), *Origins of Christian Church Art* (1923); Ch. Diehl, *Manuel de l'Art byzantin*[2] (1925–6); O. M. Dalton, *East Christian Art* (1925), *Byzantine Art*; A. Baumstark, *Liturgie comparée* (1939).

penetration which reached beyond Gandhara as far as India, central Asia, and the Far East, military stations were established in all the conquered areas and the more important positions in the government entrusted to Greek officials. An attempt was made to Hellenize the whole of the Near East, but the policy was only rigorously and successfully pursued along the Mediterranean coast and where roads or rivers led inland. Away from the main roads and in the interior the native Eastern civilization was able to hold its own against that imposed by the ruling classes, and shortly after Alexander's death a reaction set in, culminating in an anti-Seleucid union between the newly formed Parthian Empire and Bactria, the farthest outpost of Hellenism in the East. The influence of this union extended over an area beyond the Hindu-Kush and the Pamir plateau, right into the steppes of Mongolia, and put an end to Greek ascendancy in the Near East. Thus Bactria was isolated, and obliged to face the attack of Mongolian nomad tribes which poured through the country into the Parthian Empire.

In the struggles which developed between Parthia and Rome, as heir of the Seleucids the position of Iran became increasingly important, her influence reaching its height when the Arsacid dynasty was replaced by the Sassanids, who consciously modelled their policy on the old Persian tradition of the times of the Achaemenids. The religious ideas of Iran spread westwards over the whole Mediterranean basin. The result was the inter-reaction of various cults which preceded the rise of Christianity and prepared the ground for its development.

While the supporters of the Oriental hypothesis rightly stressed the important role of Eastern and particularly Syro-Hellenistic elements in the formation of Byzantine civilization, they tended to underestimate the penetration of ideas from the West. In fact, the influences from both East and West were considered too much in isolation, without allowing for the assimilation and transformation of the heterogeneous foreign elements in the new ideas and conditions which were arising in the Empire itself.

It is now the generally accepted view that Byzantine civilization was essentially a fusion of Western and Eastern elements.[1] The legal and administrative machinery was Roman; Latin was the official language in Constantinople from its foundation up to

[1] Cf. D. Talbot Rice, *Byzantine Art* (1935), and Steven Runciman, *Byzantine Civilization* (1936).

the sixth century, when it was replaced by Greek. The city was built after the Roman pattern, with its temples and the Imperial court and its circus, theatres, baths, and other public buildings. Even its palaces are supposed to have been replicas of the Roman homes of the wealthy families which Constantine had induced to settle in the new capital.

Greek tradition, however, was preserved in all forms of cultural life. Greek classical literature was the basis of education and the Attic idiom had to be acquired with the aid of lexicon and grammar.[1] The libraries of Constantinople were filled with Greek manuscripts, the museums with art treasures drawn from all over the Greek Orient. Thus the citizen of the Eastern Empire was continually reminded of his Hellenic inheritance. But Greek classical civilization had lost its generative power. The heritage could be preserved; it could no longer be preserved alive. With the growth of Christianity and its establishment as the State religion under the Emperor as head of the Church, High-Priest of the Empire, the Greek way of life came definitely to an end. This new civilization, which had developed from the fusion of Graeco-Roman tradition with ideas infiltrating from the East, had a character of its own. The citizen of the Empire no longer considered himself a Hellene, but a Christian and a Byzantine.[2]

II. THE COMPOSITE CHARACTER OF BYZANTINE CIVILIZATION

Christianity began in Syria, one of the provinces on the outskirts of the Roman Empire, whose sphere of influence came to an end immediately behind the Lebanon. The province was administered by a Graeco-Roman governing class, the population including Aramaeans, Cappadocians, and Armenians, as well as the Jews. Differences in dogma and practice were to be found not only among the various Jewish sects but also in Orthodox Judaism itself, and in addition, the whole Jewish population was influenced by Hellenistic and Persian ideas. Hence, when the Jews and Gentiles of Palestine and Syria adopted the new teaching, which related religious ideas to the conduct of daily life, the civilization which arose was composed of many heterogeneous elements. This new Christian civilization spread to the east across Syria into Armenia and Mesopotamia, to the south into

[1] N. Baynes, *The Byzantine Empire*, The Home Univ. Libr. (1939), p. 165.
[2] Cf. S. Runciman, *Byzantine Civilization*, pp. 28–9.

Egypt, to the north into Asia Minor, attracting elements of the orientalized Hellenism of these countries, as well as others, purely Semitic and Iranian. Since the Eastern Empire was based on Christian principles, the blend of Hellenistic with Semitic and Iranian conceptions became more powerful as the Western influence declined after the collapse of the Empire in the West in the fifth century.

We shall have to bear in mind the composite character of Byzantine civilization in attempting to give a survey of the history of its music. We may say now that this will have to be principally an outline of Byzantine hymnography, since only in this most important branch of ecclesiastical music is there abundant documentary evidence at our disposal.

III. THE VOCAL CHARACTER OF BYZANTINE MUSIC

Byzantine ecclesiastical music was entirely vocal[1] and, whether chanted by one or more singers or by a choir, was always homophonic.[2] The liturgical books with musical signs can be divided into two groups: (1) those intended for the chanting of the Lessons, and (2) those containing chants to be sung during the Mass and Office. The pieces of the first group, the Lessons, had normally to be performed in a kind of chanting called *ekphonesis*, midway between recitation and singing. On very solemn feasts actual singing could replace this cantillation.

The second group comprises the entire *corpus cantilenarum* which, from Early Christian times to the apogee and right on to the decline of the Empire, played an ever-increasing role in Byzantine liturgy. The most important parts of the Mass and Office to be sung were (1) the psalms and canticles; (2) verses from psalms, or short poems composed on the same pattern; (3) the hymns, poems of various length, comparable in form and content to the Sequences and Tropes of the Western rites; and (4) the Alleluias. In addition to these main types of liturgical chants there were (5) the litanies and processional songs.

We shall have to study the different forms of Ecclesiastical

[1] The use of organs and other instruments was forbidden inside the churches. Portable organs were carried in processions, but had to be left outside the doors when the procession went into the church. On certain solemn occasions, however, the appearance of the Emperor in the church was celebrated by a brass band, which accompanied the *Polychronia*, i.e. the Acclamations of the singers wishing him a long life. Cf. Codinus Curopalates, *de Officiis*, ch. 6, *C.S.H.B.*, p. 149.

[2] Homophony is the technical term for music composed and performed in one single melodic line.

Chant in later chapters. Here we shall try to see how the various types may be classified into groups whose development is dependent on the development of Eastern liturgy. The investigation takes us back to the beginnings of Christianity.

In a passage of the Epistle to the Ephesians (v. 19) St. Paul tells the followers of Christ to speak to themselves 'in psalms and hymns and spiritual songs' (*ψαλμοῖς καὶ ὕμνοις καὶ ᾠδαῖς πνευματικαῖς*); similar advice is given in Col. iii. 16. It is clear from these passages that St. Paul considered music a proper means of worship. His authority was a strong argument against the hostile attitude adopted by Athanasius, and a certain ascetic tendency in Oriental monasticism which was the result of Monophysite ideas derived from the Persian Christians. It should be observed, however, that in both passages the Apostle speaks of 'singing in your hearts to the Lord', or, according to St. Chrysostom, 'from the heart' (*ᾄδοντες ἐν τῇ καρδίᾳ ὑμῶν τῷ κυρίῳ* Col. iii. 16, *ᾄδοντες καὶ ψάλλοντες τῇ καρδίᾳ ὑμῶν τ. κ.* Eph. v. 19).[1] He makes it clear that he does not mean singing for pleasure, but as the expression of a virtuous state of mind.

The meaning of the three terms *ψαλμοί, ὕμνοι*, and *ᾠδαὶ πνευματικαί* has been widely discussed ever since Origen, Basil, and Augustine first tried to explain them. It has been suggested by modern scholars that the three terms were used almost synonymously, and that Paul 'had no clear distinction in mind when he wrote', though they have to admit that since St. Jerome's day persistent efforts have been made to differentiate them.[2] However, from the context of the passage in the Epistle to the Colossians it is evident that St. Paul refers to a liturgical usage with which the readers of the epistle were well acquainted. The suggestion that psalm, hymn, and spiritual song were used synonymously for the same form of chant originated in patristic writings which date from a time when Christians no longer took part in the Jewish service, and had begun to compose hymns and odes on the pattern of the psalms and canticles. It should, however, be observed that these writers differentiate between *ode* and *ode pneumatike*. The term *ode* was eventually used for psalm or hymn, but *ode pneumatike*, the special kind of jubilant song to which St. Paul refers, has always its distinct meaning.

[1] Cf. L. B. Radford, *The Epistle to the Colossians*, Westminster Comment. (1931), pp. 285 sqq.

[2] Cf. A. B. Macdonald, *Christian Worship in the Primitive Church* (1934), pp. 113–14.

The individuality of psalm, hymn, and spiritual song is obvious to the student of comparative liturgiology. The three groups of chants of which the Apostle speaks correspond to the three different kinds of singing customary in the Byzantine ritual, as throughout the Eastern and Western Churches. It derived from the Jewish liturgy of the Synagogue which the followers of Christ used to attend daily, though, of course, the Christian community of Jerusalem went also to the Temple. From the Acts of the Apostles we know that after the descent of the Holy Spirit the newly baptized continued 'daily with one accord in the Temple, and breaking bread from house to house did eat their meat with gladness and singleness of heart, praising God, and having favour with all the people' (ii. 46, 47).

That the Christians continued to pray with the other members of the Jewish community is confirmed by another passage of the Acts: 'Peter and John went up together into the Temple at the hour of prayer, being the ninth hour' (iii. i). This shows that the Apostles attended the evening prayer,[1] the second of the two daily services of prayer and sacrifice, as described in Exod. xxix. 39, 40 and Lev. vi. 20. But it was from the Synagogue[2] that the Christian communities took over the tradition of reciting, chanting, and singing, as more fitting for their simple service than the elaborate rite of the Temple, with its great choirs and instrumental music.[3]

For training Christian congregations in singing, converted readers (*ἀναγνῶσται*) and precentors from the synagogues were chosen.[4] The *schola cantorum* sang from the Psalter which Esdras is said to have compiled for the Levites. The people answered with responses taken from a collection of short verses and liturgical formulae made for the use of the Jewish congregation. The acceptance of the Jewish institution of readers and precentors, specially trained for their office, made it possible to introduce into Christian worship antiphonal singing (as described in Exod. xv. 1 and 21 and Judges v. 1–31), and psalms sung by a soloist with responses from the congregation (as described in the second book

[1] Cf. *The Beginnings of Christianity*, ed. by F. J. Foakes Jackson and Kirsopp Lake, iii. 24–5. The reading of Cod. Bezae *ἀνέβαινον εἰς τὸ ἱερὸν τὸ δειλινὸν ἐπὶ τὴν ὥραν ἐνάτη⟨ν⟩* contains the addition *τὸ δειλινόν*, which is lacking in Cod. Vatic.

[2] Cf. L. Duchesne, *Origines du Culte chrétien*[5] (1925), pp. 48–9

[3] Cf. F. Leitner, *Der gottesdienstliche Volksgesang* (1906), p. 71.

[4] F. Leitner, op. cit., p. 195.

of the Apostolic Constitutions: 'after the reading of the two lections some one else must chant the hymns of David and the people must answer with the responses').[1]

Another kind of singing was taught in the schools of the prophets, referred to in 1 Sam. x. 5: ecstatic songs to the accompaniment of instruments, inspired chanting which filled with the Spirit of God the singers and those who listened, so that they received the gift of prophecy.

IV. THE LEGACY OF THE SYNAGOGUE

(*a*) *Psalmody*

In the early days of Christianity psalms were sung in the way customary in the Jewish Synagogue. The precentor sang the whole psalm, and the congregation responded after each verse with an interpolated phrase.[2] The performance varied from simple recitation to elaborate cantillation with the character of the feast and in accordance with the liturgical prescription for the particular part of the service. The service of the Temple, with its big choirs of singers, required a different and more splendid performance; there the psalms were sung by alternating choirs, accompanied by instruments, as we learn from various passages in the Old Testament.

The earliest evidence that the Psalter was sung by alternating choirs in Christian churches is to be found in the patristic writings of the fourth century, but we may assume that this was so from the beginning, since we know from Philo (b. *c.* 30 B.C.) that the

[1] *ἀνὰ δύο δὲ γενομένων ἀναγνωσμάτων, ἕτερός τις τοὺς τοῦ Δαυὶδ ψαλλέτω ὕμνους καὶ ὁ λαὸς τὰ ἀκρόστιχα ὑποψαλλέτω. Const. apost.* ii. 57. The term *ὑποψάλλειν* is used by patristic writers for singing responses; other terms are *ὑπηχεῖν* and *ὑπακούειν*. The terms for the substantive Response are: *ἀκροτελεύτιον, ἀκρόστιχον, ὑπακοή, ἐφύμνιον*. The phrase *ὁ λαὸς ἀκρόστιχα ὑποψαλλέτω* seems to indicate that the congregation answered with the first verse of the psalms, in which, in some cases, each verse began with a letter of the alphabet in order. From the *Lectionaria* we know that this kind of response with the repetition of the first verse of the first strophe was prescribed for the singing of certain hymns.

[2] The Byzantine Church took over the practice of inserting between the psalm verses short phrases which were called *ὑπόψαλμα*. The Antiphon (*ἀντίφωνον*) consists of verses, taken from a psalm, each of them answered by a recurring phrase. This can be shown from the Antiphon from the first psalm, sung by the lectors, the *ἀναγνῶσται*, during the Vigil of the Nativity. Cf. *Prophetologium*, i, p. 49.

στιχ. α′ Μακάριος ἀνήρ, ὃς οὐκ ἐπορεύθη ἐν βουλῇ ἀσεβῶν: (v. 1)
ἀντιλαβοῦ μου, Κύριε:
στιχ. β′ ὅτι γινώσκει Κύριος ὁδὸν δικαίων: (v. 6)
ἀντιλαβοῦ μου, Κύριε:
στιχ. γ′ καὶ ὁδὸς ἀσεβῶν ἀπολεῖται: (v. 6)
ἀντιλαβοῦ μου, Κύριε, κ.τ.λ.

practice was not confined to the service in the Temple. In a famous passage in the *De Vita Contemplativa* he speaks of the religious customs of the sect of the Therapeutae, who used to celebrate the vigil of the 'great festival' by singing first in two choirs of men and women, and finally uniting their voices, 'the high tones of the women blending with the deep ones of the men in antiphonal and alternating singing'.[1] Whether the Therapeutae were really Christians is irrelevant in this context; but it is important to learn that Eusebius, referring in his *Ecclesiastical History* to Philo's treatise, considers the description of the ceremony an obvious allusion to Christian worship, to 'the first heralds of teaching according to the Gospel and the customs handed down from the beginning by the Apostles'.[2]

The musical structure of the psalms consists of four elements: (1) an initial clausula leading to the note on which the verse is chanted; (2) the *tenor*, the repeated, or slightly changed note of recitation; (3) an occasional *mediant*, or half-cadence; (4) the *finalis*, a cadence, marking the end of the verse. The Church, trying to preserve as much as possible of the traditional way of singing, was particularly conservative in preserving the formulae of the psalm-tunes. The same applies to the Jewish liturgy as far as psalm-singing is concerned. The initial formulae and cadences of the psalm-tunes have changed so little that some of the *toni psalmorum*, sung to-day by Jews from Arabia, Persia, or Morocco are practically identical with those of the Roman Church in the tenth century, and only slightly different from the version now used. This can be seen from the following examples. The first is taken from the cantillation of Ps. lxxxi by Arabian Jews, the second gives the psalmody of two verses (1 and 2, first phrase) of Ps. xliv, according to the anonymous *Commemoratio brevis*, formerly ascribed to Hucbald (tenth century):[3]

[1] Cf. my *East. Elem.* i, ch. 4.

[2] Eusebius, *Eccles. Hist.* ii. 17. 24.

[3] The connexion between Jewish and Western liturgical melodies was discussed for the first time by A. Z. Idelsohn in an essay 'Parallelen zwischen gregorianischen und hebräisch-orientalischen Gesangsweisen', *Z.M.W.* iv (1921–2). It should be noted that the Plainchant versions do not correspond to the melodies of the new *Editio Vaticana*, and are not always rendered correctly. In the present case, for example, Idelsohn has not noticed that P. Wagner, from whose *Gregor.*

(2) α β γ
E - ru - cta -vit cor me - um ver-bum bo-num: dico &c.

α β δ_1
Lin - gu - a me - a ca - la - mus scri-bae: velociter &c.

In both melodies we find the same *initium* (α), the *tenor* on *a* (β), and the same mediant (γ); the final cadence of the Jewish psalm (δ) corresponds to the mediant of the second verse of the Latin psalm (δ_1). The fact that the final cadence of the Jewish chant occurs as a half-close in the Latin version needs a word of explanation. In Eastern melodies the formulae are not treated as rigidly as in Gregorian Chant, particularly in Gregorian psalmody. We shall see in the course of our investigations that in Byzantine melodies the same formulae can be used at the beginning, in the middle, and at the end of a chant. The relationship between the two melodies is the result of the same formulae being used in both psalms.

In the Byzantine Psalter a set of nine canticles was appended to the Psalms under the title 'The Nine Odes' (*Αἱ Ἐννέα ᾨδαί*). In the Early Christian liturgy a larger number of canticles was available for the Divine Service than when the Byzantine liturgy was fully developed. The Codex Alexandrinus of the early fifth century contains the following canticles:*

(1) The song of Moses after the passage through the Red Sea (Exod. xv. 1–19): *ᾌσωμεν τῷ Κυρίῳ, ἐνδόξως γὰρ δεδόξασται . . .*
(2) The song of Moses before his death (Deut. xxxii. 1–43): *Πρόσεχε, οὐρανέ, καὶ λαλήσω . . .*
(3) The prayer of Hannah (1 Sam. ii. 1–10): *Ἐστερεώθη ἡ καρδία μου ἐν Κυρίῳ . . .*
(4) The prayer of Isaiah (Isa. xxvi. 9–19): *Ἐκ νυκτὸς ὀρθρίζει τὸ πνεῦμά μου πρὸς σέ, ὁ Θεός . . .*

Formenlehre, p. 92, he takes the psalm-tune of *Eructavit*, does not print the full verse, but only the first semi-cola of each verse and the beginning of the second colon. Nevertheless, Idelsohn's article, illustrated by many examples, is a very important contribution to studies connected with the origin of Early Christian music. More examples are given in E. Werner's 'Preliminary notes for a comparative study of Catholic and Jewish musical punctuation', *Hebrew Union College Annual*, vol. xv (1940), pp. 335–66.

(5) The prayer of Jonah (Jonah ii. 3–10): *'Εβόησα ἐν θλίψει μου πρὸς Κύριον τὸν Θεόν μου . . .*
(6) The prayer of Habakkuk (Hab. iii. 2–19): *Κύριε, εἰσακήκοα τὴν ἀκοήν σου καὶ ἐφοβήθην . . .*
(7) The prayer of Hezekiah (Isa. xxxviii. 10–20): *'Εγὼ εἶπα ἐν τῷ ὕψει τῶν ἡμερῶν μου . . .*
(8) The prayer of Manasses (Apocrypha): *Κύριε παντοκράτορ . . .*
(9) The prayer of Azariah (Dan. iii. 26–45): *Εὐλογητὸς εἶ, Κύριε ὁ Θεὸς τῶν πατέρων ἡμῶν . . . ὅτι δίκαιος εἶ ἐπὶ πᾶσιν . . .*
(10) The song of the Three Children (Dan. iii. 52–88): *Εὐλογητὸς εἶ, Κύριε ὁ Θεὸς τῶν πατέρων ἡμῶν . . . καὶ εὐλογημένον τὸ ὄνομα . . .*
(11) The prayer of Mary, the Theotokos (Luke i. 46–55): *Μεγαλύνει ἡ ψυχή μου τὸν Κύριον . . .*
(12) The prayer of Simeon (Luke ii. 29–32): *Νῦν ἀπολύεις τὸν δοῦλόν σου, Δέσποτα . . .*
(13) The prayer of Zacharias (Luke i. 68–79): *Εὐλογητὸς Κύριος ὁ Θεὸς τοῦ 'Ισραήλ . . .*
(14) The Morning Hymn: *Δόξα ἐν ὑψίστοις Θεῷ . . .*

From these canticles[1] a few were selected for the daily service. The first to be used was the Song of Moses from Exodus and the Song of the Three Children. In the Church of Jerusalem in the fifth century they were introduced after the sixth and twelfth Lessons which were read during the Vigil of Easter Day.[2]

We do not know when the 'Nine Odes' were introduced as a set into the Office of Lauds, the *"Ορθρος*; there are liturgical reasons for believing that they were adopted in the Byzantine Church before the year 550.[3]

The 'Nine Odes' are:

(1) *"ΑΙσωμεν* (Exod. xv. 1–19).
(2) *Πρόσεχε* (Deut. xxxii. 1–43).
(3) *'Εστερεώθη* (1 Sam. ii. 1–10).
(4) *Κύριε, εἰσακήκοα* (Hab. iii. 2–19)
(5) *'Εκ νυκτός* (Isa. xxvi. 9–19).
(6) *'Εβόησα* (Jonah ii. 3–10).
(7*a*) *Εὐλογητὸς εἶ . . . ὅτι* (Dan. iii. 26–45).
(7*b*) *Εὐλογητὸς εἶ . . . καί* (Dan. iii. 52–6).
(8) *Εὐλογεῖτε πάντα* (Dan. iii. 57–88).
(9*a*) *Μεγαλύνει* (Luke i. 46–55).
(9*b*) *Εὐλογητὸς Κύριος* (Luke i. 68–79).

[1] Cf. H. Schneider, 'Die biblischen Oden im christl. Altertum', *Biblica*, xxx (1949), 52–7.
[2] A. Baumstark, *Liturgie comparée*, pp. 37–8.
[3] J. Mearns, *The Canticles*, p. 2.

The canticles were sung by a soloist, the people responding after each verse, or group of two verses, with a refrain taken from the first line of the canticle. It can be seen from the rubrics in the *Prophetologium*[1] how the Song of Moses from Exodus was sung on Good Friday. One of the chanters (*ψάλτης*) goes up to the pulpit (*ἄμβων*) and announces: 'The Song from Exodus'. And then the deacon: 'Attention'. And the Psaltes immediately says:

Ὠδὴ τῆς Ἐξόδου.

ὁ ψάλτης: Ἄσωμεν τῷ Κυρίῳ, ἐνδόξως γὰρ δεδόξασται:
ὁ λαός: Ἄσωμεν τῷ Κυρίῳ, ἐνδόξως γὰρ δεδόξασται:
ὁ ψάλτης: Ἵππον καὶ ἀναβάτην ἔρριψεν εἰς θάλασσαν:
Ἐνδόξως γὰρ δεδόξασται:
Βοηθὸς καὶ σκεπαστὴς ἐγένετό μοι εἰς σωτηρίαν:
Ἐνδόξως γὰρ δεδόξασται:
ὁ λαός: Ἄσωμεν τῷ Κυρίῳ, ἐνδόξως γὰρ δεδόξασται.

(*the precentor:* Let us sing unto the Lord, for he hath triumphed gloriously:
the people: Let us sing unto the Lord, for he hath triumphed gloriously:
the precentor: The horse and the rider hath he thrown into the sea:
the people: For he hath triumphed gloriously:
the precentor: The Lord is my strength and my protector, and he is become my salvation:
For he hath triumphed gloriously:
the people: Let us sing unto the Lord, for he hath triumphed gloriously.)

All eighteen verses of the canticle are sung in this way. To the last verse is appended the 'Little Doxology', followed by the refrain of the chanter, and the response of the congregation:

ὁ ψάλτης: Δόξα Πατρὶ καὶ Υἱῷ καὶ ἁγίῳ Πνεύματι:
Ἐνδόξως γὰρ δεδόξασται:
ὁ λαός: Ἄσωμεν τῷ Κυρίῳ, ἐνδόξως γὰρ δεδόξασται:
ὁ ψάλτης: Καὶ νῦν καὶ ἀεὶ καὶ εἰς αἰῶνας τῶν αἰώνων, ἀμήν:
Ἐνδόξως γὰρ δεδόξασται:
ὁ λαός: Ἄσωμεν τῷ Κυρίῳ, ἐνδόξως γὰρ δεδόξασται:
ὁ ψάλτης: Ἄσωμεν τῷ Κυρίῳ, ἐνδόξως γὰρ δεδόξασται:
ὁ λαός: Ἐνδόξως γὰρ δεδόξασται.

(*the precentor:* Glory be to the Father and the Son and the Holy Spirit:
For he hath triumphed gloriously:

[1] Cf. MSS. Laud. gr. 36 fol. and Barocc. 99 fol. of the Bodl. Oxford. A critical edition of the *Prophetologium* has been started by C. Höeg and G. Zuntz in *Monumenta Musicae Byzantinae: Lectionaria*, edited by C. Höeg and Silva Lake: vols. i (1939), ii (1940), iii (1952).

the people: Let us sing unto the Lord, for he hath triumphed gloriously:
the precentor: Now and ever, and to ages of ages, amen:
For he hath triumphed gloriously:
the people: Let us sing unto the Lord, for he hath triumphed gloriously:
the precentor: Let us sing unto the Lord, for he hath triumphed gloriously:
the people: For he hath triumphed gloriously.)

The combination of each half-verse of the Doxology with *Ἐνδόξως γὰρ δεδόξασται*, the refrain of the Ode, created a new poetical form, in which text and music were of equal importance. The performance of the Ode by a precentor with responses from the congregation seems to have been the liturgical usage for smaller churches; the rubrics of other *Lectionaria* show that the canticles were also performed by a group of chanters. *

(*b*) *Hymns*

The hymns were sung to melodies ranging from a simple syllabic type to chants in which two or three groups of notes could be sung to one syllable of the text. In the Byzantine, as in the other branches of the Eastern Church, ecclesiastical poetry gave the *melōdos* or poet-composer the opportunity to exercise his talents in the writing of hymns. He could either write new words to already existing chants, adapting them melodically and rhythmically to the new poem, or he could compose a new melody. It is only in this group, the hymns, that the names of the composers are preserved.

We shall have to go into the rather involved question of the origin of the genre in the chapter on the texts of Byzantine ecclesiastical poetry. It does not present such a simple problem as in the case of the psalms, since the texts of the greater part of the group were subject to changes, and new poems, written on the pattern of the old, were constantly replacing them. It is obvious from the hymns, or fragments of hymns, preserved in the New Testament that their original purpose was the praise of God. Like the chanting of psalms, the singing of hymns was a religious custom deeply rooted in the practice of Temple and Synagogue and consequently familiar to the first generation of Christians. But because these hymns were free paraphrases of the text, and were not based exclusively on the words of the Scriptures, there was an orthodox reaction against them in the middle of the third century. All new hymns were condemned, and only those to be found in the Scriptures were tolerated. This measure explains why so few hymns survive from the beginnings of Christianity. But they played too large and important a part in religious life to be completely suppressed. They had embellished the liturgy; their loss was felt to decrease its splendour. The Church, particularly the Church in the East, had to change its attitude. By altering passages containing heretical doctrines, and by putting new words to melodies of pagan or gnostic poetry, the old practice was restored, and hymnography developed more richly than before.

(*c*) *Spiritual Songs*

The third group comprises chants of the melismatic type, the most important part of which are the Alleluias. In his exposition of the ninety-ninth Psalm St. Augustine describes the character of the songs of exultation: 'He who jubilates, speaks no words; it is a song of joy without words.'[1] The *ᾠδαὶ πνευματικαί*, the 'spiritual songs' of which St. Paul speaks, were obviously the melismatic melodies of the Alleluias and other exultant songs of praise, which, again, the Jewish Christians brought with them from the Temple and the Synagogue into the Christian Church. The Hebrew word itself has not been translated by either the Greek or the Latin Church, and it has always been assumed that the chants derived from the Jewish liturgy. Isidore of Seville, as early as 636, suggested a Hebrew origin for the singing of the *Alleluia-iubili*: 'Laudes, hoc est alleluia, canere, canticum est Hebraeorum.'[2] This view is supported by the musical structure of the Alleluias of the Ambrosian rite, the oldest specimens of the type which survive in manuscripts.

V. CONCLUSION

From all these considerations it is evident that the groups of chants of which St. Paul speaks correspond to actual liturgical usages, and that the Christians to whom the Epistles were addressed would have understood the meaning of each term and

[1] 'Qui iubilat, non verba dicit, sed sonus quidam est laetitiae sine verbis: vox est enim animi diffusi laetitia, quantum potest exprimentis affectum, non sensum comprehendentis. Gaudens homo in exsultatione sua ex verbis quibusdam, quae non possunt dici et intellegi, erumpit in vocem quandam exultationis sine verbis; ita ut appareat, eum ipsa voce gaudere quidem, sed quasi repletum nimio gaudio, non posse verbis explicare quod gaudet.' *Enarr. in Ps. xcix.* 4, *P.L.* xxxvii, c. 1272.

[2] *De off. eccl.* i. 13; *P.L.* xxxiii, c. 750.

have been able to differentiate between them. The continuity in the development of Eastern Chant from Early Christian times to the apogee of hymnography allows us to adopt the same classification, and to divide Byzantine liturgical chant into the following three groups:

(1) Psalmody (Psalms and Canticles).
(2) Hymns (Verses, Stanzas and Hymns, Litanies and Processional songs).
(3) Spiritual Songs (Alleluias, Songs of Praise).

It should be understood that, musically, no absolute differentiation between the three groups is possible. Psalmody includes recitation by alternating choirs and the singing of simple psalm-tunes; even, on special occasions, melodies of a more ornamented type sung by a soloist. Hymns range from simple syllabic songs to richly embellished chants. Finally, there are some Spiritual Songs which are similar to the more elaborate hymns, sung at solemn feasts, while others are so richly ornamented that the words, drawn out over long groups of melismata, are no longer intelligible.

This kind of melismatic ornamentation, which is found in the earliest group of Spiritual Songs, should not be confused with the lavish *coloraturas* of late Byzantine and Neo-Greek melodies. The process of melodic development which ultimately changed the character of Byzantine Chant by indulging a tendency towards ever-increasing embellishment until the structure of the original melody is made unrecognizable by the exuberance of the ornamentation, will have to be discussed in a later chapter. From the point of view of musical composition, the difference between melismatic style and *coloratura* can be defined as follows: the melismata are organic elements of a melody, they form part of the structure. The *coloraturas* are embellishments, deriving from an originally simpler melodic structure; they can be reduced or extended, without affecting the main structure of the chant.

When we consider these three main forms of ecclesiastical music it is obvious that, from the very beginning of Christian worship, liturgical chant was an integral part of the service. Its development is inseparably bound up with that of the liturgy, and, although only a few fragments of music are preserved in documents of Early Christian times, we may assume that a core of Byzantine chant, as of Plainsong, goes back to the early days of the Church and therefore to the practice of the Christian communities in Palestine and Syria. This has been only recently accepted by students working on the development of Christian music. For a long time the view was held that Byzantine chant derived from Greek classical music and that Plainsong originated in Rome or, according to a modified theory, in the Eastern Empire.

As we noticed in the Introduction, most of the work on this subject has been done by scholars who approached the problem from the point of view of Western chant. No theory of the origin of Plainsong can be conclusive which does not take into account its relationship to Byzantine music, but we must bear in mind that even such a preliminary investigation as the comparison of manuscripts of Byzantine melodies with specimens of Western chant[1] was impossible until the problem of Byzantine notation was solved. Once these Byzantine melodies were considered in relation to the oldest stratum of Western chant, the so-called Ambrosian melodies, previous theories became untenable. It is obvious that the oldest versions of both Byzantine and Gregorian melodies go back to a common source, the music of the Churches of Antioch and Jerusalem, which in their turn derived from the music of the Jews. On the pattern of these melodies both the Eastern and Western Churches developed their own ecclesiastical music, adding to and transforming their originals as the necessities of their different rites demanded.

In view of these facts we shall have to consider, in the course of this book, how far this oldest layer was preserved in Byzantine hymnography, and what kind of alterations occurred when the melodies sung to Syriac texts were adapted to Greek. We shall expect to find that new Byzantine hymns were not, in fact, new compositions, but were made on the pattern of older melodies, though hymns were added to the Byzantine treasury from pagan, heretical, and, later, European sources. Originally, like Plainsong in the West, Byzantine music was a foreign element in the Greek-speaking parts of the Eastern Empire. It was the remarkable achievement of Byzantine Christianity that the chants of the Early Church became an intrinsic part of Byzantine civilization.

[1] The first attempt to tackle a problem which needs more extensive investigation can be seen in the present writer's *Eastern Elements in Western Chant*.

We may conveniently consider here what foundation there is for the view, which still finds advocates, that Byzantine Chant was an offspring of Greek classical music. There are three main reasons for the misconception: (1) the fact that the melodies were sung to Greek words; (2) the existence of the Byzantine musical modes, the eight *echoi*, which were thought to be derived from the Greek modes; (3) the aesthetic conceptions of Early Christian and Byzantine theorists, who based their views on Greek philosophers, particularly Plato and his school.

We have already dealt briefly with the first argument and we shall have to return to it when we are discussing the origins of Byzantine ecclesiastical poetry. A. Baumstark's studies on the translations of Syriac liturgical poetry into Greek and P. Maas's investigations into Early Byzantine poetry finally disposed of it.[1]

The second argument is equally ill founded. The Byzantine system of eight modes, the *Oktoëchos*, ascribed to John Damascene (born towards the end of the seventh century), actually goes back to the *Oktoëchos* of Severus, the Monophysite Patriarch of Antioch (512–19).[2] The choice of eight for the number of modes may have been due to Hellenistic influences in Antioch. In all rites of the Eastern Church the character of a chant is determined by the occurrence of certain melodic formulae, rather than, as in Greek music, because it is based on a particular mode.[3]

The third argument is only valid if we ignore those Greek theorists who were no longer familiar to the monks composing for and singing in the Byzantine Church, and limit our comparison to those writers on music who discussed its essence and its effect on the listener. We shall consider, in later chapters, the survival of ancient Greek musical theory in Early Christian times, and the attitude towards music in the pagan world, in the midst of which Byzantine Christian civilization developed. We shall see that Christian music, deriving from a Syriac-speaking province, was quickly assimilated into Byzantine civilization. It was

[1] P. Maas, 'Das Kontakion', *B.Z.* 1910; A. Baumstark, 'Vom geschichtlichen Werden der Liturgie', *Ecclesia Orans*, x (1923), 103–9.

[2] Dom J. Jeannin and Dom J. Puyade, 'L'Octoëchos syrien', *O.C.*, N.S. iii (1913), 87.

[3] The occurrence of certain formulae as typical elements of the modal system was first pointed out by Jeannin and Puyade in their study on the Syrian Oktoëchos, op. cit., p. 278, by A. Idelsohn in his article 'Die Maqamen der arabischen Musik', *S.I.M.* xv (1914), 1 sqq., and by the present writer in 'Die Struktur d. serbischen Oktoëchos', *Z.M.W.* ii (1919), 140 sqq. The combination of formulae as the leading principle of Byzantine musical composition is widely discussed in the present writer's *Eastern Elements in Western Chant*, Part II A, ch. 2, 'The Technique of Musical Composition'.

judged by patristic writers by the same standards which Platonic and Neoplatonic philosophers applied to manifestations of divine Beauty. The rigid attitude of the ascetic monastic communities, which condemned the use of music, was overcome by the efforts of the Emperor and the high ranks of the clergy, who wanted to adorn the Divine Office with all the splendour which architecture, the arts, music, and poetry could provide. The ascendancy of this point of view can be seen from Paul the Silentiary's poetical description of St. Sophia. The poet describes in ornate language every part of the interior and finally the Narthex, where the singers chant the psalms:

ἔνθα δέ τις κατὰ νυκτὰ διαμπερὲς ἦχος ἀνέρπων
εὐκέλαδος Χριστοῖο βιαρκέος οὔατα θέλγει,
ὁππόθι τιμήεντα θεουδέος ὄργια Δαυὶδ
ἀντιπόροις ἰαχῇσιν ἀείδεται ἀνδράσι μύστηις
Δαυὶδ πρηϋνόοιο. . . .

(Here, through the night, without a break, springs up a melodious chant, pleasing to the ears of the life-giving Christ, where the precious rites of David the God-fearing are sung in alternating strains by the initiates of David the gentle minded.)

The passage shows clearly—and, indeed, typically—the approach of an author in Early Byzantine times to that part of Christian liturgy which was regarded as a legacy from the Jewish religion. Here the nocturnal singing of the Davidic Psalter is described in words which would be equally appropriate to a Greek song in the days of Homer. The subject is Christian, but the cultural background of the poet is still that of the Greek classical tradition. On the other hand, we shall find that the spirit of the poetry no longer produces in the listener the immediate effect of Greek classical verse. The style is elaborate and involved. The author makes use of that kind of Graeco-Oriental versification which originated and was developed in the rhetorical schools of the Hellenistic cities of Syria. Similar stylistic features can be found in all Byzantine art, demonstrating the complex character of the new civilization which, far from being sterile, combined elements from the past and the present in a new synthesis, perfected through the link of a common tongue, the Greek language.

CHAPTER II

THE SURVIVAL OF GREEK MUSICAL THEORY

I. THE PRINCIPLES OF GREEK MUSICAL THEORY

THE starting-point of Greek musical theory is the Pythagorean assertion that the soul is a kind of harmony (*ἁρμονίαν γάρ τινα αὐτὴν λέγουσι*), since harmony is 'a blending and combining of opposites' (*κρᾶσις καὶ σύνθεσις ἐναντίων*).[1] This blending is identical with *harmonia*, the fundamental principle in Greek musical theory. Here the term stands for the proper building up and arranging of the intervals constituting one of the musical modes. Since all the intervals of a mode had to be put together in an appropriate order, the term *harmonia* is also used for the mode itself. It is by the properly organized succession of intervals that the *ethos* (*ἦθος*) or character of a mode is defined. According to the *Pseudo-Aristotelian Problems*, an important source of our knowledge of Greek musical theory, *ethos* can be found only in an organized progression of intervals, not in the sounding together of two tones of different pitch, since the simultaneous sound of tones does not produce *ethos* (*ἡ συμφωνία οὐκ ἔχει ἦθος*).[2] Each mode has its own character and moral significance.[3] This ethical conception of music is already to be found in Pythagorean philosophy, where the faculty of improving character (*ἐπανόρθωσις τῶν ἠθῶν*) is associated with this art.[4]

The ethical conception of the modes is not confined to Ancient Greek music. It can also be found in Chinese, Indian, and Arabic musical treatises. Each Indian mode (*rāga*), for example, is con-

[1] Aristotle, *de Anima* 407b–408a. J. Burnet, referring to this view in *Early Greek Philosophy*[4], pp. 295–6, writes that it cannot have belonged to the earliest form of Pythagoreanism; for, 'as shown in Plato's *Phaedo* (86c–92B), it is quite inconsistent with the idea that the soul can exist independently of the body'. The earliest reference to the use of *ἁρμονία* and *ἦθος* (see n. 4, p. 38) as musical terms is to be found in a fragment of Damon quoted by Aristides Quintilianus in *de Musica*, ii. 14 (Meib., p. 95), ed. A. Jahn, p. 58: *ἐν γοῦν ταῖς ὑπ' αὐτοῦ* [i.e. Damon] *παραδεδομέναις ἁρμονίαις τῶν φερομένων φθόγγων ὁτὲ μὲν τοὺς θήλεις, ὁτὲ δὲ τοὺς ἄρρενας ἔστιν εὑρεῖν ἤτοι πλεονάζοντας, ἢ ἐπ' ἔλαττον ἢ οὐδ' ὅλως παρειλημμένους, δῆλον ὡς κατὰ τὸ ἦθος ψυχῆς ἑκάστης καὶ ἁρμονίας χρησιμευούσης*. Cf. H. Diels, *Die Fragmente der Vorsokratiker*[6], i. 384.

[2] *Probl.* 27, ed. Jan, p. 93.

[3] Cf. Plato, *Rep.* iii. 398 C–9 D and Aristotle, *Pol.* viii. 7. 1342 a, b.

[4] *καὶ διὰ τοῦτο μουσικὴν ἐκάλεσε Πλάτων καὶ ἔτι πρότερον οἱ Πυθαγόρειοι τὴν φιλοσοφίαν, καὶ καθ' ἁρμονίαν τὸν κόσμον συνεστάναι φασί, πᾶν τὸ μουσικὸν εἶδος θεῶν ἔργον ὑπολαμβάνοντες· . . . ὡσαύτως δὲ καὶ τὴν τῶν ἠθῶν κατασκευὴν τῇ μουσικῇ προσνέμουσιν, ὡς πᾶν τὸ ἐπανορθωτικὸν τοῦ νοῦ τοῖς θεοῖς ἐγγὺς ὄν*. Strabo Geographus, x. 3. 10, ed. A. Meineke, Bibl. Teubn., vol. ii, p. 658, ll. 8 sqq.

nected with a god or goddess, and images of deities, representing the different *rāgas*, are a favourite subject of Indian miniature-painting.[1] The rules given in the Chinese *Book of Ceremonies* are even more rigid than those of Plato in his *Republic*: certain melodies must be played in the morning, others only in the evening, otherwise they cause disorder. Certain instruments can be used only by a restricted number of persons of high rank.[2] From comparative studies in Eastern musical theory we may conclude that the scales which have been accepted as basic formulae of the modes must have been abstracted from songs or melodies of a certain type, all of them built up on the same sequence of intervals. Taking the scale of a mode for the mode itself we may speak of it 'as the epitome of stylized song'.[3] We may also accept the definition of the Lydian *harmonia* as 'the anatomy of the Lydian *melodia*'.[4] Investigations in other fields of the history of music have shown that the theory which regarded 'scale' or mode as the basis of musical composition can no longer be maintained. The original meaning of *harmonia* in musical practice, therefore, must have been connected with the correct relationship of musical formulae in a group of melodies built up on the same modal scheme. The use of *harmonia* for the mode itself in Platonic philosophy and musical theory should not obscure the fact that musical theory always tries to reduce musical practice to a scheme, as the practice becomes complicated and it is found necessary to draw up rules in order to prevent confusion. We shall have to come back to this question when we deal with the modes in Byzantine music.

Nicomachus of Gerasa[5] ascribes to Pythagoras the discovery that the perfect consonances, which are the basic intervals in a mode, are expressible in terms of the ratios of the numbers 1, 2, 3, 4. If the string is divided in the ratio of 2 : 1 it gives the octave, of 3 : 2 the fifth, of 4 : 3 the fourth.[6] By adding up the four numbers $1+2+3+4 = 10$ the *tetractys* of the decade was reached, that by which the Pythagoreans swore.[7]

The doctrine of the Pythagoreans having originated from

[1] Cf. R. Lachmann, *Musik d. Orients* (1929), pp. 54–64.
[2] Cf. L. Laloy, *La Musique chinoise*, pp. 11 sqq.
[3] R. P. Winnington-Ingram, *Mode in Ancient Greek Music*, p. 3.
[4] M. I. Henderson, 'The Growth of the Greek *ἉΡΜΟΝΙΑΙ*', *C.Q.* xxxvi. 97.
[5] *Harmonikon Encheiridion*, ed. Jan in *Mus. Script. Gr.*, p. 244. 14.
[6] Cf. T. Heath, *A History of Greek Mathematics*, i. 69.
[7] Cf. J. Burnet, *Early Greek Philosophy*[4], p. 102, and Aristotle's *Metaphysics*, i. 145–6, ed. Ross.

speculations in the field of music, we may well understand the conclusion to which they came, referred to by Aristotle in his *Metaphysics* that 'numbers are the substance of things in the whole of nature' and the whole heaven is 'a *harmonia* and a number'.[1] This theory was developed in the *Timaeus* of Plato by combining the Empedoclean theory of the 'four roots of all things', the elementary bodies—fire, air, earth, and water—with the Pythagorean system of geometrical figures.[2] The school of medicine, which regarded Empedocles as its founder, and which was still flourishing in the days of Plato, identified the four elements with the 'opposites', the hot and the cold, the moist and the dry. By mingling the four elements in different proportions the organic world was created. But while the innumerable forms of being are always passing away, these ultimate forms of reality are immortal.[3]

According to the *Timaeus* the World-Soul was blended by the Demiurge from three ingredients: (1) an intermediate form of Existence (οὐσίας εἶδος), compounded out of indivisible Existence 'that is ever in the same state', and the divisible Existence 'that becomes in bodies'; (2) an intermediate Sameness, and (3) an intermediate Difference, both compounded on the same principle. Having compounded these constituents, the Demiurge divided the mixture in the proportions of a musical *harmonia*. Out of the material so compounded and divided he then constructed a system of circles representing the principal motions of the stars and planets.[4]

Human souls are made in the same mixing-bowl, from what remained of the material. They are blended from the same ingredients, but it is a fresh brew, 'no longer so pure as before, but second or third in degree of purity. And when he had mixed the whole, he divided it into souls equal in number with the stars, and distributed them, each soul to each several star.'[5] The human soul, therefore, is divided in the ratios of the same *harmonia* as the World-Soul; it is in a constant motion, regulated according to the same ratios as the stars.[6]

[1] Aristotle, *Meta.* i. 5. 986a.

[2] Cf. J. Burnet, *Early Greek Philosophy*[4], 1930, pp. 228–30. A. E. Taylor points out 'that the formula for the physics and physiology of the dialogue is that it is an attempt to graft Empedoclean biology on the stock of Pythagorean mathematics' (*A Commentary on Plato's Timaeus*, p. 18).

[3] Cf. Burnet, *Early Greek Philosophy*[4], pp. 205–6, 239 sqq.

[4] Cf. F. M. Cornford, *Plato's Cosmology, The Timaeus of Plato*, pp. 59–67.

[5] *Timaeus*, 41 D.

[6] Cf. Aristotle, *De Anima*, 407a.

The compounding of the ingredients, both of the World-Soul and of the human soul in conformity with definite mathematical ratios, produces an attunement of the parts and, as 'like is known by like', a harmony between the World-Soul and the human soul which is in perfect order. As the ratios of the circles in our souls correspond to the melodic intervals, music, as far as it uses audible sound, was bestowed upon mankind as a gift from heaven for the sake of harmony. 'And harmony, whose motions are akin to the revolutions of the soul within us, has been given by the Muses to him whose commerce with them is guided by intelligence, not for the sake of irrational pleasure (which is now thought to be its utility) but as an ally against the inward discord that has come into the revolution of the soul, to bring it into order and consonance with itself. Rhythm also was a succour bestowed upon us by the same hands to the same intent, because in the most part of us our condition is lacking in measure and poor in grace.'[1]

Music, therefore, is a most excellent training, because rhythm and harmony find their way into the inner parts of the soul 'imparting grace, and making the soul of him who is rightly educated graceful'.[2] Our souls resound with the same harmonies as the cosmos, because the circles in our souls can execute revolutions answering those of the cosmos. But it is only through philosophy that we are able to attain to this highest music, as our circles are thrown out of gear by birth.[3] Consequently music has the power to lead back the soul from the state of unrest to that of harmony,[4] to correct the character,[5] to heal mental diseases.[6] On this power Greek philosophers from Plato onwards laid particular stress; for the same reason they considered music to be a perfect instrument of education. Plato grants music an important role in the education of the young in the ideal State.[7] Training in music is a

[1] *Timaeus* 47 D–E, trans. Cornford. Plato contrasts the ideal task of music with the debased use which is made of it in his times (*οὐκ ἐφ' ἡδονὴν ἄλογον καθάπερ νῦν εἶναι δοκεῖ χρήσιμος*).

[2] *Rep.* iii. 401 D, trans. Jowett.

[3] Cf. A. E. Taylor, *Commentary on Plato's Timaeus*, p. 296.

[4] Aristotle, *Pol.* 1342ᵃ. Cf. Ptolemy, *Harm.* iii. 7.

[5] Strabo i. 2. 3 and x. 3. 10. Cf. Philodem. *de Mus.* 100. 30; Arist. Quintil. *de Mus.*, p. 64 (ed. Jahn, p. 41): *τί δὴ θαυμάζομεν εἰ συνέβη τοὺς παλαιοὺς πλείστην ἐπανόρθωσιν πεποιῆσθαι διὰ μουσικῆς;*

[6] Iamblichus, *V. Pyth.* 110, calls this kind of treatment of mental diseases *κάθαρσις*. Cf. H. Abert, *Die Lehre vom Ethos in der griechischen Musik* (Leipzig, 1899). Abert's book is still the best source for the study of the ethical side of Greek musical theory.

[7] *Rep.* iii. 398 C–401 A; *Laws*, ii. 653 A sqq., 656 C, 660 E sqq., 668 A, C sqq., 671 D, vii. 800 A sqq., 813 A.

preparation for the study of philosophy.[1] The State, therefore, cannot tolerate arbitrary innovations,[2] for any musical innovation may prove to be dangerous for the whole State.[3]

The conception of a correspondence between Cosmic and musical harmony, as expounded in the *Timaeus*, makes a purely aesthetic appreciation of music, as an art, impossible. This attitude is of importance for the understanding of Platonic and Neoplatonic musical theory. Music of the highest quality must of necessity be beautiful, because the creative artist imitates the *harmoniai* according to which the circles of the soul revolve. But his work could never transmit the perfection of the cosmic *harmoniai*, because the human soul is blended of a mixture inferior in quality to that from which the World-Soul was compounded. In other dialogues Plato has expounded more fully his view of the artist as an imitator,[4] but these various discourses on imitation (*μίμησις*) do not make the question less obscure, as he uses the term *μίμησις* and its cognates in two senses, a good and a bad. The artist imitates in the good sense if he imitates the ideal model; in the bad, if he copies external characteristics.[5] Plato stresses the dangerous influence of art, especially music, if it aims at giving pleasure by imitating the world of appearances. It is not this type of music to which we should aspire 'but that other which retains its likeness to the model of the noble (*τῷ τοῦ καλοῦ μιμήματι*)'. The citizens of Plato's State 'will also have to aim not at a music which is pleasing, but at one which is right'.[6] They are helped in this noble aspiration by the mysterious connexion which Plato and the Pythagoreans believed to exist between the ratios on which the musical *harmoniai* are based and those regulating the motions of the circles of the human soul. This fact explains the prominence given in Greek philosophy and musical theory to minute discussions of numbers and proportions.

1 *Rep.* iii. 398 C sqq., iv. 424 C; *Laws*, ii. 664 B sqq., 667 B sqq., 669 C sqq., vii. 812 B.

2 *Rep.* iv. 423 E; *Laws*, ii. 656 D sqq., vii. 797 A sqq.

3 Plato refers (*Rep.* iv. 424 C) to a saying of Damon that when the style of music (*μουσικῆς τρόποι*) is disturbed, the fundamental laws of the State are always disturbed also. Damon's saying corresponds to many similar utterances, which can be found in the classical books of Chinese philosophy, above all in the *Lī Kī*, the *Memorial of the Rites* (compiled in the first century B.C.). Legends showing the pernicious effect on the State of changes in musical style are given in the *Memoirs* of Sēu-mà Ts'iên, ch. 28 (French translation by M. Chavannes).

4 Cf. J. Tate, '"Imitation" in Plato's *Republic*', *C.Q.* xxii (1918), 16 sqq., and 'Plato and Imitation', *C.Q.* xxvi. 161 sqq.

5 Id., *C.Q.* xxvi. 162.

6 *Laws*, ii. 668 A sqq. (trans. A. E. Taylor).

Plato is the strongest advocate of the ethical function of music as an art. His restricted view had already been opposed by Aristotle in the famous passages in the eighth book of the *Politics* (1339^{b} sqq.), where he speaks of the fourfold function of music as (1) an amusement (παιδιά), (2) an education (παιδεία), (3) an intellectual enjoyment (διαγωγή),[1] and (4) a purification (κάθαρσις). The most important part of Aristotle's theory is the doctrine of the healing effect of music on persons in a state of frenzy, and its influence, in general, on the emotions.[2] The priesthood had made use of certain melodies of a ritual character to raise the state of ecstasy to a crisis, at which a violent paroxysm was inevitable, followed by the re-establishment of a normal state of mind.[3] Aristotle, deviating from Plato, transferred the doctrine of *Katharsis* from the limited domain of religious frenzy to that of the emotions in general. He believed that art, and above all Tragedy, had the power to bring about the proper purification of these emotions. The language of Tragedy being embellished (ἡδυσμένον) by rhythm, harmony, and song (μέλος),[4] it is obvious that music had a prominent part to play in purifying 'those who are influenced by pity and fear and every emotional nature'.[5]

The Platonic conception of harmony as regulating the movements of the universe and of the human soul, together with Aristotle's view of music as a valuable means of forming the character of the individual through intellectual enjoyment (διαγωγή) and purification (κάθαρσις), influenced Greek and Early Christian musical theory both in the East and in the West. It also became the basis of medieval speculations on the three *genera* into which Boëtius, writing at the beginning of the sixth century A.D., divided the *scientia musicae*, viz. (1) *musica mundana* dealing with the harmony in the universe; (2) *musica humana* with the harmony between soul and body; (3) *musica, quae in quibusdam constituta est instrumentis*, music as an art.[6] A survival of the Platonic conception of music as a preparation for philosophy can be seen in Boëtius's definition of the musician as a man

1 Music as an intellectual enjoyment comes nearest to the modern view of the function of art it belongs to those activities 'which are desirable in themselves'. Cf. Arist. *Ethica Nicom.* x. 6 1176^{a} sqq., trans. W. D. Ross.

2 Arist. *Pol.* viii. 7. 1342^{a}.

3 Cf. H. Abert, *Die Lehre vom Ethos*, p. 16.

4 Arist. *Poetics*, ch. 6. 1449^{b}.

5 Arist. *Pol.* viii. 7. 1342^{a}.

6 Boëtius, *de institutione musica*, p. 187, ed. G. Friedlein.

'qui ratione perpensa canendi scientiam non servitio operis sed imperio speculationis adsumpsit'.[1]

II. THE DOCTRINE OF 'ETHOS' IN GREEK MUSICAL THEORY

The greater part of the extant treatises on Greek music[2] deal with the theory of acoustics, the modes, scales, rhythm, and musical notation, some with the history and the development of ancient Greek music, as, for example, the treatise, *About Music*, ascribed to Plutarch. Occasional reference to the *ethos* theory is made in many of them, but nothing new is added to the views expounded by Plato and Aristotle. A general feature of all the treatises is the praise of the simple style of the music of the past, as opposed to the fashionable innovations of modern composers. Complaints of this kind can already be found in the collection of convivial discussions, *Symmikta Sympotika*, by Aristoxenus of Tarentum, fragments of which are preserved in Plutarch's *About Music*.[3] Aristoxenus' attitude, favouring the restitution of the solemn and simple music of earlier days, can be explained by the fact that he was a pupil of Aristotle and believed, like his teacher, in the ethical and purifying power of music; a view which made it impossible for him to approve of innovations, and led him to repeat Plato's demand that music should be preserved in its original form.[4]

Platonic and Aristotelian influence may also be found in the treatise *Eisagoge harmonike* ascribed to Cleonides (*c.* second century A.D.), a follower of Aristoxenus. Cleonides speaks of three kinds of character (ἦθος) in music: (1) exciting (διασταλτικόν), (2) depressing (συσταλτικόν), and (3) soothing (ἡσυχαστικόν).[5] Music of the exciting character is used in Tragedy and other similar poetry; music of the depressing character in lamentations, or to express the passions of love. Music of the soothing character is used to express tranquillity of the soul or a carefree and peaceful state of the mind, and is to be found in hymns, paeans,

[1] Boëtius, *de institutione musica*, p. 224, ed. G. Friedlein.

[2] A clear and precise survey of the present state of knowledge in this field is given in the second chapter of G. Reese's book, *Music in the Middle Ages*.

[3] Cf. R. Westphal, *Πλουτάρχου περὶ μουσικῆς* (1866), p. 20.

[4] Plato, *Rep.* iv. 424 c. The passage from Aristoxenus' *Symmikta Sympotika* is quoted by Athenaeus 14. 632 A. The *Harmonics* of Aristoxenos, the most important source for our knowledge of Ancient Greek musical theory, refers to the aesthetical doctrine in only a few passages.

[5] Cleonides, *Eisag.*, *Mus. Script. Gr.*, ed. Jan, p. 206.

songs of praise (ἐγκώμια), and other similar songs.[1] The same division can be found in the treatise *About Music* by Aristides Quintilianus (*c.* first or beginning of the second century A.D.), except that here music of a soothing character (ἦθος ἡσυχαστικόν) is called moderate, as it leads the soul to tranquillity (μέσην, δι' ἧς εἰς ἠρεμίαν τὴν ψυχὴν περιάγομεν) (Meib., p. 30, A. Jahn, p. 20).

The treatise Περὶ μουσικῆς by Aristides Quintilianus is the most lucid and comprehensive dissertation on Greek music we possess, yet his name is not mentioned by any other late-classical author writing on the subject. This does not mean that the treatise remained unnoticed. M. Meibom, who published *About Music* in the second volume of the *Antiquae musicae auctores septem* in 1652, discovered large sections of it in *De Nuptiis Philologiae et Mercurii* by Martianus Capella, an author of the late fourth to early fifth century. Through him the musical theories of Aristides became known to the West. In the same way the content of *About Music* was copied by Greek writers on music, particularly Bacchius, Cleonides, and Gaudentius and through them made known to the leading Byzantine theoreticians, Pachymeres* and Bryennius, both of whom drew extensively on his *Harmonics*.[2]

The adherents of the Neo-Pythagorean philosophy worked out a system of musical theory in which speculations on the mystical character of numbers played a predominant part. The outstanding figure among these philosophers is Nicomachus of Gerasa, who lived in the second century A.D. It was he who, in his philosophical system, associated music with mathematics, and

[1] H. Abert, *Die Lehre*, p. 20, referring to the three genera of Cleonides, misquotes the author in speaking of τρόποι = *Stilarten* and making him differentiate between τρόπος διασταλτικός, τ. συσταλτικός, and τ. ἡσυχαστικός. Cleonides speaks of ἦθος διασταλτικόν, συσταλτικόν, and ἡσυχαστικόν. *Ethos* means the effect of music of a certain character on the listener. Greek theorists make a clear distinction between ἦθος and τρόπος. *Tropos* has an ambiguous significance. Relating to the (formal) features of a melody it means 'mode'. Thus Bacchius the Elder, an Aristoxenian theorist, discussing the various successions of intervals in the tetrachords, speaks of the Lydian, Phrygian, and Dorian mode, approaching them from the technical and formal side of the question (οἱ οὖν τοὺς τρεῖς τρόπους ᾄδοντες τίνας ᾄδουσι;—Λύδιον, Φρύγιον, Δώριον: Bacch. *Introductio*, p. 12 M.). Aristides Quintilianus, on the other hand, speaks of three *tropoi* in Greek music: (1) the style of the Nomos (τρόπος νομικός), (2) a dithyrambic (διθυραμβικός), and (3) a tragic (τραγικός). Here the term refers to the different emotional qualities of certain melodies, which make each group applicable to a different genre of poetry. In this case 'style' is the best translation of τρόπος, as we speak of a tragic style, dithyrambic style.

[2] When, at the beginning of the nineteenth century, studies in Greek music were systematically resumed, the recognition of Aristides Quintilianus as an original author by Boeckh, G. Hermann, and T. Gaisford was in the end forced to give way to the adverse criticism of R. Westphal, then the great authority on metrics. It is only lately that the position of A.Q. has been re-established by H. Weil, C. E. Ruelle, H. Abert, and R. Schäfke.

astronomy with geometry, the former two dealing with multitudes (πλήθη), the latter with magnitudes (μεγέθη). The origin of the *quadrivium* seems to go back to Pythagorean doctrine, as Porphyry refers to a passage in the *About Mathematics* of Archytas, containing the classification of astronomy, music, geometry, and arithmetic.[1] But it was through Nicomachus that this classification became generally known and accepted as the basis of medieval musical aesthetics.

Naturally, as a Neo-Pythagorean, Nicomachus was concerned more with the metaphysical than the mathematical significance of numbers. He discussed the divine nature of the numbers one to ten, seeing in them the symbols of gods and goddesses. The classes of the *quadrivium* are four, because in the doctrines of arithmetical theology great significance is attached to this number. Nicomachus tells us that no one can penetrate into this arithmetical theology who is not exercised in musical theory and in the playing of instruments (. . . *καὶ μὴν καὶ τοῖς μουσικοῖς θεωρήμασι καὶ δὴ καὶ ὀργάνοις ἐγγεγυμνάσθαι*).[2] Nicomachus, who assigned such an important place in his writings on music to metaphysical speculations on numbers, dealt also with the passages on harmony in the *Timaeus*, combining Platonic and Aristotelian ideas with Pythagorean. Thus he became an authority for the Neoplatonists, who took over his views on music and preserved them in quotations from his writings.

Among the theorists of the second century A.D. who dealt with the elements of music, Claudius Ptolemy of Alexandria holds the first place: his *Harmonics* are rightly considered 'the most scientific and best arranged treatise'[3] on the subject that we possess in Greek.[4] But it was a commentary of the third century,

[1] παρακείσθω δὲ καὶ νῦν τὰ Ἀρχύτα τοῦ Πυθαγορείου, οὗ μάλιστα καὶ γνήσια λέγεται εἶναι τὰ συγγράμματα. λέγει δ' ἐν τῷ Περὶ μαθηματικῆς εὐθὺς ἐναρχόμενος τοῦ λόγου τάδε· "Καλῶς μοι δοκοῦντι τοὶ περὶ τὰ μαθήματα διαγνῶναι καὶ οὐθὲν ἄτοπον ὀρθῶς αὐτοὺς περὶ ἑκάστου θεωρεῖν. περὶ γὰρ τᾶς τῶν ὅλων φύσιος καλῶς διαγνόντες ἔμελλον καὶ περὶ τῶν κατὰ μέρος, οἷά ἐντι, ὄψεσθαι. περί τε δὴ τᾶς τῶν ἄστρων ταχυτᾶτος καὶ ἐπιτολᾶν καὶ δυσίων παρέδωκαν ἁμῖν διάγνωσιν καὶ περὶ γαμετρίας καὶ ἀριθμῶν καὶ οὐχ ἥκιστα περὶ μουσικᾶς. ταῦτα γὰρ τὰ μαθήματα δοκοῦντι ἦμεν ἀδελφεά." I. Düring, *Porphyrios Kommentar zur Harmonielehre des Ptolemaios*, p. 56. Cf. H. Diels, *Fragm. d. Vorsokratiker*[5], i. 431–2.

[2] Phot. *Biblioth.* cod. 187. Cf. H. Abert, *Die Musikanschauung des Mittelalters*, p. 31, and C. Jan, *De Nicomacho eiusque libris*, *Mus. Script. Gr.*, pp. 219 sqq.

[3] Cf. J. F. Mountford, 'The Harmonics of Ptolemy', *Trans. of the Amer. Philol. Assoc.* lvii (1926), 71.

[4] Until recently the importance of Ptolemy's *Harmonics* was not sufficiently emphasized in books and essays on Greek music; this omission may have been due to the lack of a modern edition of the work. We now possess the excellent critical edition by I. Düring, who edited Porphyry's

by Porphyry, the former pupil of Plotinus, rather than the original work, that was important as an influence on the development of musical theory in Early Christian times and in the Byzantine Empire.

III. NEOPLATONIC INFLUENCES ON MUSICAL THEORY

Setting forth his doctrine of the Intelligible Beauty (*περὶ τοῦ νοητοῦ κάλλους*) in *Enneads* v. 8. 1, Plotinus writes: 'If any think meanly of the Arts, on this ground, that when they create they do no more than mimic Nature, we have a threefold answer. First, we shall remark that all Nature is in its turn an imitation of some other thing. In the second place, we are not to conceive that the Arts imitate merely the thing seen: they go back to the principles of Form out of which Nature is generated. Thirdly, in many of their creations they go beyond imitation: because they possess beauty, they supply from themselves whatever is lacking in the sensible object.'[1] From this passage we can see the great change that had taken place in Greek philosophy since Plato had made the statement in the tenth book of the *Republic* (602 B)—so difficult to reconcile with the views on music expressed elsewhere in his dialogues—, that art, being an imitation, can only be considered as a kind of pastime, not a serious pursuit. The artist is no longer considered as a 'manufacturer of images, far removed from truth', but, according to Plotinus' essay on *Dialectic* in *Enneads* I. iii. 1–3, his aim is to produce an object which contains some reflection of the Divine Beauty. The musician is particularly well equipped for the task, being 'sensitive to tones and the beauty they convey'. He is repelled by discords, and seeks for 'properly ordered rhythm and well-planned form' (*τὸ εὔρυθμον καὶ τὸ εὔσχημον διώκειν*).[2] If the truths of Philosophy (*λόγους τοὺς*

commentary on the *Harmonics* in 1932, and ended his work with a German translation of Ptolemy's *Harmonics* and a commentary on both treatises.

[1] *εἰ δέ τις τὰς τέχνας ἀτιμάζει, ὅτι μιμούμεναι τὴν φύσιν ποιοῦσι, πρῶτον μὲν φατέον καὶ τὰς φύσεις μιμεῖσθαι ἄλλα· ἔπειτα δεῖ εἰδέναι ὡς οὐχ ἁπλῶς τὸ ὁρώμενον μιμοῦνται, ἀλλ' ἀνατρέχουσιν ἐπὶ τοὺς λόγους ἐξ ὧν ἡ φύσις· εἶτα καὶ ὅτι πολλὰ παρ' αὐτῶν ποιοῦσι. καὶ προστιθέασι γὰρ ὅτῳ τι ἐλλείπει, ὡς ἔχουσαι τὸ κάλλος.* *Plotini Enneades*, ed. R. Volkmann (Bibl. Teubn. 1883), ii, p. 232. The translation of the passage is taken from E. R. Dodds, *Select Passages illustrating Neoplatonism* (S.P.C.K.), pp. 104–5.

[2] *πρῶτον δὴ διασταλτέον τοὺς ἄνδρας τούτους ἡμῖν ἀρξαμένους ἀπὸ τοῦ μουσικοῦ ὅστις ἐστὶ λέγοντας τὴν φύσιν. θετέον δὴ αὐτὸν εὐκίνητον καὶ ἐπτοημένον μὲν πρὸς τὸ καλόν, ἀδυνατώτερον δὲ παρ' αὐτοῦ κινεῖσθαι, ἕτοιμον δὲ ἐκ τῶν τυχόντων οἷον κτύπων, ὥσπερ οἱ δειλοὶ πρὸς τοὺς ψόφους, οὕτως καὶ τοῦτον πρὸς τοὺς φθόγγους καὶ τὸ καλὸν τὸ ἐν τούτοις ἕτοιμον, φεύγοντα (δὲ) ἀεὶ τὸ ἀνάρμοστον καὶ τὸ μὴ ἓν ἐν τοῖς ᾀδομένοις καὶ ἐν τοῖς ῥυθμοῖς τὸ εὔρυθμον καὶ τὸ εὔσχημον διώκειν.* Ibid. i. 3. 1, p. 58.

φιλοσοφίας) are implanted in him he may pass beyond the state of a *mousikos*—which is the first degree of spiritual development—into the higher one of a lover (ἐρωτικός). He can even reach the third and highest degree of the philosopher, who advances within the sphere of the Intelligibles (τοῖς ἐν τῷ νοητῷ γενομένοις) 'until the summit of the Intellectual Realm is won'.[1] In describing the three degrees—*mousikos, erotikos, philosophos*—Plotinus follows up an idea from the opening speech of Socrates in the *Phaedo* (61 A) that 'philosophy is the highest music', and another, in the *Phaedrus* (249 C), that our 'learning is nothing else but reminiscence'. It is also clear from Plotinus' description of the path leading to the perception of Divine Beauty that in the melodies which we hear with our human ears beauty exists in a weaker form than in their models, just as, according to the *Timaeus*, the ingredients compounded in the World-Soul appear in a weaker blend in human souls.[2]

Plotinus' conception of music perceptible to the senses as an echo of divine harmonies, and the musician as a being particularly fitted for the task of reproducing these harmonies, became a doctrine generally accepted in Neoplatonic philosophy. From this view it followed that the musician, aiming at the Divine, had to abstain from sensual emotions, just as Socrates declares 'that those who pursue philosophy rightly abstain from all bodily desires'.[3] Only music in the service of religion should be regarded as an art worthy to be pursued; secular music can only distract from the higher, spiritual achievements.

Proclus (410–85) was the last of the Neoplatonists to deal extensively with the theory of music. He was particularly devoted to these studies, since a dream had revealed to him that he possessed the soul of Nicomachus of Gerasa. His views on music are not brought into a homogeneous system, but are scattered through his commentaries on Plato's dialogues. Proclus took over and developed Plotinus's concept of the three degrees of conversion from the material world to the peak of the Intellectual Realm. In his commentary on the first book of Euclid's *Elements* he describes the process as a progression from visible to invisible Beauty, a kind of initiation into a mystery religion. The musician, the 'born lover', and the philosopher are raised above the

[1] Plotinus, *Enneads*, I. iii. 1–3.
[2] *Timaeus* 41 D.
[3] *Phaedo* 82 C.

world of sense, because they fulfil and accomplish the primary life of the soul. 'The beginning and path of elevation for the lover is a progression from apparent beauty, using as steps the middle forms of beautiful objects. To the musician, to whom the third place is assigned, the way consists in a transition from harmonies perceptible to the senses to those that are imperceptible and to the principles existing in these.'[1]

The Christian author of the *Heavenly Hierarchy* who wrote under the pseudonym of Dionysius the Areopagite was a pupil or adherent of Proclus. Dionysius speaks of an echo (ἀπήχημα) of the divine harmony and beauty which can be observed in everything existing in the realm of the material world.[2] The Hierarchy means 'a certain Holy Order, an image of the Divine Beauty'. Each rank of this Order 'is led in its own degree to the co-operation with the divine by performing, through grace and God-given power, those mysteries which are essentially and super-essentially in the Godhead, and are accomplished by It supernaturally, and are manifested to us through our Hierarchy for the imitation of God-loving minds to the highest possible extent'.[3]

The Neoplatonic teaching of the three degrees of initiation which lead towards the highest point of the Intellectual Realm had to give way to the mystical conception of the Celestial Hierarchy with its earthly counterpart, the Ecclesiastical Hierarchy. Together they form the rungs of a ladder, leading from the lowest grade of clerics to the highest rank of the triad, where the Seraphs dance around God, singing with never silent lips the Hymn of Praise, 'Holy, holy, holy, Lord of Sabaoth. The whole earth is full of Thy glory.'[4]

The beauty of these hymns, which is imperceptible to the lower ranks of the triad, is revealed to them by the Seraphs and thence to the inspired prophets and saints. Thus, an angel taught the prophet Isaiah the hidden mysteries of 'the divine and highly reverenced heavenly Hymn of Praise, the angel who

[1] *ἀλλὰ τῷ μὲν ἐρωτικῷ τῆς ἀναγωγῆς ἀρχὴ καὶ ὁδὸς ἐντεῦθεν ἀπὸ τοῦ φαινομένου κάλλους ἐπαναβασμοῖς χρωμένῳ τοῖς μέσοις εἴδεσι τῶν καλῶν, τῷ δὲ μουσικῷ τρίτην λαχόντι τάξιν ἀπὸ τῶν ἐν αἰσθήσεσιν ἁρμονιῶν ἐπὶ τὰς ἀφανεῖς ἁρμονίας καὶ τοὺς λόγους τοὺς ἐν ταύταις ἡ μετάβασις. Procli in Primum Euclidis Elementorum Librum Commentarii*, ed. G. Friedlein (Bibl. Teubn.), p. 21, ll. 8–13.

[2] *ἔστι τοιγαροῦν οὐκ ἀπᾳδούσας ἀναπλάσαι τοῖς οὐρανίοις μορφάς, κἀκ τῶν ἀτιμοτάτων τῆς ὕλης μερῶν, ἐπεὶ καὶ αὐτή, πρὸς τοῦ ὄντως καλοῦ τὴν ὕπαρξιν ἐσχηκυῖα, κατὰ πᾶσαν αὐτῆς τὴν ὑλαίαν διακόσμησιν ἀπηχήματά τινα τῆς νοερᾶς εὐπρεπείας ἔχει. Cael. Hier.*, c. 2, § 4.

[3] Ibid., c. 3, § 2.

[4] Cf. ibid., c. 7, § 4.

formed the vision imparting as far as possible his own divine knowledge to the prophet'.[1]

A passage in the *Ecclesiastical Hierarchy* throws an even clearer light on the significance of the divine songs for the Church. The hymns and canticles of the Church are the reflection of the spiritual chants, transmitted from the Celestial Hierarchy to mankind and made audible to human ears in the form of the Psalms. When the singing of the hymns (*ὑμνολογία*) has brought our souls 'into harmony with the ritual which is to follow' and has brought our hearts 'into concord with the divine, with ourselves and with one another', the poetic imagery of the Psalms is further explained by the reading of the divine Lessons.[2]

This passage illustrates well the difference between Plotinian philosophy and Dionysian theology. In the former the musician was depicted as emotional, easily moved and passionately drawn to material beauty (*εὐκίνητος καὶ ἐπτοημένος μὲν πρὸς τὸ καλόν*)[3] and consequently it is easy to lead him by means of philosophy to the perception of the Intelligible Beauty. The Dionysian theology regards him as a recipient of the hymns sung in heaven and transmitted from one order to the next,[4] until they become perceptible to human ears in the ranks of the Ecclesiastical Hierarchy.

Henceforth the musician is simply a humble hymn-writer, his faith making him an instrument of the divine grace. He knows that he can only compose and sing melodies which came into the world of matter as an imperfect echo of the heavenly hymns, but, Dionysius states, 'it is possible through these to be led to the immaterial archetypes'.[5] This assertion is based on propositions in Proclus' *Elements of Theology*, particularly on the famous Seventh: that 'every productive cause is superior to that which it produces',[6] and on the Twenty-first: 'Every order has its beginning in a monad and proceeds to a manifold co-ordinate

[1] *Cael. Hier.*, c. 13, § 4.

[2] *ὅταν οὖν ἡ περιεκτικὴ τῶν πανιέρων ὑμνολογία τὰς ψυχικὰς ἡμῶν ἕξεις ἐναρμονίως διαθῇ πρὸς τὰ μικρὸν ὕστερον ἱερουργηθησόμενα, καὶ τῇ τῶν θείων ᾠδῶν ὁμοφωνίᾳ τὴν πρός τὰ θεῖα καὶ ἑαυτοὺς καὶ ἀλλήλους ὁμοφροσύνην ὡς μιᾷ καὶ ὁμολόγῳ τῶν ἱερῶν χορείᾳ νομοθετήσῃ τὰ συντετμημένα καὶ συνεσκιασμένα μᾶλλον ἐν τῇ νοερᾷ τῶν ψαλμῶν ἱερολογίᾳ διὰ πλειόνων καὶ σαφεστέρων εἰκόνων καὶ ἀναρρήσεων εὐρύνεται ταῖς ἱερωτάταις τῶν ἁγιογράφων συντάξεων ἀναγνώσεσιν.* *Eccles. Hier.*, c. 3, § 5.

[3] *Enneads*, I. iii. I.

[4] Cf. *Cael. Hier.*, c. 7.

[5] *δυνατόν ἐστι δι' αὐτῶν ἀνάγεσθαι πρὸς τὰς ἀΰλους ἀρχετυπίας.* Ibid., c. 2, § 4.

[6] Proclus, *The Elements of Theology* (a revised text with translation by E. R. Dodds, 1933), p. 9. For the Oriental influences in Proclus' theology see Dodds's Introduction, § 3, 'Proclus and his Predecessors', pp. xviii–xxvi.

therewith; and the manifold in any order is carried back to a single monad.'[1] But the author of the *Hierarchies* succeeded in adapting the Neoplatonic doctrine to Christian dogma, and it became one of the main pillars upon which the liturgical order of the Eastern Church was built. The artist in the service of the Orthodox Church was not permitted to treat his subject freely. The painter of an icon of a saint had to copy the features handed on to him by his predecessors, because the portrait was regarded as the earthly manifestation of the immaterial being; in other words, the painter had to give the 'idea' of the saint, not a resemblance of the human being who became a saint. The hymnographer, too, had to follow a model, a hymn already existing for the feast of the saint or martyr in whose praise it was written. This model was considered an echo of the hymn sung by the angels in his praise. This can be seen from several Kontakia written by Romanus, the 'prince of melodes'. Glorifying the *Hymn of the three Children in the Furnace* in the Kontakion for the 27th of December,[2] Romanus sings:

Στήσαντες οὖν οἱ παῖδες
χορὸν ἐν μέσῳ καμίνου,
οὐρανίαν ἐκκλησίαν
ἀπειργάσαντο τὴν κάμινον,
ψάλλοντες μετ' ἀγγέλου
τῷ ποιητῇ τῶν ἀγγέλων,
καὶ πᾶσαν τὴν ὑμνῳδίαν
τῶν ἀσάρκων ἐκμιμούμενοι.

(In the midst of the furnace the Children formed a chorus, and made the furnace a heavenly Church, singing with the angel to the Maker of the angels and imitating the whole hymnody of the Immortals.)

We must realize that it is a vision of the Dionysian theology presented in a poetical form, not a mere poetical phrase, when Romanus begins his Kontakion for the feast of the Presentation of Our Lord[3] with the following parallelism:

Χορὸς ἀγγελικὸς
ἐκπληττέσθω τὸ θαῦμα,

[1] *πᾶσα τάξις ἀπὸ μονάδος ἀρχομένη πρόεισιν εἰς πλῆθος τῇ μονάδι σύστοιχον, καὶ πάσης τάξεως τὸ πλῆθος εἰς μίαν ἀνάγεται μονάδα. ἡ μὲν γὰρ μονάς, ἀρχῆς ἔχουσα λόγον, ἀπογεννᾷ τὸ οἰκεῖον ἑαυτῇ πλῆθος· διὸ καὶ μία σειρὰ καὶ μία τάξις, ἣ ὅλη παρὰ τῆς μονάδος ἔχει τὴν εἰς τὸ πλῆθος ὑπόβασιν.* Ibid., p. 24.

[2] *de tribus SS. pueris in fornace*, str. 27 in J.-B. Pitra, *Analecta Sacra*, i, p. 195.

[3] Romano il Melode, *Inni*, ed. G. Cammelli, p. 128.

βροτοὶ δὲ ταῖς φωναῖς
ἀνακράξωμεν ὕμνον
ὁρῶντες τὴν ἄφατον
τοῦ θεοῦ συγκατάβασιν.

(Let the Choir of Angels be astonished at the wonder, and let us mortals raise our voices in a hymn, beholding the ineffable condescension of God.)

The musician whose task is to supply the Divine Service with melodies is limited still more by liturgical directions reflecting the spirit of pseudo-Dionysian theology. The vast treasury of Byzantine melodies was developed from a limited number of archetypes, transmitted by the angels to prophets and inspired saints. Thus the heavenly hymns became perceptible to human ears. The Byzantine musician is bound to keep as closely as possible to these models. He can only make slight changes in the melodies, in order to fit them to the words of a new poem, or, at a later stage, he can introduce some embellishments. It would be mistaken to see in this strict adherence to prescribed patterns a lack of musical imagination on the part of the musicians. The artist felt himself, in company with all other artists, as a link in a chain, with his place in the ranks of the faithful, where his position was determined by the measure of his piety.

IV. THE BYZANTINE CONCEPTION OF MUSIC

Byzantine musical theory did not have any development of its own after the essence of Neoplatonic philosophy had been assimilated to the doctrine of Pseudo-Dionysius at the end of the fifth or the beginning of the sixth century. This can best be seen from a letter on music written by Michael Psellus (1018–*c.* 1080), and probably addressed to the Emperor Constantine Monomachus (1042–55).[1] Speaking after a short Platonic introduction about the various classes and forms of music, Psellus asserts that these are given to us by the Higher Powers (*τῶν κρειττόνων*) which weave together indissolubly in heaven eternal life, unceasing movement, and productive powers. We finally discover that 'the movements of the created beings follow a rhythmical, their voices a harmonic order, and that the dances composed from both are well constructed: we proceed to the artful devising of all sorts of instruments, tunefully made: and

[1] Cf. H. Abert, 'Ein ungedruckter Brief des Michael Psellus über die Musik', *S.I.M.* ii, p. 334.

then we observe that that the power emanating from music is extended to everything. Music is the scientific knowledge, both theoretical and practical, of perfect singing and playing; the art of mastering what is fitting in melody and rhythm, directed to training the character.'[1] Psellus then mentions the view of some philosophers that music leads the soul from beautiful things on earth to the idea of Beauty (*ἐπ' αὐτὸ τὸ νοητὸν κάλλος*). He speaks of the healing effects of music, taking his examples from well-known passages of Platonic writers. After a concise treatment of vocal and instrumental music, based on Aristides Quintilianus, Psellus deals with the relationship of music and astronomy, and comes to the conclusion that there exist 'connexions between the order in our chants, rhythms, or dances and divine music' (*οἰκειότητές εἰσιν τῆς ἡμετέρας ἁρμονίας πρὸς τὴν θείαν μουσικήν*). Hence the Greeks introduced various kinds of hymns, odes, and dances to be performed at the feasts of their gods, and similar songs and dances were performed during the ceremonies accompanying the most important events of human life, such as the bridal procession and the wedding-feast. But he ends the letter regretfully, 'the kind of music which occupies our minds to-day is only a faint echo of the former' (*αὕτη ἀπήχημα οἷον ἐκείνης ἐστίν*).

Psellus' letter is very characteristic of many other treatises on music, both Eastern and Western, written before or after it. It becomes a habit to allude to the grandeur of Greek music, which had completely disappeared since the sixth century. Everywhere we find regrets for this lamentable fact. Towards the close of the tenth century in Byzantium, as the Hellenistic renaissance of the eleventh century draws nearer, they become still more outspoken. No mention is made in any of the treatises of the rise and development of Byzantine ecclesiastical music. This lack of information on the subject may be explained as follows. Byzantine ecclesiastical music, being part of the Divine Service, could not be a matter for aesthetic speculation: Byzantine ceremonial music, approved by the Emperor, could not be subject to criticism. There remains only secular music in general,

[1] *ἐπειδὰν δὲ τελευτῶντες ἀνεύρωμεν τὰς τῶν συνθέτων ζῴων κινήσεις εὐρύθμους συνισταμένας καὶ τὰς φωνὰς εὐαρμόστους καὶ τὰς ἀπ' ἀμφοτέρων τούτων συμμιγνυμένας χορείας τεταγμένας, ἔτι δὲ, ὀργάνων μουσικῶν παντοίων ἐμμελεῖς ποιήσωμεν εὐτεχνίας, τότε δὴ τὴν ἀπὸ τῆς μουσικῆς δύναμιν προσερχομένην ἐπὶ τὰ ὅλα καὶ διατείνουσαν ἐπ' αὐτὰ θεωροῦμεν, καὶ ἔστι ἐν τούτοις ἡ μουσικὴ ἐπιστήμη θεωρητική τε καὶ πρακτικὴ μέλους τελείου τε καὶ ὀργανικοῦ καὶ τέχνη πρεπόντων ἐν μέλεσι καὶ ῥυθμοῖς, συντείνουσα πρὸς ἠθῶν κατασκευήν.* Ibid., p. 335.

and it is this kind of music to which Psellus evidently refers, as it was condemned equally by the educated, brought up in an atmosphere of admiration for Greek civilization, and by the Church.

The technique of Byzantine ecclesiastical music, however, could be learned from treatises containing instructions about the modes, musical notation, rhythm, dynamic signs, together with some elementary exercises for the beginner. These 'grammars' are the main source of information for the deciphering of Byzantine musical notation; they also show that in the great age of Byzantine ecclesiastical music the knowledge of Greek music had entirely disappeared from music schools. Speculations on the subject, without any connexion with actual practice, were confined to students of the 'stepping-stones of wisdom' (*σοφίας ἐπιβάθραι*):[1] grammar, rhetoric, dialectic, medicine, arithmetic, and geometry.

The extent of the gap which divided Byzantine musical practice from Hellenistic theory at the end of the twelfth century can be seen from a treatise of Nicolas Mesarites on the Church of the Apostles at Constantinople.[2] In the precincts of the church quarters were provided for the classes of a school.* Here the younger children were taught the elements of grammar, the elder, dialectic and rhetoric. In close connexion with these subjects elementary training in music was given. 'On the other, western side you can see hymn-singers with children, almost babes, stammering, just taken from the breast. These infants open their mouths and talk wisdom and rehearse the praise of God the King of all, and of his saints, who imitate his Life and Passion. Going a little farther you will find boys with young men just emerged from boyhood, singing a well-shaped song and a well-sounding harmony with their throat, mouth, tongue, with their lips and teeth. They make conductor's movements with their hands in order to guide the beginner in following the mode with his voice, that he may not slip away from the melodic line, drop out of rhythm, nor fall away from the other voices, nor sing out of tune.'[3]

Continuing his description of the Church of the Apostles, Mesarites informs the reader that teaching in the theory of music

[1] Cf. Nicomachus, *Theolog. arithm.*, p. 17, Ast.

[2] Cf. A. Heisenberg, *Grabeskirche und Apostelkirche* (1908), ii. 10–96.

[3] *ἐκεῖθεν ἴδοις ὡς πρὸς δυσμὴν [ὑμνῳδοὺς] ψαλτῳδοὺς σὺν παισὶ νηπιάχοις σχεδὸν καὶ ὑποψελλίζουσιν καὶ τῆς θηλῆς ἀρτίως ἀποσπασθεῖσιν, οἳ καὶ ἀνοίγουσι στόμα καὶ λαλοῦσι σοφίαν καὶ καταρτί-*

is completely separated from elementary teaching in singing, as described above. After dealing with the school of geometry, Mesarites draws a picture of the students who debate about tones and intervals. 'They argue with each other discussing terms unfamiliar to most people or even unheard of, such as *nete*'s, *hypate*'s, and *parhypate*'s, *mese*'s and *paramese*'s instead of strings; further they say that the interval which they call *diatessaron* is denominated *epitritos*, in agreement with the arithmeticians; but the interval called *diapente* seems to them to be a kind of *hemiolios*, corresponding to the *diapente* of the arithmeticians. And also, why the octave is called *diapason*, why the first mode in it is found to be the principal, why they call the fifteenth string *disdiapason*, and why the whole instrument is named fifteen-stringed when it has sixteen strings.'[1]

From this account, which is almost entirely nonsensical, it becomes evident that Greek musical theory had no connexion whatever with Byzantine ecclesiastical music in the twelfth century. The latter was taught merely as practical singing, the former was part of mathematical science. Mesarites drew his knowledge, directly or indirectly, from passages in the pseudo-Aristotelian *Problems*, the *Eisagoge* of Gaudentius, and the *Encheiridion* of Nicomachus, without understanding the subject-matter he cited. Not only did he no longer understand the meaning of the subject he tried to explain to the reader, but we may also accept as a fact his view that in his day the terms *nete*, *hypate*, and *parhypate* were to most people mere names, or were completely unknown to them. They had no significance in actual Byzantine musical practice, and were only found in discussions on topics taken from classical authors.

ζουσιν αἶνον τῷ πάντων βασιλεῖ καὶ Θεῷ καὶ τοῖς ἁγίοις αὐτοῦ τοῖς τὴν ἐκείνου πολιτείαν μιμησαμένοις καὶ τὰ παθήματα. μικρὸν παριὼν μειρακίοις ἐντύχοις σὺν νεανίσκοις ἄρτι τὸν μείρακα παραμείβουσιν, εὔρυθμον μέλος καὶ σύμφωνον ἁρμονίαν ἐκ φάρυγγος, ἐκ στόματος, ἐκ γλώττης, ἐκ χειλέων, ἐξ ὀδόντων προπέμπουσιν. νωμῶσιν οὗτοι καὶ χεῖρα πρὸς φωνῶν καὶ ἤχων ἐξίσωσιν τὸν ἀρτιμαθῆ χειραγωγοῦσαν οἷον τοῦ μὴ τοῦ συντόνου ἐξολισθαίνειν κἀκ τοῦ ῥυθμοῦ καταπίπτειν μηδ' ἐκ τῆς συμφωνίας ἐκνεύειν καὶ διαμαρτάνειν τοῦ ἐμμελοῦς. Ibid., pp. 20–1.

[1] *κατακούσειας οὖν αὐτῶν πρὸς ἀλλήλους διαπορούντων, ἀσυνήθῆ τινα τοῖς πολλοῖς καὶ ἀκατακρόατα νήτας ἀντὶ χορδῶν ὑπάτάς τε καὶ παρυπάτας, μέσας καὶ παραμέσας προσφθεγγομένων ἀλλήλοις, καὶ πῶς ὁ μὲν διὰ τεσσάρων παρ' αὐτοῖς ἐπονομαζόμενος συμφώνως τοῖς ἀριθμητικοῖς ἐπίτριτος ὀνομάζεται, ὁ δὲ διὰ πέντε καλούμενος ἡμιόλιός τις εἶναι τούτοις δοκεῖ, τῷ τῶν ἀριθμητικῶν διὰ πέντε ἀπ' ἐναντίας ἱστάμενος. ἵνα τί τὲ ἡ ὀγδόη διὰ πασῶν ἐπικέκληται καὶ πῶς ὁ τῶν ἤχων πρῶτος ἐν αὐτῇ κυριώτατος ἐφευρίσκεται, καὶ ὅπως ἡ πεντεκαιδεκάτη τούτοις χορδὴ δὶς διὰ πασῶν ἐπωνόμασται καὶ πεντεκαιδεκάχορδον ἐν ἑξκαιδεκαχόρδῳ τὸ σύμπαν ὄργανον ὀνομάζεται.* Ibid., pp. 93–4. Cf. E. Wellesz, 'Zur Erforschung d. byz. Hymnengesanges', *Zeitschrift f. d. oesterr. Gymnasien*, 1917, pp. 33–6, and 'Die Rhythmik d. byz. Neumen', *Z.M.W.* iii (1921), 322–4.

V. MUSIC IN TREATISES OF GREEK GNOSTICS AND ALCHEMISTS

Besides the writings of Greek philosophers and theorists discussed in the course of this chapter, two other groups of written documents containing sections on music must be mentioned, viz. the works of Gnostic authors on magic, and those of Byzantine alchemists.[1] Investigations into these two groups of sources have been going on for a considerable time; but only recently have attempts been made to connect certain magic formulae which are found in fragments of Greek papyri and in speculations on music in passages of alchemical treatises, with the origins of Byzantine musical theory.[2] It therefore remains to be seen whether the hypothesis, put forward with a great deal of ingenuity, can be accepted or must be rejected as a misconception.

(*a*) *Gnostic formulae of incantation*

In a number of Greek papyri containing fragments of treatises on magic, incantations have been found beginning or ending with groups of letters consisting of the seven Greek vowels *α ε η ι ο υ ω* in various combinations, e.g.:

ὁ τῶν ὅλων δεσπότης
ἅγιε κάνθαρε: αω· σαθρεναβρασαξ: ιαωαιαεω·
ηωα: ωαη: ιαω: ιηο: ευ: αη: ευ: ιε: ιαωαι[3]

Similar combinations are also to be found on small pieces of papyrus, serving as amulets:[4]

α α α α
ο ο ο ο ο
η η η η
ι ι ι ι ι
ο ο ο ο ο ο ο
υ υ υ υ
ω ω

[1] Cf. C. E. Ruelle, 'Le Chant des sept voyelles grecques d'après Démétrius et les papyrus de Leyde', *R.É.G.* ii (1888), 38 sqq.; 'Le Chant gnostico-magique des sept voyelles grecques', *Congrès d'histoire de la musique* (Paris, 1900), pp. 15 sqq.; E. Poirée, 'Formules musicales des papyrus magiques', ibid., pp. 28 sqq.; A. Gastoué, 'Les Origines du chant romain', *Bibl. musicol.* i (1907), 24–31; Leclercq, 'Alphabet vocalique des Gnostiques', *D.A.C.L.* i. 1268 sqq.; M. Berthelot–C. E. Ruelle, *Collection des anciens Alchimistes grecs* (1887–8), ii. 219, 434; K. Wachsmann, *Untersuchungen zum vorgregorianischen Gesang* (1935), pp. 24–34; G. Reese, *Music in the Middle Ages* (1940), pp. 85–6.

[2] C. Höeg, 'La théorie de la musique byzantine', *R.É.G.* xxxv (1922), 321–34.

[3] C. Wessely, 'Neue griechische Zauberpapyri', *Denkschriften d. k. Ak. d. Wiss. i. Wien phil.-hist. Cl.* xlii (1893), 27.

[4] Ibid., p. 72.

The meaning of these groups of vowels becomes evident from formulae of invocation in the papyrus W of Leyden,[1] of which two significant examples may be given:

(1) *Σοῦ τὸ ζ̄ γραμμάτων ὄνομα πρὸς τὴν ἁρμονίαν τῶν ζ̄ φθόγγων ἐχόντων φωνὰς πρὸς τὰ κη̄ φῶτα σελήνης, Σαραφαρα, Αραφαιρα, Βρααρμαραφα, Αβρααχ, Περταωμηχ, Ακμηχ, Ιαω: ουεη: ιαω: ουε: ειου: αηω: εηου: εηου: Ιαω.* (p. 18, l. 28.)

(Thy name, composed of seven letters, according to the harmony of the seven tones, which have their sound according to the twenty-eight lights of the Moon, Saraphara, Araphaira, Braarmarapha, Abraach, Pertaomech, Akmech, Iaō: oueē: iaō: oue: eiou: aēō: eēou: eēou: Iaō.)

(2) *Ἐπικαλοῦμαί σε, Κύριε, ᾠδικῷ ὕμνῳ, ὑμνῶ σου τὸ ἅγιον κράτος, αεηιοωωω.*

(I invoke thee, Lord, in a hymnic song, I celebrate thy holy might, aeēioōōō.)

From Oriental mystery rites it is known that single vowels or groups of vowels were uttered by the initiate to intensify the effect of the incantation. The texts of the two invocations from papyrus W, however, seem to permit of another interpretation by which stress is laid on the words *ᾠδικῷ ὕμνῳ* and *ὑμνῶ σου* in the second invocation, on *ἁρμονίαν*, *φθόγγων*, and *φωνάς* in the first. It is this interpretation which É. Ruelle, and following him other scholars,[2] adopted in order to prove that the seven Greek vowels were used by the Gnostics in the place of the seven tones of the seven-stringed lyre, tuned on the two conjunct tetrachords of the Dorian scale. According to the Pythagorean doctrine each tone of this scale represented the sound of one of the seven planets; therefore, Ruelle and his followers argued, the seven Greek vowels were magical symbols of the music of the spheres.

This hypothesis is based on a passage from the treatise *On Style* (*περὶ ἑρμηνείας*) formerly ascribed to Demetrius Phalereus, which suggests that the Gnostics had adopted the Egyptian magic ritual. 'In Egypt too the priests celebrate (*ὑμνοῦσι*) the gods through the seven vowels, letting them sound one after the other; and instead of the aulos and the zither it is the sound of these

[1] C. Leemans, *Papyri graeci musei antiquarii publici Lugduni-Batavi*, tom. ii (Leyden, 1885).

[2] Cf. p. 56, n. 1. Ruelle gives in *Le Chant des sept voyelles* a summary of the theories of his predecessors on the subject.

letters which is heard in euphony.'[1] The clue which made it possible to determine the pitch of each of the tones represented by a vowel was found in a passage from the *Harmonics* of Nicomachus of Gerasa,[2] whose contribution to the development of Neo-Pythagorean musical theory has already been mentioned in the course of this chapter. Developing the Pythagorean conception of the relation between the harmony of the world and that regulating the intervals in music, Nicomachus states that the motion of each of the seven spheres produces a sound (*ψόφον ποιόν*); the first sphere producing the first tone, the second sphere the second tone, and so on. To these tones the names of the seven vowels have been given. According to the cosmological doctrine of Anaximander, adopted and elaborated by Pythagoras and a later generation of his followers,[3] the spheres carry the heavenly bodies in their revolutions round the earth. The vowels therefore are also symbols of the planets. Thus the following concordances between vowels, planets, and tones have been established by Gnostic writers:[4]

A	Moon	Nete	*d'*
E	Mercury	Paranete	*c'*
H	Venus	Paramese	*b♭*
I	Sun	Mese	*a*
O	Mars	Lichanos	*g*
Y	Jupiter	Parhypate	*f*
Ω	Saturn	Hypate	*e*

Taking *ὑμνεῖν* in the second invocation literally as 'to sing', A. Gastoué, starting from Ruelle's hypothesis, arrives at the following rendering of the vowels into musical notation:[5]

Ἐπικαλοῦμαί σε, Κύριε, ᾠδικῷ ὕμνῳ·

[1] *Ἐν Αἰγύπτῳ δὲ καὶ τοὺς θεοὺς ὑμνοῦσι διὰ τῶν ἑπτὰ φωνηέντων οἱ ἱερεῖς, ἐφεξῆς ἠχοῦντες αὐτά, καὶ ἀντὶ αὐλοῦ καὶ ἀντὶ κιθάρας τῶν γραμμάτων τούτων ὁ ἦχος ἀκούεται ὑπ' εὐφωνίας.* *Rhetores Graeci*, edited by L. Spengel (1856), iii. 278.

[2] *Mus. Script. Graeci*, ed. C. Jan, p. 276, l. 8 to p. 277, l. 9.

[3] J. Burnet, *Early Greek Philosophy*[4], pp. 306–7.

[4] *Mus. Script. Graeci*, ed. Jan, pp. 241–2, and E. Ruelle, 'Le Chant des sept voyelles grecques', op. cit., p. 20; Irenaeus, *Adv. haereses*, i. 14, *P.G.* vol. vii, c. 610, quotes Marcus (who flourished in the second century A.D., a disciple of Valentinus writing in his *Sige*), that 'the first heaven sounds the *A*, the next the *E*, the third the *H*, the fourth, in the middle, cries out the might of the *I* (*τὴν τοῦ I δύναμιν ἐκφωνεῖ*), the fifth the *O*, the sixth the *Y*, the seventh and fourth from the middle calls out the element of the *Ω* (*τὸ Ω στοιχεῖον ἐκβοᾷ*)'.

[5] A. Gastoué, *Les Origines du chant romain*, p. 29.

ὑμνῶ σου τὸ ἅγιον κράτος.

From the musical point of view such a final cadence makes a strange impression, but is not impossible. It must be considered, however, whether the formulae of incantation and the vowels were actually meant to be sung by the performer of the sacred rites, or to be pronounced mentally, according to the practice known from mystery sects in the East. From a passage in the *Excerpta* it is obvious that Nicomachus had a kind of mystical utterance in mind, and not real singing, since he says that the initiates invoke the god symbolically by hissings and sibilations, and by inarticulate and incoherent sounds.[1]

We have to bear in mind that to the Greeks the letters of the alphabet were identical with numbers, for which they had no ciphers. Since the Pythagoreans professed that the essence of all things was numbers, they attributed great importance to the correspondence of the seven Ionian vowels to the same number of planets, seeing in the equal number of both a sacred manifestation of the holy figure seven.[2] Thus they came to use the seven vowels for the planets themselves, as well as for the sound of these celestial bodies. Archytas, however, had already pointed out that these were not perceptible to the human senses.[3] The same view is found in Plato's *Timaeus*, where there is no suggestion that the music of the heavens might be audible to human ears.[4] According to Nicomachus it is number 'pre-existent in the mind of the world-creating God, number conceptual only and immaterial in every way, but at the same time the true and eternal essence' by which all things are created: time, motion, the heavens, the stars, and the whole celestial revolution.[5] Nicomachus distinguishes this divine number sharply from the other, which can be apprehended (ἐπιστημονικός); the latter being constantly found in connexion with material things.[6] It is obvious that the vowels were not meant

[1] διὸ δὴ ὅταν μάλιστα οἱ θεουργοὶ τὸ τοιοῦτον σεβάζωνται, σιγμοῖς τε καὶ ποππυσμοῖς καὶ ἀνάρθροις καὶ ἀσυμφώνοις ἤχοις συμβολικῶς ἐπικαλοῦνται. *Excerpta ex Nicomacho*, *Mus. Script. Graeci*, p. 277. 6.

[2] F. Dornseiff, 'Das Alphabet in Mystik und Magie', *Στοιχεῖα*, vii (1922), 33.

[3] H. Diels, *Die Fragm. d. Vorsokr.* i⁶. 433.

[4] F. M. Cornford, 'Plato's Cosmology', *The* Timaeus *of Plato*, p. 72.

[5] D'Ooge, *Nicom. Introduction to Arithmetic*, i. 6, pp. 189–90.

[6] Ibid., p. 98.

to be symbols of audible tones, but of the divine numbers, through which the immaterial nature of the god was revealed to the priests. In mystery rites the magic ceremonial aimed at transferring the initiate from the material sphere to the immaterial. The invocations formed part of the process of transformation, and silence was thought to be 'the first companion of the divine name'.[1]

From these theoretical considerations we must now turn back to the transcriptions of the groups of vowels into musical notation.[2] An examination of the melodic structure of the examples taken from papyrus W of the museum at Leyden and the Berlin papyrus shows that some of them were intended for amulets, others for invocations. The formulae of the amulets can be read from left to right and from right to left, with the same sequence of vowels. The second collection of formulae is built up of combinations of the seven vowels in groups of three, four, six, or seven. These formulae of incantation are often of some length. E. Poirée, following C. E. Ruelle's hypothesis, gives a sufficient number of transcriptions from the papyri to permit us to study their musical structure. The following examples are taken from his article (1 and 2) and from Gastoué's *Origines* (3).

[1] ὁ α΄ σύντροφος τοῦ ὀνόματος σιγή. K. Preisendanz, *Papyri Graecae Magicae*, ii (1931), 34. C. Wessely's transcription of this passage from Pap. London 121 in *Neue griech. Zauberpapyri*, pp. 47–8, is incorrect. The transcription and interpretation of the passage in A. Gastoué's *Les Origines du chant romain*, p. 30, can, therefore, no longer be regarded as valid.

[2] Cf. Élie Poirée's article 'Chant des sept voyelles, Analyse musicale', *Congrès internat. d'histoire de la musique*, pp. 30–7.

We can see at once that intervals of the type found in nearly all the transcriptions are not to be found in any music from which these melismata would be likely to derive, neither in Jewish, Syriac, nor Greek music. In fact, these melismata are so different from anything we should expect that it is difficult to see how anyone could have thought of accepting the transcriptions as a basis for further discussion. Even if the deductions drawn from the passages of Nicomachus' *Introduction* had left any doubt, the musical examples should make it clear that the discussions on the music of the spheres and the connexions between tones and vowels are purely symbolical. They have no reference to the domain of music proper, i.e. to music which can be perceived with our human senses.[1] We can therefore dismiss Ruelle's hypothesis as an erroneous interpretation both of the theoretical treatises on which it is based and of the formulae of incantation.

E. Werner[2] rightly drew attention to the connexion between the importance of the number eight in Gnostic writings and the introduction of the system of the eight modes on which not only classical Greek, but also Byzantine and Western medieval musical theory is based. Here we leave the field of cosmological speculations and enter that of calendaric observations which influenced the structure of Eastern liturgies. With great perspicacity E. Werner pointed out that the Oktoëchos, the liturgical book of the Eastern Churches in which the hymns for the cycle of eight consecutive Sundays are arranged in accordance with the eight modes, is a remnant of a calendaric system, consisting of forty-nine plus one days, which can be traced back to 'the Sumerians, Akkadians and other ancient nations of West Asia'.[3] It has survived in Jewish liturgy and was first introduced into Eastern Christian liturgy for the period between Easter and Pentecost. The Oktoëchos of Severus of Antioch, a monophysite monk who lived in the first half of the sixth century, consists of hymns for the Common of the Seasons which are sung on each of the eight Sundays in a different *echos* (mode), viz. on the first Sunday in

[1] The same view is expressed by K. Wachsmann in his 'Untersuchungen zum vorgregorianischen Gesang', *Veröffentl. d. gregor. Ak. zu Freiburg i. d. Schweiz*, xix. 24–34. He points out that no reference has been found to the use of melodies as amulets, whereas it is known that groups of vowels were used.

[2] E. Werner, 'The Origin of the Eight Modes of Music (Octoëchos). A Study in Musical Symbolism', *Hebrew Union College Annual*, xxi (Cincinnati, 1948), 211–55; 'The Sacred Bridge. The Interdependence of Liturgy and Music in Synagogue and Church during the first Millennium' (1959), pp. 373–406.

[3] Ibid., pp. 23–4.

the first echos, on the second Sunday in the second, and so on. These eight Sundays comprise a period of fifty days, a Pentecontade. Originally the hymns of the Oktoëchos were sung on the eight Sundays after Pentecost,[1] but soon three other Pentecontades were added on which the hymns arranged in the eight echoi were sung, and finally the custom of singing the hymns in cycles of eight weeks on all the days of the week was introduced in the Eastern Churches.[2]

Putting together the material now available, E. Werner has shown that the liturgical practice of the Oktoëchos has its origin in a calendaric system which uses a period of seven weeks plus one day as a unit and builds up the year 'of seven Pentecontades plus fourteen intercalated days. The origin of the Pentecontade Calendar rests with the conception of seven seasons and seven winds. Each wind corresponds to a God. Over these seven Gods there ruled a supreme deity.'[3] This is the *Ogdoas*.

In the so-called 'Eighth Book of Moses', or 'Moses' Book about the Great Name' from the Papyrus Magicus Leyden W, pp. 16 sqq.,[4] the anonymous author informs the adept that he will bind him by an oath to keep secret the content of its revelations, for he will soon realize what magic power the book possesses:

'Εναπόκειται γὰρ αὐτῇ τὸ κύριον □ *(ὄνομα) ὅ ἐστι "Οκδοος ('Ογδοάς), ὁ τὰ πάντα ἐπιτάσσων καὶ διοικῶν· τούτῳ γὰρ ὑπετάγησαν ἄγγελοι, ἀρχάγγελοι, δαίμονες, δαιμώνισσαι, καὶ πάντα τὰ ὑπὸ τὴν κτίσιν.*

(Stored up in it is the supreme name, which is Ogdoas, who commands and administers the whole; to him are obedient the angels, the archangels, the demons and demonissae and everything under creation.) p. 16, ll. 46–9.

Until recently the eight echoi in Byzantine music had been identified by modern scholars with the eight modes of ancient Greek musical theory. This was a mistake, because the Greek 'scales'—if we are permitted to use the term—were reckoned from the highest note downwards, whereas the Byzantine theorists built up the modes from the lowest note upwards:

[1] Cf. A. Baumstark, *Festbrevier und Kirchenjahr der syrischen Jakobiten* (Paderborn, 1910), pp. 26, 44.

[2] The name Oktoëchos is properly used only for the liturgical book which contains the hymns, arranged in cycles of the eight modes for Sundays; the book which contains hymns for the whole week is called Parakletike; but the first is also called 'the lesser Oktoëchos', and the second 'great Oktoëchos'.

[3] E. Werner, op. cit., pp. 223–4. [4] C. Leemans, op. cit., tome ii, pp. 139 sqq.

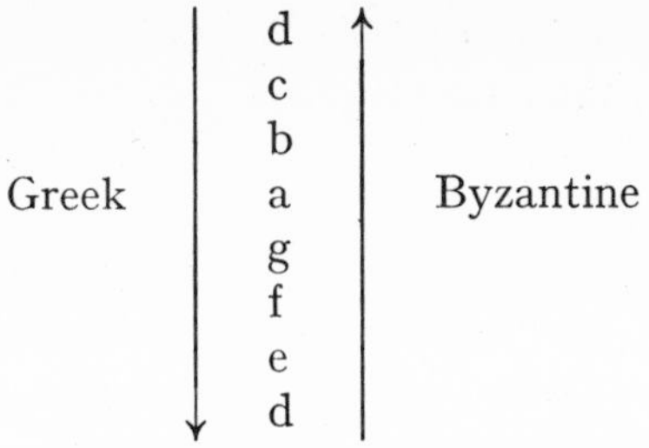

Greek ↓		Byzantine ↑
	d	
	c	
	b	
	a	
	g	
	f	
	e	
	d	

The essence of a melody sung in one of the eight echoi, however, was its musical content. By analysing the musical structure of the melodies belonging to one of the eight echoi I found that the melodies of each echos were built up of a number of formulae which were a peculiar feature of the mode,[1] or, in other words: it was not the 'scale' which was the basis of composition for the early Christian and Byzantine hymnographer, but a group of formulae which belonged together and made up the material for each mode. The composer's task consisted in adapting these melodic formulae to the words of a new hymn and in linking them together in accordance with the words.

This principle can be found as the basis of musical composition everywhere in Western Asia and down to India where the Râgas or melody types which represent different modes are depicted in miniatures as gods and goddesses. It remains to be seen whether further research will show that the musical formulae which constitute the material for each mode originally had a certain ritual significance, so that they could only be sung at certain times of the year or day. We may suspect that this was the case from the fact that the melodies of the third plagal mode, the *Barys*, or grave mode, are used primarily for hymns of a mournful character, and, as the name indicates, which had to be sung in a slow tempo. This question, however, cannot be settled until we know more about Early Byzantine and even Early Christian music, since the feeling for the peculiar character of the different modes has completely vanished in Byzantine music of the period from which we have the earliest specimens of musical notation.

[1] Cf. pp. 300–6, and pp. 417–27. The fact that the melodies of the Eastern Church were built up from a certain number of melodic formulae which gave the mode its peculiar character was first expounded by the present writer in a study on 'Die Struktur des serbischen Oktoëchos', *Zeitschrift für Musikwissenschaft*, ii (1919–20), 140–8.

(*b*) *Greek alchemists on music*

In the second book of the treatise *de magna et sacra arte* ascribed to Stephanus of Alexandria who was public professor at the time of the emperor Heraclius (610–41),[1] at the beginning, there is a short passage which refers to music. Speaking of 'the multitude of numbers compounded together' which had its existence 'from one atom and natural monad', Stephanus compares the relation of the emanating but immutable and unmoved monad with the rhythmical sound produced by Orpheus on a stringed instrument, so that the harmonious sounds 'should re-echo the co-ordinated movement of the elements and the sounding melody should be harmoniously perfected. For from the one instrument the whole composition takes its origin.'[2]

Here reference to music is only made in order to show the relation of one element, the single musical instrument, to the multitude of sounding elements, but it is significant of the Neo-Platonic attitude of the author that in the second paragraph of his treatise he already introduces music as an analogy to his statement, made in the first paragraph, that 'the symbol of every circular sphere is the centre, likewise of every triangle and plane and solid figure set out by lines'.[3] Music, for Stephanus, comes next to geometry; it forms part of the *quadrivium* which can be traced back to Pythagorean philosophy.

Musicologists have recently drawn attention to two sections on music: one in a treatise ascribed to Zosimus of Panopolis, an author of the third or fourth century A.D., the other in one ascribed to an anonymous writer of the seventh century, who was supposed to have given an augmented version of Zosimus's treatise. The sections in question form part of two chapters on music and alchemy published by M. Berthelot and C.-É. Ruelle in their *Collection des anciens alchimistes grecs* (Paris, 1887–8). It was assumed that in them the first traces of a Byzantine musical theory are to be found.[4] Recent investigations by O.

[1] Cf. F. Sherwood Taylor, 'The Alchemical Works of Stephanos of Alexandria, Part I', *Ambix*, i (1937), 117. The treatise *de magna et sacra arte* has been edited by I. L. Ideler in *Physici et medici Graeci minores*, ii (Berlin, 1847), 203 sqq.

[2] Translation by F. Sherwood Taylor, op. cit.

[3] Ibid., p. 27.

[4] C. Höeg, 'La Théorie de la musique byzantine', *Revue des études grecques*, vol. xxxv (1922); A. Gastoué, 'Über die 8 Töne', *Kirchenmusikalisches Jahrbuch*, vol. xxv (1930); K. Wachsmann, op. cit., pp. 55–77. A survey of investigations into the passage of music in alchemical treatises is given in G. Reese's *Music in the Middle Ages* (1940), pp. 85–6.

Gombosi in his 'Studien zur Tonartenlehre des Mittelalters' in *Acta Musicologica*, xii (1940), 29–52, however, have proved that both chapters belong together and form a short treatise, written for the purpose of comparing the elements of alchemy with those of music. In this study Gombosi has shown that owing to a lacuna in the text of the manuscript from which Cod. Bibl. Nat. Paris. gr. 2327 (A) was copied, the final pages of Zosimus's treatise *πρὸς Θεόδωρον κεφάλαια* (*Coll.* iii. 43, pp. 215–18) and the beginning of the next, 'On the making of Gold' by an anonymous author (*Coll.* iii. 44, pp. 219–20), were put together. The editors of the *Collection*, though acknowledging the corrupt state of the text, overlooked the fact that the chapter on music was not the work of Zosimus, but of an anonymous author, whose treatise was appended to Zosimus's *πρὸς Θεόδωρον*. Gombosi points out that the editors of the *Collection* could have observed this from the study of the oldest manuscript which contains a group of alchemical treatises, namely, the eleventh-century Codex Marcianus 299 (M) of the Marciana in Venice containing the end of Zosimus's *πρὸς Θεόδωρον* and the complete treatise of the *Anonymus*. The treatise of the 'anonymous philosopher' contains, in fact, the only complete version of the text. It should not, therefore, have been published by the editors of the *Collection* in the sixth part, among the commentators (*Coll.* vi. 15, 433–41).

The content of the treatise of the 'anonymous philosopher' still offers many difficulties to our understanding, though attempts have been made to explain the most obscure passages and to correct the text. Textual criticism of the treatise has to start by explaining the main technical term used in it, viz. the rare word *στοχός*, which we find in the oldest source, the Codex Marcianus (M). The two principal sources of the other group of manuscripts, viz. the Paris MSS., Bibl. Nat. gr. 2327 (A) and 2249 (K) use the term *στοῖχος*. Though Ruelle, the editor of the treatise in the *Collection des anciens alchimistes grecs*, has left *στοχός* in the Greek edition, he has emended it into *στοῖχος* (*ligne musicale*) = ecclesiastical mode in his translation. Accepting this emendation, C. Höeg, A. Gastoué, and, recently, A. Auda, developed the hypothesis that Zosimus—whom they considered as the author of the treatise—had twenty-four modes in view when he spoke of the *στοχοὶ κδ′*. The adherents of the modal hypothesis referred to a footnote to the Greek text (*Coll.* vi., p. 434) in which Ruelle pointed out that in Codex Paris. gr. 2329 (E) *στοχός* or *στοῖχος* is replaced by *ἦχος*, a term occurring in Byzantine musical theory and practice for the mode of a hymn-tune. E, however, cannot be accepted by us as a source for corrections in the text, since it derives from the manuscripts of group A and was written in the seventeenth century. By substituting *στοῖχος* for *στοχός* a satisfactory interpretation of the text was made impossible. This fact was already recognized by K. Wachsmann,[1] who suggested that *στοιχεῖον* (= element) should be substituted for *στοχός*. This is a considerable alteration. But recently Lagercrantz has proved convincingly[2] that the scribe of M wrote *στοχός* where other sources had *στοιχεῖον*. The main difficulties for an understanding of the text virtually disappear when *στοχός* is replaced everywhere by *στοιχεῖον*, which means the element, not only in alchemy, but also in music, where it is one of the four tones of the tetrachord. We shall see, however, that by this change the very elaborate and far-reaching conclusions drawn from the text of the Anonymous by Gastoué and Auda can no longer stand.

Let us now give a short synopsis of the text of the alchemical treatise. The anonymous author starts by explaining the nature of the mystical egg of the alchemists, which consists of four elements. Four elements, too, can be found as the constituents of music, since the elementary row, the tetrachord, is built up of four tones. There are six different kinds of tetrachords: Kentroi, Isoi, Plagioi, Katharoi, Aëchoi, and Paraëchoi, each consisting of four tones.[3] Thus, he concludes, all music is confined to twenty-four elements of different kinds. 'There is no other possible way of building up the melodies—countless within their species—of the hymns, or benedictions, or revelations, or other parts of the divine science without aberration and corruption and other musical calamities. The same can be found in the unique and true supreme matter, the generation of birds.'[4] But

[1] *Untersuch. z. vorgreg. Gesang*, p. 61, n. 9.

[2] *Catalogue des manuscrits alchimiques grecs*, iv. 424.

[3] *ὥσπερ δὲ τεσσάρων ὄντων μουσικῶν γενικωτάτων στοιχείων, α^{ου}, β^{ου}, γ^{ου}, δ^{ου}, γίνονται παρ' αὐτῶν τῷ εἴδει διάφορα στοιχεῖα κδʹ, κέντροι καὶ ἴσοι καὶ πλάγιοι, καθαροί τε καὶ ἄηχοι<καὶ παράηχοι>.* *Coll.* vi. 15, § 2, p. 434, ll. 4–6.

[4] *καὶ ἀδύνατον ἄλλως ὑφανθῆναι τὰς κατὰ μέρος ἀπείρους μελῳδίας τῶν ὑμνῶν ἢ θεραπειῶν ἢ ἀποκαλύψεων ἢ ἄλλου σκέλους τῆς ἱερᾶς ἐπιστήμης, καὶ οἷον ῥεύσεως ἢ φθορᾶς ἢ ἄλλων μουσικῶν παθῶν ἐλευθέρας. τοῦτο κἀνταῦθα ἔστιν εὑρεῖν [τὸν δυνατὸν] ἐπὶ τῆς μιᾶς καὶ ἀληθοῦς κυριωτάτης ὕλης, τῆς ὀρνιθογενίας.* *Coll.*, p. 434, ll. 7–11.

it is not only the melodies that are sung, the anonymous author continues, which are built up from the four elements, but also the music which is played on wind instruments (τὸ αὐλούμενον) and on stringed (κιθαριζόμενον). He then explains of which elements a melody can be composed and how the tetrachords can be combined without creating disorder. The same procedure has to be applied to the different stages of alchemical mixtures. Finally some wind, stringed, and percussion instruments are enumerated, some of them familiar from classical Greek authors, others, like the Achilliakon or the Rax, difficult to identify. Names like Nadion and Kabithakanthion seem to be corruptions of Arabic names for instruments: Nadion for Nafir = trumpet, καβιθακάνθιον ἑπτὰ δακτύλων for κόβουζ ἀκάνθων ἑπτὰ δακτύλων = 'a Qupûz (a kind of cither) with seven thorns (or frets) for the fingers'.[1]

The treatise is obviously a compilation from passages dating back to writers on alchemy of the third and fourth centuries, among whom Zosimus of Panopolis is the outstanding figure, though very little, if any, of his work is really original.[2] It has been proved that Zosimus was heir to the ideas of Mary and of Cleopatra,[3] two alchemical authors of the first century A.D.; the passages on music of the Ps.-Zosimus may, therefore, go back to speculations on musical theory current in the days of Philo of Alexandria, and compiled by him from alchemical writings by Zosimus and later commentators, through whose works fragments from Mary, Cleopatra, and other original authors on alchemy were scattered. This view is based on the examination of a passage in the sixth paragraph of the treatise, from which it seems rather doubtful whether this 'anonymous philosopher' of the seventh century had a clear view of the musical ideas which he inherited. After stating in § 2 that twenty-four different species (τῷ εἴδει διάφορα) of elements are obtained from the four principal elements, the author admits in § 6 the possibility of another view, viz. that the twenty-four species derive from only six, each of them consisting of four elements. But, he concludes abruptly, 'it is not fitting for us to talk about this question'.[4]

It is probable that he was an adherent of the Neo-Pythagorean School who wanted to prove the essential unity of a physical

[1] Cf. O. Gombosi, 'Studien, III', *A.M.* xii. 48.

[2] Cf. F. Sherwood Taylor, 'A Survey of Greek Alchemy', *J.H.S.* l (1930), 119.

[3] Ibid., pp. 116 and 119.

[4] Cf. *Coll.* vi. 15, § 6, p. 437, l. 9.

world which is different in its species. His reference to a passage from Zosimus that 'everything caused by nature is one, not in form, but in system' (ἑνὸς ὄντος τοῦ φυσικοῦ, ἀλλ' οὐκ εἴδους, ἀλλὰ τέχνης)[1] suggests such a line of thought. The content of the treatise in which the elements of alchemy are compared with those of music has to be considered as a whole. The two parts are of equal importance. The chemical processes described in this and other alchemical treatises are symbolical. The chemical directions for colouring the 'egg'[2] stand for the magical process through which the initiate is enabled to produce the philosopher's stone, i.e. to acquire superior powers by overcoming his bodily nature and transforming himself into a higher being. Similarly the 'elements' of music do not apply to audible tones and tetrachords but to the music of the spheres and to the harmonies which create an attunement between soul and body.

The fact that some of the names of instruments appear in a corrupt form, while others are so strange that it is doubtful whether they are not pure inventions of the author, is an additional indication that the treatise could have had no connexion with musical practice. This part of the treatise may have been added later in order to prove that the elementary principles on which all music is based can be applied to all musical instruments, though they vary in shape and quality of sound.

Any attempt, therefore, to establish connexions between the speculations on music in the alchemical treatise and actual Byzantine musical theory should proceed with great caution, particularly as the treatise consists of various parts compiled from works spread over a period of between six to eight hundred years. To assign it to a Christian author[3] is certainly wrong. Speaking of the hymns to be sung at the service of the divine knowledge (τῆς ἱερᾶς ἐπιστήμης), Ps.-Zosimus certainly does not refer to the Christian Office, but to the mystery cult of a Gnostic sect, influenced by Iranian and Chaldean ideas.[4] This becomes evident from a treatise bearing the title: 'The High Priest Komarius, the philosopher, teaches Cleopatra the divine and

[1] Ibid., p. 437, l. 5.

[2] Cf. R. Reitzenstein, 'Zur Geschichte d. Alchemie u. des Mystizismus', *Nachrichten d. Kgl. Ges. d. Wiss. zu Göttingen, Phil.-hist. Kl.*, 1919, p. 20.

[3] Cf. A. Gastoué, 'L'Origine lointaine des huit tons liturgiques', *Revue du Chant Grégorien*, xxxiv (1930), 126 sqq.

[4] R. Reitzenstein, op. cit., p. 20. Zosimus (*Coll.*, p. 114) calls the alchemical process of preparing the philosopher's stone τὸ μιθριακὸν μυστήριον.

holy art of the philosopher's stone.'[1] This art (τέχνη) is identical with that of initiation into the mystery of the 'Egg', composed of four elements, 'since it is the image of the world and contains in itself the four elements'. It is also called 'the stone which is turned by the moon', 'stone which is not stone', 'eagle-stone', and 'brain of alabaster'.[2]

There is one point still to be mentioned: the musical terms used by Ps.-Zosimus to designate the six tetrachords, Katharos, Plagios, Isos, Kentros, Aëchos, and Paraëchos are not to be found in any works on musical theory either by classical Greek or by Byzantine authors. In Byzantine theory the term Plagios, of course, commonly designates subsidiary species of the four authentic modes, but there is a fundamental difference between these modes and the rows of tones mentioned by Ps.-Zosimus. All the Byzantine modes are based on ascending scales. The difference between authentic and plagal modes is to be found in their cadences. On the contrary, of the six tetrachords mentioned by Ps.-Zosimus, three (Kentros, Katharos, Paraëchos) are ascending, the other three descending.[3]

From all these considerations we may conclude that the treatise 'On the making of gold' is a document of some value for our studies. More importance, however, may be attached to the blending of Greek cosmogonic speculations with ideas appertaining to Gnostic and other mystical sects, than to its reference to the theory of music. In fact, the allusions to music are incoherent to such a degree that it is easy to see that they were given by the author only as illustrations of the alchemical process, which he described to the initiates. These allusions are kept obscure in the same way as the descriptions of the alchemical process itself. References to musical theory are based on Greek musical thought; they do not show any development characteristic of Byzantine musical theory, the beginnings of which are still concealed from us. The treatise of the 'anonymous philosopher' forms a link in the chain of other alchemical works of a similar character, extending from the earliest days of a Christian society existing in the midst of a pagan majority, to the time when Orthodox Christianity had been fully developed, and had given to the Eastern Empire the features characteristic of the new Byzantine civilization.

1 *Catal. des MSS. alchimiques grecs*, iv. 400–1.

2 τὸ ᾠὸν ἐκάλεσαν τετράστοιχον διὰ τὸ εἶναι αὐτὸ κόσμου μίμησιν, περιέχον τὰ τέσσαρα στοιχεῖα ἐνέαυτῷ· ὃν καὶ λίθον ἐκάλεσαν ὃν κυλίει ἡ σελήνη, καὶ λίθον τὸν οὐ λίθον, καὶ λίθον ἀετίτην, καὶ ἀλαβάστρινον ἐγκέφαλον. *Coll. d. anc. Alchim. gr.* i. 4, pp. 20–1.

3 O. Gombosi, 'Studien III', *A.M.* xii. 49.

CHAPTER III

THE PAGAN BACKGROUND

I. ABSENCE OF MUSICAL DOCUMENTS

THE prominent part which music held in the daily life of the Eastern Empire can be seen from the reports of ceremonies and festivities by Byzantine historians. To these may be added the arguments of Christian writers and the decrees of councils against the pernicious effects on morality of public shows and spectacles. Yet anyone who looks for records of secular music in Byzantine manuscripts will be disappointed, since no trace of this kind of music has been discovered in any document up to the present day. This fact will not surprise the student of the history of music, as there is a similar absence of documents for secular music in the West before the twelfth century. This lack of documents for Byzantine secular music is regrettable, but we are faced with the same absence of written evidence in every other branch of Eastern secular music, and it is hardly to be expected that we should be in a more favourable position with regard to that of Byzantium alone.

Eastern secular music has been transmitted orally up to the present day, and the instrumentalists were used to accompanying the singers by heart. Byzantine musical notation was exclusively used for fixing ecclesiastical hymns and some of the acclamations (ἄκτα) sung during ceremonies of the court in honour of the Emperor and the Empress, or of the Church in honour of a visiting ecclesiastical dignitary. The specific character of this musical notation, with which we shall have to deal fully later on, would have made its use impossible for any other purpose before its final development as an interval notation at the beginning of the thirteenth century. But even at that stage its application to secular music would have been most unlikely. The clergy, the courtiers, and other members of the educated classes who collected books and ordered them to be written treated with contempt public shows, ballets, pantomimes, and other theatrical performances accompanied by music. They would never, therefore, have suggested that the system of musical signs used for the transmission of hymns or acclamations in honour of the

Imperial family and of ecclesiastical dignitaries should be used for recording profane music.

II. THE ATTITUDE OF THE CHURCH TO MUSIC IN PUBLIC LIFE

This fact, however, must not lead us to overlook the important role which secular music played in Byzantine civilization. The Eastern Empire had inherited from the Western and from the Hellenistic world many of the pagan feasts which were connected with processions, dances, pantomimes, and other theatrical performances; it had inherited from Rome the passion for the Hippodrome, which had dominated public life during the whole period of the city's growth and decline. These feasts, above all the Olympic games, the Calendae, Vota, Brumalia, and Maïoumas, were celebrated in the Eastern part of the Roman Empire, above all in Antioch, Ephesus, Miletus, Pergamum, and Alexandria, in their original pagan form during the first centuries of our era.[1] From the beginning they were vigorously attacked and condemned by Christian writers, and when the Christian faith became the State religion of the newly founded Byzantine Empire the attacks became even more violent, as they were backed by the authority of the *Basileus*, whom Byzantine Christianity regarded as God's delegate on earth, as *Isapostolos*, the prince 'equal to the Apostles'. But when the clergy became convinced that it was impossible to abolish the feasts, which were too deeply rooted in the minds of the people, they changed their policy, taking all the performances under their control and gradually christianizing them.

The hostile attitude of the Church is easy to understand. From the second to the fourth centuries the members of Christian communities lived in the midst of a highly developed pagan civilization and were tempted to take part in the theatrical performances, dances, and processions they were constantly witnessing. This fact explains the warning voices which many Christian writers raised against the 'theatre of the Devil',[2] which destroyed the modesty of family life.[3] The warnings can be

[1] Cf. V. Cottas, *Le Théâtre à Byzance* (Paris, 1931), pp. 6 sqq. Vénétia Cottas's book is largely based on the copious study of K. N. Sathas, *Ἱστορικὸν δοκίμιον περὶ τοῦ θεάτρου καὶ τῆς μουσικῆς τῶν Βυζαντινῶν* (Venice, 1878); it makes part of the material collected by Sathas easily accessible to the Western reader.

[2] *καὶ οὐ παύσομαι, ἕως ἂν διασκεδάσας τοῦ διαβόλου τὸ θέατρον, καθαρὸν ποιήσω τῆς ἐκκλησίας τὸν σύλλογον.* St. John Chrysostom, *Homiliae in Matth.* (7th Hom., c. 7), *Bibl. Patr.* i. 100, l. 1, ed. F. Field.

[3] *ἐκεῖθεν μὲν γὰρ εὐθέως πῦρ δέχεται ἔρωτος ἄτοπον ὁ ἀκροατής.* Ibid. ii (68th Hom., c. 4), 299 l. 2, ed. F. Field.

found as early as the writings of the Apologists. Tatian in his controversial discussion of Hellenic civilization, *Address to the Greeks* (λόγος πρὸς Ἕλληνας), denounces (22–4) the dangers of assemblies, which take place under the patronage of 'wicked demons'. Athenagoras in his *Supplication concerning the Christians* (πρεσβεία περὶ Χριστιανῶν, 35) tries to persuade Christians not to go to the amphitheatre, and states that those who fail to prevent murder are as guilty as those who commit murder. Theophilus, Bishop of Antioch, brings forward the same arguments in *Ad Autolycum*, 3. 15. Clement of Alexandria asks in the last chapter of the *Paedagogus* whether there exists any shameful thing which was not to be seen in a theatrical show. The peril had obviously become so serious by the end of the second and the beginning of the third centuries that two Christian writers found it necessary to deal with it in special pamphlets. Both authors belonged to the Church of Carthage, and both wrote in Latin: they were Tertullian and either Cyprian himself or one of his contemporaries known to-day as Pseudo-Cyprian.

Tertullian, after giving a survey of the historical development of the theatre which he shows to have always been connected with the cult of the gods, comes to the conclusion that it is a place of idolatry and immodesty: 'quae vero voce et modis et organis et lyris transiguntur Apollines et Musas et Minervas et Mercurios mancipes habent.'[1] He addresses his reader and asks whether anyone could imagine that the angels in heaven would be ignorant of what was going on in *diaboli ecclesia*. 'Non ergo fugies sedilia hostium Christi, illam cathedram pestilentiarum, ipsumque aerem, qui desuper incubat, scelestis vocibus constupratum?' What a difference, Tertullian concludes, between these spectacles and that of the triumphant coming of Christ, or of the Last Judgement: 'ille ultimus et perpetuus judicii dies, ille nationibus insperatus, ille derisus, cum tanta saeculi vetustas, et tot eius nativitates uno igni haurientur. quae tunc spectaculi latitudo!'[2] The second pamphlet, dating from the middle of the third century, refutes those who look to the Old Testament to provide an excuse for attending theatrical performances and ballets:

Non pudet, inquam, non pudet fideles homines et christiani sibi nominis auctoritatem vindicantes superstitiones vanas gentilium cum spectaculis mixtas de scripturis caelestibus vindicare et divinam auctoritatem

[1] *De spectaculis*, c. 10; *P.G.* i, col. 643.

[2] Ib., c. 30; *P.G.* i, col. 660.

idololatriae conferre. Nam quando id quod in honore alicuius idoli ab ethnicis agitur a fidelibus christianis spectaculo frequentatur, et idololatria gentilis asseritur et in contumeliam Dei religio vera et divina calcatur. Pudor me tenet praescriptiones eorum in hac causa et patrocinia referre. 'ubi', inquiunt, 'scripta sunt ista, ubi prohibita? alioquin et auriga est Israel Helias et ante arcam David ipse saltavit. Nabla cynaras aera tympana tibias citharas choros legimus.'[1]

To argue in this way, Ps.-Cyprian says, is to misinterpret the text. 'For then harps, cymbals, flutes, drums, and zithers sounded in honour of God, and not of idols; whereas now through the skill of the devil these instruments have become forbidden things.'

No Christian writer, however, has used more violent language against the theatre than John Chrysostom, who served the Church of Antioch as deacon and presbyter from A.D. 381 to 398. At this time Antioch was, after Alexandria, the chief theatrical centre of the Eastern Empire. It had four theatres, the theatre of Dionysos, the theatre of Zeus Olympius, the so-called 'Plethron', and 'the Oblong theatre' (*πρόμηκες θέατρον*), where classical tragedies and comedies, and also lighter comedies, ballets, pantomimes, and all sorts of scenic shows were performed.

From a passage in the seventh homily *in Matthaeum* it is clear what kind of shows the theatres of Antioch presented at the end of the fourth century. Chrysostom asks his reader: 'Tell me, then; if anyone offered to take you to the palace and show you the king on his throne, would you really choose to see the theatre instead of the king? And yet there is nothing to be gained in the palace. But here there is a spiritual well of fire that gushes up from this Table, and you abandon this and run down to the theatre to see women swimming and nature put to open dishonour, leaving Christ sitting by the well.'[2] He warns his audience that they risk shipwreck of soul by deserting the fountain of blood, the awful cup, for the fountain of the devil: 'For that water is a sea of lasciviousness, not drowning bodies but working shipwreck of souls. And whereas she swims with naked body, you, beholding, are sunk in the deep of lasciviousness.'[3]

[1] Ps.-Cyprian, *De spectaculis*, *C.S.E.L.*, vol. iii, Appendix i, p. 5.

[2] *εἰπὲ γάρ μοι, εἴ τίς σε εἰς βασίλεια εἰσαγαγεῖν ἐπηγγέλλετο, καὶ δείξειν τὸν βασιλέα καθήμενον, ἆρα ἂν εἵλου τὸ θέατρον ἀντὶ τούτων ἰδεῖν; καίτοιγε οὐδὲν οὐδὲ ἐκεῖθεν κερδᾶναι ἦν. ἐνταῦθα δὲ πηγὴ πυρὸς πνευματικὴ ἀπὸ ταύτης ἀναβλύζει τῆς τραπέζης καὶ σὺ ταύτην ἀφεὶς κατατρέχεις εἰς τὸ θέατρον, ἰδεῖν νηχομένας γυναῖκας καὶ φύσιν παραδειγματιζομένην, καταλιπὼν τὸν Χριστὸν παρὰ τὴν πηγὴν καθήμενον;* *Hom. in Matth.*: *Bibl. Patr.* i. 96.

[3] *τὸ γὰρ ὕδωρ ἐκεῖνο πέλαγος ἀσελγείας ἐστίν, οὐ σώματα ποιοῦν ὑποβρύχια ἀλλὰ ψυχῶν ναυάγια*

In another passage, in the thirty-seventh homily *in Matthaeum*, Chrysostom gives a masterly picture of the corruption of the spectacles which he had obviously seen in his youth in Antioch: 'Yea, and in that place there are foul words and fouler gestures, and the dressing of the hair has the same purpose, and the gait, and the costume, and the voice, and the languishing movement of the limbs, and the rollings of the eyes, and the flutes, and the pipes, and the action, and the plots, and everything, in short, is full of the utmost licentiousness.'[1]

He implores the Christian congregation not to behave worse than the barbarians, who cannot understand how the civilized citizens of the Empire can enjoy such spectacles: 'What excuse, then, can there be for us, since we who are citizens of heaven, and have our part in the chorus of the Cherubim, and are the companions of the angels, degrade ourselves lower than even the barbarians in this respect, and that when there are innumerable other better pleasures within our reach.'[2]

At the climax of the thirty-seventh homily he introduces a dialogue between himself and an imaginary questioner, who asks what is to be done; should the theatres be closed, and everything turned upside down? Chrysostom answers that society is already turned upside down: marriage and family life are completely corrupted by the bad example of the stage. He is asked whether in that case the theatres should not be pulled down altogether. He replies that it would, indeed, be best: 'Nevertheless, I do not command it, but, standing as these places are, I bid you make them of no effect, which were a greater praise than pulling them down.'[3]

As we read these homilies we must try to envisage the situation of the Christian community to which they were addressed. They were a minority in a pagan city, by whose laws they were obliged to live. Any violent action on their part would have been immediately and easily suppressed. They were forced, therefore,

ἐργαζόμενον. ἀλλ' ἡ μὲν νήχεται γυμνουμένη τὸ σῶμα, σὺ δὲ ὁρῶν καταποντίζῃ πρὸς τὸν τῆς ἀσελγείας βυθόν. Ibid., p. 96.

[1] *καὶ γὰρ τὰ ῥήματα αἰσχρὰ αὐτόθι, καὶ σχήματα αἰσχρότερα, καὶ κουρὰ τοιαύτη, καὶ βάδισις, κα στολή, καὶ φωνή, καὶ μελῶν διάκλασις, καὶ ὀφθαλμῶν ἐκστροφαί, καὶ σύριγγες, καὶ αὐλοί, καὶ δράματα, καὶ ὑποθέσεις, καὶ πάντα ἁπλῶς τῆς ἐσχάτης ἀσελγείας ἀνάμεστα.* Ibid., p. 523.

[2] *τίς οὖν ἡμῖν ἔσται ἀπολογία λοιπόν, ὅταν ἡμεῖς οἱ τῶν οὐρανῶν πολῖται, καὶ τῶν Χερουβὶμ συγχορευταί, καὶ τῶν ἀγγέλων κοινωνοί, καὶ τῶν βαρβάρων χείρους ταύτῃ γινώμεθα, καὶ ταῦτα ἐξὸν μυρίας ἑτέρας τούτων βελτίους τέρψεις εὑρεῖν;* Ibid., p. 525.

[3] St. John Chrisostom, ibid. xxxvii. 525.

to defend themselves against corruption by withdrawing from the scenes where it was enacted, not by abolishing them.

Chrysostom's attitude to the theatre is summed up for us in the sixth homily *in Matthaeum*:

'It is not for us, then, to be continually laughing, and to be dissolute and luxurious, but it is for those upon the stage, for the harlot women, the men who are gelded to this intent, parasites and flatterers, not for those who bear spiritual arms but for those who belong to the devil. For it is he, yea, it is he, who even made this thing an art, so that he might weaken Christ's soldiers, and soften the sinews of their zeal. For this cause he also built theatres in the cities, and, having trained these buffoons, by means of their wretched condition he hurls this terrible pestilence on the whole city, persuading men to follow those things which Paul commanded us to flee, foolish talking and jesting.'[1]

Chrysostom is fighting against the 'mortiferi cantus et acroamata scenicorum, quae mentem emolliunt ad amores', as St. Ambrose calls them.[2] He follows the same line of argument as Tertullian, Cyprian, Clement of Alexandria, the Cappadocian Fathers Gregory Nazianzen and Basil the Great, Ambrose, Augustine, and Jerome.[3] In fact, we already find in Chrysostom's homilies the distinction, which was made later by St. Augustine between *musica luxuriantis*, creating *luxuriosa aurium voluptas*, and *musica sapientis*; a distinction of great importance for the development of the art of music in the Middle Ages.

III. ECCLESIASTICAL EDICTS AGAINST PAGAN MUSIC

The legislation of the Church dealt extensively with the danger arising from theatrical displays. The Council of Laodicea (A.D. 360) denounced people who jumped about and danced on their way to a wedding as behaving in a way improper for Christians (Canon 53).[4] Priests or clerics were forbidden to remain at a wedding-feast when the actors entered to perform a theatrical show: they had to leave before the actors came (Canon 54).[5] But we may ask if there is any difference between the attitude of the Church in condemning theatrical shows and that of

[1] *Hom. in Matth.*: *Bibl. Patr.* vi. 84.

[2] *Hexaëmeron*, iii. 1.

[3] Cf. T. Gérold, *Les Pères de l'Église et la Musique* (Paris, 1931), ch. ii.

[4] *ὅτι οὐ δεῖ χριστιανοὺς εἰς γάμους ἀπερχομένους βαλλίζειν ἢ ὀρχεῖσθαι, ἀλλὰ σεμνῶς δειπνεῖν ἢ .ἀριστᾶν ὡς πρέπει χριστιανοῖς.* J.-B. Pitra, *Iuris Eccles. Graec. Monumenta*, i. 502.

[5] *ὅτι οὐ δεῖ ἱερατικοὺς ἢ κληρικούς τινας θεωρίας θεωρεῖν ἐν γάμοις, ἢ δείπνοις, ἀλλὰ πρὸ τοῦ εἰσέρχεσθαι τοὺς θυμελικούς, ἐγείρεσθαι αὐτοὺς καὶ ἀναχωρεῖν ἐκεῖθεν.* Ibid.

civilized pagan society. While the Council of Laodicea was being convoked the Emperor Julian was making a last effort to reorganize pagan religion. In a letter written to the High Priest of the province of Asia[1] at the beginning of A.D. 363 he issued the following orders:

'No priest should, in any place, attend these licentious theatrical shows, . . . nor introduce (an actor) into his own house, for that is altogether unfitting. Indeed, if it were possible to expel such shows completely from the theatres and give back a pure stage to Dionysus I should certainly have attempted zealously to carry this out; but since I thought that this was impossible, and that even if it were possible it would, for other reasons, not be expedient, I abstained entirely from this ambition. I do expect, however, that priests should withdraw themselves from the obscenity of the theatres and leave them to the crowd. Therefore let no priest enter a theatre, or have an actor or a charioteer for his friend; and let no dancer or mime approach his door. I only permit him to go, if he likes, to the sacred games in which women are forbidden not only to participate in the competitions, but even to have seats in the theatres. With regard to the hunting shows with dogs which are arranged by the cities inside the theatres, need I say that not only priests but even the sons of priests must abstain from them?'[2]

This edict shows clearly that Julian saw the same dangers as the Church did. But the Church had not merely to guard against the dangers to the morals of the Christian population which arose from the indecency of public shows: she had an even more important reason for prohibiting her adherents from attending anything connected with theatrical displays. Such displays were sacred to the gods. Therefore, in the course of the following centuries, the attitude of the Church became increasingly hostile to scenic performances and every kind of public display.

No less than four canons of the Council *in Trullo* (A.D. 691),* Canons 24, 51, 62, and 71, have as their object the anathematizing

[1] Cf. *Iuliani Imperatoris epistulae et leges*, ed. J. Bidez et F. Cumont (Paris, 1922), p. 127, and J. Bidez, 'L'Empereur Julien', *Œuvres complètes*, tome i, 2e Partie (Paris, 1924), pp. 102–5.

[2] *τοῖς ἀσελγέσι τούτοις θεάτροις τῶν ἱερέων μηδεὶς μηδαμοῦ παραβαλλέτω . . . μήτε εἰς τὴν οἰκίαν εἰσαγέτω τὴν ἑαυτοῦ· πρέπει γὰρ οὐδαμῶς. καὶ εἰ μὲν οἷόν τε ἦν ἐξελάσαι παντάπασιν αὐτὰ τῶν θεάτρων, ὥστε αὐτὰ πάλιν ἀποδοῦναι τῷ Διονύσῳ καθαρὰ γενόμενα, πάντως ἂν ἐπειράθην αὐτὸ προθύμως κατασκευάσαι· νυνὶ δὲ οἰόμενος τοῦτο οὔτε δυνατὸν οὔτε ἄλλως, εἰ καὶ δυνατὸν φανείη, συμφέρον αὐτὸ γενέσθαι, ταύτης μὲν ἀπεσχόμην παντάπασι τῆς φιλοτιμίας. ἀξιῶ δὲ τοὺς ἱερέας ὑποχωρῆσαι καὶ ἀποστῆναι τῷ δήμῳ τῆς ἐν τοῖς θεάτροις ἀσελγείας. μηδεὶς οὖν ἱερεὺς εἰς θέατρον ἐξίτω, μηδὲ ποιείσθω φίλον θυμελικὸν μηδὲ ἁρματηλάτην, μηδὲ ὀρχηστὴς μηδὲ μῖμος αὐτοῦ τῇ θύρᾳ προσίτω. τοῖς ἱεροῖς ἀγῶσιν ἐπιτρέπω μόνον τῷ βουλομένῳ παραβάλλειν, ὧν ἀπηγόρευται μετέχειν οὐκ ἀγωνίας μόνον ἀλλὰ καὶ θέας ταῖς γυναιξίν. ὑπὲρ δὲ τῶν κυνηγεσίων τί δεῖ καὶ λέγειν, ὅσα ταῖς πόλεσιν εἴσω τῶν θεάτρων συντελεῖται, ὡς ἀφεκτέον τούτων ἐστὶν οὐχ ἱερεῦσι μόνον, ἀλλὰ καὶ παισὶν ἱερέων; Iuliani Imp. epist. et leg.*, epist. 89 b, ed. J. Bidez, pp. 172–3.

of public shows and theatrical performances. The late-twelfth-century commentators on the canons, Zonaras and Balsamon suggest, however, that these canons were directed not so much against the usual celebration of festivals and theatrical representations in general, as against their abuse. But from the text of Canon 62 we can see that the popular feasts, viz. the Calendae, Vota, Brumalia, Lupercalia, and Dionysia, should 'once and for all be excluded from the association of the faithful'. Public dances by women, 'which meant so much outrage and harm', were also forbidden, as well as ballets and rites of men and women 'following pagan customs and alien to Christian life'. No man was allowed to dress as a woman, no woman to appear in a man's dress. It was forbidden to put on either comic or satyric or tragic masks, or to take part in the Dionysia. The canon ends by ordering clerics who disobeyed these orders to be deposed, laymen to be excommunicated.[1]

The Council *in Trullo* marked the climax of resistance against the maintenance of celebrations rooted in pagan customs and rites. It went so far as to ban the acclamations (*ἄκτα*) which had been sung at the other councils. Thus it came about that no acclamations were sung at the Council *in Trullo*, though it was presided over by the Emperor himself, who was accustomed to be greeted on such occasions by the clergy with carefully prepared sentences executed in the same manner as in the Hippodrome. It was, as a matter of fact, the only council at which acclamations were not sung.

IV. THE THEATRE

The sixty-second canon of the *Concilium in Trullo* contains the prohibition of comic, satyric, or tragic masks (*προσωπεῖα κωμικὰ ἢ σατυρικὰ ἢ τραγικά*). In this passage more distinct reference is made to the theatre* proper than in the homilies of

[1] *τὰς οὕτω λεγομένας Καλάνδας καὶ τὰ λεγόμενα Βῶτα καὶ τὰ λεγόμενα Βρουμάλια καὶ τὴν ἐν τῇ πρώτῃ τοῦ Μαρτίου μηνὸς ἡμέρᾳ ἐπιτελουμένην πανήγυριν, καθ' ἅπαξ ἐκ τῆς τῶν πιστῶν πολιτείας περιαιρεθῆναι βουλόμεθα· ἀλλὰ μὴν καὶ τὰς τῶν γυναίων δημοσίας ὀρχήσεις, καὶ πολλὴν λύμην καὶ βλάβην ἐμποιεῖν βουλομένας, ἔτι μὴν καὶ τὰς ὀνόματι τῶν παρ' Ἕλλησι ψευδῶς ὀνομασθέντων θεῶν, ἢ ἐξ ἀνδρῶν καὶ γυναικῶν γινομένας ὀρχήσεις καὶ τελετὰς κατά τι ἔθος παλαιὸν καὶ ἀλλότριον τοῦ τῶν χριστιανῶν βίου ἀποπεμπόμεθα, ὁρίζοντες μηδένα ἄνδρα γυναικαίαν στολὴν ἐνδιδύσκεσθαι, ἢ γυναῖκα τὴν ἀνδράσιν ἁρμόδιον· ἀλλὰ μήτε προσωπεῖα κωμικὰ ἢ σατυρικὰ ἢ τραγικὰ ὑποδύεσθαι, μήτε τοῦ βδελυκτοῦ Διονύσου τὸ ὄνομα τὴν σταφυλὴν ἀποθλίβοντας ἐν τοῖς ληνοῖς ἐπιβοᾷν, μηδὲ τὸν οἶνον ἐν τοῖς πίθοις ἐπιχέοντας γέλωτα ἐπικινεῖν, ἀγνοίας τρόπῳ ἢ ματαιότητος τὰ τῆς δαιμονιώδους πλάνης ἐνεργοῦντας. τοὺς οὖν ἀπὸ τοῦ νῦν τι τῶν προειρημένων ἐπιτελεῖν ἐπιχειροῦντας, ἐν γνώσει τούτων καθισταμένους, εἰ μὲν κληρικοὶ εἶεν, καθαιρεῖσθαι προστάσσομεν, εἰ δὲ λαϊκοί, ἀφορίζεσθαι.* *P.G.* cxxxvii, c. 727.

the Fathers of the Church or in other manifestoes of Christian writers who, speaking of the 'pomp of the devil' (πομπὴ διαβόλου),*[1] contrast the passion for the stage (θεατρομανία) and for athletic games and races with 'that for the theatre above'. It is, in fact, to the repertory of the ancient Greek theatre that the sixty-second canon refers, as is evident from the commentary on the canons of the council by Balsamon, a Byzantine writer of the second part of the twelfth century. He gives, as examples of comedy, the plays of Aristophanes; of the satyric drama the rites in honour of Dionysus; of tragedy the iambic poems of Euripides.[2] Whether the classical drama was still acted on the stage in the twelfth century, or whether Balsamon speaks merely from a knowledge gained by reading, cannot be decided from the passage. We know, however, from Joannes Lydus,[3] a Byzantine writer of the sixth century, that Byzantium had inherited from Rome seven different genres of light comedy. These are: (1) the *palliata*, with plots taken from scenes of Greek life; (2) the *togata*, giving pictures of Roman life; (3) the *Atellana*, attached as an *exodium* to the tragedies, similar to the satyric drama; (4) the *tabernaria*, comedies accompanied by music and dance; (5) the *Rhinthonics* (Ῥινθωνική), comedies in hexameters, and with improvised verses, accompanied by dances; (6) the *planipedaria*, short pieces, executed by the *planipedes*, mimes without masks and cothurnus, wearing thin-soled boots; (7) and finally the mimic comedies which, according to Lydus, were the only surviving type. These were plays without any high artistic merits, whose sole purpose was to make the crowd laugh.[4]

The indecency of the spectacles was, it seems, not the only evil against which Christian writers and the Church had to

[1] Cyril of Jerusalem, *Catechetical Oration*, 19. 6. πομπὴ δὲ διαβόλου ἐστὶ θεατρομανίαι καὶ ἱπποδρομίαι, κυνηγεσία καὶ πᾶσα τοιαύτη ματαιότης. *P.G.* xxxiii, c. 1069.

[2] ζητητέον οὖν τίνα εἰσὶ τὰ κωμικὰ προσωπεῖα, τίνα τὰ τραγικά, καὶ τίνα τὰ σατυρικά. καὶ κωμικὰ μέν εἰσι τὰ γελωτοποιὰ καὶ ἐφύβριστα, ὡς τὰ συγγραφέντα παρὰ τοῦ Ἀριστοφάνους· τραγικὰ τὰ περιπαθῆ καὶ τὰ θρηνώδη, ὡς τὰ τοῦ Εὐριπίδου ἰαμβεῖα· καὶ σατυρικά, τὰ εἰς ὕμνον τοῦ Διονύσου τελούμενα ὄργια παρὰ Σατύρων καὶ Βακχῶν. Cf. *Balsamonis, Zonarae, Aristeni Commentaria in Canones SS. Apostolorum, Conciliorum, et in Epistolas canonicas SS. Patrum. P.G.* cxxxvii, c. 730.

[3] ἡ μέντοι κωμῳδία τέμνεται εἰς ἑπτά, εἰς παλλιᾶταν τογᾶταν Ἀτελλάνην ταβερναρίαν Ῥινθωνικὴν πλανιπεδαρίαν καὶ μιμικήν· καὶ παλλιᾶτα μέν ἐστιν ἡ Ἑλληνικὴν ὑπόθεσιν ἔχουσα κωμῳδία, τογᾶτα δὲ ἡ Ῥωμαϊκήν, ἀρχαίαν· Ἀτελλάνη δέ ἐστιν ἡ τῶν λεγομένων ἐξοδιαρίων· ταβερναρία δὲ ἡ σκηνωτὴ ἢ θεατρικὴ κωμῳδία· Ῥινθωνικὴ ἡ ἐξωτική· πλανιπεδαρία ἡ καταστολαρία· μιμικὴ ἡ νῦν δῆθεν μόνη σῳζομένη, τεχνικὸν μὲν ἔχουσα οὐδέν, ἀλόγῳ μόνον τὸ πλῆθος ἐπάγουσα γέλωτι. *De magistratibus*, i. 40, ed. Wuensch, Bibl. Teubn., pp. 41–2.

[4] Cf. K. N. Sathas, *Ἱστορικὸν Δοκίμιον περὶ τοῦ θεάτρου καὶ τῆς μουσικῆς τῶν Βυζαντινῶν* (1878), p. 367, and V. Cottas, *Le Théâtre à Byzance*, p. 36.

fight. In the early days of Christianity the theatre was apparently used as a means of ridiculing Christian religion and its rites. This may be gathered from a legend transmitted in Syriac. It is called 'The Tale of the Actors',[1] and cannot have been a mere fiction of a Christian writer. The legend runs as follows. Pagan actors in Oxyrhynchus set out to amuse the crowd with a play imitating and turning to ridicule the ceremony of the Mass, the symbols of the Church, and Christian martyrdom. But the play had the opposite effect. Some of the actors who were 'baptized' on the stage were really converted and professed their new religious belief with great sincerity. Glaukus, the pagan actor, who performed the role of the priest, surprised by their attitude, tried to convince them that it was only a play they were acting. But wonders happened; the cross on his breast began to shine, and he too, together with the other actors and many of the crowd, joined them in the new belief. Igorius, King of the Goths, sent for them. They were summoned before him and interrogated. He tried to persuade them to give up their new belief, but in vain, and they were imprisoned and finally executed. Though the historical background of the legend is full of inaccuracies—there was, for example, no Gothic king called Igorius in Oxyrhynchus—, the 'Tale of the Actors' cannot be regarded as mere invention. The calendar of the Eastern Church contains several names of actors who suffered martyrdom, and it seems very likely from this account that pagan authorities encouraged the performances of such plays and used them as propaganda to check the spread of the new belief.

V. THE PANTOMIME

The Byzantine theatre had also adopted from Rome another kind of scenic performance, the pantomime. We learn how it was performed from an essay of Libanius about dancers.[2] A poem was sung, and the actor had to expound its meaning mimically. Some actors had developed the art of the mimic dance to such a degree that they were able to perform 'loquente gestu, nutu, crure, genu, manu, rotatu'[3] whole tragedies. Libanius reports that

[1] J. Link, *Die Geschichte der Schauspieler, nach einem syrischen MS. der kgl. Bibliothek in Berlin* Inaug. Diss., 1904). The MS. is no. 75 (222) of Sachau's *Catalogue*.

[2] Libanius, *Oratio pro Saltatoribus*, 94–8: *Opera*, ed. R. Foerster, iv. 481–5, Bibl. Teubn.

[3] C. Sollius Apollinaris Sidonius, carmen 23, Bibl. Teubn., p. 344.

one of them, the dancer Xenophon, was admired for his mimic performance of the *Bacchae* of Euripides. The mimic dancer, the τραγῳδός, as he is now called, is the favourite actor of the Byzantine stage, and he maintains his position until the end of the Empire.[1] But his social status remains as low as that of the other actors. Once his name was entered in the register of mimes he became deprived of the right to inherit or to appear as a witness in court. The Church refused him the last sacrament and excluded him from baptism and holy communion. This decree can be traced back as far as the *Canones Hippolyti*[2] at the end of the fourth century and the Apostolic Constitutions.[3] Actors, therefore, had to remain pagans, or give up their career, although if they did so they could be forced by Byzantine civil law to reappear on the stage, which naturally led to their excommunication.[4] There were short periods in which these severe rules were relaxed—such humane intervals occurred under some of the Isaurian emperors and especially during the reign of the Macedonian dynasty—but as a whole the low social position of the actors contrasted strongly with the high appreciation of the public for their art. Here, too, however, Byzantine society—pagan in the beginning and Christian after the victory of the Church—did not institute a new social order but followed the principles expounded in the third book of the *Republic* of Plato and developed by Neoplatonic philosophy. There is, in fact, no great difference between Plato's attitude, which accords every kind of honour to the pantomimic artist and worships him 'as holy, wonderful, and delightful being', but also informs him 'that in our State such as he are not permitted to exist',[5] and that of Byzantine legislation described above; except that the latter is more lenient and accepts the more modified view expounded by Aristotle in his *Politics* and *Poetics*.

[1] Cf. V. Cottas, *Le Théâtre à Byzance*, p. 50.

[2] Canon 12, see W. Riedel, *Kirchenrechtsquellen des Patriarchats Alexandrien*, p. 206.

[3] *Constitutiones Apostolorum*, 8. 32. 9: τῶν ἐπὶ σκηνῆς ἐάν τις προσίῃ ἀνὴρ ἢ γυνὴ ἢ ἡνίοχος ἢ μονομάχος ἢ σταδιοδρόμος ἢ λουδεμπιστὴς ἢ χοραύλης ἢ κιθαριστὴς ἢ λυριστὴς ἢ ὁ τὴν ὄρχησιν ἐπιδεικνύμενος ἢ κάπηλος, ἢ παυσάσθωσαν ἢ ἀποβαλλέσθωσαν.

[4] V. Cottas, p. 51.

[5] ἄνδρα δή, ὡς ἔοικε, δυνάμενον ὑπὸ σοφίας παντοδαπὸν γίγνεσθαι καὶ μιμεῖσθαι πάντα χρήματα, εἰ ἡμῖν ἀφίκοιτο εἰς τὴν πόλιν αὐτός τε καὶ τὰ ποιήματα βουλόμενος ἐπιδείξασθαι, προσκυνοῖμεν ἂν αὐτὸν ὡς ἱερὸν καὶ θαυμαστὸν καὶ ἡδύν, εἴποιμεν δ' ἂν ὅτι οὐκ ἔστιν τοιοῦτος ἀνὴρ ἐν τῇ πόλει παρ' ἡμῖν οὔτε θέμις ἐγγενέσθαι, ἀποπέμποιμέν τε εἰς ἄλλην πόλιν μύρον κατὰ τῆς κεφαλῆς καταχέαντες καὶ ἐρίῳ στέψαντες . . .. *Rep*. iii. 398 A.

VI. PAGAN FEASTS

(*a*) *Olympic Games*

Musical performances also played an important part in the Olympic games, which were revived in several towns of the Eastern Roman Empire. Our information is most complete for the Olympic games at Antioch. In the time of Claudius (A.D. 41–54) the Emperor was asked by the Antiochenes to renew the Olympic games, for which the money had been provided by the legacy of a rich citizen, Sosibius; they were instituted by an Imperial edict and consisted of theatrical shows, musical and dramatic performances, athletic games, horse-races, and fighting of gladiators. It was originally intended to hold them on a large scale every fifth year, in October, and they were to last for thirty days; but wars, an earthquake, and fires prevented this plan from being fully carried out. Only the horse-races were maintained and took place in June.

In the reign of Commodus (A.D. 180–92) the Antiochenes again asked the Emperor to reinstitute the Olympic games. Commodus agreed, and ordered the games to be held every fourth year in July at the Feast of Offerings for forty days (ἑορτὴ τῶν ἀναθημάτων ἤτοι θυσιῶν). For the first time Olympic games took place in the new gymnasium built by Commodus. According to Malalas all sorts of athletic contests took place here, and also performances on instruments and singing of dramatic cantilenas (οἱ δὲ ἐφωνάσκουν τραγικὰ μέλη). In these contests young girls also participated, candidates of philosophy devoted to a virtuous life, some of them performing mimic dances, others singing Greek hymns (καὶ τραγῳδοῦσαι καὶ λέγουσαι ὕμνους τινὰς Ἑλληνικούς). All the victors in these games, both men and girls, were obliged to preserve chastity until their death.

The Olympic games at Antioch seem to have acquired such fame that Diocletian came expressly from Egypt to Antioch in order to attend them, not as Emperor, but as an Alytarches of Antioch, i.e. as the master of ceremonies at the Olympic games. This dignitary, who had to distribute the prizes, deputized for Zeus, and divine honours were conferred upon him. In the Olympic games the Hellenic spirit was preserved in its pure essence; nevertheless it could not prevail against the new Christian civilization, and the Olympic games at Antioch were forbidden by the Emperor Justinian.

(*b*) *The Maïoumas*

Among the feasts already mentioned the 'Orgies of Maïoumas' seem to have occupied a prominent place at Antioch. They were ordered by Commodus in the same edict by which he had instituted the Olympic games. The Orgies of Maïoumas were a nocturnal feast connected with scenic performances in honour of Dionysus and Aphrodite. The feast was celebrated every third year in May. In the reign of Theodosius I, the Great (379–95) it was forbidden on account of its orgiastic character, but reinstituted by his son and successor Arcadius in A.D. 396.[1] It spread over all the provinces of the Empire and left many traces in several feasts, which were celebrated throughout the whole period of the Byzantine Empire.[2] According to V. Cottas the *λαχανικὸν ἱπποδρόμιον*, the 'Hippodrome of Vegetables', described in Constantine Porphyrogennetus, *De Ceremoniis,* had absorbed some of the features characteristic of the Maïoumas, and of the 'Feast of the Roses'—called *τῆς Γάστρης*—a variant of the Maïoumas. On the day of the 'Hippodrome of Vegetables' the races were followed by performances by the mimes (*οἱ τοῦ λογίου*).[3] The Hippodrome was adorned for the occasion with a cross of roses, and vegetables and sweets were distributed among the crowd.

(*c*) *The Calendae*

Another feast, taken over, as it seems, directly from Rome, and christianized by Byzantium, was the Calendae. John Chrysostom had written his Sermon concerning the Calendae (*Λόγος ταῖς Καλάνδαις*) against the pagan form of the feast because the celebrations on the 1st of March—the beginning of the new year in Rome—were accompanied by masques. The habit of wearing masks on this feast spread so widely that even clerics had to be warned not to take part.[4] The Calendae were

[1] 'Clementiae nostrae placuit, ut Maïumae provincialibus laetitia redderetur, ita tamen, ut servetur honestas et verecundia castis moribus perseveret. DAT. VII KAL. MAI. CONSTAN(TINO)P(OLI) ARCAD(IO) IIII ET HONOR(IO) III AA. CONSS. (A.D. 396, 25 Apr.).' *Codex Theodosianus*, lib. xv, tit. vi, *de Maïuma*, ed. Th. Mommsen, i. 2, pp. 820–1.

[2] See V. Cottas, *Le Théâtre à Byzance*, pp. 10, 11.

[3] Cf. *Le Livre des Cérémonies*, edited by A. Vogt, tome ii, Commentaire (Paris, 1940), p. 160.

[4] *ἀλλὰ καί τινες κληρικοί, κατά τινας ἑορτάς, πρὸς διάφορα μετασχηματίζονται προσωπεῖα καὶ ποτὲ μὲν ξιφήρεις ἐν τῷ μεσονάῳ τῆς ἐκκλησίας μετὰ στρατιωτικῶν ἀμφίων εἰσέρχονται, ποτὲ δὲ καὶ ὡς μοναχοὶ προοδεύουσιν ἢ ὡς ζῷα τετράποδα.* W. Beveridge, *Pandectae Canonum* (Oxford, 1672), i. 230–1.

finally abolished by Canon 62 of the Council *in Trullo*, along with the other feasts mentioned above, the *Vota* and *Brumalia*. But it seems that this interdict either had no effect at all or was only effective for a short time in Constantinople. Constantine VII Porphyrogennetus for example gives, in his *De Ceremoniis*, a detailed description of the Brumalia and points out that he reintroduced the feast, whose celebration had been forbidden by his co-regent Romanus Lecapenus.[1] Another feast described by Constantine, the *Τρυγητικὸν Δεῖπνον*, the 'Banquet of the Vintage', or *Γοτθικόν*, the 'Gothic pageant', has preserved features of the Calendae. It took place on the ninth day of the Dodekaimeron, the days between Christmas and Epiphany. Members of the two main factions in Constantinople, the Blues and Greens, were dressed up as Goths and performed a warrior dance, accompanied by musicians playing on lutes, and singing in a gibberish which professed to be Gothic but which was in fact, as has recently been discovered, a corrupted Latin.[2]

VII. INSTRUMENTAL MUSIC

In the early days of the Eastern Empire the social position of professional musicians was hardly better than that of actors or mimes. Both pagan and Christian writers looked down upon them with equal contempt. John Chrysostom's description of an actor disguised in woman's clothes, wearing his hair long, and striving both in aspect and gesture to look like a tender girl,[3] is no more severe than Lucian's derision of those who went to entertainments in order to see effeminate singers, imitating lecherous women to the accompaniment of flutes.[4]

Again, we have to distinguish two reasons for the condemnation of instrumental music by Christian writers: its pernicious effect on morals, and its connexion with pagan religious ceremonies. The playing of certain instruments during the immola-

[1] *De Ceremoniis*, ii. 186–7.

[2] Ibid. i. 83. Cf. J. Handschin, *Das Zeremonienwerk Kaiser Konstantins u. die sangbare Dichtung* (1942), pp. 34–6.

[3] *Homil. in Matth.* 37, ch. 5: ὁ μὲν γὰρ ὄπισθεν ἔχει κόμην νέος ὤν, καὶ τὴν φύσιν ἐκθηλύνων, καὶ τῷ βλέμματι, καὶ τῷ σχήματι, καὶ τοῖς ἱματίοις, καὶ πᾶσιν ἁπλῶς εἰς εἰκόνα κόρης.

[4] Lucian, *de Saltatione* 2: Ἀνὴρ δέ τις ὤν, ὦ λῷστε, καὶ ταῦτα παιδείᾳ σύντροφος καὶ φιλοσοφίᾳ τὰ μέτρια ὡμιληκώς, ἀφέμενος, ὦ Λυκῖνε, τοῦ περὶ τὰ βελτίω σπουδάζειν καὶ τοῖς παλαιοῖς συνεῖναι, κάθησαι καταυλούμενος, θηλυδρίαν ἄνθρωπον ὁρῶν ἐσθῆσι μαλακαῖς καὶ ᾄσμασιν ἀκολάστοις ἐναβρυνόμενον καὶ μιμούμενον ἐρωτικὰ γύναια, τῶν πάλαι τὰς μαχλοτάτας, Φαίδρας καὶ Παρθενόπας καὶ Ῥοδόπας τινάς, καὶ ταῦτα πάντα ὑπὸ κρούμασι καὶ τερετίσμασι καὶ ποδῶν κτύπῳ καταγέλαστα ὡς ἀληθῶς πράγματα καὶ ἥκιστα ἐλευθέρῳ ἀνδρὶ καὶ οἵῳ σοὶ πρέποντα;

tions and libations was an essential part of the ceremonies, in both Greek and Roman rites. In mystery-cults the rites of initiation were accompanied by dances and the sounding of percussion instruments. Ecstatic rites, deriving from the Orient, were accompanied by the sound of cymbals, drums, and Phrygian flutes, as we learn from Catullus:[1]

simul ite, sequimini
Phrygiam ad domum Cybelles, Phrygia ad nemora Deae
Ubi cymbalum sonat vox, ubi tympana reboant,
Tibicen ubi canit Phryx curvo grave calamo,
Ubi capita Maenades vi iaciunt hederigerae,
Ubi sacra sancta acutis ululatibus agitant,
Ubi suevit illa divae volitare vaga cohors
Quo nos decet citatis celerare tripudiis.

Drums (τύμπανα), cymbals (κύμβαλα), clappers (κρόταλα), horns (κέρατα), and flutes (αὐλοί) were the instruments mainly used in orgiastic rites. Under the influence of the sound those who attended the orgies passed into a state of holy frenzy (ἱερομανία). Lucian, describing in *De Syria Dea* a ceremony in honour of Cybele, makes us realize how powerful the effect of this kind of music could be, even on people who had only come to the ceremony out of curiosity. He says that on certain days the priests and a crowd of the Initiated gather in the Temple in order to perform the holy rites. A large crowd gathers outside the Temple, playing flutes, beating drums, or singing ecstatic songs. Many who only came to see the ceremony go into a trance. A raving youth tears off his clothes, jumps forward, seizes one of the swords prepared for that purpose, and castrates himself.[2]

The ecstatic element in Oriental rites did not merely survive in the Eastern cities of the Empire; it increased in intensity. The Fathers of the Church had to take up the struggle against the seductive influence of instrumental music. Thus, two hundred years after Catullus, Clement of Alexandria, in his *Paeda-*

[1] Carmen lxiii, ll. 19–26.

[2] The state of frenzy caused by the sound of certain instruments and ecstatic singing is a phenomenon widely commented on by writers who have observed the reaction of an Eastern audience to any kind of exciting music. Lucian's description in *De Syria Dea* may also throw some light on the passages in the *Republic* of Plato and the *Politics* of Aristotle concerned with the ethical significance of the Modes in Greek music (cf. H. Abert, *Die Lehre vom Ethos in der griechischen Musik*, Leipzig, 1899). Aristotle is certainly right in objecting to the Socrates of the *Republic* who wants to retain the Phrygian mode, but rejects the flute, as both of them are exciting and emotional (cf. *Politics*, 8. 7. 1342^{b}).

gogus (ii. 4), wrote his brilliant argument against the participation of instrumentalists in festivities:

'If people occupy their time with flutes and psalteries, and choirs and dances, and Egyptian clappers and such amusements, they become disorderly fools and unseemly and altogether barbarous. They beat cymbals and drums and make a loud noise on the instruments of deceit. Certainly, such a banquet—as it seems to me—is a theatre of drunkenness. . . . Let the pipe be given back to the shepherds, and the flute to the superstitious who are engrossed in idolatry. For, in truth, such instruments are to be banished from a temperate banquet, being more suitable to beasts than to men, and to the more irrational portion of mankind. For we have heard of stags being charmed by the pipe, and, when they are pursued by the huntsman, being lured into the toils. . . .'[1]

Clement of Alexandria then proceeds to explain what kind of music is permissible to Christians, basing his prescriptions on Matt. xxii. 37 and 39; Col. iii. 16 and 17; Ps. xxxii; Eph. v. 19, and other passages taken from the Scriptures. Only the more austere melodies are permitted; those that are weak and effeminate are forbidden. Therefore melodies which use chromatic intervals should not be employed.[2]

The dangerous effect on Christians of exciting instruments was obviously very strong. The Fathers of the Church had to fight continually against the use of instruments in Christian ceremonies. Their struggle was made even more difficult by the fact that the Jews made abundant use of instruments in their service,[3] and that in many passages of the Psalms the Christians found themselves invited to praise God with the sound of trumpets, psalteries, zithers, drums, stringed instruments, organs, and with dances. Theodoret of Cyrus, quoting Amos v. 23 'Take thou away from me the noise of thy songs; for I will not hear the melody of thy instruments', tries to explain that the Israelites had learnt to use instruments in their service from the Egyptians. He argues that God permitted them to use instruments

[1] Clem. Alex., ed. O. Stählin (1905), i. 181.

[2] καὶ γὰρ ἁρμονίας παραδεκτέον τὰς σώφρονας, ἀπωτάτω ὅτι μάλιστα ἐλαύνοντας τῆς ἐρρωμένης ἡμῶν διανοίας τὰς ὑγρὰς ὄντως ἁρμονίας, αἳ περὶ τὰς καμπὰς τῶν φθόγγων κακοτεχνοῦσαι εἰς θρύψιν καὶ βωμολοχίαν ἐκδιαιτῶνται· τὰ δὲ αὐστηρὰ καὶ σωφρονικὰ μέλη ἀποτάσσεται ταῖς τῆς μέθης ἀγερωχίαις. καταλειπτέον οὖν τὰς χρωματικὰς ἁρμονίας ταῖς ἀχρώμοις παροινίαις καὶ τῇ ἀνθοφορούσῃ καὶ ἑταιρούσῃ μουσικῇ. Ibid., p. 184.

[3] Cf. J. Quasten, *Musik und Gesang in den Kulten der heidnischen Antike und christlichen Frühzeit.* iv, § 3. 'Die Auseinandersetzung des Christentums mit dem jüdischen Tempelkult', *Liturgiegeschichtliche Quellen und Forschungen*, Heft 25.

in His honour in their ceremonies and services, not because He liked their sound, but in order to put an end to the madness of idolatry.[1] The same view is taken by Chrysostom. He too thinks that God, knowing the weakness of the Jews, had allowed them to use instruments in order to temper their minds to perform with joy what would be useful to them.[2] And Gregory of Nazianzus is obliged to exhort his audience: 'Let us take up hymns instead of drums, chanting of psalms instead of indecent writhings of the body and songs.'[3]

VIII. MUSICA PERNICIOSA AND THE CHRISTIAN IDEAL

To avoid the morally pernicious effect of the highly emotional Graeco-Roman music was a difficult task for Christians, particularly for those living in the great cities in close contact with the ruling pagan society. It was not only the music performed in the theatres and at public festivities, or connected with the various cults, which influenced the mind. Here the danger was obvious, and could therefore be eliminated to a certain degree. A more difficult task was to avoid the music at private entertainments, as this involved a limitation of the Christian's contact with his fellow citizens. It was the habit of pagan society to engage musicians to sing and play at their meals. The music was performed by girls, who played the flute, and often also the cithara, the lyre, or some other instrument.

As has already been mentioned, Clement of Alexandria was compelled to speak at some length against this practice in the *Paedagogus*.[4] Basil of Caesarea condemns the custom of playing the lyre during *symposia*. Psalteries and zithers, he says, increase the drunkenness caused by wine and hinder people from meditating on the works of the Lord.[5] The same view is expressed

[1] Theodoret, *Graecarum affectionum curatio* 7. *De sacrificiis*, § 21: τὰ τῶν εὐήχων ὀργάνων ἠνέσχετο, οὐ τῇ τούτων ἁρμονίᾳ τερπόμενος, ἀλλὰ κατὰ βραχὺ παύων τῶν εἰδώλων τὸν πλάνον. Cf. J. Quasten, op. cit., pp. 86–7.

[2] Chrysostom, *Homil. in Ps. 150*; *P.G.* lv, c. 497: καὶ τὰ ὄργανα δὲ ἐκεῖνα διὰ τοῦτο ἐπετέτραπτο τότε, διά τε τὴν ἀσθένειαν αὐτῶν, καὶ διὰ τὸ κιρνᾶν αὐτοὺς εἰς ἀγάπην καὶ συμφωνίαν.

[3] Gregory Naz., *Oratio* 5. 25; *P.G.* xxxv, c. 708–9: μηδὲ πρόθυρα καλλωπίσωμεν· μὴ τῷ αἰσθητῷ φωτὶ καταλαμπέσθωσαν αἱ οἰκίαι, μηδὲ συναυλίαις καὶ κρότοις περιηχείσθωσαν. οὗτος μὲν γὰρ Ἑλληνικῆς ἱερομανίας ὁ νόμος. . . . ἀναλάβωμεν ὕμνους ἀντὶ τυμπάνων, ψαλμῳδίαν ἀντὶ τῶν αἰσχρῶν λυγισμάτων τε καὶ ᾀσμάτων.

[4] Cf. *Paedagogus*, ii. 4.

[5] εἶτα πόρρω προϊόντος τοῦ πότου, αὐλοὶ καὶ κιθάραι καὶ τύμπανα κατὰ μὲν τὴν ἀλήθειαν ἀποθρηνοῦνται τοὺς ἀπολλυμένους, κατὰ δὲ τὴν ἐπιτήδευσιν τῶν μεθυόντων, ὥστε αὐτοῖς πάσας τῆς ψυχῆς τὰς ἡδονὰς τῇ μελῳδίᾳ διεγερθῆναι. *Comment. in Isai.* 5. 158; *P.G.* xxx, c. 372. σοὶ δὲ χρυσῷ καὶ ἐλέφαντι πεποικιλμένη ἡ λύρα ἐφ' ὑψηλοῦ τινος βωμοῦ ὥσπερ τι ἄγαλμα καὶ εἴδωλον δαιμόνων ἀνάκειται. καὶ γυνή τις ἀθλία, ἀντὶ τοῦ τὰς χεῖρας ἐρείδειν πρὸς ἄτρακτον διδαχθῆναι, διὰ τὴν ἐκ τῆς δουλείας

by John Chrysostom in the first *Homily on the Epistle to the Colossians.* He contrasts the pagan with the Christian *symposium*: 'For there, indeed, are flutes, citharas, and Panpipes (*σύριγγες*); but here there is no discordant melody, but instead, hymns and psalm-singing. There the demons are celebrated in songs, but here God, the Lord of all. . . . For these songs to the lyre (*τὰ γὰρ διὰ τῶν πηκτίδων*) are none other than songs to Demons (*δαιμόνων ᾄσματα*).'[1]

These ideas are followed up by Chrysostom in the chapter on *symposia* in the *Expositio in Psalmum 41*, where he contrasts pagan drinking-parties with meals in a truly Christian household. There wanton songs (*ᾄσματα πορνικά*) which attract heathen demons; here spiritual chants (*ᾄσματα πνευματικά*) to which the Spirit flies, and blesses mouth and soul.[2] Chrysostom urges his hearers not only to sing hymns of praise themselves, but to teach their children and wives to sing them too; not only at the looms and during their other work, but above all at their meals.

'For it is mostly at meals that the devil lurks. There he has as allies drunkenness and gluttony, laughter and disorder, and dissipation of soul. Therefore it is particularly necessary at meals and after meals to build a stronghold against him through the security which comes from the psalms, and to sing sacred hymns in praise of the Lord, by standing up with one's wife and children after the *symposia*. . . . Just as these invite mimes, dancers, and indecent women to their meals and call up demons and the devil, and fill their houses with innumerable brawls, so those invite Christ into their houses, and call upon David with the zither. Where Christ is, there is no place for a Demon; he would not even dare to look in. . . . These people make their house a theatre; you shall make your dwelling a church. For nobody would fail to call a gathering a church, where there are psalms, and prayers and dances of the prophets, and God-loving thoughts in the singers. . . . No charge will be made against anybody for the way he sings, whether he be old or young, hoarse, or even lacking rhythm. What is required here is an uplifted soul, a watchful mind, a contrite heart, a powerful reasoning, a purified conscience. If you enter the holy choir of God possessing these, you will be able to stand next to David. There is no need of zithers, nor of taut strings, nor of a plectrum,

ἀνάγκην ἐπὶ λύραν ἐκτείνειν ἐδιδάχθη παρὰ σοῦ ἴσως καὶ μισθοὺς τελέσαντος, τάχα καὶ προαγωγῷ τινι γυναικὶ παραδόντος· ἢ μετὰ τὸ πᾶσαν ἀσέλγειαν ἐν τῷ ἰδίῳ σώματι ἀπαθλῆσαι ταῖς νέαις προκάθηται τῶν ὁμοίων διδάσκαλος. Ibid., c. 376.

[1] *ἐκεῖ μὲν αὐλοὶ καὶ κιθάραι καὶ σύριγγες, ἐνταῦθα δὲ οὐδὲν ἀπηχὲς μέλος, ἀλλὰ τί; ὕμνοι, ψαλμῳδίαι. ἐκεῖ μὲν οἱ δαίμονες ἀνυμνοῦνται, ἐνταῦθα δὲ ὁ πάντων δεσπότης θεός. . . . τὰ γὰρ διὰ τῶν πηκτίδων οὐδὲν ἄλλο ἐστίν ἢ τῶν δαιμόνων ᾄσματα.* *In epist. ad Coloss.*, *Hom.* i. 8; *Bibl. Patr.*, ed. F. Field, p. 182.

[2] *P.G.* lv, c. 157.

nor skill, nor any instruments. But if you will, you can make yourself into a zither, mortifying the limbs of the flesh, and forming a great concord (*συμφωνία*) between body and soul.'[1]

Here the music permitted to Christians is clearly indicated. It is, according to the Pauline precept, to speak in psalms, and hymns, and spiritual songs,[2] rather than in drunkenness and excess.[3] This line is taken by most of the Christian writers. There is another, more austere view, to be found in the writings of some Eastern monks, who are opposed to any kind of singing, even during the service, as preventing the *κατάνυξις*, the spirit of contrition. These voices, however, represent only a small minority. They are not typical of the attitude of the Church in general, particularly after its victory in the fourth century.

From the pronouncements of the Fathers of the Church on music suitable for Christians we can trace the ideological basis from which their conceptions arose. It is not to be expected that this basis should be homogeneous. It is not only that a gradual change took place in the leading ideas, from the Apostolic age until the time when a fully developed dogma was formed into a kind of *summa* in the writings and hymns of John Damascene: there is also variation according to the individual writer's standard of education. Some of them were drawn from a society highly trained in Greek philosophy; others came from provincial centres of the East which despised Hellenic civilization, and based their concepts, in the main, on passages from the Old and New Testaments.

In spite of their various theological views, Early Christian writers were agreed on one point. Music was treated by them not as an aesthetic but as an ethical problem. This conception of the art of music, as has been shown in the first chapter, is closely associated with the ideas of the Greek philosophers who dealt with music—Pythagoreans, Empedocleans, Plato and his followers, Neo-Pythagoreans, and Neoplatonists—and with the views of the Greek musical theorists.

It is a well-known fact that the revival of Platonism in the second century, the so-called Middle Platonism, facilitated the entry of Christianity into the world of Graeco-Roman civiliza-

[1] Ibid.

[2] *ὁ λόγος τοῦ Χριστοῦ ἐνοικείτω ἐν ὑμῖν πλουσίως, ἐν πάσῃ σοφίᾳ διδάσκοντες καὶ νουθετοῦντες ἑαυτούς, ψαλμοῖς ὕμνοις ᾠδαῖς πνευματικαῖς ἐν τῇ χάριτι ᾄδοντες ἐν ταῖς καρδίαις ὑμῶν τῷ θεῷ.* Col. iii. 16.

[3] In Eph. v. 18.

tion. Platonic musical theory could be adapted without difficulty to the teaching of the theologians, as will be shown in the next chapter. The connexion between Greek philosophy and the Christian ideal of music becomes even closer under the influence of Neoplatonism, which had absorbed elements of the Pythagorean and Gnostic systems. In both these systems emphasis is laid on the task which music must fulfil of producing harmony between soul and body,[1] tempering passions,[2] giving grace and dignity to manners,[3] elevating the soul.[4] Gradually the ascetic attitude of the Pauline doctrine, represented in Chrysostom's *Expositio in Psalmum 41*, is replaced by the Neoplatonic, which aims at a perfect rendering of the chants. Thus Augustine admits that he feels more pleasure in hearing the melodies animating the word of God, when they are sung by a beautiful voice in a perfect way.[5]

This famous passage of the *Confessions* is significant of the aesthetic attitude towards music in the West at the end of the fourth century. It explains the growing importance of, and the demand for, an increased use of music in the service of the Church, both in the West and in the East. Byzantine musical theory, which has been preserved only in relatively late documents, has maintained in an even more obvious way elements of Gnostic, Neo-Pythagorean, and Neoplatonic doctrine. These remnants of Pagan philosophical systems in Early Christian times furthered the appreciation of Eastern Ecclesiastical Chant, but were not associated with the stylistic development of Byzantine ecclesiastical music, since this was closely connected with the evolution of the Eastern service, and regulated by the requirements of liturgy.

[1] Athanasius of Alexandria, *Epistula ad Marcellinum de interpretatione Psalmorum*, 27: *ὥσπερ ἁρμονία τοὺς αὐλοὺς συντιθεῖσα μίαν τὴν συμφωνίαν ἀποτελεῖ, οὕτως ἐπειδὴ καὶ ἐν τῇ ψυχῇ διάφορα κινήματα φαίνεται καὶ ἔστιν ἐν αὐτῇ τὸ λογίζεσθαι καὶ τὸ ἐπιθυμεῖν καὶ τὸ θυμοειδές, ἐκ δὲ τῆς τούτων κινήσεως καὶ ἡ τῶν μελῶν γίνεται τοῦ σώματος ἐνέργεια, βούλεται ὁ λόγος μὴ ἀσύμφωνον εἶναι τὸν ἄνθρωπον ἑαυτῷ μηδὲ διίστασθαι πρὸς αὐτόν.* Cf. Plato, *Rep.* iii. 401 D; Ptolemy, *Harmonica*, iii. 7, &c.

[2] Basil the Great, *Homil. in Ps. 1*; *P.G.* xxix, c. 212 B: *ἐπειδὴ γὰρ εἶδε τὸ Πνεῦμα τὸ ἅγιον δυσάγωγον πρὸς ἀρετὴν τὸ γένος τῶν ἀνθρώπων, καὶ διὰ τὸ πρὸς ἡδονὴν ἐπιρρεπὲς τοῦ ὀρθοῦ βίου καταμελοῦντας ἡμᾶς. τί ποιεῖ; τὸ ἐκ τῆς μελῳδίας τερπνὸν τοῖς δόγμασιν ἐγκατέμιξεν, ἵνα τῷ προσηνεῖ καὶ λείῳ τῆς ἀκοῆς τὸ ἐκ τῶν λόγων ὠφέλιμον λανθανόντως ὑποδεξώμεθα.* Cf. Ptolemy, *Harmon.* iii. 7; Iamblichus, *V. Pythag.*, c. 114, &c.

[3] Clement of Alexandria, *Stromateis*, vi. 11; *P.G.* ix. 312: *ἁπτέον ἄρα μουσικῆς εἰς κατακόσμησιν ἤθους καὶ καταστολήν.* Cf. Plato, *Rep.* iii. 398 C; Aristotle, *Pol.* viii. 5, 1339b, &c.

[4] Chrysostom, *Expos. in Ps. 41*; *P.G.* iv, c. 156. Cf. Plato, *Laws*, ii. 659 E; Aristotle, *Pol.* viii. 7, 1341b, &c.

[5] *Confess.* x. 33.

CHAPTER IV

MUSIC IN CEREMONIES

I. ORIGIN AND DEVELOPMENT OF THE ACCLAMATIONS

A FEATURE characteristic of all Byzantine ceremonies, secular as well as ecclesiastical, was the acclamations. It was with these panegyric salutations that the factions of the Blues and the Greens[1] used to greet the public appearances of the Emperor, the Empress, the Porphyrogenneti—the children of the Emperor, born in the Purple Chamber of the Palace—, other members of the Imperial family, and high officials and dignitaries. Similar acclamations were sung in church when the Emperor as head of the Church, or a high ecclesiastical dignitary, came to visit it. The stylized form of these panegyrics, which were apparently intended to give the impression of the spontaneous outburst of feelings of loyalty, devotion, gratitude, or admiration, reflects the highly organized system of Byzantine public life, in which the Emperor and his family played the foremost part. 'The task of applause was not abandoned to the rude and spontaneous voices of the crowd. The most convenient stations were occupied by the bands of the Blue and Green factions of the Circus; and their furious conflicts, which had shaken the capital, were insensibly sunk to an emulation of servitude.'[2]

The origin of the acclamations has not been fully investigated. Rehearsed cheering was already customary in Imperial Rome. When the Forum, formerly the scene of turbulent outbursts of passion, was reduced to order at the end of the Civil Wars, it was to the Circus, with its chariot-races, games, and fights, that the emotions of the populace were diverted.[3] The Roman Caesars, some of whom were passionately interested in the races, favoured the faction to which their own charioteer belonged. Since not more than four chariots took part in one race, and each charioteer was dressed in the colour of his party, Rome had already the factions of the Blues, Greens, Whites, and Reds, of

[1] Cf. J. B. Bury, *History of the Later Roman Empire*, i. 84 sqq. An excellent study on 'The Acclamations of Emperors in Byzantine Ritual' has been published by H. J. W. Tillyard in *A.B.S.* xviii (1911–12), 239–60.

[2] Gibbon, *Decline and Fall*, vi, Bury's ed., p. 85.

[3] Cf. A. Rambaud, *Études sur l'histoire byzantine*, pp. 5–6.

which the Blues and the Greens were the most prominent. They cheered the Imperator when he appeared in the Circus, and, at a later date, on certain occasions when he entered the Senate. *Laudes* in praise of Caligula, Nero, Domitian, and Trajan are reported by Latin and Greek historiographers. These acclamations were composed in a kind of metrical prose.[1] They had to be carefully rehearsed, and were performed like the *Sprechchöre* by which modern dictators used to be acclaimed. Thus, for example, the senators, among them Dio Cassius—from whom we have the report—were commanded to greet Commodus in the following way:[2]

Καὶ κύριος εἶ
Καὶ πρῶτος εἶ
Καὶ πάντων εὐτυχέστατος
Νικᾷς, νικήσεις
Ἀπ' αἰῶνος, Ἀμαζόνιε, νικᾷς.

(Thou art Lord. Thou art First. Thou art most favoured. Thou conquerest, Thou wilt conquer. From old Thou conquerest, Amazonius.)[3]

It was due to Nero's passion for display and theatrical effects that he first built up an ordered system of applause by creating the bands of the Augustiani, into which Roman Knights were enlisted.[4] The elaborate form of salutations introduced by Nero was obviously modelled on patterns from the Greek East.[5] Thus the Roman form of organized applause may have derived from Oriental court ceremonies* and have been used from the same motives, which, six hundred years later, induced the Byzantine autocrators to introduce a repertory of acclamations for State occasions, differing in content for each of the major secular and ecclesiastical ceremonies.

When Constantine transplanted the entire system of Roman administration to the city destined to be the 'New Rome', the Hippodrome and its factions found an even more fertile ground for their activities in the capital of the Eastern Empire. Here the Hippodrome acquired a political significance which the Roman Circus had never possessed.[6]

From its elder sister New Rome had taken over the system of the four groups or *dēmes* into which the people of Constantinople

[1] Cf. Dio Cassius lxxiii. 2. 3.
[2] Ibid. lxii (lxi), 20. 2.
[3] Ἀμαζόνιος, epithet of Apollo.
[4] Tacitus, *Annals* xiv. 15. 4.
[5] Cf. M. P. Charlesworth, 'Pietas and Victoria', *J.R.S.* xxxiii (1943), 5.
[6] Cf. J. B. Bury, *Hist. of the Later Roman Empire*, i. 85.

had been organized. Here, too, the Blues or *Veneti* (*Βένετοι*) and Greens or *Prasini* (*Πράσινοι*)[1] were the two most powerful factions, each of them headed by a captain (δήμαρχος) and organized as a city militia. The main place of their activities was the Hippodrome, which was more than a race-course; it was 'an assembly—a substitute for the vanished Comitia, the last asylum of the liberties of the Populus Romanus'.[2] In the Byzantine Empire, particularly in its first period, the shouts and cries of the crowd were not confined to salutations: they reflected the attitude of the population towards all pending internal and external questions. They could express equally well approval towards, or hostility against, decisions made by the Emperor or the Patriarch. *ἄκτα*, the Greek transliteration of the Latin *acta*, originally used for shouts of all kinds, had this double meaning.[3]

In their desire to consolidate the system of administration the Emperors tried to bring the factions under their control by instituting a ceremonial which followed the calendar of the court, just as the ecclesiastical year was regulated by the calendar of the Church: nothing was left to chance. The elaborate form of panegyric formulae and poems sung by the alternating choirs of the Blues and Greens obviously developed under Oriental influences from the days of Heraclius onwards.[4] It was actually after the decisive defeat of the Persians in 629 that the Empire gradually became orientalized. The Emperor changed the title Imperator into Basileus. Latin ceased to be the official language of the Empire. The Roman organization of the provinces was given up, and foreign policy was directed mainly towards the East. The Christian character of the Empire was accentuated by the introduction of passages from the Bible into the texts of the Laws. Veneration of holy relics and miracle-working icons was favoured by the Emperors.[5] The Council *in Trullo*, convoked on the initiative of Justinian II, repudiated, in 691, representations of Christ which followed the Hellenistic, idealized type, and ordered that icons of the Lord should be

[1] Cf. F. Dvornik, 'The Circus Parties in Byzantium', *Byzantina-Metabyz.* i (1946), 119–33.

[2] N. H. Baynes, *The Byz. Empire*[3] (1939), p. 31.

[3] The verb ἀκταλογεῖν, however, is always used synonymously with εὐφημεῖν. Cf. J. J. Reiske's *Comment. ad Const. Porph. de Cer.* ii. 86.

[4] L. Bréhier, 'Les Origines des titres impériaux', *B.Z.* xv. 171–2. See also S. Runciman, *Byz. Civilisation*, p. 62.

[5] Cf. A. Grabar, *L'Empereur dans l'art byzantin* (1936), p. 164.

painted in His human appearance (κατὰ τὸν ἀνθρώπινον χαρακτῆρα),[1] i.e. realistically, according to the Syrian type known to us from the Rabula-Codex.[2]

With regard to the music used in ceremonies, a striking resemblance can be observed between performances at the court of Baghdad and those at Constantinople. From descriptions of festivities at the court of Baghdad we know that the music was performed by choirs of Persian singers and players, hidden from the assembly by curtains.[3] A similar ceremony is reported from the court at Constantinople when the Emperor entertained foreign ambassadors in the octagonal reception-hall of the Imperial Palace, the so-called Chrysotriclinium. During the meal, choirs from the two main churches, Hagia Sophia and Holy Apostles, sang hymns in honour of the Basileus (τὰ βασιλίκια).[4] They were placed in the niches behind curtains, which were drawn 'according to custom' (εἰσήχθησαν κατὰ τὸν εἰωθότα τύπον τὰ βῆλα),[5] so that the performers remained invisible to the guests. In the intervals between the *Basilikia* music was played on portable organs and other instruments. We shall have to return in the course of this chapter to the use of instruments, particularly of organs, in ceremonies.

The term generally used for a chant of greeting was *Euphemia* (εὐφημία), or—for a special acclamation, in which the singers addressed the person they greeted with wishes for a long life—*Polychronion* (πολυχρόνιον) and *Polychronisma* (πολυχρόνισμα).[6] These latter terms are taken from the first word of the typical formulae used on such occasions:

Πολυχρόνιον ποιήσαι ὁ Θεὸς τὴν ἁγίαν καὶ κρατείαν βασιλείαν σας εἰς πολλὰ ἔτη.

Πολυχρόνιον ποιήσαι ὁ Θεὸς τὴν θεοπρόβλητον, θεόστεπτον καὶ θεοφρούρητον, κρατείαν καὶ ἁγίαν βασιλείαν σας εἰς πολλὰ ἔτη.[7]

(Long may the Lord extend your holy, mighty reign, through many years.

Long may the Lord extend your heaven-appointed, heaven-crowned, heaven-protected, mighty and holy reign, through many years.)

1 *Concilium Quinisextum*, Canon 82.

2 Cf. C. Diehl, *Manuel d'art byzantin* (1910), p. 305.

3 Kraemer, *Kulturgeschichte des Orients*, ii. 71 sqq. Cf. E. Wellesz, 'Die Kirchenmusik im byz. Reiche' *O.C.*, N.S. vi. 120–3.

4 Const. Porph. *de Cer.* i, *C.S.H.B.*, p. 585, l. 14.

5 Ibid., p. 583, l. 22.

6 Cf. Cod. Curop. *de Off.*, *Gretseri et Goari comment.*, *C.S.H.B.*, p. 277.

7 *de Off.*, ch. vi, p. 46.

The *Euphemiai* which have come down to us range from poems of a certain artistic quality to conventional versifications. As an example of this kind of poetry a charming 'Hymn of Spring' may serve. This poem was sung annually by the Blues and Greens in the Hippodrome at the 'Races of Carnival' (*Μακελλαρικὸν ἱπποδρόμιον*), which took place in the week before Sexagesima Sunday.[1] The verses were sung antiphonally by the choirs of the two factions, and the adherents of the two *demes* gave the response to the verses of their respective choirs.[2]

Ἴδε τὸ ἔαρ τὸ γλυκὺ
πάλιν ἐπανατέλλει
χαράν, ὑγείαν καὶ ζωὴν
καὶ τὴν εὐημερίαν,
ἀνδραγαθίαν ἐκ θεοῦ
τῷ βασιλεῖ Ῥωμαίων,
καὶ νίκην θεοδώρητον
κατὰ τῶν πολεμίων.

(See sweet Spring sends out for the Emperor of the Romans happiness, health and life, well-being, and strength from God and victory, god-given, over his enemies.)

In the later days of the Empire a distinction was made between the terms *Polychronion* and *Euphemia*. We find *Polychronion* applied to acclamations in honour of the Emperor, his family, or a member of the court, while *Euphemesis* (*εὐφήμησις*) was used for those in honour of an ecclesiastical dignitary. After the end of the Empire in 1453, however, both terms were used for ecclesiastical dignitaries.[3] *Euphemeseis* are still sung in Greek churches in honour of a visiting archbishop at the present day.[4]

II. THE PERFORMANCE OF MUSIC IN THE CEREMONIES

Concerning the ceremonies during which acclamations were sung ample evidence can be gathered from Byzantine historiographers. Among the books which provide us with information about the organization of the choirs, their participation in the ceremonies, and their way of singing, the famous *De Ceremoniis*

[1] Cf. A. Vogt's commentary to his edition of *de Cer.*, vol. ii, pp. 172–4.

[2] The metrical form of this and other acclamations has been restored by P. Maas in his article on 'Metrische Akklamationen der Byzantiner', *B.Z.* xxi, pp. 28–51, who, going back to the version of the MS., substituted in line 3 *ὑγείαν* for *ὑγιείαν*, and in line 6 *τῷ βασιλεῖ* for *τοῖς βασιλεῦσι*.

[3] Cf. H. J. W. Tillyard, 'The Acclamations of Emperors', *A.B.S.* xviii. 241.

[4] An example of a modern *Euphemesis* is given in J. B. Rebours's *Traité de Psaltique*, pp. 234 sqq.

by Constantine VII Porphyrogennetus (913–59)[1] holds the first place; next to it comes *De Officiis*, a handbook ascribed to George Codinus Curopalata.[2] From these books we learn that the acclamations prescribed for the ceremonies were performed by two groups of singers, according to the character of the ceremony. Acclamations in honour of the Emperor, the Empress, the Imperial family, or court dignitaries were sung by the two choirs of *Kractae* (κράκται), those for ecclesiastical dignitaries by the *Psaltae* (ψάλται). The *Kractae* were court officials and laymen. Each choir of the *Kractae*[3] was conducted by a *domesticus scholarum*, one being the captain (δημοκράτης) of the Veneti, the other of the Prasini. The *domesticus* was the precentor and chief of the musicians and singers. It was his task to rehearse the music, and to take care that the *acta* were sung in the right order.[4] The procedure was as follows: the Emperor was received by the two factions, each headed by the *domesticus*, who stood before the Emperor, his head bowed down and his hands crossed on his breast,[5] while the singers sang the first of the acclamations. When they had finished, the members of the faction sang the response, which consisted in repeating either the whole strophe or its last phrase.[6] During the singing of the refrain by the crowd the *domesticus* signed the Emperor three times with the sign of the Cross. While the *Kractae* sang the second part of the *actologia* the *domesticus* again assumed the attitude of reverence, and when the response was again sung by the crowd he again made the sign of the Cross, and this was repeated as long as the singing lasted.[7]

[1] Constantine VII Porphyrogennetus' book about the ceremonies is in the main a compilation from older treatises on court ceremonies; only a part of it was written by Constantine himself. Cf. A. Vogt's Introduction to his *Commentaire*, vol. i of *Constantin Porphyrogénète, Le Livre des Cérémonies* (1935).

[2] According to J. B. Bury, *De Officiis* dates from the fifteenth century.

[3] In a very learned study on the subject J. Handschin, *Das Zeremonienwerk Kaiser Konstantins und die sangbare Dichtung* (Basel, 1942), pp. 72 sqq., assumes that the *Kractae* were the precentors of the factions, two for each faction. No conclusive proof, however, is given to support the hypothesis, and on p. 77 Handschin himself takes the view that the *Kractae* were a choir, alternating with the people (the λαός).

[4] *εἶτ' οὖν ἀρχῳδὸς καὶ ἐπιστάτης μελῳδιῶν καὶ τῶν μελῳδῶν, οἷα εἰς ῥυθμὸν καὶ τάξιν καθιστῶν αὐτούς τε καὶ τὰ μελῳδήματα.* John Citrus, quoted by J. J. Reiske in his commentary to *de Cer.* ii. 153.

[5] The attitude used when standing before the Emperor, the head inclined, the hands crossed over the breast, is that prescribed by the ritual at the courts of the Kings of Persia and Armenia, as J. J. Reiske points out in his commentary to *de Off.* ii. 89.

[6] Ibid., p. 90.

[7] *ἰστέον ὅτι τοῦ δήμου ἀκτολογοῦντος κατὰ τὴν ἀκολουθίαν τῆς ἀκτολογίας, ἤγουν τοῦ λαοῦ ἀποκρινομένου τοῖς κράκταις, κατασφραγίζει ὁ δομέστικος τῶν σχολῶν κατ' ἄκρον τῆς αὐτοῦ χλανίδος πρὸς τὸν βασιλέα τρίτον· καὶ τῶν κρακτῶν λεγόντων ἔχει δεδεμένην ταῖς χερσί· πάλιν τοῦ λαοῦ λέγοντος, κατασφραγίζει μέχρις ἂν πληρωθῇ πᾶσα ἡ ἀκτολογία. Schol. ad de Off.* i. 1, p. 12.

The *Psaltae*, on the other hand, were members of the clergy and had taken holy orders. They, too, were divided into two choirs, each of them under a *domesticus*, but both together under the direction of the *Protopsaltes* (πρωτοψάλτης),[1] who stood between them when they sang.[2]

When the Emperor took part in a procession, or went to church, both groups of singers, the *Kractae* and *Psaltae*, sang the *Euphemiae* together, the responses being made by the crowd. At the ceremony on Christmas Eve[3] instruments (ὄργανα) accompanied the singers. The players, the so-called *paegniotae* (οἱ λεγόμενοι παιγνιῶται), stood behind the clergy and were separated from the crowd by the standard-bearers. The Imperial band consisted only of trumpeters (σαλπιγκταί), horn-players (βουκκινάτορες), cymbal-players (ἀνακαρισταί), and pipers (σουρουλισταί); none of the weak-sounding instruments (τῶν λεπτῶν ὀργάνων) were used. The Emperor mounted a dais. Curtains were drawn to hide him and his suite from the eyes of the crowd. When they were opened again the Emperor, who had changed his vestment, was seen standing alone and visible to all. At that moment the singers, accompanied by all the various instruments, intoned the *Polychronion*. When the singers had finished their hymn of praise the instruments still continued to play for a while until the Emperor, waving a handkerchief, gave them a sign to cease. Now the *Psaltae* began to sing again, this time the verses[4] appointed for the feast, and, soon after, 'Christ is born, who crowned thee as King'.[5] After this they sang the rest of the verses, and the instruments played for a time. Then the Emperor and Empress were praised by name. While the *Psaltae* sang the *Polychronia* for the occasion, the curtains were closed, and when they had finished and only the band was left playing, the standard-bearers started to leave the church.

[1] In *de Off.*, ch. 1, a list of the officials of 'The Great Church', i.e. Hagia Sophia, is given. The offices are divided into groups, each containing five ranks. The seventh group (πεντάς) contains the following: ὁ πρωτοψάλτης,—οἱ δύο δομέστικοι, τοῦ πρώτου καὶ τοῦ δευτέρου χοροῦ,—ὁ λαοσυνάκτης,—πριμμικήριος τῶν ταβουλαρίων,—ὁ ἄρχων τῶν κοντακίων. *de Off.*, p. 6. 6. An explanation of the functions of these officials is given in Reiske's commentary, pp. 153–5.

[2] ὁ πρωτοψάλτης ἵσταται μέσον τῶν δύο χορῶν, δεξίου τε καὶ εὐωνύμου. ἄρχεται δὲ καὶ τὴν ἔναρξιν τῆς ψαλμῳδιας· μετὰ δὲ ταῦτα καὶ ψάλται ὅλοι. Ibid., p. 153. These explanatory lines are taken from Allatius (Allacci) (1586–1669). From them we learn that it was the function of the *protopsaltes* to start the chanting of the psalms, which was continued by the choirs of the *Psaltae*.

[3] A description of the ceremony is given in *de Officiis*, *C.S.H.B.*, pp. 43–55; the part dealing with the acclamations is to be found on pp. 49–53.

[4] The text has προσφόρους στίχους τῇ ἑορτῇ. Stichoi are verses from the psalms.

[5] Χριστὸς ἐγεννήθη ὁ στέψας σε βασιλέα. *de Off.*, p. 53, l. 3.

III. THE ORGAN

From this and other passages in *De Ceremoniis* and *De Officiis*, describing the use of instruments in secular and ecclesiastical celebrations, some conclusions can be drawn about the use of the organ. Organs were played in the Hippodrome in processions, and during banquets and receptions in the Imperial Palace. In the Early Empire hydraulic organs may have been used, since instruments of that type were well known in Rome. The earliest description of the water-organ is to be found in the *Pneumatica* of Hero of Alexandria, who flourished about 150 B.C.[1] The next oldest, 'and practically the only other ancient description' of the hydraulic organ is by Vitruvius (about A.D. 70) in the tenth book of his *De Architectura*, chapter 13. From these descriptions, and from the drawing of Hero's hydraulic organ in MS. Harl. 5589 of the British Museum, it can be assumed that the water-organ was a large instrument of some weight, the sound of which could be heard all over the Roman Circus.

A different kind of organ is represented on a relief, dating from the end of the fourth century, on the obelisk of Theodosius I, the Great (379–95), in Constantinople.[2] In the centre of the relief the Emperor is shown in the Hippodrome waiting with a garland in his hand for the victor of the races. Under his throne are two rows of spectators, and beneath them a row of female dancers. On both sides of them two small organs are placed, looking like gigantic pan-pipes. We can also see the players (*οἱ ὀργανάριοι*) and two youths who work the blast-bags[3] with their feet.

This is the new type of the instrument, the portable pneumatic organ, which seems to have displaced the hydraulic organ in the East at an earlier date than hitherto was thought. A description of the Byzantine pneumatic organ can be found in the reminiscences of Harun-ben-Jahja, who was made a prisoner of war

[1] Cf. C. Maclean, 'The Principle of the Hydraulic Organ', *S.I.M.* vi (1904), 187. According to W. Schmidt, the editor of the *Πνευματικά*, Hero lived a century or two later. The invention of the instrument is variously ascribed to Archimedes of Syracuse, Ctesibius of Alexandria, and Hero. The Greek text of Hero's description of the water-organ, together with an English translation, is to be found in the Appendix to Maclean's article, *S.I.M.* vi. 217–20. A facsimile of Hero's organ from Cod. Harl. 5589 of the Brit. Mus. is given in Appendix C, p. 223.

[2] A reproduction of the relief can be seen on p. 82 of my *Byzantische Musik*, Jedermann's Bücherei (1927).

[3] Cf. Maclean's article, pp. 184–6, where he gives the reasons for substituting 'blast-bag' for 'bellows'.

at Ascalon and brought to Constantinople in 867. Describing a banquet for the prisoners held at Christmas in the presence of the Emperor he wrote:[1]

'Then they bring a thing which is called *al-urgana* (=τὰ ὄργανα). This is an object made out of a square of wood after the manner of an oil-press, covered with strong leather, into which sixty pipes of copper are put. The part of the pipes outside the leather is covered with gold, so that only a little of them can be seen, because each pipe is only a little longer than the one before. At one side of the square object is a hole; into this a pair of bellows is put, like the bellows of a forge....[2] Two men now start to blow the organ, and the master comes and plays the pipes; and each pipe sings according to its length, sounding in honour of the Emperor, while all the people sit at their tables. After this enter twenty men, holding *chulbag*s (cymbals) in their hands. These men play as long as the banquet lasts.'

The same ceremony is repeated on the following eleven days.[3]

The golden organ, mentioned by Harun-ben-Jahja, is the instrument of the Emperor.[4] Occasionally two golden organs were used to accompany the ceremonies in honour of, or performed by, the Emperor, for example those which took place at the reception of foreign ambassadors.[5] On the side of each of the factions the silver organs of the Greens and Blues were placed.[5] The organs were mainly used to provide a harmonious background to the most solemn moments of a ceremony. They usually began to play when the singers had finished a Polychronism, and the same seems to be true of the other instruments mentioned in the books of ceremonies.[6] But reference is also made in the ceremonials to occasions on which organs or other instruments were played, while the *Kractae* and *Psaltae* sang, either separately or together. It has already been mentioned that the Imperial band played while the *Basilikia* were sung, and continued to play in the interval between two or more subsequent *Polychronia*. Another case of simultaneous singing and playing is mentioned in the sixty-ninth chapter of the first book

[1] Cf. J. Marquardt, *Osteurop. und ostasiat. Streifzüge* (1903), pp. 217 sqq.

[2] From this part of the description we may gather that the pneumatic organ was not known to the Arabs.

[3] From Christmas Day to Epiphany.

[4] *ἐν δὲ τῷ πόρτικι τοῦ χρυσοτρικλινίου, ητοι ἐν τῷ ὡρολογίῳ, ἔστησαν τὰ δύο χρυσᾶ ὄργανα τὰ βασιλικὰ καὶ τὰ δύο ἀργυρᾶ ὄργανα τῶν μερῶν.* *de Cer.* i. 580, l. 3.

[5] Ibid., p. 571.

[6] John Cantacuzene, *Hist.*, vol. ii, p. 588.

of *De Ceremoniis*, dealing with the ritual for the day before the opening of the chariot-races in the Hippodrome. On that occasion *Euphemeses* were sung, among other chants, praising the Holy Trinity, the Emperor, and the Imperial family. Here the following direction for the singers is to be found: 'While the organ plays the Trisagion (καὶ τρισαγιάζοντος τοῦ ὀργάνου), the *Kractae* chant: Thrice Holy, succour the Lords.'[1] Another passage of *De Ceremoniis* describes the ritual which must be observed when a bride, belonging to the nobility, is conducted to the house of the bridegroom. The two factions, with their organs, go to the house of the bride, who receives them at the door, accompanied by tambourine-players and cymbalists (ὑπὸ πληθίων καὶ χειροκυμβάλων). She then mounts on horseback and is acclaimed by the two factions. To this description of the ceremony the Scholiast of *De Ceremoniis* adds that the organs are played while the bride descends to leave her house and during the singing of the acclamations (ἐν τῷ ἀκτολογεῖν τὰ μέρη αὐλοῦσι τὰ ὄργανα).[2]

There are no indications of the way in which the accompaniment of the chants was performed by the organ or the other instruments, but the kind of playing and singing that are heard nowadays in the Orient gives us some guidance. The organists certainly did not use harmonies, though some concords may have been occasionally introduced. They probably used both hands, and played in octaves. The instrumentalists may have introduced, from time to time, a kind of heterophony. It is a question still open to controversy whether the medieval term *organum*, used for singing in parallel fifths, fourths, and octaves, does not refer to an accompaniment by the organ which, according to P. Wagner, 'was known to the Franks and Germans only through the Byzantines'.[3] There are too few indications in the sources of the way in which organs and other instruments were used for us to be able to draw any far-reaching conclusions regarding the extent to which the instruments accompanied the singers; yet it seems permissible to assume that, as a rule, acclamations were sung unaccompanied. This hypothesis is connected with another, which has now to be discussed.

1 *de Cer.* i, ch. 69, p. 315, l. 10.

2 Ibid., ch. 81, p. 379, ll. 21–2.

3 Cf. P. Wagner, *History of Plain-Chant*, The Plainsong and Medieval Music Society (1901), p. 232.

The question has often been raised as to whether organs were used in church in the days of the Byzantine Empire or whether they were excluded from liturgical use as they are to-day. There is a passage which might be interpreted as answering the question in a positive sense; it occurs in the 'Dissertation about the Imperial Banquets' by the *Protospatharius* Philotheos, appended as chapter 52 to *De Ceremoniis*, ii. Here it is said that on Holy Saturday the court, the nobility, and the patricians attend the evening service in the church of the Theotokos of Pharus. When it is finished and a 'secret organum' has given the sign (μετὰ τὴν ἐκφώνησιν τοῦ μυστικοῦ ὀργάνου), they all take off their ceremonial garments and put on their usual cloaks. They then leave the church and go to the banquet, which is given by the Emperor in his palace. This passage, however, does not contribute anything in favour of the view that organs were used in church. 'Organon' is the term both for instrument and for the 'king of instruments', *the* instrument, viz. the organ. From the wording of the passage it is not clear whether it refers to the sudden signal given by an instrument of the band or to the organ. This, however, is of secondary importance. The essential point in Philotheos's account is the statement that the *organon* was played after the Divine Office, and therefore did not accompany the liturgical chants or the liturgical action between them.* On that occasion the sound of the instrument was used to mark the beginning of a new, secular, ceremony which followed the liturgical. From every other passage which refers to liturgical singing it is clear that the organ was excluded from use in the church. The use of the instrument in the Western Church may be explained in the following way. In 757 Constantine Copronymus sent an organ as a present to King Pippin. In 812 Michael I presented Charlemagne with another instrument. The gift was accompanied by musicians who knew how to play the organ, and who obviously taught their art to Frankish musicians.[1] It is also reported that the instruments were copied by Frankish craftsmen and the new organs used to assist the teaching of Plainchant. Since all this work was done by the monks, it follows that the organ was gradually introduced inside the church and spread all over the West[2] as a church instrument. Organs of a

[1] *History of Plain-Chant*, p. 210.

[2] C. Sachs, *Handbuch d. Musikinstrumentenkunde* (1920), p. 354.

larger size were built, and the Byzantine portable organ was replaced by instruments of the size we know nowadays, one of the earliest being the great organ at Winchester, built in 980.

IV. USE OF THE ACCLAMATIONS

Acclamations were sung when a new Emperor was crowned.[1] The ceremony took place in Hagia Sophia, where the Patriarch of Constantinople, after having blessed the crown, himself puts it on the head of the Basileus. At that moment the singers shout 'Worthy', and the whole assembly does reverence. After this the singers chant: 'Glory to God in the highest, and on earth peace.' This is repeated three times by the congregation. Again the singers chant: 'Good will towards Christian men', to which the congregation responds three times with the same acclamation. The singers continue: 'For God had mercy upon His people.' The people respond three times with the same chant. Thus the *actologia* continues, the people always repeating three times the verses sung by the *Kractae*:

Αὕτη ἡ ἡμέρα Κυρίου ἡ μεγάλη.
Αὕτη ἡ ἡμέρα τῆς ζωῆς τῶν Ῥωμαίων.
Αὕτη ἡ χαρὰ καὶ ἡ δόξα τοῦ κόσμου·
ἐν ᾗ τὸ στέφος τῆς βασιλείας
τῆς κορυφῆς σου ἀξίως περιετέθη.
Δόξα θεῷ τῷ Δεσπότῃ πάντων.
Δόξα θεῷ τῷ στέψαντι τὴν κορυφήν σου.
Δόξα θεῷ τῷ ἀναδείξαντί σε βασιλέα.
Δόξα θεῷ τῷ δοξάσαντί σε οὕτως.
Δόξα θεῷ τῷ εὐδοκήσαντι οὕτως.
Ἀλλ' ὁ στέψας σε, ὁ δεῖνα βασιλέα, αὐτοχείρως
φυλάξῃ σε εἰς πλήθη χρόνων ἐν πορφύρᾳ,
σὺν ταῖς Αὐγούσταις καὶ τοῖς πορφυρογεννήτοις,
εἰς δόξαν καὶ ἀνέγερσιν τῶν Ῥωμαίων.
Εἰσακούσῃ ὁ θεὸς τοῦ λαοῦ ὑμῶν.
Πολλά, πολλά, πολλά. [*ὁ λαός*] *Πολλὰ ἔτη εἰς πολλά.*
Πολλοὶ ὑμῖν χρόνοι, ὁ δεῖνα καὶ ὁ δεῖνα αὐτοκράτορες Ῥωμαίων.
[*ὁ λαός*] *Πολλοὶ ὑμῖν χρόνοι.*
Πολλοὶ ὑμῖν χρόνοι, οἱ θεράποντες τοῦ Κυρίου.
[*ὁ λαός*] *Πολλοὶ ὑμῖν χρόνοι.*[2]

[1] *de Off.*, pp. 86–97 and *de Cer.*, i. 191–6.
[2] Ibid., p. 195.

(This is the day of the Lord, the great day. This is the day of life for the Romans. This is the joy and the glory of the world, on which the crown of kingship, worthy of your head, was put on.

Glory to God the Master of all. Glory to God who has crowned your head. Glory to God who has marked you out as king. Glory to God who has thus glorified you. Glory to God who has been pleased to do this thing. And He who crowned you, N.N., to be king, with His own hand, may He guard you in the purple your full time, together with the Augustae and Princes, for the glory and encouragement of the Romans. May God listen to your people (*shouting*): Many, many, many! (*the assembly*) 'Many years; for many years.' May your life be long, N.N. and N.N., Emperors of the Romans! (*the assembly*) 'May your life be long'. May your life be long, Servants of the Lord! (*the assembly*) 'May your life be long!')

Similar acclamations salute the Empress and the Porphyrogenneti. At the end of the *actologia* another group of acclamations follows in honour of the Emperor and his co-regent. Acclamations were also sung to welcome the Imperial bride, who came to Constantinople by sea or by land, and to praise her when she was crowned by the Basileus after the crown had been blessed by the Patriarch.[1]

According to the court ceremonial the Empress had to take a bath on the third day after her marriage. As she returned from the bath she was acclaimed, on her way back to her apartments, by the court and all the dignitaries. Three organs were posted at different places along her route, and the Blues and Greens greeted her with chants in the customary way.[2] Extended *actologiae* were sung on the third day after the birth of a prince in the Purple Chamber,[3] and at the receptions on the anniversaries of the coronation of the Emperor or of his birthday. Apart from the texts of the *Polychronia* a poem has been preserved celebrating the coronation day. It gives an idea of the kind of court poetry which flourished in Byzantium, and served as a model for the sycophantic glorification of Eastern and Western rulers. We should, however, bear in mind that these poems were not written in order to flatter an individual, but the bearer of the Imperial crown. This is clearly indicated by the fact that we do not find the names of Emperors in these poems, but instead the words ὁ δεῖνα (so-and-so), which had to be replaced by the name of the Emperor actually reigning at the time when they

[1] *de Cer.*, pp. 208 sqq. [2] Ibid., pp. 214–15.
[3] Ibid., pp. 216–17.

are sung. This poem[1] was chanted by the two factions after they had performed a dance with torches:

Χαίρει ὁ κόσμος ὁρῶν σε αὐτοκράτορα δεσπότην
καὶ ἡ πόλις σου τέρπεται, θεόστεπτε ὁ δεῖνα·
ὡραΐζεται ἡ τάξις σε βλέπουσα ταξιάρχην,
καὶ εὐτυχοῦσι τὰ σκῆπτρα σκηπτοῦχόν σε κεκτημένα.
Κατακοσμεῖς γὰρ τὸν θρόνον τῆς πατρῴας βασιλείας
σὺν τῇ Αὐγούστῃ προπέμπων μαρμαρυγὰς εὐταξίας·
ὅθεν εὐημεροῦσα διὰ σοῦ ἡ πολιτεία
τῆς σῆς αὐτοκρατορίας ἑορτάζει τὴν ἡμέραν.

(At the sight of you, the Lord Emperor, the world rejoices, and your city is gladdened, God-crowned N.N. Seeing you as its leader the army is enriched, and with you as their bearer the sceptres are happy. For you adorn the throne, the Kingdom of your fathers, sending forth, together with the Empress, rays of harmony. Therefore the State, flourishing through you, celebrates this day of your rule.)

The diversity of the acclamations is not exhausted by the enumeration of all those which were written for the solemn feasts and celebrations of the Byzantine calendar, for the christianized pagan feasts, for the Hippodrome, and for the triumphant return of the victorious Emperor. The ceremonial also contains acclamations for celebrations of minor importance, for example for the promotion of court officials, and in addition for the seasonal feasts such as the 'Vintage Feast' (*ἡμέρα τοῦ τρυγητοῦ*). This feast was celebrated in the middle of September and took place in an open space in the vineyard of the Emperor's summer-palace. After the blessing of the grapes by the Patriarch of Constantinople the Emperor presented each of the assembled officials, senators, and patricians with a cluster of grapes. During the ceremony hymns were sung by the factions of the Blues and Greens, the first of which, composed in the first Mode, runs as follows:

Ἐκ τοῦ λειμῶνος τῆς γνώσεως
τοῦ δεσπότου τῆς σοφίας
τρυγήσαντες ἄνθη,
ἱερὰ τάξις τῶν ἐντίμων πατρικίων
ἐν τῷ προσφέρειν τῶν ᾀσμάτων τὰ πλήθη,
κεφαλὴν καταστέψωμεν,

[1] Ibid., i. 279. The metrical form of the poem has been restored by P. Maas in 'Metrische Akklamat.', *B.Z.* xxi (1912), 37 sqq. Cf. A Vogt, *Constant. Porphyr.*, *Le Livre des cérémonies, Comment.* ii. 196.

ὡς οἶκον τῆς εὐωδίας τῶν νοημάτων,
ἀντιλαμβάνοντες τοῦ ἐκείνου τερπνῶν χαρίτων.
Ἀλλά, ἀθάνατε βασιλεῦ τῶν ἁπάντων,
σὺ δίδου ἐπὶ πολὺ ταύτην τὴν ἑορτὴν
τῷ κόσμῳ τῆς αὐτοκράτορος ἐξουσίας
ὁ δεῖνα τοῦ θεοστέπτου χρισθέντος βασιλέως.

(From the field of knowledge of the Master of Wisdom, we, the sacred order of the honourable patricians, have gathered flowers and, offering many songs, having participated in his pleasant graces, we will crown the head, like a fragrant house of thoughts.

Hence, immortal King of the Universe, grant that the world may for long enjoy this festival of the Imperial power, of N.N., the God-crowned and anointed Emperor.)

V. FUNCTION OF THE ACCLAMATIONS

From the descriptions of ceremonies during which acclamations were sung their main function becomes evident. They were primarily intended to increase the pomp of the appearance of the Emperor and his court, or of the Patriarch and his clergy, or of both. They had the further object of regulating the order of rites, processions, games, receptions, entertainments, and representations performed in the presence of the Emperor. They also served to impress foreigners with a demonstration of the splendour of the capital and the power of the Eastern Empire.

The descriptions given in the two Ceremonials of the reception of Oriental ambassadors give us a vivid picture of the theatrical apparatus with which such an effect was accomplished. Cooler minds, however, seem to have seen through the artificiality of these spectacular shows. The famous report of Liutprand of Cremona to Otto I on his mission to Nicephorus in June 968 gives us an idea of how these ceremonies failed to impress an unfavourably biased spectator. Describing the procession of Nicephorus from the palace to Hagia Sophia he wrote:

'As Nicephorus, like some crawling monster, walked along, the singers began to cry out in adulation: "Behold the morning star approaches: the day star rises: in his eyes the sun's rays are reflected: Nicephorus our prince, the pale death of the Saracens". How much more truly might they have sung:—"Come, you miserable burnt-out coal, old woman in your walk, wood devil in your look; clodhopper, haunter of byres, goat-footed, horned, double-limbed; bristly, wild, rough, barbarian, harsh, hairy, a rebel, a Cappadocian!" So, puffed up by these lying ditties, he entered St. Sophia, his masters, the emperors, following at a distance and doing him homage on the ground with the kiss of peace.'[1]

Besides these there were the acclamations sung by the *Psaltae* which formed part of the religious ceremonies. They were of a different character, as can be seen from the examples given above. The splendour of the singing of the *Euphemeses* in Hagia Sophia certainly surpassed anything of that kind in Western ritual, since we may assume that the 110 *Anagnostae* of the days of Justinian, who were increased in number to 160 under Heraclius,[2] had the office not only of chanting the Epistles but also the acclamations, while the twenty-five *Psaltae*, mentioned by both Justinian and Heraclius, had to sing the hymns and to intone the acclamations. Otherwise it would be impossible to explain why such a great number of 'Readers' were needed, amounting under Justinian to more than four times, under Heraclius to more than six times, the number of the singers. The function of the Readers, the *Anagnostae*, could not have been confined to the chanting of the lessons from the Prophets and the Epistles; it was obviously their task to do all the chanting required at a solemn service in the 'Great Church', as Hagia Sophia was called by the people of Constantinople. John Cantacuzene's description of the funeral of Andronicus Palaeologus the Younger gives an idea of the singing in Hagia Sophia on such an occasion. He writes that so many priests came to Constantinople to attend the ceremony that the Great Church seemed too small to hold them all; yet the rites were performed in such perfect order that it seemed as if only a select number of officiants had taken part in them. There was no murmur to be heard from the crowd, as is often the case on such occasions, but a perfect and harmonious performance was given, when the whole congregation sang the sacred hymns antiphonally. 'Seeing the enormous assembly of priests with their bishops, adorned with the holy vestments, led by the one Patriarch, performing the same rites, was a spectacle producing not only amazement but also delight.'[3] We may assume that the singing at the funeral was conducted by the *domestici* of the two choirs of *psaltae*,

[1] *The Works of Liudprand of Cremona*, translated by F. A. Wright (1930), pp. 240–1.

[2] Cf. *de Off.*, p. 112.

[3] John Cantacuzene, *Hist.* iii, ch. i; *P.G.* cliii, col. 707.

reinforced by those of the Blues and Greens, and by the *anagnostae*, while the responses were sung by the congregation.

These massed choirs, however, were used only on rare occasions, as John Cantacuzene points out, and yet even the normal service at Hagia Sophia, on solemn festivals, exceeded in pomp that of all other Byzantine churches, where a much smaller number of singers was used. Originally only two *anagnostae* were required for the reading of the Lessons, as can be seen from another regulation of Heraclius, and this custom was retained in the small churches. The fact that 160 *anagnostae* took part in the liturgical service from the seventh century onwards, in addition to the *psaltae*, gives an idea of how far Eastern liturgy had developed from the monastic ideal of the early days of Christianity, which was still preserved in anchoretic communities of the fifth century, which abstained from any form of singing even from the chanting of the psalms.[1] We shall have to refer in a later chapter to the tendency of the Eastern Church to heighten the solemnity of the Divine Office by introducing more and more music into the service. The history of Byzantine ecclesiastical music, as a matter of fact, shows a slow but gradually increasing preponderance of the music over the words.

VI. THE MUSIC OF THE ACCLAMATIONS

The music of all the *actologiae* and poems contained in the books of ceremonies is lost, but fortunately some *Polychronia* and *Euphemeseis* sung during religious ceremonies in honour of the Emperor and the Patriarch are preserved in liturgical manuscripts. Though the versions of the melodies belong to the final period of the Empire, these documents give us a clear idea of the kind of music that was sung to the text of the acclamations.

The acclamation which follows here was performed in honour of the Emperor John VIII Palaeologus (1425–48) and of the Patriarch Joseph II (1425–39). The manuscript, belonging to the monastery of Pantocrator on Mount Athos, seems to be dated 1433.[2] The rubrics of the manuscript indicate that each of the

[1] Cf. J.-B. Pitra, *Hymnogr. de l'égl. gr.*, p. 43.

[2] Cf. H. J. W. Tillyard's article on 'The Acclamation of Byzantine Emperors', *A.B.S.*, no. xviii, p. 241, from which music and text of the acclamation are taken. Tillyard visited the monastery of Pantocrator in September 1912, his transcriptions of the music from MS. Pantocr. 214 are contained on pp. 247 and 250–1 of his article. I have adapted the rhythmical rendering of the

three parts of the *Euphemesis* is first sung by a Precentor[1] in the Sanctuary, and then repeated by the *psaltae*, standing in the Solea.

(i) *Εὐφήμησις τῶν Βασιλέων· λέγει δὲ πρῶτον ὁ ἐν τῷ βήματι.*

(ii) *Ἀποκρίνονται οἱ ἐκτὸς τὸ αὐτό· καὶ πάλιν οἱ ἐντὸς ἕτερον εἰς τοὺς Βασιλεῖς.*

(iii) *Καὶ οἱ ἐκτὸς πάλιν ὁμοίως τὸ αὐτό, καὶ πάλιν οἱ ἐντὸς εἰς τὸν Πατριάρχην.*[2]

(i)
acc.
acc.
Πολ - λὰ . . . . τὰ ἔ - τη τῶν βα - σι - λέ - ων
acc.
acc.
Πολ - λὰ . . . . τὰ ἔ - τη τῶν βα - σι - λέ - ων
acc.
Πολ - λὰ . . . . τὰ ἔ - τη τῶν βα - σι - λέ - ων
(ii)
Ἰ - ω - άν - - - νου τοῦ εὐ - σε - βεσ - τά - του βα - σι - λέ - ως
καὶ αὐ - το - κρά - το - ρος Ῥω - μαί - ων τοῦ Πα - λαι - ο - λό - γου·
καὶ Μα - ρί - ας τῆς εὐ - σε - βεσ - τά - της Αὐ - γού - στης πολ - λὰ τὰ ἔ - τη

melodies to the methods agreed on by us at a conference at Copenhagen in July 1931, at which the foundation of the *Monumenta Musicae Byzantinae* was decided upon, and the rules for the transcriptions set up by the Editorial Committee.

1 In some of the rubrics the *Domesticus*, in others the *Protopsaltes* is specified as precentor.

2 *A.B.S.*, no. xviii, p. 246.

(iii)

The *Polychronisma* proper, viz. the phrase πολλὰ τὰ ἔτη τῶν βασιλέων, is set to a florid musical passage; the part containing the names and the titles of the Emperor and the Patriarch keeps to a kind of cantillation or chanting.

Another example taken from the same manuscript shows a richer style throughout the whole composition. It contains the most familiar formula of the acclamations: πολυχρόνιον ποιήσαι ὁ Θεὸς τὴν ἁγίαν βασιλείαν σας εἰς πολλὰ ἔτη.[2]

acc.

Πο - λυ - χρό - - - - νι - ον ποι · ή - σαι - - -

ὁ Θε - - - ὸς

τὴν ἁ - γί - αν βα - - - σι - λεί - αν

σας εἰς πολ - λὰ ἔ - -

χε - χε - χε - ε - τη καὶ εἰς πολ - λὰ ἔ - - - τη.

[1] *A.B.S.*, no. xviii, p. 247.

[2] Ibid., pp. 250–1.

Tillyard's suggestion, nearly half a century ago, that the acclamations for the Emperor John VIII and the Patriarch Joseph might be an adaptation of earlier music, was confirmed by O. Strunk. In his study on 'The Byzantine Office in Hagia Sophia'[1] Strunk refers to acclamations in Codex 2061 of the National Library at Athens which are addressed to the Emperor Manuel II Palaeologus (1391–1425) and his wife, the Serbian princess Helena, when they visited an archi-episcopal church, probably Saint Sophia in Thessalonica. For political reasons this event must have taken place shortly after 1403, when Sultan Bajezid had given back Thessalonica to the Byzantine Emperor.

Strunk refers further[2] to the acclamations in Codex 2062 which also 'has come to Athens from the Gymnasium in Salonika', and is of an earlier date than Cod. 2061, because it contains the acclamations for John V, Palaeologus (1341–91) and his wife Helena, followed by those for his son Andronicus IV Palaeologus and his wife Maria. These acclamations must belong to the period between 1379 and 1383, because these were the only years in which a kind of peace existed between the rebellious Andronicus and the old Emperor John who had made him Coregent.

Stylistically these two groups of acclamations are of the same type as those addressed to John VIII and the Patriarch. They consist of (1) a group of liturgical formulae, followed (2) by the acclamations proper in which the Emperors and Empresses were addressed by their names, and (3) the repetition of the liturgical formulae. Between the chants are prayers by the bishop. The chants were intoned alternately by one of the two Domestici, the precentors of the two choirs, and repeated by the choirs, as can be seen from the rubrics in e.g. Cod. 2062, fol. 56, where the response of the left choir (ὁ ἀριστερὸς χορός) and the right choir (ὁ δεξιὸς χορός) is indicated in red ink. The people (ὁ λαός) answered with short stereotyped formulae. The acclamations proper and their responses were repeated several times, as can be seen from Codd. Athens 2061 and 2062; but only Cod. 2061, fol. 72 v. contains the Polychronion which we know already from

[1] Cf. *Dumbarton Oaks Papers*, ix and x (1956), 180.

[2] Ibid., p. 199.

the acclamations in honour of John VIII, though in a slightly different version:

Whereas the liturgical formulae are composed in the ornamented psalmodic style, the acclamations proper in which the names of the emperors and empresses are chanted are in the simplest type of musical declamation, like the Western *laudes regiae*.[1] The chanting occurs on a repeated note, the so-called *legetos*, the reading note, which is *g*, but changes with recitation on the higher fifth, on *d*; in some instances only the interval of a second upwards occurs to mark a short, accentuated syllable.

There now follow the transcription of the acclamations in honour of John V and Andronicus IV when they and the empresses entered the church:

The Domesticus:

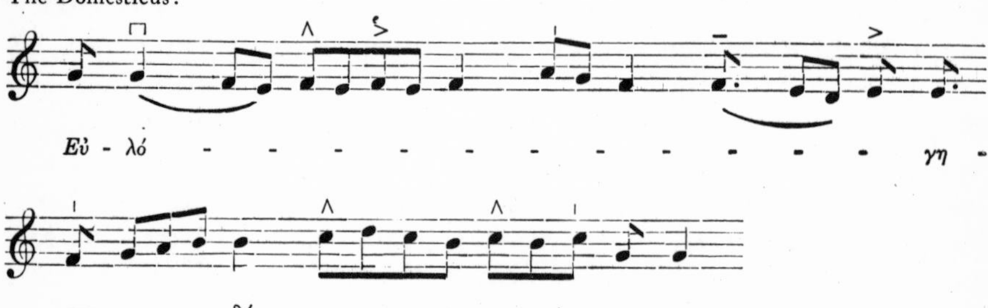

[1] Cf. E. H. Kantorowicz, *Laudes Regiae*, with a study of the music of the *Laudes* and musical transcriptions by M. F. Bukofzer, Univ. of Calif. Press (1946). Here too the liturgical formulae like *Exaudi Christe*, *Christus vincit*, *Salvator mundi*, &c. are melodies, whereas the acclamation (p. 220) *Domino nostro regi Friderico magnifico et triumphatori ac invictissimo vita perpetua* is a recitative with cadences on *triumphatori* and *perpetua*.

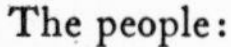
The people:

Ἀ - μή - - - - - - - ν.

The Domesticus:

Εἰς πολ - λὰ . . . . , ... ἔ - τη . . . .

δέ - - - - σπο - τα.

Σῶ - σον Θε - ὸ - - ς τὴν ἁ - γί - αν καὶ δι - καί -

rit.
- αν καὶ ὁ - λό - φω - τόν σου ψυ - χή - - - - ν,

ἅ - γι - ε ἡ - μῶν δέ - σπο - τα εἰς αἰ - ῶ - - νας.

The Domesticus: (The people repeat these words)

Πολ - λὰ τὰ ἔ - τη τῶν βα - σι - λέ - ων: .

The Domesticus:

Ἰ - ω - άν - νου τοῦ εὐ - σε - βε - στά - του βα - σι - λέ - ως καὶ αὐ - το -

- κρά - το - ρος 'Ρω - μαί - ων τοῦ Πα - λαι - ο - λό - γου καὶ 'Ε - λέ - νης τῆς

The people: Πολλὰ τὰ ἔτη κτλ.

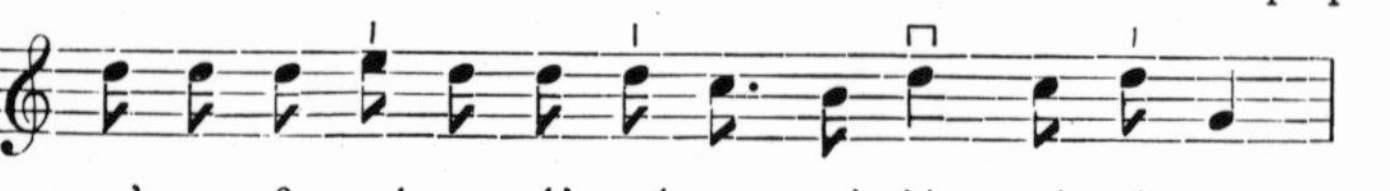

εὐ - σε - βε - στά - της Αὐ - γού-στης· πολ - λὰ τὰ ἔ - τη:

The Domesticus

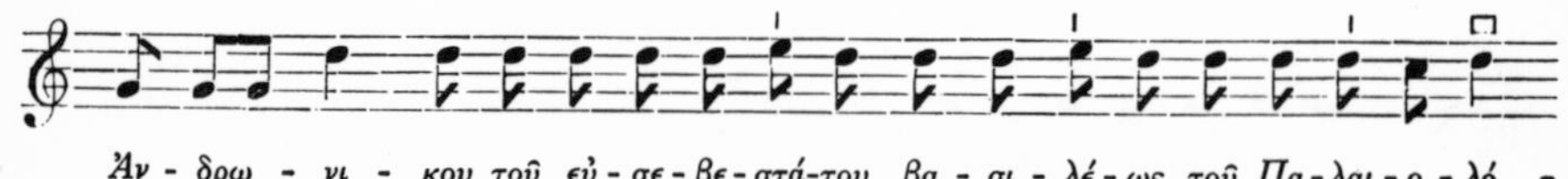

Ἀν - δρω - νι - κου τοῦ εὐ - σε - βε - στά-του βα - σι - λέ - ως τοῦ Πα - λαι - ο - λό -

The people: Πολλὰ τὰ ἔτη κτλ.

- γου· καὶ Μα - ρί - ας τῆς εὐ - σε - βε - στά-της Αὐ-γού-στης πολ - λὰ τὰ ἔ - τη.

The Domesticus:

The people repeat.

Πολ - λὰ τὰ ἔ - τη τῶν βα - σι - λέ - ων·

Εὐ - λό - γη - σον δέ - - - - - σπο - τα

Evidently the acclamations belonged to the liturgical repertory and may have been introduced into the Byzantine ritual at a very early date. In a review of the first edition of this book Dom M. Huglo[1] showed the striking similarity between the acclamation to John VIII and the Kyrie *Jesu Redemptor*, dating from the tenth century. We give here a synopsis of (1) the Polychronion in honour of Manuel II (1391–1425), (2) the Acclamation in honour of John VIII (1425–48), and (3) the Kyrie *Jesu Redemptor* (Ed. Vat., no. XIV).

[1] Cf. *Revue grégorienne*, xxx (1951), 35–40.

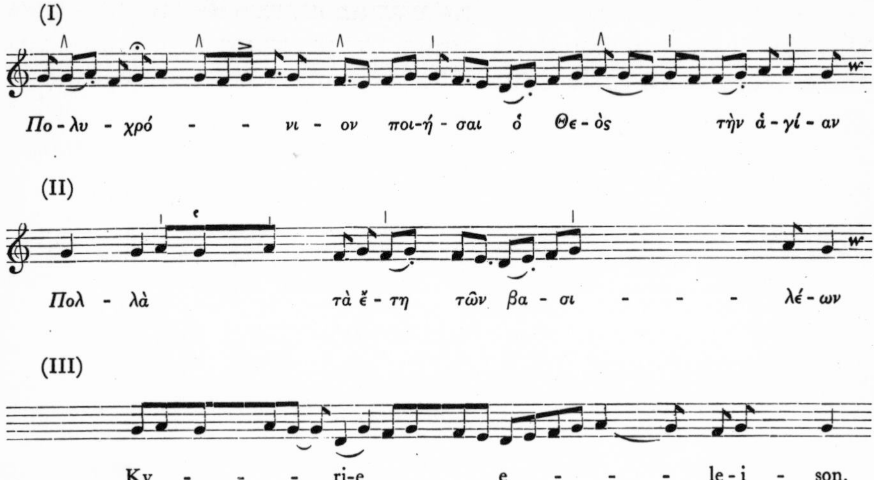

We may assume, therefore, that the melody belongs to that old stratum, common to the Eastern and Western Churches, which goes back to Syro-Palestinean worship.[1]

In the Polychronion on p. 116, last line, the word ἔτη is extended by three inserted χε. Such inserted syllables or vowels are regular features in the so-called *kalophonic* chant, and they are particularly frequent in richly ornamented music from the thirteenth century onwards.[2] The practice of inserting syllables, however, is much older and not confined to Byzantine texts. One finds the inserted vowels *â* and *î* and the syllables *ygâ* in fragments of Manichean hymns from caves in Turfân. These texts date from the seventh century and are written in Sogdic.[3] Similar insertions can be found in songs of Bedouins, Roumanians, Caucasians, Tartars, &c. The Manichean hymns are written in a Syriac script and have a kind of ecphonetic notation, consisting of a system of dots for the *lectio solemnis* which was introduced in Syria itself about A.D. 500. We may assume therefore that this system of ecphonetic notation was in use in the Syro-Palestinean

[1] Undoubtedly the common archetype was simpler; this is made evident by the two different Byzantine versions, but we need not consider a direct Byzantine influence in the *Kyrie*; the process of ornamentation is in keeping with similar melismatic developments both in Eastern and Western Chant.

[2] Cf. E. Wellesz, *The Akathistos Hymn*, *M.M.B. Transcripta*, vol. ix, pp. xxxvii–xxxviii.

[3] Cf. E. Wellesz, 'Probleme der musikalischen Orientforschung', *Jahrbuch der Musikbibliothek Peters*, 1917, pp. 15–18, and 'Early Christian Music' in the *New Oxford History of Music*, ii. 10–13; C. Höeg, *La Notation ekphonétique*, *M.M.B. Subsidia*, i. 2 (1935), 142–5.

churches of the Byzantine Empire at an early date and also that the way of singing which demanded the insertion of syllables was the custom at an early date. The breaking up of the melisma in groups of two and three notes made the singing of extended phrases easier for the soloist. The practice of inserting syllables is even now to be found in printed books of the Greek Church.

CHAPTER V

BYZANTINE LITURGY

I. THE LITURGIES OF ST. BASIL AND OF ST. CHRYSOSTOM AND THE LITURGY OF THE PRESANCTIFIED

BEFORE giving a survey of Early Christian and Byzantine Hymnography we must first say a few words about the development of the Byzantine rite and the service-books which contain the liturgical texts. Among the latter we shall find a group of books which contain either the words of the hymns alone or both the words and the melodies written down in Byzantine musical notation. Since this group of books is the basis for the study of Byzantine Hymnography, we shall have to give a summary of the contents of the two of them which are most important sources for our studies.

The principal part of Early Christian worship consisted in the celebration of the Mass. Its liturgical origin can be traced back to the moment when the two distinct elements of the worship of the Primitive Church were combined into a single, henceforth inseparable, liturgical action: they were, (1) the service of the Temple or the Synagogue on Saturday morning, in which the Jewish Christians of the Apostolic age used to participate, and (2) the common meal, the *Agape* or 'Love-feast', which was held in the private houses of some wealthier members of the Christian community in order to commemorate the Lord's Supper.[1]

In the early days of the Byzantine Church, as has already been said, Mass was celebrated frequently, but not daily; the same practice existed originally in the Western Church. But while the Latin Church introduced into the service of the Mass elements peculiar to the feast of the Saint for the day, the Eastern Church maintained the liturgical custom of Early Christianity by celebrating Mass without variation throughout the ecclesiastical year and refraining from inserting into the Canon of the Mass prayers or songs proper to the day's celebration. Thus only three texts were used by the Byzantine Church: (1) the Liturgy

[1] Cf. A. Baumstark, *Vom geschichtlichen Werden der Liturgie* (Freiburg i. B., 1923), pp. 13–21; *Liturgie comparée* (Amay à Chevetogne, 1939), pp. 33–56; A. B. Macdonald, *Christian Worship in the Primitive Church* (Edinburgh, 1934), pp. 11–12; C. W. Dugmore, *The Influence of the Synagogue upon the Divine Office* (O.U.P., 1944).

of St. Basil, (2) the Liturgy of St. Chrysostom, and (3) the Liturgy of the Presanctified.

Eastern tradition is unanimous in ascribing the first liturgy to the great Cappadocian Father. There is no reason to question this belief, as in his writings St. Basil several times mentions the difficulties which he encountered in reforming the liturgy and as the text bears the marks of an outstanding theologian and a master of Greek rhetoric.[1] The Liturgy of St. Basil seems to be an adaptation of a Syrian text which had been in use in Cappadocia up to this time. From Caesarea, the metropolitan see of Basil, where it first came into use, the new liturgy spread widely and was finally introduced into Constantinople. Here it was celebrated on certain solemn festival days in addition to the shorter local service, viz. the Liturgy of St. Chrysostom, which also derived from a Syrian source.[2] The third text, the Liturgy of the Presanctified, was celebrated during the sixth and seventh centuries on a few weekdays only, especially on Wednesdays and Fridays in Lent, i.e. on days for which the gifts were consecrated before, on the Sunday. When the regulations of the Council *in Trullo* (A.D. 691) came into force the use of the Liturgy of the Presanctified was extended to all weekdays in Lent.[3] At present, however, the old custom of celebrating the Mass of the Presanctified only on Wednesdays and Fridays in Lent has been restored.

II. THE COMMUNITY AND THE SERVICE

The role played by music in the Byzantine Mass was determined by its rigid structure. The Mass of the Eastern Church retained the Jewish form of congregational service. It can be seen from the *Apostolic Constitutions* that the chanting of the psalm by the *Anagnostes* was accompanied by the congregation, who sang the responses after each verse.[4] The congregation respond with the singing of *Kyrie eleison* to each summons to prayer by the deacon.[5] In the Byzantine liturgy before the seventh century, the episcopal blessing 'Peace be to you all' is

[1] A. Baumstark, *Die Messe im Morgenland* (1906), p. 53.

[2] S. Salaville–J. M. T. Barton, *An Introduction to the Study of Eastern Liturgies* (1938), p. 15.

[3] J. Pargoire, *L'Église byzantine de 527 à 847* (Paris, 1905), p. 231.

[4] *Ἀνὰ δύο λεγομένων ἀναγνωσμάτων ἕτερός τις τοῦ Δαβὶδ ψαλλέτω ὕμνους καὶ ὁ λαὸς τὰ ἀκροστίχια ὑποφαλλέτω.* *Apostolic Constitutions*, ii, ch. 57.

[5] Ibid. viii. 6, § 9.

answered by the people, who sing 'And with thy spirit', and the same responses are used when the bishop enters the church before the sermon, at the ceremony of the Kiss of Peace, and before the dismissal of the congregation at the end of the service.[1] As the liturgy developed, these formulae increased in number and were repeated more frequently during the service, which, accordingly, took on the character of a corporate action between the celebrant and the clergy on one hand and the congregation on the other.

Apart from a large number of responses, the Byzantine Mass included from the earliest days a certain number of hymns. Though the Mass-formularies of the fifth to the ninth centuries are transmitted in fragmentary form, we can see that the place for singing the Divine Songs (*τὰ θεῖα ᾄσματα*)[2] was in the 'Mass of the Catechumens', between the Lections. These 'Divine Songs' were the Prokeimenon, sung before the lesson from the 'Apostle', and the Alleluia, sung before the Gospel. At the beginning of the Mass the 'Trisagios Hymnos' was sung. Already in the days of Justin II (565–78), according to Cedrenus, the 'Cherubic hymn', accompanying the 'Great Entrance' (*ἡ μεγάλη*, or *ἡ τῶν ἁγίων μυστηρίων, εἴσοδος*) was sung. Of the same date seems to be the Communion Chant (*Κοινωνικόν*). The reading of the Gospel was followed by a homily in poetical prose.* The dramatic character[3] of the Byzantine Mass, however, did not permit the accumulation of too many chants, which would have clogged the liturgical action and introduced a static element. This less dramatic type of worship had its place in the Morning and Evening Service.

III. THE OFFICE

By a decree of Justinian I in 528 the daily singing of the three main offices, i.e. Matins (*Μεσονυκτικόν*), Lauds (*Ὄρθρος*), and Vespers (*Ἑσπερινός*), was made compulsory for all the clergy who were attached to a church.[4] The obligation was confined to the

[1] S. Chrysostom *in Col.* iii. 3 (348 c). Cf. F. E. Brightman, *Liturgies Eastern and Western*, pp. 527–30.

[2] Cf. F. E. Brightman, op. cit., pp. 3–4 and p. 535.

[3] Cf. P. Hendrix, 'Der Mysteriencharacter der byzantinischen Liturgie', *B.Z.* xxx. 334.

[4] *ἔτι θεσπίζομεν πάντας τοὺς κληρικοὺς τοὺς ἐν ἑκάστῃ ἐκκλησίᾳ δι' ἑαυτῶν ψάλλειν τά τε νυκτερινὰ καὶ τὰ ὀρθρινὰ καὶ τὰ ἑσπερινά, καὶ μὴ μόνον ἐν τῷ δαπανᾶν τὰ ἐκκλησιαστικὰ πράγματα κληρικοὺς φαίνεσθαι, ὄνομα μὲν ἔχοντας κληρικῶν, μὴ ἐπιτελοῦντας δὲ τὸ πρᾶγμα τοῦ κληρικοῦ πρὸς τὴν λειτουργίαν τοῦ δεσπότου θεοῦ.* *Codex Iustinianus*, i. 3. 42, § 10; ed. P. Krueger, p. 28. The decree refers not to the entire cycle of the Canonical Hours but only to the three most important parts of the Office, to those which had their origin in the ancient Vigils. In the days of Justinian only Egypt and the Sinai adhered to the old use of celebrating these Hours only. Everywhere else, for nearly a century, Prime (*Ὥρα πρώτη*), Terce (*Ὥρα τρίτη*), Sext (*Ὥρα ἕκτη*), and None (*Ὥρα ἐννάτη*) had been

sanctuary alone. Neither a monk outside his monastery nor a member of the clergy outside his church was obliged to say the prayers of the *Horae diurnae*. This rule remained in force in the Eastern Church from the sixth century to the present day. On the other hand, the recitation of the Psalter, the main part of the Office, was not confined to the choir but could also be performed by laics. This practice goes back at least to the sixth century, since, in the decree, Justinian contrasts the zeal of many laics in performing the psalmody with the laxity of some clerics who do not fulfil the duties to which they are appointed.[1]

From the decree in the *Codex Iustinianus* it can be seen that the Imperator, acting as head of the Church, was anxious to strengthen the tendency to preserve the oldest form of Christian worship, the daily corporate morning and evening prayers, whose principal elements can be traced back to Jewish liturgical usage in the times of the Apostles.[2]

Daily prayers following a prescribed ritual were not alien to the earlier, pagan, Greek society. From inscriptions on stelae it is known that a kind of pagan Breviary was in use in the time of the Roman Emperors.[3] This evidence is strengthened by a passage from a letter of Julian the Apostate, in which he prescribed that men should pray 'many times to the Gods both privately and as a community, preferably three times daily, but if not, certainly in the morning and evening'.[4] Thus the Imperial edict appealed both to those who had been brought up in the Christian spirit and to those in whose mind the memory of the pagan faith of their ancestors was still alive. The terms of the edict, however, are entirely based on Early Christian tradition.

The edict of Justinian is a reaffirmation of prescriptions which date back to the *Apostolic Constitutions* (viii, c. 34) and to the rule of St. Basil. There, however, not only the participation in the ancient, tripartite cycle of Matins, Lauds, and Vespers is prescribed, but also in Terce, Sext, and None. Chrysostom even goes a step farther by imposing the duty of attending the Mid-

introduced between the Morning and Evening Office. Cf. J. Pargoire, *L'Église byzantine de 527 à 847*, p. 103.

[1] *εἰ γὰρ πολλοὶ τῶν λαϊκῶν διὰ τὸ τὴν οἰκείαν ὠφελῆσαι ψυχὴν ταῖς ἁγιωτάταις ἐκκλησίαις προσεδρεύοντες σπουδαῖοι περὶ τὴν ψαλμῳδίαν δείκνυνται, πῶς οὐκ ἄτοπον τοὺς κληρικοὺς τοὺς ἐπὶ τούτῳ τεταγμένους μὴ πληροῦν τὸ οἰκεῖον ἐπάγγελμα; Cod. Iust.* i. 3. 25.

[2] Cf. S Bäumer, *Geschichte des Breviers*, pp. 31 sqq.

[3] Cf. footnote to Chapter vi, p. 146.

[4] *εὔχεσθαι πολλάκις τοῖς θεοῖς ἰδίᾳ καὶ δημοσίᾳ, μάλιστα μὲν τρὶς τῆς ἡμέρας, εἰ δὲ μὴ πάντως ὄρθρου γε* [*τε*] *καὶ δείλης. Iulian. ep.* 89 b.

night Office (*Μεσονυκτικόν*) not only on clerics but also on laics.[1] From the edict of Justinian we can gather that such a rigorous performance of religious duties could not be reconciled with the normal life of the citizen, particularly in the big towns. But even among the clergy a remarkable slackening of religious activity seems to have taken place in consequence of the growing wealth of monasteries and churches, as can be seen from Justinian's warning that the clerics should not only profit from the goods of the churches but should discharge their duties towards the service of God, their Lord.[2] After the reorganization of monastic discipline the daily attendance at all the canonical Hours became compulsory for the clergy.[3]

From the early days of Christianity the Divine Office was composed of four elements: (1) Psalms, (2) extracts from the Scriptures, (3) prayers, and (4) songs, all of them deriving from the Jewish Service. To these, homilies and sermons must be added. As the calendar of the ecclesiastical year developed it became necessary to celebrate the various feasts of the cycle and the commemorations of the saints. Here there is a divergence from Western liturgical development: the place for celebrating the Proper of the Season and the feasts of Our Lord, the Blessed Virgin, the Apostles, Saints, and Martyrs, was not the Mass but the Office. Here prayers and hymns for special purposes were inserted. Intent on augmenting the splendour of the service, the Byzantine Church introduced songs into the Office in an ever-increasing number, until in the eleventh century a richness and variety was achieved, which could not be increased without lengthening the *Horae diurnae* out of all proportion. Byzantine liturgy, therefore, was codified, and the form given to it in the eleventh century remained practically unchanged until the present day. With the exception of a few hymns which were added after the codification, ecclesiastical poetry came to a standstill. But the musical development could not be stopped. We shall see that the musicians embellished the melodies to which the poems—written in a strict form or in poetical prose—were sung, until it became necessary to shorten the texts, since in many instances the ornamentation of the music made it

[1] Cf. P. A. Couturier, *Cours de liturgie grecque-melkite*, ii. 9.

[2] *Cod. Iustin.* i. 3. 42, § 10; cf. p. 109, n. 5.

[3] Exceptions from the rule are given by P. A. Couturier, op. cit., pp. 12–13.

impossible for the words to be understood. The process of embellishing the melodies began in the last period of the Byzantine Empire; it gained ground in the course of the sixteenth, seventeenth, and eighteenth centuries. It is best to refrain from any aesthetic conclusions which may prove unjustified and false in the light of later investigations. It is, however, accepted by nearly all students of Byzantine music that this latest phase, whose beginning coincides with the decline of the Byzantine Empire and which continues during the influx of foreign elements in a time of foreign domination, has all the features of a superficial development. Here we shall have to concentrate on the development of hymnography in the great period of Byzantine civilization, from the early days of the Empire to the fourteenth century. The destruction of all musical manuscripts prior to the end of the Iconoclastic controversy makes it impossible for us to follow the development of the music from the beginning of the Empire to the end of the ninth century; but we can give a survey of the poetical development, from which it can be seen that this period was one of the great epochs in the history of music. Moreover, we shall be able to show that the treasury of melodies which were sung in that period did not vanish together with the books which have perished, but was preserved in later manuscripts, though in slightly changed form, when the melodies, originally sung to the words and stanzas of the Kontakia, were set to new texts and sung as melodies of the Odes, the Kanons, and the Stichera.

The codification of the Office restored the preponderance of the two ancient Hours, Lauds (*Ὄρθρος*) and Vespers (*Ἑσπερινός*). Between the two stand a liturgical night prayer, *Apodeipnon*, corresponding to *Compline*, to be said after supper, and the *Mesonyktikon* prayers at midnight, which were practically combined with the *Orthros*.

The Office of Vespers (*Ἑσπερινός*), for example, is built up of eighteen, in Lent of nineteen, parts as follows:[1]

Vespers

I. Initial prayers.
   (1) Sacerdotal benediction.
   (2) Invocation of the Holy Spirit.
   (3) Trisagion. Dominical prayer.

[1] The structure of Vespers is given according to F. Mercenier and F. Paris, *La Prière des églises de rite byzantin*, tome i (1937), pp. 3–4.

II. Introductory Psalm (Ps. 103) and sacerdotal prayers in silence.
III. Great Collect.
IV. Lection from the Psalter and short Collect.
V. Vesper Psalms (140, 141, 129, 116) with Stichera (versicles) inserted between the last few lines of the Psalms.
VI. Procession (on feasts) and Evening Song.
VII. Prokeimenon (response) and Lections of prophecies from the Old and New Testaments.
VIII. Litany (on feasts) or prayer by the Superior.
IX. Litany (on Vigils) or Procession.
X. Aposticha (short hymns).
XI. The Hymn of Simeon 'Nunc dimittis' (Luke ii. 29–32).
XII. Trisagion.
XIII. Apolytikion (Hymn before the Dismissal), Troparion followed by its Theotokion.
XIV. Artoklasia (Breaking of Bread at Vespers, preceding a Vigil).
XV. Litany of the feast.
XVI. Benediction.
XVII. Prayer.
(XVIII. Lenten prayers.)
XIX. Apolysis (final benediction).

The central group of the *Hesperinos* is formed by the Vespertine Psalms (*οἱ Λυχνικοί*) of the fifth part (Pss. 140, 141, 129, 116), preceded by Ps. 103 (*Εὐλόγει,· ἡ ψυχή μου, τὸν Κύριον*), and followed by the Evening Song 'Hail, gladdening Light' (*Φῶς ἱλαρόν*) and the prayer of Simeon (*Νῦν ἀπολύεις*). These psalms and songs obviously constitute the oldest poetical layer of the *Hesperinos*. Part IV, which according to the *Typikon*, the Ritual of the Eastern Church, contains a reading from the Psalter, was added when psalms having a special reference to the feast of the day were inserted. The hymns and short stanzas, placed between the last verses of the *Psalmi Lucernarii*, or sung during the processions or other ceremonies, also had the function of connecting the Office with the movable feasts.

IV. THE LITURGICAL BOOKS

The complex structure of the Office required the use of a number of liturgical books in which the fixed and movable parts of the ritual for the ecclesiastical year were collected. The celebration of the Byzantine rite was, as we have learned, incumbent on monasteries and churches, but not on individuals.

The Byzantine Church, therefore, did not possess books comparable to the Western breviaries or missals. The texts needed for the service were distributed in various books, each of which was handed over to clerics, whose function it was to read or sing a special part of the Office. These liturgical books varied in number and content from the great period of the Byzantine Empire to the present day. They are divided into two groups: those which contain the regularly recurring items, as e.g. the prayers during Mass, and others which contain the variable items of the Service, as e.g. the Lessons. Both groups include the order for the movable and fixed feasts of the year. Each day of the ecclesiastical year is related to both the movable and the fixed feasts. In the first group each day is related to Easter, in the second group, which represents the year of the Calendar, each day is dedicated either to the memory of the Lord, or the Theotokos or a Saint, and therefore has its special Service for that occasion. The two services are combined and the Typikon, the Ritual of the Eastern Church, gives instructions in procedure when it is difficult to decide which feast of the day, the fixed or movable one, has precedence.

The Byzantine rite derived from that of Jerusalem as can be seen from the journal of the pilgrimage of the nun Etheria to the holy places[1] toward the end of the fourth century, between 383 and 385. The detailed description she gives of the feasts in the Holy Land—e.g. Epiphany, which was not yet detached from the Nativity of Our Lord—makes her journal an invaluable source for the study of pre-Byzantine liturgy. The description of the Liturgy of the Holy Week in Jerusalem is verified by several documents. The first is the Old Armenian Lectionary published by Conybeare in his *Rituale Armenorum* (Oxford, 1905), pp. 507–27, translated from MS. Anc. Fonds Armen. 20 of the

[1] The MS. of the *Peregrinatio* was discovered by J. F. Gammurini in a convent at Arezzo and published in 1887 in *Biblioteca dell'Accademia storico-guiridica*, vol. iv (Rome), under the title *S. Silviae Aquitanae peregrinatio ad loca sancta.* P. Geyer published a textual-critical edition of the *Peregrinatio* in 'Itinera Hierosolymitana saeculi IV–VIII' in *Corpus script. eccles. lat.*, vol. xxxix (Vienna, 1898). In his article, 'Le Véritable auteur de la "Peregrinatio Silviae", la vierge espagnole Étheria', *Revue des questions historiques*, lxxiv (1903), 367–97, Dom M. Férotin attributed the journal of the pilgrimage to a Spanish nun, Etheria. The riddle of the name of the pilgrim has not yet been completely cleared up, nor that of the exact date of her journey. K. Meister in his study 'De itinerario Aetheriae abbatissae perperam nomini s. Silviae addicto', *Rheinisches Museum für Philologie*, N.S. lxiv (1909), 337–92, tried to fix the journey between 533 and 540. H. Pétré, in her Latin–French edition of the 'Journal de voyage' in *Sources chrétiennes* (Paris, 1948), accepts the name Etheria and suggests as date *c.* 400. A. Baumstark, however, in a penetrating liturgiological study 'Das Alter der Peregrinatio Aetheriae', *O.C.*, N.S. i. 32–76, has shown convincingly that the *Peregrinatio* must have taken place between 383 and 385.

Bibl. Nat. in Paris. The manuscript, a translation from a Greek original written in the ninth or even eighth century,[1] contains, according to Baumstark,[2] the liturgy practised in the Churches of Jerusalem in the late fifth century.

The second document, and in fact the most important source for the knowledge of the old liturgy of Jerusalem, is a Georgian Kanonarion, i.e. Rule or *Ordo anni circuli* of the seventh century, published in Georgian and Russian from two manuscripts by K. S. Kekilidze (Tiflis, 1912).[3] The particular value of the Georgian Kanonarion for the study of Byzantine Chant was seen by A. Baumstark and other scholars in the fact that the rubrics, connected with the lessons, contain the *Incipits* of the poems which were sung. Thus it was not only possible to find out that a great number of Byzantine Troparia originally belonged to the local rite of Jerusalem, but also that they were written in pre-Islamic days.

To these manuscripts must be added an even more important source, the Georgian Codex no. 3 of the Bibl. Nat. in Paris. This is a complete Lectionary with the rubrics 'according to the rule of the very holy city of Jerusalem'. It contains not only the Incipits, but the full texts of the chants. In an article, which appeared in 1923 in a small German journal, H. Goussen drew first attention to the Lectionary as another source for studying the liturgy and the Calendar of the Saints in Jerusalem in early Christian days.[4] A translation of the Georgian Lectionary would enable us to study in detail the early phase of Christian hymnography. Already from the excerpts from Kekilidze's Kanonarion in Kluge–Baumstark's articles can be seen that some of these early chants turn up in Byzantine manuscripts of the tenth century. Unfortunately the liturgical melodies cannot be deciphered from that early type of musical notation and in that of the thirteenth they have acquired already a richly ornamented shape. The

[1] Cf. F. C. Conybeare, *Rituale Armenorum*, p. 507.

[2] Cf. A. Baumstark, 'Das Alter d. Peregrinatio Aetheriae', *O.C.*, N.S. i (1911), 64.

[3] The sections referring to Lent, Easter, Pentecost have been translated into German by T. Kluge, that referring to the Nativity by G. Peradze, and published with a commentary by Baumstark. See Kluge-Baumstark, *O.C.*, N.S. v (1915), 201–33 and 359–63; *O.C.*, N.S. vi (1916), 223–39; Peradze-Kluge, *O.C.*, Ser. III, vol. i (1926–7), pp. 310–18. See also A. Baumstark, 'Nichtevangelische syrische Perikopenordnungen des ersten Jahrtausends', *Liturgiegeschichtliche Forschungen*, Heft 3 (Münster, 1921), pp. 133–72; and F. C. Burkitt, 'The Old Lectionary of Jerusalem', *J.T.S.*, xxiv (1923), 415–24.

[4] 'Über georgische Drucke und Handschriften die Festordnung und den Heiligen Kalender des altchristlichen Jerusalems betreffend', *Liturgie und Kunst*, iv (1923), 3–42.

original simple structure, however, is preserved, as I have shown in a detailed analysis,[1] in a number of Beneventan manuscripts of the twelfth and thirteenth centuries. Here one finds the melodies in bilingual versions, first with the Greek text, followed by that in the Latin, preserved as venerable relics. These versions date from the time when the chants were introduced in Italy directly from Palestine. Here they were kept in the liturgy particularly in those parts which were occupied by Belisar in the days of Justinian and which remained for centuries under Byzantine domination.

The role of Constantinople differed, according to A. Baumstark,[2] from that of Jerusalem in the same way as that of Rome differed from the Gallican rite under the Merovingians. In the first centuries of the Empire Jerusalem was the religious centre of the East, as Rome was that of the West, and it was the spiritual importance of Jerusalem with its holy places which made its rite the model for the monasteries of the Eastern Empire. Constantinople, the Imperial City, took its liturgy from Antioch and developed a rite which took account of the presence of the Emperor and the Patriarch at the Divine Service in the 'Great Church' in Hagia Sophia; it is the solemn rite for the high dignitaries of the Clergy.

In the first phase of the Iconoclastic controversy the monasteries in Palestine, particularly that of St. Saba in Palestine, bore since 727 the brunt of the fight directed against the veneration of the Icons. In 787 this first phase had come to an end. The seventh Oeconumenic Council had virtually put an end to the attempts of the Isaurian emperors to place the Church under the power of the State.[3] At that moment, however, the leadership in the struggle between Church and State had shifted from St. Saba in Jerusalem to the Studios Monastery in Constantinople.

When in the second phase of the Iconoclastic controversy, the opposition of the monks of the Studios triumphed over the

[1] See my *Eastern Elements in Western Chant*, *M.M.B. Subsidia*, vol. ii, Amer. Ser., no. 1 (1947), pp. 19–31 and pp. 92–110.

[2] Cf. his two studies 'Denkmäler der Entstehungsgeschichte des byzantinischen Ritus', *O.C.*, Ser. III, vol. ii (1927), pp. 1–32 and 'Das Typikon der Patmos-Handschrift 266 und die altkonstantinopolitanische Gottesdienstordnung', *J.L.*, vi (1926), 90–111, and *Liturgie comparée*, 2nd ed., Chevetogne, 1953, p. 7.

[3] Cf. J. D. Mansi, *Sacrorum Conciliorum nova et amplissima collectio*, Florence, 1767, vols. xii and xiii, *Concilium Nicaenum II*.

Patriarch, who supported the Iconoclastic tendencies of the Emperor, the pro-Palestinian sympathies of monasticism led to the introduction of certain forms of the cult from Jerusalem, particularly of hymns into the rite of Constantinople. The most significant fact of the victory of the Image-worshippers can be seen in the introduction of the 'Sunday of Orthodoxy' by the Synod of 843, which was first celebrated on 19 February of that year. Henceforth a *Synodikon* was chanted annually from the pulpit on the Sunday of Orthodoxy, for which the first Sunday of *Quadragesima* was chosen,[1] in which the defenders of Orthodoxy, emperors, members of the Imperial family, saints, patriarchs, abbots, and monks, were enumerated and praised by a thrice repeated *Αἰωνία ἡ μνήμη* (eternal be their memory), whereas the names of the offenders of the true faith and heretics were followed by a thrice repeated Anathema (*Ἀνάθημα*).[2]

From the end of the Iconoclastic controversy the mixed rite, embellishing the Office with Troparia from the rite of Jerusalem and Kanons of the Studios monks became the official rite of Constantinople and of the Empire.

(1) *Typikon* (*τὸ Τυπικόν*). This book contains the Rule for the Service, arranged according to the Calendar of the year and the movable feasts; to these are added the rules for the celebration of the feasts and of special offices. The oldest example of such an *Ordo anni circuli* is the Typikon of the Patmos Codex 266, dating from the ninth or tenth century, published by A. Dmitrievsky in vol. I of his 'Description of the liturgical MSS. in the Libraries of the Orthodox Orient',[3] pp. 1–152. It is the Typikon of Hagia Sophia in Constantinople and refers to Patriarch of Constantinople as head of the officiating clergy and represents,

[1] Cf. N. Nilles, *Kalendarium Manuale*, ii (Innsbruck, 1897), 101–21.

[2] An eleventh-century copy of the Synodikon has been acquired lately by the Bodleian Library from the Holkham Library (MS. Holkham 172). Prof. A. Raes, S.J., whom I informed of the content of the MS. replied that it represented the original text of the Russian Synodikon which was thought lost. Dr. Cyril Mango, of Harvard University and Dumbarton Oaks, whom I had asked to give me his opinion about the MS., told me (letter of 14 Feb. 1958) that the date of the Synodikon 'can be determined quite accurately (1050–55) on the basis of the commemoration of dead emperors, empresses and patriarchs, and the acclamation of those alive at that time'. That the text was chanted can be seen from the signs of the Ecphonetic notation (see pp. 251–60) which are set even to the quotations of the titles of the Synods to which the lector refers. It must be noted that the Synodikon contains not only the praises and curses of the Council of Chalcedon, read on Orthodoxy Sunday but also those of the five other Councils, read on the 'Sunday of the holy fathers of the six Oecumenical Councils', i.e. on the Sunday after 13 July.

[3] *Opisanie liturgicheskikh rukopisei*, vol. i (Typika), Kiev, 1895.

as A. Baumstark points out,[1] the state of the liturgy before the end of the Iconoclastic controversy, i.e. before the introduction of Palestinean elements and, with it, of the richly flowering monastic Hymnography. There is, further, no mention of the procession on Palm Sunday, nor of the Office *τῶν Ἁγίων Παθῶν* in the night from Maundy Thursday to Good Friday, nor of the Lessons during the Offices of the Hours on Good Friday, to which Etheria already refers in her description of the Holy Week Service in Jerusalem towards the end of the fourth century.[2] The most important instance, however, for assigning the main body of the Patmos Typikon to the second half of the ninth century is the attribution of the first Sunday of Quadragesima to the 'memory of the holy prophets Moses, Aaron and Samuel', whereas soon after 843 on that Sunday the feast of Orthodoxy was celebrated.[3]

The influence of the rite of Constantinople upon that of Palestine can be seen from the Typikon for Lent and Easter of the Church of the Anastasis in Jerusalem, published by A. Papadopoulos-Kerameus from Codex 43 of the Holy Cross Monastery, written in 1122.[4]

The Typikon represents, as Baumstark has shown from topographical evidence, the rite of Jerusalem at about 1009.[5] It is, for our purpose, one of the most important sources, since it contains the liturgical texts—and among them the poetical ones—in full. From a comparison with the Patmos Typikon it can be seen that a number of poems which are of Constantinopolitanean origin are to be found in this Typikon of Jerusalem, which, therefore, is the copy of an older one, which must have dated from the beginning of the eleventh century.

The mixed rite of Constantinople and Jerusalem which, as mentioned before, was accepted throughout the major part of the Empire, has come down to us in the eleventh- or twelfth-century Typikon of the Euergetis Monastery in Constantinople, Codex 788 of the University Library in Athens.[6]

[1] Cf. A. Baumstark, 'Das Typikon d. Patmos-Handschrift 266 &c.', *J.L.W.* vi. 99.

[2] Cf. Éthérie, *Journal de voyage*, ed. H. Pétré, pp. 236–8.

[3] Cf. A. Michel, 'Die jährliche Eucharistia nach dem Bildersturm', *O.C.*, N.S. xiii–xv (1925), 151–61. A Baumstark shows that the Patmos MS. is not a pure Typikon, but composed of a Typikon, written between the death of the Empress Irene in 802 and that of the Patriarch Tarasios in 806, and of a Synaxarion (Martyrologium) written between 878 at the earliest and 893 at the latest.

[4] Cf. *Ἀναλέκτα Ἱεροσολυμιτικῆς Σταχυολογίας* II, Petersbourg, 1894, pp. 1–254.

[5] Cf. *O.C.* v. 229–58.

[6] See A. Dmitrievski, *Opisanie*, i. 256–614.

Though the manuscript derives from a monastery, its content no longer represents the Order and Rule of a single monastery but the general 'Byzantine rite' of the mid-eleventh century. Since no Typika from the Studios monastery have survived, the history of the synthesis of the two main rites remains hidden from our knowledge. The fully developed new composite rite occurs first in the Typikon of the St. Sabas-Lavra,[1] representing that type of the liturgy 'which was celebrated at the tomb of St. Saba by the Palestinean monks in the ages of the Crusades'.[2]

The St. Sabas Typikon exists in a great number of manuscripts, classified by Dmitrievski in vol. iii of his 'Description of the Liturgical MSS.' The first printed edition of the Typikon appeared in Venice in 1545, and this edition was followed down to 1771 by seven new editions.[3]

(2) *Menaia*[4] (*τὰ Μηναῖα*). A series of twelve volumes, one for each month of the year, beginning on 1 September and comprising the Proper of the Saints, i.e. the Offices commemorating the Saints. The Menaia contain the lives of the saints, special hymns with or without musical notation, and prayers. In some editions two months are bound in one volume. The history of this collection has not yet been investigated. We may assume that the Calendar of the lives of the saints which are nowadays collected in the Synaxarium, originally formed the kernel of the Menaia. The best extant manuscripts date from the eleventh to the fourteenth centuries. Printed editions exist since the sixteenth century. The first printing was made in Venice from 1528 to 1596.

(3) *Menologion* (*Μηνολόγιον*). This is a kind of Martyrologium; it contains the description of the lives of the saints in the order of the Calendar of the Eastern Church and its compilation is attributed to Symeon Metaphrastes who lived in the second half of the tenth century,[5] though manuscripts of Menologia of an

[1] Documents of this type are collected by A. Dmitrievski in vol. iii of his *Opisanie*, pp. 1–508

[2] Baumstark, 'Denkmäler d. Entstehungsgeschichte d. byz. Ritus', *O.C.*, Ser. III, vol. ii, p. 28.

[3] A recent edition is that by M. Saliveros, Athens, 1913.

[4] A reliable explanation of this and the other terms used for the liturgical books of the Byzantine Church is given in L. Clugnet's *Dictionnaire grec-français des noms liturgiques en usage dans l'Église grecque* (Paris, 1895), and in R. Ll. Langford-James's *A Dictionary of the Eastern Orthodox Church* (London, 1923). In his *L'antica melurgia bizantina*, pp. 58–63, P. Lorenzo Tardo gives a list of MSS. of Menaia and other liturgical books, but he constantly confuses the two terms Menaion and Menologion; in nearly all cases in which he speaks of a Menologion we have to substitute the term Menaion.

[5] H. Delehaye, 'Le Ménologe de Métaphraste', *Analecta Bollandiana*, xvii (1898), 450–1.

earlier date, and also others, independent of his collection, have come down to us.[1]

According to their size and content the manuscripts of Menologia before Symeon Metaphrastes are divided into three groups:

(1) the great Menologia, or Menologia proper, which contain the complete and full texts of the lives of the saints;[2]

(2) the abridged Menologia, which are composed of short narratives;

(3) the Synaxaria in which each life of the saint is condensed to half a page. The most famous manuscript of a Menologium of the Synaxarium type is the Menologium made for the Emperor Basil II (976–1025) towards the end of the tenth or beginning of the eleventh century, illustrated by seven painters with more than 400 miniatures. A textual critical edition of a complete Menologium of group 3 from a manuscript in the Berlin Library, Codex 219, was made by H. Delehaye.[3]

(4) *Euchologion* (*Εὐχολόγιον*). J. Goar made in 1647 an edition with commentary of this book, which is still a most valuable source for our knowledge of the Greek Service. Here he defines it for the Western reader as *Rituale, Manuale* and *Sacerdotale* of the Greek Church. It exists in two versions: the 'Great Euchologium' contains (1) the ceremonies to be performed by the priest and deacon during the Office, and the prayers prescribed for them; (2) the texts of the three liturgies;[4] (3) the rites and prayers for the sacraments, benedictions, and other ceremonies. The 'Little Euchologion' contains parts of it. The prayers of the Euchologium represent the oldest layer of Christian liturgy; they can be traced back to those which are written on Papyrus[5] as can be seen from the fragment of an Euchologium from Dêr-Balizeh,[6] dating from the seventh century.

[1] 'Les Ménologes grecs', ibid. xvi (1897), 323–9.

[2] Cf. the edition of the lives of the saints commemorated in February and March from an illuminated tenth-century Athos MS., now Codex Mosquensis bibl. Synod. 376 by B. Latyšev in *Menologii anonymi Byzantini saeculi X quae supersunt*, Petropoli, 1911.

[3] 'Synaxarium ecclesiae constantinopolitanae e codice Sirmondiano', *Propylaeum ad Acta Sanctorum Novembris*, Brussels, 1902.

[4] Cf. P. N. Trempelas, *Αἱ τρεῖς λειτουργίαι*, Athens, 1935.

[5] Cf. Cabrol-Leclerq, 'Releliquiae liturgicae vetustissimae', i. 2, in *Monumenta Ecclesiae liturgica*, Paris, 1913, pp. cxxxvii–ccx.

[6] Cf. C. H. Roberts and Dom B. Capelle, 'An Early Euchologium', *Bibliothèque du Muséon*, vol. xxiii (Louvain, 1949) and the literature given on p. 7.

A critical edition of the 'Little Euchologium' has been made by P. N. Trempelas.[1] For the student of liturgical chant the section about the 'chanted' Office at Lauds and Vespers[2] is of particular interest. It is largely based upon the treatise *Περὶ τῆς θείας προσευχῆς*[3] (*On the divine Prayer*) by Symeon, Archbishop of Thessalonika 1410–29, and two music manuscripts of the National Library in Athens, MSS. 2061 and 2062, the first written between 1391 and 1425, the second not later than 1385.[4] These manuscripts contain the music for the psalms and canticles which will be discussed in the section on melismatic chant.

(5) *Prophetologion* (*Προφητολόγιον*). The reading of the lessons from the Old Testament is a direct continuation of the practice of the Synagogue by the Early Christian Church and *Incipits* of lessons from the Pentateuch, the Proverbs and Prophets are attested in the Old Armenian, the Syro-Palestinean, and Georgian lectionaries in Jerusalem in the late fifth century.[5] The manuscripts, approximately 160, dating from the ninth to the sixteenth centuries, show a marked uniformity both in text and liturgical instructions, which are much fuller here than in the two other lectionaria, the Praxapostoloi and Evangelia.[6] The uniformity of the text points at a centre where the Prophetologion took its present shape, blending elements of the use of Jerusalem with those of the Byzantine one,[7] and this centre must have been the Studios Monastery in Constantinople.[8]

The lessons were read by a Reader (*Ἀναγνώστης*) in a mixture between speech and chanting, called *Ekphonesis*. In order to fix the reading musical signs, the so-called ecphonetic signs, were set

[1] *Μικρὸν Εὐχολόγιον*, 2 vols., Athens, 1950 and 1955.

[2] Ibid. ii. 147–274.

[3] *P.G.* clv, c. 535–670.

[4] The dates are given in O. Strunk's article on 'The Byzantine Office at Hagia Sophia' in *Dumbarton Oaks Papers*, vols. ix and x (1956). Independently of Trempelas Strunk had made the chanted office the subject of a most valuable paper which he read at the Symposium on Byzantine Liturgy and Music at Dumbarton Oaks, 29 April–1 May 1954. In the enlarged article, printed in 1956, Strunk was able to refer to P. N. Trempelas' work which confirmed the correctness of his solution of the problems with which he had to deal. I am grateful to Prof. Strunk for having provided me with microfilms of MSS. 2061 and 2062 to which I am able to refer in this second edition of my book.

[5] Cf. A. Rahlfs, 'Die alttestamentlichen Lektionen der griechischen Kirche', *Nachrichten von der Kgln. Gesellschaft der Wiss. zu Göttingen, Philol.-histor. Kl.* (1916), pp. 28–136, particularly pp. 59–69 and 78–84.

[6] Cf. C. Höeg and G. Zuntz, 'Remarks on the Prophetologium', *Quantulacumque. Studies presented to Kirsopp Lake* (London, 1937), p. 191.

[7] A. Rahlfs, op. cit., pp. 70–1.

[8] Höeg–Zuntz, op. cit., p. 221.

to the text (see pp. 254–6). An edition of the Prophetologion with added ecphonetic notation is now in progress in connexion with the *Monumenta Musicae Byzantinae*.[1]

(6) *Apostolos* (*Ἀπόστολος*). A similar book, containing the pericopes from the Acts of the Apostles and the Epistles, arranged as they are to be read during the course of the year. The greater part of the pericopes are taken from the Epistles of St. Paul. The reading from the Apostolos was preceded by three antiphons and the Prokeimenon, called *Προκείμενον τοῦ Ἀποστόλου*, now reduced to a refrain and a verse. Since each day of the week had a particular devotional significance, apart from their function in the feasts of the ecclesiastical year, there was a standing list of six Prokeimena referring in their text to the dedication of the day of the week on which no liturgical feast was celebrated. Monday was the day of the Angels, Tuesday that of St. John the Baptist, Wednesday the day of the Theotokos, Thursday of the Apostles, Friday of the Crucifixion, Saturday of the Dead. The Apostolos gives also the standing Koinonikon, i.e. Communion Chant, for the days of the week. On Mondays and Thursdays it is identical with the Prokeimenon for that day. Thus, e.g. the Prokeimenon—Koinonikon for Monday, the day of the Angels, runs as follows:

Προκείμενον. ἦχος δ΄.

Ὁ ποιῶν τοὺς Ἀγγέλους αὐτοῦ πνεύματα, καὶ τοὺς λειτουργοὺς αὐτοῦ πυρὸς φλόγα·

Verse *Εὐλόγει ἡ ψυχή μου τὸν Κύριον· Κύριε ὁ Θεός μου ἐμεγαλύνθης σφόδρα·*

Ἀλληλουΐα. ἦχος β΄.

Αἰνεῖτε τὸν Κύριον ἐκ τῶν οὐρανῶν.

Verse *Αἰνεῖτε αὐτὸν πάντες οἱ Ἄγγελοι αὐτοῦ.*

Κοινωνικόν

Ὁ ποιῶν τοὺς Ἀγγέλους αὐτοῦ πνεύματα, καὶ τοὺς λειτουργοὺς αὐτοῦ πυρὸς φλόγα.

On a high feast, however, e.g. on Easter Day, the cantillation of the pericope from the Apostolos was preceded by three antiphons, each followed by a Doxology, and the second also by the Troparion *Ὁ μονογενὴς υἱὸς καὶ λόγος τοῦ Θεοῦ*. The singing of the antiphons was followed by *Ὅσοι εἰς Χριστόν*[2] and the Prokei-

[1] *M.M.B. Lectionaria*, vol. i, *Prophetologium*, ed. C. Höeg et G. Zuntz fasc. i–iv (1939–60).
[2] i.e. the verse replacing on high feasts the Trisagion.

menon appointed for that feast. After the reading from the Acts of the Apostles an Alleluia was sung.

(7) *Evangelion* (τὸ Εὐαγγέλιον). This book contains the sections, or pericopes (αἱ περικοπαί), from the four Gospels which are to be read during the year, both during Mass and the Offices, and some other sections taken from the Gospel for certain special occasions. There are two groups of manuscripts: one containing the pericopes taken from the four Gospels arranged according to the four Evangelists, and another appointing the lessons to be read from 1 September during the whole cycle of the ecclesiastical year. The Evangelia are mostly calligraphically written on parchment of the best quality; the leather cover is often covered with gold and jewels. The reading of the text is regulated by musical signs written above it, the so-called ekphonetic notation.[1]

(8) *The Psalter* (τὸ Ψαλτήριον) contains the 150 psalms, divided into twenty sections or Kathismata (*Καθίσματα*). Every kathisma is subdivided into three parts, called stanzas (στάσεις), of from one to five psalms. Attached to the Psalter were, from the fifth century, the biblical Odes or Cantica, a group of fourteen Odes which were in liturgical use at that time both in Alexandria and Jerusalem,[2] and this number was kept in certain rites, e.g. in that of Constantinople until the ninth century. But from the sixth century Jerusalem reduced the Odes to nine, a number which first appears in the Uspensky-Psalter, Codex gr. 216 of the Leningrad Public Library, written in 862 by a monk of the Anastasis Church in Jerusalem.[3]

From the first half of the eighth century Troparia were added to each of the nine Odes and at a later date the name Odes was transferred to these.

(9) *Parakletike* (ἡ *Παρακλητική*). One of the most important liturgical books for the study of Byzantine Hymnography. It contains the Proper of Vespers (*Ἑσπερινός*), Matins (*Μεσονυκτικόν*), Lauds (*Ὄρθρος*), and Mass (*Λειτουργία*) for all the days of the year. It is divided into eight parts, each containing the Offices for a week. Each of the eight parts is sung in one of the eight ecclesiastical modes (ἦχοι); i.e. the first section in the first mode (ἦχος α′), the second in the second mode (ἦχος β′), &c.

[1] See pp. 251–60.

[2] H. Schneider, 'Die biblischen Oden im Christlichen Altertum', *Biblica*, xxx (1949), 52–65.

[3] Ibid., p. 255.

When the whole cycle has been gone through a fresh beginning is made with the hymns in the first mode. The Office, which, according to the rules of the Typikon, is taken each day from the Parakletike, is combined either with the Office of a fixed feast—the parts of which are to be found in the Menaia—or with that of a movable feast, for which the lessons, hymns, and prayers are collected in the Triodion or Pentekostarion. The Parakletike has also a second name; it is called 'the Great Oktoëchos' (ἡ μεγάλη Ὀκτώηχος), i.e. the book containing the eight modes. An edition of the book is also used which contains only the eight Sunday Offices. It is called Oktoëchos (without the added words ἡ μεγάλη). The latter is generally considered to be an abridged version of the Parakletike, but this view is wrong. The Oktoëchos, a collection of songs for a cycle of eight consecutive Sundays, was already in use in the days of Severus, the Monophysite Patriarch of Antioch (512–19).[1] From the sixth century onwards the repertory of hymns which Severus had introduced was in use in the Church of Antioch. From the Syriac Church the great Byzantine hymn-writers, Andrew of Crete and John Damascene, took over the repertory of songs, collected in the Oktoëchos, and adapted it for use in Byzantine monasteries and churches. After the end of the Iconoclastic controversy during a renascence of religious activity, the monks of the Studios monastery, above all Joseph the Hymn-writer, filled in the Offices between the Sundays and composed the 'Great Oktoëchos', or the 'New Oktoëchos', i.e. the Parakletike.[2] A detailed explanation of the musical content of the Oktoëchos is given by H. J. W. Tillyard in the introduction to his transcription of the *Hymns of the Oktoëchos*, Part I, pp. xi–xxiv, and Part II, pp. xi–xx.[3]

(10) *Horologion* (Ὡρολόγιον).[4] The name is taken from the original content of the book, i.e. the prayers of the canonical 'Hours'. Thus it is comparable to the *Ordinarium divini Officii* of the Roman Church. At a later date the *Menologion* was added and hymns of a certain type, the Apolytikia (Dismissal Troparia or Post-Communion chants), Kontakia for the time from Lent

[1] J. Jeannin et J. Puyade, 'L'Octoëchos syrien', *O.C.*, N.S. iii. 85–7.

[2] J. Pargoire, *L'Église byzantine*, pp. 332–3.

[3] H. J. W. Tillyard, *The Hymns of the Octoechus*, *M.M.B. Transcripta*, vols. iii (1940) and v (1949).

[4] Cf. N. Borgia, 'Ὡρολόγιον, Diurno delle chiese di rito bizantino', *O.C.*, num. 56 (Rome, 1929).

to Pentecost, Anastasima, Theotokia, Antiphons, the Office of the 'Akathistos', certain Canons in praise of Our Lord, the Blessed Virgin, and the saints.[1]

(11) *Triodion* (Τριῴδιον). It contains the Offices of the ten weeks preceding Easter, i.e. from the Sunday of the Pharisee and the Publican up to and including Holy Saturday. The Triodion got its name from the great number of Kanons it contains, which are reduced to three Odes, on Tuesdays even to two Odes. A great part of the hymns and, above all, the redaction of the Triodion are the work of the monks of the Studios monastery in the beginning of the ninth century.

(12) *Pentekostarion* (τὸ Πεντηκοστάριον). This book is a continuation of the former, containing the Proper of the Offices from Easter Sunday to the first Sunday after Pentecost, the Sunday of All Saints (Κυριακὴ τῶν Ἁγίων πάντων). It, too, is the work of the monks of the Studios monastery, probably of Theodore and Joseph Studites themselves, or of their pupils and followers.

(13) *Hirmologion* (τὸ Εἱρμολόγιον). Exclusively destined for the chanter, this book contains the model stanzas (εἱρμοί)—with or without the melodies—according to which the stanzas of each of the nine Odes of the Kanons are to be sung. At an early date the chanting of the second Ode, modelled upon the second Song of Moses (Deut. xxxii. 1–43) was suppressed, it is said, because of its threatening character, so that the second Ode is found only in Kanons of the early period. It seems, however, more likely that the great length of the Canticle was the reason, since we find the second Ode in a Nativity Kanon by Kosmas[2] and in another anonymous one. Manuscripts of Heirmologia with musical notation, which date as far back as the tenth or even the ninth century, have come down to us; they are most valuable sources for our knowledge of the earliest phase of Byzantine music and hymnography. A facsimile edition of a Heirmologion from the monastery of the Georgians on Mount Athos (ἡ μονὴ τῶν Ἰβήρων) no. 470 (in Lambros, *Catalogue of the Greek MSS. on Mount Athos*, vol. ii, Cambridge, Mass., 1900, no. 4590), dating from the twelfth century, has been published in *Monumenta Musicae Byzantinae*,

[1] Cf. the 2nd ed. of the *Horologion*, edited at Grottaferrata: Ὡρολόγιον (Rome, 1937).

[2] Cf. S. Eustratiades, *Εἱρμολόγιον* (Chennevières-sur-Marne, 1932), p. 6, see also pp. 8, 11, 12, 13, 15, &c.

vol. ii (1938), and C. Höeg followed up the publication of the facsimile by editing the transcription of the Heirmoi of the first Echos, made some twenty years ago by Dr. Aglaïa Ayoutanti and Dr. Maria Stöhr, and introducing the transcription by a study of the various phases of the notation.[1] A second facsimile edition was made by Dom L. Tardo of the Grottaferrata Heirmologion *E γ* ii, written in 1281[2] (*Musicae Byzantinae Monumenta Cryptensia*, vol. i, *Hirmologium e Codice Cryptensi E γ* ii, Rome, 1950). In a separate volume, published in 1951, Dom L. Tardo gave an introduction to the facsimile edition and a list of the beginnings of all the 1959 Heirmoi which Codex *E γ* ii contains.

(14) *Sticherarion* (*Στιχηράριον*). A bulky volume, the main part of whose contents are the Stichera (*στιχηρά* sc. *τροπάρια*) of the Evening and Morning Office, arranged according to the cycle of the ecclesiastical year, the Stichera of the movable feasts from Lent to Trinity, those of the Oktoëchos, and, in addition, several groups of Stichera for special occasions.

While much has been written about the Hirmologion in works commenting on the liturgical books of the Orthodox Church, no reference to the Sticherarion can be found in them. No explanation of either the title or the contents of the Sticherarion can be found in the books on the subject by Neale, Nilles, Clugnet, or Langford-James. Even Thibaut gives no explanation of the term in his *Monuments de la notation ekphonétique et hagiopolite de l'Église grecque*, though he publishes pages from various *Sticheraria*. Only Gastoué in his *Catalogue des manuscrits de musique byzantine* and Tillyard in his *Byzantine Music and Hymnography* give a summary of the contents of this important service-book.

The omission of the Sticherarion in all the older books dealing with the liturgical manuscripts of the Eastern Church is obviously due to the fact that it fell into disuse in the course of the fifteenth century, when the melodies became richly ornamented. A single volume which contained all the hymns in the florid style would have been too bulky for use. The contents of the Sticherarion, therefore, were split up into several volumes, each of which was given a separate name. This happened long before

[1] *The Hymns of the Hirmologium*, Part I; transcribed by A. Ayoutanti and M. Stöhr, revised and annotated by C. Höeg, *M.M.B. Transcripta*, vol. vi (1952).

[2] Cf. A. Rocchi, *Codices Cryptenses* (Rome, 1884), p. 427. The reproduction of the original is so perfect that with the Codex and the facsimile side by side, the difference was hardly noticeable.

Leo Allatius wrote his *Dissertatio de libris et rebus ecclesiasticis Graecorum* (1646), the main source for all modern works on Greek liturgy, and it explains why in these works which are based on second-hand information, no mention of the Sticherarion can be found.

(15) *The Psaltikon* (*Ψαλτικόν*) differs in style from the foregoing books of chants; it is destined for the Protopsaltes, the Soloist, and contains chants in a richly ornamented style, whereas those of the Hirmologion were of a more or less syllabic type and those of the Sticherarion in a syllabic and slightly ornamented style. The Psaltikon has come down to us in a small number of manuscripts which contain the Kontakia,[1] the Hypakoai,[2] Prokeimena,[3] the Allelouiaria,[4] and the other ornamented chants at Mass and Vespers.

The collection of Kontakia is called Kontakarion (*Κοντακάριον* or *Κονδακάριον*) and this name is usually given to the whole collection since the main part of the Psaltikon is made up of Kontakia.

The fact that the Psaltikon is the Soloist's book and that the melodies in it were never intended for the choir explains why the refrains of the Kontakia are missing in all Psaltika: they were sung by the choir or by the congregation. The omission of the responses by the choir is even more disturbing in the Allelouiaria and Doxologies, since it was the custom to let the two or three last words of a verse be sung by the choir. Thus, e.g. the two verses of Psalm 18 on fol. 200 r. and v. of Cod. Ashburnham. L 64 are written down as follows:

Soloist.	*Οἱ οὐρανοὶ διηγοῦνται δόξαν θεοῦ,*
	ποίησιν δὲ χειρῶν αὐτοῦ ἀναγγέλλει
Choir.	*τὸ στερέωμα.*
Soloist.	*Ἡμέρα τῇ ἡμέρᾳ ἐρεύγεται ρῆμα,*
	καὶ νὺξ νυκτὶ
Choir.	*ἀναγγέλλει γνῶσιν.*
(*Soloist*:	The heavens shew forth the glory of God.
	And the work of his hands declareth *Choir*: the firmament
Soloist:	Day to day uttereth speech
	And night to night *Choir*: showeth knowledge.)

[1] Cf. pp. 329–39. [2] Hypakoe is a Troparion inserted in certain Kanons after the third Ode.

[3] Prokeimena are verses, mostly from the Psalms, which are sung before the reading of a Lesson from the Acts and the Epistles.

[4] These are Prokeimena which are sung at Mass before the Lesson from the Gospel.

The omission of the last musical phrase and cadence of each verse makes the transcribing of these richly melismatic lines a difficult task.

(16) *The Asmatikon* (τὸ Ἀσματικόν) is the book for the choir.[1] O. Strunk has shown in a paper, read at the Byzantine Congress at Salonika in 1953,[2] that certain manuscripts of the thirteenth and fourteenth centuries, written at Messina in the Monastery San Salvatore, e.g. Codd. San Salvatore 129, Grottaferrata *Γ γ* v, Vatic. gr. 1606 and San Salvatore 1200, combine in one volume, together with other chants, the contents of both the Psaltikon and Asmatikon.

In the Psaltika the Kontakia are reduced to two stanzas, to the Prooemium (or Koukoulion) which is now called Kontakion and the first stanza, which is called Oikos. There is only one Kontakion which has come down to us with the music of all its twenty-four stanzas, this is the 'Akathistos' hymn, of which the Laurenziana at Florence possesses one complete copy in Codex Ashburnham. L 64, and another one in Grottaferrata, Codex Cryptense *E β* vii, a most important Palimpsest, badly damaged through chemicals which were used by the Cardinals Mai and Pitra in order to read the underlying Latin text. Cod. *E β* vii is, as the title says, a Psaltikon for the whole year, ascribed to Romanos (*Ψαλτικὸν σὺν θεῷ τοῦ ἐνιαυτοῦ ὅλου. ποίημα Ῥωμανοῦ τοῦ μελῳδοῦ*). A. Rocchi,[3] in his Catalogue of the manuscripts in the Library of Grottaferrata, came to the conclusion that the Codex was written between 1214 and 1230, whereas Codex Ashburnham. L64 was written in 1289.[4]

The ornamented style of the melodies, originating in the fourteenth century, made a new form of musical notation necessary, with which we shall have to deal later on. The old codices fell into disuse and new were written, containing many more signs, some of them in red ink, directing the singer where to breathe, and how to sing groups of notes. These new books were written in an ever-increasing variety from the fifteenth century onwards,

[1] Cf. B. di Salvo, 'Qualche appunto sulla chironomia nella musica bizantina', *Orientalia Christiana Periodica*, xxiii (Rome, 1957), 198.

[2] *Πεπραγμένα τοῦ θ' διέθνους βυζαντινολογικοῦ Συνεδρίου*, tom. ii (Athens 1956), p. 274.

[3] Cf. *Codices Cryptenses*, Rome, 1884, p. 422.

[4] Cf. C. Höeg's Introduction to the facsimile edition in *M.M.B.*, vol. iv; E. Wellesz, 'The "Akathistos". A Study in Byzantine Hymnography', *Dumbarton Oaks Papers*, vols. ix/x (1956), and *The Akathistos Hymn*, *M.M.B. Transcripta*, vol. ix (1957).

and were given different names. This fact explains the great number of new names for books which we find in the last period of Byzantine music, in that of the Maïstores who embellish the existing melodies in the 'calophonic' (καλόφωνον, καλοφωνικόν) manner.[1]

Some of the new titles are colourless, e.g. *Anthologia*, a title which occurs frequently in the catalogues, others point to the kind of liturgical poetry they contain, e.g. Kekragarion, Cheroubikon, Dogmatikon. It may suffice to mention the titles of some of the chant books since this late period of Byzantine music and the period of transition from Byzantine to Neo-Greek music is beyond the scope of our investigation. A discussion of it would, indeed, be wholly out of place in this book since it marks the end of a great tradition and the replacement of the Byzantine melodies by compositions of the Maïstores[2] written in an entirely different style.

[1] Thus, e.g. Cod. Vatopedi 1498, a fifteenth-century MS., has the title: *Στιχηράριον καλοφωνικὸν τοῦ ὅλου ἐνιαυτοῦ.*

[2] The period of the Maïstores has been dealt with by: L.-A. Bourgault-Ducoudray, *Études sur la musique ecclésiastique grecque* (Paris, 1877); J. B. Rebours, *Traité de psaltique* (Paris, 1906); Dom L. Tardo, *L'antica melurgia bizantina* (Grottaferrata, 1938), pp. 76–109. Cf. also: Dom L. Tardo, 'La musica bizantina e i codici di melurgia della Biblioteca di Grottaferrata', *Accademie e biblioteche*, anno iv (1931); 'I codici melurgici della Vaticana', *Archivio storico per la Calabria e la Lucania*, anno i (1931), pp. 225–48; Emm. G. Pantelakis, 'Les Livres ecclésiastiques de l'Orthodoxie', *Irenikon*, xiii. 11.

CHAPTER VI

EARLY CHRISTIAN HYMNS

I. THE PAGAN AND JEWISH BACKGROUND

THE singing of hymns was an adequate expression of the enthusiastic mood of the Early Christians. To the outside world it was the most remarkable aspect of their meetings. Thus Pliny, the governor of Bithynia, could state in his report to Trajan that the adherents of the new creed gathered before sunrise 'carmenque Christo quasi deo dicere secum invicem'. Christians of the Apostolic age were accustomed to the singing of hymns from their worship in the Synagogue, though it acquired for them a greater significance as a thanksgiving for the fulfilment of the Messianic prophecies. When they ceased to take part in the Jewish ritual, and developed their own service, new hymns were added to those which were in use in the Apostolic age.

From the very beginnings of an independent Christian poetry, however, one of the most characteristic features of the liturgy was its tendency to preserve the connexion with the traditional Jewish treasury of psalms and hymns, and new hymns were modelled on patterns known to the Christian community from the Jewish Service. Later on, when Christians came into closer touch with the surrounding pagan civilization, a new type of hymn was added, modelled on Hellenistic pagan poetry. To converts from Greek paganism, the singing of hymns at certain hours of the day was not an alien custom, as the Epidaurian inscriptions show.[1] One of the *stelae* contains fragments of hymns in the form of a breviary for the six daily hours of prayer.[2] Another of the inscriptions refers to the performance of daily rites in the liturgy of the temple of Epidaurus. Morning and evening hymns were sung, incense was burnt, lamps were lighted.[3] Among the Gnostics, especially, hymns were composed to an

[1] *IG.* iv. 2.

[2] Cf. P. Maas, 'Epidaurische Hymnen', *Schriften d. Königsberger gelehrten Ges.* ix, geisteswiss, Kl., vol. v (1933). The headline *ὥρᾳ τρίτῃ* on top of the hymn on the second column of stele B indicates that the missing title of the *Paean* of Ariphron on the first column must have been *ὥρᾳ πρώτῃ*.

[3] For this and other examples of the pagan ritual see M. P. Nilsson, 'Pagan Divine Service in Late Antiquity', *The Harvard Theol. Review*, xxxviii (1945), 63–9.

ever-increasing extent: Basilides, Valentinus, Bardesanes, and other authors were famous not only in exegesis but also in hymn-writing. The Church, which at first favoured this kind of ecstatic worship, soon recognized the danger of its taking a preponderant place in religious life, and of the introduction of ideas not consistent with the dogma. Towards the end of the fourth century the Council of Laodicea prohibited the singing of private (ἰδιωτικούς) psalms in churches, admitting only 'the book of the hundred and fifty psalms'.[1] This step was taken to check the spread of heretical ideas, but apparently it did not prevent hymnographers from writing poetry which was the expression of their own religious feelings. The order, therefore, had to be renewed by the Council of Braga in 563 in a more precise, though less rigorous, form.[2] All hymns which were not based on passages from the Scriptures were excluded from use in the liturgical service.

As a result of both edicts the activity of the hymnodists was restricted to the reiteration and elaboration of certain poetical ideas from the canticles and psalms. We must bear this in mind if we are to understand the artistic vigour and skill of the hymn-writers, who, undeterred by the difficulty of their task, succeeded in producing an uninterrupted flow of inspired poetry.

Because of the hostility of the Church to freely composed songs of praise, hymn-writing lost the element of personal worship which it had had in the early days of Christianity, and became more stylized. Anyone seeking in the hymns the sort of personal expression which is to be found in classical poetry will be disappointed. For this reason Byzantine poetry failed to attract or to impress classical scholars of the last century. The first impulse to take up the study of Byzantine ecclesiastical poetry came, indeed, from liturgiologists, men like Cardinal Pitra[3] and J. M. Neale[4] who regarded the hymns as part of the liturgy, and, instinctively, recognized the greatness of their poetry. W. Christ, on the other hand, when he edited his *Anthology of Greek Ecclesiastical Poetry*,[5] still found it necessary to apologize for deserting 'the elegance and fine freedom of the poets of Greece and Rome for the thorny bypaths of Medieval

[1] Can. 59. J. D. Mansi, *Sacr. Concil. nova et ampl. coll.* (1759–67), ii. 574 c.

[2] Can. 12. Mansi, op. cit. ix. 778 c–d.

[3] *L'Hymnographie de l'église grecque* (1867); *Analecta Sacra*, i (1876).

[4] *Hymns of the Eastern Church* (1862).

[5] *Anthologia Graeca carminum Christianorum* (1871).

Christian verse'. His cautious defence of the undertaking can easily be understood.

The attitude towards art in the nineteenth and early twentieth centuries was marked by a determination to find either evidence of a progressive stylistic development or the unmistakable expression of personal and original ideas. The art critic of that period was therefore bound to underrate any poetry in which he could not discover signs of these two factors. To him the greatest poet was the man who could apply to himself the words of Horace:

> Libera per vacuum posui vestigia princeps,
> non aliena meo pressi pede. qui sibi fidet
> dux reget examen.

Such an attitude cannot be maintained if we are to attempt to understand Byzantine ecclesiastical poetry. The inspiration of the Byzantine hymn-writer came from a different source. His mind, directed towards the Divine, contemplating the mysteries of the Holy Trinity, the Immaculate Conception, the Nativity, the Life, Passion, and Resurrection of our Lord, the Acts of the Apostles, the deeds and martyrdoms of the saints, was bound to work within the limits prescribed for him by dogma and the requirements of the liturgy. These theological ideas did not derive from the teachings of Christ and his Apostles, but from Neoplatonic philosophers, especially Plotinus and Proclus, and were brought into conformity with the Christian dogma by Denys the Areopagite. According to this conception every work of art must be considered as an emanation of the Superessential (ὑπερούσιος), made apprehensible through the inspiration of the artist. Thus, to the Orthodox Christian, the hymns sung in the liturgy are a reflection of the songs of praise sung by the angels; the icons of the saints are the image of their superessential existence in heaven. The artist is a man capable of producing a faint copy of the original which he sees or hears in a moment of inspiration; the superessential alone is the model for the artist who paints his icon in the likeness of Christ or the Apostles, and the same is true of the hymn-writer.

II. SYNESIUS

Of the rich treasury of hymns in use in the first centuries of the Christian era a small fraction only has come down to us.

Most of them are composed in poetical prose, some, however, in classical metres. From the first century A.D. we possess the 'Odes of Solomon' discovered in 1909 in a collection of hymns in Syriac. The ecstatic diction of these poems is reminiscent of their Hebrew prototypes, the Canonical Psalter, the Sapiential books, and Isaiah.[1] From the 'Odes' a direct line can be drawn to the hymns of Bardesanes, the author of a new psalter, and of his son Harmonius.[2] They became so famous that Ephraem, the great orthodox opponent of Bardesanes, had to use the metre and the melodies of the hymns of Bardesanes in his own poems in order to introduce into the ritual poems in accordance with the doctrines of the Church.[3]

Hymns are further to be found in the Apocryphal Acts, especially of St. John and St. Thomas. They are transmitted in Greek, but the diction shows the characteristics of Semitic poetry to such a degree that a translation from Syriac may be assumed. A legacy from the pre-Constantinian period is a morning and evening hymn, both still in use in the services of the Greek Church. The first, *Δόξα ἐν ὑψίστοις θεῷ*, is an extended version of the original on which the Western 'Gloria in excelsis' is based;[4] the second, *Φῶς ἱλαρὸν ἁγίας δόξης* (Joyous light of the holy glory), already attested as an old song by St. Basil, is part of the evening prayer.

The hymns composed in classical metres represent an attempt by educated men to preserve Greek civilization. The hymn of praise to Christ by Clement of Alexandria shows how the master of the Catechetical School (*c.* 190–203) tried to combine the spirit of Greek poetry with Christian theology. The hymn stands at the end of the 'Paedagogus'.[5] Its theme is a thanksgiving of the children, i.e. the newly baptized, to Christ the Good Shepherd, who saved them from the 'Sea of Evil'. The hymn begins as follows:

Στόμιον πώλων ἀδαῶν,
Πτερὸν ὀρνίθων ἀπλανῶν,
Οἴαξ νηῶν ἀτρεκής,
Ποιμὴν ἀρνῶν βασιλείων·
τοὺς σοὺς ἀφελεῖς

1 Rendel Harris and A. Mingana, *The Odes and Psalms of Solomon* (1920), ii. 159.

2 Sozomen, *Hist. Eccles.* iii. 16.

3 Ibid. iii. 16.

4 Cf. A. Baumstark, 'Hymns (Greek Christian)' in J. Hastings, *Encycl. of Relig. and Ethics.*

5 *P.G.* viii, col. 681. The translation is taken from W. Wilson's English version of Clement's writings in *A.-N.C.L.* iv (1867), 345

παῖδας ἄγειρον,
αἰνεῖν ἁγίως,
ὑμνεῖν ἀδόλως
ἀκάκοις στόμασι
παίδων ἡγήτορα Χριστόν.

(Bridle of untamed colts, Wing of unwandering birds, sure Helm of ships, Shepherd of royal lambs, assemble Thy simple children to praise in holiness, to hymn in guilelessness with innocent mouths, Christ the Guide of children.)

Even in the first lines the style is more highly wrought than that of Greek poetry, and, as the poet continues in praise of the Saviour, his style becomes more and more ecstatic and turns from Greek to Semitic diction. Indeed, the aggregation of attributes in the following passages sounds more like a litany, a type of euchological prayer deriving from the Jewish liturgy, than a Greek poem:

Βροτέας γενεᾶς
Σῶτερ Ἰησοῦ,
Ποιμήν, ἀροτήρ,
Οἴαξ, στόμιον,
Πτερὸν οὐράνιον
Παναγοῦς ποίμνης . . ..

(Jesus, Saviour of the human race, Shepherd, Husbandman, Helm, Bridle, Heavenly Wing of the all-holy flock . . ..)

Short anapaestic verses follow each other, almost without interruption. It is the metre of the Hellenistic poets imbued with Oriental thought, and we learn from Clement's hymn how deeply Christianity spreading from the Orient had infiltrated Greek civilization.

This view is further confirmed when we read the hymns of Synesius, Bishop of Cyrene (*c.* 409), who brought Neoplatonic ideas into unison with Christianity.

The first verses of the ninth Hymn[1] evoke the spirit of classical Greek poetry:

Ἄγε μοι, λίγεια φόρμιγξ,
μετὰ Τηΐαν ἀοιδάν,
μετὰ Λεσβίαν τε μολπὰν
γεραρωτέροις ἐφ' ὕμνοις
κελάδει Δώριον ᾠδάν,

[1] Synesius Cyrenensis, *Hymni et opuscula*, vol. i, *Hymni*, ed. N. Terzaghi (Rome, 1939). In W. Christ's *Anthologia Gr. carm. Christ.* this hymn is the first of the series of ten hymns.

ἁπαλαῖς οὐκ ἐπὶ νύμφαις
ἀφροδίσιον γελώσαις,
θαλερῶν οὐδ' ἐπὶ κούρων
πολυηράτοισιν ἥβαις·
θεοκύμονος γὰρ ἁγνὰ
σοφίας ἄχραντος ὠδὶς
μέλος ἐς θεῖον ἐπείγει
κιθάρας μίτους ἐρέσσειν,
μελιχρὰν δ' ἄνωγεν ἄταν
χθονίων φυγεῖν ἐρώτων.

(Sound forth, clear-tongued lyre, after the Teian cadence, after the Lesbian movement; sing to me in more time-honoured strains a Dorian ode, not one for dainty love-laughing girls or for the adolescence of flowering youths that compelleth desire; for it is a sacred travail of divine wisdom and one unsullied that prompts me to strike the strings of my lyre to a divine refrain, and bids me flee from the honied infatuation of earthly loves.) Translation by A. Fitzgerald.

But it is the frequent use of antitheses, characteristic of Semitic poetry, which adds a new element to that of Greek thought. Thus Synesius introduces the language of the Prophets when he sings in the first Ode[1] (verses 191–6):

Σὺ τὸ τίκτον ἔφυς,
σὺ τὸ τικτόμενον,
σὺ τὸ φωτίζον,
σὺ τὸ λαμπόμενον,
σὺ τὸ φαινόμενον,
σὺ τὸ κρυπτόμενον . . ..

(Thou art the Generator, Thou the Generated; Thou the Light that shineth, Thou the Illumined; Thou what is revealed, Thou that which is hidden . . ..)

The words of the hymns can convey to us, however, only a part of the impression that they must have made upon the audience when they were sung to the kithara. Synesius frequently refers to the singing of the hymns. He also says proudly that he was the first who introduced a new 'Nomos', i.e. melody-type for the praise of Christ:[2]

Πρῶτος νόμον εὑρόμαν
ἐπὶ σοί, μάκαρ, ἄμβροτε,

[1] No. iii in Christ's *Anthologia*. The following translations are taken from A. Fitzgerald, *Synesius of Cyrene, The Essays and Hymns*, vol. ii.

[2] No. vi; No. vii in the *Anthologia*. Nomos, a term of Greek musical theory, rendered by A. Fitzgerald as 'measure', means 'melody-type'.

γόνε κύδιμε παρθένου,
Ἰησοῦ Σολυμήϊε,
νεοπαγέσιν ἁρμογαῖς
κρέξαι κιθάρας μίτους.

(I was the first to find the measure established in new harmonies to strike the strings of the zither in praise of Thee, Blessed One, Immortal, illustrious Offspring of the Virgin, Jesus of Solyma.)

We know from his letters that he practised music and we also know[1] a song which he used to sing, the Hymn to Nemesis, one of the few pieces of Greek music which have come down to us. Synesius quotes in a letter (Epist. 95) three lines from the hymn.* But we do not know anything about the character of the music, nor about its melodic structure. Indeed, we should know nothing at all about the character of Early Christian music if a fragment of a Christian hymn with musical notation had not been discovered in 1918 and published by A. S. Hunt in the fifteenth volume of the *Oxyrhynchus Papyri* in 1922.[2]

III. THE CHRISTIAN HYMN WITH MUSIC

The strip of papyrus which has come down to us contains the music and words of the close of a hymn dating from the end of the third century. The melody has a compass of eight notes, designated by eight letters: R φ σ ο ξ ι ζ ϵ. These letters are used for the Diatonic Hypolydian key, as handed down to us in the *Isagoge* of Alypius,[3] an author of the fourth century; they are set for the following row of tones:

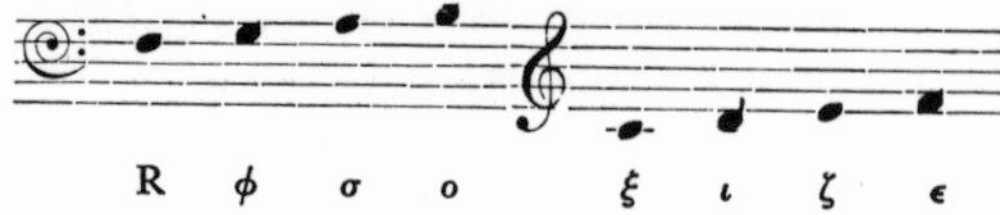

R φ σ ο ξ ι ζ ϵ

[1] Wilamowitz-Moellendorff, 'Die Hymnen des Proklos und Synesius', *Sitzber. d. Kgl. Preuss. Ak. d. Wiss.*, 1907, pp. 277–8.

[2] The 'Christian hymn in Greek with musical notation' is published under No. 1786, pp. 21–5, and rendered into modern staff notation by H. Stuart Jones. The problem of the musical notation of the hymn was widely discussed in the years following its publication in the fifteenth volume of the *Oxyrhynchus Papyri.* The principal studies on the subject are: T. Reinach, 'Un Ancêtre de la musique d'église', *Revue musicale*, 1922; H. Abert, 'Ein neu entdeckter frühchristlicher Hymnus mit antiken Musiknoten', *Z.M.W.*, iv (1921–2), 524–9; R. Wagner, 'Der Oxyrhynchus Hymnus', *Philologus*, lxxix, N.F.B., xxxiii (1923); H. Abert, 'Das älteste Denkmal der christlichen Kirchenmusik', *Die Antike*, ii (1926). The transcriptions into modern staff notation by Wagner and Abert are based on H. Riemann's rhythmical theories; T. Reinach has his own theory. Though all these scholars, including H. Stuart Jones, recognized the importance of the rhythmical signs in the papyrus, none of them made any attempt to render them in the transcription of the music of the hymn. Cf. E. Wellesz, 'The Earliest Example of Christian Hymnody', *C.Q.* xxxix (1945), 34 sqq.

[3] *Musici Scriptores Graeci*, ed. C. Jan, *Bibl. Teubn.*, p. 370.

Apart from the signs fixing the pitch, five additional signs are used which regulate the rhythm and the execution of the melody:

(1) – A horizontal stroke of varying length above one, two, or three notes, lengthening their duration.

(2) ᵕ The *hyphen*, a slur, binding two or three notes together.

(3) ⌒ The *leimma*, a sign for a rest. It can be lengthened by a horizontal stroke.

(4) : The colon, obviously marking a short interruption of the melodic flow by taking breath.

(5) · A dot, placed above the letter, or, if the tone is lengthened, above the horizontal stroke. It indicates arsis.

Taking these signs into consideration, we arrive at the following rendering of the text and music of the fragment into modern stave-notation:

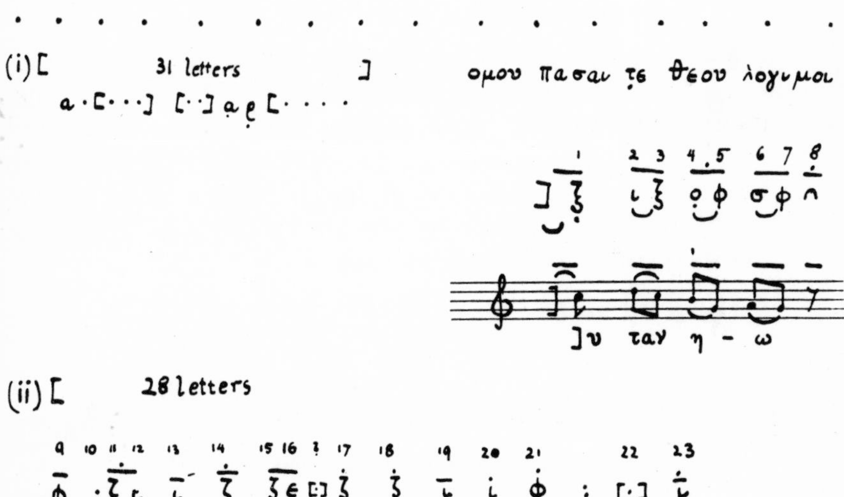

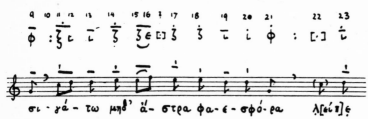

(iii)

[σ]θ̣ων[·] · λει · [· · · · ·]ϱ̣ [· · · · · · · · · · · ·] πο-τα-μῶν ῥο-θί-ων

πᾶ-ṣαι. ὑ-μνούν-των δ' ἡ-μῶν

(iv)

[π]α-τέ-ρα χυἱ-ὸν χἅ-γι-ον πνεῦ-μα.

πᾶ-σαι δυ-νά-μεις ἐ-πι-φω-νούν-των· ἀ-μὴν

ἀ-μήν· κρά-τος, αἶ-νος

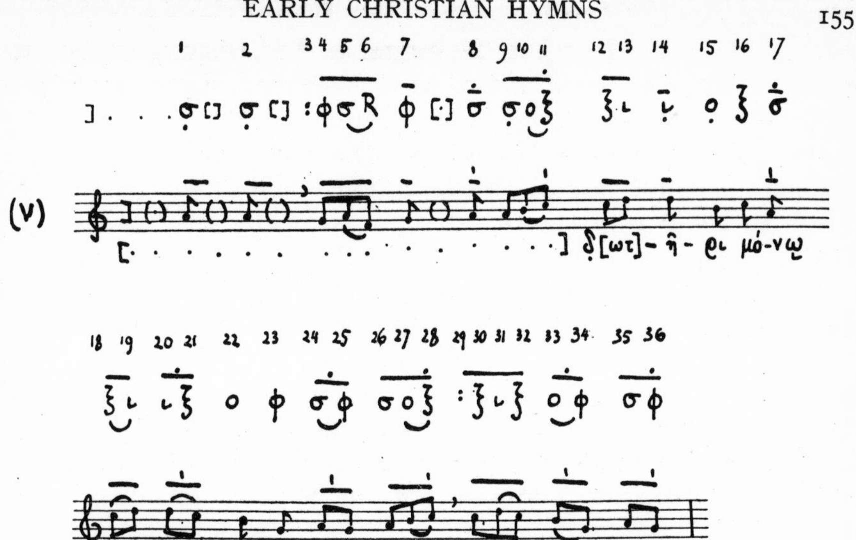

The doxological formula: *ὑμνούντων δ' ἡμῶν* | *πατέρα χυἱὸν χἅγιον πνεῦμα* (and we sing a song of praise to the Father, and the Son, and the Holy Spirit) shows that we have before us the close of a hymn to the Holy Trinity. The metre of the text of the fragment is based on an anapaestic system handled in a free, even irregular, manner, especially in the doxological formula. The metre, therefore, is not the result of the archaizing tendency of an individual poet of the Alexandrian School, as was assumed by some scholars, but of the highly wrought diction to which the Hellenistic hymn-writer was accustomed from other hymns which he knew from the service. He either translated a Jewish or Syrian hymn into Greek, or he wrote a new hymn on the pattern of an older one. Setting the words to music he tried to write anapaests, the popular metre of the Hellenistic age. But when he came to insert the doxological formula, the wording of which could not be altered except in slight details, as its text, prescribed by the liturgy, was sung to a stereotyped cadence, he had to abandon the anapaestic metre and to introduce rhythmical prose.

Comparing the music of the hymn with the other documents of Greek music which have come down to us we can see an important difference between the remnants of classical Greek music on the one hand and the Christian hymn on the other. With the exception of the *Paean* from the Berlin papyrus, dating from the end of the second or the beginning of the third century A.D., no other piece of Greek music shows so rich a flow of melody as that of the Hymn to the Holy Trinity. With the exception of a few passages all the Greek melodies are syllabic, i.e. a single note corresponds to a syllable or a monosyllabic word of the text. Even in the *Paean* the florid style is mostly restricted to the cadences and is of a more ornamental than structural character.

The music of the Christian hymn is structurally florid. It is built up from a number of melodic formulae linked together by varying short passages in the manner of a recitative. This principle of composition is to be found everywhere in the Middle East, but is unknown in old Greek music; it is the same principle of composition which has been discovered in both Gregorian and Byzantine melodies, and some of the melodic formulae of the fragment of the hymn actually show a close relationship to Byzantine melody-types. We may assume, therefore, that the melodic formulae, particularly that sung to the words of the doxology, derive from the Service of the Primitive Church, and were taken over by the hymn-writer who either composed the hymn to the Holy Trinity on the pattern of an older song of praise, or made a translation of a Syriac hymn which he adapted to the already existing melody.

In spite of its Greek notation the hymn is an example—the oldest one which has come down to us in writing—of the new kind of ecclesiastical music modelled on patterns deriving from Oriental sources. The scholars who first transcribed the hymn into modern staff-notation were wrong in trying to adapt the rhythm of the music to the metre of the text, since the hymn does not belong to the group of archaizing songs of praise of which the hymns of Synesius represent the acme. Its execution is regulated by the system of rhythmical signs mentioned above. In interpreting the hymn according to the rhythmical nuances indicated by these signs we obtain a melody whose structure and expression already show the features characteristic of Byzantine ecclesiastical music. Thus the importance of the Oxyrhynchus find is greater than was at first assumed. 'The Christian hymn with music' is the earliest document of Christian music we possess, and we learn from it—as will be proved explicitly in the following chapters—that the music of the Byzantine Church developed in an unbroken tradition from the music of the Primitive Church.

CHAPTER VII

ORTHODOX THEOLOGY AND BYZANTINE HYMNOGRAPHY

I. THE CHARACTER OF BYZANTINE HYMNS

BYZANTINE hymnography extended over a period of six centuries. It began in the second part of the fifth century and came to a close in the eleventh, when the introduction of new hymns into the service was forbidden by the ecclesiastical authorities. The development of Byzantine hymnography is divided into two periods, each of them marked by the introduction into the service of a new poetical form. The first, dating from the middle of the fifth century to the seventh, produced as its main feature the *Kontakion*; the second, beginning towards the end of the seventh century, is characterized by the almost complete replacement of the *Kontakion* by the *Kanon*, a poetical form of greater structural variety and length. In the western sphere of Byzantine authority it was only in Italy, where Nilus the Younger founded the Basilian monastery of Grottaferrata near Rome, that the local school of hymn-writers gave rise to a belated flowering of ecclesiastical poetry, which continued until the twelfth century. This Western school, however, had no influence upon liturgical practice in other parts of the Empire, and the singing of the Basilian hymns was confined to monasteries of the Greek colonies in Italy.

Byzantine hymnography is the poetical expression of Orthodox theology, translated, through music, to the sphere of religious emotion. It mirrors the evolution of the dogmatic ideas and doctrines of the Orthodox Church from the early days of the Eastern Empire to the full splendour of the service at the height of its development. Neither the poetry nor the music, therefore, can be judged independently of each other; verse and voice are intimately linked together. Nor, since they are part of the liturgy, can they be judged according to the aesthetical standards which we are used to apply to works of art which are the expression of individual feeling. The monks who composed the hymns had to bear in mind that their artistic contributions to the service must fit into the place for which they were destined. A great proportion of hymn-writers were humble artisans, whose talent just sufficed for the unobtrusive adornment of the liturgy. Some of the monks, however, towering above the rest, produced hymns of outstanding value, though through the special needs of the liturgy their task was made more difficult than that of secular poets, who could choose their subject freely and follow their own ideas in working it out.

On the other hand, the restriction on the free play of imagination induced the hymn-writers to pay special attention to elevated diction, metrical variety, and elaborate structure. This tendency coincided with the predilection of the public for formal perfection. But whereas in secular Byzantine poetry this tendency produced artificiality and sophistication, sacred poetry achieved real greatness through the spiritual qualities of the hymn-writers. Combining a colourful style, rich in images and bold similes, with sensitiveness to structural balance, they succeeded in producing poems which reflect to a remarkable degree the spirit of Byzantine worship.

The days of Early Christendom were gone, and with them disappeared the expression of individual religious feeling with which the faithful had originally participated in the liturgical action. The Orthodox Church, in building up a highly organized hierarchical system, regulated the life of the citizen by the uninterrupted succession of ceremonies which formed the cycle of the ecclesiastical year. For this purpose more hymns were needed, and to adorn the feasts of the Church with verse and music the hymn-writers strove to keep pace with the splendour and solemnity of the ritual. Byzantine hymnography now heralds the victory of Orthodoxy and proclaims the triumph of the State Church. Before giving an outline of this development a few words must be said about the events which led to the unification of the Eastern dioceses into one body, the Orthodox Church, and of the establishment of an ecclesiastical organization which 'to the last remained a copy of the secular state'.[1] These events take us back to the closing stage of Early Christian hymnography which is, at the same time, the opening phase of Byzantine hymnography.

[1] S. Runciman, *Byzantine Civilisation*², 1936, p. 111.

II. THE ORTHODOX CHURCH

The Council of Constantinople,[1] summoned in 381 by Theodosius I, the Great, achieved two aims: it crushed the Arian heresy and established the pre-eminence of Constantinople in the East. These far-reaching decisions were instigated by the Emperor. Resolved to pursue with the greatest energy his constitutional obligations as head of the Church and the 'Equal to the Apostles', Theodosius seized the opportunity offered by the Arian contest to unify, centralize, and govern the Eastern Church. From the days when she was Byzantium, a city of little importance in ecclesiastical affairs, Constantinople, now the capital, was under the jurisdiction of the diocesan of Heraclea.[2] The status of the Bishop of Byzantium had long ago been transformed into that of Patriarch of Constantinople, but in practice this change was not recognized by the older sees of Alexandria and Antioch. Now, the Council declared that the Bishop of the capital should have the first place after the Bishop of Rome 'because Constantinople is New Rome'.[3] Well aware that he could only establish his rule on a firm basis with the co-operation of a powerful group of the clergy, Theodosius sought support from the bishops of the Asiatic provinces, who like himself were adherents of the Neo-Orthodox party. His policy strengthened the links between the Churches of Antioch and Constantinople, but aroused the jealousy of Alexandria, anxious to maintain her prominent position.

For some time changes of reign favoured Alexandria in her struggle for ecclesiastical supremacy. Theodosius I was followed by Arcadius (395–408), under whom Chrysostom was defeated and banished by the Patriarch of Egypt. Arcadius was succeeded by his seven-year-old son Theodosius II (408–50), who was faced with the outbreak of a new dogmatic contest. Nestorius, a representative of the School of Antioch, became Patriarch of Constantinople in 428. He taught that in the one Person of Christ two

[1] For a general picture of the dogmatic controversy and of the relation between Church and State see A. Harnack, *History of Dogma* (Engl. tr.), vol. iv; C. Diehl, *Justinien et la civilisation byzantine au VIe siècle* (1901), pp. 315–16 and 497–531; J. Pargoire, *L'Église byzantine de 527–847* (1905); J. B. Bury, *History of the Later Roman Empire* (1923), vol. i, pp. 348–88, vol. ii, pp. 360–94; N. H. Baynes, *The Byzantine Empire*, pp. 75–98; A. A. Vasiliev, *History of the Byzantine Empire* (1958), i. 80–1.

[2] Cf. F. Kattenbusch, *Lehrbuch der vergleichenden Confessionskunde* (1892), pp. 84–5.

[3] Canon iii.

substances and natures—the Godhead and the manhood—were united. 'Christ is indivisible in His being Christ, but He is twofold in His being God and His being man.'[1]

Cyril, Bishop of Alexandria (412–44), declared the Nestorian doctrine of the Incarnation a heresy. The clash between the Church and School of Antioch represented by Nestorius and Alexandrian theology ended with the victory of orthodoxy. At the Council of Ephesus in 431 Cyril, acting as papal legate, secured the condemnation and deposition of Nestorius. Thus Alexandria, becoming the stronghold of orthodoxy, again strengthened her position. But Dioscurus, Cyril's successor, went too far by supporting the Monophysite doctrine of Eutyches, and by condemning at the 'Robber Synod' of Ephesus (449) Flavian, Bishop of Constantinople, who had the support of Leo I. Once more Alexandria seemed all-powerful, but her triumph was short-lived. Theodosius II died, and was followed by Marcian (450–7), who was determined to achieve the complete unification of all the Eastern Churches under his administration. Turning against the man whom two years ago Theodosius II had supported against the Pope, Marcian summoned the Council of Chalcedon (451), at which Dioscurus was deposed and exiled.

By accepting at Chalcedon the Christological formula of Leo I the clergy reversed their own former decision at the Council of Ephesus and submitted to the will of the Emperor. The power of Alexandria was broken for ever and the struggle within the Eastern Church came to an end. The Monophysite party, however, rejected the decisions of the Council of Chalcedon. Basing itself in the main upon the doctrine of Cyril, and withdrawing from the exaggerated conclusions of Eutyches, the party gained a large number of adherents in Egypt, in parts of Syria, and in Armenia. Attempts of the Emperors to bring them back into the Orthodox Church failed; they could be influenced neither by concessions nor by menaces, and during the reign of Justinian they finally formed the independent Jacobite Church. The enmity of the Monophysites to the Byzantine Empire was so strong that when the Musulmans conquered Palestine, Syria, and Egypt (633–43), they greeted the Arabs as liberators.

[1] *Sermo* xii. For the Nestorian controversy see J. F. Bethune-Baker, *Nestorius and his Teaching* (1907); F. Loofs, *Nestorius and his Place in the History of Christian Doctrine* (1914); A. Harnack, *Lehrbuch der Dogmengeschichte*[5], vol. ii, pp. 339 sqq.

Rome, on the other hand, though victorious on the dogmatic issue, protested against the juxtaposition of Constantinople as 'New Rome' with 'Old Rome' in the cautiously worded twenty-eighth canon of Chalcedon. Rome had never recognized the third canon of the Synod of Constantinople, where the position of the Patriarch of Constantinople was based on the political argument that the Eastern capital was New Rome. The *cathedra Petri* could not accept the existence of a second city equally privileged. 'Alia tamen ratio est rerum secularium, alia divinarum', wrote Leo I in his Epistle to Marcian (*Ep.* 104). The Council, summoned to end heresy, he continued, had been misused by the Patriarch to increase the power of Constantinople. Anatolius ought not to disdain 'regiam civitatem, quam apostolicam non potest facere sedem'.[1] Here *civitas* and *sedes* are contrasted. The capital of the Eastern Roman Empire cannot be made an Apostolic see; this position can be occupied only by Rome, 'una cathedra in uno Petro fundata'. In Pope Leo's conception Rome is not a secular but a spiritual city.[2] The Western dogmatic view is strictly opposed to the Eastern constitutional formula: two Emperors, two capitals, two supreme bishops. It was from this formula that the Roman Emperor in the East—the only Roman Emperor after the fall of the Western Empire in 476—derived his right to establish a monarchy on Oriental lines. Like his opponent the Persian King, the Byzantine Basileus became undisputedly High Priest of the Empire.

Eastern Christianity had now reached the peak of its interest in dogmatic questions. Though passions were not to subside during the second part of the fifth century—even causing over the question of Zeno's 'Henoticon' a temporary schism with Rome (484), and, in the Eastern provinces, an increase of Monophysite activities—the Orthodox Church, henceforth included in the administration of the State, consolidated its position and gained in power. This was due to the diplomacy of Leontius of Byzantium, the greatest theologian of the sixth century, who had removed dogmatic problems from the sphere of hotly contested discussion to that of a philosophical treatment, based on Aristotelian definitions.[3]

1 *S. Leonis Magni Epistolae*, *Ep.* 104; *P.L.* liv, c. 995.
2 Kattenbusch, *Vergl. Confessionskunde*; pp. 90–101.
3 Harnack, *Lehrbuch d. Dogmengesch.*[5] ii. 407–10.

The Christological orthodoxy inaugurated by Leontius put an end to dogmatic evolution. Questions of dogma were expounded according to scholastic methods; deviations from the accepted doctrines treated as heresies. This conservative outlook became the starting-point of Justinian's ecclesiastical policy. In his decree of 18 October 530 Justinian ordered that the ecclesiastical canons of the four Oecumenical Councils should have the same validity as Imperial laws.[1] Heresy became a crime against the State. Heretics were deprived of all the privileges of citizenship. In practice, however, heresy was defined in accordance with the doctrinal views of the reigning Emperor. Justinian himself was the first to evade his own decree by his continued efforts to come to terms with the Monophysites. The problem remains unsolved as to whether his conciliatory attitude was determined by the great number of the sect's adherents or by the influence of the Empress Theodora who openly sympathized with them. Whatever the reason may have been, the Monophysites found protection even at the Imperial Court, and gained increasing power in Constantinople. Severus, ex-Patriarch of Antioch who had been from the beginning of their reign repeatedly invited to come to Constantinople by Justinian and Theodora, at last gave way, and in 535 left his exile. On his arrival in the capital he was lodged in the palace. Soon he began to influence the new Patriarch Anthimus, whose Monophysite tendencies became more and more open. At that moment Pope Agapetus arrived in Constantinople, and was reverently received by Justinian and Theodora. Informed by Ephraem, Patriarch of Antioch, of the alarming situation, he refused to see Anthimus, deposed him in March 536, and consecrated his successor. Justinian submitted to the decision of the Pope. The Synod of Constantinople in May 536 anathematized Anthimus, Severus, and their followers. Three months afterwards Justinian issued a Novel, confirming the decision of the Church by Imperial decree.[2] Widespread persecution of the Monophysites followed the Imperial enactment. They lost all but three of the episcopal sees; their bishops were either imprisoned or exiled. But the

[1] *θεσπίζομεν τοίνυν, τάξιν νόμων ἐπέχειν τοὺς ἁγίους ἐκκλησιαστικοὺς κανόνας τοὺς ὑπὸ τῶν ἁγίων τεσσάρων συνόδων ἐκτεθέντας ἢ βεβαιωθέντας, . . . τῶν γὰρ προειρημένων ἁγίων συνόδων καὶ τὰ δόγματα καθάπερ τὰς θείας γραφὰς δεχόμενα καὶ τοὺς κανόνας ὡς νόμους φυλάττομεν.* *Nov.* 131. *Imp. Iustiniani Novellae*, ed. K. E. Zachariä von Lingenthal, ii. 267.

[2] Cf. C. Diehl, *Justinien*, pp. 336–8.

population persevered in their faith in the Monophysite doctrine. Secretly helped by Theodora, Monophysite bishops and monks came back to the capital. Here Jacob Baradaeus[1] was consecrated Bishop of Edessa by the Monophysite bishops (543). Disguised as a beggar he travelled through Syria, Armenia, and Asia Minor, consecrating bishops, installing priests, and creating a secret organization. In 550 he ordained the Patriarch of Antioch. This investiture marked the beginning of a separate Eastern Church, called by the name of its founder, the Jacobite Church.[2]

The religious enthusiasm of the Monophysites, indomitable in withstanding all persecutions, is mirrored in the rich treasury of their hymns. From Antioch comes the oldest extant hymnal of a non-biblical character, dating back to the beginning of the sixth century: the so-called *Oktoëchos* of Severus.[3] In its original form the service-book was a collection of hymns in Greek for the main feasts of the ecclesiastical year, similar to the Western Breviary. It not only survived the deposition of Severus as Patriarch of Antioch, but was enlarged and translated into Syriac in the seventh or eighth century, and introduced throughout the whole domain of the Jacobite Church. Another group of hymns, originally written in Greek, are the *ʿEnjānē*, translations of Greek Kanons.[4] The greater part of these hymns came from Jerusalem, some probably from Constantinople.[5] Future investigations into the oldest manuscripts of the Octoechus of Severus may prove that in these hymns the oldest layer of Byzantine hymnography has been preserved. But the study of the *ʿEnjānē* of the Syro-Jacobite Church will certainly throw light on the texts of the Greek Kanons of the first period, i.e. from the end of the seventh to the middle of the eighth century, and further, on the structure of the Byzantine liturgy at that period.

Justinian, while wavering in his attitude towards the Monophysites—lenient at the beginning of his reign, aggressive in the middle, and compromising at the end—was resolute in combat-

1 The surname Burdĕʿānā, which was given to Jacob bar Theophilus 'because his dress consisted of a bardaʿthā or coarse horse-cloth', was corrupted into Baradaeus. Cf. W. Wright, *A Short History of Syriac Literature* (1894), p. 85.

2 Ibid.

3 Cf. A. Baumstark, *Festbrevier u. Kirchenjahr d. syr. Jacobiten* (1910), p. 45.

4 Cf. O. Heiming, 'Syrische 'Eniânê und griechische Kanones', *Liturgiegesch. Quellen und Forschungen*, Heft xxvi (1932), 40–52.

5 Cf. A. Baumstark, *Festbrevier*, p. 95.

ing paganism. The most significant act in a series of drastic measures to extinguish Hellenism was his edict of 529 ordering the closing of the Academy at Athens, which had flourished from the days of Plato and Aristotle until the death of Proclus (A.D. 485) and still had 'teachers of considerable metaphysical ability'.[1] Consequently all schools in Athens and in the provincial cities in which the pagan tradition of teaching survived were closed. Thus the last obstacles to establishing the Christian faith as the religion of the State were removed. High dignitaries at the court, suspect as pagans, were condemned to death, books and statues of the gods were burned, and the study of philosophy forbidden. The closing of the Academy at Athens 'marks the moment at which the Greco-Latin world gives way to the Byzantine world'.[2]

With great energy Justinian began to build up this new world. His aim was to strengthen the religious life of the Empire by creating a powerful ecclesiastical administration, by furthering the building of churches and monasteries, and by connecting secular life to a hitherto unprecedented extent with ecclesiastical ritual.

As a visible sign of the centralization of all ecclesiastical power in the capital of the Empire, Justinian ordered the building of a church whose magnitude and splendour should surpass that of all others. During the riots of 532[3] a church was burnt down which had been built by Constantine and dedicated to the Divine Wisdom. Instead of repairing the damaged building Justinian ordered two architects from Asia Minor, Anthemius of Tralles and Isidore of Miletus, to build a church capable of holding the court, the Senate, the patricians, and a huge crowd. For four years 10,000 craftsmen were at work and on 27 December 537 Hagia Sophia was solemnly inaugurated. Justinian, overwhelmed by the realization of his dream, is said to have rushed to the ambo under the vast dome and to have cried: 'Glory to God who has deigned to find me worthy to achieve such a work. O Solomon, I have conquered thee.'[4] The whole Empire had contributed to the splendour of Hagia Sophia, and when, twenty years after the inauguration, on 7 May 558, the dome collapsed,

[1] J. B. Bury, *History of the Later Roman Empire*, ii. 369.
[2] C. Diehl, *Justinien*, p. 564.
[3] Cf. Bury, *Hist. of the Later Rom. Empire*, vol. ii, ch. xv, § 5, 'The Nika Revolt'.
[4] Malalas, *Chronogr.* 479; Theophanes Cont., *Script. rer. byz.* 217; Ps.-Codinus, 143.

consternation swept over the whole Empire and the destruction of the dome was mourned by the poets. Justinian instantly ordered the construction of a new, more solid dome, and on 24 December 562 the Emperor inaugurated Hagia Sophia for the second time. During the festivities held on that occasion Paul the Silentiary recited the proem of his famous 'Description of Sancta Sophia' in the presence of the Emperor, praising the building as the greatest of all his achievements.[1]

The pomp of the liturgy in the days of Justinian can be inferred from a decree (535) ordering[2] that the number of the clergy of Sancta Sophia and of the three churches annexed to it should not exceed the figure of 425, that is to say, 60 priests, 100 deacons, 40 deaconesses, 90 subdeacons, 110 lectors, and 25 singers. To these must be added 100 doorkeepers, who did not belong to the clergy. But the influx of priests from the provinces could not be stopped, and their number must have increased beyond control. In the days of Heraclius (610–41), therefore, a new decree had to be issued reducing the number of 'Hagiosophitae' to 80 priests, 150 deacons, 40 deaconesses, 70 subdeacons, 160 lectors, and 25 singers.[3] These figures show that even the reduced number of clergy at Sancta Sophia under Heraclius exceeded the total number decreed by Justinian for the four churches. The dimensions of Sancta Sophia and the large number of the clergy celebrating Mass and Office made an increased number of hymns and other chants necessary to fill up the time required for the various entrances and processions. One of these new hymns was the Troparion *Ὁ μονογενὴς υἱός*, composed, according to Sophronius and Cedrenus, by Justinian in 535 or 536.[4]

The extension of the liturgical ceremonies at Sancta Sophia was copied by all the principal churches throughout the Empire. The splendour of the ritual was to the faithful the visible manifestation of the establishment of Orthodoxy, and the spirit of

[1] . . . *ἔστι δ' αὖ τῶν πράξεων|τὸ παμμέγιστον ἡ κτίσις τοῦ σοῦ νεώ*, Friedländer, *Paulus Silentiarius*, 108–11.

[2] *ὥστε θεσπίζομεν, μὴ περαιτέρω μὲν* sexaginta *πρεσβυτέρους κατὰ τὴν ἁγιωτάτην μεγάλην ἐκκλησίαν εἶναι, διακόνους δὲ ἄρρενας* centum, *καί* quadraginta *δὲ θηλείας, καὶ ὑποδιακόνους* nonaginta, *ἀναγνώστας δέ* centum decem, *καὶ ψάλτας* viginti quinque, *ὡς εἶναι τὸν πάντα ἀριθμὸν τῶν εὐλαβεστάτων κληρικῶν τῆς μεγάλης ἐκκλησίας ἐν τετρακοσίοις εἰκοσιπέντε προσώποις, καί* centum *πρὸς τούτοις τῶν καλουμένων πυλωρῶν*. *Nov.* 3, § 1, ed. Z. v. Lingenthal, vol. i, p. 71.

[3] J. Pargoire, *L'Église byzantine*, pp. 60–1.

[4] Ibid., p. 100. The hymn is printed by W. Christ and M. Paranikas in *Anthol. Gr.*, p. 52.

the Church Triumphant found its expression in the 'Cherubic Hymn', sung by the choir at the Great Entrance since 574:[1]

Οἱ τὰ χερουβὶμ μυστικῶς εἰκονίζοντες
καὶ τῇ ζωοποιῷ τριάδι τὸν τρισάγιον ὕμνον προσᾴδοντες
πᾶσαν τὴν βιωτικὴν ἀποθώμεθα μέριμναν
Ὡς τὸν βασιλέα τῶν ὅλων ὑποδεξόμενοι
ταῖς ἀγγελικαῖς ἀοράτως δορυφορούμενον τάξεσιν
ἀλληλούϊα ἀλληλούϊα ἀλληλούϊα.[2]

(We who mystically represent the Cherubim and sing the thrice-holy hymn to the lifegiving Trinity let us lay aside all worldly cares
That we may receive the King of the Universe invisibly attended by the angelic orders.
Alleluia, Alleluia, Alleluia.)[3]

Here the appearance of Christ, invisible to human eyes, is brought near to the minds of the faithful by the vision of the anonymous poet, who sees the Lord attended by the hosts of the angels like the Imperator with his bodyguard. The hymn reveals also the element of mystery-initiation in Eastern liturgy.[4] When they exhort the people to listen to the Cherubic Hymn, the singers are no longer the *psaltae* of the Choir;[5] they impersonate the Cherubim, angels of the second order of the ninefold celestial hierarchy, whose utterance is no mere speaking (*λέγειν*) but exultant singing (*ὑμνεῖν*).[6]

The mystical element in Eastern Christianity found its purest expression in the religious attitude of those who fled from the world into the seclusion of monastic life. Justinian professed his admiration for them not only because they were virtuous and would become 'citizens of Heaven'[7] but because their way of life would have a favourable influence on the life of society in general. He, therefore, encouraged the foundation of monasteries throughout the Empire by private acts and legislation, working out the most detailed plans for them.[8]

It was in the monasteries that the liturgical movement began

[1] Cf. Cedrenus, *Hist. Compend.*; *P.G.*, vol. cxxi, c. 748 b.
[2] Cf. F. E. Brightman, *Liturgies Eastern and Western* (1896), pp. 377–8.
[3] Cf. H. A. Daniel, *Codex Liturgicus*, iv (1853), 400.
[4] Cf. P. Hendrix, 'Der Mysteriencharakter der byz. Liturgie', *B.Z.* xxx. 3.
[5] *εἶτα οἱ ψάλται ὡς μιμηταὶ ἀγγέλων προτρέπουσι τὸν λαὸν εἰς τὸν χερουβικὸν ὕμνον.* Ps.-Sophronius, *Commentarius Liturgicus*, ch. 20, *P.G.* lxxxvii, c. 4000.
[6] H. Koch, *Pseudo-Dionysius Areopagita* (1900), pp. 46 sqq.
[7] *Nov.* 133 (A.D. 539).
[8] Cf. C. Diehl, *Justinien*, pp. 502 sqq.

which made the Office the principal regular service of prayer and singing of psalms and hymns. Mass was celebrated frequently, but not daily; but Office had to be held daily, particularly in all the larger monasteries.[1] As a consequence of the enlargement of the Office more hymns were required for the service. Thus the liturgical development in Eastern monasticism led to the growth of Byzantine hymnography.

From the time of the establishment of the State Church onwards Byzantine ecclesiastical legislation aimed at eliminating the peculiarities of the various Eastern rites and at establishing its own supremacy in all questions of ecclesiastical discipline. These aspirations were fulfilled by the decrees of the Council *in Trullo*, summoned by Justinian II in the capital in the autumn of 691. The entire organization of Eastern religious life was codified in 102 canons. Though really only an Oriental Synod, the *Concilium Trullanum* assumed the authority of an Oecumenical Council, and gave proof of Eastern independence of the West by its criticism, in the fifty-fifth canon, of the Roman usage of quadragesimal fasting. Henceforth the divergencies in ritual between East and West became more important than their common viewpoint in dogmatic questions, and it was differences concerning ritual and ecclesiastical discipline which caused the estrangement between Constantinople and Rome; the dogmatic difference on the question of the Procession of the Holy Ghost, raised by Photius, was only the final cause of the breach in 867; the liturgical controversy between Cerularius and Leo IX in 1054 was the final inducement to a permanent schism.

Before the first schism Byzantine orthodoxy had passed through a crisis more dangerous than that caused by the Monophysite or Monothelete heresies; this was the Iconoclastic controversy, which threatened the foundations of Orthodoxy for more than a hundred years. In its outset a conflict over the popular custom of paying reverence to sacred pictures, the Iconoclastic controversy passed at a later stage into the sphere of politics and finally assumed the character of a social movement directed against the wealth of the monasteries. The struggle was conducted with passion on both sides; it is difficult to reconstruct the situation, since the writings of the Image-Breakers have perished and we have to rely on the treatises of

[1] Cf. Pargoire, *L'Église byzantine*, pp. 103–4.

the Image-Worshippers. Rationalistic writers see in Iconoclasm a Puritan reaction against superstition; ecclesiastical authors, on the other hand, see in it the intrusion of Imperial ambition into the domain of the Church. The unbiased historian, who collects and studies the facts, refrains from taking part on one side or the other; he sees in the conflict a tragic clash of principles.[1] For our task a short delineation of the inner causes of the controversy may suffice to explain its reflection in Byzantine hymnography.

Jewish Christians and members of those Churches whose observances were particularly strict had always been hostile to the representation of Christ in Early Christian art. They saw in such representations a breach of the Mosaic Commandment. This attitude found expression in the thirty-sixth Canon of the Council of Elvira (306), which forbade pictures in churches or paintings of objects of worship on the walls.[2] With the spread of Christianity among the Gentiles, to whom the mystery of the Invisible God had to be made accessible in a familiar form, the material representation of Christ, the Virgin, the Apostles, and the Saints became inevitable, and was favoured by both State and Church, particularly since the reign of Justinian. From the middle of the sixth century Eastern piety showed a tendency to dedicate churches and monasteries to the Theotokos, the angels, and the saints; to place in these sanctuaries icons of the Divine Persons and the saints and martyrs to whom they were consecrated; and to preserve in them relics to which pilgrimages and processions were arranged at local feasts. Soon the veneration of the icons took the form of adoration. The theology of Dionysius the Areopagite had developed the Neoplatonic conception that the human manifestations of the Supernatural Beauty are reflections of the invisible Divine Essence, revealed to inspired artisans. It was only necessary to carry these ideas a step farther for Byzantine piety to see in the icons the earthly personifications of the Theotokos or of the saint, and to confer on them the same adoration as on their divine, invisible proto-

[1] Cf. K. Schwarzlose, *Der Bilderstreit* (1890), pp. 42–50; A. Lombard, *Études d'histoire byzantine* (1902), pp. 124–8; L. Bréhier, *La Querelle des images* (1904), pp. 3–4; H. Leclercq, in *D.A.C.L.* vii (1926), col. 180–302. See also the masterly outline of the Iconoclastic controversy by N. H. Baynes in his *The Byzantine Empire*, pp. 88–93.

[2] 'Placuit picturas in ecclesia esse non debere, ne quod colitur et adoratur in parietibus depingatur.' Mansi, *Concil. Coll.* ii. 11, *Concil. Illiberitanum*, Can. 36.

types.[1] The icons are, according to Dionysius, 'predeterminations' (*προορισμοί*);[2] they are pre-existent in God, just as a house that is to be built is created first in the imagination of the architect.[3] There was a strong tendency in Byzantine theology to encourage the adoration of the icons for the sake of religious education; they were considered as a means of approach to the mysteries of the Church for the uneducated who could not read. 'The Icon is an aid to the memory (*ὑπόμνημα*)', writes John Damascene; 'it means to the uneducated and uncivilized what the book means to those who can read.'[4]

The conflict broke out in 725 under Leo III (717–41), the first of the Isaurian dynasty. Born in the mountainous country of the Taurus, at the eastern border of the Empire, Leo was influenced by Paulician ideas, which spread in the middle of the seventh century and gained many followers in Armenia, Mesopotamia, and Syria.[5] As the Paulician sect was an offshoot of the Manichaeans,* the representation of the Divine in human form was regarded by them as blasphemous. Leo's decree in 726 against icon-worship led to a revolt which was suppressed by force, and the see of Constantinople was handed over to a patriarch who supported the Iconoclastic policy of the Emperor. Thus a struggle began between the Emperor and the army on the one hand, and orthodoxy represented by the monks on the other, which was continued by Leo's successors and lasted, not counting a short interval of peace under the Empress Irene, until the death of Theophilus in 842. Resistance of the monks, who were courageous in opposing the intervention of Imperial power in matters of faith, was everywhere quelled. Monasteries were closed or secularized, the monks were persecuted, exiled, imprisoned, or put to death. Images and statues were destroyed; codices, particularly those with miniatures, were burnt.[6] In Constantinople the frescoes of the church at Blachernae, representing scenes from the life of Christ, were destroyed, and the mosaics and frescoes of the Patriarchate disappeared together with many other famous works of Christian art.[7] The long period

[1] *Εἶτα πάλιν εἰκόνες εἰσὶ τὰ ὁρατὰ τῶν ἀοράτων, καὶ ἀτυπώτων, σωματικῶς τυπουμένων πρὸς ἀμυδρὰν κατανόησιν.* John Damascene, *De imaginibus oratio* i. 11; *P.G.* xciv, c. 1241.

[2] *De div. nom.*, cap. 5.

[3] *De imag. or.* i. 10; *P.G.* xciv, c. 1241.

[4] Ibid. i. 17; *P.G.* xciv, c. 1247.

[5] Cf. Pargoire, *L'Église byzantine*, p. 181.

[6] Cf. Mansi, *Concil. Coll.* xiii, col. 329.

[7] Cf. Ch. Diehl, *Manuel d'art byz.* (1910), p. 338.

of destruction explains the loss of all manuscripts containing the music of hymns prior to the ninth century. Not a single composition of the greatest of all Byzantine hymn-writers, St. Romanus, has come down to us in a manuscript of his period; we do not even know whether the writers of *Kontakia* wrote down their melodies in neumatic notation, as was the custom later, or transmitted them orally.

After the death of Theophilus on 20 January 842 his widow Theodora reigned for her son Michael III, who was under age. Suddenly all persecution came to an end and orthodoxy was restored. To commemorate the triumph of the Church the new Patriarch of Constantinople, Methodius, introduced in 843 the Feast of Orthodoxy,[1] which is celebrated on the first Sunday of Lent.[2] Image-worship, the cult of relics, pilgrimages to sanctuaries which possessed miracle-working icons and relics flourished even more than before the outbreak of the Iconoclastic controversy. To repair the damage done to the decoration of churches and monasteries, a wave of artistic activity set in, and they were adorned with mosaics, frescoes, and icons. In the scriptoria of the monasteries schools of calligraphers copied the manuscripts which had escaped destruction, and illuminated them. The reaction against the period of puritanism was, in fact, so strong that it led to a second golden age of Byzantine art, which lasted for nearly three centuries from the beginning of the Macedonian to the end of the Comnenian dynasty in 1204. From that period a number of manuscripts have come down to us, containing both texts and music of the liturgical hymns. These manuscripts transmit the rich treasury of hymnody in all the various stages of musical notation from the earliest to the most fully developed, and they are the source for the study of Byzantine ecclesiastical music.

[1] The text chanted at the feast was a kind of 'Blessing and cursing Litany'. It has come down in a unique MS. from the Library of the Duke of Leicester, now in the Bodleian Library, [MS. Holkham 172]. Cf. 'Die jährliche Eucharistia nach dem Bildersturm', *O.C.*, N.S., xii–xiv (1925), 151–61.

[2] N. Nilles, *Kalendarium Manuale*, ii (1897), 102.

CHAPTER VIII

THE POETICAL FORMS: (I) TROPARION AND KONTAKION

I. TROPARION

THE rise of the Byzantine Church from an episcopal see to a dominating position in the East under Justinian and, finally, to independence from Rome, was reflected in the ever-increasing activity of Byzantine hymn-writers. Taking their models from the Churches of Jerusalem, Antioch, and Alexandria, they gradually built up a characteristically Byzantine style by introducing successively, in addition to the mass of originally monostrophic hymns, the two great poetic forms characteristic of Eastern piety: Kontakion and Kanon. Before we discuss these genres of liturgical poetry, which first attracted the interest of students in Eastern liturgy and ecclesiastical poetry, we must speak about the Troparia:[1] from the aesthetic point of view, these hymns are as important as the longer forms which developed later; from the musical point of view they are of even greater importance, because their texture is richer than that of the melodies which are sung to the stanzas of the Kanons.

The name Troparion (τροπάριον) was given to short prayers which, in the earliest stage of hymnography, were written in poetic prose and inserted after each verse of a psalm. In the fifth century, when the Troparia were composed in strophic form and became longer, these poetical prayers were sung only after the three to six last verses of a psalm. Hymns of this kind are known to have formed part of Matins and Vespers in churches and monasteries of the fifth century. In this period the liturgy consisted of psalms, of the nine Odes or *Cantica*, of certain formulae dating back to the earliest times of Christianity, and of the Troparia, added by contemporary hymnodists. This usage, however, did not apply to monastic congregations living in seclusion, such as those of monasteries in the desert. Monks of this strict rule, anchorites and hermits, rejected, as we know from reports which have come down to us, every kind of singing.

[1] See the article τροπάριον in L. Clugnet's *Dictionnaire grec-français des noms liturgiques* (1895), pp. 153–5.

The oldest of these reports,[1] referring to the practice of the fifth century, is that of Abbot Pambo, who had sent his disciple from the monastery in the desert to Alexandria to sell some of the products of their manual labour. The disciple returned after sixteen days, having spent his nights in the vestibule of the Church of St. Mark, where he saw the ceremonies and heard the singing of the Troparia. The abbot, observing that the disciple was troubled by something, asked for the reason. The young monk answered that he felt they wasted so many days in the desert singing neither Kanons nor Troparia such as he had heard at Alexandria. To these complaints the abbot answered in despair that he saw the time coming when the monks would abandon their rigid discipline pronounced by the Holy Spirit, and would give themselves over to songs and melodies. What kind of contrition, what kind of tears could result from the Troparia..., when the monk stands in his church or his cell and raises his voice like the oxen? . . . 'The monks did not emigrate into this desert in order to perform before God, and to give themselves airs, and to sing songs, and to compose tunes, and to shake their hands and move from one foot to the other', but we should offer our prayers to God in great fear and trembling, with tears and sighings, in reverence and in the spirit of contrition with moderate voice.[2]

Another report, dating from the sixth century, describes the

[1] The text of the report, first published by Gerbert in his collection of *Scriptores eccles. de musica*, and quoted by J.-B. Pitra in *L'Hymnographie de l'église grecque* is given in full in Christ–Paranikas, *Anthologia graeca carm. christ.*, pp. xxix–xxx. A free and rather inaccurate rendering of the Greek text is given in E. Bouvy's *Poètes et mélodes* (1886), pp. 238–9. Reference to the report is made in H. J. W. Tillyard's *Byzantine Music and Hymnography* (1923), p. 9, and in O. Tiby's *La Musica Byzantina* (1938), pp. 127–8.

[2] *λέγει οὖν αὐτῷ ὁ γέρων· οὐαὶ ἡμῖν, τέκνον, ὅτι ἔφθασαν αἱ ἡμέραι, ἐν αἷς ὑπολείψουσι οἱ μοναχοὶ τὴν στερεὰν τροφὴν τὴν διὰ τοῦ ἁγίου πνεύματος ῥηθεῖσαν καὶ ἐξακολουθήσουσιν ᾄσματα καὶ ἤχους· ποία γὰρ κατάνυξις, ποῖα δάκρυα τίκτονται ἐκ τῶν τροπαρίων; ποία γὰρ κατάνυξις τῷ μοναχῷ, ὅταν ἐν ἐκκλησίᾳ ἢ ἐν κελλίῳ ἵσταται καὶ ὑψοῖ τὴν φωνὴν αὐτοῦ ὡς οἱ βόες; εἰ γὰρ ἐνώπιον τοῦ θεοῦ παριστάμεθα, ἐν πολλῇ κατανύξει ὀφείλομεν ἵστασθαι καὶ οὐχὶ ἐν μετεωρισμῷ· καὶ γὰρ οὐκ ἐξῆλθον οἱ μοναχοὶ ἐν τῇ ἐρήμῳ ταύτῃ, ἵνα παρίστανται τῷ θεῷ καὶ μετεωρίζονται καὶ μελῳδοῦσιν ᾄσματα καὶ ῥυθμίζουσιν ἤχους καὶ σείουσι χεῖρας καὶ μεταβαίνουσι πόδας, ἀλλ' ὀφείλομεν καὶ μετρίας [ταπεινῆς] φωνῆς τὰς προσευχὰς τῷ θεῷ προσφέρειν.* Ibid., pp. xxix–xxx. The reference to the singing of the hymns accompanied by clapping of the hands and rhythmical steps reminds us of the description of the ecstatic gesticulations and movements of the Ethiopian saint Jārēd (*Corpus script. christ. orient.*, *Scriptores Aethiopici*, Ser. II, vol. xvii, p. 4), and of the present Ethiopian custom of accompanying the singing of the Mass by drums and rhythmical gesticulations. Cf. E. Wellesz, 'Studien zur aethiopischen Kirchenmusik', *O.C.*, N.S. ix. 81–4. Since the Ethiopian practice goes back to that of the Coptic Church, this kind of ecstatic singing may have been customary in Alexandria in the days of Pambo, and we may well understand that monks of strict discipline rejected a kind of singing which they considered as a relapse into paganism, or, as Pambo puts it: *χυθήσεται ὁ νοῦς εἰς τρόπους καὶ εἰς τοὺς λόγους τῶν Ἑλλήνων.*

visit of the Abbots John and Sophronius to Nilus, abbot at Mount Sinai.[1] John and Sophronius came to see Nilus on a Sunday. They found him with two disciples at the top of the mountain. When they arrived it was the hour for Vespers. The abbot began the service with the Doxology (*Δόξα Πατρί*), followed by the first Psalm (*Μακάριος*) and the hundred and fortieth (*Κύριε, ἐκέκραξα*), without singing the customary Troparia (*χωρὶς τῶν τροπαρίων*); he continued with the prayers *Φῶς ἱλαρόν* and *Καταξίωσον*[2] and ended with Symeon's prayer *Νῦν ἀπολύεις* (Luke ii. 29–32). After Vespers a meal was served. When they had finished they began to celebrate Matins. They said first the Hexapsalm (Psalms iii, xxxvii, lxii, lxxxvii, cii, and cxlii) and the Lord's Prayer; then, with subdued voice, they recited the entire cycle of the 150 Psalms, divided into three groups (*στάσεις*) of fifty Psalms. After the first group the abbot said the Lord's Prayer and the *Kyrie eleison*. Then they sat down and one of the disciples read the Epistle of St. James. The same order of prayers and lessons was repeated after the second and third group of Psalms; after the second an Epistle of St. Peter was read, after the third an Epistle of St. John. The recitation of the Psalms was followed by the nine Odes, again repeated in a subdued voice, without the Troparia (*ἄνευ τροπαρίων*); they sang no Mesodion (*μεσῴδιον*)[3] after the third and sixth Ode, but said the Lord's Prayer and the *Kyrie eleison*. After having said the Lauds (*αἶνοι* = Psalms cxlviii, cxlix, and cl) without the Troparia, they ended with the Doxology, the Lord's Prayer, the *Kyrie eleison*, and a short prayer.

John and Sophronius were astonished by the omission of all the hymns and asked Nilus why he did not follow the practice of the 'catholic and apostolic Church'. Nilus tried to convince them that he did. But they asked: 'Why do you sing Troparia at the Vespers of the holy Sunday neither to *Κύριε, ἐκέκραξα* (Psalm cxl), nor to *Φῶς ἱλαρόν*; nor at Matins the *Θεὸς Κύριος*,[4] nor to the recitation of the Psalms the Sabbath-*Kathisma*-

[1] Cf. J.-B. Pitra, *Iuris eccles. graec. historia*, ii. 220, and Christ–Paranikas, *Anthol. graeca carm. christ.*, pp. xxx–xxxii.

[2] The first word of the prayer: *Καταξίωσον, Κύριε, ἐν τῇ ἑσπέρᾳ*, read in the Greek Church during the second part of Vespers.

[3] *μεσῴδιον* apparently means a short hymn, sung between the third and fourth, and the sixth and seventh, Canticle.

[4] *Θεὸς Κύριος καὶ ἐπέφηνεν ἡμῖν· εὐλογημένος ὁ ἐρχόμενος ἐν ὀνόματι Κυρίου* has its place before the Hexapsalm and is followed by the Troparion of the feast.

ta,[1] nor the Troparia of the Three Children to the Canticles; nor the *Πᾶσα πνοή* to *Μεγαλύνει*,[2] nor *'Ανάστασιν τοῦ σωτῆρος* to the Doxology?'[3]

From this report the following facts can be ascertained about sixth-century liturgy: (1) In early Byzantine liturgy Vespers and Matins already contained most of the elements they contain to-day. (2) The singing of Troparia formed part of the ritual of the Orthodox Church. (3) The Troparia had their fixed position in the Canonical Hours; this fact can be inferred from the surprise of John and Sophronius at the liturgical practice of the abbot of Mount Sinai. Nilus obviously adhered to the rigid rule of fourth- and fifth-century solitaries, who rejected singing as harmful to the spirit of contrition, the state of mind essential to monastic piety, as can be seen from the anecdote about Pambo and his disciple.

The first Byzantine hymn-writers to be mentioned by name are Anthimus and Timocles, who flourished in the middle of the fifth century, in the days of Leo I (457–74). Both Anthimus, the Orthodox poet, and Timocles, the Monophysite, had a large following in Constantinople.[4] But none of the Troparia of these hymnodists have come down to us, or at any rate not under their names. Among the large number of anonymous Troparia which the Byzantine service-books contain, some compositions of the poets of Early Byzantine hymnography may have survived, but no convincing proof of the fact is possible.

We should have no information about the state of fifth-century hymnography if a group of Troparia of Auxentius had not been transmitted in a *Vita* of the saint.[5] In the days of Theodosius II Auxentius came from his native land, Syria, to Constantinople to take up military service in the Imperial Guard. He became a member of a circle to which John Monachus, Marcian, Setus,

[1] Kathisma: (1) one of the twenty sections into which the Psalter is divided, apart from the three Staseis; (2) a Troparion which is sung sitting. The term Sabbath-*Kathismata* obviously refers to the Troparia sung during the third part of the Orthros.

[2] *μεγαλύνει ἡ ψυχή μου τὸν Κύριον* is the beginning of the ninth Canticle; the antiphon *Πᾶσα πνοὴ αἰνεσάτω τὸν Κύριον* is sung in the present service before Lauds.

[3] According to present-day usage the Resurrection-Troparion of the Great Doxology is sung after the Trisagion.

[4] *τῷ η' ἔτει . . . Ἄνθιμος καὶ Τιμοκλῆς οἱ τῶν τροπαρίων ποιηταὶ ἐγνωρίζοντο.* Cedrenus, *Compendium Historiarum*, i. 612 (*C.S.H.B.*). According to Theodore the Lector's *Excerpta ex Eccl. Hist.*, *P.G.* lxxxvi, cc. 173–5, Anthimus introduced the Vigils *τὰς παννυχίδας* into the Service.

[5] Cf. *Vita S. Auxentii*, *P.G.* cxiv, c. 1412. According to Pitra, *Analecta Sacra*, p. xxii the *Vita* was written by Georgius, a pupil of Auxentius.

and other citizens of high rank belonged, all of whom led a strict Christian life. Many of them gave up their private occupation, took orders, and retired from the world. Auxentius lived as a solitary on a mountain near Chalcedon in Bithynia, but had to leave his seclusion for a time by order of the Emperor Marcian to take part in the Council of Chalcedon. He became a famous preacher, and pilgrimages were made to his cell on Mount Oxia. Here, according to the *Vita*, Auxentius received the pilgrims one by one, gave advice, and taught them to chant simple Troparia, consisting of two or three phrases (τροπάρια ἀπὸ δύο ῥητῶν ἢ τριῶν). When they had learned them, they all chanted together, and the singing of the crowd went on for several hours. Finally the Saint intoned in the following manner the 'Song of the three Holy Children', which forms the eighth Ode of the Byzantine Psalter. He sang the first hemistich of each line, and the crowd responded with the second, as the author of the *Vita* indicates:

Auxentius: Εὐλογεῖτε, πάντα τὰ ἔργα Κυρίου τὸν Κύριον.
The people: Ὑμνεῖτε καὶ ὑπερυψοῦτε αὐτὸν εἰς τοὺς αἰῶνας.

(O all ye works of the Lord, bless ye the Lord: praise Him and magnify Him for ever.)

The Troparia of Auxentius, transmitted in the *Vita*, were rearranged by Pitra in the form of a hymn consisting of seven stanzas.[1] From the text of the *Vita* we learn that each Troparion formed a short prayer, interspersed between the parts of his address to the pilgrims, but that an inner connexion existed between the Troparia, since Auxentius taught the pilgrims to sing them in their proper order (κατὰ τάξιν).

This breaking up of a hymn consisting of a number of stanzas is in conformity with the liturgical practice mentioned above of singing a short hymn after each verse of a psalm. In this first stage of Troparion-writing the stanzas were loosely linked together. Later on, however, all the Troparia are linked by a common thought and have the same unity as a lyrical poem built up from a number of stanzas. We also learn from the *Vita* that a Troparion need not necessarily be performed by a single person, but could also be sung by a choir. The fragment of the hymn of Auxentius runs as follows:

[1] Cf. Pitra, *Analecta Sacra*, p. xxiii.

(1) Πτωχὸς καὶ πένης
ὑμνοῦμέν σε, Κύριε·

δόξα τῷ Πατρὶ
δόξα τῷ Υἱῷ
δόξα τῷ ἁγίῳ Πνεύματι,
τῷ λαλήσαντι διὰ τῶν
προφητῶν

(2) Στρατιαὶ ἐν οὐρανοῖς
ὕμνον ἀναπέμπουσιν,
καὶ ἡμεῖς οἱ τῆς γῆς
τὴν δοξολογίαν·

ἅγιος, ἅγιος, ἅγιος Κύριος,

πλήρης ὁ οὐρανὸς
καὶ ἡ γῆ τῆς **δόξης** σου.

(3) Δημιουργὲ πάντων,
εἶπας καὶ ἐγεννήθημεν,
ἐνετείλω καὶ ἐκτίσθημεν·
πρόσταγμα ἔθου
καὶ οὐ παρελεύσεται·
σῶτερ, εὐχαριστοῦμέν σοι.

(4) **Κύριε τῶν δυναμέων,**
ἔπαθες ⟨καὶ⟩ ἀνέστης,
ὤφθης **καὶ ἀνελήφθης.**
ἔρχῃ κρῖναι κόσμον[1]
οἰκτείρησον καὶ σῶσον ἡμᾶς.

(5) Ἐν ψυχῇ **τεθλιμμένῃ**
προσπίπτομέν σοι
καὶ **δεόμεθά** σου,
Σῶτερ τοῦ κόσμου·
σὺ γὰρ εἶ **Θεὸς**
τῶν μετανοούντων.

(6) **Ὁ καθήμενος ἐπὶ τῶν Χερουβὶμ**

καὶ τοὺς οὐρανοὺς ἀνοίξας

οἰκτείρησον καὶ σῶσον ἡμᾶς.

(7) **Ἀγαλλιᾶσθε,**
δίκαιοι, ἐν Κυρίῳ,
πρεσβεύοντες ὑπὲρ ἡμῶν·
δόξα σοι, Κύριε,
ὁ Θεὸς τῶν ἁγίων.

(1) We, the poor and the needy, praise thee, O Lord; glory to the Father, and to the Son, and to the Holy Spirit, who spake by the Prophets.
(2) The Heavenly Hosts send up a hymn, and we upon earth the song of praise: Holy, holy, holy Lord, heaven and earth are full of Thy glory.
(3) Creator of all, Thou didst speak, and we were begotten; Thou didst ordain, and we were created; Thou gavest the command, and it shall not pass away. Saviour, we thank Thee.
(4) Lord of hosts, Thou didst suffer and Thou didst arise; Thou didst appear, and Thou didst ascend. Thou art coming to judge the world, have pity upon us and save us.
(5) With contrite heart we fall down before Thee and beseech Thee, O Saviour of the world, for Thou art the God of the penitent.
(6) Thou who sittest above the Cherubim and hast opened the heavens, have pity upon us and save us.
(7) Rejoice, ye righteous, in the Lord and intercede for us.
Glory to Thee, O Lord, the God of the saints.

[1] This line from the text in the *Vita* is omitted in Pitra's version of the hymn.

In a study on the hymn T. M. Wehofer[1] pointed out that Auxentius was inspired by Hebrew poetry both in form and style. He therefore published the hymn in a form which made apparent the correspondence of the stanzas 2, 6, and 7 as antistrophes to 1, 4, and 5. The third stanza, consisting of two verses of equal length, has no antistrophe. The correspondences in thought between strophes and antistrophes are emphasized by bolder type.

The hymn consists of two parts: an invocation, comprising the first three stanzas, and a prayer, comprising the last four stanzas. The first two stanzas are contrasted by means of antithesis. The 'poor and needy' (Ps. cviii. 22) in the first stanza are contrasted with the 'multitude of the heavenly host' (Luke ii. 13) in the second. The common thought in both is the praise of God; the words of praise in the first stanza are taken from the doxological formula and the Nicene Symbol; in the second from Isaiah's vision of the Seraphim (Isa. vi. 3). The third stanza, standing by itself, is connected with the second by *concatenatio*: *ὁ οὐρανὸς καὶ ἡ γῆ* are the works of the Creator of the universe, who is addressed, with a term occurring in the Symbol of the Synod of Sirmium (359), as *Δημιουργὲ πάντων*. With the exception of this invocation, these lines are an echo of Psalm cxlviii. 5 and a paraphrase of *δι' οὗ τὰ πάντα ἐγένετο* from the Nicene Symbol. The following lines are based on Ps. xxxii. 9. The last line *Σῶτερ, εὐχαριστοῦμέν σοι* links the invocation with the prayer.

In the second part the fourth and fifth stanzas together form the antithesis to the sixth and seventh. The first line of the fourth stanza *Κύριε τῶν δυνάμεων* (Ps. lxxix. 8) corresponds to the first line of the sixth *Ὁ καθήμενος ἐπὶ τῶν Χερουβίμ* (Ps. lxxix. 2). The second and fourth lines of the fourth stanza are influenced by the *Nicaeno-Constantinopolitanum*: *παθόντα καὶ ταφέντα, καὶ ἀναστάντα . . . καὶ πάλιν ἐρχόμενον μετὰ δόξης κρῖναι ζῶντας καὶ νεκρούς*; but *ἀνελήφθης* has its origin either in the Symbol of Sirmium or in the *Nicaenum*: both have the same formula (*καὶ τεσσαράκοντα ἡμερῶν πληρουμένων ἀναληφθέντα εἰς τοὺς οὐρανούς*), which does not occur in the *Nicaeno-Constantinopolitanum*. The invocation *Οἰκτείρησον* (Ps. iv. 2) *καὶ σῶσον ἡμᾶς* is identical in both the fourth and sixth stanzas, whereas the contrast between

[1] 'Untersuchungen zum Lied des Romanos auf die Wiederkunft des Herrn', *Sitzungsber. d. Ak. d. Wiss. in Wien, Phil.-Hist. Kl.* cliv, part 5 (1907), pp. 11–15.

the 'poor and needy' on the one hand, and the 'righteous' on the other, is continued in the fifth and seventh stanzas. The sinners cry to God in contrition, *ἐν ψυχῇ τεθλιμμένῃ* (Ps. xxxiii. 6, 19 or l. 19); the righteous, who rejoice in God, *ἀγαλλιᾶσθε, δίκαιοι, ἐκ Κυρίῳ* (Ps. xii. 5–6 or Ps. xciv. 1) are asked to intercede for the sinners. The antithesis between the 'poor and needy' and the 'righteous' is maintained up to the last lines of the corresponding stanzas; but the last invocations, *σὺ γὰρ εἶ Θεὸς τῶν μετανοούντων* and *δόξα σοι Κύριε, ὁ Θεὸς τῶν ἁγίων*, express the assurance of the preacher that there is hope for all, because the Lord is not only *Θεὸς τῶν ἁγίων* (the mention of the saints points to the religious attitude of the post-Nicene period), but also *Θεὸς τῶν μετανοούντων.*

The analysis of the hymns shows that Auxentius drew heavily on the Psalms for both thought and diction; to a lesser extent on passages from other parts of the Scriptures, from the Symbols, and, finally, on liturgical formulae. From the *Vita* we know that the Troparia were sung to simple melodies which the pilgrims were able to learn quickly.[1] Even without that information it would be reasonable to assume that the Troparia were sung in a kind of psalmody; either to the usual psalm-tunes or to those of a paraphrase. It is certain that neither the text nor the melody showed any signs of artistic individualism, but followed the usual liturgical pattern.

From the sixth century a monostrophic Troparion *Ὁ μονογενὴς υἱός* has come down to us, attributed, as has already been said, to Justinian.* The hymn is a poetical paraphrase of the *Constantinopolitanum*, of which, in his decree of 533, Justinian speaks as 'the holy Creed or the Symbol':[2]

Ὁ μονογενὴς υἱὸς καὶ λόγος τοῦ θεοῦ,
ἀθάνατος ὑπάρχων,
καὶ καταδεξάμενος διὰ τὴν ἡμετέραν σωτηρίαν
σαρκωθῆναι ἐκ τῆς ἁγίας θεοτόκου
καὶ ἀειπαρθένου Μαρίας,
ἀτρέπτως ἐνανθρωπήσας, σταυρωθείς τε, Χριστὲ ὁ θεός,
θανάτῳ θάνατον πατήσας,
εἷς ὢν τῆς ἁγίας τριάδος
συνδοξαζόμενος τῷ πατρὶ καὶ τῷ ἁγίῳ πνεύματι,
σῶσον ἡμᾶς.[3]

[1] *P.G.* cxiv, c. 1415.

[2] . . . *τὸ ἅγιον μάθημα ἤτοι τὸ σύμβολον.* *Cod. Iustin.* I. i. 7.

[3] The text of the Troparion is taken from *Anthologia graeca carm. christ.*, p. 52.

(Only-begotten Son and Word of God, Thou who art Immortal,
Who wast pleased, for our salvation, to become flesh from the holy Mother of God
And ever-Virgin Mary, Thou who, immutable, puttedst on man's nature
And wast crucified, Christ our God, crushing death through death,
Who art One of the Holy Triad, glorified with the Father and the Holy Spirit,
Save us.)

Here, too, the work of the hymn-writer is limited to paraphrasing passages from the Symbol, and to adding the doxological formula and the prayer for salvation. The style of the music, we may assume, followed the pattern of syllabic psalmody, with groups of notes at the half- and full closes of each line.

Besides the Troparia another genre of ecclesiastical poetry, the Kontakion, began to flourish at the beginning of the sixth century, more independent of the Scriptures in its content and more extended in form. Its growth coincides with the increase of Byzantine piety in the Justinianic era.

II. KONTAKION

The rise of the new poetical form is associated with the names of the great *Melodoi* Anastasius, Kyriakos, and, above all, of Romanus. No evidence is available to determine the date at which the Kontakion was received into Byzantine liturgy. No reference to it is to be found in Byzantine documents or writings during the time it was in use. Even the name Kontakion only occurs for the first time in the ninth century; the monk who composed a hymn of that kind called it Hymn (ὕμνος), Psalm (ψαλμός), Poem (ποίημα or ἔπος), Song (ᾠδή or ᾆσμα), Laud (αἶνος), or Prayer (προσευχή or δέησις).[1]

The Kontakion (κοντάκιον or κονδάκιον) consists of from eighteen to thirty, or even more, stanzas all structurally alike. The single stanza is called Troparion; its length varies from three to thirteen lines. All the Troparia are composed on the pattern of a model stanza, the Hirmus (εἱρμός). A Kontakion is built either on the pattern of a Hirmus specially composed for it, or follows the metre of a Hirmus already used for another Kontakion, or group of Kontakia. At the beginning of the Kontakion stands a short Troparion, metrically and melodically independent of

[1] Cf. E. Mioni, *Romano il Melode* (1937), p. 10.

it: this is the Prooemium (*προοίμιον*) or Kukulion (*κουκούλιον*), which, at a later stage, often consists of two or three stanzas. Prooemium and Kontakion are linked together by the refrain, the Ephymnium (*ἐφύμνιον*), with which all the stanzas end, and by the musical mode (*ἦχος*).[1] The occurrence of the refrain at the end of each stanza indicates that the Kontakia were sung by a soloist, the choir singing the refrain.

The stanzas of the Kontakion are connected either alphabetically or by an acrostic, in the following way. The first letters of the stanzas either are the letters of the alphabet in its usual order, or form a short sentence containing the name of the hymn-writer and the title of the poem. The acrostic is indicated in the title of the Kontakion. From the title we learn (1) the day of the feast on which the Kontakion is sung, (2) the feast for which it is composed, (3) the acrostic, (4) the musical mode of the melody. Let us take for example the Kontakion 'Joseph the Chaste' by Romanus which the Orthodox Church sings on Easter Monday. The title runs as follows:[2]

Τῇ ἁγίᾳ καὶ μεγάλῃ δευτέρᾳ. Κοντάκιον εἰς τὸν Ἰωσὴφ φέρον ἀκροστιχίδα τήνδε· Ἀλφάβητον Ῥωμανοῦ. Πλάγιος δ΄. Πρὸς τὸ Ὁ υἱός σου παρθένε πανάμωμε.

From the title we learn that the Kontakion in honour of Joseph was sung on the second day of Easter; further, that each stanza began with a letter of the alphabet, followed by an acrostic consisting of the two words *Ἀλφάβητον Ῥωμανοῦ*, that the melody was written in the fourth plagal mode and modelled on an already existing hymn beginning with the words *Ὁ υἱός σου παρθένε πανάμωμε*. The Kontakion consists of forty stanzas, each beginning with one of the following letters.

α β γ δ ε ζ η θ ι κ λ μ ν ξ ο π ρ σ τ υ φ χ ψ ω   α λ φ α β η τ ο ν   ρ ω μ α ν ο υ.

The acrostic most frequently to be found indicates that 'the humble Romanus' is the author of the poem: *φέρον ἀκροστιχίδα τήνδε· τοῦ ταπεινοῦ ῥωμανοῦ*, or *τοῦ ταπεινοῦ ῥωμανοῦ τοῦτο τὸ ποίημα*, or *τοῦ ταπεινοῦ ῥωμανοῦ ὁ ψαλμός*.

It sometimes happened that the hymn-writer wanted to write more stanzas than there were letters in the acrostic. In that

[1] J.-B. Pitra, *Analecta Sacra*, i, pp. liv–lxxviii; G. Cammelli, *Romano il Melode* (1930), pp. 51–72; E. Mioni, *Romano*, pp. 11–17.

[2] K. Krumbacher, 'Studien zu Romanos', *Sb. B.A.* (1898), p. 135.

case he had to use some of the letters of the acrostic twice for two consecutive strophes, e.g.:

ττοῦ ταπεινοῦ γαβριὴλ ὁ ὕμνος οὗτος ἀμήν ἀμμήν.[1]

In another case, in the poem of an anonymous hymn-writer in memory of St. John Chrysostom, the principle of doubling letters is carried even farther. The direction from the title:

φέρον ἀκροστιχίδα τήνδε· εἰς τὸν χρυσόστομον

is executed as follows: *εις τον χχρρυυσσοοσσττομον.*[2]

At the time when the Kontakia were written the Greek language had already lost the difference between long and short vowels, the basis of the quantitative metre of classical poetry; *ω* had become equal to *ο*; *η*, *ει*, and *οι* were pronounced as a short *ι*, *αι* as *ε*. A new system of versification had developed based on the principle that all the stanzas had to have the same number of syllables as the Hirmus on which they were modelled and that the stress accents had to have the same place in all the stanzas as in the verses of the Hirmus.

The discovery that the hymns, which were transmitted in Byzantine liturgical manuscripts and in the printed Service-books of the Greek Church as prose texts, were composed in an elaborate rhythmical scheme of lines of varying length was made by Pitra in 1859,[3] and expounded in detail in his *Hymnographie de l'église grecque* (Rome, 1867). He also drew attention to the following passage from an unpublished treatise on prosody by the grammarian Theodosius,[4] in which the two main principles of Byzantine hymnography are laid down: 'He who wants to compose a Kanon, has first to set the Hirmus to music; then he shall let the Troparia follow, which must have the same number of syllables as the Hirmus, and the stress-accents on the same syllables (i.e. in all the lines corresponding to the leading line of the Hirmus), and preserve [the features of] the model.'[5]

The composition of a Kontakion, or, at a later date, of a Kanon, was a task which a poet could not achieve who was not

[1] K. Krumbacher, 'Die Akrostichis in der griech. Kirchenpoesie', *Sb. B.A.* (1903), p. 613.

[2] Ibid., p. 597.

[3] Cf. the Introduction to the present book, pp. 3 sqq.

[4] *Analecta Sacra*, p. xlvii.

[5] *ἐάν τις θέλῃ ποιῆσαι κανόνα, πρῶτον δεῖ μελίσαι τὸν εἱρμόν, εἶτα ἐπαγαγεῖν τὰ τροπάρια, ἰσοσυλλαβοῦντα καὶ ὁμοτονοῦντα τῷ εἱρμῷ, καὶ τὸν σκοπὸν ἀποσῴζοντα.* Theodosius of Alexandria, quoted by Pitra, op. cit., p. xlvii.

also a skilled musician.[1] Music and poetry had to make a single entity. To adapt the Troparia to the melody of the Hirmus it was not sufficient to make each line, corresponding to a line of the model strophe, of equal length, i.e. with the same number of syllables, but the stress accents must also fall on the same syllable as in the Hirmus, in order to make the accentuated notes of the melody coincide with the accentuated syllables of the stanzas.

The Kontakion makes its appearance suddenly, without antecedents. Byzantine hagiography attributes its introduction into Eastern liturgy to Romanus, who is praised by Germanus, the author of a hymn in honour of the saint, as

Πρώτη καλῶν ἀπαρχὴ
ὤφθης, σωτηρίας ἀφορμή,
Ῥωμανὲ πατὲρ ἡμῶν·
ἀγγελικὴν γὰρ ὑμνῳδίαν συστησάμενος,
θεοπρεπῶς ἐπεδείξω τὴν πολιτείαν σου.[2]

(Earliest first-fruit of beautiful (hymns), thou wast manifested a means of salvation, Romanus our father, composing the angelic hymnody, thou hast shown thy conversation meet for God.)

This monostrophic hymn was sung on 1 October, the day on which the Eastern Church celebrates the feast of St. Romanus. In order to show the combination of 'Voice and Verse' in a Byzantine panegyric poem we give the hymn in full, according to the version of a thirteenth-century Sticherarion, Codex 1499 of the Vatopedi Monastery on Mount Athos.[3] The melody, composed in the second plagal mode,[4] runs as follows:

Πρώ - τη κα - λῶν . . ἀπ - αρ - χὴ ὤ - - - - φθης, σω -
- τη - ρί - ας ἀφ - ορ - μή, Ῥω - μα - νὲ πα - τὲρ ἡ - μῶν·

[1] *Δεῖ δὲ τὸν ποιητὴν ἔμπειρον εἶναι τῆς μουσικῆς, ἵνα μελίζῃ καλῶς τὰ ποιήματα.* Ibid., p. xlvii.

[2] Cf. Pitra, *Analecta sacra*, p. xxvi.

[3] The term *Sticherarion* has been explained in p. 142. Cf. also the Introduction to the present writer's edition of 'Die Hymnen des Sticherarium für September', in *M.M.B. Transcripta*, vol. i (1936), pp. xi–xiii, and xxix–xxxvii.

[4] Cf. H. J. W. Tillyard, 'Signatures and Cadences of the Byzantine Modes', *A.B.S.*, No. xxvi (1923–5), pp. 83–4.

ἀγ - γε - λι - κὴν . . γὰρ ὑ - μνῳ - δί - αν συ - στη -
- σά - με - νος, θε - ο - πρε - πῶς ἐ - πε - δεί - ξω τὴν πο - λι -
τεί - αν σου· Χρι - στὸν τὸν θε - ὸν ἱ- κέ - τευ - ε πει -
ρα - σμῶν καὶ κιν - δύ - νων λυ - τρω - θῆ - ναι τοὺς ἀ - νυ - μνοῦν - τάς σε.

The association of the name of Romanus with the rise of the Kontakion makes it possible to fix the date of its reception into Byzantine liturgy within the first decades of the sixth century. Romanus was a Jew by birth. He was born at Emesa on the Orontes, became deacon at Berytus in northern Phoenicia, and went to Constantinople in the days of Anastasius I (491–518)[1] to join the clergy of the Theotokos Church. Here, according to the legend, he was given the gift of hymn-writing by a miracle and composed more than a thousand Kontakia. In August 555 part of Constantinople was destroyed by an earthquake. The disaster was commemorated every year on the day it had happened by hymns and prayers. Romanus, who in his Kontakia frequently alludes to contemporary events, mentions the earthquake in a 'Psalm', which was sung on Wednesday of the third

[1] The feast of St. Romanus is celebrated on 1 October. From the *Vita* of the Saint in the famous *Menologion* of Emperor Basilius II (Cod. Vatic. 1613) we learn that Romanus lived in the days of Emperor Anastasius (ἐπὶ τῶν χρόνων Ἀναστασίου τοῦ βασιλέως); but there were two Emperors of that name, Anastasius I (491–518) and Anastasius II (713–16). Pitra, Grimme, De Boor, Maas, Papadopoulos-Kerameus were in favour of the earlier date; Christ, Gelzer, Vailhé, and Petrides of the later. Krumbacher changed his opinion several times. In 1905 Papadopoulos-Kerameus succeeded in solving the problem by discovering in a hagiographical MS. containing the Life of St. Artemius, a passage, stating that the hymns of Romanus were sung in the days of Heraclius (610–41). At the same time P. Maas published an article, 'Die Chronologie der Hymnen des Romanus', *B.Z.* (1906), pp. 1–44, in which he proved from references in the hymns to contemporary events that Romanus lived in the sixth century. A survey of the controversy about the chronology of Romanus is given in G. Cammelli's *Romano il Melode* (1930), pp. 11–18.

week of Lent.[1] Since the Kontakion was obviously written under the immediate impression of the disaster,[2] and no event later than it is mentioned in a poem by Romanus, it may be assumed that he died shortly after 555.

The maturity of diction in the Kontakia of Romanus, his mastery of the problems which the form offered to the Melode make it difficult to accept the tradition that he invented the new poetical genre in a moment of inspiration. We can, however, hardly disregard the fact that Romanus was considered by Byzantine hagiographers as the first hymn-writer to compose Kontakia, and that no Kontakia earlier than his have been found in Byzantine liturgical manuscripts. The answer to these apparently contradictory facts is that antecedents of the Kontakion existed in Syriac ecclesiastical poetry, and that Romanus, being of Syrian origin, was well acquainted with them. It was his great achievement to have adapted them to the spirit of Byzantine hymnography, and to have introduced the new form of ecclesiastical poetry into the liturgy of Constantinople.

Investigations carried out by Grimme, Meyer, Maas, Emereau, and Baumstark[3] have shown that the essential features of the Kontakion derive from the main forms of Syriac poetry in the fourth and fifth centuries, viz. Memrâ, Mâdrâshâ, and Sôgithâ. Of these three forms, the Memrâ, the poetical homily, must be regarded as the most important for the development of the Kontakion. Like the Memrâ, the Kontakion had its place in the Morning Office after the reading of the Gospel and paraphrased the text of the Scriptures. There is, however, a noticeable difference between Memrâ and Kontakion. The Memrâ invariably has the character of a sermon, while the Kontakion in the most perfect hymns of Romanus loses the homiletic character and, by assimilating elements from Mâdrâshâ and

[1] Cf. E. Mioni, *Romano*, p. 86.

[2] *Ψαλμοῖς ἐγέραιρον ποτὲ*
Σοφίαν καὶ Εἰρήνην,
δυνάμεις τὰς ἐνδόξους
τῆς ἄνω πολιτείας
οἱ τοῦ βαπτίσματος υἱοί.
ἔβλεπον δὲ ἄρτι
τοὺς ναοὺς τοὺς ἱεροὺς
κειμένους εἰς τὸ ἔδαφος.
(Ibid., pp. 100–1.)

[3] Cf. H. Grimme, *Der Strophenbau in den Gedichten Ephraems des Syrers* (1898); W. Meyer (Speyer), 'Anfang u. Ursprung der lat. u. griech. rythm. Dichtung', *Abh. B.A.* xvii. 2 (1884); P. Maas, 'Das Kontakion', *B.Z.* (1910), pp. 290 sqq.; C. Emereau, *Saint Ephrem le Syrien* (1919), pp. 97 sqq.; A. Baumstark, 'Festbrevier u. Kirchenjahr der syrischen Jakobiten', *Studien z. Geschichte u. Kultur des Altertums*, iii (1910).

Sôgithâ, develops into a poetical description of the object of the feast on which it is sung.[1]

The hypothesis of the Syrian origin of the Kontakion has recently been strengthened, but at the same time set in the right perspective, by the discovery of the Greek text of the *Homily on the Passion* by Melito, Bishop of Sardis, dating from the middle of the second century.[2] Fragments of the homily in Syriac have been known for a long time, but were regarded as being written in prose. Investigations[3] into the style and structure of both the Greek and Syriac texts, however, have shown that Melito's *Homily on the Passion* is composed in oratorical prose, which makes use of all the features typical of Semitic poetry. The entire homily is written in lines of from four to seventeen syllables. Lines of from seven to nine syllables are most common.[4] Rhyme is frequent, both in the Greek and Syriac texts, not as a formal element, but as a means of emphasizing certain lines of either parallel or antithetic content.

The discovery of Melito's homily makes it evident that the creation of the poetical sermon can no longer be attributed to Ephraem the Syrian († 373) or his immediate predecessors. This form goes back to the early days of Christianity and has developed from sermons in oratorical prose. Let us illustrate the development from the Early Christian sermon in the days of Melito to the Kontakion by giving a few examples showing the connexion of the poetical homily with the preceding Lesson.

Second century

Melito, Homily on the Passion:[5]

(1) *Ἡ μὲν γραφὴ τῆς Ἑβραϊκῆς ἐξόδου ἀνέγνωσται,*
καὶ τὰ ῥήματα τοῦ μυστηρίου διασεσάφηται,
πῶς τὸ πρόβατον θύεται
καὶ πῶς ὁ λαὸς σῴζεται.

[1] Cf. C. Émereau, op. cit., p. 100.

[2] Campbell Bonner, 'The Homily on the Passion by Melito Bishop of Sardis', *Studies and Documents*, xii (1940).

[3] Cf. E. Wellesz, 'Melito's Homily on the Passion. An Investigation into the Sources of Byzantine Hymnography', *J.T.S.* xliv (1943), 41–52; P. Kahle, 'Was Melito's Homily on the Passion originally written in Syriac?', ibid., pp. 52–6.

[4] The heptasyllabic line is the typical scheme in Ephraem's homilies. Cf. C. Emereau, *Saint Ephrem*, pp. 40 sqq. and pp. 50–1; he also makes use of tetrasyllabic and heptasyllabic lines (*τοῦ αὐτοῦ λόγου τετρασύλλαβα, τοῦ αὐτοῦ λόγου ἑπτασύλλαβα*). Ibid., pp. 39 and 52–3.

[5] *Studies and Documents*, xii. 87. Cf. E. Wellesz, 'Melito's Homily', *J.T.S.* xliv. 45.

(2) *Τοίνυν ξύνετε, ὦ ἀγαπητοί·*
οὕτως ἐστὶν καινὸν καὶ παλαιόν,
ἀΐδιον καὶ πρόσκαιρον,
φθαρτὸν καὶ ἄφθαρτον,
θνητὸν καὶ ἀθάνατον
τὸ τοῦ πάσχα μυστήριον.

((1) The Scripture of the Hebrew Exodus has been read, and the words of the mystery have been explained; how the sheep is sacrificed and how the people are saved. (2) Therefore, hear ye, beloved: thus the mystery of the Passover is new and old, eternal and transient, corruptible and incorruptible, mortal and immortal.)[1]

Fourth century

Ephraem, 'Encomium in honour of Basil the Great':[2]

Κλίνατέ μοι ἀκοάς,
ἀδελφοὶ ἀγαπητοί,
διηγήσομαι ὑμῖν
καλλίστην διήγησιν.

(Listen to me, beloved brethren. I will relate to you a beautiful tale.)

Fifth century

Basil of Seleucia, *Oratio in Herodiadem*:[3]

Τὴν τῆς Ἡρωδιάδος ὄρχησιν
ἡ τῶν Εὐαγγελίων σήμερον
ἡμῖν στηλιτεύει φωνή.

(The voice of the Gospel to-day proclaims to you the dance of Herodias.)

Sixth century

Romanus, *Kontakion of the Ten Virgins*:[4]

Τῆς ἱερᾶς παραβολῆς
τῆς ἐν εὐαγγελίοις
ἀκούσας τῶν παρθένων
ἐξέστην, ἐνθυμήσεις
καὶ λογισμοὺς ἀνακινῶν,
πῶς τὴν τῆς ἀχράντου
παρθενίας ἀρετὴν
αἱ δέκα μὲν ἐφύλαξαν

[1] *Studies and Documents*, xii. 168 (C. Bonner's translation). Cf. G. Zuntz, 'On the opening sentence of Melito's Paschal Homily', *The Harvard Theological Review*, xxxvi (1943), 299–315.

[2] *S. Ephraemi Syri Opera*, i, ed. S. J. Mercati (Rome, 1915), p. 143.

[3] *P.G.* lxxxv, c. 225. Other examples are given by P. Maas in his study on the Kontakion, *B.Z.* xix. 289.

[4] Pitra, *Analecta Sacra*, p. 78.

ταῖς πέντε δὲ παρθένοις
ἐγένετο
ἄκαρπος ὁ πόνος.

(Hearing the holy parable of the Virgins from the Gospel, I was distraught, revolving thoughts and reasonings: how it came about that the ten virgins preserved the virtue of undefiled virginity, while for five their toil was barren.)

The influence of Ephraem on Romanus has been shown in a study already mentioned by Wehofer on the 'Hymn on the Second Coming of Christ', by Romanus. Both were firm adherents of the Orthodox Church and held the same views on the much discussed dogmatic questions of Early Byzantine theology: Christology and Mariology. In his Kontakion on the *δευτέρα παρουσία* Romanus drew largely on Ephraem's sermons on the same subject. His dependence on Ephraem goes so far that some of the stanzas of his Kontakion are paraphrases of passages from Ephraem's homilies, and he follows his model so closely that not only the same thoughts but even the same words are used. The technique of Romanus can be studied, as has been done by Wehofer, by setting side by side a stanza of Romanus, the sixteenth Troparion, based on Matt. xxiv. 30–1, and the corresponding passage from Ephraem's homily:

Romanus[1]

Νύμφιε θεῖε, σωτὴρ ἡμῶν,
ἵνα δείξῃς[(2)] σου
τὴν ἀνείκαστον[(1)] δύναμιν[(2)]
ἀγγέλων[(4)] πάντων[(6)] τὰ τάγματα[(3)]
καὶ τῶν ἀρχαγγέλων[(5)]
ἀνυμνοῦντα προτρέχουσι[(7)]
πρὸ τοῦ θρόνου σου, κύριε·
φλὸξ[(8)] δὲ πέλουσιν[(9)] οὗτοι
πυρὸς[(10)] κατακαίουσα
καὶ τὴν γῆν ἐκκαθαίρουσα·
καὶ ποταμὸς[(11)] δὲ
πεπληρωμένος[(12)]
φρικτοῦ[(14)] πυρὸς[(13)] προτρέχει·[(7)]
Χερουβεὶμ[(15)] καὶ Σεραφεὶμ[(16)] δὲ

Ephraem

μετὰ δόξης[(2)] ἀνεικάστου[(1)]
προτρεχόντων[(7)] τῶν ταγμάτων[(3)]
ἐνώπιον τῆς δόξης αὐτοῦ
ἀγγέλων[(4)], ἀρχαγγέλων[(5)]
πάντες[(6)] φλόγες[(8)] πυρὸς[(10)] ὄντες[(9)]
καὶ ποταμὸς[(11)] πλήρης[(12)] πυρὸς[(13)]
ἐν φοβερῷ[(14)] ῥοιζήματι.
Χερουβὶμ[(15)] ἔχοντα τὸ βλέμμα κάτω
καὶ Σεραφὶμ[(16)] ἱστάμενοι
καὶ κρύβοντα τὰ πρόσωπα(17)
καὶ τοὺς πόδας ἐν τέσσαρσι πτέρυξι
τῶν πυρίνων[(16)] κεκραγότα μετὰ φρίκης

[1] Cf. T. W. Wehofer, 'Untersuchungen zum Lied des Romanos auf die Wiederkunft des Herrn', *Sitzber. d. Ak. d. Wiss. i. Wien, phil.-hist. Kl.* cliv (1907), 1–195. The *Canticum de Iudicio Extremo* was first published by Pitra in *Anal. Sacra*, pp. 35–43. A textual-critical edition was made by K. Krumbacher in 'Studien zu Romanos', *Sb. B.A.* (1898), pp. 163–83; G. Cammelli's edition of the Kontakion, op. cit., pp. 215–49, is based on Krumbacher's edition. The sixteenth Troparion is analysed by Wehofer in his study, pp. 82–8.

μετὰ τρόμου[17] *λειτουργοῦσι·*
καὶ δοξολογοῦσι
λέγοντες[18] *ἀπαύστως*
τὸν ὕμνον τὸν τρισάγιον·[19]
τὰ πρόσωπα κρύπτουσι[17]
κραυγάζοντα· Δόξα σοι,
Κριτὰ δικαιότατε.

καὶ λέγοντα[18] *ἕτερον πρὸς ἕτερον·*
τρισάγιος,[19]
τρισάγιος,[19]
τρισάγιος[19] *ὁ κύριος.*

(*Romanus*:

Divine Bridegroom, our Saviour, that Thou mayest show Thine incomparable power, all the ranks of the Angels and Archangels, praising Thee in song, run forth before Thy throne, O Lord: They flit as a flame of fire which burns and cleanses the world; and a stream runs forth filled full of awful fire. Cherubim and Seraphim serve Thee in fear and glorify Thee, singing incessantly the thrice holy hymn. They cover their faces and cry aloud: glory to Thee, most righteous Judge.)

There is, however, a marked difference between the two poets: Ephraem is verbose, Romanus concise; he uses half as many words as his predecessor to describe the same situation. There is further, at least by Western aesthetic standards, a difference of poetical quality between the hymn-writers: Ephraem has written, for example, most excellent hymns on the Nativity; but they cannot match the effect of the famous hymn of Romanus, beginning with the words:

Ἡ παρθένος σήμερον
τὸν ὑπερούσιον τίκτει
καὶ ἡ γῆ τὸ σπήλαιον
τῷ ἀπροσίτῳ προσάγει.
ἄγγελοι μετὰ ποιμένων
δοξολογοῦσι,
μάγοι δὲ μετὰ ἀστέρος
ὁδοιποροῦσι·
δι' ἡμᾶς γὰρ ἐγεννήθη
παιδίον νέον
ὁ πρὸ αἰώνων θεός.

(The Virgin to-day bears the Superessential and the earth brings the cave to the unapproachable. Angels give praise with shepherds and Magi journey with a star. For the God who is before the ages was born for us a young child.)

Romanus is the *poeta vere Christianus* of the age of Justinian. His Christology is closely related to that which was made the basis of civil law by the Emperor in his *Codex*. He glorifies the Nativity, the Life, and Passion of Christ, the mystery of the relation of the two Natures in Christ. His religious practice is that of the average Byzantine Orthodox Christian, whose adoration includes an ever-increasing circle of saints and martyrs;[1] but he shares with him the polemic spirit against heretics and pagans. His Kontakia contain violent outbursts against Nestorius and Eutyches, as well as against the spirit of ancient Greek poetry and philosophy; they occur suddenly and most effectively, and demonstrate the homiletical character of the Kontakion far more convincingly than investigation on historical or philological lines could do.

Let us take as an example the Hymn on Pentecost,[2] based on Acts ii, describing the miracle of the descent of the Holy Spirit. In dramatic language Romanus assures his listeners that all who believe in Christ shall 'speak one word, not many and proclaim one God, not many'.[3] The Kontakion seems to have come to an end with the profession of the Creed. But with the eighteenth Troparion Romanus suddenly changes the subject. He asks, should not those who speak 'with other tongues' rank before all others? And he continues:[4]

(18) *Τί φυσῶσι καὶ βαμβαίνουσιν*
οἱ Ἕλληνες;
τί φαντάζονται πρὸς Ἄρατον
τὸν τρισκατάρατον;
τί πλανῶνται πρὸς Πλάτωνα;
Δημοσθένην τί στέργουσι
τὸν ἀσθενῆ;
τί μὴ ὁρῶσιν Ὅμηρον
ὄνειρον ἀργόν;
τί Πυθαγόραν θρυλοῦσι
τὸν δικαίως φιμωθέντα;
τί δὲ καὶ μὴ τρέχουσι
καὶ σέβουσιν οἷς ἐνεφανίσθη
τὸ πανάγιον Πνεῦμα;

[1] A complete edition of the poetical works of Romanus by P. Maas is still unpublished. For the time being the collections by Pitra, Christ, Krumbacher, Maas, Cammelli, and Mioni must be consulted. Prose translations in English of the 'Ode for a dead Brother' and the 'Death of S. John the Baptist' by Tillyard have been published in his *Byz. Music and Hymnography*.

[2] *Analecta sacra*, pp. 157–64.

[3] Ibid., p. 163.

[4] Ibid., p. 164.

(19) Ὑμνήσωμεν, ἀδελφοί,
τῶν μαθητῶν τὰς γλώσσας,
ὅτι οὐ λόγῳ κομψῷ,
ἀλλ' ἐν δυνάμει θείᾳ
ἐζώγρησαν πάντας· . . .

(Why do the Greeks boast and puff themselves up? Why do they dream of Aratos the thrice accursed? Why do they err after Plato? Why do they love Demosthenes the feeble? Why do they not see that Homer is a vain dream? Why do they prate of Pythagoras who rightly has been silenced? And why do they not hasten and honour those to whom the All-holy Spirit appeared?—Let us praise, brethren, the voices of the disciples, because they captured all men by divine power, and not by fine words.)

Romanus, in his revolt against the greatest minds of the Classical world, is not unaware of their greatness. But it must be remembered that he does not address his audience as a rhetorician but as a preacher speaking from the pulpit, like his predecessors the three Cappadocians or John Chrysostom. Like the latter he contrasts the Christian ideas and ideals with those of the Greek thinkers, orators, and poets, and tries to create in the minds of his audience appreciation of the divine truth, conveyed by the words of the Apostle, which Romanus takes from the Gospel and paraphrases in a diction no less poetical than that of the greatest classical authors.[1]

Romanus is the outstanding figure in Byzantine hymnography. Until the twelfth century his Kontakion on the Nativity was sung every year at Christmas, during dinner in the Imperial Palace, by a double choir of singers from Sancta Sophia and the Church of the Apostles.[2] His fame was, indeed, so great that he was considered the paramount Melodos, and more Kontakia than he wrote were ascribed to him in order to heighten their value. Thus, as has already been mentioned, we read in the title of Codex Grottaferrata *E β* vii—which in its main part is a Kontakarion, a cycle of Kontakia for the ecclesiastical year—that this Psaltikon (i.e. the book for the Soloist) is the work of the 'Melode

[1] The polemic spirit in the poems of Romanus has been criticized by P. Maas in his study 'Die Chronologie der Hymnen des Romanos', *B.Z.* (1906), pp. 1–44. We may, however, understand the attitude of Romanus better by comparing his passages against the Greeks with those of a great contemporary poet, Paul Claudel, when the author speaks in his 'Magnificat' as *defensor fidei* in an age filled with the spirit of religious indifference: 'Restez avec moi, Seigneur, parce que le soir approche et ne m'abandonnez pas! — Ne me perdez point avec les Voltaire, et les Renan, et les Michelet, et les Hugo, et tous les autres infâmes!' *Cinq Grandes Odes* (1907), p. 108.

[2] Pitra, *Anal. sacra*, p. xxi.

Romanus'. The ascription of all the Kontakia to Romanus is obviously an exaggerated tribute, as can be seen from the large number of Melodoi whose names appear in the Kontakaria, and the figure of thousand Kontakia mentioned in the Synaxaria should be understood merely to indicate his great productivity [1]

The uncertainty of authorship is particularly embarrassing in the case of the most famous hymn of the Byzantine Church, the 'Akathistos' (*Ἀκάθιστος ὕμνος*).*[2] We learn from the Patmos Codex of the Typikon of Constantinople, which represents the Ritual of the tenth century,[3] that the hymn was sung either during the Vigil of the Saturday in the middle of Lent or during that of the following Saturday.[4] The titles of the hymn in the Kontakaria, however, indicate that the Akathistos was originally sung on the feast of the Annunciation, on 25 March. It is now sung in four sections during Matins of the first, second, third, and fourth Sunday in Lent, and *in toto* during the Vigil of the fifth Saturday in Lent. That day, the 'Sabbath of the Akathistos Hymn', has a special office.[5]

The Akathistos hymn has in early manuscripts two Prooemia, one which serves as an introduction to the content, the other which praises the Theotokos as saviour of Constantinople and commemorates her victory by this hymn of thanksgiving. In the 'Office of the Akathistos' the first Prooemium *Τὸ προσταχθὲν μυστικῶς* . . . (the Angel, understanding the secret command . . .) is first separated from the hymn and placed as Apolytikion (*ἀπολυτίκιον*) at the end of Vespers. In the Office of the Orthros, i.e. Matins, it precedes the second Prooemium *Τῇ ὑπερμάχῳ στρατηγῷ τὰ νικητήρια* (To the invincible Leader I, thy City, freed from danger, dedicate the thanksgiving for victory . . .) which, as will be seen, is of a later date than the first one.

[1] See the Index of Melodoi in N. B. Tomadikis's edition of the works of Romanos, *Ῥωμανοῦ τοῦ Μελῳδοῦ ὕμνοι*, ii (Athens, 1954), 363 sqq.

[2] The name Akathistos (α *privativum* and *καθίζειν*) means that the hymn was sung not sitting, i.e. standing.

[3] Cf. A. Baumstark, 'Das Typikon der Patmos Hs. 266 und die altkonstantinopolitanische Gottesdienstordnung', *J.L.* vi. 98–111.

[4] *καὶ οἵαν ἑβδομάδα τῶν νηστειῶν κελεύει ὁ πατριάρχης εἴτε τῇ μέσῃ, εἴτε τῇ μετὰ ταύτην ἑβδομάδι γίνεται ἡ παννυχὶς ἐν Βλαχέρναις οὕτως.* A. Dmitrievsky, *Opisanie liturgicheskikh rukopisei*, i (Typika), Kiev, 1895, p. 124.

[5] Cf. P. de Meester's Greek and Latin edition of the *Ἀκολουθία τοῦ Ἀκαθίστου ὕμνου εἰς τὴν ὑπεραγίαν θεοτόκον—Officio dell'inno Acatisto in onore della Santa Madre del Dio*, Rome, 1903.

The Akathistos[1] has a form unique in Byzantine hymnography. It is a Kontakion of twenty-four stanzas, forming an acrostic of the letters of the alphabet. The Kontakion is divided into two main sections, each of twelve stanzas. The content of the first group is the story of Christ from the Annunciation to the flight into Egypt and Simeon's recognition of God in the Child Jesus. The second part contains the praise of the Mystery of the Incarnation and a comment on its effect upon mankind, ending with a prayer to the Mother of God. The formal uniqueness of the Akathistos consists in the blending of the Kontakion with a garland of Salutations (*χαιρετισμοί*) which are appended to the odd stanzas. These odd stanzas have the same refrain as the Prooemium:[2] 'Hail, Bride unwedded' (*Χαῖρε, νύμφη ἀνύμφευτε*), the even stanzas the refrain 'Alleluia' (*Ἀλληλούια*).

In his narrative of the events from the message of the Angel to the flight into Egypt the poet makes extensive use of direct speech in the dialogues between the Angel and the Virgin, in the salutations of John the Baptist, the shepherds, the Magi, Simeon, the crowds of the strangers and the faithful and, finally, of the poet himself. Two heterogeneous elements of poetry are blended together with great skill and effect: the dramatic in the description of events and situations, and the lyrical in the panegyrics to the Virgin.[3] The formal problem is handled with great ingenuity. Twelve Troparia, each consisting of nineteen lines and the refrain *Χαῖρε, νύμφη ἀνύμφευτε*, alternate with an equal number of shorter stanzas consisting of seven lines and the refrain *Ἀλληλούια*. Each of the twelve Troparia of twenty lines consists of two equal parts. In the first seven lines the poet describes the events and introduces the *dramatis personae*, frequently by direct speech; in the second part he praises the Theotokos through the voices of the Angel, of the saints, of the narrator, and the crowd, in the style of the Early Christian litanies.[4] The Troparia of seven lines and the Alleluia-refrain correspond in their content to the first parts of the extended Troparia.

[1] The problems of the form of the Akathistos, its origin, and background, are discussed in my paper 'The "Akathistos". A Study in Byzantine Hymnography', *Dumbarton Oaks Papers*, ix and x (1956), 141–74, and my book *The Akathistos Hymn*, *M.M.B. Transcripta*, vol. ix (1957), Introduction, pp. vii–xcii, Transcription, pp. 3–88.

[2] Both Prooemia have, in fact, the same refrain; but I refer to the original Prooemium (Koukoulion) *Τὸ προσταχθέν*, whereas the second one took the already existing refrain from the hymn.

[3] The adoration of the Virgin in Byzantine poetry is the subject of a study by J.-B. Thibaut, *Panégyrique de l'Immaculée* (1909).

[4] Cf. A. Baumstark, 'Ein frühchristliches Theotokion', *O.C.*, N.S. ix (1920), 36–61.

By addressing the Theotokos with an unending stream of attributes the poet created a poem[1] which combines the features of the Kontakion with those of the Litany, as can be seen from the first Troparion, describing the appearance and salutation of the Angel:

Ἄγγελος πρωτοστάτης
οὐρανόθεν ἐπέμφθη
εἰπεῖν τῇ θεοτόκῳ τὸ Χαῖρε.
καὶ σὺν τῇ ἀσωμάτῳ φωνῇ
σωματούμενόν σε θεωρῶν, Κύριε,
ἐξίστατο καὶ ἵστατο,
κραυγάζων πρὸς αὐτὴν τοιαῦτα·
Χαῖρε, δι' ἧς ἡ χαρὰ ἐκλάμψει·
Χαῖρε, δι' ἧς ἡ ἀρὰ ἐκλείψει·
Χαῖρε, τοῦ πεσόντος Ἀδὰμ ἡ ἀνάκλησις·
Χαῖρε, τῶν δακρύων τῆς Εὔας ἡ λύτρωσις·
Χαῖρε, ὕψος δυσανάβατον ἀνθρωπίνοις λογισμοῖς·
Χαῖρε, βάθος δυσθεώρητον καὶ ἀγγέλων ὀφθαλμοῖς·
Χαῖρε, ὅτι ὑπάρχεις βασιλέως καθέδρα·
Χαῖρε, ὅτι βαστάζεις τὸν βαστάζοντα πάντα·
Χαῖρε, ἀστὴρ ἐμφαίνων τὸν ἥλιον·
Χαῖρε, γαστὴρ ἐνθέου σαρκώσεως·
Χαῖρε, δι' ἧς νεουργεῖται ἡ κτίσις·
Χαῖρε, δι' ἧς βρεφουργεῖται ὁ Κτίστης·
Χαῖρε, νύμφη ἀνύμφευτε.

(A captain of the angels was sent from heaven to say to the Virgin 'Hail!', and seeing Thee, Lord, become corporeal, he was amazed and stood still and cried out to her with incorporeal voice: 'Hail, thou through whom joy will shine forth! Hail, thou through whom the curse will be lifted. Hail, Restoration of the fallen Adam. Hail, Redemption of the tears of Eve. Hail, Summit inaccessible to human minds. Hail, Depth scarce visible even to angels' eyes. Hail, because thou art the seat of the King. Hail, because thou bearest the Bearer of all. Hail, Star who makest visible the Sun. Hail, Womb of the divine Incarnation. Hail, thou through whom the creation is regenerated. Hail, thou through whom the Creator becometh a babe. Hail Bride unwedded.')

[1] For parallels to the blending of narrative and panegyric elements in earlier homiletical prose-poetry see, e.g., the *Encomium in S. Mariam Deiparam*, by Cyril of Alexandria, *P.G.* lxxvii, c. 1032 D.

Χαίροις Μαρία τὸ κειμήλιον τῆς οἰκουμένης·
Χαίροις Μαρία ἡ περιστερὰ ἡ ἀμίαντος·
Χαίροις Μαρία ἡ λαμπὰς ἡ ἄσβεστος· κτλ.

The question whether the hymn is the work of Romanus or of another Melodos has been widely discussed during the past fifty years, i.e. from the moment the question of the date of Romanus had been settled and it was an established fact that he came to Constantinople during the reign of the Emperor Anastasius I (491–518).[1] The attribution of the Akathistos to Romanus was questioned on the basis of two arguments. The first one was that in some manuscripts the hymn is ascribed to the Patriarch Sergius,[2] in others to George Pisides,[3] in the Latin version to the Patriarch Germanus,[4] and by Papadopoulos-Kerameus even to Photius.[5] In a single manuscript only, in Cod. Thessalonic. Blataion 41, fol. 193, the name of Romanus appears as an alternative to Sergius:

οὗτοι οἱ θεῖοι οἶκοί εἰσιν ὥς τινες λέγουσι Σεργίου τοῦ τηνικαῦτα τὸν . . . Κωνσταντινουπόλεως· ἄλλοι δὲ τοῦ θείου Ῥωμανοῦ [διακόνου] τοῦ μελῳδοῦ. δῆλον δέ ἐστιν ἀπὸ τῶν ἐλ. . . .[6]

(These divine stanzas are, as some say, the work of Sergius, at that time . . . of Constantinople; according to others, however, the work of the divine Romanus, deacon and hymn-writer. . . .)

The second argument in favour of one of the three Patriarchs of Constantinople—Sergius in the seventh, Germanus in the eighth, Photius in the ninth century—was the fact that the 'Akathistos' was regarded as a 'Hymn of Victory' because of its Prooemium in which Constantinople praises the Theotokos for having saved 'Her City'[7] from deadly peril. The hymn, therefore,

[1] A. Papadopoulos-Kerameus found in Codex 30 of the University Library in Messina the report of a miracle which happened during the reign of the Emperor Heraclius (611–41): a boy was healed while he sang the Troparia of the 'humble Romanus'. Cf. his article "Ὁ χρόνος τῆς ἀκμῆς τοῦ Ῥωμανοῦ", *Νέα Ἡμέρα*, xxix (Sept. 1905). Romanus must have lived in the sixth century, since he was known in the seventh century. Papadopoulos's discovery made it impossible to place Romanus in the eighth century.

[2] Cf. W. Christ–M. Paranikas, *Anthologia gr. carm. christ.*, p. 140; J.-B. Pitra, *Analecta Sacra*, i. 250.

[3] Migne, *P.G.* xcii, c. 1353 sqq.

[4] Cf. M. Huglo, 'L'Ancienne version latine de l'hymne acathiste', *Muséon*, lxiv (1951), 44–61. Huglo ascribes the Prooemium to Germanus, but points out that his investigation into the Old Latin version produced no argument against Romanus's authorship.

[5] A. Papadopoulos-Kerameus "Ὁ Ἀκάθιστος ὕμνος, οἱ Ῥῶς καὶ ὁ πατριάρχης Φώτιος", *Βιβλ. Μαρασλῆ*, vol. ccxiv (Athens, 1903).

[6] Cf. C. Émereau, 'Hymnographi Byzantini. Acathisti Auctor', *E.O.* xxi (1922), 259–63.

[7] Cf. N. Baynes, 'The Supernatural Defenders of Constantinople', *Mélanges Paul Peeters I*, *Analecta Bollandiana*, lxvii (1949), 172. The article is reprinted in N. Baynes, *Byzantine Studies and other Essays* (London, 1955), pp. 248–60.

was connected with one of the sieges which threatened Constantinople. In the Synaxar[1] for the Akathistos the singing of the hymn is mentioned in connexion with the following three sieges: (1) in 626 by the Avars, Persians, and Slavs in the days of Heraclius when, in the absence of the Emperor, the Patriarch Sergius raised the spirit of the defenders and, after the miraculous liberation of the City, intoned the Akathistos in the Church of the Theotokos in the Blachernae-quarter. (2) 673–7 by the Arabs in the reign of the Emperor Constantine Pogonatus. (3) 717–18 under Leo III, the Isaurian, which ended with the destruction of the fleet of the Arabs and the lifting of the siege on 15 August 718. According to the Synaxar the Patriarch Germanus sang the hymn in the night after the victory in the same church and the people responded with the refrain. In commemoration of the victory it is said the singing of the Akathistos was repeated every year during the Vigil of the feast of the Annunciation on 25 March. The Russian siege of 860 is not mentioned in the Synaxar, and it was chiefly A. Papadopoulos-Kerameus who supported the Photian authorship. But his pamphlet[2] was rejected by M. Thearvic in an article for which P. V. Winterfeld had provided material from his at that time unpublished study of the old Latin version of the Akathistos in a ninth-century St. Gall MS.[3] Printed, however, in journals which were not easily accessible to Byzantinists Thearvic's article and Winterfeld's study, which was soon afterwards published,[4] passed practically unnoticed; we shall see later how important the evidence from the Latin version turned out to be.

The first decade of this century proved to be the most fertile for the investigation of the poetical and theological background of the Akathistos, and it became clear that the Christological problems of the Akathistos were those of the age of Romanus, expounded by him in some of his other Kontakia.[5]

1 Printed in Migne, *P.G.*, xcii, c. 1348–53. The Synaxaria are the equivalent to the Western *Acta Sanctorum*.

2 Cf. p. 194 note 5.

3 M. Thearvic, 'Photius et l'Acathiste', *E.O.* vii (1904), 293–300.

4 Cf. P. V. Winterfeld, 'Ein abendländisches Zeugnis über den *ὕμνος ἀκάθιστος* der griechischen Kirche', *Zeitschrift f. deutsches Altertum u. deutsche Litteratur*, Bd. 47 (1904), pp. 81–8.

5 The main articles in which these questions have been discussed are: P. Maas's review of P. de Meester's articles on the Akathistos in *Bessarione*, Ser. II, vols. vi (1904), vii (1905), in *B.Z.*, xiv (1905), 644. See also P. Maas, 'Die Chronologie d. Hymnen d. Romanos', *B.Z.* xv (1906), 1–45; 'Das Kontakion', *B.Z.* xix (1910), 285–306; A. Baumstark's review of J. Strzygowski's book *Der serbische Psalter*, *B.Z.* xvi (1907), 656–8; P. F. Krypiakiewicz, 'De hymni Acathisti auctore',

Although, as work progressed, the scales turned more and more in favour of Romanus's authorship of the Akathistos, it needed evidence on which to base a new approach to the question, i.e. to disprove the view, suggested by the Synaxaria, that the Akathistos was composed as a 'Hymn of Victory'. In his study *De Hymni Acathisti auctore*, P. F. Krypiakiewicz had clearly shown[1] that of the two Prooemia of the Akathistos, the *Τὸ προσταχθὲν μυστικῶς λαβὼν ἐν γνώσει* (understanding the secret command) must be the original one; first, it follows the usual pattern and gives the *argumentum*, the content in brief, of the following Kontakion; secondly, it has the same refrain as the Kontakion; thirdly, it is composed of words and phrases to be found in the Kontakion. Krypiakiewicz' argument was, indeed, so conclusive that it was accepted by C. del Grande in his study and edition of the Akathistos.[2]

It was Dom Huglo's publication of the Latin version[3] of the Synaxarium, the Prooemium and the twenty-four stanzas of the Akathistos from Codex Paris, Bibliothèque Mazarine 693, foll. 109 v.–115 v. which made it evident that Photius and the Russian siege of 860 had to be discarded, because the Patriarch Germanus and details of the siege are mentioned in the Latin version which, on the evidence of its vocabulary, must have been made 'between the third-fourth of the eighth century and the middle of the ninth', though the manuscript dates from the end of the eleventh or the beginning of the twelfth century. This date is supported by the old Latin version in the St. Gall MS. which, as has already been mentioned, was published by Winterfeld in 1904, but remained unnoticed, until Dom Huglo referred to it. The St. Gall MS. C.78 has only the Synaxarium and the beginning of the Hymnus; but since the text in this ninth-century manuscript corresponds to that of the later manuscripts, Dom Huglo is correct in assuming that all these manuscripts go back to an even earlier manuscript which is lost.

Comparison of the Latin text with the Greek text provided

B.Z. xviii (1909), 357–82. A survey of these articles is given in my paper 'The "Akathistos". A Study in Byzantine Hymnography', *Dumbarton Oaks Papers*, ix–x (1956), 143–74, and in my book *The Akathistos Hymn*, *M.M.B. Transcripta*, vol. ix (1957), pp. xx–xxxiii.

[1] *B.Z.* xviii. 361.

[2] C. del Grande, *L'Inno acatisto* (Florence, 1948), p. 17.

[3] Dom M. Huglo, 'L'Ancienne version latine de l'hymne acathiste', *Muséon*, tome lxiv (1951), pp. 27–61.

further evidence for an early dating of the Akathistos. The examination of the Latin text showed that it differed from that of the best Greek manuscripts in exactly the same words and phrases as the manuscripts written in the Basilean monasteries in south Italy and Sicily. This peculiar version of the Akathistos, however, did not originate in south Italy and Sicily, as was the general opinion, but came from the St. Catherine's monastery on Mount Sinai[1] as can be seen from the text of the Akathistos in the tenth-century Kontakarion, Codex Vindob. suppl. gr. 96, which came from Mount Sinai and has the same divergencies from the text based on the Constantinopolitanean version, as the south Italian Greek Codices and, consequently, that of the Bibliothèque Mazarine in Paris, which contains the Latin text.

If we take into account (1) the time which must have passed before the Latin copies were made from the lost original, (2) the time it must have taken for the hymn to become so famous that a Latin translation was considered desirable, (3) the fact that the translation was made from the Sinaitic version—which differs so widely from the original that considerable time must have passed for these variants to arise—we must come to the conclusion that the Akathistos hymn itself—without the Prooemium *Τῇ ὑπερμάχῳ στρατηγῷ* must belong to the period in which the Kontakion flourished; this was the age of Romanus.

[1] Cf. E. Wellesz, 'The Akathistos', *Dumbarton Oaks Papers*, ix and x (1956), 165; *The Akathistos Hymn*, *M.M.B. Transcripta*, ix (1957), pp. xxiii–iv.

CHAPTER IX

THE POETICAL FORMS: (II) KANON

I. ORIGIN AND DEVELOPMENT

THE last period of Byzantine hymnography began towards the end of the seventh century, with the introduction of the Kanon (κανών) into the *Orthros*, the Morning Office. The Kanon is a complex poetical form, made up of nine Odes (ᾠδαί), each of which originally consisted of from six to nine Troparia. At a later date, owing to the introduction of a number of additional monostrophic stanzas, only three of the Troparia of each Ode were used in the service. Structurally, therefore, the Ode is no different from a short Kontakion; the difference between the two forms lies in their content. The Kontakion is a poetical homily; the nine Odes of every Kanon are modelled on the pattern of the Nine Canticles from the Scriptures and have the character of hymns of praise. Whatever the object of a Kanon may be—the celebration of a feast of Christ or the Theotokos, or the commemoration of a saint or a martyr—the hymn-writer had to allude in each of the nine Odes to its scriptural model.

Originally Kanons were composed only for Lent; at a later date, for the period between Easter and Pentecost.[1] The new hymns replaced the singing of the canticles, which from now onwards were only recited and were followed by the singing of the Kanons. At a later date, when Kanons were composed for all the feast days of the ecclesiastical year, the custom of reciting the Canticles before the singing of the Kanons was maintained during Lent and between Easter and Pentecost; on other days the canticles were omitted and replaced by the Kanons.[2] The second Ode, modelled on the canticle 'Give ear, O ye heavens' (Deut. xxxii. 1–43), was, on account of its mournful character, only used in Lent, and in consequence Kanons destined for other parts of the ecclesiastical year were subsequently composed without the second Ode.

[1] Cf. A. Baumstark, 'Psalmenvortrag und Kirchendichtung des Orients', *Gottesminne*, vii. 8 (1912–13), p. 551.

[2] Cf. A. Baumstark, *Liturgie comparée* (1939), pp. 28–9.

Before entering into a more detailed examination of the new poetical genre we shall try to explain the reasons for the replacement of the Kontakion by the Kanon. In all the histories of Byzantine literature the view is put forward that, artistically, the Kontakia rank higher than the Kanons. Western scholars, therefore, find it difficult to understand how it was possible for the Kanon to displace the older form of ecclesiastical poetry in such a short time and so completely that only a few isolated stanzas from Kontakia remained in liturgical use. It was Pitra alone, whose judgement on all questions of Byzantine hymnography can still be regarded as the most authoritative, who provided an explanation. He pointed out that the new Melodes composed most of their hymns in the dark days of the Iconoclastic controversy. The hymn-writers of this period, threatened with persecution, exile, and death, were no longer preoccupied with the elegance of their diction, but only with the expression of the sombre mood of their age in their 'rough and passionate songs'.[1]

From the days of Justinian, and the development of monasticism on a broader basis, the mystical element in Byzantine theology penetrates every form of Byzantine piety. It permeates the works in the new poetical form, the Kanons, which obviously reflected the religious ideas and the atmosphere of the Byzantine Church at its height better than the poems of earlier generations of hymn-writers. Instead of the homiletic style of the narrator, heightened by the introduction of direct speech, which is characteristic of the Kontakion, we now find hymns of praise in an exultant or eschatological mood, expressing dogmatic ideas by the means of reiteration and variation. These highly elaborate repetitions produce in the listeners a mystical mood, which was intensified by the solemnity of the ritual, and the visual impression of the icons. Direct speech, already known from the Kontakia, now occurs to such an extent that the effect of this kind of poetry on the listener is sometimes almost that of a mystery play. On the feast of the Annunciation of Our Lady on 25 March, for example, the Pericope from the Gospel (Luke i. 26–38) is turned by Theophanes Graptos into a Kanon, composed—except for the first stanza of the first Ode and the whole of the ninth Ode—in the form of a dialogue between the Angel and the

[1] Pitra, *Anal. sacra*, p. xxxvii.

Theotokos.[1] The dialogue, opened by the Angel, begins with the second stanza of the first Ode:

ᾠδὴ α΄.

Ἀδέτω σοι, δέσποινα,
  κινῶν τὴν λύραν τοῦ πνεύματος
Δαυῒδ ὁ προπάτωρ σου·
  ἄκουσον, θύγατερ,
τὴν χαρμοσύνην
  φωνὴν πρὸς τοῦ ἀγγέλου·
χαρὰν γὰρ μηνύει σοι
  τὴν ἀνεκλάλητον.

Ὁ ἄγγελος.

Βοῶ σοι γηθόμενος·
  κλῖνον τὸ οὖς σου καὶ πρόσχες μοι
θεοῦ καταγγέλλοντι
  σύλληψιν ἄσπορον·
εὗρες χάριν γὰρ
  ἐνώπιον κυρίου
ἣν εὗρεν οὐδέποτε
  ἄλλη τις, πάναγνε.

Ἡ θεοτόκος.

Γνωσθήτω μοι, ἄγγελε,
  τῶν σῶν ῥημάτων ἡ δύναμις·
πῶς ἔσται ὃ εἴρηκας;
  λέγε σαφέστατα,
πῶς συλλήψομαι
  παρθένος οὖσα κόρη;
πῶς δὲ καὶ γενήσομαι
  μήτηρ τοῦ κτίσαντος;

Ὁ ἄγγελος.

Δολίως με φθέγγεσθαι
  διαλογίζῃ, ὡς ἔοικε,
καὶ χαίρω θεώμενος
  τὴν σὴν ἀσφάλειαν·
θάρσει, δέσποινα·
  θεοῦ γὰρ βουλομένου
ῥᾳδίως περαίνεται
  καὶ τὰ παράδοξα.

[1] Cf. *Κανὼν εἰς τὸν εὐαγγελισμὸν τῆς θεοτόκου.* Christ and Paranikas, *Anth. gr.*, pp. 236–42.

(David, thy forefather, O lady, shall sing to thee, plucking the lyre of the spirit; listen, O daughter, to the joyful voice of the angel, for he announces to thee an inexpressible joy.

The Angel: In joy I cry to thee. Incline thine ear and listen to me announcing the unbegotten conception of God. For thou hast found favour before the Lord as no other has ever found, O immaculate.

The Mother of God: Make known to me, O Angel, the meaning of your words, how shall what you have said come to pass. Speak plainly: how am I, being a maid, to conceive, and how am I to become the mother of the Creator?

The Angel: It appears that you believe me to be speaking deceitfully, and yet I rejoice to see your circumspection. Take courage, O lady, for, through the will of God, even the incredible is easily accomplished.)

The first, third, fourth, fifth, and sixth Odes are built up of four stanzas. Each stanza begins with a letter of the alphabet (*Ἡ ἀκροστιχὶς κατ' ἀλφάβητον*), in order. The last two Odes, the eighth and ninth, each of them built up of six stanzas, have their own alphabetic acrostic. In the eighth Ode the scheme is as follows. The stanzas have eight lines. In the first stanza the second letter of the alphabet is put at the beginning of the third line, the third letter at the beginning of the fourth, the fourth letter at the beginning of the fifth:

Ἄκουε, κόρη παρθένε ἁγνή,
εἰπάτω δὴ ὁ Γαβριὴλ
Βουλὴν ὑψίστου ἀρχαίαν ἀληθινήν.
Γενοῦ πρὸς ὑποδοχὴν ἑτοίμη θεοῦ·
Διὰ σοῦ γὰρ ὁ ἀχώρητος
βροτοῖς ἀναστραφήσεται·
διὸ καὶ χαίρων βοῶ·
(*Refrain*) *εὐλογεῖτε πάντα τὰ ἔργα Κυρίου τὸν Κύριον.*

(Listen, O pure Virgin, let Gabriel announce the old and true counsel of the Most High. Prepare for the reception of God; for, through thee the Boundless is to dwell among mortals. Therefore joyfully I cry: praise ye the Lord, all ye works of the Lord.)

The same scheme is used throughout the Ode.

In the ninth Ode, too, each stanza contains four letters of the acrostic, but the scheme is a different one: the stanzas are built up of seven lines, and the order of the letters is reversed. The acrostic begins with *Ω* and ends with *A*, as can be seen from the first stanza of the ninth Ode:

῾Ως ἐμψύχῳ θεοῦ κιβωτῷ
Ψαυέτω μηδαμῶς χεὶρ ἀμυήτων·
Χείλη δὲ πιστῶν τῇ θεοτόκῳ ἀσιγήτως
Φωνὴν τοῦ ἀγγέλου ἀναμέλποντα
ἐν ἀγαλλιάσει βοάτω·
(*Refrain*) Χαῖρε κεχαριτωμένη·
ὁ Κύριος μετὰ σοῦ.

(The hand of the uninitiated must not touch the living Ark of the Lord. The lips of the faithful shall cry in ecstasy to the Mother of God, and never cease, echoing the voice of the angel: 'Hail, full of grace, the Lord is with thee.')

The introduction of a different type of acrostic into the two last Odes is contrary to the custom of Byzantine hymnographers. W. Christ, therefore, maintains that these two last Odes were added by John Monachus.[1] This fact, however, would not explain the ending of the first acrostic at the close of the seventh Ode, which is not in conformity with the general practice of extending the acrostic over the whole poem. The problem, therefore, remains open for further investigation.

The most significant difference between Kontakion and Kanon lies in the increased use, and the greater variety, of the music in the new poetical genre. All the stanzas of a Kontakion are sung to the melody of the Hirmus, which is kept, as far as we can gather, to a simple syllabic type, in which preponderance is given to the words of the hymn. The Kanon had originally nine, but in later usage mostly eight, different Hirmi, sung to a small number of Troparia in each Ode. This fact alone may be taken as a sign that in the new genre the weight had shifted from the words to the music. But the music itself was of a different type. Originally there may have been no marked difference between the music of the Hirmus of a Kontakion and that of a Kanon. But Byzantine music shows such a marked tendency to become increasingly florid[2] that we are entitled to assume that the music of the Hirmi of the Kanons changed at a relatively early date from its originally strictly syllabic structure to a more ornamented style, which made use of groups of two or three notes set to a single syllable of the text.

[1] Cf. *Anth. gr.*, p. 236, footnote.

[2] See the study of the present writer on Ὅτε τῷ σταυρῷ—*O quando in cruce* in 'Eastern Elements in Western Chant', *M.M.B.*, Amer. Ser., vol. i.

The Odes of the Annunciation Kanon were sung to melodies from Odes of other Kanons. The first Ode was sung to the melody of the first Ode of the Kanon *Ἀνοίξω τὸ στόμα μου* on the feast of the anniversary of the death of the Theotokos; it runs, according to Cod. Iviron 470, fol. 65r., as follows:

If the four stanzas of the first Ode of the Annunciation Kanon are sung to this melody, it will be seen how admirably the words fit the music.

The tendency of the Orthodox Church to transfer the emphasis from the words to the music, which had its origin in the increasing splendour of the service, may explain why the study of the Kanons is less attractive from the literary point of view than that of the Kontakia. From the liturgical point of view, however, words and music form an indissoluble whole, and the examination of the music will show that the melodies cannot be studied and appreciated without the texts from which they receive their expression and rhythmical nuances. But the question still remains to be answered of why the Orthodox Church eliminated the Kontakia at the end of the seventh century and replaced them by the Kanons.[1] The reason for this change may be found in the development and the expansion of the liturgy.

[1] See the present writer's paper 'Kontakion and Kanon', *Atti del Congresso Internazionale di Musica sacra Rome 1950* (Tournai, 1952), pp. 131–3.

The great period of homiletics came to an end in the fourth century and was followed, as is generally accepted, by the decline of the art of rhetoric. Its place in liturgy was taken by the poetical homily which finally developed into the Kontakion. By the nineteenth Canon of the Council *in Trullo* (692) the daily preaching, especially on Sundays, was made obligatory for all the higher clergy.[1] This is exactly the date of the replacement of the Kontakion by the Kanon. We may assume that the Kontakion sung after the reading of the Gospel in the Morning Office had to make way for the sermon of the preacher. But as the liturgy needed the embellishment of hymns, the singing of the Kanons, which had hitherto been customary only during Lent and between Easter and Pentecost, was introduced throughout the entire ecclesiastical year. This liturgical change, caused by the reintroduction of the spoken sermon, seems to have been the decisive factor in eliminating the Kontakion and in introducing the Kanon.

Byzantine hagiography ascribes the invention of the Kanon to Andrew of Crete, who was born at Damascus *c.* 660 and died as Bishop of Crete *c.* 740.[2] Though his orthodoxy was doubted on account of his monotheletic tendencies, the Eastern Church admitted his Kanons into the liturgy and made him a saint after his death.

The Kanons of Andrew of Crete, most of them of an exceptional length, show the genre fully developed. His main work is the 'Great Kanon' (*ὁ μέγας κανών*) of the Mid-Lent week, consisting of 250 Troparia, divided into four sections: a stanza of the Kanon corresponds to nearly every verse of the canticles.[3] The 'Great Kanon' is a penitential hymn and must be sung in a spirit of contrition (*μετὰ συντετριμμένης καρδίας καὶ φωνῆς*), each Troparion being followed by three prostrations.[4] The Eastern Church holds this hymn in the highest esteem and regards it as 'the King of Kanons'. Andrew of Crete is certainly one of the greatest hymn-writers and, like Romanus, indefatigable in turning scriptural examples to the purpose of penitential confession.[5] He owes much to Romanus, and his technique can best be illustrated by showing how he worked on the pattern of his

[1] *ὅτι δεῖ τοὺς τῶν ἐκκλησιῶν προεστῶτας ἐν πάσαις μὲν ἡμέραις, ἐξαιρέτως δὲ ταῖς κυριακαῖς, πάντα τὸν κλῆρον καὶ τὸν λαὸν ἐκδιδάσκειν τοὺς τῆς εὐσεβείας λόγους* . . .. Mansi, *Sacr. concil. coll.*, *Conc. Quinisextum*, Can. xix.

[2] Cf. S. Vailhé, 'André de Crète', *Échos d'orient*, 1902.

[3] Christ and Paranikas, *Anth. gr.*, p. xlii.

[4] Cf. Nilles, *Kalend. Man.* ii. 148.

[5] J. M. Neale, *Hymns of the Eastern Church*[2] (1863), p. 23.

model in paraphrasing the Proemium *Ψυχή μου* by Romanus in the fourth Ode of his 'Great Kanon'.

Ψυχή μου, ψυχή μου,
ἀνάστα, τί καθεύδεις;
τὸ τέλος ἐγγίζει
καὶ μέλλεις θορυβεῖσθαι·
ἀνάνηψον οὖν,
ἵνα φείσηταί σου Χριστὸς ὁ θεός,
ὁ πανταχοῦ παρὼν
καὶ τὰ πάντα πληρῶν.

(Romanus)[1]

(My soul, my soul arise; why sleepest thou? The end is coming, and thou wilt be confounded. Be sober, that Christ the Lord may spare thee; for He is everywhere and filleth all things.) Transl. by H. J. W. Tillyard.

Ἐγγίζει, ψυχή, τὸ τέλος,
ἐγγίζει καὶ οὐ φροντίζεις,
οὐχ ἑτοιμάζῃ·
ὁ καιρὸς συντέμνει, διανάστηθι·
ἐγγὺς ἐπὶ θύραις ὁ κριτής ἐστιν·
ὡς ὄναρ, ὡς ἄνθος ὁ χρόνος
τοῦ βίου τρέχει·
τί μάτην ταραττόμεθα;

Ἀνάνηψον, ὦ ψυχή μου,
τὰς πράξεις σου, ἃς εἰργάσω,
ἀναλογίζου,
καὶ ταύτας[2] *ἐπ' ὄψεσι προσάγαγε*
καὶ σταγόνας στάλαξον δακρύων σου·
εἰπὲ παρρησίᾳ τὰς πράξεις,
τὰς ἐνθυμήσεις
Χριστῷ, καὶ δικαιώθητι.

(Andrew of Crete)[3]

(The end is near, O Soul, it is near, and you take no heed. You make no preparation. The time is growing short; arise. Near, at the door, stands the Judge.

Like a dream, like a flower the time of life is running out. Why are we confused by vain thoughts?

Be sober, my soul, consider the works which you have done, and put them before your eyes, and let your tears run down. Confess your works and thoughts freely to Christ and be justified.)

[1] *Anth. gr.*, p. 90.
[2] *Ταύταις* in Christ–Paranikas is obviously a misprint.
[3] Ibid., p. 150. Cf. K. Krumbacher, *Geschichte d. byz. Lit.*[2], p. 667.

The first school of Kanon-writers flourished in the monastery of St. Sabas, near the Dead Sea, in the middle of the eighth century. The leading masters among a group of Greek, Syrian, Armenian, and Coptic monks were John Damascene and his foster-brother Kosmas of Jerusalem. Byzantine literary criticism considered the Kanons of these hymnographers as matchless,[1] and this judgement has been confirmed by Neo-Greek writers on the history of Byzantine hymnography.[2]

John Damascene (*c.* 675–*c.* 748) lived during the first period of the Iconoclastic controversy. His position in the Eastern Church can be compared to that which Thomas Aquinas holds in the Western. His *De fide orthodoxa* has rightly been called 'the greatest theological effort of Eastern scholasticism',[3] his adherence to orthodoxy made him a powerful defender of the Icons in his three apologetical orations *De imaginibus*,[4] and his editorial work on the Oktoëchos gave him a prominent place in the history of Byzantine liturgy.[5]

II. THE STRUCTURE OF THE KANON

(*a*) *The Resurrection Kanon*

Among the hymns of John Damascene the Kanon for Easter Day, called 'The Golden Kanon' or 'The Queen of Kanons', holds the most prominent place.

In order to give the reader an idea of the style and the technique of the first group of Kanon-writers, the full text of the Greek hymn is given, together with the prose translation by Neale,[6]

[1] *οἱ γοῦν ᾀσματικοὶ κανόνες Ἰωάννου τε καὶ Κοσμᾶ σύγκρασιν οὐκ ἐδέξαντο οὐδὲ δέξαιντο ἄν, μέχρις ὁ καθ' ἡμᾶς βίος περαιωθήσεται.* Suidas, *Lexicon*, ed. Bernhardy, i. 2, p. 1028.

[2] Cf. G. Papadopoulos, *Συμβολαὶ εἰς τὴν ἱστορίαν παρ' ἡμῖν ἐκκλησιαστικῆς μουσικῆς* (1890), pp. 154–62.

[3] H. B. Swete, *Patristic Study* (1909), p. 113.

[4] *P.G.*, vol. xciv, cc. 1232–1420.

[5] Cf. Tillyard, *Byz. Music and Hymnography*, p. 21.

[6] The Greek text follows the version of Christ and Paranikas in the *Anthologia graeca*, pp. 218–21. The translation is taken from J. M. Neale's *A History of the Holy Eastern Church*, vol. i, pp. 880–5. Neale handled the Greek text with great freedom, but his translation has the advantage over other attempts at finding English equivalents for the Greek words, since he drew on the language of the Authorized Version of the Bible just as John Damascene drew on that of the Greek New Testament. In consequence the modern reader who does not know Greek is able to see the close connexion between the language of John Damascene, and all other hymn-writers, and that of the Scriptures. From the earliest days of investigations into the music of Byzantine hymns the words and the melodies of the Hirmi of *Ἀναστάσεως ἡμέρα* have been made the object of studies by Western scholars. The most detailed of these is Dom H. Gaisser's *Les 'Heirmoi' de Pâques dans l'Office grec* (Rome, 1905), first published in *O.C.* iii (1903), 416–510. H. J. W. Tillyard has given a literal

who has also made the famous poetical version of the hymn,[1] beginning with:

'Tis the Day of Resurrection:
Earth! tell it out abroad![2]

It should be noted that the Kanons were not sung without a break, but with Troparia and short Responses of the choir, sung after each of the Odes.

Κανὼν εἰς τὴν κυριακὴν τοῦ Πάσχα
ἦχος α′
ᾠδὴ α′.

Ἀναστάσεως ἡμέρα,
λαμπρυνθῶμεν λαοί·
πάσχα κυρίου, πάσχα·
ἐκ γὰρ θανάτου πρὸς ζωὴν
καὶ ἐκ γῆς πρὸς οὐρανὸν
Χριστὸς ὁ θεὸς
ἡμᾶς διεβίβασεν,
ἐπινίκιον ᾄδοντας.

Καθαρθῶμεν τὰς αἰσθήσεις
καὶ ὀψόμεθα
τῷ ἀπροσίτῳ φωτὶ
τῆς ἀναστάσεως Χριστὸν
ἐξαστράπτοντα, καὶ
'χαίρετε' φάσκοντος
τρανῶς ἀκουσόμεθα,
ἐπινίκιον ᾄδοντες.

Οὐρανοὶ μὲν ἐπαξίως
εὐφραινέσθωσαν,
γῆ δὲ ἀγγαλλιάσθω·
ἑορταζέτω δὲ κοσμος
ὁρατός τε ἅπας
καὶ ἀόρατος·
Χριστὸς γὰρ ἐγήγερται,
εὐφροσύνη αἰώνιος.

translation of the Hirmi and a transcription of the music from an early-fourteenth-century MS., Cod. Cantab. Trin. 1165 in his study 'The Canon for Easter', *Laudate*, vol. i (1923), pp. 61–71. I have published a transcription from Cod. Iviron 4590 in *Trésor de musique byzantine*, i (Paris, 1934), 3–6.

[1] See Neale, *Hymns of the Eastern Church*[2] (1863), pp. 33–48.

[2] This poetical version (abridged) has been included in the repertory of hymns of the Anglican Church; see, e.g., *Hymns Ancient and Modern*.

First Mode. First Ode

On the day of the Resurrection let us, O people, be clothed with gladness; it is the Pascha, the Pascha of the Lord: for from death to life, and from earth to heaven, hath Christ our Lord caused us to pass over, singing the Hymn of Victory.

Cleanse we our souls, and we shall behold Christ, glittering in the unapproachable light of the Resurrection; and we shall clearly hear Him exclaiming, Hail! and singing the Hymn of Victory.

Let the Heavens, as it is meet, rejoice, and let the earth exult: and let the whole universe, visible and invisible, keep festival. For Christ hath arisen, and there is eternal joy.

ᾠδὴ γʹ.

Δεῦτε πόμα πίωμεν καινὸν
οὐκ ἐκ πέτρας ἀγόνου τερατουργούμενον,
ἀλλ' ἀφθαρσίας πηγὴν
ἐκ τάφου ὀμβρήσαντος Χριστοῦ,
ἐν ᾧ στερεούμεθα.

Νῦν πάντα πεπλήρωται φωτός,
οὐρανός τε καὶ γῆ καὶ τὰ καταχθόνια·
ἑορταζέτω δὲ πᾶσα κτίσις
τὴν ἔγερσιν Χριστοῦ,
ἐν ᾧ στερεούμεθα.

Χθὲς συνεθαπτόμην σοι, Χριστέ,
συνεγείρομαι σήμερον ἀναστάντι σοι·
συνεσταυρούμην σοι χθές·
αὐτός με συνδόξασον, σωτήρ,
ἐν τῇ βασιλείᾳ σου.

Third Ode

Come, and let us drink the new drink, not produced by miracle from the barren rock, but the fountain of immortality, bursting from the tomb of Christ, in whom we are established.

Now are all things filled with light; earth and heaven, and that which is under the earth. Now then let all creation keep festival for the Resurrection of Christ, in whom we are established.

Yesterday, O Christ, I was buried together with Thee; to-day with Thee arising, I arise. Yesterday I was crucified together with Thee: glorify me, O Saviour, together with Thyself in Thy Kingdom.

ᾠδὴ δ′.

Ἐπὶ τῆς θείας φυλακῆς
 ὁ θεηγόρος Ἀββακοὺμ
  στήτω μεθ᾽ ἡμῶν καὶ δεικνύτω
φαεσφόρον ἄγγελον
 διαπρυσίως λέγοντα·
σήμερον σωτηρία τῷ κόσμῳ
  ὅτι ἀνέστη Χριστὸς ὡς παντοδύναμος.

Ἄρσην μὲν ὡς διανοίξας
 τὴν παρθενεύουσαν νηδὺν
  πέφηνε Χριστός· ὡς βροτὸς δὲ
ἀμνὸς προσηγόρευται·
 ἄμωμος δὲ ὡς ἄγευστος
κηλῖδος τὸ ἡμέτερον πάσχα,
  καὶ ὡς θεὸς ἀληθὴς τέλειος λέλεκται.

Ὡς ἐνιαύσιος ἀμνὸς
 ὁ εὐλογούμενος ἡμῖν
  στέφανος Χριστὸς ἑκουσίως
ὑπὲρ πάντων τέθυται
 πάσχα τὸ καθαρτήριον,
καὶ αὖθις ἐκ τοῦ τάφου ὡραῖος
  δικαιοσύνης ἡμῖν ἔλαμψεν ἥλιος.

Ὁ θεοπάτωρ μὲν Δαυῒδ
 πρὸ τῆς σκιώδους κιβωτοῦ
  ἥλατο σκιρτῶν· ὁ λαὸς δὲ
τοῦ θεοῦ ὁ ἅγιος,
 τὴν τῶν συμβόλων ἔκβασιν
ὁρῶντες, εὐφρανθῶμεν ἐνθέως,
  ὅτι ἀνέστη Χριστὸς ὡς παντοδύναμος.

Fourth Ode

Upon thy divine watch-tower, Habakkuk, Prophet of God, stand with us and show the Angel of light continually proclaiming, To-day is salvation to the world, for Christ, as Almighty, hath arisen.

Christ appeared as a male, opening the Virgin's womb; and, as mortal, He is named a Lamb. Spotless is our Pascha called, as being without taste of blemish, and, as true God, He is named perfect.

As a yearling lamb, our blessed Crown, Christ, was of His own accord sacrificed as the expiatory Pascha for all; and again shone forth to us from the tomb, the beautiful Sun of Righteousness.

David, the Divine Father, leapt and danced before the mystic Ark; but we, the holy people of God, beholding the forthgiving of the symbols, let us rejoice in God, for that Christ, as Almighty, hath arisen.

ᾠδὴ ε′.

Ὀρθρίσωμεν ὄρθρου βαθέος
καὶ ἀντὶ μύρου τὸν ὕμνον
προσοίσωμεν τῷ δεσπότῃ·
καὶ Χριστὸν ὀψόμεθα
δικαιοσύνης ἥλιον,
πᾶσι ζωὴν ἀνατέλλοντα.

Τὴν ἄμετρόν σου εὐσπλαγχνίαν
οἱ ταῖς τοῦ ᾅδου σειραῖς
συνεχόμενοι δεδορκότες
πρὸς τὸ φῶς ἠπείγοντο,
Χριστέ, ἀγαλλομένῳ ποδί,
Πάσχα κροτοῦντες αἰώνιον.

Προσέλθωμεν λαμπαδηφόροι
τῷ προϊόντι Χριστῷ
ἐκ τοῦ μνήματος ὡς νυμφίῳ,
καὶ συνεορτάσωμεν
ταῖς φιλεόρτοις τάξεσι
Πάσχα θεοῦ τὸ σωτήριον.

Fifth Ode

Let us arise very early in the morning, and instead of ointment let us bring a hymn to our Lord. And we shall behold Christ, the Sun of Righteousness, causing life to spring forth to all.

They that were held by the chains of Hades, when they beheld Thy gentle pity, O Christ, hurried onward to light, applauding, with joyful foot, the Eternal Pascha.

Let us draw near with lamps in our hands, to Him that as a Bridegroom comes forth from the tomb. And let us, with the company that loves the Feast, celebrate together the saving Pascha of the Lord.

ᾠδὴ ς′.

Κατῆλθες ἐν τοῖς κατωτάτοις τῆς γῆς
καὶ συνέτριψας μοχλοὺς
αἰωνίους κατόχους
πεπεδημένων, Χριστέ,
καὶ τριήμερος
ὡς ἐκ κήτους Ἰωνᾶς
ἐξανέστης τοῦ τάφου.

Φυλάξας τὰ σήμαντρα σῶα, Χριστέ,
ἐξηγέρθης τοῦ τάφου,
ὁ τὰς κλεῖς τῆς παρθένου
μὴ λυμηνάμενος
ἐν τῷ τόκῳ σου,
καὶ ἀνέῳξας ἡμῖν
παραδείσου τὰς πύλας.

Σωτήρ μου ζῶν τε καὶ ἄθυτον
ἱερεῖον ὡς θεὸς
σεαυτὸν ἑκουσίως
προσαγαγὼν τῷ πατρὶ
συνανέστησας
παγγενῆ τὸν Ἀδάμ,
ἀναστὰς ἐκ τοῦ τάφου.

Sixth Ode

Thou didst descend into the lowest parts of the earth, O Christ; and having broken the eternal bars which held the prisoners, Thou didst on the third day, as Jonah from the whale, rise again from the tomb.

Thou didst preserve inviolate the seals, O Christ, when Thou didst rise from the tomb: Thou didst not burst the bars of virginity in Thy birth, and didst open to us the gates of Paradise.

My Saviour, Who didst offer Thyself to the Father, a living and unsacrificed victim, as God, Thou didst raise, together with Thyself, Adam and all his race, when Thou didst arise from the tomb.

ᾠδὴ ζ'.

Ὁ παῖδας ἐκ καμίνου ῥυσάμενος
γενόμενος ἄνθρωπος
πάσχει ὡς θνητὸς
καὶ διὰ πάθους τὸ θνητὸν
ἀφθαρσίας ἐνδύει εὐπρέπειαν,
ὁ μόνος εὐλογητὸς τῶν πατέρων
θεὸς καὶ ὑπερένδοξος.

Γυναῖκες μετὰ μύρων θεόφρονες
ὀπίσω σου ἔδραμον·
ὃν δὲ ὡς θνητὸν
μετὰ δακρύων ἐζήτουν,
προσεκύνησαν χαίρουσαι ζῶντα θεόν,
καὶ Πάσχα τὸ μυστικὸν σοῖς, Χριστέ,
μαθηταῖς εὐηγγελίσαντο.

Θανάτου ἑορτάζομεν νέκρωσιν,
ᾅδου τὴν καθαίρεσιν,
ἄλλης βιοτῆς
τῆς αἰωνίου ἀπαρχήν,
καὶ σκιρτῶντες ὑμνοῦμεν τὸν αἴτιον,
τὸν μόνον εὐλογητὸν τῶν πατέρων
θεὸν καὶ ὑπερένδοξον.

Ὡς ὄντως ἱερὰ καὶ πανέορτος
αὕτη ἡ σωτήριος
νὺξ καὶ φωταυγής,
τῆς λαμπροφόρου ἡμέρας
τῆς ἐγέρσεως οὖσα προάγγελος,
ἐν ᾗ τὸ ἄχρονον φῶς ἐκ τάφου
σωματικῶς πᾶσιν ἐπέλαμψεν.

Seventh Ode

He that delivered the children from the furnace became man, and suffered as a mortal, and by suffering, endued the Mortal with the beauty of immortality, He, the God of our Fathers, that is only blessed and most glorious.

The holy women followed after Thee with their ointments. But Him whom they sought with tears as a mortal, they worshipped with joy as the Living God, and announced to Thy Disciples, O Christ, the glad tidings of the mystic Pascha.

We celebrate the death of death, the destruction of hell, the first-fruits of another and eternal life. And with exultation we hymn the Cause, the God of our Fathers, that is only blessed and most glorious.

How truly holy, and all-celebrated is this night of salvation and glory! This night that precedes the splendour-bearing day! in which the Eternal Light burst in His Body from the tomb, and shone upon all.

ᾠδὴ η′.

Αὕτη ἡ κλητὴ καὶ ἁγία ἡμέρα,
ἡ μία τῶν σαββάτων,
ἡ βασιλὶς καὶ κυρία,
ἑορτῶν ἑορτὴ
καὶ πανήγυρίς ἐστι πανηγύρεων,
ἐν ᾗ εὐλογοῦμεν
Χριστὸν εἰς τοὺς αἰῶνας.

Δεῦτε τοῦ καινοῦ τῆς ἀμπέλου γεννήματος,
τῆς θείας εὐφροσύνης,
ἐν τῇ εὐσήμῳ ἡμέρᾳ

τῆς ἐγέρσεως
βασιλείας τε Χριστοῦ κοινωνήσωμεν,
ὑμνοῦντες αὐτόν
ὡς θεὸν εἰς τοὺς αἰῶνας.

Ἆρον κύκλῳ τοὺς ὀφθαλμούς σου, Σιών, καὶ ἴδε·
ἰδοὺ γὰρ ἥκασί σοι
θεοφεγγεῖς ὡς φωστῆρες
ἐκ δυσμῶν καὶ βορρᾶ
καὶ θαλάσσης καὶ ἑῴας τὰ τέκνα σου,
ἐν σοὶ εὐλογοῦντα
Χριστὸν εἰς τοὺς αἰῶνας.

Πάτερ παντοκράτορ καὶ λόγε καὶ πνεῦμα,
τρισὶν ἑνιζομένη
ἐν ὑποστάσεσι φύσις,
ὑπερούσιε
καὶ ὑπέρθεε, εἰς σὲ βεβαπτίσμεθα
καὶ σὲ εὐλογοῦμεν
εἰς πάντας τοὺς αἰῶνας.

Eighth Ode

This is the chosen and holy day, the first of all Sabbath-days, the Feast that is lady and queen of Feasts, and the solemn Festival of solemn Festivals, in which we bless Christ for ever and ever.

O come, and let us participate in the new fruit of the Vine, heavenly joy, in the glorious day of the Resurrection, of the kingdom of Christ, honouring Him as God, for ever and ever.

Lift up thine eyes round about thee, O Sion, and see; as lights, illumined of God, thy children come to thee, from the East and from the West, from the Sea and from the North, blessing in thee Christ for ever and ever.

Father Almighty, and Word, and Spirit, united nature, and three Persons, superessential, and God Most High, in Thee have we been baptized, and we bless Thee for ever and ever.

ᾠδὴ θʹ.

Φωτίζου, φωτίζου, ἡ νέα Ἱερουσαλήμ·
ἡ γὰρ δόξα Κυρίου
ἐπὶ σὲ ἀνέτειλε·
χόρευε νῦν καὶ ἀγάλλου, Σιών·
σὺ δέ, ἁγνή,
τέρπου, θεοτόκε,
ἐν τῇ ἐγέρσει τοῦ τόκου σου·

Ὢ θείας, ὢ φίλης, ὢ γλυκυτάτης σου φωνῆς.
μεθ' ἡμῶν ἀψευδῶς γὰρ
ἐπηγγείλω ἔσεσθαι
μέχρι τερμάτων αἰῶνος, Χριστέ·
ἣν οἱ πιστοὶ
ἄγκυραν ἐλπίδος
κατέχοντες ἀγαλλόμεθα.

Ὢ Πάσχα τὸ μέγα
καὶ ἱερώτατον, Χριστέ·
ὢ σοφία καὶ λόγε
τοῦ θεοῦ καὶ δύναμις,
δίδου ἡμῖν ἐκτυπώτερον
σοῦ μετασχεῖν
ἐν τῇ ἀνεσπέρῳ
ἡμέρᾳ τῆς βασιλείας σου.

Ninth Ode

Arise and shine, New Jerusalem; for the glory of the Lord hath risen upon thee. Rejoice and exult, O Sion! and thou, pure Mother of God, joy in the Resurrection of thy Son.

O heavenly and dear and most sweet word! Thou hast promised, O Christ, to be with us, and Thou canst not lie, until the end of the world! We, the faithful, exult, holding that Thy word as an anchor and hope.

O great and most holy Passover, Christ! O Wisdom and Word and Power of God! grant us more expressly to partake of Thee, in the day of Thy kingdom that hath no evening.

The relation of the eight Odes of the Resurrection Kanon—the second Ode is, of course, omitted on Easter Day— to the eight Canticles can easily be traced, though the leading theme running through all the Odes is the idea of the liberation of the soul through the Resurrection of Christ from the bondage in which it is kept in the body. The feast of the Resurrection inspired John Damascene with a Hymn of Victory, similar to that which Moses sang after the passage of the Red Sea (Exod. xv). The trend of thought of the first Ode is: Moses led the children of Israel through the Red Sea, Christ led us from earth to heaven; Moses from the bodily captivity to freedom, Christ from the enslavement in which the soul was held before His appearance, to the freedom of spiritual life.

In the third Ode, John Damascene uses a bold simile: Hannah, the wife of Elkanah, was barren, yet through the grace of God she became the mother of Samuel. Moses smote the barren rock and brought forth water for the 'thirsty congregation and their beasts'. We, John says, do not need water 'produced by miracle from the barren rock'; through Christ we drink the new drink from 'the fountain of immortality'.

The fourth Ode is modelled on the Prayer of Habakkuk (Hab. iii). The Prophet stood upon the watch-tower (Hab. ii. 1) and saw the Holy One coming (Hab. iii. 3). Thus we pray that we may stand with the Prophet and see the Angel of light coming; for Christ has 'shone . . . from the tomb'. The fourth stanza of the Ode evokes the vision of David dancing 'before the mystic Ark' and exhorts us to 'rejoice in God for that Christ, as almighty, has arisen'. This line is based upon the last three verses of the fourth Canticle: *'Εγὼ δὲ ἐν τῷ Κυρίῳ ἀγαλλιάσομαι κτλ.*

The fifth Ode takes up the idea of the first line of the Prayer of Isaiah (xxvi. 9): *'Εκ νυκτὸς ὀρθρίζει τὸ πνεῦμά μου πρὸς σὲ, ὁ Θεός*; but instead of shutting ourselves up in our chambers, as Isaiah advises the Jews to do (Isa. xxvi. 20–1), because 'the Lord cometh out of His place to punish the inhabitants of the earth for their iniquity', we are to welcome Christ with lamps in our hands, Him who has left the tomb and has arisen as victor. This thought is followed up in the sixth Ode, and related to the Prayer of Jonah (ii. 2–9) in the fish's belly.

While the connexion between the Hymn of the Three Holy Children, which forms the content of the seventh Canticle, and the seventh Ode of the Kanon can be seen from the first line of the Ode 'He that delivered the children from the furnace', the connexion between the Hymn of the Three Holy Children and the eighth Ode is not clearly worked out. An allusion to the Canticle may be seen in the words of the third verse of the Ode: 'as lights, illumined of God, Thy children come to Thee'; but since the eighth Ode of a Kanon generally refers to the object of the feast for which the Kanon is written, it is rather the exultant mood of both hymns which links them together than a common trend of thought.

The theme of the ninth Ode of a Kanon had to be the praise and adoration of the Theotokos; it is based on the *Magnificat* (Luke i. 46) and bears in the Byzantine Psalter the title: *'Ωδὴ τῆς Θεοτόκου*. In the Resurrection Kanon, however, John Damascene wanted to confine his words of praise to the subject of the 'queen of feasts'; he begins with Isa. lx and addresses Mary only in the last line of the first stanza: 'and thou, pure Mother of God, joy in the Resurrection of thy Son!'. Next in one of his most inspired stanzas John Damascene evokes the picture of the City of God, the city of the kingdom 'that hath no evening', and returning to the praise of Christ, he ends the Kanon in the same exultant mood in which he began it.

The melodies of the eight Odes of the Resurrection Kanon have come down to us in many musical manuscripts, dating from the tenth century to the fifteenth, most of them providing slight variants, but some of them showing a structure substantially different from that in the bulk of the Hirmologia. In order to show the extent of the divergencies the melody of the first Ode is given in three versions: the first is taken from a Hirmologion of the Iviron monastery (Cod. Iviron 470, fol. 5r.), the second from a Saba manuscript in the library of the Patriarchate in Jerusalem, dating from the end of the thirteenth or the beginning of the fifteenth century (Cod. Saba 599, fol. 2r.), the third from an autograph manuscript by the musician John Koukouzeles, written in 1302 (Cod. Koukouzeles). The transcription of the other Odes is based on Cod. Iviron; the versions of Cod. Saba are added in the case of the fifth and sixth Odes.

I

Easter Day

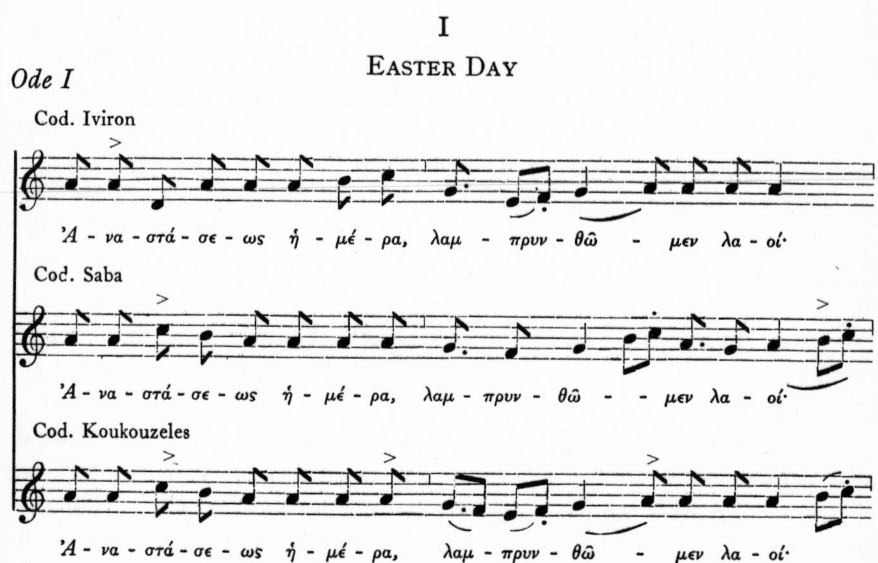

I.
Πά - σχα Κυ - ρί - ου, Πά - σχα· ἐκ γὰρ θα - νά - του πρὸς
S.
Πά - σχα Κυ - ρί - ου, Πά - σχα· ἐκ γὰρ θα - νά - του πρὸς
C.
Πά - σχα Κυ - ρί - ου, Πά - σχα· ἐκ γὰρ θα - νά - του πρὸς
I.
ζω - ήν, καὶ ἐκ γῆς πρὸς οὐ - ρα - νόν, Χρι - στὸς ὁ Θε - ὸς
S.
ζω - ήν, καὶ ἐκ γῆς πρὸς οὐ - ρα - νόν, Χρι - στὸς ὁ Θε - ὸς
C.
ζω - ήν, καὶ ἐκ γῆς πρὸς οὐ - ρα - νόν, Χρι - στὸς ὁ Θε - ὸς
I.
ἡ - μᾶς δι - ε - βί - βα - σεν, ἐ - πι - νί - κι - ον ᾄ - δον - τας.
S.
ἡ - μᾶς δι - ε - βί - βα - σεν, ἐ - πι - νί - κι - ον ᾄ - δον - τας.
C.
ἡ - μᾶς δι - ε - βί - βα - σεν, ἐ - πι - νί - κι - ον ᾄ - δον - τας.

Ode III
Δεῦ - τε πό - μα πί - ω - μεν και - νόν, οὐκ ἐκ πέ - τρας ἀ - γό - νου τε -
- ρα - τουρ - γού - - - με - νον, ἀλλ' ἀ - φθαρ - σί - ας πη - γήν,
ἐκ τά - φου ὀμ - βρή - σαν-τος Χρι - στοῦ, ἐν ᾧ στε - ρε - ού - - με - θα.
Ode IV
Ἐ - πὶ τῆς θεί - ας φυ - λα - κῆς ὁ θε - η - γό - ρος Ἀβ - βα - κοὺμ
στή-τω μεθ' ἡ - μῶν, καὶ δει-κνύ - τω φα - εσ - φό - ρον ἄγ - γε - λον δι - α -
- πρυ - σί - ως λέ - γον - τα· σή - με - ρον σω - τη - ρί - α τῷ
κόσ-μῳ, ὅ - τι ἀ - νέ - στη Χρι - στὸς ὡς παν - το - δύ - να - μος.
Ode V
I.
Ὀρ - θρί - σω - μεν ὄρ - θρου βα - θέ - ος καὶ ἀν - τὶ μύ - ρου
S.
Ὀρ - θρί - σω - μεν ὄρ - θρου βα - θέ - ος καὶ ἀν - τὶ μύ - ρου

I.
τὸν ὕ - μνον προσ - οί - σο - μεν τῷ Δε - σπό - τῃ
S.
aco.
τὸν ὕ - μνον προσ - οί - σο - μεν τῷ Δε - σπό - τῃ . .

I.
καὶ Χρι - στὸν ὀ - ψό - με - θα, δι - και - ο - σύ - νης ἥ - -
S.
καὶ Χρι - στὸν ὀ - ψό - με - θα, δι - και - ο - σύ - νης ἥ - -

I.
- - λι - ον πᾶ - σι ζω - ὴν ἀ - να - τέλ - λον - τα.
S.
- - λι - ον πᾶ - σι ζω - ὴν ἀ - να - τέλ - λον - τα.

Ode VI

I.
Κατ - ῆλ - θες ἐν τοῖς κα - τω - τά - τοις τῆς γῆς,
S.
Κατ - ῆλ - θες ἐν τοῖς κα - τω - τά - τοις τῆς γῆς,

I.
καὶ συν - έ - τρι - ψας μοχ - λοὺς αἰ - ω - νί - ους, κατ - ό - χους πε -
S.
καὶ συν - έ - τρι - ψας μοχ - λοὺς . . αἰ - ω - νί - ους, κατ - ό - χους πε -

I.
- πε - δη - μέ - νων, Χρι - στέ, καὶ τρι - ή - με - ρος . . ὡς ἐκ
S.
- πε - δη - μέ - νων, Χρι - στέ, καὶ τρι - ή - με - ρος ὡς ἐκ

I.
κή - τους Ἰ - ω - νᾶς ἐξ - α - νέ - στης τοῦ τά - φου.
S.
accel.
κή - τους Ἰ - ω - νᾶς, ἐξ - α - νέ - στης τοῦ τά - φου.

Ode VII

Ὁ παῖ - δας ἐκ κα - μί - νου ῥυ - σά - με - νος, γε - νό - με -
- νος ἄν - θρω - πος πά - σχει ὡς θνη - τός, καὶ δι - ὰ πά - θους

τὸ θνη - τὸν ἀ - φθαρ - σί - ας ἐν - δύ - ει εὐ - πρέ - πει -

- αν, ὁ μό - νος εὐ - λο - γη - τὸς . . τῶν πα - τέ - - ρων

Θε - ός, καὶ ὑ - περ - έν - δο - ξος.

Ode VIII

Αὕ - τη ἡ κλη - τὴ καὶ ἁ - γί - α ἡ - μέ - - ρα,

ἡ μί - α τῶν σαβ - βά - των, ἡ βα - σι - λὶς καὶ κυ - ρί - α,

ἑ - ορ - τῶν . . ἑ - ορ - τή, . . καὶ παν - ή - γυ - ρίς ἐ -

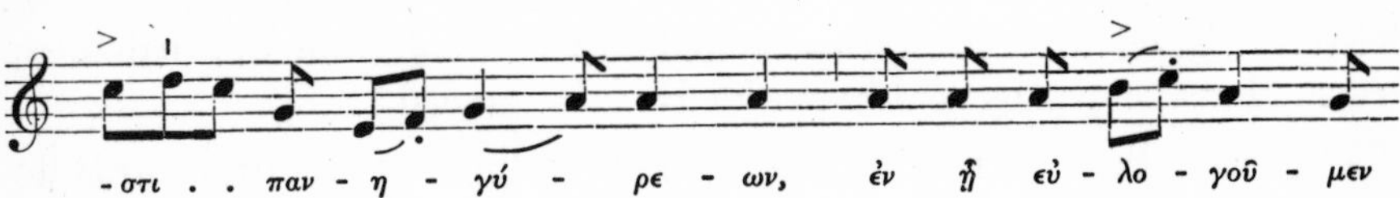
- στι . . παν - η - γύ - ρε - ων, ἐν ᾗ εὐ - λο - γοῦ - μεν

Χρι - στὸν εἰς τοὺς αἰ - ῶ - νας.

Ode IX

Φω - τί - ζου, φω - τί - ζου, ἡ νέ - α Ἰ - ε - ρου - σα - λήμ· ἡ γὰρ
δό - ξα Κυ - ρί - ου ἐ - πὶ σὲ ἀν - έ - τει - - λε.
χό - ρευ - ε νῦν καὶ ἀ - γάλ - λου, Σι - ών· σὺ δέ, ἁ - γνή,
τέρ - που, Θε - ο - τό - κε, ἐν τῇ ἐ - γέρ - σει τοῦ τό - κου σου.

(b) *Canticle and Ode*

The connexion between the words of the Canticles and those of the Odes is more apparent in John Damascene's Kanon for the first Sunday after Easter, the *Κυριακὴ τοῦ Ἀντιπάσχα*, which is also the feast of St. Thomas the Apostle. The Hirmus of the first Ode runs as follows:[1]

(1) *Ἄσωμεν πάντες λαοὶ*
τῷ ἐκ πικρᾶς δουλείας
Φαραὼ τὸν Ἰσραὴλ ἀπαλλάξαντι,
καὶ ἐν βυθῷ θαλάσσης
ποδὶ ἀβρόχῳ ὁδηγήσαντι,
ᾠδὴν ἐπινίκιον,
ὅτι δεδόξασται.

(Let us sing, all ye people, a hymn of victory unto Him who hath delivered Israel from the bitter bondage of Pharaoh, and who led them dry-shod in the depths of the sea: for He is magnified.)

The prototype of the stanza is the first lines of the first canticle (Exod. xv. 1–4):

Ἄσωμεν τῷ Κυρίῳ, ἐνδόξως γὰρ δεδόξασται· ἵππον καὶ ἀναβάτην ἔρριψεν εἰς θάλασσαν.

[1] The melodies of this and the following eighteen Hirmi, transcribed from Cod. Iviron, are given in Appendix I, 1–19.

Βοηθὸς καὶ σκεπαστὴς ἐγένετό μοι εἰς σωτηρίαν· οὗτός μου Θεός, καὶ δοξάσω αὐτόν· Θεὸς τοῦ πατρός μου, καὶ ὑψώσω αὐτόν.

Κύριος συντρίβων πολέμους, Κύριος ὄνομα αὐτῷ.

Ἅρματα Φαραὼ καὶ τὴν δύναμιν αὐτοῦ ἔρριψεν εἰς θάλασσαν· ἐπιλέκτους ἀναβάτας τριστάτας κατεπόντισεν ἐν Ἐρυθρᾷ θαλάσσῃ.

(Let us sing unto the Lord, for He is gloriously magnified.

The horse and the rider He has thrown into the sea.

The Lord is my strength and my protector, and He is become my salvation: He is my God, and I will glorify Him; the God of my father, and I will exalt Him.

The Lord breaks the battle; the Lord is His name.

Pharaoh's chariots and his host He has thrown into the sea; He has drowned the chosen captains of his horsemen in the Red Sea.

This is not an isolated case. The study of the Hirmologion[1] shows that a great number of Hirmi of the first Odes by Andrew of Crete, John Damascene, Kosmas of Jerusalem, and of later hymn-writers are paraphrases of the first lines of the Hymn of Victory, e.g.:

(2) *Ἄσωμεν τῷ Κυρίῳ ᾠδὴν ἐπινίκιον·*
τὸν Φαραὼ γὰρ πόντῳ ἐκάλυψε
καὶ ἐποδήγησε[2] *λαὸν ὃν ἐρρύσατο*
ἐν ὑψηλῷ βραχίονι
καὶ ἐν χειρὶ κραταιᾷ,
ὅτι δεδόξασται.

Kosmas (Hirmol., p. 9)

(Let us sing unto the Lord a hymn of victory, for He has drowned Pharaoh in the sea and led the people whom He set free with mighty arm and strong hand: for He is magnified.)

(3) *Ἄσωμεν ᾆσμα καινὸν τῷ Θεῷ*
τῷ ἐκ δουλείας Φαραὼ
λυτρωσαμένῳ τοὺς υἱοὺς Ἰσραὴλ
καὶ ἐν ἐρήμῳ τούτους διαθρέψαντι,
ὅτι ἐνδόξως δεδόξασται.

Andrew of Crete (Hirmol., p. 13)

(Let us sing a new song unto God, who has released the sons of Israel from the bondage of Pharaoh, and fed them in the wilderness: for He is gloriously magnified.)

1 Reference is made in the following quotations to the *ΕΙΡΜΟΛΟΓΙΟΝ*, edited by Sophronios Eustratiades (Chennevières-sur-Marne, 1932).

2 The MSS. use *ἐποδήγησε*, *ἐποδήγησας* (p. 227) for *ἐφωδήγησε*, *ἐφοδήγησας*.

(4) Ἄσωμεν ᾠδὴν τῷ Θεῷ
τῷ μόνῳ νικητῇ τοῦ θανάτου
ὅτι ἐξήγαγε λαόν,
ὡς ἐκ δουλείας Φαραώ,
τῶν τοῦ ᾅδου ταμείων.

Elias the Patriarch (Hirmol., p. 15)

(Let us sing a hymn unto the Lord, who alone has conquered death, for He led out the people from the chambers of Hades, as from the bondage of Pharaoh.)

(5) Ἄσωμεν τῷ Κυρίῳ
τῷ ἐν θαλάσσῃ πάλαι
λαὸν καθοδηγήσαντι
καὶ ἐν αὐτῇ τὸν Φαραὼ
πανστρατὶ βυθίσαντι
ᾠδὴν ἐπινίκιον,
ὅτι δεδόξασται.

Ioannes Monachus (Hirmol., p. 38)

(Let us sing a hymn of victory unto the Lord, who of old guided the people through the sea, and sunk therein Pharaoh with all his host: for He is magnified.)

(6) Ἄσωμεν τῷ Κυρίῳ ᾆσμα καινὸν
ὅτι παραδόξως τὸν Ἰσραὴλ διέσωσε
δουλείας λυτρωσάμενος,
καὶ τυραννοῦντας ἐχθροὺς
ἐκάλυψε θάλασσα.

Ioannes Monachus (Hirmol., p. 41)

(Let us sing a new song unto the Lord, for He preserved Israel marvellously, releasing them from bondage, and the sea covered their imperious foes.)

(7) Ἄσωμεν ᾆσμα καινὸν
τῷ λυτρωτῇ καὶ Θεῷ ἡμῶν,
οἱ διὰ σταυροῦ ῥυσθέντες
τοῦ νοητοῦ Φαραὼ
καὶ οἰκειωθέντες τῇ στρατιᾷ
τῶν ἀΰλων οὐσιῶν,
ὅτι ἐνδόξως δεδόξασται.

Damianus Monachus (Hirmol., p. 77)

(Let us sing a new song unto our God and Redeemer, we who are delivered through the Cross from the spiritual Pharaoh, and have become companions of the army of the immaterial essences: for He is gloriously magnified.)

(8) Ἄσωμεν τῷ Κυρίῳ τῷ ποιήσαντι
θαυμαστὰ τέρατα
ἐν Ἐρυθρᾷ θαλάσσῃ·
πόντῳ γὰρ ἐκάλυψε
τοὺς ἐναντίους,
καὶ ἔσωσε τὸν Ἰσραήλ·
αὐτῷ μόνῳ ᾄσωμεν
ὅτι δεδόξασται.

Germanus the Patriarch (Hirmol., p. 78)

(Let us sing unto the Lord who worked wondrous signs in the Red Sea, for He covered the enemy with the waters and saved Israel: to Him alone let us sing, for He is magnified.)

(9) Ἄσομαί σοι, Κύριε, ὁ Θεός μου
ὅτι ἐξήγαγες λαὸν
δουλείας Αἰγύπτου,
ἐκάλυψας δὲ ἅρματα
Φαραὼ καὶ τὴν δύναμιν.

Germanus the Patriarch (Hirmol., p. 103)

(I will sing unto Thee, O Lord my God, for Thou hast led out the people from the bondage of Egypt, and hast drowned the chariots of Pharaoh and his host.)

(10) Ἄσωμεν ᾠδὴν ἐπινίκιον
τῷ μόνῳ Θεῷ,
τῷ ποιήσαντι παράδοξα·
πάλαι γὰρ τὸν Φαραὼ
πανστρατὶ ἐν θαλάσσῃ ἐβύθισεν.

Andrew of Crete (Hirmol., p. 105)

(Let us sing a hymn of victory to the one God, who performed marvels, for of old He sank Pharaoh with all his army in the sea.)

(11) Ἄσωμεν τῷ Κυρίῳ τῷ ποιήσαντι
θαυμαστὰ τέρατα
ἐν Ἐρυθρᾷ θαλάσσῃ
ᾠδὴν ἐπινίκιον,
ὅτι δεδόξασται.

Germanus the Patriarch (Hirmol., p. 135)

(Let us sing a hymn of victory unto the Lord, who worked wondrous signs in the Red Sea: for He is magnified.)

(12) Ἄσωμεν τῷ Κυρίῳ
τῷ τὸν λαὸν δουλείας

Αἰγύπτου ἀπαλλάξαντι
καὶ Φαραὼ βυθίσαντι.

Germanus the Patriarch (Hirmol., p. 168)

(Let us sing unto the Lord who has delivered the people from the bondage of Egypt and sank Pharaoh in the deep.)

(13) *Ἄισωμεν τῷ Κυρίῳ,*
ἐνδόξως γὰρ δεδόξασται·
ὅτι διέσωσε λαὸν
χειρὸς Φαραωνίτιδος.

Ioannes Monachus (Hirmol., p. 200)

(Let us sing unto the Lord, for He is gloriously magnified; He preserved the people from the hand of the Egyptian.)

(14) *Ἀισώμεν τῷ Κυρίῳ πάντες λαοὶ*
τῷ ἐν θαλάσσῃ Ἐρυθρᾷ
τὸν Φαραὼ βυθίσαντι
ἐπινίκιον ᾠδὴν
ᾄδοντες, ὅτι δεδόξασται.

Ioannes Monachus (Hirmol., p. 227)

(Let us sing, all ye people, singing a hymn of victory unto the Lord, who sank Pharaoh in the Red Sea, for He is magnified.)

In some of the Hirmi the influence upon the hymn-writer of the first verses of the ninety-seventh Psalm of the Byzantine Psalter is noticeable, particularly of the first and second lines:

Ἄισωμεν τῷ Κυρίῳ ᾆσμα καινόν, ὅτι θαυμαστὰ ἐποίησεν ὁ Κύριος.
Ἔσωσεν αὐτὸν ἡ δεξιὰ αὐτοῦ, καὶ ὁ βραχίων ὁ ἅγιος αὐτοῦ.

(Let us sing unto the Lord a new song, for the Lord has worked miracles: His right hand and His holy arm have saved Him.)

In other Kanons the connexion with the Hymn of Victory is worked out in a more subtle way, e.g.:

(15) *Τὸν Φαραὼ σὺν ἅρμασιν ἐν τῇ θαλάσσῃ*
Χριστὸς κατεπόντισε
καὶ διήγαγε λαὸν
ὑμνοῦντα καὶ λέγοντα·
ᾄσωμεν τῷ Κυρίῳ,
ἐνδόξως γὰρ δεδόξασται.

Germanus (Hirmol., p. 16)

(Christ has drowned Pharaoh with his chariots in the sea, and He has led the people through, singing and saying: 'Let us sing unto the Lord, for He is gloriously magnified.')

(16) Ἐξάρχει πάλαι νεανίδων ᾄδουσα
Μαριὰμ ἡ προφῆτις
ᾆσμα καινὸν
τῷ ἐν θαλάσσῃ Ἐρυθρᾷ
διαγαγόντι λαόν·
ἐξάρχει δὲ νῦν
τῶν ἀπ' αἰῶνος κτισμάτων
ᾄδουσα καινότερον
τῷ τὴν ἁγνὴν θεόπαιδα
ἐξ ἀγόνου καὶ στείρας
προαγαγόντι γαστρός.
in Nativitatem Deiparae, Georgius Sikeliotes (Hirmol., p. 18)

(Miriam the prophetess of old took the lead among the maidens, singing a new song to Him who led the people through the Red Sea. But now she takes the lead of all the creatures created from the beginning, singing a song more new to Him who led forth the pure maiden whose child is divine, from a barren and unfruitful womb.)

(17) Ἐπὶ τὴν ἄβυσσον μολὼν
ὁ Ἰσραηλίτης λαὸς
ᾠδὴν ἀνέμελπε
τῷ ἐν χειρὶ κραταιᾷ
δυνατῶς συντρίψαντι πολέμους
Φαραὼ τοῦ τυράννου.
ᾄσωμεν τῷ Κυρίῳ,
ἐνδόξως γὰρ δεδόξασται.
Cyprianus Monachus (Hirmol., p. 49)

(Descending into the abyss, the people of Israel raised a hymn unto Him who broke the battle of King Pharaoh mightily with His strong hand. Let us sing unto the Lord, for He is gloriously magnified.)

(18) Θαυμάσια τὰ ἔργα σου, Κύριε,
καὶ ἡ ψυχή μου γινώσκει σφόδρα·
ἐκάλυψας γὰρ Φαραὼ
καὶ τὴν δύναμιν αὐτοῦ
εἰς θάλασσαν Ἐρυθρὰν
καὶ ἐποδήγησας λαὸν
ὕμνον σοι βοῶντα·
[τῷ Κυρίῳ ᾄσωμεν,
ἐνδόξως γὰρ δεδόξασται.]
Elias the Patriarch (Hirmol., p. 240)

(Wonderful are Thy works, O Lord, and my soul knoweth it right well. Thou hast covered Pharaoh and his host in the Red Sea and Thou hast guided the people, singing a hymn to Thee. [Let us sing unto the Lord, for He is gloriously magnified.])

(19) *Τῷ ἐν νεφέλῃ φωτεινῇ*
τὸν Ἰσραὴλ ὁδηγήσαντι
ᾠδὴν ἐπινίκιον
λαοὶ πάντες ᾄσωμεν.

Anon. (Hirmol., p. 140)

(To Him who led Israel in the shining cloud, let us sing a hymn of victory, all ye people.)

It often happened that the hymn-writer had to compose a Kanon for a feast whose object could not easily be connected with the Hymn of Victory. In such a case the poet had to work out a solution which was satisfactory from both the liturgical and the artistic point of view. The solution could rarely be achieved in a short stanza; more space was needed to connect the object of the feast with the Passage of the Red Sea. The Hirmus was generally composed upon a paraphrase of the 'Passage', and in the following stanzas of the Ode the hymn-writer had to effect the transition to the object of the feast. There are only a few Kanons in which the hymn-writer succeeded in combining both the allusion to the Canticle and that to the feast in the Hirmus itself. An example of such a combination can be found in the Kanon for the feast of the Exaltation of the Holy Cross (*εἰς τὴν ὕψωσιν τοῦ τιμίου σταυροῦ*) by Kosmas of Jerusalem.

Τὸ πέλαγος Ἐρυθρᾶς
διατμήξας πάλαι
διὰ ξηρᾶς διήγαγε
τὸν Ἰσραὴλ ῥυσάμενος·
νῦν δὲ Χριστὸς σαρκωθεὶς
ἐκ Παρθένου εἵλκυσε
λαὸν ἐθνῶν τὸ πλήρωμα
δομήσας ἐκκλησίαν
οὐρανότυπον τάγμα·
διὸ αὐτῷ ᾄσωμεν
ὡς Θεῷ ἡμῶν, ὅτι δεδόξασται.

(Hirmol., p. 224)

(Of old, dividing the Red Sea, He led Israel over dry land and rescued them. Now Christ, incarnate of the Virgin, has rescued the people, the fullness of the Gentiles, by building the Church, ordered according to the heavenly pattern. Therefore let us sing unto Him, unto our God, for He is magnified.)

III. THE LATER DEVELOPMENT OF HYMN-WRITING

From the beginning of the ninth century the Studios* monastery at Constantinople became the centre of Byzantine hymnography. The community belonged to the Order of 'the Sleepless' (οἱ Ἀκοίμητοι), so called from the unceasing recitation of the Office, night and day, instituted by its first Hegumen, Alexander. The monastery was founded in 462 by a Roman Consul, Studios, and became a stronghold of orthodoxy, particularly in the days of the Iconoclastic controversy. Its most famous abbot was Theodore, who established its famous school of calligraphy. Theodore Studites (759–826) joined the community together with his two brothers Joseph and Euthymius and, at the age of thirty, was elected Hegumen of the great abbey in succession to his uncle St. Plato. Through his sufferings for the cause of orthodoxy and his defence of the images he became one of the great figures of the Iconoclastic controversy: under Leo the Armenian he was exiled, imprisoned, scourged, and left for dead; under Michael Curopalata he enjoyed more liberty, but he was an exile at the time of his death.[1] The Eastern Church raised Theodore to the rank of a saint, and celebrates his memory on the 11th of November, the day of his death.

Theodore, together with other hymn-writers of the Studios, inaugurated a second great period of the Kontakion. His poetical diction is more elaborate than that of Romanus, who was his chief model, but is a no less convincing expression of religious ardour. The dependence of Theodore on Romanus in some of his hymns can be seen by setting side by side the eighth Troparion from the *Canticum de mortuis* by Romanus and the second Troparion from the Kontakion *In monachorum exsequiis* by Theodore.[2]

Romanus

Ἐξιστάμενος βλέπω τὸ ὅραμα
ὅτι ἄπνους ὁ χθές μοι συνόμιλος·
ἀπεπαύσθη φωνὴ ἀγορεύουσα,
ὀφθαλμὸς θεωρῶν ἀπελήλατο·[3]
τὰ πάντα ὄργανα ἐσίγησαν·
ὁ Θεὸς γὰρ συνέκλεισε τούτους, ὡς
γράφει,

Theodore

Φρικτὸν βλέπω καὶ ξένον τὸ ὅραμα·
ὅτι ἄπνους ὁ χθές μοι συνόμιλος,
ἀπεπαύθη[3] φωνὴ ἀγορεύουσα
ὀφθαλμὸς θεωρῶν ἀπελήλατο,
πάντα τὰ ὄργανα σεσίγηκαν·
ὁ Θεὸς ἀπέκλεισε κατὰ αὐτοῦ, ὡς
γράφει,

[1] Cf. Neale, *Hymns*², p. 99.

[2] Cf. Pitra, *Anal. sacra*, p. 373.

[3] ἀπεπαύθη, ἀπελήλατο: see Pitra's note 2, op. cit., p. 374.

Romanus (*cont.*)	*Theodore* (*cont.*)
καὶ οὐκέτι ἐπαναστρέψειαν λοιπόν· ἔνθεν ᾄδωμεν πάντες μετ' ἤχου Θεῷ τὸ ἀλληλούϊα.	καὶ οὐκέτι λοιπὸν ἐπιστρέψειεν· ἔνθα ᾄδωμεν πάντες μετ' ἤχου βροτοὶ τὸ ἀλληλούϊα.
(*Anal. sacra*, p. 46)	(*Anal. sacra*, p. 374)

(I see an awful and strange spectacle: without breath is he who yesterday conversed with me; the speaking voice is stopped, the sight of the eyes has failed, all the senses are silent. God has hedged him in, as it is written (Job iii. 23), and he may never turn again. Therefore, let us mortal men all sing in melody our 'Alleluia'.)

According to modern aesthetic standards such a close imitation of a pattern would be called a pastiche. But, as has been said, we must refrain from comparing Byzantine ecclesiastical poetry with that of classical or modern times; we should rather think of the icons, which often differ only in slight details. The changes of phrase which Theodore introduced into his version are few, but they are sufficiently important to make it a work of his own.[1] From the study of this and other Kontakia it seems, indeed, that these hymns are bound to contain the same similes as their models, just as the icons, representing the saints in whose honour the Kontakia are composed, must all show the same features.

The poetical strength of Theodore Studites becomes apparent from the study of his Kanons. The first Ode of his Kanon for the Sunday of Apokreos, our Sexagesima, may be taken as an example of his poetic powers:

(1) Τὴν ἡμέραν τὴν φρικτὴν
τῆς παναρρήτου σου παρουσίας
φρίττω ἐννοῶν,
δεδοικὼς προορῶ,
ἐν ᾗ προκαθίσεις
κρῖναι ζῶντας καὶ νεκρούς,
Θεέ μου παντοδύναμε.

(2) Ὅτε ἥξεις ὁ Θεός
ἐν μυριάσι καὶ χιλιάσι
τῶν ἀγγελικῶν
οὐρανίων ἀρχῶν,

[1] We must remember that Handel added a second part to Arias of contemporary composers and did not hesitate to include these Duets in his own Oratorios.

κἀμὲ ἐν νεφέλαις
ὑπαντῆσαί σοι, Χριστέ,
τὸν ἄθλιον ἀξίωσον.

(3) Δεῦρο λάβε μοι, ψυχή,
αὐτὴν τὴν ὥραν καὶ τὴν ἡμέραν,
ὅτε ὁ Θεὸς
ἐμφανῶς ἐπιστῇ·
καὶ θρήνησον, κλαῦσον,
εὑρεθῆναι καθαρὰ
ἐν ὥρᾳ τῆς ἐτάσεως.

(4) Ἐξιστᾷ με καὶ φοβεῖ
τὸ πῦρ τὸ ἄσβεστον τῆς γεέννης,
σκώληξ ὁ πικρός,
τῶν ὀδόντων βρυγμός·
ἀλλ' ἄνες μοι, ἄφες,
καὶ τῇ στάσει με, Χριστέ,
τῶν ἐκλεκτῶν σου σύνταξον.

(5) Τῆς εὐκταίας σου φωνῆς,
τῆς τοὺς Ἁγίους σου προσκαλούσης
ἐπὶ τὴν χαράν,
εἰσακούσω κἀγὼ
ὁ τάλας, καὶ εὕρω
βασιλείας οὐρανῶν
τὴν ἄρρητον ἀπόλαυσιν.

(6) Μὴ εἰσέλθῃς μετ' ἐμοῦ
εἰς κρίσιν, φέρων μου τὰ πρακτέα,
λόγους ἐκζητῶν,
καὶ εὐθύνων ὁρμάς·
ἀλλ' ἐν οἰκτιρμοῖς σου
παρορῶν μου τὰ δεινά,
σῶσον με, παντοδύναμε.

(7) Τρισυπόστατε μονὰς
ἀρχικωτάτη Κυρία πάντων,
τελεταρχική,
ὑπεράρχιε,
αὐτὴ ἡμᾶς σῶσον,
ὁ Πατήρ, καὶ ὁ Υἱός,
καὶ Πνεῦμα τὸ πανάγιον.[1]

[1] *Triodion* (Rome, 1879), p. 34.

(1) That fearful day, that day of speechless dread,—When Thou shalt come to judge the quick and dead—I shudder to foresee,—O God! what then shall be!

(2) When Thou shalt come, angelic legions round,—With thousand thousands, and with trumpet sound;—Christ grant me in the air—With saints to meet Thee there!

(3) Weep, O my soul, ere that great hour and day,—When God shall shine in manifest array,—Thy sin, that thou may'st be—In that strict judgement free!

(4) The terror! hell-fire fierce and unsufficed:—The bitter worm: the gnashing teeth: O Christ—Forgive, remit, protect;—And set me with the elect!

(5) That I may hear the blessed voice that calls—The righteous to the joy of heavenly halls:—And, King of Heaven, may reach—The realm that passeth speech!

(6) Enter Thou not in judgement with each deed,—Nor each intent and thought in strictness read:—Forgive, and save me then,—O Thou that lovest men!

(7) Thee, One in Three blest Persons! Lord o'er all!—Essence of essence, Power of power, we call!—Save us, O Father, Son,—And Spirit, ever one!

(Transl. by J. M. Neale, *Hymns of the Eastern Church*[2], pp. 104–5.)

Here, too, the dependence on Romanus can be seen by comparing Theodore's Kanon on the Last Judgement with Romanus' famous Kontakion on the same subject. But we have to remember that both the Kontakion and the Kanon were destined for the Apokreos Sunday; Theodore, therefore, was bound to follow Romanus as closely as Romanus had followed Ephraem the Syrian, his great forerunner. Theodore's great achievement is the adaptation of the poetical vision of the Last Judgement to the structure of the Kanon, and, from the musical point of view, the adjustment of the stanzas of his Odes to the melodies of nine already existing Hirmi. From the words *Βοηθὸς καὶ σκεπαστής* in the title of the Kanon it can be seen that the Hirmi of the Odes were *Prosomoia*; they were set to the melodies of the 'Great Kanon' (*τοῦ μεγάλου κανόνος*) by Andrew of Crete, which is sung on Friday of the first week of Lent. The original words of the Hirmi, composed by Andrew of Crete, are used by Theodore for the *Katabasiae*; consequently the text of the Hirmus of the first Ode *Βοηθὸς καὶ σκεπαστής* appears in the last stanza of Theodore's first Ode. Since Codex Iviron does not contain the

Hirmi of Theodore's Kanon, but only those of Andrew of Crete, a transcription of the melodies of the first and third Ode with the text from the 'Great Kanon' may follow here. We have added underneath the words from Theodore's Kanon. It may be noted that the text of Andrew's Hirmus is taken, word for word, from the second verse of Moses' Hymn of Victory (Exod. xv), which is used as a Troparion without alteration of a single word except for the usual addition of the refrain: ἐνδόξως γὰρ δεδόξασται.

First Ode

Mode II Plag.

Βο - η - θὸς καὶ σκε - πα - στής ἐ - γέ - νε - τό μοι εἰς σω - τη -
Τὴν ἡ - μέ - ραν τὴν φρι - κτὴν τῆς παν - αρ - ρή - του σου παρ - ου -

- ρί - αν· οὗ - τος μου Θε - ός, καὶ δο - ξά - σω αὐ - τόν·
- σί - ας φρίτ - τω ἐν - νο - ῶν, δε - δοι - κὼς προ - ο - ρῶ,

Θε - ὸς τοῦ πα - τρός . . μου· καὶ ὑ - ψώ - σω αὐ -
ἐν . . ᾗ προ - κα - θί - σεις κρῖ - ναι ζῶν - τας καὶ

- τόν, ἐν - δό - ξως γὰρ δε - δό - ξα - σται.
νε-κρούς, Θε - έ μου παν - το - δύ - να - με.

Third Ode

Mode II Plag.

Στε - ρέ - ω - σον, Κύ - ρι - ε, ἐ - πὶ τὴν πέ - τραν τῶν
Ὁ Κύ - ρι - ος ἔρ - χε - ται, καὶ τίς ὑπ - οι - σει αὐ -

ἐν - το - λῶν σου . . σα - λευ - θεῖ - σαν τὴν καρ - δί - αν μου,
- τοῦ τὸν φό - βον; . . τῷ προσ - ώ - πῳ τίς ὀφ - θῇ αὐ - τοῦ;
ὅ - τι μό - νος ἅ - γι - ος ὑπ - άρ - χεις καὶ δί - και - ος.
ἀλλ' ἑ - τοί - μη γε - νοῦ, ὦ ψυ - χή, πρὸς ὑπ - άν - τη - σιν.

(Cod. Iviron, fol. 107r.)

The Odes of this and of the other Kanons of Theodore are no longer paraphrases of the Canticles, as were those of the hymn-writers of the School of St. Sabas. This is the new achievement of the School of the Studios. In the first period of hymn-writers the Odes were loosely linked together. Now the Kanon becomes a unity. With great skill a single thought is worked out and varied in all the Odes, as may be seen from another example, the first Ode of the Kanon commemorating the Holy Martyrs Proclus and Hilarius on 12 July. The Kanon is composed by Joseph of the Studios, a Sicilian by birth, who left his country in 830 when it was invaded by the Arabs, took holy orders in Thessalonica, and later joined the monastery of the Studios.

Συνόντες τῷ Θεῷ
καὶ ταῖς θείαις ἀκτίσι
πυρσευόμενοι ἀεί,
γενναῖοι Ἀθληταί,
τὴν ψυχήν μου φωτίσατε
μέλποντες τὴν φωτοφόρον
καὶ σεπτὴν ὑμῶν ἄθλησιν
κατανύξει καρδίας, μακάριοι.

Ἐπτέρωσεν ὑμᾶς
ὁ οὐράνιος πόθος
ὅθεν πάντα τὰ τερπνὰ
τοῦ βίου Ἀθληταί,
ἐλογίσασθε σκύβαλα,
νεύσεσι ταῖς πρὸς τὸ θεῖον
θεωθέντες, καὶ ἅπασαν
τῶν ἀθέων ἰσχὺν ταπεινώσαντες.

Πυρὶ θεαρχικῆς
ἀναφθέντες Τριάδος,
δυσσεβείας τὴν πυρὰν
ἐσβέσατε, Σοφοί,
τῶν αἱμάτων τοῖς ῥεύμασιν·
ὅθεν ταῖς τῶν ἰαμάτων
καθαραῖς ἐπομβρήσεσι
τῶν παθῶν ἡμῶν ῥύπον ἐκπλύνατε.

Τὴν ἄλυπον ζωήν,
τὴν οὐράνιον δόξαν,
παραδείσου τὴν τρυφήν,
τὸ φῶς τὸ νοητόν,
τὴν τερπνὴν ἀγαλλίασιν,
Μάρτυρες, ἐπιζητοῦντες,
τῶν δεινῶν ὑπηνέγκατε
τρικυμίαν γενναίῳ φρονήματι.

Οὐράνιοι χοροὶ
τὴν ὑμῶν καρτερίαν
κατεπλάγησαν, Σοφοί·
αἰκίσεις γὰρ σαρκὸς
καὶ πολύπλοκα βάσανα,
Μάρτυρες, γενναιοφρόνως
ὑπηνέγκατε χαίροντες,
καὶ ἐχθροῦ τὴν κακίαν συντρίβοντες.

Ἰὸν τῶν ἀκοῶν
τῆς προμήτορος Εὔας
Γαβριὴλ σοι προσφωνῶν
τὸ Χαῖρε ἀληθῶς
ἐξετίναξε, Δέσποινα·
μόνη γὰρ τὸν ἀναιρέτην
τῆς κακίας τοῦ ὄφεως
ὑπὲρ νοῦν τε καὶ λόγον ἐκύησας.[1]

J. M. Neale gives the following free translation:

Thrice-noble athletes, that had fellowship with God, and were enlightened by the divine rays! illuminate my soul, O blessed ones! who with compunction of heart sing your life-giving and venerable passion.

Of heavenly love ye had the wings: wherefore, O athletes, accounting the pleasant things of this life as dross, and rapt with desire towards God, ye humbled all the strength of the godless.

[1] *Menaià*, vol. vi (Rome, 1902), pp. 92–3.

Radiant with the fire of the Divine Trinity, ye quenched, O wise ones, by the streams of your blood, the fire of our ungodliness. Wherefore wash out the filth of our passions with the pure dews of your healings.

Ever seeking, O Martyrs, the life that is without grief, the glory of Heaven, the intellectual light, the joyous exultation, ye bore up against the surges of peril with dauntless resolution.

Valiant deeds of us men the choirs of Heaven admired. For gallantly and joyfully, O Martyrs, ye bore up against the insults of the flesh, and divers kind of torments, trampling on the malice of the enemy.

Theotokion

Rightly did the salutation addressed to thee, O Lady, by Gabriel, atone for the poison of the words that our general mother Eve gave ear to. For thou only, beyond word and imagination, didst bring forth the destroyer of the malice of the serpent.[1]

The literary history of this second great period of the Kontakion and of the new development in Kanon-writing has still to be written. The names of a great number of the hymnographers of the period have been transmitted in the various service-books, but little is known about their lives and their works. We can therefore only give a rough outline of this important phase in Byzantine ecclesiastical poetry, and must content ourselves with mentioning a few of the most prominent hymn-writers.

The first of them is Joseph of Thessalonica, Theodore's brother. Less prominent as a poet, but an even more voluminous writer than the famous Hegumen, he collaborated with Theodore in composing a great number of hymns for the *Triodion*. Another pair of brothers, Theophanes (759–*c.* 842) and Theodorus, 'the branded ones' (οἱ γραπτοί), and Methodius (†846) fought and suffered for the cause of orthodoxy, and composed Kanons, hymns, and Stichera for the feasts of the Saints. St. Methodius, who came from a family of Sicilian patricians, became Patriarch of Constantinople; having been mutilated by the Iconoclasts, he dictated his hymns, some of which were written in an iambic measure of twelve syllables, a metre favoured by John Damascene.

In the second half of the ninth century this group of hymn-writers from the Studios was followed by another generation of

[1] Transl. by Neale in *History of the Eastern Church*, Part I, ii, pp. 833–4.

monks, among whom Joseph of the Studios (†883) and Metrophanes (†*c.* 910) were the most famous.

Two Emperors also contributed to the service-books: Leo VI (886–912), who wrote eleven *Eothina* or Morning Resurrection Hymns,[1] and Constantine Porphyrogennetus (913–59), who composed a set of eleven short hymns, called *Exaposteilaria*, referring to the appearances of Christ after the Resurrection.[2]

From the middle of the ninth century we possess a few hymns and Kanons composed by the nun Kasia,[3] whose name is familiar to us from a passage in Gibbon describing the presentation of brides to the Emperor Theophilus (829–42). She was equally gifted as a poet and as a composer,[4] and seems to have written the music for some hymns the words of which were composed by Byzantius, Georgius, Cyprianus, and Marcus Monachus.[5] The last of this group of hymn-writers was John Mauropus (*c.* 1081), Metropolitan of Euchaita. A number of the hymns bearing the name of *Ἰωάννης Μόναχος* may have been written by him and not by John Damascene, to whom they were formerly attributed.[6]

With John Mauropus, sometimes called 'the last of the Greek Fathers',[7] the rich production of Byzantine hymns came to an end in the Eastern part of the Empire. The immense number of hymns introduced into the service made it necessary for the ecclesiastical authorities to prohibit the addition of new hymns to the repertory, and the artistic activity of the monks from that time onwards was concentrated upon the embellishment of the music, which, in the following centuries, and even after the fall of the Empire, became increasingly rich and elaborate, until the

[1] The words and the music of these hymns have been published and commented upon by H. J. W. Tillyard in his study '*ΕΩΘΙΝΑ ΑΝΑΣΤΑΣΙΜΑ*. The Morning Hymns of the Emperor Leo', in *A.B.S.*, vols. xxx and xxxi.

[2] Cf. H. J. W. Tillyard, *Byz. Music and Hymnography*, p. 35.

[3] Gibbon refers to her as Icasia (*Decline and Fall*, ch. 48). In the MSS. of chronicles and service-books the following variants of the name are found: *Κασσία*, *Κασία*, *Κασσιανή*, *Εἰκασία*, *Ἰκασία*. In his study on the hymns of the nun Krumbacher suggests that the forms *Εἰκασία* and *Ἰκασία* are due to the error of a scribe who mistook *ἡ κασία* for *ἰκασία* or *εἰκασία*, which, in fact, do not exist. Cf. K. Krumbacher, 'Kasia', *Sb. B.A.* (1897), pp. 316–17.

[4] See H. J. W. Tillyard, 'A Musical Study of the Hymns of Casia', *B.Z.* xx (1911), 420–85. In this study Tillyard still adhered to Riemann's rhythmical hypothesis, which he abandoned in his later studies. Revised transcriptions of two hymns of Kasia can be studied in Tillyard's *Byzantine Music and Hymnography*. A transcription of *Αὐγούστου Μοναρχήσαντος* by O. Strunk is published in G. Reese's *Music in the Middle Ages* (1940), p. 82.

[5] Cf. Tillyard, op. cit., pp. 422–3.

[6] Cf. Tillyard, *Byz. Music*, p. 35.

[7] Cf. Neale, *Hymns of the Eastern Church*², p. 160.

originally simple structure of Byzantine melodies was transformed into an ornamented style and the words of the text made unrecognizable by extended coloraturas. This musical style developed in the thirteenth and fourteenth centuries. The musicians who either embellished the older simple melodies or composed new ones in the elaborate style of the day were called *Melurgi* (μελουργοί), or, if they also taught the new kind of composition and gave instruction in singing, *Maïstores* (μαϊστῶρες). The most famous of these 'Masters' were Ioannes Glykys, Manuel Chrysaphes, Theodulos Hieromonachus, Ioannes Koukouzeles, Ioannes Lampadarius. They did not improvise their rich, often abundant, coloraturas, but worked them out according to certain rules, which had to be strictly observed. Even in the days of the foreign domination, when Byzantine ecclesiastical music was influenced by the scales and musical formulae of the Turkish overlords, this process of 'variation'—to use a modern technical term—was not musical improvisation, but followed certain accepted rules. The study of this musical development, however, is outside the scope of the present outline of Byzantine music, as it would require comparative studies in the whole field of the music of the Near and Middle East, from the sixteenth to the end of the eighteenth century, a task for which the preliminary investigations have not yet been accomplished.

After hymn-writing in the East had come to an end there was still some poetical activity in the Greek colonies and monasteries in Sicily and southern Italy in the eleventh and up to the middle of the twelfth century. Though nominally dependent on the Church of Rome, Sicily, on account of its large Greek population, was, after its conquest by the Byzantines in 535, virtually under the influence of the Patriarchate of Constantinople, and the Eastern influence became even stronger in the days of the Iconoclastic controversy. Sicilian and Calabrian monasticism, which originally followed the Benedictine rule, became 'Basilian'. When, in 827, the Arabs conquered Sicily, many of the monks, together with some of the Greek population, emigrated from Sicily into Calabria and so extended Byzantine civilization, which continued to flourish in this part of Italy during the tenth and eleventh centuries. In 1004 a Basilian monk, Nilus the Younger, founded a monastery at Grottaferrata, near Rome, which became the centre of Byzantine ecclesiastical life in Italy. Both its founder Nilus, the first Abbot of Grottaferrata, and his successor Paulus, inaugurated a rich poetical activity, by composing Kontakia, Kanons, and Stichera.[1] The School of Grottaferrata flourished up to the twelfth century. Its most prominent representatives were St. Bartholomaeus, Clemens, Arsenius, Germanus, Ioannes, Joseph, Pancratius, Procopius, and Sophronius.[2] Untouched by the troubles which foreign domination caused in the East, the School of Grottaferrata preserved the great tradition of Byzantine hymnography without major changes up to the present day.

IV. MINOR BYZANTINE HYMNOGRAPHY

Side by side with the Kontakion and the Kanon, the oldest form of Christian poetry, the Troparion, remained in use in Byzantine liturgy. As a result of the extension of the service and the introduction of new feasts of the saints, the number of these short hymns had increased considerably. New hymns were added to the oldest layer of Troparia, and were either sung to new melodies or composed and sung to already existing ones. They were sung between the stanzas of the Kontakia, and, at a later date, between the Odes of the Kanons, and also at the beginning and the end of the longer forms. They range from stanzas consisting of from one to three lines, written in poetical prose, to poems of a lyrical character.

These hymns, widely differing in character and poetical value, have their fixed places in the service and a special name which indicates their function. The main groups of hymns which were inserted between the Odes of a Kanon are the following: Hypakoe (ὑπακοή), Katabasia (καταβασία), Kathisma (κάθισμα), Kontakion (κοντάκιον), Oikos (οἶκος), Theotokion (θεοτόκιον), Staurotheotokion (σταυροθεοτόκιον).

Hypakoë[3] is originally the liturgical term for a Troparion which was chanted in the Morning Office after Ps. cxviii Μακάριοι οἱ

1 Cf. D. Sofronio Gassisi, 'Innografi Italo-Greci. Poesie di S. Nilo Iuniore e di Paolo Monaco Abbati di Grottaferrata', *O.C.* v (1905), 26–81.

2 Pitra, *L'Hymnographie*, p. 62. See also L. Tardo, *L'Antica Melurgia Bizantina* (1938), pp. 130–40.

3 The explanations of this and the following terms are based on: J. Goar, *Euchologium Graecorum* (1730); Neale, *A History of the Holy Eastern Church*, Part I, ii. 819–942; Christ-Paranikas, *Anthol. Graeca*; Nilles, *Kalendarium Manuale*, i, pp. liv–lxv; L. Clugnet, *Dictionnaire grec-français des noms liturgiques* (1895); and Langford-James, *A Dictionary of the Eastern Orth. Church* (1923). But it is impossible to gather even a superficial knowledge of this extremely complicated matter without studying the service-books themselves.

ἄμωμοι; it seems that it was sung by the whole congregation as a response to the chanting of the psalm by a single precentor. At a later date the name was given to a Troparion which was sung after the third Ode of a Kanon. In the Resurrection Kanon, for example, the Hypakoë runs as follows:

Προλαβοῦσαι τὸν ὄρθρον
αἱ περὶ Μαριάμ,
καὶ εὑροῦσαι τὸν λίθον
ἀποκυλισθέντα
τοῦ μνήματος,
ἤκουον ἐκ τοῦ ἀγγέλου·
Τὸν ἐν φωτὶ ἀϊδίῳ ὑπάρχοντα,
μετὰ νεκρῶν
τί ζητεῖτε ὡς ἄνθρωπον;
βλέπετε τὰ ἐν τάφῳ σπάργανα·
δράμετε, καὶ τῷ κόσμῳ κηρύξατε,
ὡς ἐγέρθη ὁ Κύριος
θανατώσας τὸν θάνατον·
ὅτι ὑπάρχει Θεοῦ Υἱός
τοῦ σώζοντος τὸ γένος τῶν ἀνθρώπων.[1]

(They who came with Mary, preventing the dawn, and finding the stone rolled away from the Sepulchre, heard from the Angel: 'Why seek ye as a man among the dead Him that dwelleth in everlasting light? See the swaddling clothes in the tomb, hasten and tell the world that the Lord hath arisen, having been the death of death; that He is the Son of God that saveth the race of men.') Transl. by Neale.[2]

Katabasia is the liturgical term for the Hirmus repeated at the end of the Ode. It is sung by the two groups of singers who descend (καταβαίνουσι) from their seats and sing it together in the centre of the choir. If the Hirmus is a *Prosomoion*, i.e. following an already existing metrical and melodic model, the Katabasia may use the words of the original stanza. In the Kanon *Τὴν ἡμέραν τὴν φρικτήν* by Theodore Studites, as has been said, the Katabasia is sung to the words of the original Hirmus *Βοηθὸς καὶ σκεπαστής*.

Kathisma is a Troparion which is sung while the community remains seated.

Kontakion is, in later hymnography, the liturgical term for a Troparion of a Kanon at the end of the sixth Ode, built upon a

[1] *Pentekostarion* (Rome, 1883), p. 7.
[2] *A History of the Holy Eastern Church*, Part I, ii. 881.

Hirmus differing from that of the Ode, as can be seen from the Kontakion of the Resurrection Kanon:

Εἰ καὶ ἐν τάφῳ
κατῆλθες, ἀθάνατε,
ἀλλὰ τοῦ Ἅδου
καθεῖλες τὴν δύναμιν·
καὶ ἀνέστης ὡς νικητής,
Χριστὲ ὁ Θεός,
γυναιξὶ μυροφόροις
φθεγξάμενος, Χαίρετε,
καὶ τοῖς σοῖς Ἀποστόλοις
εἰρήνην δωρούμενος,
ὁ τοῖς πεσοῦσι
παρέχων ἀνάστασιν.[1]

(Though, O immortal, Thou didst descend into the tomb, yet didst Thou overthrow the might of Hades, O Christ our God; and Thou didst arise as Victor, saying to the Ointment-Bearers, Hail! Thou didst give peace to Thine Apostles, who dost cause them that are fallen to arise.) Transl. by Neale.[2]

Oikos is the term for stanza. The Oikos always follows a Kontakion at the end of the sixth Ode. Structurally it differs little from the Kontakion, except in its greater length, as can be seen from the following stanza by Romanus, taken from the Resurrection Kanon:

Τὸν πρὸ ἡλίου Ἥλιον
  δύναντά ποτε ἐν τάφῳ
προέφθασαν πρὸς ὄρθρον
  ἐκζητοῦσαι ὡς ἡμέραν
μυροφόροι κόραι,
  καὶ πρὸς ἀλλήλας ἐβόων·
Ὦ φίλαι, δεῦτε,
  τοῖς ἀρώμασιν ὑπαλείψωμεν
σῶμα ζωηφόρον
  καὶ τεθαμμένον·
Σάρκα ἀνιστῶσαν
  τὸν παραπεσόντα Ἀδάμ,
κειμένην ἐν τῷ μνήματι·
  ἄγωμεν,
  σπεύσωμεν

[1] *Pentekostarion*, p. 9.
[2] *A History of the Holy Eastern Church*, Part I, ii. 882.

ὥσπερ οἱ Μάγοι,
  καὶ προσκυνήσωμεν,
καὶ προσκομίσωμεν
  τὰ μύρα ὡς δῶρα
τῷ μὴ ἐν σπαργάνοις,
  ἀλλ' ἐν σινδόνι
ἐνειλημένῳ·
καὶ κλαύσωμεν,
  καὶ κράξωμεν·
Ὦ Δέσποτα,
ἐξεγέρθητι,
ὁ τοῖς πεσοῦσι
  παρέχων ἀνάστασιν.[1]

(The women with their ointment came very early, before the sun, seeking the Sun that had set in the tomb. And they said one to the other, O friends, let us hasten to anoint with spices the quickening and buried Body, the Flesh that raiseth again Adam after his fall, lying in the tomb; let us go on, let us hurry like the Wise Men, and let us worship, and let us offer myrrh as a gift to Him that is wrapped, not in swaddling clothes, but in fine linen; and let us weep and cry, Arise, O Lord, Thou that affordest resurrection to the fallen.) Transl. by Neale.[2]

*Theotokion** is, in the first place, the term for the ninth Ode of a Kanon which contains an invocation to the Mother of God. This change of the character of the ninth Ode was made by John Damascene, and was due to the increased veneration of the Virgin in the service of the Eastern Church in the eighth century. In the second place it is the term for a Troparion in honour of the Mother of God, which follows each Ode of a Kanon composed for a special festival in honour of the Theotokos. The Theotokia were mostly of a lyrical character, and are 'at least as strong as any corresponding expression of the Latin Church',[3] as can be seen from the following Theotokion for the Vespers of the Sunday of Tyrophagus (*Κυριακὴ τῆς Τυροφάγου*), corresponding to the Quinquagesima of the Western Church:

Μυστικῶς ἀνυμνοῦμέν σε,
  Θεοτόκε Μαρία·
ἀνεδείχθης γὰρ θρόνος
  τοῦ μεγάλου Βασιλέως,
σκηνὴ παναγία,
  τῶν οὐρανῶν πλατυτέρα,

[1] *Pentekostarion*, p. 9.
[2] *A History of the Holy Eastern Church*, Part I, ii. 883.
[3] Ibid., p. 832, footnote.

Χερουβὶμ ἅρμα,
ἀνωτέρα δὲ τῶν Σεραφίμ,
νυμφὼν δόξης·
ἐκ σοῦ γὰρ προῆλθε
σαρκωθεὶς ὁ πάντων Θεός.
Αὐτὸν ἱκέτευε,
σωθῆναι τὰς ψυχὰς ἡμῶν.

(Mystically we hymn thee, Mary, Mother of God! for thou hast been made the throne of the Great King. Most holy tabernacle! more spacious than the heavens! chariot of the Cherubim, and more exalted than the Seraphim! Bridal chamber of glory! For from thee came forth Incarnate the God of all. Supplicate Him for the salvation of our souls.) Transl. by Neale.[1]

Staurotheotokion is a Troparion in honour of the Blessed Virgin at the Cross, as can be seen from the Staurotheotokion in the Kanon for the Martyrs Proclus and Hilarius at Vespers on 12 July:

Ἐν τῷ σταυρῷ παρεστῶσα
τοῦ σοῦ υἱοῦ καὶ Θεοῦ,
καὶ τὴν μακροθυμίαν
τούτου ἀποσκοποῦσα
ἔλεγες θρηνοῦσα
μῆτερ ἁγνή·
Οἴμοι, τέκνον γλυκύτατον,
τί ταῦτα πάσχεις ἀδίκως,
Λόγε Θεοῦ,
ἵνα σώσῃς τὸ ἀνθρώπινον;

(Standing by the Cross of thy Son and the Son of God, and beholding His long-suffering, with tears, pure Mother, thou saidst, Woe is me! Why sufferest Thou thus unjustly, my dearest Son, Word of God, to save man?)

The most important and numerous independent group of Troparia are the *Stichera* (στιχηρά). Originally they were verses sung after a verse (στίχος) of a psalm; in this strict sense the term *Sticheron* (στιχηρόν) still applies to a Troparion sung after Pss. cxli, cxxix, and cxvi in the Evening Office. Later the Stichera increased in length and were sung in various parts of the Evening and Morning Office; in their function and musical structure they can best be compared to the Antiphons of the Latin Church. Like the Hirmi they have either their own melody—*Stichera*

[1] Ibid., Part I, ii. 859. Greek text: *Triodion*, (Rome, 1879), pp. 100–1.

Idiomela—or follow a melody, already used in a Sticheron—*Stichera Prosomoia*.

The Stichera, words and music, are collected, as has been said in the fifth chapter, in a single bulky volume, the *Sticherarion*. A facsimile edition of a complete *Sticherarion*, Cod. theol. gr. 181 of the National Library in Vienna, written in 1221 by John Dalassenos, was published in *Mon. Mus. Byz.*, vol. i (1935). A complete *Sticherarion* contains:

(1) The *Stichera Idiomela* or *Automela* from the Menaia for the fixed days of the ecclesiastical year, which, in the East, begins on the 1st of September (*ἀρχὴ τῆς Ἰνδίκτου ἤτοι τοῦ νέου ἔτους*.)

(2) The *Stichera Idiomela* from the Triodion and Pentecostarion for Lent, Easter, and Pentecost up to Trinity Sunday inclusive (*ἀπὸ τοῦ Φαρισαίου καὶ τοῦ τελώνου μέχρι τῶν Ἁγίων Πάντων*).

(3) The *Stichera Anastasima* and *Anatolika*, or Resurrection Verses from the Oktoëchos, the latter ascribed to the Patriarch Anatolius.[1]

(4) The twenty-four *Alphabetical Stichera* from the Oktoëchos for the Evening Office on Saturday.

(5) The *Anabathmoi* (*τροπάρια ἀναβαθμοί*) from the Oktoëchos for Morning Office on Sundays, divided into eight sections, each of which is sung in one of the eight modes. Each section is made up of three groups of Antiphons (*ἀντίφωνα*) with the exception of that in the fourth plagal Mode, which is made up of four. The third Sticheron of each Antiphon is in praise of the Holy Spirit and invariably begins with the words *Ἁγίῳ Πνεύματι*.

(6) The *Stichera Prosomoia* for Lent from the Triodion, belonging to the Evening Office.

(7) The *Heothina Anastasima* (*τὰ Ἑωθινὰ Ἀναστάσιμα*) of Leo VI (886–911), sung at the end of the Sunday Morning Office.

(8) The *Stichera Dogmatika* by John Damascene in honour of the Blessed Virgin; other *Theotokia* are often added to these, and also the *Staurotheotokia* of Leo VI.

[1] In most Codices these are called *Stichera Anastasima Anatolika*, but as Dom Tardo points out in his article 'L'Ottoèco nei manoscritti di antica melurgia bizantina', *Bollettino della Badia Greca di Grottaferrata*, N.S. I (1947), pp. 37–8, the best MSS. distinguish between the two groups.

(9) A group of *Stichera* connected with the special feasts of the monastery or the church to which the Sticherarion belonged.

A number of Stichera taken from these groups will be found in the Appendix. It can be seen at once that most of them differ widely from the Hirmi in length, compass, and extent of the ornamentation. But the analysis of the structure of both Hirmi and Stichera in the last chapter will show that the principle underlying their formal structure is the same: the combination of a number of melodic formulae, connected by simple transitional passages.

CHAPTER X

BYZANTINE MUSICAL NOTATION I

I. THE TWO SYSTEMS: ECPHONETIC SIGNS AND NEUMES

IN Byzantine manuscripts of service-books for the use of lectors and singers two systems of musical signs occur: one regulating the cantillation of the Lessons from the Prophets, Epistles, and the Gospel; the other fixing the flow and execution of the melodies of the model stanzas of the Kanons, the Stichera, Kontakia, and other poetical texts. Psalms, Alleluias, and Doxologies appear in thirteenth- and fourteenth-century manuscripts only.

The first system of signs, regulating the recitation (ἐκφώνησις) of the Lessons, comprises the ecphonetic signs;[1] the second the musical signs proper. Both systems derive from the Greek prosodic signs, but have a different development: the ecphonetic signs are set, in the main, at the beginning and at the end of a group of words; the musical signs correspond to the syllables of the text. The function of the ecphonetic signs, therefore, is equivalent to that of the system of Syriac accents whose introduction is ascribed to Joseph Hûzâjâ (*c*. A.D. 500),[2] though their shape is very like that of the prosodic signs.

The system of the ecphonetic signs seems to have been introduced towards the end of the fourth century;[3] it appears fully

[1] Attention was first drawn to the signs in Byzantine lectionaries by Montfaucon in his *Palaeographia Graeca* (Paris, 1708), pp. 234 and 260, and by Wattenbach in *Schrifttafeln zur Geschichte der griechischen Schrift* (Berlin, 1876–7). Sabas in his *Specimina Palaeographica cod. graec. et slavon. bibliothecae mosquensis synodalis saec. vi–xvii* (Moscow, 1863) and Gardthausen in the first edition of his *Griechische Palaeographie* (Leipzig, 1879) gave the first account of the function of the signs. The term 'ecphonetic' was first used by I. Tzetzes in his essay *'Η ἐπινόησις τῆς παρασημαντικῆς τῶν Βυζαντινῶν*, *Parnassos*, ix (1885), 441; but it is through J.-B. Thibaut's 'Étude de musique byzantine. Le chant ekphonétique', *B.Z.* viii (1899), 122 sqq., that the term was made known to western scholars. For the study of the ecphonetic notation see J.-B. Thibaut, *Monuments de la notation ekphonétique et hagiopolite de l'église grecque* (1913); E. Wellesz, 'Die byzantinischen Lektionszeichen', *Z.M.W.* xi (1929), 513–34; id., 'Ein griechisches Evangelium der Wiener Nationalbibliothek', *Kirchenmusikalisches Jahrbuch*, 1930, pp. 9–24; C. Höeg, *La Notation ekphonétique*, *M.M.B.*, Subs. i. 2 (1935); P. L. Tardo, *L'Antica Melurgia Bizantina* (1938), pp. 45–53.

[2] Cf. Th. Weiss, 'Zur ostsyrischen Laut- und Akzentlehre', *Bonner Orientalistische Studien*, v (1933). A similar system, consisting of single dots, or a combination of two or three, was discovered and described by the present author from Manichean and Christian texts, written in 'Soghdic', a Middle-Persian dialect; cf. E. Wellesz, 'Die Lektionszeichen in den soghdischen Texten', *Z.M.W.* i (1919), 505 sqq.

[3] Cf. C. Höeg, *La Notation ekphon.*, pp. 38–9.

developed in eighth-century manuscripts.[1] The number of the signs and their shape are maintained, practically unchanged, from the eighth century to the end of the thirteenth. From the beginning of the fourteenth to the end of the fifteenth centuries the texts show a slow disintegration of the ecphonetic system, and by the end of the fifteenth century the meaning of the signs has become obscure.[2]

An exact dating of manuscripts containing ecphonetic signs is difficult, not only because the shape of the signs remained the same for practically five centuries, but also because it was the habit of the scribes to copy the script with meticulous care. The lectionaries were the most precious books, particularly the *Evangeliaria*, with their richly jewelled covers, and therefore had to be written calligraphically with an archaizing tendency. A script composed of capital letters was more legible in the darkness of the church before dawn or after dusk than the complex forms of minuscule script which developed later. These two causes contributed to make the scribes intensely conservative.

It is, however, possible to date these manuscripts. When the scribe reached the end of a column he was often forced to compress the letters to make the material fit the column, and at this point he utilized the cursive forms that were in common use in his day.

This can be seen, for example, from examining the script of Codex Sinaiticus 204 (Plate II), written about A.D. 1000. Here the scribe imitated, as is usual in liturgical manuscripts of that period, the script of the fifth and sixth centuries, the so-called 'Old Parchment Uncial'[3] which is of unsurpassed perfection. Nearly all the letters of the alphabet of that script can be brought into the shape of a square or a circle, or inscribed into one of them. The full circle occurs as a rule in O and Θ, the half circle in Є and C. The letters ΑΒΓΔΖ, &c., can be placed into a square. Furthermore all letters are of equal height and have no additional ornaments.

Glancing, however, at the second line of the first column one instantly sees that in the two words ΟΥΚ ΟΙ(ΔΑΤΕ) the two omikron's are written differently each time. The scribe was obliged to do so. He had reached the end of the line with the Κ

[1] Cf. Thibaut, *Monuments de la notation ekphon.*, p. 32; Höeg, ibid., p. 137.

[2] Cf. Höeg, ibid., p. 137.

[3] Cf. V. Gardthausen, *Griechische Palaeographie* (Leipzig, 1913), pp. 119 sqq.

of OUK. He, therefore, had not much space left in the margin and wrote OI in the script of the 'Liturgical Uncial' of his day. This means that he no longer imitated the 'Old Parchment Uncial' with its letters in the shape of □ and ○, but turned to the familiar forms of the 'Younger Parchment Uncial' in which the square was replaced by the rectangle ▯, and the circle by the oval 0.

The same tendency to imitate an older script can be observed in manuscripts in minuscule script. I take as an example the Gospel-Lectionary, *Codex suppl. gr.* 128 of the Vienna National Library. As can be inferred from the covers, this is a manuscript which belonged to one of the monasteries in Constantinople or its surroundings, for the covers each consist of two thin wooden plates, glued together and covered with red leather. On the cross-sides and the protruding front-sides are small grooves in the shape of a half circle which are made only by craftsmen in Constantinople. The text is calligraphically written on yellow-white parchment of a very good quality; it is nearly faultless. The parchment was prepared from calf hides, the material customarily used for liturgical books after the tenth century. The lines for the script were made on the flesh side of the parchment with a leaden wheel which leaves deep grooves.[1] The letters are written with dark brown ink—this too is customary in liturgical books—the ecphonetic signs, however, by the music master in a light brown ink. In this Codex the columns, consisting of twenty-two lines, each containing ten to twelve letters, are carefully planned so that each line has exactly the length of the others. This often makes it necessary to compress, or reduce in size, the last letters or, if it is the case of an *ου*, to place the *υ* on top of the *ο*: ȣ. The script normally tries to imitate that of the ninth century but in such cases the scribe gives himself away by unexpectedly using shapes of letters which do not occur in liturgical manuscripts of the ninth century. Nevertheless, the dating of Greek liturgical manuscripts remains a very difficult task, because as has already been mentioned, it is less a matter of writing as in Western manuscripts, than a kind of drawing which aims at following as closely as possible an old and venerable model.

Late in the twelfth century the straight lines of the neumes were converted into curved. At the same time a number of new dyn-

[1] Cf. E. Wellesz, 'Ein griechisches Evangelium der Wiener National Bibliothek mit ekphonetischen Lesezeichen', *Kirchenmusikalisches Jahrbuch*, xxv (1930), 9–24.

amic and rhythmical signs were added, until, in the first half of the fifteenth century—when the melodies had become florid—all the signs were revised and a new group of subsidiary signs in red ink, called the 'Great Signs' (*μεγάλα σημάδια*) or 'Great Hypostases' (*μεγάλαι ὑποστάσεις*), was introduced. This system survived the end of the Empire and remained in use up to the beginning of the nineteenth century, when a reformed system of notation was introduced by Chrysanthus, who retained a small number of the old signs and added some new ones. Consequently all manuscripts containing the original Byzantine notation fell into disuse, and the ability to read them was completely lost.

The development of Byzantine music after the fall of Constantinople, and its transformation into Neo-Greek music is not within the scope of the present outline; we shall therefore exclude the latest development of Byzantine musical notation and its replacement by the Chrysanthean notation, and may refer to the *Traité de Psaltique* (Paris, 1906) by J.-B. Rebours, from which all the necessary information for the study of the modern system can be obtained. Here we shall restrict ourselves to giving a brief survey of the development of Byzantine neumes from a ninth-century Hirmologion, the earliest musical manuscript which has come down to us, up to manuscripts from the fifteenth century, which show a richly developed system of subsidiary signs.

II. ECPHONETIC NOTATION

The invention of the prosodic signs (*προσῳδίαι*) or accents, is ascribed to the grammarian Aristophanes of Byzantium (*c.* 180 B.C.). They were introduced in the Hellenistic age as a guide for declamation when Greek became the predominating language in the East.

In Byzantine manuscripts the accents are set according to the teaching of Herodianus and other Greek grammarians of the second and the following centuries.[1] There are four groups of prosodic signs:[2]

[1] Cf. G. Zuntz, 'The Ancestry of the Harklean New Testament', *Brit. Acad. Suppl. Papers*, vii (1945), pp. 89 sqq.

[2] It may be noticed that a similar system of signs is found in the ancient Hindu scriptures. Cf. M. Haug, 'Über das Wesen und den Wert des Vedischen Accents', *Abh. d. Akad. d. Wiss.* (Munich, 1873), and O. Fleischer, 'Über Ursprung und Entzifferung der Neumen', *Neumen-Studien*, i (Leipzig, 1895), 56–64. Originally the Pathe were not included in the Prosodiai, as can be seen e.g. from a paragraph in the treatise *Περὶ προσῳδίων* by Georgius Choiroboscus: *Ἔνιοι δὲ τὰ καλούμενα πάθη προστιθέασι ταῖς προσῳδίαις, ἅπερ ἐστὶν ἀπόστροφος, ὑφέν, ὑποδιαστολή. Ἰστέον δὲ ὅτι ταῦτα οὐ καλοῦνται κυρίως προσῳδίαι κτλ. Scholia in Dionysii Thracis artem grammaticam*, ed. A. Hilgard, *Grammatici Graeci*, iii. 125.

I *Τόνοι. Tones*

(1) *προσῳδία ὀξεῖα*, the high tone = acute ′
(2) *προσῳδία βαρεῖα*, the low-pitched tone = grave ‵
(3) *προσῳδία περισπωμένη*, the ligature consisting of acute and grave = circumflex ^

II *Χρόνοι. Time-units*

(1) *προσῳδία μακρά*, sign for the long syllable = long -
(2) *προσῳδία βραχεῖα*, sign for the short syllable = breve ◡

III. *Πνεύματα. Breathings*

(1) *προσῳδία δασεῖα*, rough breathing = spiritus asper ⊢
(2) *προσῳδία ψιλή*, smooth breathing = spiritus lenis ⊣

IV. *Πάθη. Declamatory signs*

(1) *ἀπόστροφος*, apostrophe ..?..
(2) *ὑφέν*, *coniunctio* ..◡..
(3) *διαστολή*, *separatio* ..ɔ...

The musical character of Greek declamation is clear, first from the very term 'accent' (*προσῳδία*), indicating the element of chant in speech, secondly from the remark of the rhetor Dionysius of Halicarnassus (*c.* 30 B.C.): 'The melos of speech is measured approximately by the one interval, called *diapente* (fifth). The voice does not ascend beyond three and a half tones, nor does it descend by more than this interval.'[1] The musical character of the prosodic signs made it possible later on to use them as a system of signs for the guidance of the Anagnostes, whose duty was the *lectio solemnis* of the pericopes from the *Prophetologion*, *Apostolos*, and *Evangeliarion*.

A small number of tables of the ecphonetic signs have come down to us,[2] the best known on a leaf of Cod. Leimon (Lesbos) 38, fol. 318r. (see Pl. I). This table is, as I have pointed out in my study on the ecphonetic notation, a kind of primer showing all the possible combinations of ecphonetic signs, and their technical

[1] *De compositione verborum*, ch. 11.
[2] A complete list of the tables and three facsimiles are given in Höeg's *La Notation ekphon.*

names, in the form of a pericope.[1] There is, in effect, one principal rule for the *lectio solemnis* of a pericope. The cantillation followed the syntactical structure of the phrase in every detail, as the ecphonetic signs in the manuscripts show. The final verse of every lesson, however, shows a peculiar notation, characterized by the use of doubled signs, which never occur in the main part of the lesson. Unlike the rest of the lesson the ending was given special emphasis by a kind of chanting which came near to emotional singing. This prepared the congregation for the ending of the lesson to which they had to respond by the formula Δόξα τῷ Θεῷ. The transcription of the table runs as follows:

Ὀξεία πρὸς ὀξείαν βα
ρίαι βαρίαι· καθισταὶ
καθισταὶ· συρματικῆ
καὶ τελεία + παρακλιτι
κῆ καὶ τελεία + ὑπόκρι
σις ὑπόκρισις ὑπό
κρισις κρεμασταὶ κρε
μασταί· ἀπέσω ἔξω· ὀ
ξεία καὶ τελεία + κεντή
ματα κεντήματα· ἀ
πόστροφος· ἀπόστρο
φος ἀπόστροφος· συν
έμβα καὶ τελεία + ὀξεῖ
αι διπλαῖ· διπλαὶ βα
ρίαι· κεντήματα· καὶ ἀ
πόστροφοι + +

[1] Papadopoulos-Kerameus was the first to draw attention to the table of the Leimon Codex in his *Μαυροκορδάτειος Βιβλιοθήκη*, p. 50, no. 35, and gave a lithographic facsimile of the first lines, followed by a printed version of the rest of the table. But, as he did not understand the meaning of the signs, he made some mistakes in reproducing them. J.-B. Thibaut's studies on ecphonetic notation are all based on this faulty reproduction of the table, and the lists of ecphonetic signs which he drew up, and which were taken over by some scholars, make no sense. The majority of Thibaut's mistakes are so obvious that I succeeded in correcting nearly all of them in my study 'Die byzant. Lektionszeichen', *Z.M.W.* (1929), though I was not able to get a photographic reproduction of the table. The authentic text could only be obtained when, in 1931, C. Höeg presented me with a photograph of fol. 317 v. of the Leimon Codex, the facsimile of which is also given in his book on ecphonetic notation.

From the table we get the following list of signs:

Simple Signs	*Compound Signs*
Oxeia	Oxeiai
Syrmatikē	Bareiai
Bareia	Kentemata
Kathiste	apeso exo
Kremaste	Apostrophoi
Apostrophos	Hypokrisis
Synemba	
Paraklitike	
Teleia	

The guiding principle[1] in setting the ecphonetic signs was the following: each sentence, or part of a sentence, each word or part of a word to be 'cantillated' in a certain manner, was encompassed at the beginning and at the end by a sign that was immediately followed by another sign for the next sentence or phrase or word. The encompassing signs were either the same or different ones. This was regulated either through the meaning of the signs or through the meaning of the words which formed a rhetorical unity.

The *Oxeia* (ὀξεῖα) indicates that the voice should rise and remain on a higher pitch until the end of the phrase, marked by a second Oxeia. The *Syrmatikē* (συρματική) demands an undulating movement like the shape of the sign.

The *Bareia* (βαρεῖα) stands for lowering the pitch of the voice and giving emphasis to the words encompassed by the two signs.

The *Kremaste* (κρεμαστή) marks a rise of the voice with slight accentuation.

The *Apostrophos* (ἀπόστροφος) seems to indicate a somewhat low pitch of the voice without giving emphasis to the words

[1] Cf. my 'Die byzantinischen Lektionszeichen', *Z.M.W.* xi. 527–8; J.-B. Thibaut, *Origine byzantine de la notation neumatique*, p. 24.

which the two Apostrophoi enclose, but it seems also to have retained the original meaning which the grammarians had given it as one of the *Pathē* or declamatory signs where it means to take breath and to begin to read. We shall have to come back to the function of the Apostrophos because we find it in Early Byzantine notation (1) at the beginning of a phrase where, at a later stage, the *Ison* is written; (2) in the course of a melodic movement where it is connected either with a falling or a rising second. At that early stage, however, we should not take the Apostrophos for the Interval sign itself, a meaning which the Apostrophos acquired in the Coislin and Round notation when it was set only to mark a falling second; it was a sign for the execution of the note.

The *Synemba* (*συνέμβα*) is a kind of slur, combining two words in one breath.

The *Paraklitike* (*παρακλιτική*). In his study on the Ecphonetic notation Thibaut[1] refers to the spelling Paraklētikē (*παρακλητική*), mentioned by Tzetzes and points out that the Paraklitike of the Ecphonetic notation looks like the Parakletike of Byzantine musical notation. Since Byzantine scribes often write phonetically, and *η* was pronounced as *ι*, the wrong spelling may be overlooked and we can accept the identity of both signs. Parakletike, therefore, indicates a phrase executed in an entreating, praying manner.

The *Hypokrisis* (*ὑπόκρισις*) has the opposite meaning to the *Synemba*;[2] it is a sign of separation. Since it may consist of two or three hooks, it can indicate a shorter or longer pause.

The *Teleia* (*τελεία*) means a full stop.

The *Kathiste* (*καθιστή*) marks the narrative style without emphasis and is always found at the beginning of a lesson from the Gospel, introduced by *Τῷ καιρῷ ἐκείνῳ* (at that time). It sometimes needed more than alteration of first words of the text in order to open the Lesson with this stereotyped phrase as can be seen from the Gospel of St. Luke xxiv, 36–48 to be read on Sundays at Matins as the sixth of the eleven 'Resurrection Evangelia' (*Εὐαγγέλια ἑωθινὰ ἀναστάσιμα*).

[1] Cf. op. cit. *B.Z.* viii. 130.

[2] See later.

Gospel	*Lesson*[1]
Ταῦτα δὲ αὐτῶν λαλοῦντων	*Τῷ καιρῷ ἐκείνῳ ἀναστὰς ὁ 'Ιησοῦς*
αὐτὸς ἔστη ἐν μέσῳ αὐτῶν.	*ἐκ νεκρῶν ἔστη ἐν μέσῳ τῶν Μαθη-*
καὶ λέγει αὐτοῖς· εἰρήνη ὑμῖν.	*τῶν*
	αὐτοῦ καὶ λέγει αὐτοῖς + Εἰρήνη ὑμῖν +
And while they were speaking these things, He stood in the midst of them, and said to them: Peace be to you.	At that time Jesus was risen from the dead, and stood in the midst of his disciples, and said to them: Peace be to you.

The two segments of the phrase *Τῷ . . . ἐκείνῳ* and *ἀναστὰς . . . νεκρῶν* are to be read in the simple way of a narration. The next section *ἔστη . . . αὐτοῦ* have the Apostrophos which seems to indicate lowering the voice, but without any emphasis. In the phrase *καὶ λέγει αὐτοῖς* (and said to them) there is an Oxeia at the beginning and Teleia at the end, which means that these words should be said or chanted on a high pitch with a certain emphasis, and that the reader should make a stop where the Teleia demands it. The Syrmatikē, which originated from the circumflex and indicates an undulating movement of the voice, has here a peculiar significance. The apparition of Jesus risen from the dead and standing in the midst of the disciples must have frightened them. Therefore the voice of the Anagnostes must come soft and serene when Jesus greets them with *Εἰρήνη ὑμῖν*, 'Peace be to you'.

Another stereotyped opening is *Εἶπεν ὁ κύριος* (the Lord said), encompassed in many cases by Oxeia and Teleia, but in some cases by Kathiste and Kathiste, when the narration continues:

Εἶπεν ὁ Κύριος +
Εἶπεν ὁ Κύριος τοῖς ἑαυτοῦ μαθηταῖς + [2]

A third alternative can be seen on plate 21 of Thibaut's *Monuments*,[3] taken from a ninth-century Evangelium, Cod. Petropol. gr. XLIII, fol. 1 r. Here, too, the first sentence from Luke xv. 11 had to be changed considerably for use as a lesson:

[1] Text and ecphonetic signs are taken from a ninth-century Evangelium, Cod. Petropol. gr. XXXVI, a MS. from Mount Sinai, reproduced in J.-B. Thibaut's *Monuments de la notation ekphonétique et hagiopolite de l'Église grecque* (St-Pétersbourg, 1913), p. 39.

[2] See C. Höeg, *La Notation ekphon.*, p. 46

[3] *Monuments de la notation ekphon. et hagiopol.*, p. 41.

Gospel	*Lesson*
Εἶπεν δέ· ἄνθρωπός τις εἶχεν δύο υἱούς.	*Εἶπεν ὁ Κύριος τὴν παραβολὴν ταύτην + ἄνθρωπός τίς εἶχεν δύο υἱούς.*
(He said: A man had two sons).	(The Lord told this parable: A man had two sons.)

For the close of a pericope a verse is always chosen which makes a good ending, and can therefore take a special emphasis. The reading from the Gospel on Easter Monday, for example, ends with verse 28 from John i: *Ταῦτα ἐν Βηθανίᾳ ἐγένετο πέραν τοῦ Ἰορδάνου, ὅπου ἦν Ἰωάννης βαπτίζων* (These things were done in Bethania beyond Jordan, where John was baptizing). (*Vide* Plate II.) The emphasis, however, was not conditioned by the sentence itself but by its position at the end of the pericope. This can be seen when the same verse which bears a special emphasis at the end of a short lesson appears in the middle of a longer one containing the same text. This happens frequently in the Orthodox Church where during the week, or on lesser feasts, a short extract from a chapter from the Gospel is read, whereas on Sundays or on major feasts a longer extract from the same chapter is read. The same thing may even happen on two primary festivals, one of which has a short service, as e.g. Easter Sunday. On the evening of that day the Lesson from the Gospel is taken from John xx. 19–25; on the following Sunday, *Κυριακῇ τοῦ Ἀντίπασχα*, however, the lesson is extended to verse 31. In the first place (1) the verse 'and thrust my hand into his side, I will not believe' has strong emphasis; in the second (2) it is accentuated in the usual way, and the emphasis is shifted to the end of the pericope, to verse 31 but these are written that ye might believe that Jesus is the Christ the Son of God, and that believing ye might have life through His name' (3).

(2) καὶ βάλω τὴν χεῖρά μου εἰς τὴν πλευρὰν αὐτοῦ
οὐ μὴ πιστεύσω +

(3) ταῦτα δὲ γέγραπται, ἵνα πιστεύητε ὅτι Ἰησοῦς
ἐστιν ὁ Χριστός ὁ υἱὸς τοῦ θεοῦ + καὶ ἵνα
πιστεύοντες ζωὴν ἔχετε ἐν τῷ ὀνόματι
αὐτοῦ +

Investigation into the *Lectionaria*[1] has shown that hardly any two codices containing the same pericopes have exactly the same ecphonetic notation throughout the text: there are many divergencies to be found, but only in small details. In the main there must have been, from the beginning, a single tradition for chanting the pericopes. The execution may have been different in small monasteries or in one of the metropolitan churches.[2] In the former the service must have been less elaborate and the reading of the Lessons would have been a simple cantillation; in the latter, on the contrary, it may have developed into real singing.

It cannot be affirmed that the *ecphonesis* had the character of a cantillation with distinct intervals and melodic cadences in the Early Byzantine Service in general,[3] but it was certainly the case

[1] Cf. the table in E. Wellesz, 'Die byz. Lektionszeichen', *Z.M.W.* xi. 525; C. Höeg, *La Notation ekphon.*, pp. 86–102. The divergencies in the setting of ecphonetic signs can be studied in the two volumes of the *Prophetologium*, *M.M.B.*, edited by G. Zuntz (Copenhagen, 1939 and 1940).

[2] Dr. G. Zuntz, who has been engaged on the edition of the *Prophetologion* for the *M.M.B.*, since 1935, informs me that MSS. of the *Prophetologion* written for use in the Patriarchal Church of Hagia Sophia use the standard ecphonetic notation with greater precision and give a more detailed version of the cadences in the middle of a phrase than any other MS.

[3] Though no MS. with ecphonetic signs of an earlier date than the tenth century has come down to us, we may assume that the Lessons from the Gospel were sung in the Eastern Church in the same way as they were sung in the West. For a series of lectures on 'Christian Chant', which I delivered in 1952–3 in the Third Programme of the B.B.C., recordings were made in Jerusalem of the chanting of lessons from the Pentateuch by Jews who had just arrived from Yemen where they had lived in enclosures since the Diaspora. These cantillations of the Lessons were very much akin to those which Greek deacons can be heard chanting nowadays in the churches. In a most valuable paper on 'The Common Ground in the Chant of Church and Synagogue', *Atti del Congresso Internazionale di Musica Sacra 1950* (Rome, 1952), pp. 134–48, E. Werner drew attention to these parallels, particularly to the fact 'that the version of the *Tonus Peregrinus* of the *Antiphonare Sarisburiense* is identical, note for note, with the *Hallel*-tune of the Yemenite Jews'.

in the tenth century. This can be proved from a table of Codex Sinaiticus 8, fol. 303 r., a *Prophetologion* dating from the tenth or eleventh century, which shows groups of neumes in Early Byzantine notation superimposed upon the ecphonetic signs. This important document has been reproduced by C. Höeg as Plate III of his *La Notation ekphonétique* and commented upon in detail on pp. 26–35. The difficulty of reaching a satisfactory solution lies, as Höeg rightly pointed out, in the fact that the Early Byzantine notation does not provide us with the exact interval-value of the melodic steps; but it is obvious that the practice which is indicated by the musical signs in Codex Sinaiticus 8 must have come very near to the present cantillation, of which Thibaut has given two examples in his study on ecphonetic notation.[1] The first is a reconstruction by Thibaut showing how the ecphonetic signs might have been chanted, the second the transcription of the actual singing of the same pericope by an ex-deacon.[2] Thibaut gives the last three verses of the pericope from Luke xxi. 34–6. The modern way of singing, according to the ex-deacon's transcription, is less stereotyped, but, in the main, does not differ very much from Thibaut's reconstruction.

[1] *B.Z.* viii (1899), pp. 139–43. The second of these examples is also printed in Höeg's *La Notation ekphon.*, pp. 128–32.

[2] Höeg gives in *La Notation ekphon.*, pp. 132–5, a transcription from a recording of the voice of the Metropolitan of Samos, made by Mme Humbert Sauvageot in conformity with the method of transcribing used by the Institut de Phonétique at the University of Paris.

(And take heed to yourselves, lest at any time your hearts be overcharged with surfeiting, and drunkenness, and cares of this life, and so that day come upon you unawares. For as a snare shall it come on all them that dwell on the face of the whole earth. Watch ye therefore, and pray always, that ye may be accounted worthy to escape all these things that shall come to pass, and to stand before the Son of man.)

There can be no doubt that the titles of the Lessons were chanted as well, as was the practice in the Latin Church, though the titles of the pericopes from the Prophets, Epistles, and Gospels have no ecphonetic signs; but since these titles had prescribed formulae it was not necessary to write them down. A few years ago, however, the manuscript of a *Synodikon* (*Συνο-*

δικόν *scil.* βιβλίον) passed from private ownership into the Bodleian Library. This manuscript contains not only the well-known *Makarismoi* and *Anathema*'s read on Orthodoxy Sunday, the first Sunday of *Quadragesima*, but also those of the Sunday of the commemoration of the six oecumenical synods (*Κυριακὴ τῶν ἁγίων πατέρων τῶν ἐν ταῖς ἓξ οἰκουμενικαῖς συνόδοις*). The first 'exposition or memorial', however, is that of the Council of Constantinople in July 920,[1] supported by the Grand Admiral Romanus Lecapenus, who governed for the young Emperor Constantine VII. In this Synodikon the titles are supplied with ecphonetic signs:

fol. 1 r. Ἔκθεσις ἤτοι ἀνάμνησις· τῆς γενομένης

τῆς ἐκκλησίας ἑνώσεως· ἐπὶ κωνσταν

τίνου καὶ ρωμανοῦ· τοῦ μὲν βασιλεύοντος·

fol. 1 v. τοῦ δε. τὸ τηνι||καῦτα· τῷ τοῦ βασιλεω-

πάτορος ἀξιώματι διαπρέποντος

(Exposition or memorial of the union of the Church under Constantine and Romanus, the one who is Emperor, the other who at that time shines forth through the honour of the title 'father of the Emperor'.)

The combination ⁊ . . . . . ⁄ is called *apeso exo* and indicates a beginning on a low pitch and rising to the Oxeia (⁄) at the end of the phrase. The next phrase is enclosed by ✓. . . . ✓, the two Kremastai, which indicate, as was said, a slightly accentuated rising of the voice. The words ἐπὶ Κωνσταντίνου καὶ Ῥωμανοῦ are enclosed by two Apostrophoi (⁊ . . . . ⁊). Höeg has given several examples[1] which show that proper names and titles are often given a narrative delivery where one would expect a stronger accentuation. As a contrast 'the one who is Emperor' has the strongest emphasis, whereas the following phrases referring to Romanus Lecapenus—who had just arrogated to himself the title Basileopater by marrying the child-Emperor to his daughter—are kept in a rather repressed expression. Should we assume that the Synodikon was compiled and the notation added at a time when Romanus lived in exile as a monk and the Emperor

[1] Op. cit., pp. 47–53.

Constantine Porphyrogenitus had triumphed over the Lecapeni?

The discovery of the *Synodikon* is at any rate of great importance, because the ecphonetic notation reflects the emotional character of its content; thus when one reads in the *Synodikon* of the Council of Chalcedon Cod. Holkham. fol. 44 v.:

῞Ολοις τοῖς αἱρετικοῖς· ἀνάθεμα Γ′

῞Ολοις τοῖς νεστοριανοῖς· ἀνάθεμα Γ

῞Ολοις τοῖς ἰακωβίταις· ἀνάθεμα Γ′

(On all heretics: Anathema [thrice])
(On all Nestorians: Anathema [thrice])
(On all Jacobitae[1]: Anathema [thrice])

The end of the Synodikon has the same intensified notation as the end of a pericope

and one may well assume that this last paragraph was not only chanted, but sung.

[1] Followers of the Monophysite Jacobus Tzantzalus.

CHAPTER XI

BYZANTINE MUSICAL NOTATION II
THE NEUMES

(1) THE THREE PHASES OF NEUMATIC NOTATION

THREE different kinds of Byzantine musical notation can be clearly distinguished, though all of them develop from the same roots, the prosodic signs: (1) an early stage in which the signs have no distinct interval value; (2) a later, in which the signs give clear indication of the size of the intervals; and (3) a final development, in which subsidiary signs in red ink are added to the musical notation in black ink. J.-B. Thibaut, the first scholar to make a systematic investigation of Byzantine musical notation and to try to deduce the origin of Latin neumes from Constantinople,[1] gave the following names to the three groups:

(1) Notation Constantinopolitaine (11th century)
(2) Notation Hagiopolite (13th century)
(3) Notation de Koukouzélès (13th–19th century).

By this division Thibaut intended to emphasize his theory that the first phase originated in Constantinople, the second in Jerusalem, and that the last, according to the view of Neo-Greek theorists, was invented by Koukouzeles. In the same year A. Gastoué's *Catalogue des manuscrits de musique byzantine* (Paris, 1907) appeared, in which he divided the earliest phase into two groups: (*a*) Notation Paléobyzantine (10th century), and (*b*) Notation Byzantine mixte Constantinopolitaine (11th century). He used the same names for the second and third phases as Thibaut had done.

The most comprehensive study on the subject, H. Riemann's *Die byzantinische Notenschrift* (Leipzig, 1909), was partly based on Fleischer's *Neumen-Studien*, partly on Gastoué's *Catalogue*. Riemann arrived at the following division:

(1) Oldest notation (*c*. A.D. 1000).
(2) Transition to (3) (fragment from Chartres, Cod. 1754, 11th–12th century).

[1] *Origine byzantine de la notation neumatique de l'église latine* (Paris, 1907).

(3) The fine 'stroke-dot' notation (12th–13th century).
(4) The round notation without hypostases (13th–14th century).
(5) The notation with hypostases (from 1300 onwards).

Neither Gastoué's nor Riemann's schemes are fully satisfactory, because their knowledge of the earliest phase was restricted to a small number of manuscripts, and the names which they gave to the different phases of notation were inconsistent. Some of the terms referred to the supposed place of origin, others to the shape of the signs, the last to a person. Starting from the term 'Late-Byzantine notation', coined by Fleischer, I proposed in my essay 'Die Kirchenmusik im byzantinischen Reich' (*Oriens Christianus*, Ser. II, vol. vi) a scheme which was based exclusively on the dates of the three main phases. It was later accepted by the editors of *M.M.B.*[1] We divide the development of Byzantine neumes into the following three groups which will, of course, need further subdivisions when more of the early manuscripts have been classified:

(1) Early Byzantine notation (palaeobyzantine, 'Stroke-dot' or linear notation): 9th–12th century.
(2) Middle Byzantine notation (hagiopolite, round): 12th–14th century.
(3) Late Byzantine notation (Koukouzelean, hagiopolite-psaltique): 14th–19th century.

In the earliest manuscripts the musical signs are not set to every syllable of the text. This can either mean that the preceding tone had to be repeated on the syllable without a musical sign, or that some of the signs had originally only a rhythmical significance. The latter hypothesis is based on the fact that the singers had to know the melodic formulae by heart and were helped by the signs to adapt the melodies to the words of the text. Musical signs indicating an upward or downward movement were used where two consecutive formulae had to be connected by a transitional passage.

Investigations into the different phases of notation have shown that the changes in the signs were due to the development of the music of the hymns, from a small group of melodic types to an

[1] O. Tiby has also accepted our classification in his *La Musica Bizantina* (Milan, 1938).

immense number of richly ornamented melodies. But these investigations have also made it quite clear that a melodic continuity existed from the earliest manuscripts which could be investigated, lasting to the end of the Empire.

This can be seen from the following table, containing the melody of the Easter hymn *Ἀναστάσεως ἡμέρα* in five different stages of notation together with its rendering into modern staff notation. The transcription is made from Codex Grottaferrata E *γ* ii (GF), written in 1281.[1] Under it is set the neumatic notation from Codex 4590 of the Iviron monastery on Mount Athos (I), dating from the middle of the twelfth century.[2] The two codices represent two different phases of Middle Byzantine notation. The neumes in Cod. Iviron still have the fine lines of the 'Stroke-dot' notation; in Cod. Grottaferrata they already show the thick curved lines which led to the introduction of the term 'Round Notation'.

The third type of notation is taken from Cod. Laurae *Γ*9[3] (L2) of Mount Athos, dating from the twelfth century. The character of the notation is similar to that of Cod. Iviron. This notation represents the final development of Early Byzantine neumes; they have no distinct interval value, but a comparison of L2 and I shows that it was only necessary to make slight changes to transform the relative pitch of the last stage of Early Byzantine notation into the absolute interval-value of Middle Byzantine notation. Both systems were for a short time used simultaneously, in the first half of the twelfth century, until all the Hirmologia were rewritten in the new type of notation.

The fourth type is taken from Cod. Coislin 220 of the Bibl. Nation. at Paris (C), dating from the end of the eleventh or beginning of the twelfth century.[4] The shape of the signs in Cod. Coislin is very similar to those in Cod. Iviron; but it has fewer signs to indicate the flow of the melodic line; we may therefore

[1] Cf. L. Tardo, 'La musica bizantina e i codici di melurgia della Biblioteca di Grottaferrata', *Accademie e biblioteche*, iv (1931), 8 and 13.

[2] Cf. Hirmologium Athoum, *M.M.B.* ii. 11.

[3] Since the new *Catalogue of the Greek MSS. in the Library of the Laura on Mount Athos* by Spiridon and Eustratiades was published the Hirmologion is quoted as Cod. Laurae 249.

[4] Cf. A. Gastoué, *Catalogue des manuscrits de mus. byz.*, p. 89. Facsimiles from this codex are given in Riemann's *Die byz. Notenschrift* and in Petresco's *Les Idiomèles et le Canon de l'office de Noël*, pls. 26–8.

assume that this stage of notation goes back to the end of the eleventh century.

The fifth type of notation is taken from Cod. Laurae B 32 from Mount Athos (L1). It represents the earliest stage of Byzantine notation of which only a few manuscripts and some fragments have come down to us. Thibaut, describing two folios of the manuscript, brought to the former Imperial Library of St. Petersburg by Archimandrite Porphyry Ouspensky[1] and catalogued as Cod. graec. Petropolit. 361, attributed the manuscript to the ninth century. Riemann, who gives reproductions of six pages from Cod. Laurae B 32 in *Die byzantinische Notenschrift,* dates them 'circa 1000'.[2] We may ascribe the manuscript to the late tenth century.

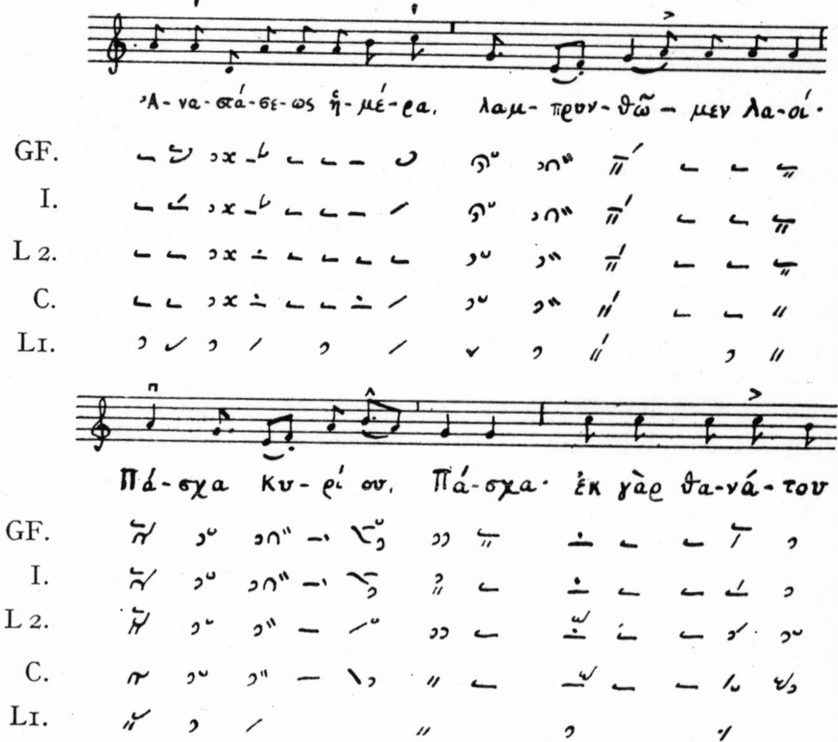

[1] Spiridon–S. Eustratiades, *Catalogue of the Greek MSS.*, register the MS. on p. 16 under no. 152. They ascribe the Hirmologion to the thirteenth century. This is obviously a mistake. C. Höeg in his introduction to 'The Hymns of the Hirmologium. Part I', *M.M.B. Transcripta*, vol. vi (1952), ascribes the MS. to the late tenth century, and I agree with him in his dating.

[2] The two folios of Cod. graec. Petropolit. 361 were cut out of Cod. Laurae B 32 by Ouspensky, who ruthlessly mutilated codices in order to get one or two leaves for the Imperial Library. It

was possible to prove this in the present case. Thibaut's *Monuments de la notation ekphonétique et hagiopolite* have reproductions of the four pages of Cod. graec. Petropolit. 361. I compared the script of fol. 1 with that of Cod. Laurae, of which I possess, thanks to Prof. C. Höeg, a complete reproduction; it proved to be identical. Further investigation showed that fol. 1v. of Cod. graec. Petropolit. contains three Odes of the Resurrection-Kanon *Τῷ διαβιβάσαντι* by Kosmas; the first page of Cod. Laurae starts with the fourth Ode of the same Kanon and gives the rest of the Odes on this and the following page.

An examination of the five manuscripts will make it clear even to the reader who knows nothing of musical palaeography that L2, I, GF and C show a great similarity. It is not so easy to see how L1, the oldest manuscript, fits into the scheme. The divergencies between C and L1 are obvious; but a comparative study of L1 on the one hand, L2 and I on the other, shows that the signs of these three manuscripts are closely related. These facts which seem to contradict each other are not difficult to explain.

L1 dates, as we have pointed out, from a time when the singers knew by heart the formulae of which the melodies were built up. Most of the signs of L1 can be found in I and GF, where they have the function of rhythmical and dynamic nuances added to interval signs. This explains why some of the signs which we find in the other four manuscripts are missing in L1. On the other hand, there are some signs in L1 which obviously have an interval-value, and which seem to indicate a melodic movement opposite to that in C and the three other manuscripts.

From these observations we may draw the following conclusions: with two notational versions of the same melody before us, the one in Early, the other in Middle Byzantine notation, and both showing great similarity, we are justified in assuming that the early melodic version is virtually identical with the later one provided that both derive from the same monastic tradition. We are, of course, wholly justified in assuming identity in the case of Codex Saba 83 of the library of the Patriarchate in Jerusalem. Here the early stage of ninth- or tenth-century notation was amended in the thirteenth century by a scribe who turned the neumes written approximately two centuries before into the shape of the Middle Byzantine notation, added new signs to the old ones, and filled in the gaps where the first scribe had left an empty space. One can see both hands on Plate III. The first line is the closing line of the eighth Hirmus of the Kanon for the feast of the Holy Apostles by Cyprianus *Συνεπάγη πρὸς ἑαυτήν*[1] (the substance of the water drew together), and on the following four lines is the ninth Hirmus (*Ὠδὴ θ′*) in Middle Byzantine notation. The following five Hirmi of the Kanon *Ἆσμα καινόν* (A new song) by Andrew of Jerusalem are left in the original Early Byzantine notation. The reason is obvious. The Kanon was taken out of

[1] See S. Eustratiades, *Εἱρμολόγιον* (1932), p. 40; *Hirmologium Athoum*, *M.M.B.*, vol. ii, fol. 28 v. *Cod. Grottaferrata E γ* ii (*Hirmologium Cryptense*), *M.M.B.*, vol. iii, fol. 40 v.

the repertory, probably in the course of the eleventh century, when the repertory was stabilized. There was no need to bring the notation up to date.

When C. Höeg visited the Library of the Patriarchate in Jerusalem, where Cod. Saba 83 is now kept, he saw that the Hirmi were written partly in Early Byzantine notation, partly in Middle Byzantine notation. He instantly recognized that the Middle Byzantine notation had been written over the notation of the early phase, and therefore took two photographs of each page: one in the usual way, the other taken with a red filter, by which process the Middle Byzantine notation faded and the Early Byzantine was brought out. We mark the older layer as S(aba) I, the later one as S(aba) II, and, following the practice of the *M.M.B.*, leave out the accents of the words to give prominence to the neumes.

S I

S II

Εποιησεν μετα σου μεγαλεια αχραντε· ο των απαντων ποιη

S I

S II

της· τεχθεις γαρ εκ σου· παλιν σωαν εφυλαξεν·

S I

S II

την σην γαστεραν παναμωμε· διο απαυστως σε

S I

S II

θ[εοτο]κε βροτων το γενος μεγαλυνομεν·

(The Creator of All performed with you mighty deeds, Undefiled One. For he who was born from you, left your womb intact, All-blameless. Therefore, Mother of God, we mortals praise you incessantly.)

Though it must be left to a later part of this chapter to speak of the significance of the neumes and to explain their development, it can be assumed as evident even from a glance at the two systems that S I represents a much more primitive stage than S II. However, it is also quite clear that the melody, represented by the signs in S I, must be fundamentally the same as that represented by those in S II. The absence of signs over many syllables in S I requires an explanation. Does this mean that on syllables without a sign the preceding note should be repeated?

Judging from our comparative notational studies we may say that sometimes the gap should be filled by a repetition of the note, but in other cases by an interval, mostly a step, upwards or downwards. The omission of a notational sign does not mean that the preceding note should be repeated, but that it was unnecessary from the point of view of execution to write a sign.

This early stage of signs was, as I have explained in some detail,[1] introduced as an *aide-mémoire* for the conductor of the choir, or for the soloist, who sang from a chant-book. The singers had to know the repertory by heart, but they needed guidance when they performed the music, particularly when a new text was sung to the melody of an older hymn. They had to be informed about the rhythmical and dynamic changes required when the words of the new text had to be fitted to the existing melody. This early system, though often indicating the up- and downward movements of the melody, was mainly intended to give the melody its expression, prolonging a note, giving it different shades of emphasis, and so on; it is in fact not very different from that of ecphonetic notation.[2]

In the study on 'Early Byzantine Neumes'[3] I referred to the Alexandrian system of accentuation which shows the changes between high- and low-pitched syllables by giving several accents to a word,[4] a custom which survived in Byzantine times.[5] Here I pointed out that the Apostrophos (ɔ), which at a later stage became the sign for an unaccentuated downward move-

[1] E. Wellesz, 'Early Byzantine Neumes', *M.Q.* xxxviii (1952), 68–79.

[2] I suggested, loc. cit., p. 77, calling the one group 'ecphonetic signs' and the other 'rhetorical neumes' (*neumes oratoires*) in order to avoid the misleading term notation; but it is difficult to change a terminology which was only established a few decades ago.

[3] Cf. op. cit., pp. 76–7, particularly p. 77, ll. 2 sqq.

[4] Cf. B. Laum, 'Das alexandrinische Akzentuationssystem', *Studien zur Geschichte und Kultur des Altertums*, Paderborn, 1928.

[5] In the Sala Gregorii XVI of the Vatican, Showcase I, there is a Byzantine ivory-carving (sec. X?) representing the Nativity. It has the title carved in with two accents: Ἡ ΓΈΝΝΗϹΊϹ.

ment, was in the first stages still a 'prosodic sign that corresponds to the apostropha in the Western system of neumes', i.e. at the beginning a kind of taking breath before one starts singing, and in the middle an indication for a weak note.[1] This interpretation solves the difficulties which one encounters in finding the ɔ definitely in an upwards movement of the melody,[2] and also—this is the most frequent case down to the beginning of the 'Coislin' system—on the first note of the melody, but turned at a later stage into an Ison (˪).[3]

Though the Saba I notation leaves gaps, there can be no doubt that the ninth–tenth-century notation reveals the same melody as Saba II from the beginning of the twelfth century. Both represent the melodic tradition of Jerusalem in the same monastery, and we may even reconstruct the old melodic version of Saba I from a close study of both notations.

Codex Saba 83—we may mention it in this context—is another proof for the thesis which I expounded in the introduction to the transcription of the *Akathistos Hymn*,[4] namely, that the manuscript tradition of the Basilean monasteries in Sicily and south Italy derives from Mount Sinai and ultimately from Jerusalem. If we compare the version of Saba II with that of Codex Crypt. *E γ* ii[5] we see that both melodies are identical in shape, whereas that of Codex Iviron 470,[6] which belongs to the Constantinopolitanean class of manuscripts, varies considerably from the Saba type, as can be seen from the following transcription:

Saba 83 II

[1] Cf. C. Höeg, *The Hymns of the Hirmologium*, Part I, *M.M.B.* (1952), p. xxvi.

[2] O. Strunk came to the same conclusion about the Apostrophos in his article, 'The Notation of the Chartres Fragment', *Annales musicologiques*, tome iii (1955), p. 19, where he writes: 'Is it not possible that the *Apostrophos* was at first a sign without melodic meaning, used to distinguish secondary syllables, and that in the course of time it gradually acquired melodic meaning through association—first in terms of direction, then in terms of interval?' I fully agree with Strunk's view, which is in fact the view which I have held for nearly forty years.

[3] Cf. my article, 'Early Byzantine Neumes', p. 75, and C. Höeg, *The Hymns of the Hirmologium*, vol. i (1952), pp. xxiii–iv.

[4] Cf. *M.M.B. Transcripta*, vol. ix (1957), pp. xxxv–vi.

[5] Cf. the facsimile edition, *M.M.B.*, vol. iii, fol. 42 r.

[6] Cf. *Hirmologium Athoum*, *M.M.B.*, vol. ii, fol. 29 v.

(a) (b) (c)
των ποι - η - τής· τε-χθεὶς γὰρ ἐκ σοῦ· πά-λιν σῶ - - αν ἐ - φύ - λα -
(d)
- ξεν τὴν σὴν γα - στέ - ρα, παν - ά - μω- με. δι - ὸ ἀ - παυ - - στῶς
(e)
θε - ο - τό - κε, βρο-τῶν τὸ γέ - νος με - γα - λύ - νο - μεν.

Hirm.
Athoum

Variants
(a) (b) (c)
τε-χθεὶς πά - λιν ἀν - έ - δει - ξε τὴν σὴν γα - στέ - ρα

(d) (e)
δι - ὸ ἀ - παυ - στῶς σε τὸ γέ - νος

Our study of the music of the hymns must therefore be based upon manuscripts in the Middle Byzantine notation, in which the interval value is given. But since these manuscripts are of a relatively late date, a survey of the various phases of Early Byzantine notation must precede it. Though, as we have said, it is impossible to transcribe with complete accuracy the melodies, handed down in the early phases of that notation, without the help of manuscripts in Middle Byzantine notation, the later stages, particularly the fully developed 'Coislin'-notation,[1] are already so near to the notation with fixed intervals that the exact shape and expression of Byzantine Chant is known to us

[1] The name 'Coislin'-notation was given by Tillyard to the last phase of Early Byzantine notation, before the interval value had been fixed. It derives from Cod. Coislin 220 of the Paris Bibl. Nat. Tillyard has drawn attention to this important MS. in 'Early Byzantine Neumes', *Laudate*, xiv (1936), 183–7, and in his fundamental study 'Byzantine Neumes: The Coislin Notation', *B.Z.* xxxvii (1937), 345–58.

from the beginning of the twelfth if not from the eleventh century.

This view can already be found in the present writer's *Eastern Elements in Western Chant:*[1]

I am convinced that anybody who knows the cadences of the *Echoi* by heart, as the Byzantine singers did, will be able to sing the melodies from manuscripts in the Early musical notation, without the help of manuscripts of the Middle period. This knowledge also enables us to detect scribal errors, and to correct them. We have often been obliged to make such corrections in our transcription, and having compared them with the notation of a manuscript containing a faultless version of the melody, we have always found them to be accurate.

II. EARLY BYZANTINE NOTATION

In his *Monuments de la notation ekphonétique et hagiopolite de l'Église grecque*, J.-B. Thibaut rightly begins his description of manuscripts with a definition of the three melodic styles which are reflected in the notation.[2] These are:

(1) The style of the melodies of the Hirmologion:[3] short, preferably syllabic. The notation consists of few signs and is rhythmically simple.

(2) The style of the melodies of the Sticherarion: more expressive and ornamented than the first one. A greater number of signs and combinations of signs is employed.

(3) The melismatic style of the liturgical chants and the melodies for the soloists. This style developed from the middle of the thirteenth century and is called psaltic, or kalophonic style.

The dating of Byzantine liturgical manuscripts is, as has already been said, much more difficult than that of Western manuscripts. There is no *ductus*, characteristic of a province or

[1] Cf. op. cit., p. 91, where some of the 'formulae' of Byzantine Chant are structurally analysed. I am most grateful to Prof. O. Strunk for having drawn attention to these passages in his article on 'The Notation of the Chartres Fragment', to which frequent reference will be made in these pages. Strunk's article marks an important step forward in clarifying the question of how far it was possible to bring the early stages of Byzantine music within the scope of our studies. This is, as Strunk rightly points out, important from the liturgical point of view because a large proportion of the early Hirmi and Stichera fell into disuse in the eleventh century, and can only be found in MSS. of Early Byzantine notation. My studies during these last years were on the same lines, particularly during my work in 1954 and 1956–7 at the Research Institute of Dumbarton Oaks in Washington, where I discussed with M. Velimirović the deciphering of old Slavonic neumes for his Harvard Doctorate thesis *The Byzantine Elements in Early Slavic Chant*.

[2] p. 65.

[3] Cf. ch. v, *Byzantine Liturgy*, pp. 141–2.

a Scriptorium as in the West; the scribes work like copyists and try to produce a replica of the original. Nothing, however, speaks against the assumption (1) that chant-books for the use of the soloists or the choirmasters existed in the eighth century, (2) that many of them perished in the Iconoclastic struggle, and (3) that in the ninth and tenth centuries the signs were more developed. The different systems of signs in manuscripts of the eleventh century suggest the idea of a long and slow development, but also that some rare musical signs were given up when musical manuscripts were produced on a large scale and sent from the Scriptoria to remote monasteries which were in need of chant-books. The increased production of Hirmologia and Sticheraria may coincide with the formation of a distinct Byzantine rite, resulting from the fusion of the rite of St. Saba in Jerusalem with that of Hagia Sophia in Constantinople.[1] This happened after 950, when the rite of St. Saba in Jerusalem had been taken up by the Studios Monastery in Constantinople, and this in turn being the centre of hymnography since the days of Iconoclasm, had influenced the clergy of Hagia Sophia to increase the sung parts of the liturgy.[2]

In his study on 'The Stages of Early Byzantine Musical Notation',[3] H. J. W. Tillyard divides the 'Archaic Systems' into three phases, each of them named after the place where a manuscript characteristic of the type of notation was found. Accordingly, Tillyard calls the earliest phase 'Esphigmenian notation', from a manuscript at the monastery Esphigmenou on Mount Athos;[4] the following one he calls 'Chartres notation', referring to a few folios from a Mount Athos manuscript which came to the Library of Chartres, and were destroyed during the last war. The last phase Tillyard calls 'Andreatic notation', from Codex 18 of the Skete of St. Andrew on Mount Athos.

[1] Cf. A. Baumstark, 'Denkmäler der Entstehungsgeschichte des byzantinischen Ritus', *O.C.*, Ser. III, vol. ii (1927), pp. 23–4.

[2] No Typikon from the Studios Monastery has survived, only the Rule of the *Μονὴ τῆς ὑπεραγίας Θεοτόκου τῆς Εὐεργέτιδος*, published by A. Dmitrievsky in *Opisanie liturgicheskikh rukopisei*, i (Typika), 256–614.

[3] *B.Z.* xlv (1952), 29–42.

[4] Tillyard informs me by letter (10 Jan. 1958) that the Esphigmenian MS. to which he refers is that Codex from which fols. 1–16 v. were cut out (probably again by Ouspensky) and brought to Leningrad. These folios are reproduced in Thibaut's *Monuments de la notation ekphon. et hagiopol.*, pls. vi–xxiii. Other specimens of the Esphigmenian notation are Codex Athoum Laura 152 (B32), of which reproductions are in Riemann's *Die byzant. Notenschrift* (1909), pls. i–iii, and Cod. Petrop. CCCLXI, of which reproductions are in Thibaut's *Monuments*, figs. 32–5.

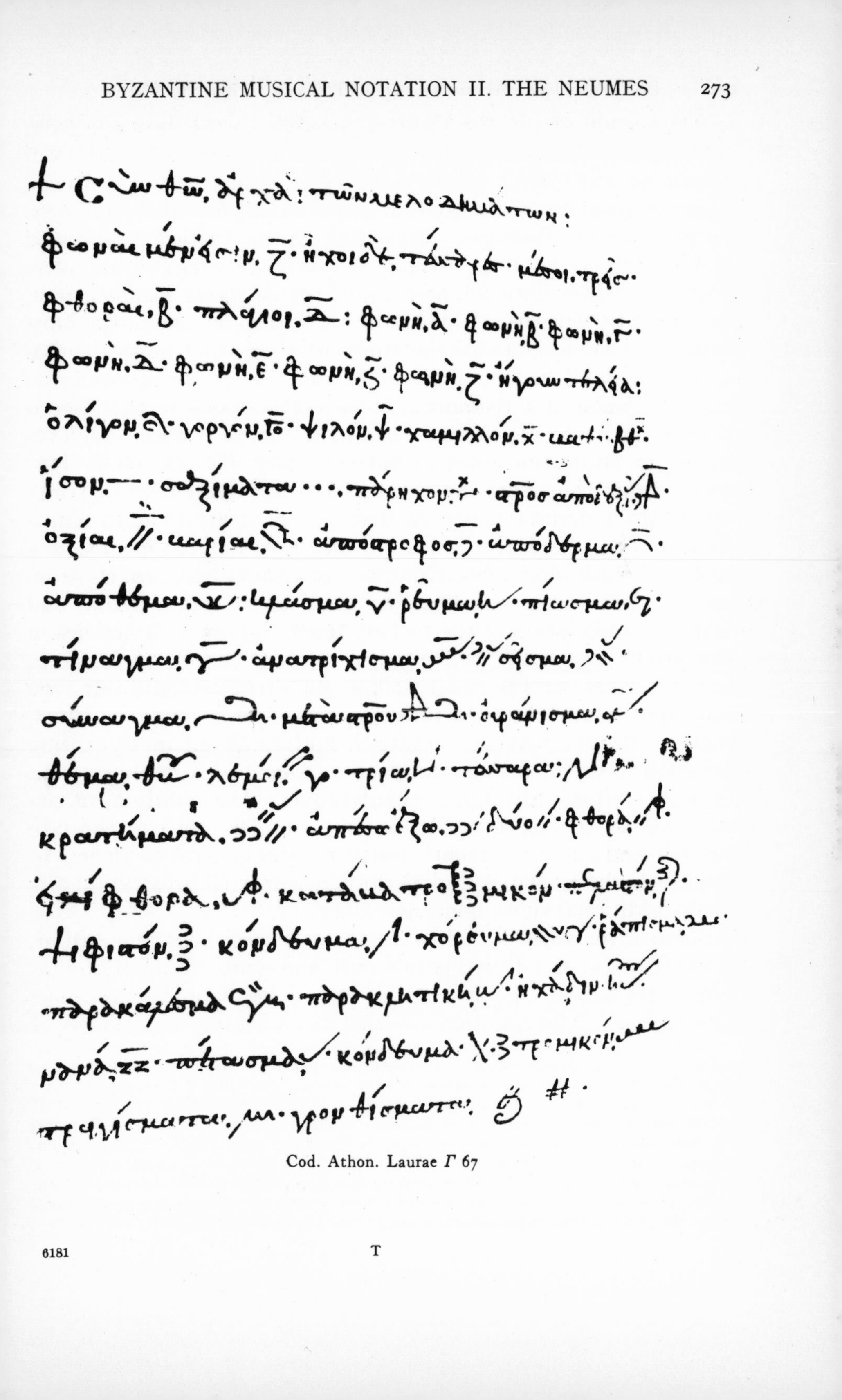

Cod. Athon. Laurae Γ 67

The second phase, the Chartres system, takes its name from a few folios (fols. 61–6) which were cut out from Codex Athoum Laura 67 and given to the Library of Chartres.[1] They were photographed by A. Gastoué, who published fols. 62 v. and 63 r. on pl. iii of his *Catalogue*. Mme Palikarova Verdeil reproduced the plate in her book *La Musique byzantine chez les Bulgares et les Russes* together with fol. 61 r. and *Liste de signes Kontakariens*, provided by Tillyard. This list of musical signs, one of the most important documents for the study of Byzantine musical notation, was published by Tillyard as early as 1913 in his study on the 'Fragment of a Byzantine Musical Handbook in the Monastery of Laura on Mt. Athos',[2] one of the most brilliant achievements in Byzantine musical palaeography. (Cf. fig. on p. 273.) In his study 'The Notation of the Chartres Fragment',[3] O. Strunk went into a minute study of that phase of notation to which he added besides MSS. Laura Γ67 and Γ72, the Vatopedi Codex 1488.[4] Strunk also gives a number of comparative tables from manuscripts of the 'Chartres' notation of the same hymn, and adds a transcription of the melody from Codices with neumes in the Middle Byzantine, or Round, notation. The facsimiles from the 'Chartres' group clearly show, as Strunk points out, the tendency to provide signs for groups of notes, a tendency which remains in Old Slavonic notation, and turns up in Byzantine notation in the melismatic manuscripts, i.e. the Kontakaria, and in manuscripts of liturgical chant proper. The notation, otherwise, shows the tendency to become simpler, until in the late twelfth and early thirteenth centuries the general tendency to embellish the melodies and perform them with great emphasis made additional signs again necessary.

Some of the signs are taken over from the ecphonetic notation, in other cases, as Tillyard points out, 'the symbol is an abbreviation of its name', e.g. *ολ* = *ὀλίγον* Ψ = *ψιλόν*, X or X = *χαμηλόν*, Γ = *γόργον*.[5] The question whether the Chartres notation is of

[1] Cf. A. Gastoué, *Catalogue des mss. de musique byz.*, pp. 96–8. Gastoué writes: 'Recueillis par P. Durand, voyageur chartrin, à la laure de St. Athanase au Mont Athos.'

[2] *A.B.S.*, xix (1912–13), 95–117, and pls. xiii, xiv.

[3] *Annales Musicologiques*, iii (1955), 7–37.

[4] O. Strunk's article contains facsimiles from the still unpublished Princeton MS., Codex Koutloumousi 412 (pl. i), Vatopedi 1488 (pls. ii, iii, vi, and vii), Laura 67 (pls. iv and viii), Laura 72 (pl. v), Laura 74 (pl. x), Laura B32 (pl. ix), and Sinai 1219 (pl. xi).

[5] Tillyard gives, op. cit., an explanation of every sign. Mme Palikarova Verdeil gives on pp. 105–25 lists of the signs of the *notation paléobyzantine archaïque* together with the corresponding signs of the Old Slavonic notation and a commentary on both groups of signs and their combinations.

an earlier date than that of Codex Esphigmenon, or simultaneous, or of a later date, has occupied the minds of all scholars who have worked in that field, but has not been answered satisfactorily. In fact, if the question is to be answered it is not enough to study the musical signs alone, important though the evidence gained from the shape of the signs may be. We must follow Mabillon's advice: 'Non ex sola scriptura, neque ex uno solo characterismo, sed ex omnibus simul de vetustis chartis pronuntiandum.'[1] It will be necessary to approach the solution of the question from the liturgical side: to take into account the feasts of the saints, the contributions of the hymn-writers, the replacement of older Kanons by new ones, to make a detailed analysis of the Typika, published and unpublished, in order to support the palaeographical evidence for the dating of manuscripts by that gained from hagiographical, liturgical, and literary sources.

Let us illustrate this[2] by an example from Codex Coislin 220 of the Bibl. Nat. in Paris, the famous Hirmologium, written in the twelfth century in what Tillyard has called 'Coislin' notation, taking the name from this Codex.

The Hirmologium comes to an end on fol. 235; the script on the next two folios is erased. On fol. 238 the *στιχηρὰ τῆς ἁγίας τεσσαρακοστῆς*, the Prosomoia and Theotokia of Lent are added; they comprise the whole sequence from Monday of the first week of Lent to Friday of the sixth week. Then follows *Δεῦτε ἅπαντες πιστοὶ τὰς τῶν ὁσίων πατέρων*, a Sticheron from the Saturday of Sexagesima[3] (*τῆς τυρινῆς* i.e. of Cheese week) which the scribe had forgotten to insert at the right place. It begins on fol. 261 v. and covers seven lines on fol. 262 r.; the rest of the page, nearly two-thirds, remained empty. But in the middle of the page are the first two words of the Kontakion *Ἄγγελος πρωτοστάτης* in an archaic script and archaic notation. What is the explanation of the occurrence of two systems of notation, separated by some 200 years, on one page?

First it is necessary to state that the set of Stichera Prosomoia on fols. 238 r.–262 r., and the following Stichera Dogmatika

[1] *De re diplomatica*, p. 241. I found the quotation in E. A. Lowe's article, 'An Unknown Latin Psalter on Mt. Sinai', *Scriptorium*, 1955, p. 188.

[2] O. Strunk, in his 'Chartres Fragment' study, has successfully followed up this line of thought, for the elaboration of which we are all indebted to A. Baumstark. [3] In the *Triodion* (Rome, 1879), p. 82, its place on Friday evening, during the first part (*Λυχνικόν*) of Vespers.

did not originally belong to the Hirmologium. They are part of the collection of monostrophic poems which belong to the Sticherarium;[1] it is by chance that they were added to the Hirmologium. We must therefore regard the Stichera Prosomoia as a separate group which has nothing to do with the main content of the Codex.

It is possible to reconstruct what the scribe did. He wrote the set of Stichera down to Friday of the sixth week of Lent, i.e. down to the Saturday preceding Palm Sunday, and finished the set by adding the *Δεῦτε ἅπαντες πιστοί* from the Saturday of the Cheese week which he had omitted. Having two-thirds of the

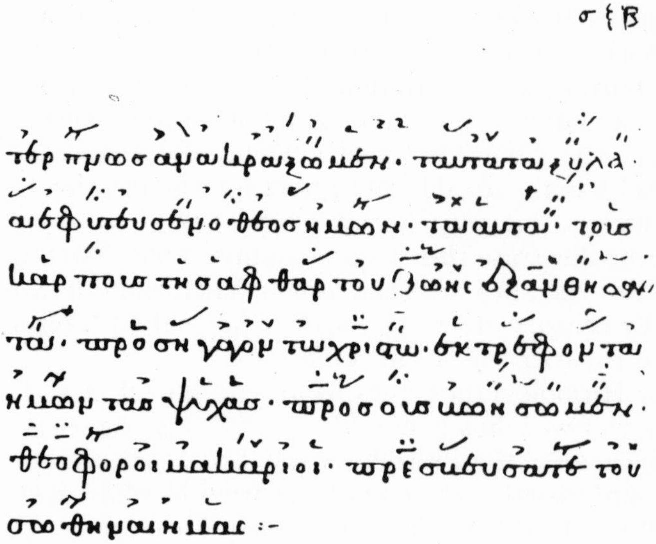

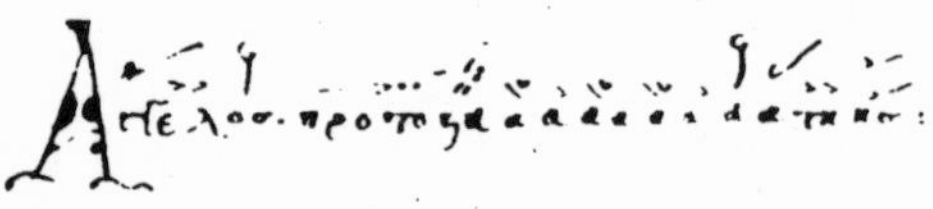

[1] Thus, e.g. the Stichera Prosomoia can be found in the facsimile edition of the *M.M.B.*, vol. i, *Sticherarium*, on fols. 312 sqq.; in Cod. Vatop. 1492, fol. 249 v. sqq.; in Cod. Vatop. 1499, fols. 38 v. sqq.

page free, he must have thought that since the Akathistos was sung during the Friday night of the fifth week, a note should be made on the page which was left empty. A copy of the Akathistos hymn dating from the ninth or early tenth century must have been on his desk, and the scribe imitated script and notation from the old manuscript. It is evident that he copied the first words of the first stanza *Ἄγγελος πρωτοστάτης* as a kind of *aide-mémoire* from a very old copy of the hymn, because the Katabasma, the sign on top of [*Αγγε*]*λος* and of [*προτοσταααααααα*]*α* [*ατηης*], belongs to the earliest phase of Byzantine notation which disappears already at the end of the tenth century from Byzantine manuscripts.[1] Through the care of the scribe we possess, as far as our present knowledge goes, the earliest example of a fragment of a Kontakion melody.[2] See example on p. 276.

The original of Tillyard's 'Andreatic' notation, Codex 18 of the Skete of St. Andrew, must be regarded as lost; Tillyard, however, provided me with a photograph of fol. 114, containing a Nativity Sticheron from which I copied the following two lines.[3]

Π αραδοξομ μυστηριομ οικονομει πλ̄ Α:

ται σημερομ· καιμο το μουνται

They are the beginning of a Sticheron Idiomelon for the Vespers of 26 December[4] by John the Monk, composed in the fourth plagal Mode, which runs as follows:

Παράδοξον μυστήριον οἰκονομεῖται σήμερον·
καινοτομοῦνται φύσεις, καὶ θεὸς ἄνθρωπος γίνεται·
ὅπερ ἦν μεμένηκε, καὶ ὃ οὐκ ἦν προσέλαβεν,
οὐ φυρμὸν ὑπομείνας οὐδὲ διαίρεσιν.

An astonishing mystery is accomplished today.
Nature has been renewed and God becomes man.
What He was, He remained, and He took on what He had not been,
Without being submitted to confusion or to division.

Let us compare the Andreatic notation (A) with that of Codex Dalassenos (*M.M.B. Facsimilia*, vol. i), fol. 99 r. (D), which is

[1] The Katabasma, however, survives in Old Slavonic MSS.; cf. Mme Palikarova Verdeil, *La Musique byzantine*, *M.M.B. Subsidia*, iii. 108, 129, 147, 224.

[2] Cf. E. Wellesz, *The Akathistos Hymn*, *M.M.B. Transcripta*, vol. ix, pp. liii–v.

[3] Cf. H. J. W. Tillyard's article 'Byzantine Music about A.D. 1100' in *The Musical Quarterly* xxxix (1953), for a full account of the notation and a complete transcription of the Nativity Sticheron. The present analysis though based on somewhat different evidence reaches the same conclusions.

[4] Cf. Menaion for December, *Menaia*, ii (Rome, 1889), 677.

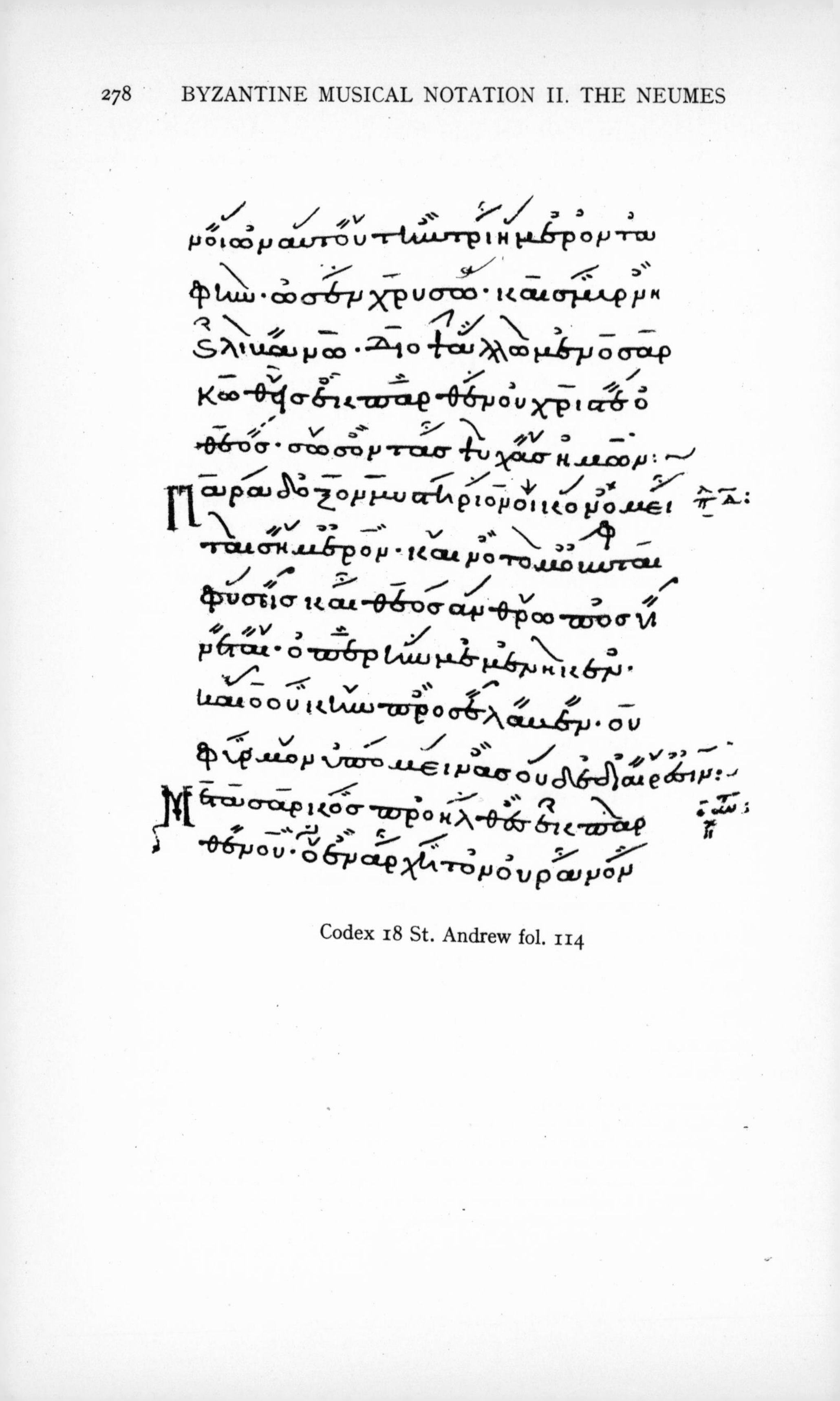

Codex 18 St. Andrew fol. 114

virtually identical with the versions of Codd. Vatopedi 1492 (V), fol. 74 v., Vatopedi 1499, fol. 102 r., Bibl. Nat. and Coislin 41, fol. 70 r., reproduced in J. D. Petresco's *Les Idiomèles et le Canon de l'Office de Noël* (Paris, 1932).[1]

The musical signs above the first two words are so different that the first impression is of two different versions. This view is not changed by the study of other manuscripts in which one finds the Early Byzantine system, e.g. Codex Saba (J) 610, fol. 73 r. and Codex Sinai (S) 1214, fol. 67 v., both of the eleventh century. As can be seen from the notation to the first words, they are much more in conformity with Cod. Dalass. than with the St. Andrew MS.

[1] The transcription of the melodies of the Christmas cycle, of which the present Sticheron forms part, was made in 1932 in Vienna by Dr. Maria Stöhr.

[2] In the Middle Byzantine notation of D a mistake occurs towards the end of line 3. The neume on top of ἦν is ↄ⌣, but not ↄ∩⌣; that means a fourth downwards is required, but not a third, as written. This is a frequent mistake in MSS. of the thirteenth century. Its explanation is that the MS. was copied from one in the Coislin system, in which the Apostrophos was used to indicate the movement downwards, either of a third or of a fourth.

S 1214

J 610

Πα-ρά-δο-ξον μυ-στή-ρι-ον οἰ-κο-νο-μεῖ-ται σή-με-ρον

If, however, the signs of the Andreatic system are considered as deriving from the ecphonetic system, with additions from the Esphigmenian notation, a different view must be taken. It will become apparent that the notation in the St. Andrew Codex serves practically the same purpose as the notations in the other manuscripts, as an *aide-mémoire*. But in the Andreatic notation the main emphasis is laid upon fixing the correct execution. It can therefore happen that the repetition of a note may have different signs, though in other phases of the Early and the Round notation these notes have the same sign, because from the musician's point of view they are of fairly equal value; they must be sung quickly without emphasizing the accented syllables and therefore they all have the Ison (⌐). In the St. Andrew MS. they are given rhetorical signs, which one would expect in cantillated texts rather than in those which are destined to be sung. To explain the Andreatic system it may suffice to give the beginning of the Sticheron *Παράδοξον μυστήριον*

πα- The stroke represents an Ison, the sign which in its hooked form (⌐) is often found as the first sign of the melody, if the first syllable is unaccentuated.

-ρα- The sign of the acute, which as a rule indicates a higher note, indicates here a slight emphasis, and is not different from the accent.

-δο- The Apostrophos is the sign of a weak syllable, but does not here indicate a lower note, though it may indicate a slight dropping of the voice.

-ξον The straight Ison indicates another unaccentuated note.

μυ- Straight Ison.

-στη- The sign is an acute / as that above on the second syllable, because the syllable *στη* carries an accent. If the sign would mean an Oxeia, an ascending second, as in the round notation, an ascending second would also be required on the *ρα* of *παράδοξον*; the compass of the melody would be changed and the cadence would end on *a* instead of *g*.

-ρι-	This sign, a dotted acute ⩵, seems to sharpen the emphasis of the acute.
-ον	A straight Ison.
οἰ-	The Psilon is, according to Tillyard,[1] the same as the Hypsile of the Middle Byzantine notation and takes its shape from the ψ. It indicates, as the name says (ὑψηλός = high) an upwards movement.
-κο-	The Petasma is, as Tillyard points out,[2] the forerunner of the Petaste of the Middle Byzantine system. It gives a sharp accent to the note to which it is related.
-νο-	The Chamelon takes its form from the letter *x*. Tillyard rightly sees in it a forerunner of the Chamile of the Middle Byzantine notation. χαμηλός means 'creeping on the ground'; the symbol, therefore, stands for a low note, or for a leap downwards.
-μει-	The compound sign ⁘ is mentioned by Thibaut in his *Monuments*, p. 68 (notules composées), and in Mme Verdeil's *La Musique byzantine*[3] as a combination of the Oxeia with semicircle and dot. This group occurs in Old Slavonic manuscripts and Mme Verdeil calls the combination 'Oxeia with *stopica s očkom*'. (The *stopica* is the Russian form of the Ison.) An explanation of the combination is not given. It seems to me that the combination is set up from a dotted Oxeia, i.e. a sharpened acute and a semicircle, which indicates a lengthening of the note.
-ται	The sign is the Bareia of the ecphonetic notation which gives a strong, downward leading accent to a group of two notes.
ση-	Diple plus Klasma indicates that very strong emphasis should be given to the note and that its value should be doubled.
-με-	Two consecutive Apostrophoi, i.e. two unaccentuated notes.
-ρον.	The —" consists of two symbols; the first gives some accent to the last note of the phrase; the second, the two strokes, have the value of a Teleia (+) and indicate that the last note should be lengthened.

We see from the analysis of the signs that the melody written

[1] Cf. H. J. W. Tillyard, 'Fragment of a Byzantine Musical Handbook', op. cit., p. 103.

[2] Op. cit., p. 108. [3] *M.M.B. Subsidia*, iii. 111.

down in the Andreatic system need not have been different from that in the other Codices which have been consulted. It is the archaic type of notation—with its mixture of simple ecphonetic signs, letters, and composite signs—which makes us believe that we have before us two different melodies. The question must be left open whether the Andreatic notation actually forms the third stage of notation, as Tillyard assumes, or represents an independent system of an archaic character. At present the 'Coislin' notation proves to be the most promising field of research, because its deciphering will make it possible to study the large number of melodies which have been preserved only in that stage of notation.

Let us add finally an example of Andreatic notation from a Vatican MS., Cod. Reg. gr. 54, fol. 46 r., and compare it with the notation of the same Sticheron in Cod. Vindob. theol. gr. 181, *M.M.B. Facsimilia*, vol. i, fol. 122 v. It is the beginning of the second of four Stichera on 25 January in honour of Gregory Theologus.

Ἐνθέοις πράξεσι τὸ σῶμα σὺν τῇ ψυχῇ νομίμως προκαθηράμενος. . . .

(Through divine actions the body is purified with the soul in a natural way. . . .)

The Vatican MS. is abbreviated R, the Vienna MS. D. The figures 1–22 refer to single or compound signs above a syllable.

1 2 3 4 5 6 7 8 9 10 11 12 13

Ενθεοιc πραξεσι το σωμα συν ψυχη

14 15 16 17 18 19 20 21 22

νομιμωc προκαθηραμενοc

The notation of R is in red ink like the titles. This is unusual; the colour of the ink of the musical signs varies from light brown to black. On first pages gold may be used as in Cod. Coislin 220.

(1) The hooked Ison was originally a straight stroke. The sign on top is a Parakletike indicating a slight accentuation. (2) The Oxeia, here and on πρά (4), corresponds to the prosodic sign of the grammarians. On 2 it is connected with the repeated note, on 4 with the step upwards. (3) The Apostrophos marks a

downward movement; here it is the interval of a fourth, whereas in 5 and 6 a second. (7) The Bareia accentuates, as we learn from D, the upward leap of a seventh, followed by a second downwards. (D and other manuscripts obviously make a mistake; it should be only the leap of a sixth, otherwise the phrase would end on a wrong note.) (8) The compound sign always stands for a long note, followed by a higher accented one. (9) The Oxeia marks a higher accent; in Middle Byzantine manuscripts the note is without accent, repeated and lengthened. (10) The Apostrophos stands, according to Middle Byzantine notation, for a Chamile, a fifth downwards. (11), (12), and (13) are Apostrophoi turned into straight Isons. In D, however, 11 and 12 stand for a second, 13 for a third upwards. (14) A dotted Bareia. The dot does not correspond in D to a Kentema, but seems to indicate a strongly accentuated Bareia. (15) is identical with (8). (16) indicates the lengthening of the note to which it belongs. One sees from D that the note is an Ison. (17) Here the Apostrophos received the additional sign of a Chamile. It cannot be decided when the *x* was added. (18) Ison with two dots, which should not be regarded as the Dyo Kentemata of Middle Byzantine notation, since they do not occur in D and other thirteenth-century manuscripts. (19) The Bareia stands for the prosodic sign. In D the syllable -*θη*- has the leap of a third, followed by a second downwards. (20) The Xeron Klasma is an agogic sign, indicating that the two notes to which it refers, should be sung separately, in a kind of staccato. (21) The Diple is used as in 8 and 15 as a sign to indicate doubling the duration of the note. (22) Apostrophos turned into Ison.

We shall now give the transcription, based on D. The Sticheron has the Martyria of the fourth mode with the sign of an ascending fifth. This means a fifth upwards from the starting point *g* of the fourth mode, i.e. *d*ˡ.

'Εν - θέ - οις πρά- ξε - σι τὸ σῶ - μα σὺν τῇ ψυ - χῇ· νο - μί - μως προ-
- καθ - η - ρά - με - νος· πλ.α' τὸ . . .

At + the leap of a seventh, consisting of the combination of

Hypsile plus Kentema, has been corrected into that of a sixth. Thus the two falling fifths (*d*'–*g*) are on the Finalis and the Dominant of the melody. Furthermore, the phrase ends on *a*, the Martyria πλ. α′ which one finds in Cod. Vatopedi 1492, fol. 95 v., indicates that the following phrase, marked by an Ison, should start on *a*. Thus it is evident that the scribe of the manuscript from which several others besides D were copied had made a mistake, and that the leap should be a sixth upwards, not a seventh.

Again, it must be emphasized, neither philological considerations alone, nor conclusions drawn from a number of manuscripts, are sufficient evidence for making emendations. The decisive evidence comes from the study of the run of the melody, and particularly from that of the formulae, as will be shown in the chapter on the structure of Byzantine melodies.

III. THE SYSTEM OF MIDDLE AND LATE BYZANTINE NEUMATIC NOTATION

The survey of Early Byzantine notation has shown that the study of Byzantine Chant must be based upon manuscripts in the Middle Byzantine notation, because in that phase the exactness in fixing the intervals precisely, the rhythmic and dynamic nuances and the modifications of tempo, have reached a degree of perfection which has no parallel in Western Chant, nor in Western medieval music, or that of the Renaissance; similar minuteness in fixing every detail will be found only in modern scores, where words explaining the execution play the same part as the red signs in Byzantine musical manuscripts.

It would be even more correct to say that studies in Byzantine music must begin with a thorough study of the theoretical treatises in which the significance of the numerous signs is explained. Though these treatises were written in the fifteenth and sixteenth centuries and referred therefore to Late Byzantine notation, they are reliable for explaining the Middle Byzantine notation, since the latter stage represents only an amplification of the former.

The following description of Middle and Late Byzantine notation is, in the main, an interpretation of the Papadike, the most concise introduction to the last phase of Byzantine notation. We must, however, bear in mind that the explanation of the complicated combination of signs which the theorists try to give has no historical background. They did not understand the early phases of notation, from which they are separated by from four to six hundred years. We have seen that neumes, deriving from the prosodic signs and letters, gradually acquired indistinct, and finally distinct, Interval value. The explanation of the theorists reverses the process, saying that in certain combinations Interval signs lose their Interval value and no longer count as notes. Such a sign is now *ἄφωνον*, i.e. without the quality of a note. This does not mean, the Papadike continues, that it is 'soundless' (*οὐχ ὅτι φωνὴν οὐκ ἔχει*), but it is not counted as a note (*ἄριθμον φωνῆς οὐκ ἔχει*). It is sung, but is not counted (*φωνεῖται μὲν οὐ μετρεῖται δέ*).

By this involved explanation the Papadike is trying to say that such a sign in a combination remains what it originally was, a symbol, indicating a rhythmic nuance.

In other combinations, or when used alone, these symbols of five different rhythmic nuances have in addition acquired the Interval value of an ascending second. This has been proved by the comparative study of all the relevant stages in the development of Byzantine notation.

There is virtually no divergency between the two methods of explaining the system of combinations in Middle Byzantine notation, since both arrive at the same results. Moreover, it is certainly easier to expound the system to the reader as it is described by the Byzantine theorists, because the terminology of these theorists has been the basis of all our attempts to solve the problem of Middle and Late Byzantine notation. The study of these treatises is, in fact, still a most valuable help; they give us an idea of the scope of the musical theory with which the musician had to be acquainted.

According to the teaching of the Papadikai, the elementary text-books on music, the interval signs are divided into two groups: the *Σώματα* (bodies) and the *Πνεύματα* (spirits). The Somata move in steps, the Pneumata in leaps. The Somata execute the interval of an ascending or descending second, the Pneumata the intervals of the third or fifth. In addition to these there are signs which are neither Soma nor Pneuma. These are: two consecutive descending seconds, producing the interval of a third, but reaching it by steps in a kind of *glissando*, and the Ison, the sign for the repetition of a note. Since it is neither a step nor a leap, it is neither a Soma nor a Pneuma.

In the course of the fifteenth century a new group of signs was added to these, called the 'Great Signs' (*μεγάλα σημάδια*) or the 'Great Hypostases' (*μεγάλαι ὑποστάσεις*). They have no interval-value—although a few of them had such a value in the earlier stages of the notation—but they regulate the expression and the dynamic and rhythmical nuances of the melody.

The following table shows the interval signs and the most important Hypostases. It comprises (A) the interval signs (*φωνητικὰ σημάδια* or *ἔμφωνα σημάδια*) and (B) the additional signs (*μεγάλα σημάδια* or *ἄφωνα σημάδια*). The Ison (*ἶσον*) is ascribed to both groups by the theoreticians.

Ison — Repeated Note

A.

(1) Somata

Ascending Second

Oligon | Oxeia | Petaste | Dyo Kentemata | Pelaston | Kouphisma

Descending Second

Apostrophos | Dyo Apostrophoi

(2) Pneumata

Ascending		Descending	
Kentema (third)	Hypsele (fifth)	Elaphron (third)	Chamele (fifth)

(3) neither Soma nor Pneuma

Aporrhoë (descending third) | Kratemo hyporrhoon

B. Bareia | Diple | Parakletike | Kratema | Kylisma | Gorgon | Argon | Antikenoma | Tzakisma | Xeron Klasma | Piasma | Apoderma ( ) | Thematismos eso | Thematismos exo | Thema haploun

It can be seen from this table that there are six signs for the interval of the ascending second, but only two signs for the descending second and only one for the third and fifth, ascending and descending. There are also two signs for a kind of *glissando* in the third downwards. All other intervals must be expressed by a combination of two of the already existing signs.

All the earlier investigators passed over the striking fact that there are six different signs for the ascending second, and yet it is precisely this fact that gives the clue to the explanation of the otherwise inexplicable rule of the *Papadike*. Each of the six signs for the ascending second represents, in fact, a particular way of singing the interval. In combination with a Pneuma, set after or under it, the interval of the Soma is cancelled, and it indicates the way in which the Pneuma with which it is combined is to be sung.

IV. THE INTERVAL SIGNS

Since the Byzantine neumes originated in the prosodic signs, their shape imitates, more or less, the movements of the melody produced by the human voice, and, consequently, the movements of the hand of the conducting precentor. This way of conducting, called Cheironomia (χειρονομία), which is said to go back to the time of Kosmas and John Damascene,[1] was brought to a high degree of perfection in the Byzantine Church. A good explanation of the Cheironomia is given by Goar in a note on p. 435 of his *Euchologium* (Paris, 1647):

> post κόμματα τροπαρίων a Canonarchâ e libro suggesta, cantus moderatorem in omnium conspectu, variis manus dextrae motibus et gestibus, erectis nimirum, depressis, extensis, contractis, aut combinatis digitis diversas cantus figuras et vocum inflexiones characterum musicorum vice designare: atque ita hunc cantus ducem reliqui attente respicientes, velut totius modulationis regulam sequuntur.

After the *Kanonarches* (Master of the Kanon) had intoned the first verse of the Troparion from the hymn-book, the Domestikos,[2] who could be seen by all, directed the singers with the movements

[1] *Χειρονομία ἐστὶ νόμος παραδεδομένος τῶν ἁγίων πατέρων· τοῦ τε ἁγίου Κοσμᾶ τοῦ ποιητοῦ, καὶ τοῦ ἁγίου Ἰωάννου τοῦ Δαμασκηνοῦ, ἡνίκα γὰρ ἐξέρχεται ἡ φωνὴ τοῦ μέλλοντος ψάλλειν τι, παραυτίκα καὶ ἡ χειρονομία, ὡς ἵνα παραδεικνύῃ ἡ χειρονομία τὸ μέλος.* MS. 811, p. 51. Cf. Thibaut, 'Étude de musique byzantine' *Izvestija russk. archeol. Instituta* vi (1901), p. 366.

[2] There were two δομεστικοί: the second precentor of the right choir and the first of the left. 'Watching the right hand of the Domestikos we sing all together (συμφωνοῦμεν) and for that reason the *Cheironomia* is very useful' (MS. 811, p. 181).

of his right hand and with certain gestures: raising, lowering, extending, contracting, or putting together his fingers, and instead of the musical signs he formed the various melodic groups and the inflections of the voice in the air. And everyone watched the leader of the choir attentively and followed, as one might say, the structure of the whole composition.

The Cheironomia which the leader of the choir executed with his music before him was, therefore, a combination of conducting in the modern way with gestures which were a mnemonic guide for the singers, who sung by heart. In a transferred sense the term Cheironomia is used by the theoreticians for the system of musical signs itself, as is clear from the treatise by Michael Blemmides,[1] written in the usual form of a dialogue between teacher and pupil (ἐρωταπόκρισις), in which the cheironomic execution of all the signs is given. The teaching of the Cheironomia starts with the Ison.

The normal movement of the melody without any special rhythmical or dynamic nuance on any note is expressed by the Ison, Oligon, and Apostrophos. They are called *τόνοι κύριοι* (notes *par excellence*) by the theoreticians. The best account of them is given in the so-called *Papadike,* which first explains the double nature of the Ison and then goes on to explain the function of these three basic signs.

> The beginning, middle, end, and integration of all the signs of the psaltic art is the Ison. Without it no singing can succeed. It is called 'aphonon' not because it is soundless, but because it is not counted as a note: it is sung, but not measured. All the time the tone remains on the same level the Ison is sung. Whenever the voice rises the Oligon, whenever it falls the Apostrophos is sung.[2]

If the neumes are to realize their function of intervals of a third and fifth, they must be combined with a Soma: if there is no special nuance of rhythmical or dynamic expression, with an

[1] *Ἀρχὴ σὺν Θεῷ τῶν σημαδίων ἑρμηνευομένων καθ' ἕκαστον, ποιηθὲν παρὰ τοῦ σοφωτάτου κυροῦ Μιχαὴλ τοῦ Βλεμμίδου.* The treatise was discovered by V. Beneševič in Cod. 310 of the monastery of S. Catherine at Mount Sinai and was published by him in his *Catalogus codicum graec. qui in monasterio S. Catharinae in Monte Sina asservantur* (Petropoli, 1911), i. p. 159. It has been re-edited by Tardo in *L'Antica mel. biz.*, pp. 245–7.

[2] *Ἀρχή, μέση, τέλος, καὶ σύστημα πάντων τῶν σημαδίων τῆς ψαλτικῆς τέχνης τὸ ἶσόν ἐστι· χωρὶς γὰρ τούτου οὐ κατορθοῦται φωνή· λέγεται δὲ ἄφωνον οὐχ ὅτι φωνὴν οὐκ ἔχει, ἀλλ' ὅτι ἀριθμὸν φωνῆς οὐκ ἔχει· φωνεῖται μέν, οὐ μετρεῖται δέ. διὰ μὲν οὖν πάσης τῆς ἰσότητος ψάλλεται τὸ ἶσον, διὰ δὲ πάσης τῆς ἀναβάσεως τὸ ὀλίγον, καὶ διὰ δὲ πάσης τῆς καταβάσεως ὁ ἀπόστροφος.* Cf. O. Fleischer, *Neumen-Studien III, Die spätgriechische Tonschrift* (1904), p. 18; E. Wellesz, 'Die Rhythmik der byzant. Neumen', *Z.M.W.* ii (1920), p. 629.

Oligon or Apostrophos. This is clear from a passage of the Anonymous A in MS. 811 of the Patriarchal Library of Constantinople.[1] After a long discussion of the Pneuma and the etymology of the word he says, of the relationship between Soma and Pneuma: 'Without the Somata the Pneumata cannot come into existence, and the Somata cannot be set in motion without the Pneumata.'

Later on in the same treatise the author gives another definition of the difference between Pneuma and Soma: the Pneumata produce a flowing up or down of the voice; but the Somata make the voice ascend or descend a little (*ἀνιοῦσι καὶ κατιοῦσιν μικρὸν τῇ φωνῇ*).

The normal movement of the melody, therefore, is expressed by the Ison, Oligon, and Apostrophos, and by the Pneumata in combination with Oligon and Apostrophos:

Interval	ascending	descending
Repetition		
Second		
Third		
Fourth		
Fifth		
Sixth		...
Seventh		...
Octave		...

But to obtain one of the special nuances of expression which, according to the theoreticians, belong to the four ascending Somata, viz. Oxeia, Petaste, Kouphisma, and Pelaston, the Somata are used as aphonic signs, added to the Ison, the descending Somata, and the Pneumata.

When we read in the *Papadike* '*Πρόσχες οὖν, ὅτι πᾶσαι αἱ ἀνιοῦσαι φωναὶ ὑποτάσσονται ὑπὸ τῶν κατιουσῶν*', the seemingly strange statement that all rising signs are ruled by the falling ones is to be understood in this sense, that the more complete

[1] Edited by J.-B. Thibaut in the *Revue de l'Orient Chrétien*, vi. 596 sqq. and by L. Tardo, *L'Antica Mel. Biz.*, based on Cod. 1656 of the Laura, pp. 207 sqq.

repertory of nuances contained in the four ascending Somata can also be utilized when the movement is a descending one, since the ascending Somata can be used as aphonic additional signs in combination with the signs of the descending movement. This is a considerable economy in an already sufficiently complicated system of notation. In practice, however, a relatively small number of compound signs was used since leaps with a particular expression occur mostly in the ascending movement of the melody up to a fifth; other intervals are very rare. Downwards, leaps of a fourth and fifth are most common, but they are rarely marked by an aphonic sign.

It may also have been noticed that no mention has been made of the Dyo Kentemata, though they are included in the tables of the *Papadikai*. In practice, the Dyo Kentemata were used exclusively as interval signs, indicating originally the rise of the voice to the interval of a half-tone, viz. *e–f*, or *a–b* flat. In combination with other signs, therefore, the Dyo Kentemata do not produce a leap, but keep their separate interval value (*ἀποτελοῦσι φωνὴν μίαν*).[1]

The Ison (*ἴσον*) occupies a special position. It is considered the most important sign (*ἀρχή, μέση, τέλος καὶ σύστημα πάντων*) because, in Byzantine Church music as in Gregorian Chant, the repetition of the *tenor*, the tone of recitation, plays an important part in the structure of the melodies.[2] It is the most humble sign, because it indicates that the melodic line is static, and because it subordinates itself to the Pneumata. But it is also the king, because it is the beginning and the foundation (*ἀρχὴ καὶ θεμέλιον*) not merely of the notation but of the melody itself. For the Ison is, in fact, the opening of the mouth in order to sing a melody, a Sticheron, or a Hirmus. It is therefore the beginning of all song, but it is also the end, because all songs close with the Ison.[3]

The end of the treatise is particularly instructive; it explains the meaning of the terms *ἔμφωνον* (sounding) and *ἄφωνον* (sound-

[1] Cf. Tardo, *L'Antica Mel. Biz.*, p. 269.

[2] *Ἐπεὶ τὴν ἀρχὴν ἐξ αὐτοῦ ποιούμεθα, καὶ ἄνευ τούτου οὐκ ἔστι δυνατὸν εὑρεῖν ἡμᾶς φωνήν, οὔτε ἀνιοῦσαν οὔτε κατιοῦσαν. δέον εἶναι τοῦτο καὶ φωνὴν καθὼς καὶ ἔστι· καὶ ἔχει μὲν φωνήν, ποίαν δὲ ἤτοι ἀριθμὸν οὐκ ἔχει. καὶ ἄκουσον τί ἐστι· ποία φωνή ἐστιν ἡ ἀποδεικτική. καὶ οὐκ ἔστιν ἄλλως εὑρεῖν φωνήν, εἰ μὴ τὸ ἴσον κατ' ἀρχὴν ὑποβάλλει. ἡ δὲ ῥυθμικὴ φωνή ἐστιν, ἡ μετὰ τάξεως ἐμμελῶς καὶ κατ' ἀκολουθίαν τοῦ εἱρμοῦ ἐναρμονίως ᾀδομένη, οἷον τὸ εὐτάκτως ᾀδόμενον μέλος* (Anon. A. MS. 811).

[3] Ibid., p. 88.

less). When the Ison is considered as a sign for the repetition of a note, with the ability to rule other signs, it is *ἔμφωνον*; in so far as it is counted as one of the Hypostases it is *ἄφωνον*.

The Ison rules, in fact, all ascending and descending signs with the exception of the Oligon, 'for the Oligon is like another self in relation to the Ison and one does not command oneself'. In other words, the Oligon is rhythmically equivalent to the Ison, it can add nothing to it by the *ἄφωνον γίγνεσθαι*, the process of becoming soundless, whereas the Oxeia, the Petaste, and the Kouphisma can transfer their special nuance to the Ison.

In the course of the discussion of the Oligon (ὀλίγον) in *Hagiopolites*[1] it is carefully explained, as a point which must cause surprise, that among the various nuances of expression there are three signs (here the author refers only to the three most frequently used signs for the ascending Second and omits the three others) and not one for the interval of the ascending Second. The Anon. A., too, states that these three signs are of equal pitch (isophonic), but that each has its characteristic cheironomic value: Oligon and Oxeia have the same sound, or note, but, according to the cheironomic system, the Oligon has less strength. Oligon, Oxeia, and Petaste are, as far as the interval is concerned, equivalent signs, but they convey different nuances of expression. And now a characteristic of the Oligon is mentioned, which it shares with the Ison and Apostrophos. This important passage was long ago quoted by Thibaut in his article on the Late Byzantine notation: 'The Oligon has an advantage over the Oxeia and Petaste, that it can be combined with all the aphonic signs, that is, the cheironomic signs; we do not find the Oxeia or the Petaste combined with the Kratema, the Bareia, the Piasma, or the Antikenoma or the Apoderma; these signs can only be combined with the Ison, the Oligon, and the Apostrophos.'[2]

This passage, too, confirms the theory and explanation of the signs given here. By means of the cheironomic signs, Ison, Oligon, and Apostrophos receive a special significance which the other signs do not need. These three signs are, therefore, tran-

[1] Cf. Thibaut, *Monuments*, p. 60.

[2] *Ἔχει δὲ τὸ ὀλίγον χάρισμα πλέον τῆς ὀξείας καὶ τῆς πεταστῆς, ὅτι τίθεται καὶ εἰς ὅλα τὰ ἄφωνα, ἤγουν τὰ τῆς χειρονομίας καὶ οὐχ εὑρίσκομεν ὀξεῖαν, ἢ πεταστὴν εἰς κράτημα, οὔτε βαρεῖαν, οὔτε εἰς πίασμα, οὔτε εἰς ἀντικένωμα, οὔτε εἰς ἀπόδερμα, εἰ μὴ τὰ τρία ταῦτα, τὸ ἶσον, τὸ ὀλίγον καὶ τὸν ἀπόστροφον* (MS. 811, p. 88). Cf. Thibaut, 'La Notation de S. Jean Damascène', *Bulletin de l'Institut archéol. russe de Cple* (1898), p. 171.

scribed by us as the standard signs of the notation with the quaver, since this was taken as the basis of the rhythmical system.

In the same treatise, MS. 811, p. 83, it is also said that the Oxeia (ὀξεῖα) is a more emphatic sign than the other two. It raises the tone abruptly and lets it fall again in the same way without lengthening it (ἡ δὲ ὀξεῖα θρασύτερόν ἐστι σημάδιον, ἐπάνω γὰρ κρούει τὴν φωνὴν καὶ καταβαίνει χωρὶς ἀργείας ὑποκάτω). This is not very clearly expressed. It is clear, however, from the repeated statements of the theoreticians, that the Oligon, Oxeia, and Petaste have the same interval value, so that this καταβαίνειν is not produced by a fall in the voice but by a reduction in dynamic strength after a Second abruptly sung.

The Petaste (πεταστή) means a Second sung quickly and with *élan*. It implies an increase in intensity beyond the Oxeia. Two Oxeiae can, therefore, follow one another but not two Petaste in the same direction, as this would mean too great an increase in emphasis. Its cheironomic sign is the movement of the hand through a curve.[1]

A further increase in intensity is produced by the Dyo Kentemata (δύο κεντήματα). According to the Anon. E this is a hybrid sign because its value is never subordinated to that of another sign, while, on the other hand, it leaves the value of the sounds with which it combines unchanged. It implies a rise of one note and, in accordance with the etymology, the shortening of the note. The Anon. E compares the Dyo Kentemata to a small double flute which was highly esteemed by the Oriental Fathers: 'These two flutes together give only one note, though in reality each gives one; this note therefore is much stronger.' It is at the same time much shorter than that of the Oligon and Petaste. From these definitions it is clear that the Dyo Kentemata occupy an exceptional position among the signs marking an ascending Second: they cannot be made aphonic, though we always find them in combination with another sign. They never occur alone, set over a syllable, but are sung as the second tone, or, if a group of notes is set to a syllable, as the last tone of the group.

The Kouphisma (κούφισμα) is a rarely used sign, whose significance is disputed by the theoreticians. It was frequently interpreted as the interval of a half-tone rather than as the halving of

[1] Τῆς δὲ πεταστῆς ἡ ἐτυμολογία ἀπὸ τῆς χειρονομίας ἐλήφθη. οἱονεὶ γάρ πέταται ἡ φωνὴ καὶ κινεῖ τὴν χεῖρα ὡς πτέρυγα. (MS. 811, p. 72.)

the rhythm. A passage in MS. 811, however, tells against this interpretation.[1] According to the rather naïve interpretation of the theoreticians the Kouphisma derived its form from the fact that a *κ*[2] was placed after a Petaste as a sign that it was reduced as far as sound and expression were concerned (*κατὰ τὴν φωνὴν καὶ κατὰ τὴν χειρονομίαν*). The Kouphisma means, accordingly, the raising of the voice by a note, but 'hesitantly, and with a very restrained and weak intonation'. Because of its weakness it is not easy to combine it with other notes. In the light of this statement the Kouphisma may be best compared with the 'liquescent notes' of Plainchant.

The Pelaston is found even less frequently. It is similar to the Petaste, to which it was later added, and meant an intensification of it.[3]

The Apostrophos (*ἀπόστροφος*) is the first of the descending signs and corresponds rhythmically to the Oligon, as has already been said. It is the sign for the interval downwards. When the Apostrophos is placed under an Ison it naturally keeps its value, and two separate notes are obtained. Its use in combination with the rhythmical cheironomic signs is always the same as that of the Oligon. It combines with the Diple, the Kratema, the Bareia, and with all the sounding and soundless signs of the Cheironomia, just as the Ison and the Apostrophos do.[4]

The Kentema (*κέντημα*), third upwards, Hypsele (*ὑψηλή*), fifth upwards, Elaphron (*ἐλαφρόν*), third downwards, Chamile (*χαμιλή*), fifth downwards, have, as Pneumata, the rhythmical value of the Ison, Oligon, and Apostrophos, and no special rhythmical significance of their own. They are transcribed by the quaver. The Kentema and the Hypsele can only be combined with the Oligon, Oxeia, and Petaste. The Elaphon combines with the Apostrophos, Oligon, and Petaste; the Chamile principally with the Apostrophos, but often with the Kouphisma, Oligon, and Petaste.

[1] *Καὶ ὁ λέγων, ὅτι τὸ κούφισμα ἡμίφωνόν ἐστι, σφάλλεται, καὶ οὐ νοεῖ τί λέγει, ἀλλὰ τελείαν μὲν φωνὴν ἔχει ἐλαφροτέραν δὲ τῆς πεταστῆς, ὥσπερ καὶ τὸ ὀλίγον ἐλαφροτέρ αν τῆς ὀξείας* (MS. 811, p. 92).

[2] *κ*: abbreviation for *κούφισμα* = lightening.

[3] *Τὸ δὲ πελαστὸν πεταστὸν ἢ κρεῖττον λέγεται· εἰς ὅσα γάρ ἐστι χρήσιμος ἡ πεταστή, εἰς τοσαῦτα καὶ τὸ πελαστόν* (MS. 811, p. 172).

[4] *Ἔνθα τίθεται τὸ ὀλίγον, τίθεται καὶ ὁ ἀπόστροφος, ἤγουν εἰς τὴν διπλῆν, εἰς το κράτημα, εἰς τὴν βαρεῖαν, καὶ εἰς πάντα τὰ σημάδια τῆς χειρονομίας φωνήεντά τε καὶ ἄφωνα, ὁμοίως καὶ ὅπου τίθεται τὸ ἶσον ἐκεῖ καὶ ὁ ἀπόστροφος* (MS. 811, p. 133).

The Hyporrhoe (ὑπορροή), also called Skolex (σκώληξ = worm) and Melos, is, according to the theoreticians, a 'little melody'. It is defined as a 'twisting', as a 'throwing out of the voice from the throat' (ἔκβλημα τοῦ γουργούρου). This melodic movement comprises two consecutive Seconds downwards. Like the Dyo Kentemata it is a hybrid sign.[1] In this ambiguous role it can be combined at will with ascending or descending signs. It is also an essential part of the Seisma, one of the 'Great Signs', which indicates a *tremolo* of the note to which it is set.

The Kratema-Hyporrhoon (κράτημα ὑπόρροον) is related to the Hyporrhoe. It has the same significance, but doubles the length.

V. THE 'GREAT HYPOSTASES'

The Bareia (βαρεῖα) is one of the most important cheironomic signs. In the Early Byzantine period it had an interval value[2] and meant the opposite to the Oxeia. It lost this significance and became a sign that the voice, starting a movement downwards, should be produced with emphasis.[3] Since the Bareia marks an *ictus* it combines neither with the Oxeia nor the Petaste.[4]

The Diple (διπλῆ) means, as well as the doubling of the Apostrophos, a rhythmical lengthening of the note under which it is set.[5] It doubles the duration of the interval sign and is therefore transcribed with a crotchet.

In the same way, the Kratema (κράτημα) means a doubling of the rhythmical value of the note under which it is placed, but it has a special cheironomic significance.[6] It means a note produced with great emphasis.

The Dyo Apostrophoi (δύο ἀπόστροφοι), or Syndesmoi (σύνδεσμοι), also belong here, according to the theoreticians, although, like the simple Apostrophos, they mean a descent of one note. They have, however, this difference that they imply lengthening.[7]

[1] Ἡ ἀπορροὴ τί ἐστι, πνεῦμα ἢ σῶμα;—Οὔτε πνεῦμά ἐστιν, οὔτε σῶμα, ἀλλὰ ἔκβλημα τοῦ γουργούρου (Cod. Laura 1656). Cf. Tardo, *L'Antica mel. biz.*, p. 228. Tardo suggests the reading from MS. 811: διὰ γαργαρεῶνος, 'through the soft palate'.

[2] Cf. Tillyard, 'Studies in Byz. Music', *Musical Antiquary*, 1913, pp. 203, 207–13.

[3] Ἡ δὲ βαρεῖα ἀπὸ τοῦ βαρέως καὶ τοῦ μετὰ τόνου προφέρειν τὴν φωνήν (MS. 811, p. 180).

[4] Cf. Thibaut, 'Étude de musique byz.', *Bulletin de l'Institut archéol. russe*, vi. 381.

[5] Πάλιν δὲ διπλασιαζόμενα, καὶ διπλῆ καλούμενα ἀποτελεῖ κράτημα, ὁμοίως καὶ ἡ ἀπόστροφος ἐνεργεῖ, διπλασιαζομένη γὰρ αὐτὸ ἀποτελεῖ (*Hagiopol.* 219 v.).

[6] Τὴν αὐτὴν δὲ δύναμιν ἔχει καὶ τὸ κράτημα, καὶ τοῦτο γὰρ δι' ἀργίαν τίθεται, διαφέρον δὲ μόνον κατὰ τὴν χειρονομίαν (MS. 811, p. 177).

[7] Οἱ δὲ δύο ἀπόστροφοι, εἰ καὶ μία ὑπόστασις ἐγένετο, ἀλλ' ἔχουσι καὶ φωνὴν καὶ ἀργείαν, καὶ χειρονομιάν (MS. 811, p. 129).

These three signs, Diple, Kratema, and Dyo Apostrophoi, produce the three main rhythmical lengthenings. The Tzakisma (*τζάκισμα*), or Klasma mikron (*κλάσμα μικρόν*), together with the Seisma (*σεῖσμα*) and Parakletike (*παρακλητική*), produce a lengthening which is less by a half. They are described as *ἡμίτονα*, half-tones, in *Hagiopolites*, not because of their interval value, but because of their rhythmical significance.[1]

The Tzakisma combines with all the cheironomic signs. When it stands above an Oxeia, the Oxeia is sung with greater emphasis than it would be if it stood alone.[2] It is transcribed with a dotted quaver.

The Seisma corresponds to a kind of *tremolo*. It is etymologically derived from *σείω*, 'tremble', and its cheironomic sign is a tremor of the hand. It is expressed in writing by a combination of two Bareiai and a Hyporrhoe. The Seisma usually stands at the beginning of Hirmi, most frequently of those of the second plagal mode.

The Kylisma (*κύλισμα*) signifies a 'rolling and rotating of the voice' (*κυλίει καὶ στρέφει τὰς φωνάς*). It has the same meaning as the *quilisma* in Latin neumatic notation. The Kylisma is transcribed with a shake.

Gorgon (*γοργόν*) and Argon (*ἀργόν*) have not the same fixed rhythmical value in Byzantine notation that they have in the Church music of the present day. They seem to have meant no more than an *accelerando* and *ritardando*.

The Apoderma (*ἀπόδερμα*) is the sign of a short musical division and stands at the end of a musical phrase. It divides it from what follows, and it also seems to have indicated a slight slowing down.

The Xeron klasma (*ξηρὸν κλάσμα*) indicates that the voice should rise abruptly and harshly (*τραχέως καὶ σκληρῶς*). It is set to a group of notes which are sung in a kind of *mezzo-staccato*.[3]

The Antikenoma (*ἀντικένωμα*) always unites ascending notes

[1] The same explanation of the cheironomic significance of the Tzakisma and the Parakletike is given by Anon. A in MS. 811, p. 40: *τὸ δὲ τζάκισμα κατὰ τὴν ἐπωνυμίαν αὐτοῦ τζακίζει μικρὸν τοὺς δακτύλους τῆς χειρός, ἤτοι κλᾶται, κτυπεῖται ὀλίγον, ἀργεῖται μικρόν, διὰ τοῦτο γοῦν λέγεται τζάκισμα. ἡ δὲ παρακλητικὴ καὶ αὔτη πρὸς τὴν κλῆσιν αὐτῆς κλαυσμός ἐστιν καὶ ὀδυρμὸς τοῦ μέλους αὐτῆς, καὶ κλαυμυρίζει, παρακλητεύει, παρακαλεῖ δακρύουσα, καὶ κλαίει τοὺς λόγους αὐτῆς, διὰ τοῦτο γοῦν λέγεται παρακλητική.*

[2] *Ὅτε γὰρ κεῖται τὸ τζάκισμα ἐπάνω τῆς ὀξείας, γίνεται ἡ ὀξεία στερεωτέρα τῆς ἄλλης ὀξείας τῆς ἄνευ τζακίσματος* (MS. 811, p. 93).

[3] Cf. Tillyard, *Handbook of the Middle Byz. Notation*, p. 26. Tillyard rightly warns the reader that the Xeron Klasma should be carefully distinguished from the Kratema, which it often resembles very closely in the later MSS.

with descending ones. According to the theoreticians it occurs more frequently in melodies of an ornamented type than in those of the more syllabic type. In Late Byzantine manuscripts it indicates 'the highest point of an up-and-down figure'.[1]

The meaning of the Thematismos eso (*θεματισμὸς ἔσω*) and the Thematismos exo (*θεματισμὸς ἔξω*) is not made entirely clear by the theoreticians. From the formation of the signs, however, we can see that both are the letter *θ*, the first with a curl downwards, the second with a curl upwards. The theoreticians take the signs as the initial letter of the word *θέμα*, a 'Theme' or group of notes. The descending sign accompanies two notes, the ascending three.[2]

The meaning of another sign of the same shape, the Thema haplun (*θέμα ἁπλοῦν*), is rather obscure. It is defined as indicating a simple rhythm (*θέσις ἁπλῆ, τουτέστι χειρονομία ἁπλῆ*) and stands at the end of a melodic phrase; its precise significance is uncertain.

The results of this section may conveniently be summarized in the following table, which gives the transcriptions in modern staff notation of the signs set out in the table on p. 286:

A. Ison
Oligon Apostrophos
Kentema Elaphron
Hypsele Chamile

Oxeia Petaste Pelaston Kuphisma

Dyo Kentemata

Dyo Apostrophoi

Hyporrhoe

Kratemo-Hyporrhoon

B. Bareia

Diple Kratema

Tzakisma Parakletike Seisma

Gorgon = *accel.* Argon = *rit.* Apoderma

Xeron Klasma = *mezzo stacc.* Kylisma *tr*

[1] Tillyard, *Handbook of the Middle Byz. Notation*, p. 27.

[2] *καὶ δηλοῖ ὁ ἔξω τρεῖς φωνὰς εἰπεῖν, ὁ δὲ ἔσω δύο* (MS. 811, p. 178).

With the development of the richly ornamented, so-called 'psaltic' style, a large number of new Hypostases were added. To the first layer, introduced in twelfth- and thirteenth-century manuscripts, belong, according to Thibaut,[1] the Parakalesma, the Enarxis, the Synagma, the Tromikon, the Kratema, the Psephiston, and the Psephiston Synagma; others were added later. Thibaut, after having examined a large number of manuscripts in the Late Byzantine notation, arrived at a list of forty aphonic signs, not including the Ison and the Phthorai which we shall discuss later in this chapter. To these he adds a number of composite cheironomic signs.

The meaning of many of them is very doubtful; some have fantastic names like *συνδεσμολύγισμα*, *κυλισμαντικένωμα*, *ἀντικοσύντισμα*, *κρατημοκαταβαζονάβασμα*, *κρατημοκαταβοτρομιυπόρροον*, of which it is impossible to make any sense. Since this work is only concerned with classical Byzantine music, the study of these signs falls outside its scope. It may suffice to give a list of them and to add briefly what, according to the theoreticians, their significance was. A more detailed account of them can be found in Thibaut's *Étude de musique byzantine*, Fleischer's *Neumenstudien*, iii, and Tardo's *L'Antica melurgia bizantina*.

(1) Diple

(2) Parakletike

(3) Kratema

(4) Seisma

(5) Piasma

(6) Gorgon

(7) Argon

(8) Gorgosyntheton

(9) Argosyntheton

(10) Stauros

(11) Apoderma

(12) Tzakisma

(13) Xeron Klasma

(14) Parakalesma

(15) Heteron Parakalesma

(16) Psephiston Parakalesma

(17) Homalon

(18) Antikenoma

[1] Thibaut, 'Étude de mus. byz.', *Bull. de l'Institut archéol. russe*, vi. 364.

(19) Synagma

(20) Bareia

(21) Lygisma

(22) Kylisma

(23) Antikenokylisma

(24) Tromikon

(25) Tromikon Synagma

(26) Tromikon Parakalesma

(27) Ekstrepton

(28) Psephiston

(29) Psephiston Synagma

(30) Epergema

(31) Uranisma

(32) Choreuma

(33) Thema Haplun

(34) Thes kai Apothes

(35) Thematismos eso

(36) Thematismos exo

(37) Enarxis

(38) Hemiphonon

(39) Hemiphthoron

(40) Hemargon

Combinations of the Great Hypostases

Kratema Kuphisma

Tromikon and Psephiston

Psephiston and Homalon

Psephiston and Parakalesma

Psephiston and Xeron klasma

Homalon and Xeron klasma

Tromikon and Synagma

Tromikon and Homalon

We need comment only on those signs which have not been previously discussed.

(5) Piasma (πίασμα, grasping). The sign indicates the 'compression' of the tones to which it is added.

(8) Gorgosyntheton, a double Gorgon; it doubles the rhythmical value.

(9) Argosyntheton, a double Argon.

(10) Stauros marks a *rallentando* at the end of the phrase.

(14) Parakalesma gives an 'imploring expression to the melody', i.e. it intensifies its expression.

(15) Heteron Parakalesma. Another form of the Parakalesma.

(16) Psephiston Parakalesma marks a 'rolling of the voice', a Mordent.

(17) Homalon indicates 'the rhythmical equality of the tones of the melisma'.

(19) Synagma marks a *ligato*.

(21) Lygisma (λύγισμα, a twisting) seems to have the same significance as the Kylisma.

(23) Antikenokylisma is an inverted Kylisma.

(24) Tromikon (τρομικόν, trembling) signifies a 'turn' of the voice.

(25) Tromikon Synagma signifies a soft tremolo.

(26) Tromikon Parakalesma signifies an intensified tremolo.

(27) Ekstrepton or Strepton is an inverted Tromikon.

(28) Psephiston (ψηφίζειν, to pick out) indicates that the tones have to be emitted separately (ἔνθα εἰσὶν αἱ φωναὶ κεχωρισμέναι καὶ οὐχ ὁμοῦ λεγόμεναι. MS. 811, p. 178).

(29) Psephiston Synagma, also called Gurgurisma, is 'a soft rolling of the voice in the throat'.

(30) Epergema is identical with the Antikenoma.

(31) Uranisma is a kind of Mordent or 'turn' (εἰς ὕψος αἴρει τὴν φωνήν, εἶτα καταβιβάζει.)

(32) Choreuma indicates another kind of Mordent.

(34) Thes kai Apothes accompanies the final cadence.

(37) Anarxis or Enarxis is set after the Intonation at the beginning of a melody before an Oligon. It is also called Diamphismos (διαμφισμός, separation), probably because it separates the Intonation from the beginning of the hymn-tune.

(38) Hemiphonon, 'half tone': No explanation of the sign is found in the treatises. According to Thibaut it marks the

modulation from the Third Plagal Mode into another.

(39) Hemiphthoron seems to indicate the modulation from the Fourth Plagal Mode.

(40) Hemargon seems to be related to the Argosyntheton. No explanation of the sign is found in the treatises. It is mentioned only in MS. 811, p. 38.

VI. THE MODES

The melodies of the hymns are divided into eight groups or Echoi (ἦχοι): four authentic (κύριοι) and four plagal (πλάγιοι), each of which is based on a scale corresponding to one of the eight Gregorian modes. At the beginning of every hymn of the *Hirmologion* and *Sticherarion* the number of the Echos is given and a group of signs, the Martyria (μαρτυρία) or Signature of the mode.

From the section on the Greek alchemists we have seen that the habit of giving ciphers to the Echoi, viz. α′, β′, γ′, δ′, πλ. α′, πλ. β′, πλ. γ′, πλ. δ′ instead of names, is already found in the alchemical treatises of Ps.-Zosimus. The author of the *Hagiopolites* complains that the Echoi are only counted over, and have no names like the Greek modes, and draws up the following list: α′ corresponds to the Greek Hypodorius, β′ to Hypophrygius, γ′ to Hypolydius, δ′ to Dorius, πλ. α′ to Hypodorius, πλ. β′ to Phrygius, πλ. γ′ to Lydius or Mixolydius, πλ. δ′ to Hypomixolydius. This list, however, is faulty. Correct lists of the names are given in Cod. Barberini Gr. 300 and in the *Papadike*; they correspond to those given to the Latin modes by Western medieval theorists:

	Byzantine Modes		*Gregorian Modes*
ἦχος α′	First authentic	I.	Dorius
ἦχος β′	Second authentic	III.	Phrygius
ἦχος γ′	Third authentic	V.	Lydius
ἦχος δ′	Fourth authentic	VII.	Mixolydius
ἦχος πλ. α′	First plagal	II.	Hypodorius
ἦχος πλ. β′	Second plagal	IV.	Hypophrygius
ἦχος βαρύς	Third plagal mode or Barys	VI.	Hypolydius
ἦχος πλ. δ′	Fourth plagal	VIII.	Hypomixolydius

At the beginning of every hymn the number of the Echos is given, followed by various groups of musical signs, the Martyriae or Signatures of the Mode. Apart from Mode I and Mode IV, each mode has several Signatures.

The meaning of the Martyriae was obscure and Gaisser, Gastoué, Thibaut, and Riemann tried in vain to solve the problem. We owe the solution to Tillyard, who found out 'by trial' that the various Signatures indicated the 'starting-notes' within a single mode. The table which he drew up in his study 'Signatures and Cadences of the Byzantine Modes' in the *Annual of the British School at Athens*, vol. xxv (1923–5), pp. 78–87, and his explanations of the significance of the Signatures made it possible to fix the pitch of the initial notes of the hymns. I give on p. 302 a survey of the Martyriae, based in the main on Tillyard's table, with some additional Intonation formulae from Codex Iviron.[1] The note added to the Signature (for example: = *a*) indicates the starting-point of the melody.

From this table we arrive at the following results:

Mode I. The Hypsele, added to the numeral α′, indicates that the note which is the starting-point of the first Mode is a fifth higher than *d*, the note on which we would expect the melody to begin. Most of the melodies of Mode I have the Martyria of the ascending fifth and start on *a*.

Mode II. The first Martyria (1) is only the letter β in its Byzantine shape. Since no interval sign is added, one would expect *e* as the starting-point; but from numerous transcriptions it became evident that melodies, preceded by this Martyria, had *g* as their starting-point. The fact that all the melodies of the first group begin on *g* cannot be explained palaeographically, but is confirmed by the Martyriae of the second and of the third groups. Melodies of the second group begin on *b*-natural, those of the third on *a*. The Martyria of the fourth group (4) has two consecutive seconds; in contrast to the first three groups, *b*-natural must be taken as the theoretical starting-point, and we have to intone two consecutive descending seconds in order to reach the actual beginning of the melodies of this type, on *g*. We have, therefore, to take *g* as the initial tone of the melodies of the first and of the fourth group.

Mode III. The majority of the melodies are reckoned, theoretically, from *a*; the two ascending seconds indicate *c* as the real starting-point of the melody. Another group starts on *a*, a third on *f*. Not all the interval groups which are added to the number

[1] A complete table of the Martyriae, which occur in Codex Iviron, was given by C. Höeg on p. 17 of the Facsimile edition of the MS. in *M.M.B.*, vol. ii.

Mode I = a

Mode II (1) = g (2) = b♭ (3) = a (4) = g

Mode III (1) = c′ (2) = a (3) = a

(4) = c′ (5) = c′ (6) = c′

Mode IV = d′ or g

Mode I Plagal (1) = d (2) = g

Mode II Plagal (1) = e (2) = g (3) = a
(4) = f

Mode III Plagal (1) = f (2) = a (3) = f

Mode IV Plagal (1) = g (2) = a

(3) = a (4) = c′

(5) = c′ (6) = e

of the mode (*Γ*) as intonation formulae, give the pitch of the initial note; where they could not be relied on, the starting note could only be discovered by exhaustive exploration of all the possibilities of the transcription. But once they had been found, there could be no doubt that the Martyriae of four groups, (1), (4), (5), (6), always indicated a beginning on *c′*, those of (2) and (3) a beginning on *a*. In Codex Iviron we find some other Martyriae indicating a beginning on *f*.

Mode IV. The Hypsele, added to δ′, indicates *d′* as the starting note of the fourth mode; but in order to avoid too high a pitch we have to transpose melodies of this mode a fifth downwards and begin on *g*; in that case *b* has to be flattened.

Mode I Plagal. The majority of the melodies of this mode belong to the first group (1); they start on *d* and end on *d*. Others start on *a* and end on *d*. Melodies of the second group (2) begin on *g* and end on *d*.

Mode II Plagal. To the four starting notes of Tillyard's table, viz. *e* (1), *f* (4), *g* (2), *a* (3), a fifth, *d*, must be added, which frequently occurs in the Hirmi of this mode in Codex Iviron.

Mode III Plagal. Instead of ἦχος πλάγιος γ′ we find for this mode the term Barys (βαρύς) or Grave. The Signature which precedes the intonation formula is obviously an abbreviation of this word. The melodies of this mode begin regularly on *f* or on *a*; some melodies of the third group (3), however, have an Apostrophos as the first interval sign instead of an Ison, which means a beginning on *e*.

Mode IV Plagal. This mode has four starting notes: *e* (6), *g* (1), *a* (2), (3), and *c′* (4), (5). In some of the Hirmi of Codex Iviron, however, the starting note is *d′* or *e′*; this is indicated by an Oxeia or the combination of Oxeia and Kentema as starting-points of the melody.

The various beginnings of melodies of the same mode attracted the attention of all the scholars who studied Byzantine musical notation; but it was impossible to arrive at any definite conclusions before a great number of hymns were transcribed and comparative studies into the structure of the melodies could be begun. Now, however, we can see that the variation in the beginnings was caused by the occurrence of certain melodic formulae and by their application to the words of the hymn. We shall explain this principle of composition in the following chapter on the structure of the melodies. Here we need only say that the Echoi of Byzantine music should be thought of not merely as scales in the modern sense, but as groups of melodies of a certain type, built upon a number of basic formulae which characterize the Echos. The discovery of this principle of construction will help us to understand the significance of the Martyriae, which Tillyard found by empirical demonstration, but which still needs an exact palaeographical explanation.

VII. THE INTONATION FORMULAE

Apart from the indications relating to the number of the Echos and to the various Signatures, the manuscripts and the theoretical treatises contain a number of melodic formulae, sung to words whose meaning was obscure. They were:[1]

First Mode	Ananeanes (ἀνανεανές)
Second Mode	Neanes (νεανές)
Third Mode	Nana (νάνα)
Fourth Mode	Hagia (ἅγια)
First Plagal Mode	Aneanes (ἀνεανές)
Second Plagal Mode	Neeanes (νεέανες)
Third Plagal Mode	Aanes (ἀανές)
Fourth Plagal Mode	Neagie (νεάγιε)

These intonation formulae were called either Echema (ἤχημα), Apechema (ἀπήχημα), or Enechema (ἐνήχημα). The Anonymus of Codex Laurae 1656 gives the following definition:[2]

'How do you start, if you want to begin a Sticheron or another hymn of that kind?'—'According to the Intonation' (ἐνήχημα).—'What is the Echema?'—'The layout of the Mode' (ἡ τοῦ ἤχου ἐπιβολή).—'And how do you intone?'—'Anane Anes.'—'What does that mean?'—'This is the approved and very useful beginning; when you hear it you will admire the singer who executes the Intonation. The Anane Anes is a prayer, this is to say: Ὦ **Ἄναξ** καὶ Βασιλεῦ οὐρανοῦ καὶ γῆς, καὶ **ἄνες** καὶ ἄφες τὰ παραπτώματά μου. . . .'

The interpretation of *Ananeanes*, cited above, as deriving from words of the prayer is improbable. It was pointed out that the significance of the formulae was 'to serve the singers as cue-words for the solemnization, and at the same time as mnemonic aids', and that their origin may go back to the Jewish *schola cantorum*.[3] The words and the melodic formulae must, however, be separated. They may be rudiments of verses from well-known hymns as the Anonymus from Codex Laurae suggests; some may go back to Jewish intonations. But there is also another possibility to which I first drew attention in a study on the cantillation of Manichaean hymns: the texts of the Byzantine intonation formulae, like Ananeanes, Nana, and so forth, may be compounds of meaningless syllables like the *yga* which we find fre-

[1] The list is based on Codex Chrysander, published by O. Fleischer in *Neumen-Studien*, iii. 37, but the syllables ἄνανες for the first mode are replaced by ἀνανεανές. Tillyard, *Handbook*, p. 31, gives a list of other variants.

[2] Edited by L. Tardo in *L'Antica Mel. Biz.*, pp. 207–20.

[3] Cf. E. Werner, 'The Psalmodic formula *Neannoe* and its origin', *The Musical Quarterly*, xxviii (1942), 93–9.

quently inserted in Manichaean cantillations, or in syllables like *na-na* in cantillations of the bedouins from Tunisia.[1]

The function of the intonation formulae, however, is a more interesting problem. It was examined by O. Strunk,[2] who showed that the Martyriae were abbreviations of the full intonation formulae. Their function was (1) 'to link the choral recitation of a verse taken from a Psalm or from a Canticle' with the hymn which followed it, or (2) where no verse precedes, 'to serve as a preparation and as an announcement of the mode of the melody'.[3]

Codex Ashburnham. 64 from the Laurenziana in Florence contains e.g. the Akathistos hymn with music to the Prooemium (Kontakion) and all twenty-four stanzas (Oikoi). Both the Prooemium and the first stanza are preceded by Intonation formulae:

Kontakion
fol. 108 r.

Cf. the facsimile edition of *Contacarium Ashburnhamense*, *M.M.B.*, vol. iv (1956), fols. 108 r.–112 v., and my transcription in *M.M.B. Transcripta*, ix. 3 and 4–5.

The Palimpsest Codex Cryptensis *E β* vii is another manuscript[4]

[1] Cf. my article 'Probleme der musikalischen Orientforschung', *Jahrbuch der Musikbibliothek Peters*, 1917, pp. 16–18.

[2] Cf. O. Strunk, 'Intonations and Signatures of the Byzantine Modes', *The Musical Quarterly*, xxxi (1945), 339–55.

[3] Ibid., pp. 353–4.

[4] As far as our knowledge goes Cod. Crypt. *E β* vii is the only other Kontakarion which contains the music to all the stanzas of the Akathistos. The parchment, however, is in a deplorable state, because in the second half of the nineteenth century it was treated with chemicals in order to read the underlying script.

which has the music to the Prooemium (Kontakion) and to all the twenty-four stanzas (Oikoi) of the hymn. In this Codex, however, the intonation formulae are missing and only the Martyriai are given. In Cod. Ashburnham. 64 abbreviated intonation formulae are frequently set to connect the cadential formula of a line with the beginning of the next line. These 'inner' Martyriae are less frequent in Cod. Crypt. *E β* vii. The same absence of written out Intonation formulae at the beginning and in the course of a stanza can be observed in Codd. Crypt. *Γ γ* iii and *E β* iii which contain Kontakion and Oikoi of the Akathistos.

In both stanzas the intonation formula of Mode IV Plagal precedes the melody. The formula of Oikos *A′*, however, is much longer than that of the Kontakion. The extension begins at † on an *a*, a note which plays an important part in the embellishment.

The most extended intonations in Cod. Ashburnham. 64 are those in the appended folios, particularly those in the 'Office of the Genuflexion' (*Ἀκολουθία τῆς Γονυκλισίας*) on Whit Sunday evening (*ἑσπερινοῦ τῆς Πεντηκοστῆς*). They are sung from the pulpit by the Domestikos, one of the two leaders of the choirs, who begins with the first line of Psalm lxxxv *Κλῖνον, Κύριε, τὸ οὖς σου καὶ ἐπάκουσόν μου* (Incline thy ear, O Lord, and hear me) which is followed by a Doxology, and then repeated. The first part of the line *Κλῖνον, Κύριε, τὸ οὖς σου* is missing. The beginning may have been cantillated or sung by the other Domestikos. The chant is in Mode II, but the rubric 'The Domestikos ascends the Ambon and begins thus', points at a sudden beginning with the intonation.

The syllables of the text are put under the notes as they are placed in the manuscript. The syllables which form the words are underlined. At the end of the intonation and of the verse from the psalm the word λεγετε occurs, which ought to be λέγετος and stands for the short intonation formula of Mode II, which is called *Legetos*. The correct explanation is given by Dom L. Tardo in his *L'Antica melurgia bizantina*, p. 368, where he quotes in note 2 several late manuscripts in which one reads *ἦχος β′ διατονικὸς ὅστις καὶ λέγετος καλεῖται*, i.e. the second diatonic Mode which is also called Legetos. This means *b-natural*, whereas the chromatic Mode II has b♭. The small *c* = *cito* corresponds to the Greek Γ = γοργόν. The sign Γ occurs frequently in manuscripts of melismatic chant and is rendered by the letter *c* which, as is well known, occurs in St. Gall MSS. where it has the same meaning.

Cod. Ashburnham.
fol. 258 r.

The Martyriae are indispensable in melodies which start with an interval unusual in the Mode. There is, e.g. in Cod. Ashburnham. 64 and Cod. Crypt. *Γ γ* iii, the melody of the famous poem of Romanus *Ψυχή μου* (see below) in Mode Plag. II. If there was no Martyria the transcription would have to start on *e* and end on *e*. There would be, however, a defect in the melodic line: the frequent occurrence of *b-natural–f*, which might be corrected either by introducing a *b-flat* or a *f-sharp*.

The Martyria, however, indicates *πλ. β'*, i.e. the ending of the Intonation one note higher (Oxeia ⁄) on *f*. The first sign above the first syllable *Ψυ* is an Elaphron ∩, the sign of the leap of a third downwards. This means that the melody begins on *d* and, as one will see, the melody ends also on *d*. By that lowering of the compass of the melody the augmented fourth *b-natural–f* disappears and is replaced by *a–e*. Here follow the first two lines which are sung to the same melodic phrase, a feature common in Kontakia.

The Kanonarch or Protopsaltes, whose task it was to intone, knew the formulae by heart. It was, therefore, not necessary to write them down in full. The number of the Echos was a sufficient indication for the intonation of the formula. But since the ending of the verse from the psalm, which preceded the hymn, had to be linked up with the 'starting note' of the Hirmus or Sticheron, he had to know which final cadence had to be used. For that purpose the final cadence was added in neumes to the number of the mode. The Martyria, therefore, is an abbreviation of a passage of transition from the *finalis* of the verse to the *initium* of the melody of the hymn. But, we may add, it is also, according to Byzantine musical theory, the 'layout' of the mode of the hymn; i.e. it gives the principal intervals of the melodic structure of the mode.

VIII. THE MODULATION SIGNS

For indicating the transition from one mode to another the theoreticians invented eight signs, one for each of the eight modes. They were called Phthorai (φθοραί). In manuscripts of the Late Byzantine period they were written in red ink, like the Great Hypostases, to make them more distinct. The Phthora (φθορά) is regularly set at the beginning of the new musical phrase.

Mode I

Mode II

Mode III

Mode IV

Mode I Plagal

Mode II Plagal

Mode III Plagal

Mode IV Plagal

The technical term for the transition from one mode into another is Parallage (παραλλαγή). The theoreticians give a clear definition of Parallage or modulation; it means to destroy the rule (λόγος) according to which a mode is sung, and its form (ἰδέα), and to transform its nature (φύσις) into that of another mode. The Phthora, therefore, is a sign which indicates that the mode in which a melody (μέλος) is sung should be completely destroyed (παρ' ἐλπίδα φθείρειν μέλος τοῦ ψαλλομένου ἤχου) in order to produce another melody and a particular change (ποιεῖν ἄλλο μέλος καὶ ἐναλλαγὴν μερικήν).

This definition, which is found in a treatise on the Phthorai by Manuel Chrysaphes,[1] is of importance. It shows that Byzantine composers, who only knew monophonic music, saw exactly the same musical process in modulation as we do with our training in the theory of harmonic changes.

But a further conclusion may be drawn from the definition. Manuel Chrysaphes and all the other theorists do not speak of tetrachords or scales, which are changed in order to get from one mode to another; they speak of the features of the *Melos* which are not the same in the first mode as in the second or third mode. This means that the structural formulae of a mode, laid down by the intonation, are different from those of the other modes. The theoreticians emphasize that it is no Parallage or modulation if the singer moves in the sphere of the second mode; it needs the Phthora to produce the definite change from one mode into another, and another Phthora if the composer wants to come back into the original mode. This again confirms our view that Byzantine *Melopoiia* or composition is fundamentally based upon the combination of a number of melodic patterns divided into eight groups, or Echoi, each of these groups consisting of formulae of a particular character, different from that of all the other groups. In other words: each Echos is built up of a number of melodic formulae which are interchangeable in melodies of the same mode. But if the composer wanted to introduce a section which did not belong to the patterns of the original mode, the character of the composition would be changed, and he would have to draw on a different group of formulae, those characteristic of the new mode.

[1] Thibaut, *Monuments*, p. 89.

CHAPTER XII

THE TRANSCRIPTION OF BYZANTINE MELODIES

FROM this exposition of the system of musical notation and theory the reader may have concluded that the transcription of the music into our modern staff notation is a complicated task. For the first generation of scholars the difficulties were indeed insuperable, as has been pointed out in the introductory chapter of this book; but now that the problem of the Signatures and of the rhythmical signs has been solved, the transcription of Byzantine melodies, written in Middle and Late Byzantine notation, is no more difficult than the transcription of Western Medieval music. Moreover, for the bulk of the melodies from the *Hirmologion* and the *Sticherarion* only a limited number of the signs discussed in the preceding chapter were needed. In practice, therefore, the transcription of a simple melody is, palaeographically, an easy task, provided that the neumatic version of the melody in the manuscripts is free from errors. If, however, there are mistakes, other manuscripts of the same period must be consulted, and in most cases the result of the comparison gives a satisfactory solution.

The following examples will show the method of transcription, first for a hymn from the *Hirmologion* and then for one from the *Sticherarion*. In order to give all the information which is necessary for the transcriber, we shall have to repeat a certain amount which has already been given in the preceding chapter, and, in order to make the explanation quite complete, the same amount of detail will be given for both examples.

I

The *Χαῖρε, ἁγία Θεοτόκε*, 'Hail, holy Mother of God', is the Hirmus of the ninth Ode of the Resurrection Kanon *Ἄσωμεν τῷ Κυρίῳ*, ascribed to Kosmas 'the monk', which is sung at Christmas. The neumatic version is taken from Codex Iviron, fol. 10ʳ. The codex is written in the 'mixed minuscule script'. The notation represents the earliest phase of Middle Byzantine notation. In shape the neumes are closely related to those of Early Byzantine notation: it seems, in fact, that the last stage of Early Byzantine notation and the first phase of Middle Byzantine notation were for a time used simultaneously in the first half of the twelfth century.

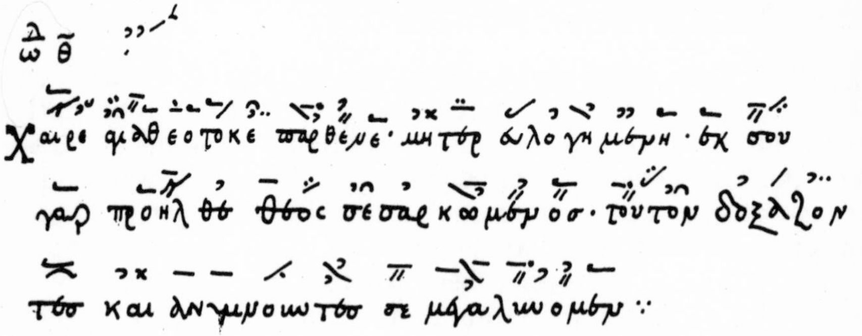

Χαῖ - ρε, ἁ - γί - α Θε - ο - τό - κε παρ - θέ - νε· μῆ - τερ

εὐ - λο - γη - μέ - νη· ἐκ σοῦ . . γὰρ προ - ῆλ - θε Θε - ὸς σε -

- σαρ - κω - μέ - νος· τοῦ - τον δο - ξά - ζον - τες καὶ ἀν - υ -

- μνοῦν - τες σὲ με - γα - λύ - νο - μεν.

(Hail, holy Virgin, Mother of God, blessed Mother; from thee came forth God who was made flesh. By glorifying and praising Him we magnify thee.)

Δ over *ω* is the usual abbreviation for ᾠδή, Ode; the letter *θ* with a dash stands for nine. Since the hymns of this section of the Codex are composed in the first mode the letter *α′* which stands for 1 is omitted. We have only the Dyo Apostrophoi of the Martyria, which indicate, as O. Strunk has pointed out,[1] that the

[1] Cf. O. Strunk, 'Intonations and Signatures', *The Musical Quarterly*, xxxi (1945), 351.

d of the Intonation formula was preceded by an *e* and has been lengthened. The Hypsele, the sign of the ascending fifth preceded by an aphonic or 'soundless' Oxeia, indicates a rise of the melody to an accentuated *a*. The Kanonarch, therefore, sang the Intonation formula as follows:

The melody of the hymn starts on *a*.

First line

Χαῖ- Ison over Kratema. Ison is the sign for the repetition of the note which precedes it. The Kratema is one of the 'Great Signs' or 'Great Hypostases'; it adds a strong emphasis to the note.

-ρε Apostrophos with added Tzakisma. The Apostrophos indicates the interval of a descending second without any particular dynamic expression. The Tzakisma lengthens the value of the note by a half.

ά- Elaphron, preceded by Apostrophos, with superimposed Dyo Kentemata. Apostrophos is a Soma, made aphonic by its combination with the Elaphron, a Pneuma, the interval of a descending third. Attached to it is an ascending second, represented by the Dyo Kentemata. This combination of two notes, *e–f*, to a syllable is very common in Byzantine music, and it is mostly the movement of a half-tone upwards, which is indicated by the Dyo Kentemata, i.e. either *e–f* or *b′* natural–*c*, provided that the melodic line continues to move upwards by a tone, as it does here by reaching *g* on *-γία*. If, however, the combination Apostrophos–Elaphron plus Dyo Kentemata, or Apostrophos plus Dyo Kentemata, is followed by an Ison, which means that the ascending movement comes to a temporary stop on the note indicated by Dyo Kentemata, or if a leap occurs, leading back to the tone reached by the Dyo Kentemata, the step can also be a full tone upwards, e.g. *g–a* on the syllable *-ζον-* in *δοξάζοντες* at the end of the second line, or *g–a* on *-κε* in *Θεοτόκε* in the first line.

-γί- Oligon over Diple. The Oligon is the Interval sign of the ascending second without any particular dynamic expression; but the Diple indicates that its rhythmical value must be doubled.

-α Ison. The *g* is to be repeated.

Θε- Oligon and superimposed Kentema. These two signs have to be added together and produce (1+2 = 3) the interval of an ascending fourth without any particular nuance.

-ο- Ison. The *c′* must be repeated.

-τό- Ison over Oxeia. In this combination the Ison is used as a Pneuma; it renders the Oxeia aphonic and receives from it its dynamic nuance, through which the repeated tone gets an expression mark. The reader may have noticed that expression marks of the music, or rhythmical signs indicating a lengthening of the tone, coincide with the accents of the words. We shall have to discuss this question in detail in the next chapter of this book, which will deal with the relation between music and words.

-κε Elaphron over Apostrophos+Dyo Kentemata. If the Elaphron is placed above the Apostrophos, the two Interval signs (2+1 = 3) have to be added together to form a descending fourth. The Dyo Kentemata are attached to the preceding note by a slur. The interval *g–a* is a full tone upwards, as has been explained above.

παρ- Bareia, Kentema, preceded by Oligon, and followed by Apostrophos, set under Kentema. The Kentema is the sign for the ascending second; the Oligon, which is rendered aphonic by it, indicates that the second should be sung without any particular rhythmical nuance, but the Bareia means that the note should be strongly emphasized. The following Apostrophos indicates that a descending second should follow on the same syllable.

-θέ- Apostrophos over Diple. A descending second, turned into a crotchet, by the Diple.

-νε Ison. The preceding note *a* is repeated.

μῆ- Apostrophos-Chamile. The Apostrophos, set before the Chamile, is made aphonic by the Pneuma, which indicates the leap of a fifth downwards.

-τερ Oligon, Dyo Kentemata. The combination of these two signs has to be read upwards. The first note of the group is the Oligon, the ascending second without any particular nuance, the second is the Dyo Kentemata.

εὐ- Petaste. This sign stands for an ascending, strongly accentuated second.

-λο- Apostrophos. Descending second without any particular nuance.

-γη- Bareia, Apostrophos. The Bareia indicates that the descending second should be sung emphatically.

-μέ- Dyo Apostrophoi. The time value of the descending second is doubled.

-νη· Ison. The preceding note is repeated.

ἐκ Ison.

σοῦ Oligon–Diple, Oxeia, Dyo Kentemata. Three notes are sung to one syllable, in order to emphasize the word. The rhythmical value of the Oligon is doubled by the Diple; two consecutive, ascending seconds are attached to it: Oxeia and Dyo Kentemata. They always mark the last note of a group, whether they are set over or under the preceding sign.

Second line

γὰρ Ison. Repetition of the preceding note.

προ- Ison.

-ῆλ- Oligon over Kratema.

-θε Apostrophos.

Θε- Oligon.

-ὸς Oxeia, Dyo Kentemata. The Dyo Kentemata are set over the Oxeia.

σε- Apostrophos–Elaphron. The Apostrophos is made aphonic and the combination represents a descending third without any particular dynamic nuance.

-σαρ- Apostrophos.

-κω- Oligon with Bareia, followed by Apostrophos.

-μέ- Apostrophos with Diple.

-νος· Ison with Diple.

τοῦ- Apostrophos–Kentema over Diple, Petaste, Dyo Kentemata. Here again a group of three notes is set to the first syllable of τοῦτον (Christ), in order to balance the setting of σοῦ, which refers to the Theotokos. The Kentema, ascending third, is a Pneuma and makes the preceding Apostrophos aphonic; its rhythmical value is doubled by the Diple. The Petaste is an ascending second, sung with *élan*; the sign is followed by Dyo Kentemata, which means the interval of a half-tone upwards.

-τον Apostrophos–Elaphron.

δο- Apostrophos.

-ξά- Oxeia.

-ζον- Apostrophos followed by Dyo Kentemata.

Third line

-τες Ison over Apoderma, which corresponds to our 𝄐, indicating a 'hold'.

καὶ Apostrophos–Chamile. A descending fifth.

ἀν- Oligon.

-υ- Oligon.

-μνοῦν- Oxeia–Kentema. The Kentema (Pneuma) renders the Oxeia (Soma) aphonic and deprives it of its dynamic expression; the combination of the two signs produces an accentuated, ascending third.

-τες Apostrophos, Bareia, Apostrophos. We read from top to bottom. The first Apostrophos gets its strong accentuation from the Bareia; the second Apostrophos follows without any particular dynamic nuance.

σὲ Oligon over Diple.

με- Oligon.

-γα- Oligon, Bareia, Apostrophos. The Bareia is combined with the Oligon, and gives it a strong accent. The Apostrophos indicates a descending second.

-λύ- Oligon–Kentema, Diple, Apostrophos. The first group of the combination has already been explained. (Cf. the first syllable of τοῦτον in the second line.) The Apostrophos indicates a descending second, which forms the second interval of the group of two notes on this syllable.

-νο- Apostrophos over Diple.

-μεν. Ison. The rhythmical value of the last note of a melody is doubled, even if there is no Diple or Apoderma, in order to produce the effect of a final stop.

II

We shall now go a step farther and transcribe a more extended hymn from the *Sticherarion*. This time the transcription is based on the photographic reproduction of a hymn from Codex theologicus graecus 181 of the National Library in Vienna. This manuscript was reproduced in full in volume i of the *Monumenta Musicae Byzantinae*, collated with Cod. Vatopedi 1492, Cod. Vatopedi 1499, and Cod. graec. 270 of the Bibl. Nation. in Paris. The Vienna Codex contains 325 folios, made of calf-skin; the size is 8¾ by 5½ inches. It was written by John Dalassenos in 1221, and was owned at one time by the hymn-writer Michael Marullas (†1500). It belonged to a group of 273 manuscripts collected between 1555 and 1562 by Augerius de Busbecq, Ambassador of the Emperor Ferdinand I at the court of Soliman II in Constantinople. The collection was sent by him to Vienna, where it was placed in 1583 in the Imperial Library.[1]

The *Sticherarion* shows the fully developed Middle Byzantine notation, for which the term 'Round Notation' has been coined. Compared with the straight strokes and fine dots of the neumes of Codex Iviron, the thick, curved neumes look rather clumsy, particularly as the script of the text consists of small, elegantly written letters. The number of the Great Hypostases has not greatly increased, but comparison with earlier manuscripts shows that the dynamics have been intensified. In many cases an Oxeia is set where in earlier manuscripts an Oligon is found, or a Petaste instead of an Oxeia.

The 'Sticheraric style' is, as has already been said, more ornamented than the 'Hirmologic'. We find five or six notes combined in a group on a single syllable, which need no longer be one which is important in the text. From now on the music has the preponderance over the text.

Let us now turn to the hymn which is found on fol. 78v. of the Codex (see Plate IV).

On the 13th of December the memory of the Saints Eustratius, Auxentius, Eugenius, Mardarius, Orestes, and Lucia of Sicily, all of whom suffered martyrdom under Diocletian, was celebrated. A note in the Menaion informs us that the *Stichera Idiomela*,

[1] Cf. my article 'Über Rhythmus und Vortrag der byzantinischen Melodien', *B.Z.* xxxii (1933), 50–4, and *M.M.B.* i, *Sticherarium*, pp. 15–16.

whose first Troparion forms the hymn reproduced here, should stand at the end of the Orthros. According to the solemnity of the feast, eight, six, or four stanzas were sung. Four are prescribed for this day: *Εἰς τοὺς αἴνους* (the Lauds come at the end of the Orthros after the *Exaposteilarion* and before the *Eothinon*) *ἱστῶμεν στίχους δ′, καὶ ψάλλομεν στιχηρὰ ἰδιόμελα.*

In deciphering the notation of this piece of music we shall use Cod. Vind. theol. gr. 181 as the basis. Codd. Vat. 1492, 1499, and Cod. Paris. gr. 270 only differ from the Vienna manuscript in unimportant melodic and dynamic readings, and we shall only draw on them in a few cases.

The hymn is introduced by the short heading *μηνὶ τῷ αὐτῷ ΙΓ′ τοῦ ἁγίου μάρτυρος Εὐστρατίου*, in red ink. In the left margin stands the Martyria *ἦχος α′*. An Oxeia (Soma) with a Hypsele, above and after it, is set over the *α*.

First line

Τὴν Chamile. Descending fifth, preceded by an aphonic Apostrophos. The Chamile is the largest interval downwards which can be expressed by a single sign. As the starting-note is *a*, this sign means that the singer should begin a fifth lower.

πεντ- Ison, the sign for the repetition of a note.

-ά- Hypsele. Ascending fifth (Pneuma), preceded by the Oligon (Soma), the second without any rhythmical nuance. This combination, which corresponds exactly to that on the syllable *τὴν*, means an unaccented ascending fifth.

-ριθ- Ison. Repetition of the preceding note.

-μον Ison over Petaste. The Ison renders the Petaste aphonic, but it assumes the dynamic value of the Petaste, which we mark with a wedge-shaped stroke (ꞌ).

χο- Apostrophos. Descending second without any particular nuance.

-ρεί- Petaste. Ascending second, sung rapidly and with *élan*.

-αν Elaphron over Dyo Apostrophoi and Oxeia. A group of two notes, since the Elaphron (descending third) and the Dyo Apostrophoi (lengthened descending second) were added together (2+1 = 3) to give a descending fourth.

τῶν Oxeia. The normal, unaccented ascending quaver.

Ἀ- Oxeia.

-γί- Kentema over Petaste. The Kentema (ascending third) is added to the Petaste (ascending second) to give a fourth, and the combination assumes the rhythmical nuance of the Petaste.

-ων Apostrophos combined with Tzakisma. The Tzakisma is one of the lengthening signs and has also the function of a division. Here it stands between this Apostrophos and the following one and prevents their being run together. At the same time it lengthens the first note, which takes the stress, by a half.

εὐ- Apostrophos and Dyo Kentemata. The melody first descends by one note, and then returns rapidly to the tone from which it started.

-φη- Oligon, Bareia, Elaphron. The Bareia lends a strong emphasis to the note to which it is set. The movement of the melody at this point is that it first rises by a strongly accented note and then falls by a third.

-μή- Oxeia.

Second line

-σω- Apostrophos.

-μεν Apostrophos.

λα- Ison.

-θοὶ Ison over Diple, which doubles the length of the note with which it is combined.

τὸν Apostrophos.

Σω- Petaste.

-τῆ- Apostrophos combined with Tzakisma.

-ρα Elaphron, preceded by Apostrophos. A descending third without special rhythmical nuance. It is joined by the indistinctly written Dyo Kentemata.

ἀν- Oligon.

-υ- Petaste.

-μνοῦν- Elaphron+Dyo Apostrophoi (descending fourth, a crotchet), followed by an Oxeia.

-τες Elaphron, preceded by an Apostrophos.

Χρι- Ison.

στόν· Ison.

Εὐ- Kentema over Oxeia, giving a descending fourth (2+1 = 3) which has the nuance of the Oxeia.

Third line

-στρά- Apostrophos.

-τι- Apostrophos.

-ον Apostrophos followed by Dyo Kentemata.

τὸν Elaphron, preceded by Apostrophos (descending third).

καρ- Kentema over Oligon (2+1), therefore an ascending fourth.

-τε- Bareia, Kentema over Oligon, Elaphron. This means a strongly accented ascending fourth, followed by a descending third.

-ρό- Oligon over Diple, which doubles the length of the note, and therefore changes a quaver to a crotchet.

-ψυ- The sign which stands above this second Diple is not clearly written; comparison with Cod. Vat. 1492, fol. 58v., shows that it must be an Elaphron, although elsewhere the sign for this interval is always a clear half-circle with the ends thicker than the centre. The Oxeia and Ison follow, both written over the Stauros, which corresponds to our *corona*. The Oxeia, an abruptly sung second, cannot, however, be lengthened. Again, Cod. Vatop. makes it clear that only the Ison is to be read over the Stauros, while the Oxeia forms a group with the preceding Elaphron.

There are no difficulties in the remainder of this and the next line. At the end of the fourth line, on the syllable -δα- we have the Kentema over the Kratema; this doubles the rhythmical value of the note and, in addition, gives it a special nuance which is expressed by ⊓ in the transcription.

Fifth line

Here we find rich melismata over *οὗτοι γάρ*, and, in consequence, the words were prolonged in the usual way: *ου τοι οι γα α αρ*.

οὗ- Hypsele, preceded by an Oligon, i.e. an ascending fifth without any nuance.

-τοι Kratema under Kentema, and, joined to it, to be read from the top downwards: Apostrophos, Apostrophos combined with Tzakisma, Dyo Apostrophoi. These

signs, however, extend over the space belonging to the next word, and it would be difficult to decide whether the Dyo Apostrophoi or the Tzakisma did not belong to the following γὰρ, if a comparison with Cod. Vatop. 1492 did not make the point clear beyond a doubt.

γὰρ Ison over Diple, followed by a faintly written Oligon over Diple, and over that an Antikenoma which, however, is lacking in Cod. Vatop.; then Kentema, preceded by Oxeia, Apostrophos, and Dyo Apostrophoi. This gives: repetition of the note, with its value doubled, ascending second with doubled value, ascending third with the rhythmical nuance of the Oxeia, descending second, and finally, another descending second with doubled value. The rest of the line, again, presents no difficulty.

Sixth line

ἀθλοῦντες. The transcription of this passage presents considerable difficulty. A Kentema combined with a Bareia, followed by an Apostrophos, comes first, then Dyo Apostrophoi. After that, however, in the facsimile, it looks as though a Kentema stands over the Ison, next to it a Tzakisma, underneath an Oxeia. Comparison with Cod. Vatop. 1492 is of no help here, because it has a variant reading. It is only when the manuscript itself is examined that it becomes clear that this Kentema was erased by the scribe, although the outline still remains. This omission of the Kentema makes possible a transcription which gives a satisfactory solution of the difficulties of the passage.

ἱλασμόν. The distribution of the signs over this word (it is correctly written ἱλασμόν in Cod. Paris. gr. 270, and in Vatop. 1492 and 1499, while Cod. theol. gr. 181 has ἱλασμῶν) is not at all clear in the Vienna Codex, as a comparison with Cod. Vatop. shows.

The signs in Cod. Vindob. are: ι- Hypsele after Oligon (ascending fifth); -λασ- Kentema (ascending third) over Kratema (strong accent); after that Apostrophos (descending second), Apostrophos combined with Tzakisma, Dyo Apostrophoi; -μόν Ison over Diple, Oligon combined with Diple, Oligon combined with Diple a second time, Kentema after Oxeia (ascending third with the nuance of the Oxeia), Apostrophos, Dyo Apostrophoi.

In Codex Vatop. 1492 these signs are more widely spaced, but we find a variant in the third group. Here we have Apostrophos, Apostrophos combined with Tzakisma, and then a sign which could be read as an Aporrhoe (two consecutive descending seconds in a kind of *glissando*). It is, however, a Tromikon, one of the Great Hypostases, which means a *tremolo* of the note by which it is set. Then follows Ison over Diple, where an Oligon stands in the Vienna Codex. The remaining signs are the same in both.

If the signs are transcribed to the end of the stanza as they stand in the Vienna Codex, the ending will be on *e*, the final note of the second Mode, and not of the first. Comparison with the Paris Codex and Vatop. 1499, however, shows that in the Vienna Codex there is one Oligon too many over the syllable -μὸν, so that from there on to the end the melody is always one tone too high. Once this obvious mistake has been corrected, there is no difficulty in reaching the right solution.

In the following transcription we have accepted this correction from Cod. Paris. and Vatop. 1499:

- δά - ρι - ον καὶ ᾿Ο - ρέ - στην. οὗ - τοι . . . γὰρ . . . . ὑ -
- πὲρ τῆς πί - στε - ως ἀ - θλοῦν - τες τὰς τρι - κυ - μί - ας κατ - ε -
- πά - τη - σαν ἐχ - θρῶν· καὶ τῷ Σω - τῆ - ρι πρεσ - βεύ - ου - σιν,
ἱ - λα - σμὸν . . . . . . καὶ ἄ - φε - σιν ἁ - μαρ - τι -
- ῶν . . . . δω - ρη - θῆ - ναι τοῖς ἐν . . πί - στει ἐκ - τε -
- λοῦ - σι τὴν μνή - μην αὐ - τῶν.

These two examples will be sufficient to give a short introduction to the actual practice of transcribing. The success of the transcription depends, of course, as we have said, largely on the quality of the manuscript and on the reliability of the scribe. But even a faulty version no longer offers the same obstacles as it did in the early days of our studies, when nothing was known about the structure of the melodies. At this early stage every melody seemed to be a new composition, and even obvious errors of the scribe could not be corrected unless other manuscripts were available for comparison. Now, however, the rules of composition are quite clear, and in most cases we are able to discover an error and to correct it.

Byzantine technique of composition is highly elaborate; indeed, hardly anything is left to free invention or improvisation. The rules according to which a new melody is composed are as strict as those which govern the writing of a new text for a hymn. This will be shown in the next chapter.

CHAPTER XIII

THE STRUCTURE OF BYZANTINE MELODIES

I. HIRMI AND STICHERA

BYZANTINE melodies, both Hirmi and Stichera, are built up from a number of melodic formulae which are linked together by short transitional passages. The discovery of this principle of composition in Byzantine music goes back to comparative studies into the form of Eastern ecclesiastical music, which began forty years ago.

Investigating the melodies of the Serbian Oktoëchos I found that they were composed of a number of musical phrases, repeated either exactly or with slight variations. Since the melodies of the Serbian Church derived from the Syrian—introduced into the Balkan countries along the pilgrim-routes which by-passed Constantinople—the occurrence of an identical principle of composition in both Syria and Serbia[1] was explained, a principle to which Idelsohn had first drawn attention in his study of the technique of Arabic music[2] and which had been confirmed by Dom Jeannin and Dom Puyade in their publications on Syrian music.[3]

The discovery of this principle of composition is of far greater importance than was at first thought. Further investigations have shown that it was not confined to the melodies of a few areas, but was the ruling principle of composition in Oriental music and, with the expansion of Christian music, spread over the whole Mediterranean basin.[4]

The transcription of the hymns collected in the *Hirmologion* and of a large number of those from the *Sticherarion* enables us to study the structure of Byzantine ecclesiastical music. The analysis of the hymns confirms our view, which has already been expressed in earlier studies on the subject, that here, too, the construction of the melody was based on the combination and

[1] Cf. E. Wellesz, 'Die Struktur des serbischen Oktoëchos', *Z.M.W.* ii (1919–20), 141–2, and the article on 'Eastern Church Music' in the Supplementary Volume of Grove's *Dictionary of Music* (1940), pp. 181–2.

[2] A. Z. Idelsohn, 'Die Maqamen der arabischen Musik', *S.I.M.* xv. 1 sqq.

[3] Jeannin et Puyade, 'L'Octoechos syrien', *O.C.*, N.S. iii. 278.

[4] I have examined some of these facts in detail in my book *Eastern Elements in Western Chant*, *M.M.B.*, Amer. Ser. i.

linking together of a certain number of melodic formulae characteristic of the mode in which the hymn was composed. The mode, we may therefore conclude, is not merely a 'scale' but the sum of all the formulae which constitute the quality of an Echos. This definition is in conformity with that given by Chrysanthus of Madytos in his *Great Musical Theory* (1832): 'Echos is the scheme (ἰδέα) of the melody, arranged according to the practice of the expert musician, who knows which tones should be omitted, which chosen on which one should begin and on which one should end.'[1]

In order to explain the structure of Byzantine hymns we give a transcription of the Hirmus of the first Ode of *Ἀναστάσεως ἡμέρα* from fol. 2r. of the *Hirmologion* Codex Saba 599, dating from about the end of the fourteenth century.[2]

[1] *Μέγα Θεωρητικὸν τῆς μουσικῆς* (Trieste, 1832), p. 19. In a footnote Chrysanthus quotes the passage in Aristides Quintilianus' *Περὶ μουσικῆς*, i, c. xi (Meib. i, p. 29), ed. A. Jahn, p. 19, from which he has taken the definition. Here, however, Arist. Quint. does not speak of the ἦχος as the scheme of the melody, but of the πεττεία ('draught-playing'), the 'planning' from which we know which tones should be omitted and which chosen, and he adds that this 'planning' becomes the expression of the ἦθος, the character of the melody (αὕτη δὲ καὶ τοῦ ἤθους γίνεται παραστατική). From a later passage of *Περὶ μουσικῆς*, ii, c. xiv (Meib. i, p. 96, Jahn, p. 58) we learn that Aristides Quintilianus took over the term πεττεία from the Pythagorean philosopher Damon, who sees in the right choice of tones the most important factor in musical composition (διὸ καὶ τῶν μερῶν τῆς μελοποιίας ἡ καλουμένη πεττεία τὸ χρησιμώτατον). Cf. R. Schäfke, Aristeides Quintilianus (Berlin, 1937), p. 207.

[2] The melodic version of the Hirmi of Codex Saba 599 differs from those of all the other Hirmologia. This fact needs further investigation.

The melody is based on *a*, which is the initial and final note of the formulae I, VI, VII, and VIII; it rises in the middle part (B) to *c′*, which is prepared by the two ascending seconds: (*a*)–*b*–*c′* at the end of the second formula (II), which would normally end on *a*. The note *c′* is made the *tenor* in III and IV. In the fifth formula (V) *c′* is still the *tenor*, but the *Initium* and *Finalis* are on *b*, leading back to *a*, which, again, is the *tenor* of the last section (C).

All the eight formulae of which the hymn is composed occur in a number of other hymns, as can be seen from the tables in Appendix III, which contain some of the most frequently used formulae from Codex Iviron and Codex Saba.

From the study of these tables it can be seen that some of the formulae, for example those of groups A and D, are, in the main, used as *Initia*, those of group G as *Mediae* and *Finales*, and those of groups B, C, F, and H as *Finales*. But the position of the formulae is not rigidly fixed: the sixth formula of Table C to the words Ὁ ἱερὸς Ἀββακούμ, for example, is used as *Initium*, the seventh of the same table to the words τῆς σῆς αἰνέσεως, as *Finalis*.

Another point should be noticed, viz. that those formulae which are regularly used as *Finales* are the most stereotyped ones. They consist, as can be seen from Tables B, C, F, G, and H, of two phrases. The first is a melodic arabesque on and round the *tenor* (*a*), often preceded by an *Initium* which leads up from *e* to *a*. The second part is, in all cases, the same cadence, which has, with a few exceptions, the identical dynamic signs on the same notes, as can be seen from Tables B, C, F, G, and H.

A table containing a list of the most frequently occurring formulae of the first mode, reduced to a bare outline in which only the essential notes are given, follows. The notes before the dotted line vary in the hymns; those after it belong to the cadences.

Investigations into the different stages of Byzantine notation have shown that these cadences were preserved, practically unchanged, from the earliest documents of musical notation which we possess to those written in the thirteenth, fourteenth, and fifteenth centuries, a fact which confirms my view, demonstrated in pp. 303–10 above, that the same principle of melody construction was maintained in Byzantine hymnography from the ninth century onwards.[1]

II. MELISMATIC CHANT

Investigation into the structure of melismatic chant is of a more complex nature, because the earliest documents of that group are thirteenth-century manuscripts in which the melismatic style is already highly developed. Since towards the end of the thirteenth and the beginning of the fourteenth century the florid passages of the same Kontakia are even more extended, we may assume that it was this genre of chant comprising Kontakia, Alleluias, Doxologies, &c., to which the Maïstores devoted particular care.

[1] Cf. also E. Wellesz, *Eastern Elements in Western Chant*, Part ii B, ch. 2; 'Über Rhythmus u. Vortrag d. byzant. Melodien', *B.Z.* xxxiii (1933), 62–4; H. J. W. Tillyard, 'Byzantine Neumes: The Coislin Notation', *B.Z.* xxxvii (1937), 356–8.

The two following examples are taken from the Akathistos Hymn. The first shows the beginning of the Kontakion Τῇ ὑπερμάχῳ στρατηγῷ[1] in the moderately ornamented version found in Cod. Ashburnham. 64 and in the Grottaferrata Codex *Γ γ* iii, and in the highly ornamented of Cod. Vatican. 1606 and Grottaferrata *E β* iii. The technique of ornamentation is akin to that in our Western music. It is therefore not difficult to understand how the musical mind of the Byzantine composer worked:

[1] Cf. *M.M.B. Facsimilia*, vol. iv, fol. 108 r., and *Transcripta*, ix. 3.

The following example shows a comparison between two versions of the opening words of the first stanza of the Akathistos *Ἄγγελος πρωτοστάτης*, the moderately ornamented one from Cod. Ashburnham. fol. 109 r., the richly ornamented from Cod. Cryptensis is *E β* iii, fol. 31 v. The beginning on *a* of the version *E β* iii is indicated by the Martyria πλ. δ in Codd. Messinens. 120, fol. 86 r. and 129, fol. 88.[1]

It is now possible to find out more about the Akathistos fragment in Codex Coislin 220, which was discussed on p. 275. The

[1] Prof. O. Strunk kindly provided me with the photographs of the Akathistos from Codd. Messina 120 and 129.

long melisma on (πρωτο)-στα-(της) particularly the combination of *a a*, which is three times repeated, may correspond to:

since the Bareia \ accentuates the first of two notes, of which the second is mostly a second lower. The Apostrophos is the symbol for the unaccentuated execution of a note, which—in the early phases of neumatic notation—may be either a higher or a lower interval, mostly of a second.

A comparison between the neumes of the Coislin fragment and the two thirteenth-century versions shows that musical signs of the Coislin fragment have a close connexion with those of Crypt. *E β* iii and Codd. Messina 120 and 129. Though the melismas in the Coislin fragment are shorter than those in the thirteenth-century manuscripts, they are fully developed and prove that the Akathistos was already sung in the ninth and tenth centuries in the same ornamented style as that of the thirteenth-century manuscripts.

We can go a step farther by saying that the melodic style of the Akathistos was not an individual one, but characteristic of the genre. We can speak of the style of the Kontakia just as we speak of the style of the Graduals and of that of the Offertories of the Western Church. It is therefore permissible to assume that the melismatic chant of the Byzantine Church had in the main the same shape in the ninth century as in the thirteenth. The great change came in the fourteenth.

The form of the Kontakion can best be studied by analysing the Prooemium and the twenty-four stanzas of the Akathistos Hymnos. The most striking feature is the regularity of the cadences. The stanza of the Prooemium (Kontakion)[1] has six melodic phrases: A, A_1, B, A_2, C, D which end with full clauses (1), (2), (3). In the middle of the melodic lines are half clauses (4), (5), (6), (7).

[1] Cf. *M.M.B.* ix. 3–4.

These cadences, and others, occurring in the 'Chairetismoi' (the 'Salutations'), are not confined to the Akathistos; they are part of the style of the Kontakia, and it is easy to learn how they developed if one glances at the following table which contains cadences from the Hirmologion, Sticherarion, and Kontakarion.

The Akathistos is in the fourth plagal Mode. The cadence regularly begins on *d′* and goes down—either directly, or in curves to *g*. In all lines the strong accents are on *d′* and *c′*.

We continue our examination of melismatic chant with the analysis of the musical structure of the Kontakion of the famous *Canticum in Christi Nativitate* by Romanus. My transcription follows the version of Cod. Ashburnham. 64, fols. 75 v.–76 v. The Kontakion is in the third Mode as can be seen from the Intonation formula preceding the first and third lines. The melody of the stanza begins and ends on *f*. The Intonation formulae, preceding the fifth, seventh, and ninth lines, indicate that the greater part of the stanza is in the first plagal and the first authentic Modes; but the melodic material of the first lines does not differ so substantially from that of the following lines that a modal change would appear to have happened. The Intonation formulae seem to have been set in the first place to make the soloist start the new melodic phrase on the right note.

Structurally the stanza of the Prooemium is built up as follows. The melodic material of lines (1) and (2) is repeated, in a slightly extended form, in lines (3) and (4). This seems to be the usual scheme for the first four lines. As can be seen from the following table, line (3) has a middle section (B) which does not occur in line (1). The half clause in lines (1) and (3) is marked by ω, the full clause by ω_1. S in lines (2) and (4) marks a sequence to which I have drawn attention in Example 3 of my article on the Akathistos.[1] Line (5) represents an extended version of line (7).

At first glance the least connexion exists between lines (6) and (8). In fact the relationship is restricted to C and D up to S, though, of course, the skeleton line of the sequence *c′ b a* has its parallel in line (8). Here the repetition of three slight variants of D on ὁδοιποροῦσιν ([*Magi*] journey) is a remarkable feature. Is the thrice repeated ὁδοιποροῦσιν intended to convey tone-poetically the idea of the three Magi 'journeying with a star'? The first sections of lines (9) and (10) are identical. In (9) the compass between *d′* and *g* is filled in by the sequence S; in line (10) a prolonged full clause is appended, beginning with C, and ending with ω'.

The following table gives the melodic line schematically in order to facilitate comparison of identical and divergent passages. NB in lines (2) and (4) marks a correction which I made in the transcription in order to achieve an ending on *e-f-a-f*, the typical cadence in the Kontakion style. The manuscript has which means a leap of a fourth. The Kentema (•), however, often resembles the Hypsile (∟) in this type of script and all difficulties disappear if the leap of the fourth is replaced by that of the sixth. A similar leap of a sixth occurs in the *Akathistos*, cf., e.g., *The Akathistos Hymn, M.M.B. Transcripta*, vol. ix, p. 11, l. 5.

In the sequence S of line 6 two notes in brackets are added. The phrase occurs so frequently in Kontakia that the completion of the sequence needs no further explanation.

In Appendix III, pp. 401–5, the Kontakion and Oikos in honour of St. Symeon Stylites is given, whose feast is celebrated on 1 September, the beginning of the Orthodox ecclesiastical year. The Kontakion is in Mode II. It is an Automelon (αὐτόμελον), i.e. it has its own melody. The scheme is:

(1) A, (2) A, (3) A, (4) A_2,
(5) B, (6) C, (7) D, (8) E

[1] *Dumbarton Oaks Papers*, ix and x (1955–6), 163.

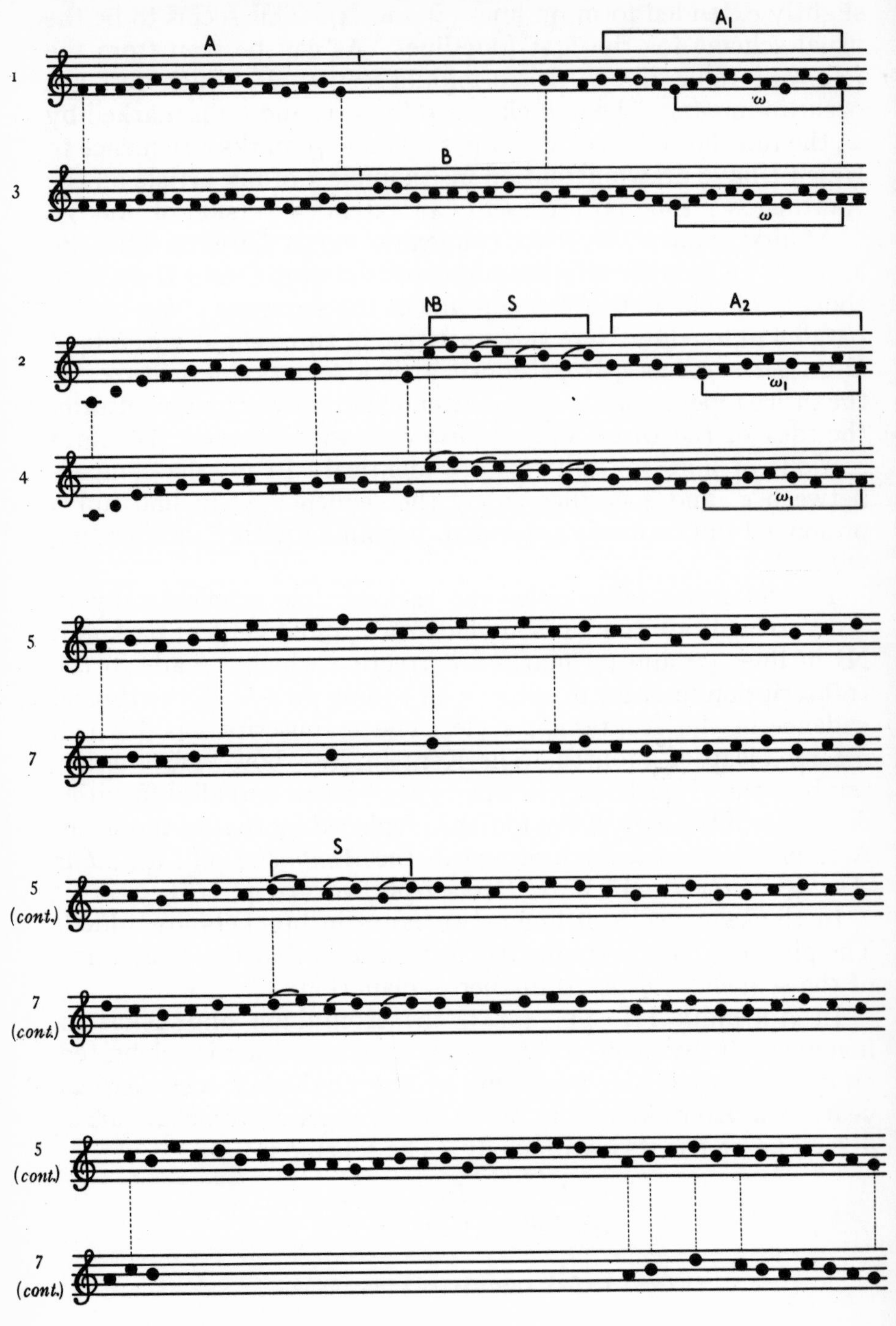
A
A1
1
ω
B
3
ω
NB
S
A2
2
ω1
4
ω1
5
7
S
5 (cont.)
7 (cont.)
5 (cont.)
7 (cont.)

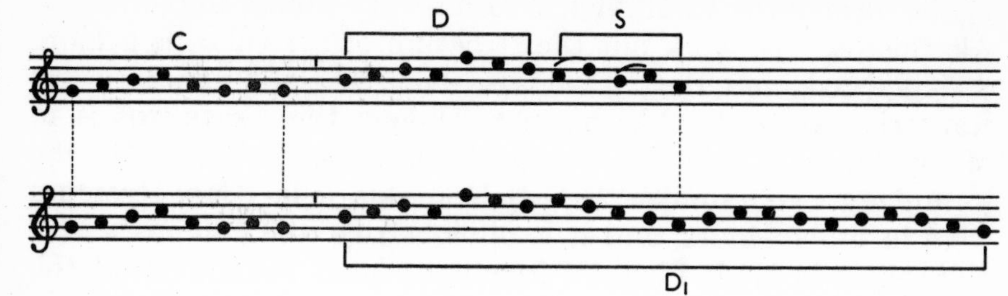
C
D
S
6
8
D_1

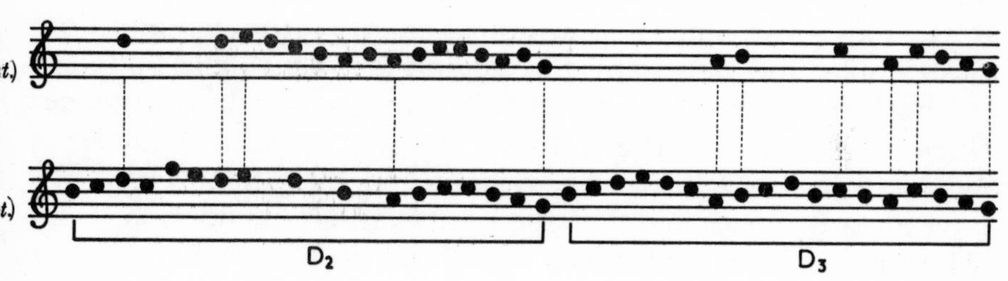
6
ont.)
8
nt.)
D_2
D_3

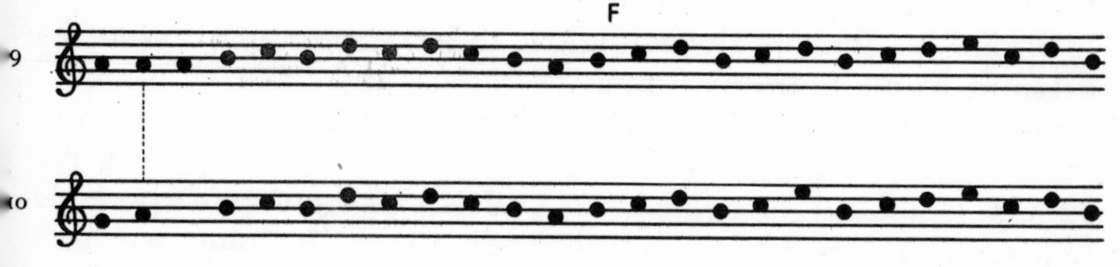
F
9
10

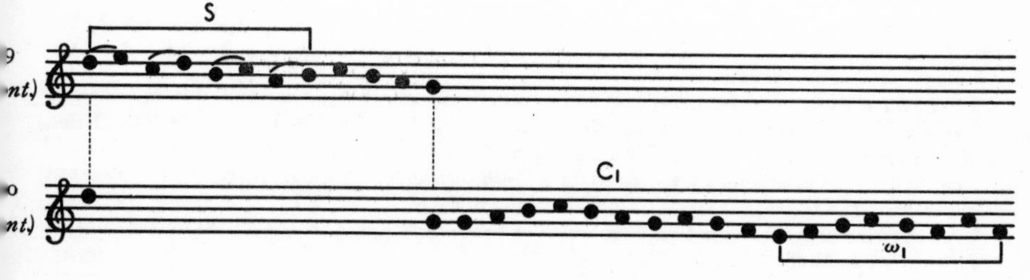
S
9
nt.)
10
nt.)
C_1
ω_1

The form of the Kontakion stanza is very similar to that of the Akathistos.[1] To work out the structure of the Oikos is a more difficult task and the method is given in the Preface to my transcription of the Akathistos.[2] Though the Akathistos is in Mode Plag. IV and the Symeon Kontakion in Mode II, the formulae are very similar. In both Kontakia, in fact, long stretches were in other Modes, and it is obvious that the composer of a Kontakion in Mode Plag. IV frequently used Mode II, and the composer of a Kontakion in Mode II has a preference for Mode Plag. IV. The astonishing similarity of formulae, however, may be taken as a proof that the technique of ornamentation was applied according to fixed rules, which must have been developed in the two great centres of liturgical chant, Jerusalem and Constantinople, and taught by the singing masters to their pupils.

The Kontakion ends on the half clause of the last sentence; there is no music to the words of line 14: πρεσβεύων ἀπαύστως ὑπὲρ πάντων ἡμῶν (towering without end over all of us).[3] We have already mentioned that the Kontakarion, Alleluiarion, Doxastarion, and other collections of melismatic chants are books for the Psaltes. They do not contain the refrain which was sung by the chorus.[4] The fact that in chants sung by the Psaltes the last words are missing makes it an unsatisfactory task to transcribe verses from the Gospel, or from Psalms, which are in the Alleluiarion,[5] because we do not know the exact ending, and any attempt at adding a final melodic phrase and full clause must remain a hypothetical solution. From the musician's point of view the response of the refrain by the chorus is perfectly understandable, but it is difficult to understand in the *Magnificat* (Appendix III, p. 408) the abrupt ending with the long melisma on (ταπείνω)-σιν (Because he has regarded the humility), and the answer by the chorus τῆς δούλης αὐτοῦ (of his handmaid).

In a similar way the last words of verses from the Psalms are

[1] Cf. E. Wellesz, 'Das Prooemium des Akathistos', *Die Musikforschung*, vi (1953), 202–5, and *The Akathistos Hymn*, *M.M.B. Transcripta*, vol. ix (1957), pp. lvi–lx.

[2] Ibid., pp. lxxxiv–lxxxviii.

[3] Symeon Stylites stood for many years on a column of stones on top of a hill near Antioch.

[4] In the twenty-four stanzas of the Akathistos the twelve odd ones have the refrain Χαῖρε, νύμφη ἀνύμφευτε which it was possible to add from the Kontakion, where the refrain is intoned by the Psaltes; the even ones have the refrain Ἀλληλούϊα which is missing, but was added from one of the Alleluias in the later part of Cod. Ashburnham. 64.

[5] A collection of Alleluias and psalm verses is in the facsimile edition of Cod. Ashburnham. fols. 200 r.–244 v., and 258 r., 265 v.

omitted in the Psaltika and handed over to the chorus. Let us take as an example of this genre the Alleluia from Nativity followed by verses 1 and 2 from Psalm xviii.[1] It will suffice to give a transcription of the Alleluia and verse 1:

> *Ἀλληλούϊα.*
> *Οἱ οὐρανοὶ διηγοῦνται δόξαν θεοῦ*
> *ποίησιν δὲ χειρῶν αὐτοῦ ἀναγγέλλει [τὸ στερέωμα]*
>
> (Alleluia.
> The heavens shew forth the glory of God:
> And [the firmament] declareth the work of his hands.)

Vatic. grec. 1606, fol. 46 v.

[1] The text is taken from Cod. Ashburnham. 64, fol. 200 r., but in the transcription of verse 1 I followed Cod. Vat. gr. 1606, fol. 46 v. At * the ∩ stands for a ʕ as often happens in south Italian MSS. The scribe copied carelessly from a 'Coislin' notation Codex.

A more extended Alleluia can be seen from the transcription of the Koinonikon, the *Communio* chant, on Palm Sunday *Εὐλόγητος ὁ ἐρχόμενος* (Matt. xxi. 9), where it follows the verse. The transcription is taken from Cod. Cryptensis *Γ γ* i, fol. 42 v. Here the number and variety of inserted vowels and syllables is particularly great and there are also two signs for which the symbols *νε* and *z* are only an approximate substitution.

The student of Western Chant will instantly be aware of the difference between a Gregorian Alleluia and the Byzantine, which always follows the pattern of one of those reproduced above.

(1) either: A - lle - - - - - - - - - - lu i a - - - ;
(2) or: A - - - - - - - lle - - - - - - - - - lu ī a - - - - .

The first type, the short Alleluia, is sung in the Orthros, the Alleluia with long melismas in the Mass. It is the syllable -lle - - - - which has the longest melismas both in Office and Mass. The last vowel *a* has a kind of cadential melisma. There is, however, no *jubilus* in any type of the Byzantine Alleluia.

Finally, a word may be said about the execution of Byzantine melismatic chant. Its various groups may be treated as a stylistic entity, because of the striking affinity between the perpetually recurring phrases and turns of the melody in all of them.

We must assume that these chants were sung slowly, with much expression. Thus the different shades of musical accents, the *glissando*'s in certain downward movements, the different nuances of lengthening a note, and many other details which the musical notation prescribes, could find adequate rendering by the soloist.

III. PSALMODY

Investigation into the music of the psalms, canticles, and other forms of liturgical chant is the most recent development in our studies. Its results will enable us to discover if the development of psalmody in the East was parallel to that in the West, and to arrive at definite conclusions about the supposed origin of the two branches in a common source, the psalmody of the Synagogue.

The question of the derivation of Western psalmody from that of the Synagogue has been virtually solved by A. Z. Idelsohn and E. Werner.[1] But it was impossible to carry these studies farther and to include the Eastern branch, because too little was known about Byzantine psalmody, which has come down to us in a small number of manuscripts of a relatively late date, mainly in an abridged form.

At present it is not possible to decide whether the psalmody and the other liturgical chants handed down in these manuscripts represent the old layer of the Justinian era, or a later one.

The early group of these manuscripts dates from the thirteenth century. They were written in the days of the Latin Empire, when Constantinople, after being sacked and pillaged by the Crusaders in 1203, was in the hands of the Frankish Knights. The Fourth Crusade had ended in the disintegration of the Byzantine Empire, and a number of small states had been founded on its territory, partly Frankish, partly Greek.[2]

The most important sources, however, for the study of liturgical chant in the Offices of Vespers and Lauds, the two Codices mentioned already above (p. 117) of the National Library at

[1] See p. 36, n. 3, and E. Werner, 'The Common Ground in the Chant of Church and Synagogue', *Atti del Congresso Internazionale di Musica Sacra* (Paris, 1952), pp. 134–48.

[2] Cf. A. A. Vasiliev, *History of the Byzantine Empire*, ch. ix, 'The Fall of Byzantium', Wisconsin, 1952.

Athens, MSS. 2061 and 2062, were written in the final phase of the Empire when the last Emperors of the Palaeologian dynasty sought in vain for help from the West against the rising tide of the Turkish conquests. In spite of the political decline of the Empire this last period showed a remarkable spiritual activity. All those qualities that symbolized the greatness of Byzantine civilization in its hey-days were manifest again in a last glorious effort.

In this connexion we may mention the treatises about the liturgical ceremonies by Symeon, Archbishop of Thessalonica (1410–29); they are 'On the holy Temple' (*περὶ τοῦ ἁγίου ναοῦ*) and 'On the holy Prayer' (*περὶ τῆς θείας προσευχῆς*).[1] In the latter a detailed description of the celebration of the Morning and Evening Office in the 'Great Church', i.e. Hagia Sophia in Thessalonica, is given.

Symeon, a fervent adherent of the old solemn celebration of Vespers and Lauds, laments that the chanted Office had come into disuse since the 'Latins' had enslaved the 'City of Constantine' and driven out the clergy; and when, after many years, they had come back, the old practice was forgotten and the secular clergy celebrated the service according to the monastic rule, where the Office was often held 'by a single monk, without singing'.[2] He states that even in Saint Sophia in Constantinople the chanted Office was celebrated only on three occasions—the feasts of the Exaltation of the Holy Cross, the Assumption, and the Commemoration of St. Chrysostom—and that the old order was celebrated now only in Thessalonica.

A few months after Symeon's death, on 29 March 1430, Thessalonica was occupied by the Turks under Sultan Murad II, who turned the Great Church into a mosque. Though incomplete, the surviving manuscripts of liturgical chant containing the chanted Office, particularly the Athens MSS. 2061 and 2062 from the Gymnasion library at Salonica[3] give us a good idea of

[1] Symeon Thessalonicensis archiepiscopus, opera omnia, *P.G.* clv, c. 3–5–61, and c. 535–669. We are indebted to O. Strunk for having drawn attention to Symeon's treatises and to the MSS. containing the music of these Offices in his valuable study on 'The Byzantine Office at Hagia Sophia'. This study is based on a paper which he read on 30 April 1954 at the 'Symposium on Byzantine Liturgy and Music' at Dumbarton Oaks in Washington, and which was published in *Dumbarton Oaks Papers*, IX and X (1956), 177–202.

[2] Ibid., c. 555 A, B, and C.

[3] O. Strunk, who has investigated the relevant MSS., regards the two MSS. Athens 2061 and 2062 as the most important sources for the study of liturgical chant in the Offices of Vespers and Lauds. The same view is expressed by P. N. Trempelas in his *Μικρὸν Εὐχολόγιον*, 2 vols. (Athens, 1950 and 1955), ii. 173 sqq., in which the description of the Offices is based upon Cod. Athens 2061.

the organization of the service, particularly in conjunction with Symeon's treatise 'On the Holy Prayer'. Both manuscripts have on the first folios 'the psalms and canticles as they are sung at the daily Vespers and Lauds'.[1]

Since in both manuscripts this section contains the regularly recurrent chants for the ferial days, i.e. the ordinary days of the week, these melodies are kept in a simple, mostly syllabic, or in a slightly ornamented psalmodic style, which makes a fluent cantillation possible. In the manuscripts they are mostly given in an abbreviated form as can be seen from the following examples, taken from Cod. Crypt. *Γ γ* i.

The first example shows the first group of Antiphons from the Feast of the Beheading of St. John the Baptist on 29 August, consisting of the first lines of Psalms xiv, xcvi, and cxi, followed by Alleluia.

Ps. xiv.
I. Mode

Κύ - ρι - ε, τίς παρ - οι - κή-σει ἐν τῷ σκη-νώ - - μα - τί σου; ἀλ - λη -

- - λού - ι - α.

Ps. xcvi
III. Mode

Ὁ Κύ - ρι - ος ἐ - βα - σί - λευ - σε, ἀγαλ - λι - ά - - - - σθω

ἡ γῆ· ἀλ - λη - - - - - λούι - α.

[1] P. N. Trempelas, ibid., p. 199.

Ps. cxi.
IV. pl. Mode

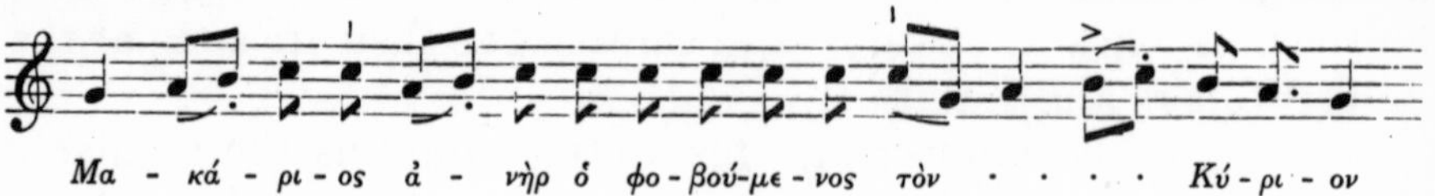

(Ps. xiv. 1. Lord, who shall dwell in thy tabernacle? Alleluia.
Ps. xcvi. 1. The Lord has reigned, let the earth rejoice. Alleluia.
Ps. cxi. 1. Blessed is the man that feareth the Lord. Alleluia.)

The following example, taken from MS. Athens 2062, fol. 20 v., shows at † a kind of shorthand abbreviation. The bracketed passage is not written out in the manuscript, because the melodic phrase was already written down.

Ps. xci. 1

Ἀλ - λη - λούι - α, ἀ - λ - λη - - λού - ι - α, ἀλ - λη - λού -
- - ι - α

(Amen. It is good to give praise to the Lord. Alleluia, it is good to give praise to the Lord, alleluia. Alleluia, alleluia, alleluia.)

The rubrics in most of the manuscripts indicate which parts of the office are to be read by the priest, which are to be sung by one of the two Domestici, and which by one of the two choirs.

I cannot here describe in detail the composition of the music of the Morning and Evening Office. I can only give in the following lines an indication of the character of the style of chanting in the daily Office, and I have chosen as an example the beginning of the Orthros, the Morning Office, on Monday. The transcription is based upon MS. 2062, fol. 3 r. and v., where we find the following rubrics:

On the second day the Priest begins the ceremony with 'Blessed be Thy Kingdom' (*Εὐλογουμένη ἡ βασιλεία*) followed by the Diakonika[1] and the 'Uphold, save, have mercy' (*Ἀντιλαβοῦ, σῶσον, ἐλέησον*). The Deacon says: 'And I slept' (*καὶ ὕπνωσα*), Ps. 3, v. 5, and the Priest: 'Of the most holy and immaculate' (*Τῆς παναγίας καὶ ἀχράντου*). Now follow the *incipits* of the chants, taken from psalms and doxologies, interspersed with rubrics which follow in Greek.

The Domesticus:

III. Plagal Mode

Καὶ ὕ - πνω - - σα. δό - ξα σοι ὁ
θε - - - - - - ός:

καὶ γένεται ἐκφώνησις· καὶ πάλιν ὁ δομεστικός.

[1] Prayers in form of a litany, recited by the deacon; the more usual term for these prayers is *Eirenika*, because they begin with the words *Ἐν εἰρήνῃ τοῦ Κυρίου δεηθῶμεν* (let us pray in peace to the Lord). To each of these prayers the people answer with *Κύριε ἐλέησον* (Lord, have mercy).

Ekphonesis (The priest)

The Domesticus (Ps. iii. 5)

(The first Choir)?

(The second Choir)?

(The Domesticus)?

fol. 3 v.

The Domesticus

καὶ ὁ ἱερεύς: Τῆς παναγίας ἀχράντου.

The Domesticus (Ps. xvii. 1)

Ἀ - μήν· Ἀ - γα - πή - - σω σε, Κύ - ρι - ε ἡ ἰ - σχύς

μου. Ἀλ - λη - λού - ι - α· Ἀ - γα - πή - σω σε, Κύ - ρι - ε

ἡ ἰ - σχύς μου· Ἀλ - λη - λού - ι - α.

Δόξα καὶ νῦν. καὶ πάλιν ποιοῦσιν τὸ αὐτό.

Ἀλ - λη - λού - ι - α· Ἀλ - λη - λού - ι - α· Ἀλ - λη - λού - ι -

- α.

Mode II

Δό - ξαν θε - οῦ· Ἐπ - ά - κου - σόν μου, Κύ - ρι - ε.
ὑπόψαλμος β''

From Symeon's treatise *De sacra precatione* it can be seen that the rubrics in MS. Athens 2062 correspond in the main to the description of the ceremony which he gives in his chapter 'On the Chanted Orthros' (*P.G.*, vol. clv, c. 636–41);[1] but we also learn from his meticulous description that the priest's part in the Office was much more extended, and that the chants were more often repeated than the rubrics of MSS. 2061 and 2062 reveal.

Even in the present, preliminary, stage of investigation the stylistic similarity between Byzantine and Latin psalmody is striking and forces upon us, as said in the beginning of this section, the need to trace both back to a common source. This is no new discovery. We may refer to the famous passage in Pope

[1] Cf. also P. N. Trempelas, *Μικρὸν Εὐχολόγιον*, ii. 202–3.

Gregory the Great's letter to John, Bishop of Syracuse, where he refutes the accusation of having extended the singing of the Alleluia outside Eastertime, and having thus followed the rite of Constantinople.[1] Gregory defends the innovation. He did not imitate, he says, the use of any other Church. 'It is an old custom, it goes back, as we know from Saint Jerome, to the rite of the Church of Jerusalem.'

[1] See my article 'Gregory the Great's Letter on the Alleluia', in *Annales Musicologiques*, ii (1954), 7–26.

CHAPTER XIV

WORDS AND MUSIC

FROM the study of the formulae we also come to understand the technique of Byzantine hymn-writers in adapting the melodies to the words of the hymns. As in Gregorian chant, a large number of texts are set to a single melody, and great skill was required to achieve a perfect union between the music and the words. A new stanza had to consist not only of the same number of syllables as the model stanza, but it also had to have the stress accent in the same places, in order to make the highest points of the melodic curves coincide with the stresses of the verses.

If a line of the new stanza had one or two more unaccented syllables before the accented one than the model stanza had had, some notes without dynamic significance were inserted, either on the same pitch as the note to which they were added or leading up to it by steps.

It must, however, be pointed out that we do not regard every syllable as accented which bears an accent in writing, but only those syllables which carry the stress in the metrical structure. In Byzantine poetry the article, for example, in all genders and cases is treated as unaccented, and the same rule applies to a number of monosyllabic words, as *καί, γάρ, μή, πῶς, ὤν*, and others.

The simplest way of setting a line to music is the recitation of a number of unaccented syllables on a repeated note, the *tenor*, followed by a cadence which starts on the note of recitation. This melodic type occurs frequently as an opening phrase in the first mode.

In the following table fourteen opening lines of hymns are collected, all of which are sung to the same melodic phrase. In two of the hymns, nos. 4 and 6, the melody starts on the first note of the cadence, in all the others one or three or five Isons on *a* precede the Ison with Oxeia, the first accented note of the cadence. In ten out of fourteen examples the musical accent coincides with the metrical accent. This accent, however, is weak. The strong accent of the line is set on the two combined notes, *g–a*, of the cadence, which coincides in thirteen out of fourteen cases with the metrical accent. The exception occurs in the fourteenth example on the word *Ἀββακούμ*, which derives from the Hebrew.

The Greek metrical rules do not apply to this word, just as in Gregorian Chant the principles of Latin metrics do not apply to Hebrew names.

Tenor Cadence

		Iviron
(1)	Σοῦ ἡ τρο - παι - οῦ - χος δε - ξι - ά	fol. 1 r.
(2)	Ἀ - κη - κο - ὼς ὁ προ - φή - της	4 v.
(3)	Τὸν ἐν σο - φί - ᾳ καὶ λό - γῳ	10 r.
(4)	Ῥῆ - μα τυ - ράν - νου	11 r.
(5)	Τῷ δι - α - βι - βά - σαν - τι	11 r.
(6)	Ἄν - θρα - κα πυ - ρὸς	12 r.
(7)	Ὡς Ἰ - ω - νᾶν τὸν προ - φή - την	14 v.
(8)	Ἐν τῷ βρον - τώ - δει κα - μί - νῳ	15 r.
(9)	Σὲ τὴν οὐ - ρα - νῶν ὑ - ψη - λο - τέ - ραν	17 v.
(10)	Τὸν τοὺς ὑ - μνο - λό - γους ἐν κα - μί - νῳ	18 r.
(11)	Χαί - ροις τὸ τῆς παρ - θε - νί - ας καύ - χη - μα	19 r.
(12)	Τὴν σὴν ἐν - αν - θρώ - πη - σιν	21 r.
(13)	Ὁ κή - τει φλοι - δού - με - νος	21 v.
(14)	Θε - ο - πτι - κῶς ὁ Ἀβ - βα - κούμ	14 r.

In another opening the recitation on *a* is interrupted by the lower fifth on *d*, which either coincides with the first accented syllable, or is used as a preparation for it. Whether the first or the second method is applied depends upon the rhythm of the lines to which the formulae are set, or upon the words which are to be emphasized by the interval of the fifth.

It also frequently happens that the lower fifth is repeated two or three times before the voice leaps up to the *tenor* on *a*.

In the following three tables a number of initial phrases are collected to show the three variants (A, B, C) of the same type.

		Iviron
(1)	Ὁ προ - φή - της	fol. 2 r.
(2)	Πα - γι - ω - θεῖ - σα ῥευ - στὴ οὐ - σί - α	3 v.
(3)	Πε - ποι - κιλ - μέ - νη τῇ θεί - ᾳ δό - ξῃ	3 v.
(4)	Νε - νί - κην - ται τῆς φύ - (σεως)	4 r.
(5)	Ἀ - να - στά - σε - ως ἡ - μέ - ρα	5 r.
(6)	Ὀρ - θρί - σω - μεν ὄρ - θρου βα - θέ - ως	5 r.
(7)	Αὕ - τη ἡ (κλητὴ)	5 v.
(8)	Ὁ θει - ό - τα - τος	5 v.
(9)	Ὀρ - θρί - ζον - τες σὲ ἀν - υ - μνοῦ - μεν	6 r.
(10)	Ἀ - πόρ - ρη - τον τὸ τῆς παρ - θέ - νου	8 r.

B
Iviron
(1) Ὁ φω - τί - σας τῇ ἐλ - λάμ - ψει fol. 1 r.
(2) Δου - λεί - ας Χρι - στοῦ 2 v.
(3) Κατ - ῆλ - θες ἐν τοῖς 5 v.
(4) Ὁ παῖ - δας ἐκ κα - μί - (νου) 5 v.
(5) Φω - τί - ζου φω - τί - (ζου) 5 v.
(6) [Θε - ὸς ὢν εἰ - ρή - (νης) 7 r.
(7) Προ - μη - νύ - ων τὴν ἔν - (σαρκον) 10 r.
C
Iviron
(1) Ὁ ὑ - ψῶν τὸ κέ - ρας τῶν εἰς σὲ fol. 2 v.
(2) Προ - ο - ρῶν σου λό - γε, τὴν φρι - κτὴν 2 v.
(3) Τῆς κα - μί - νου τὴν φλό - γα οἱ τρισ - (όλβιοι) 3 r.
(4) Κα - τα - βή - τω ὡς δρό - σος 12 v.
(5) Τὴν ᾠ - δὴν Ἀ - να - νί - ου τῷ ἀν - άρ - (χῳ) 20 r.

In a third opening passage of the first mode the melodic and metrical accents coincide in all cases. The cadence starts with a group of three notes *b♮–c–a*, as can be seen from nos. 12, 16, 17, 20, and 21; it is preceded by a *tenor* on *a* which consists of one, two, three, or six unaccented syllables; but it may be noticed that *a* is treated as an essential part of the formula when the line starts with an unaccented syllable:

		Iviron
(1)	Ἐ - κύ — κλω - σεν ἡ - μᾶς	fol. 1 r.
(2)	Ἐν σοὶ παρ - θέ - νε	3 r.
(3)	Ἀ - λι - ο - πον - το - γε - νές κη - τῶ - εν	4 r.
(4)	Ἐκ νυ - κτὸς ὀρ - θρί - ζον - τες	4 v.
(5)	Ὡς ἐν πε - λά - γει τοῦ βί - ου	4 v.
(6)	Εἰ - κό - νι λα - τρεύ - ειν	4 v.
(7)	Τὸν ἐν φλο - γὶ πυ - ρὸς	5 r.
(8)	Χρι - στὸς γεν - νᾶ - ται	6 v.
(9)	Πι - κρᾶς δου - λεί - ας	6 v.
(10)	Τῷ παντ - ά - να - κτος	8 v.
(11)	Ὡς οἱ παῖ - δες πά - λαι	9 v.
(12)	Μέ - γα τὸ μυ - (στήριον)	10 v.
(13)	Ὁ ὑ - πο - φή - της εἰς τύ - πον	10 v.
(14)	Ὅ - τι Θε - ὸς σαρ - κοῦ - ται	11 r.
(15)	Τὸ φα - ει - νὸν ἡ - μῖν ἐξ	14 r.
(16)	Ἄ - σω - μεν ᾆ - (σμα)	14 v.
(17)	Ἴ - δε - τε, ἴ - (δετε)	14 v.
(18)	Τὴν στει - ρω - θεῖ - σαν μου ψυ - χήν	15 r.
(19)	Προ - φη - τι - κῶς βο - ῶ - σι	16 r.
(20)	Δί - δα - ξον ἡ - μᾶς ποι - (εῖν)	16 v.
(21)	Ἔ - λαμ - ψεν ἡ χά - ρις	17 v.
(22)	Τὴν ἀ - κο - ὴν ὁ προ - φή - της	19 v.

These examples will be sufficient to show how Byzantine hymnodists adapted the words of new Odes to the melody of a traditional Hirmus. It would be beyond the scope of the present outline to give a more detailed account of this technique of composition. For further information about the technique of both Hirmi and Stichera I must refer to Parts II and III of my book *Eastern Elements in Western Chant*, where detailed analyses of the formal structure of Byzantine melodies and the setting of words to music will be found.

A few words must be added about the more elaborate technique which was used when words were fitted to the melody of a Sticheron. Melodies of a simple, more or less syllabic type, for example the *Anastasima Anatolika*, do not differ from the Hirmi, as can be seen from the following examples, which are taken from Tillyard's *The Hymns of the Octoechus*:[1]

(1)
Τὴν τῶν πα - θῶν θεί - αν μω - λώ - πω - σιν . .
Dalass., fol. 280 r. Tillyard, p. 8.
(2)
Εὐ - φράν - θη - τε οὐ - ρα - νοί
Dal., fol. 279 r. T., p. 3.
(3)
Ὅ - τε προσ - η - λώ - θης τῷ ξύ - λῳ
Dal., fol. 279 v. T., p. 6.
(4)
Τῷ ζῳ - ο - δό - χῳ σου τά - φῳ . .
Dal., fol. 279 v. T., p. 4.

Of the same simple type are many of the Stichera for minor feasts of saints, as can be seen, for example, from the Sticheron

[1] *M.M.B.*, vol. iii (1940).

Τῆς οὐρανίου γνώσεως in honour of St. Denys the Areopagite on 3 October, transcribed from Cod. Dalass., fol. 30r. (Appendix II, No. 1). To a slightly more ornamented type belong a large group of hymns composed partly for the Proper of the Saints, partly for the Proper of the Season. As an example of the latter type we may quote the famous hymn of the nun Kasia, 'Lord, the woman fallen in many sins', which is sung at Matins on Wednesday in Holy Week. A transcription of the melody, from Cod. Dalass., fol. 232v., is given in Appendix II, no. 9.

Κύριε, ἡ ἐν πολλαῖς ἁμαρτίαις
περιπεσοῦσα γυνὴ
τὴν σὴν αἰσθομένη Θεότητα,
μυροφόρου ἀναλαβοῦσα τάξιν,
ὀδυρομένη μύρον σοι
πρὸ τοῦ ἐνταφιασμοῦ κομίζει·
Οἴμοι· λέγουσα,
ὅτι νύξ με συνέχει
οἶστρος ἀκολασίας,
ζοφώδης τε καὶ ἀσέληνος
ἔρως τῆς ἁμαρτίας·
δέξαι μου τὰς πηγὰς τῶν δακρύων,
ὁ νεφέλαις στημονίζων
τῆς θαλάσσης τὸ ὕδωρ·
κάμφθητί μοι
πρὸς τοὺς στεναγμοὺς τῆς καρδίας,
ὁ κλίνας τοὺς οὐρανοὺς
τῇ ἀφράστῳ σου κενώσει·
καταφιλήσω τοὺς ἀχράντους σου πόδας,
ἀποσμήξω τούτους δὲ πάλιν
τοῖς τῆς κεφαλῆς μου βοστρύχοις·
ὧν ἐν τῷ Παραδείσῳ
Εὔα τὸν δειλινὸν
κρότον τοῖς ὠσὶν ἠχηθεῖσα,
τῷ φόβῳ ἐκρύβη·
ἁμαρτιῶν μου τὰ πλήθη
καὶ κριμάτων σου ἀβύσσους
τίς ἐξιχνιάσει,
ψυχοσῶστα, Σωτήρ μου;
μή με τὴν σὴν δούλην παρίδῃς
ὁ ἀμέτρητον ἔχων τὸ μέγα ἔλεος.

(Lord, the woman fallen in many sins, seeing Thy Divinity, Taking the part of myrrh-bearer, wailing bringeth to Thee myrrh against Thy burial;

'Alas!' she crieth, 'for that night is to me the wildness of sin, dusky and moonless, even the love of transgression; Accept the springs of my tears, Thou who with clouds partest the waters of the sea; Bend to the groanings of my heart, who hast brought down Heaven by Thine ineffable humiliation. I will kiss Thy stainless feet, I will wipe them with the hair of my head; Thy feet, whereof when Eve in Paradise heard their sound, she hid herself for fear; The multitude of my sins and the depths of Thy judgement who shall explore, Saviour of souls, my Redeemer? Forget not me, Thy servant, Thou, whose mercy is infinite!') Translation by H. J. W. Tillyard.[1]

The blending of words and music, however, becomes more subtle in the richly ornamented Stichera for Christmas and for Lent and Easter. For these feasts the most extended Stichera are written, as can be seen from the examples in Appendix II, Nos. 2–8, 10–11, which are representative of the greater part of the hymns sung during these feasts.

Byzantine hymnodists paid great attention to keeping the right balance between the text and the music. The words to which an ornament was set were well chosen. As in Plainchant, the ornaments were generally set to words which could be emphasized, but which were not of primary importance for the understanding of the phrase. It is essential to point out this fact, because the practice of Byzantine composers is entirely different from that of Western composers in the seventeenth and eighteenth centuries, who set the coloraturas to the most important words of the phrase.

Let us take, for example, the Christmas Sticheron (Cod. Dalassinos, fol. 91[v.]) which is transcribed in Appendix II, no. 7:

Δεῦτε χριστοφόροι λαοί, κατίδωμεν
θαῦμα πᾶσαν ἔννοιαν
ἐκπλῆττον καὶ συνέχον,
καὶ εὐσεβῶς ἀνυμνοῦντες
πίστει προσκυνήσωμεν.
Σήμερον πρὸς τὴν Βηθλεὲμ
ἐγκυμονοῦσα κόρη παραγίνεται
τοῦ γεννῆσαι τὸν Κύριον,
χοροὶ δὲ ἀγγέλων προτρέχουσι.
Καὶ ταῦτα βλέπων
ἐβόα Ἰωσὴφ ὁ μνήστωρ·
Τί τὸ ἐν σοὶ ξένον μυστήριον, παρθένε;

[1] *Byzantine Music and Hymnography* (1923), p. 30.

καὶ πῶς μέλλεις λοχεῦσαι
ἡ ἀπειρόζυγος δάμαλις;

(Come, Christ-bearing people, let us look upon the marvel which confounds thought and holds it bound, and raising a godly hymn, let us worship in faith.

To-day the Virgin who became pregnant comes to Bethlehem to bring forth the Lord, and choirs of angels run before her. And seeing this, Joseph, her betrothed, cried, 'O Virgin, what is this strange mystery within thee? and how is it possible for thee to bring forth, thou, the heifer that hath not felt the yoke?')

The Sticheron is written, for the most part, in the hirmological style: one, two, or three notes are set to a syllable. But there are three extended melismata: the first, as the opening, to the word *Δεῦτε*, the second, at the beginning of the second section, to the word *Σήμερον*, the third, at the end, to *ἀπειρόζυγος*. There are also two shorter melismata, set to *βλέπων* and *μνήστωρ*:

Here, as in so many other Stichera, a perfect setting of the poem to music is achieved. The dynamic marks on the melismata underline the ecstatic character of the music, which is in keeping with the dramatic language of the poem. But it would be a mistake to consider the setting of the words to the music in this hymn as the individual work of the composer. We find another Sticheron of exactly the same type among the Troparia sung during the sixth Hour on Good Friday:

Δεῦτε χριστοφόροι λαοί, κατίδωμεν
τί συνεβουλεύσατο
Ἰούδας ὁ προδότης
σὺν ἱερεῦσιν ἀνόμοις
κατὰ τοῦ Σωτῆρος ἡμῶν.
Σήμερον ἔνοχον θανάτου
τὸν ἀθάνατον Λόγον πεποίηκαν·
καὶ Πιλάτῳ προδώσαντες
ἐν τόπῳ Κρανίου ἐσταύρωσαν.
Καὶ ταῦτα πάσχων
ἐβόα ὁ Σωτὴρ ἡμῶν λέγων·
Ἄφες αὐτοῖς, Πάτερ, τὴν ἁμαρτίαν ταύτην,
ὅπως γνῶσι τὰ ἔθνη
τὴν ἐκ νεκρῶν μου ἀνάστασιν.

(Come, Christ-bearing people, let us see what counsel Judas the traitor took against our Saviour with the perfidious priests. To-day they condemned to death the immortal Word, they delivered Him to Pilate, and crucified Him at the place of the skull. Suffering this, our Saviour cried, saying, 'Father, forgive them this sin, so that the nations may acknowledge my Resurrection from the dead.')

On examining the music we find a surprising similarity between the melody of the Christmas hymn and that of the Holy Week service (see Appendix II, No. 8). We find extended melismata set to *Δεῦτε* and *Σήμερον*, and shorter ones to *πάσχων* (which corresponds to *βλέπων* in the Christmas hymn) and to *ἡμῶν, λέγων* (which corresponds to *ὁ μνήστωρ*). But the extended melisma to *ἀπειρόζυγος*, which emphasizes so well the striking phrase applied to the Virgin, has no parallel in the Good Friday hymn; here we only find a short melisma on the first syllable of *ἀνάστασιν*.

The dramatic element which is apparent in these Stichera becomes even more obvious in a group of Troparia from the Nativity cycle, some of which are ascribed to Sophronius, Patriarch of Jerusalem 634–8. The cycle opens with the jubilant hymn *Βηθλεέμ, ἑτοιμάζου*, 'Bethlehem, get ready! The manger shall be prepared', in which the narrator announces the Nativity of Our Lord. In the following hymn, *Τάδε λέγει Ἰωσήφ*, 'Thus speaketh Joseph to the Virgin' (Appendix II, No. 3), the narrator introduces Joseph, astonished and disturbed, demanding an explanation of the strange event which is taking place:

Μαρία, τί τὸ δρᾶμα τοῦτο
ὃ ἐν σοὶ τεθέαμαι;

She has brought forth hastily and in concealment. And again he asks: '*Μαρία, τί τὸ δρᾶμα τοῦτο;*'. In a group of antitheses he reminds her that instead of honour and happiness she has brought sorrow and shame upon him; and, for the third time, he asks her to give an explanation.

Both the words and music of the hymn are of the highest artistic quality. The repetition of the phrase, *Μαρία, τί τὸ δρᾶμα τοῦτο*, with the passionately extended melisma on *τοῦτο*, is most impressive, and shows how perfectly the composer succeeded in building up a powerful dramatic situation in a few lines.

In the following hymn, *Νῦν προφητικὴ πρόρρησις*, the narrator paraphrases the verse from Matt. ii. 6, 'And thou, Bethlehem, in the land of Juda, art not the least among the princes of Juda'. The same exultant mood is maintained in the hymns *Οὗτος ὁ Θεὸς ἡμῶν*, 'This is our God', and *Πρὸ τῆς γεννήσεως τῆς σῆς*, 'Before Thy birth, O Lord'. But the dramatic element returns in the next hymns: *Ἰωσήφ, εἰπὲ ἡμῖν*, 'Joseph, tell us', and *Δεῦτε πιστοί*, 'Come hither, ye faithful'. *Ἄκουε, οὐρανέ*, 'Hear, O heavens and give ear, O earth' follows, taking the vision of Isaiah, which begins with the same words, as the annunciation of the Incarnation of Our Lord. The content of these last hymns is summed up in *Δεῦτε χριστοφόροι*, 'Come hither, Christ-bearing people', the hymn which we have already analysed.

The next hymn, *Ἐξεπλήττετο ὁ Ἡρώδης*, 'Herod was astounded', completes the picture by introducing the hostile element which is conquered by the Incarnation. Now comes the answer of the Virgin to the reproaches of Joseph, in the hymn *Ὅτε Ἰωσήφ* (Appendix II, No. 5). In ecstasy, overwhelmed by the 'awful mystery', the Virgin comforts Joseph. She begs him to put away all fear, and tells him that 'God has descended upon earth' and has assumed flesh, 'He whom the angels unceasingly celebrate in song and worship together with the Father and the Holy Spirit'.

This hymn is, poetically and musically, the highest point of the cycle. As in the hymn of Joseph's reproaches, the narrator has only a short introductory passage, and the entire hymn consists of the words of the Virgin. The dramatic element is strongly accentuated: the melismata on *λοιπόν* and on *γάρ* create a tension by which the following words *ἀπόθου φόβον ἅπαντα* and *ἐπὶ τῆς γῆς* are emphasized. The extended *fiorituras* on *ἀγνοῶν*, *ἅπαντα*, and *πλησθείς*, on the other hand, introduce an element of mystical emotion. The tension has been raised to such a climax that a continuation of hymn-singing would produce an anti-climax. Rightly, therefore, the cycle ends abruptly with a kind of finale on the hymn *Σήμερον γεννᾶται ἐκ παρθένου*, 'To-day from the Virgin is born'.

The dramatic element in the Nativity cycle is so obvious that it is not going too far to suggest that we have before us one of the oldest specimens of a Nativity play, built around the dialogues of Joseph and the Virgin. This type of hymn goes back to the Syriac poetical genre of the Sôgithâ, hymns in the form of dialogues, which flourished in the fifth century. The ancient Sôgithâ seems to have derived from poems which were sung by the Precentor, who introduced the monologue of a Biblical person. Two precentors may have come into action when the old form of monologue was superseded by dialogue. Among the Sôgithâ for the Nativity feast, monologues of the Virgin were outstanding. They belong to the oldest layer, since from dogmatic reasons they must have been composed before the outbreak of the christological controversy.[1] Hymns in which the Virgin addresses her Child can already be found in the 'Nativity Hymns' by Ephraem the Syrian.[2]

[1] Cf. A. Baumstark, 'Die christlichen Literaturen d. Orients', *Sammlung Göschen*, i. 100.

[2] Cf. Schaff and Wace, *A Select Library of Nicene and Post-Nicene Fathers*, Second Series, xiii. 245–7.

Sophronius, who was born at Damascus and spent many years as a monk at the Theodosius monastery near Jerusalem, certainly knew either the Nativity hymns of Narsai of Edessa, who lived at the end of the fifth century, or later hymns modelled upon them in Syriac or Greek. We may regard the established cycle of the Nativity hymns, which obviously grew out of a smaller group in the early days of the Byzantine Church, as the prototype of the religious drama of the Middle Ages.

We may close our investigations into the setting of words to music with an analysis of the Sticheron *Ὦ πῶς ἡ παράνομος συναγωγή* (Appendix II, No. 11), which is sung at Vespers on Good Friday.[1] The text is a paraphrase of the Troparion *Τάδε λέγει Κύριος τοῖς Ἰουδαίοις*, sung during the sixth Hour on the same day.[2] *Τάδε λέγει Κύριος* forms part of a group of twelve Troparia which belong to the oldest layer of Byzantine hymnography; they also are attributed to Sophronius. The relation of the text of the Troparion to that of the *Improperia* of the Roman rite is striking.[3]

Like the Nativity hymns the Troparion *Ὦ πῶς* is divided into two sections: the introduction of the Narrator, and the words of Our Lord. Both sections open with a passionate outcry, which is sung to an extended melisma. But while the rest of the words of the narrator are set to music in the hirmological style, i.e. one, two, or three notes to a syllable, the 'Reproaches' are composed in a richly ornamented style. This can be shown by printing the words and syllables which are emphasized by melismatic formulae in heavy type:

Ὦ πῶς
ἡ παράνομος συναγωγὴ
τὸν βασιλέα τῆς κτίσεως
κατεδίκασε θανάτῳ,
μὴ αἰδεσθεῖσα τὰς εὐεργεσίας,
ἃς ἀναμιμνήσκων προησφαλίζετο
λέγων πρὸς αὐτούς·
Λαός μου,
τί ἐποίησα **ὑμῖν** *;*
οὐ **θαυμά***των ἐνέπλησα τὴν Ἰουδαί***αν** *;*
οὐ **νεκροὺς** *ἐξανέστησα μόνῳ τῷ λόγῳ ;*
οὐ πᾶσαν μαλακίαν

[1] *Triodion* (Rome, 1879), pp. 703–4.
[2] Ibid., pp. 692–3.
[3] Cf. *Eastern Elements in Western Chant*, pp. 22–3.

ἐθεράπευσα καὶ νόσον;
τί οὖν μοι ἀνταποδίδοτε;
εἰς τί ἀμνημονεῖτέ μου;
ἀντὶ τῶν ἰαμάτων
πληγάς μοι ἐπιθέντες,
ἀντὶ ζωῆς νεκροῦντες,
κρεμῶντες ἐπὶ ξύλου
ὡς κακοῦργον τὸν εὐεργέτην,
ὡς παράνομον τὸν νομοδότην,
ὡς κατάκριτον τὸν πάντων Βασιλέα.
Μακρόθυμε Κύριε, δόξα σοι.

(How could the lawless council condemn to death the King of the Creation, not regarding his benefactions, which he called to mind and affirmed beforetime, saying to them, 'My people, what have I done unto you? Have I not filled Judaea with miracles? Have I not raised the dead with my word alone? Have I not healed all sickness and disease? And now, what return are you making to me? Why are you unmindful of me? In return for the healings you have given me blows, for life, you are putting me to death, hanging upon the cross the Benefactor like a malefactor, the Lawgiver like a lawbreaker, the King of the universe like a condemned man.' Forbearing Lord, glory to Thee.)

An examination of the words and syllables which carry a musical ornament shows clearly the skill of the musician who worked out these embellishments so that ornaments are never placed on words which are essential for the understanding of the text. The antitheses, for example, are composed in the syllabic style; the melisma on *'Ιουδαίαν* only begins on the last syllable, so that the word can be clearly heard. In other cases the melodic line is drawn so carefully that the singer can pronounce the word distinctly before the actual ornamentation begins.

This most elaborate technique of setting words to music is one of the finest achievements of Byzantine hymnography in its best period. In fact, now that the intimate relation between words and music has been recognized, it is obvious that we should no longer consider the poems apart from the melodies, nor the music apart from the texts.

From our studies in Plainchant we are accustomed to consider words and music as a unity. The subtlety of the Byzantine technique of blending words and music surpasses even the achievements, so justly admired, of Plainchant, although both poets and composers of Byzantine hymns were forced to keep closely to a prescribed pattern, a restriction which, from the technical point of view, made their task much more difficult.

The art of a nation is generally judged by the best works it has produced. Until the present day it was impossible to do justice to Byzantine hymnography, since only one part of it, its poetry, was studied. But here too the approach was one-sided. Scholars favoured, as has been already said, the early period of Byzantine poetry, which produced the Kontakion, and rated this kind of poetry much more highly than the longer forms of the later period, the Kanon. The lesser forms of Byzantine hymnography, particularly the Stichera, were unduly neglected.[1]

From an extended study of the subject, however, it becomes evident that the peak of later Byzantine hymnography is reached in the Stichera of the Nativity cycle and in those for Lent and Holy Week. The kernel of both goes back to the days of the Early Christian Church;[2] but generation after generation of Byzantine hymnographers remodelled the old Troparia and added new ones to the original stock.

The same is true of the music. The special technique of musical composition, which consisted in connecting together certain groups of formulae and cadences, enabled the musicians to write a number of variations on a given theme. The advantage of this kind of technique is obvious. The congregation heard the well-known musical phrases in every new Sticheron, but arranged in a different way, and connected by new transitional passages. They must have taken pleasure in hearing musical phrases which were familiar but were linked together in an unexpected way, just as a modern audience takes pleasure in the recurrence of the themes in a movement of a symphony.

The repetition of a musical phrase in a slightly varied form, and the division of the melodic line by clearly worked out cadences are, as a matter of fact, the most important principles in musical composition, because by these two factors the sense of form is

[1] An exception which must be mentioned is P. Kilian Kirchhoff's translations into German of the hymns of the Triodion and Pentekostarion, and his evaluation of them in the introduction to the six volumes of his work: cf. *Die Ostkirche betet*, 4 vols., Leipzig, 1935–7, and *Osterjubel der Ostkirche*, 2 vols., Regnsburg-Münster (imprim. 1940). I wish to pay homage here to the memory of this great priest and scholar, who was executed in 1942, before he could see his work finished.

[2] Cf. my article, 'The Nativity Drama of the Byzantine Church', *J.R.S.* xxxvii (1947), pp. 145–51.

produced in the listener. These principles are worked out in an admirable way in Byzantine melography, particularly in the melodies of the Sticheraric genre.

The time has come, at last, for the recognition of the high artistic qualities of Byzantine hymnography. Those of our predecessors who did not realize the greatness of what must be considered an integral part of Byzantine liturgy are not to blame. They had access only to the texts of the hymns. Now that the music can be read again, we can appreciate Byzantine hymns as they were sung in the apogee of the Eastern Empire. We learn what an important part they played in the liturgy. We are beginning to distinguish between routine work and hymns which show the marks of an inspired mind.

But we must also realize that we are only at the beginning of the work which needs to be done. It will be the task of those who continue our work to bring to life the music which we undertook to decipher in the belief that Byzantine music, the legacy of the Early Christian Church, had an equal share of those qualities which for centuries made Byzantium the artistic centre of the Christian world.

And now, after sufficient music has been deciphered, we are satisfied that our instinct has led us right, and that the hymnography of the Orthodox Church can take its place among the great achievements of Byzantine civilization.

EXCURSUSES

Excursus p. 37

It was the Psalter of David which in the first centuries of our era slowly replaced all the other songs which Christians used to sing. But they missed chants which they had been used to hearing; thus, e.g. the Psalter did not contain the 'Song of Victory' of Moses (Ex. xv) by which the baptized used to thank God for their salvation, nor the 'Song of the Three Holy Children' (Dan. iii. 52–88), nor, from the New Testament, the *Magnificat* (Luke i. 46–55). Thus we find in Codex Alexandrinus the fourteen biblical songs which are called Odes. In four studies H. Schneider has given the history of the development of the Odes in Eastern liturgy, in *Biblica*, vol. xxx (1949): (1) 'Die biblischen Oden im christlichen Altertum', pp. 28–65; (2) 'Die biblischen Oden seit dem VI. Jahrhundert', pp. 239–72; (3) 'Die biblischen Oden in Jerusalem und Konstantinopel', pp. 433–52; (4) 'Die biblischen Oden im Mittelalter', pp. 479–500. H. Schneider shows that from the series of fourteen Odes in Codex Alexandrinus a definite series of fourteen Odes soon evolved which is found in the fifth century in Greek, Syrian, Coptic, and Armenian manuscripts and which kept for a particularly long time its liturgical place towards the end of the Evening Psalter in Constantinople.

The transformation of the fourteen Odes series to that of nine Odes was the work of monastic circles in Jerusalem during the fifth and sixth centuries. With the rise of the sung Kanons, at the end of the seventh century, which were modelled upon the nine Odes, the biblical canticles lost their liturgical significance and maintained their place only in Lent in the Morning Office.

Excursus p. 40

The practice of responding to each verse of a canticle with the repetition of the first verse in full, or its second half, can be seen from the rubrics of the *Typikon*, Cod. 43 of the Holy Cross Library in Jerusalem, dating from 1122, published by A. Papadopoulos-Kerameus in *Analecta Jerosolym. Stachyologias*, vol. ii. Here, on p. 182, it is ordered that the Song of Moses and the Song of the Three Holy Children (Dan. iii. 52–88) shall both be chanted during the Easter Vigil by three Psaltae and that after each verse the choir shall answer with ἐνδόξως γὰρ δεδόξασθαι (for He has triumphed gloriously) (Ex. xv. 1) and ὑμνεῖτε καὶ ὑπερυψοῦτε αὐτὸν εἰς τοὺς αἰῶνας (Praise and exalt Him above all for ever) (Dan. iii. 57). The *Triodion* (Rome, 1879), p. 757, has the rubric that the Anagnostes shall recite the following Canticle of the Three Holy Children 'and we sing after each verse Τὸν Κύριον ὑμνεῖτε (Praise the Lord, etc.)'.

This kind of responding must have been taken over from the Jewish Service, because we find it described in the Apostolic Constitutions (F. X. Funk, *Didascalia et Constitutiones Apostolorum* (2 vols., Paderborn, 1905), ii. 57, p. 161) which belong to the early fourth century: 'Here it is said that from an elevated place the Reader (ἀναγνώστης) should read lessons' from (the five books of) Moses, from Joshua, the Judges, the Kings, the Paralipomena, and from the Return (from the captivity in Babylon), and also from Job, from Solomon, and from the sixteen prophets. At the end of each of the two Lessons another Anagnostes shall sing the hymns of David and the people shall come in with the last part of the verse (τὰ ἀκροστίχια ὑποψαλλέτω).

The same practice was taken over in Western liturgy. It is preserved in the Roman Breviary, as can be seen from the Invitatorium in the Matins on Sundays from the Octave of Epiphany to Septuagesima: here, alternatively, after each verse either the whole first verse 'Venite, exsultemus Domino: Jubilemus Deo salutari nostro', or its second part 'Jubilemus Deo salutari nostro' is repeated. At the end is here, too, the Doxology, followed by 'Jubilemus Deo salutari nostro'. The plan obviously derives from Psalm cxxxv in which the repetition of ὅτι εἰς τὸν αἰῶνα τὸ ἔλεος αὐτοῦ—*quoniam in aeternum misericordia eius* runs from the first to the last verse.

Excursus p. 53

Pachymeres, Harmoniai; cf. P. Tannery, 'Quadrivium de Georges Pachymère', *Studi e Testi*, xciv (1940), 97–199, particularly p. 100.

Excursus p. 62

Mesarites's description of the Church of the Apostles has been the subject of a valuable study, in which particularly the borrowings from Libanius' Oration in praise of Antioch (Orat. XI) are mentioned. I refer to G. Downey's 'Nicolaos Mesarites: Description of the Church of the Holy Apostles at Constantinople', *Transactions of the American Philosophical Society*, N.S., vol. xlvii, part 6 (Philadelphia, 1957). According to Downey (p. 865, n. 1) the elementary students were installed 'in a colonnaded peribolos out of which there opened "seats of the Muses", i.e. schools'. On the western side, as part of the *Trivium*, was the teaching of the choirboys in singing. In the Pronaos (ibid., p. 894, n. 2) the advanced courses of the *Quadrivium* were taught, to which the course on arithmetical subjects belonged. In that course students discussed relations of numbers and of geometry, and next to them, others the mathematical foundations of musical theory.

Excursus p. 84

The Council *in Trullo* took place in the autumn of 691, as Pargoire, *L'Église byzantine de 527 à 847* (Paris, 1905), has shown. I have therefore corrected the date (692) of the first edition. See also S. Salaville, 'La Formation du Calendrier liturgique byzantin, etc.', *Ephemerides Liturgicae*, vol. l (Rome, 1936), p. 33, n. 8.

Excursus p. 85

L. Bréhier, in 'La Civilisation byzantine', *Le Monde byzantin*, iii (Paris, 1950), 104, rightly points out that the historians neglected the theatre because their interest was concentrated upon the Hippodrome. The best study on it is still an article by A. Vogt, 'Le Théâtre à Byzance et dans l'Empire du IVe au XIIIe siècle. I. Le Théâtre profane', *Revue des questions historiques*, lix (Oct. 1931), 257–96. Here we learn that a theatre was built in Byzantium by the order of Septimius Severus, facing the temple of Aphrodite on the cliffs near the sea. It was known as 'The Great Theatre' and remained at that place until the end of the Empire. It was the theatre the court used to visit. For the rising population, however, one theatre did not suffice—Antioch, Alexandria, Berytos, Gaza, and Caesarea had their own theatres; Constantinople, the capital, needed more than one. A second theatre was built, probably in the fifth century, and called 'The Little Theatre'; a third was built near the Blachernae quarter, and a fourth in Syke or Galata.

Excursus p. 86

Pompa diaboli. The exact meaning of the term *πομπή—pompa*, of which S. Reinach has made a study in an article 'Satan et ses pompes', published finally in *Cultes, Mythes et Religions*, i² (Paris, 1908), 347–62, has been investigated by several scholars. One of the last contributions came from H. Rahner, S.J., 'Pompa diaboli. Ein Beitrag zur Bedeutungsgeschichte des Wortes *πομπή—pompa* in der urchristlichen Taufliturgie', *Zeitschrift f. Kathol. Theol.* lv (1931), 239–73. Rahner argues that all nuances in the use of the word *pompa* can be reduced (*a*) to everything connected with the public spectacles, (*b*) to things connected with delusive splendour. J. H. Waszink, in his article 'Pompa Diaboli', *Vigiliae Christianae*, i (1947), 13–41, sums up all the existing interpretations and comes to the conclusion that all the nuances of the meaning find an explanation in the association of the term in early Christianity with *pompa circi*.

Excursus p. 99

Acclamations were shouted when a king was anointed in Israel: 'And you shall sound the trumpet, and shall say: God save King Solomon' (1 Kings i. 34). A similar enthronement ritual is found in Babylonian texts; there 'songs were sung by the rejoicing populace and by choirs of professional singers'. See C. H. Kraeling and L. Mowry, 'Music in the Bible', *The New Oxford History of Music*, i (1957), 290.

Excursus p. 108

Organs. In a series of four articles in *Revue de Musicologie*, 1929–33, Mahmoud Raghib collected excerpts from a number of Turkish sources which confirm the use of organs in Christian churches in the East. He quotes (ibid., no. 36, Nov. 1930, p. 262) the report of a Turkish traveller in 1075 who describes the organ and says that 'the instrument is played on certain days in the majority of churches'. A. Gastoué, in his *Notes sur l'orgue en Orient* in the same journal (no. 33, 1930, p. 20), rightly draws attention to the fact that the Byzantines had organs in their churches at least at the time when the Turks took possession of the country. He points out that the Turkish musicians were unable to play these instruments because they were used to different and much smaller intervals than the Byzantines. Gastoué confirms an opinion which I had expressed since 1917, namely, that the transformation of the old Byzantine tonality took place under Turkish influence, and only during these last centuries. Before that happened tonality was diatonic in Byzantium as well as in Syria. The reports, however, of Arabic and Turkish writers need not upset our former views about unaccompanied Byzantine Chant. I should like to suggest that portable organs, such as were used in the Imperial Palace, in the Hippodrome, and for processions, were used in the teaching places attached to a church as a help to the singing master. In the last phase of the Empire they may have been used in the churches as well, perhaps as a kind of 'organum', the 'Ison' of the Byzantines, i.e. a kind of drone which represents a primitive stage of polyphony, a stage which was never passed in the East.

Excursus p. 125

The preaching of a homily is mentioned, as Brightman has shown (*Liturgies Eastern and Western*, i. 531), in Socrates' *Historia Ecclesiastica*, vi. 5. It seems to have disappeared from the liturgy of the Mass after the Council *in Trullo* in 691, as can be seen from Brightman, op. cit., p. 314, where prayers follow the reading from the Gospel. The homily now seems to have found its place in Matins after the reading of the Gospel. This transfer may have caused the disappearance of the Kontakion, which until that time had followed the pericope from the Gospel and had to be dropped because a sung homily, followed by a spoken one, would have meant duplicating the same part of the liturgy, as I have pointed out in my study on 'Kontakion and Kanon', *Atti del Congresso di Musica Sacra*, Rome, 1950.

C. Chevalier mentions in his study 'Les Trilogies homilétiques dans l'élaboration des fêtes Mariales 650–850', *Gregorianum*, xviii (1957), 361–78, that in Jerusalem and Constantinople occasionally on certain high feasts three homilies were preached on the same day. But this practice was confined to a short period in the history of the Greek liturgy and the occurrence of such cycles may have had a special reason. In one of his sermons John Damascene makes reference to the two preceding ones which he had delivered. He hopes, he says, nobody will criticize him here for adding to the two sermons which he had already delivered a third 'refrain' as a final offering in praise of the Mother of God (*εἰ τρίτον τοῖς προλαβοῦσι δυσὶ τὸ παρὸν ἐποιησάμην ἐφύμνιον, τῇ Μητρὶ τοῦ θεοῦ μου, ὥσπερ τι δῶρον ἐξόδιον. P.G.* xcvi, c. 753, A 2). From this passage we may conclude that these three sermons were delivered by John Damascene during different 'Hours' of the same Vigil: the first two during the night in his capacity as Archimandrite of the monasteries of Palestine, the third one as Bishop of Jerusalem in the solemn Matins.

The Eastern Church still maintains the practice of celebrating Mass only on Sundays and feasts when the Divine Service is attended by a sufficiently large number of people. During the week Mass is celebrated for weddings, funerals, and on other special occasions. On the development of the liturgy cf. P. de Meester's article 'Grecques (Liturgy)' in *D.A.C.L.* vi, c. 1591–1662.

Excursus p. 152

The passage to which Wilamowitz refers is the following in Synesius's letter:

. . . *νέμεσιν· αὔτη μέντοι σαφῶς ἐστὶν περὶ ἧς πρὸς λύραν ᾄδομεν*:

Λήθουσα δὲ παρὰ πόδα βαίνεις 9
γαυρούμενον αὐχένα κλίνεις 10
ὑπὸ πῆχυν ἀεὶ βιοτὰν κράτεις. 11

(See R. Hercher, *Epistolographoi Hellenikoi*, Paris, 1872.)

Wilamowitz rightly points out that Synesius is quoting from memory, as one can see for oneself by glancing at the facsimiles of the Greek hymns in F. Bellermann's *Die Hymnen des Dionysius und Mesomedes* (Berlin, 1840); here the last two words in line 11 read *βίοτον μετρεῖς*. Wilamowitz, like many scholars before him, mentions the famous Mesomedes, court composer of the Emperor Hadrian, as author of the hymns. The name of Mesomedes, however, does not occur in Synesius's letter, as one might assume from Wilamowitz's reference, nor does it occur in the manuscripts reproduced by Bellermann. Here, on Plates II and III on which Codex Naples 262. III. C4 is reproduced, the three hymns (1) *εἰς μοῦσαν, ἴαμβος βακχεῖος*, (2) *ὕμνος εἰς Ἥλιον*, and (3) *ὕμνος εἰς νέμεσιν* are ascribed to one Dionysius. The title is simply *Διονυσίου*. In her chapter on 'Ancient Greek Music', in vol. i of the *New Oxford History of Music* (1957), pp. 372–3, Mrs. Henderson gives eight arguments against the almost generally accepted ascription of the music to Mesomedes. In fact this name does not occur in the first printed edition by Vincentio Galilei (1581) nor in the anonymous (John Fell) edition of Aratus (Oxford, 1672) in which Dionysius is mentioned as author. It was not before P. J. Burette's *Dissertation de la mélopée de l'ancienne musique* in 1720 that the name of Mesomedes occurs. Burette was the first scholar who drew attention to Synesius's letter with the quotation from the Nemesis hymn, and it was he also who referred to a fragment in the Bibl. Nat. in Paris in which one Mesodmes (*Μεσόδμης*) is mentioned in connexion with the poem. Since the name Mesodmes is otherwise unknown, Burette suggested it was a mistake for Mesomedes, and this was accepted during the eighteenth and nineteenth centuries by classical scholars interested in Greek music. It must, however, be stated that F. Bellermann called his famous essay *Die Hymnen des Dionysius und Mesomedes* and, on pp. 54–6, argued in favour of Dionysius, who may have been the musician of that name mentioned in a poem in some of the manuscripts which contain the hymns. This poem stands between a theoretical treatise by Bacchius and the first of the hymns and begins as follows:

Τῆς μουσικῆς ἔλεξε Βακχεῖος γέρων
τόνους, τρόπους, μέλη τε καὶ συμφωνίας·
τούτῳ συνῳδὰ Διονύσιος γράφων
τὸν παμμέγιστον δεσπότην Κωνσταντῖνον.

Bellermann assumed that it was Constantine the Great who is mentioned in the poem. Mrs. Henderson, however, has shown (op. cit., p. 372) that the *παμμέγιστος δεσπότης*—a typically Byzantine term—is the Emperor Constantine Porphyrogennetus (913–59). The music, therefore, which Synesius heard or sung was not the same as that which we have before us in the *Ottoboni Codex* and the others of its kind. There is no difficulty in explaining the use of the Alypian notation in the tenth century, particularly in the days of Constantine VII, when the Empire flourished both intellectually and economically, and Ancient Greek philosophy, literature, poetry, mathematics, and music were considered the indispensable basis of education. We must remember, however, that if we shift the date of the composition of the Nemesis hymn down to the tenth century, the same must be done with the two other hymns, that to the Muse (*Ἄειδε, μοῦσά μοι φίλη*) and to the Sun (*Χιονοβλεφάρου πάτερ Ἀοῦς*).

Excursus p. 169

In his 'Historia Manichaeorum qui et Pauliciani dicuntur' (*P.G.* civ) Peter of Sicily identified the Paulicians with the Manichaeans. His authority was questioned by K. Ter-Mkrttschian in *Die Paulikianer im byzantinischen Kaiserreiche und verwandte ketzerische Erscheinungen in Armenien*, Leipzig, 1893, and F. C. Conybeare in his *The Key of Truth*.

A Manual of the Paulician Church of Armenia, Oxford, 1898. H. Grégoire, however, in his study 'Les sources de l'histoire des Pauliciens: Pierre de Sicile est authentique et "Photius" un faux', *Bull. Acad. belge, Classe des lettres*, xxii (1936), 95–114, has shown that Peter of Sicily's report gives a reliable account of their history, doctrines, and customs. D. Obolenski, *The Bogumils* (Cambridge, 1948), pp. 42–5, fully subscribes to Grégoire's view in so far as the origins of the sect are concerned. But he finds that at a later stage Paulicianism had connexions with Marcionism, and even with other sects, the Syrian Massalians and the Armenian Borborites and Thonraki (pp. 48–53).

Excursus p. 178

According to V. Grumel, 'L'auteur et la date de composition du Tropaire *Ὁ μονογενής*', in *E.O.* xxii (1923), 398–418, the hymn may have been written either by Justinian or Severus of Antioch, to whom the Troparion is attributed in Syriac liturgy. It may be the work of Justinian I who between 535 and 536 was very near to monophysite Christology. On the other hand, the poem may equally well be the work of the monophysite Patriarch Severus who in 534 left Egypt and came to Constantinople, where he was received, particularly by the Empress, with all the honours due to a Patriarch (cf. J. Puyade, 'Le Tropaire *Ὁ μονογενής*', *R.O.C.* xvii (1912), 253–8). However, the authorship of the Emperor Justinian is attested by many reliable sources as can be seen from Christ-Paranikas's *Anthologia gr. carm. christian.*, p. xxxii, and, as V. Grumel has shown, phrases of the poem can be traced back to edicts and writings of Justinian.

Excursus p. 191

The origin of the form of the Akathistos has not yet been examined in all its details. The most interesting problem to be solved is that of the combination of twelve groups of 'Salutations' with the Kontakion. The 'Salutations' in the Akathistos can be traced back to the liturgy of the Hellenic Synagogues (cf. H. Chase, 'The Lord's Prayer in the Early Church', *Texts and Studies*, i. 3 (Cambridge, 1891), pp. 168–76). In early Christianity they were connected with the name of Christ. The prototype of the twelve *Chairetismoi*, or Salutations, in the Akathistos probably dates from the time of the Council of Ephesus in 431 at which the divine motherhood of Mary, the *Theotokos*, was defended by Cyril of Alexandria against the formula of the Orientals, who saw in her the *Theodochos*, the receptacle of God.

Excursus p. 229

Reference is generally made to 'the Studion monastery', and I have followed this practice in the first edition. H. D(elehaye), however, showed in an article 'Stoudion-Stoudios', *Analecta Bollandiana*, lii (1934), 64–5, that Byzantine authors never talked of *τὸ Στούδιον* but of *ἡ τοῦ Στουδίου μονή* or *ἡ μονὴ τῶν Στουδίου*, i.e. 'the monastery of Studios' or 'the monastery of those of Studios'. Studios, who founded the monastery, was a patrician, Consul in 454.

Excursus p. 242

Theotokion. In his study 'Die Akrostichis in der byzantinischen Kanonesdichtung', *B.Z.* xvii (1908), 1–69, W. Weyh dealt with the question of when the Theotokia became integral parts of the Kanons. Though no special investigation has been made into that question we may accept W. Weyh's preliminary suggestion that Theotokia are found in Kanons in the first part of the ninth century and are integrated into the acrostics of the Kanons of Theophanes and Joseph Studites in the second quarter of the ninth century. At a later date Theotokia were inserted in Kanons of hymnographers who flourished before Theophanes and Joseph.

APPENDIX I

HYMNS FROM THE HIRMOLOGION

A. Nineteen Hirmi modelled on the First Canticle, the 'Victory Hymn of Moses'

(1) Ἄσωμεν πάντες λαοί

ODE I
Mode I
Cod. Iviron, fol. 4 v.
Ἄ - σω - μεν, πάν - τες λα - οί, τῷ ἐκ πι - κρᾶς . δου - λεί - ας,
Φα - ρα - ὼ τὸν Ἰσ - ρα - ὴλ ἀπ - αλ - λά - ξαν - τι, καὶ ἐν βυ -
- θῷ θα - λάσ - σης πο - δὶ ἀ - βρό - χῳ ὁ - δη - γή - σαν - τι,
ᾠ - δὴν ἐ - πι - νί - κι - ον, ὅ - τι δε - δό - ξα - σται.
(2) Ἄσωμεν τῷ Κυρίῳ
Mode I
Cod. Ivir., fol. 10 v.
Ἄ - σω - μεν τῷ Κυ - ρί - ῳ ᾠ - δὴν . . ἐ - πι - νί - κι - ον, τὸν
Φα - ρα - ὼ γὰρ πόν - τῳ ἐ - κά - λυ - ψε, καὶ ἐ - πο - δή - γη

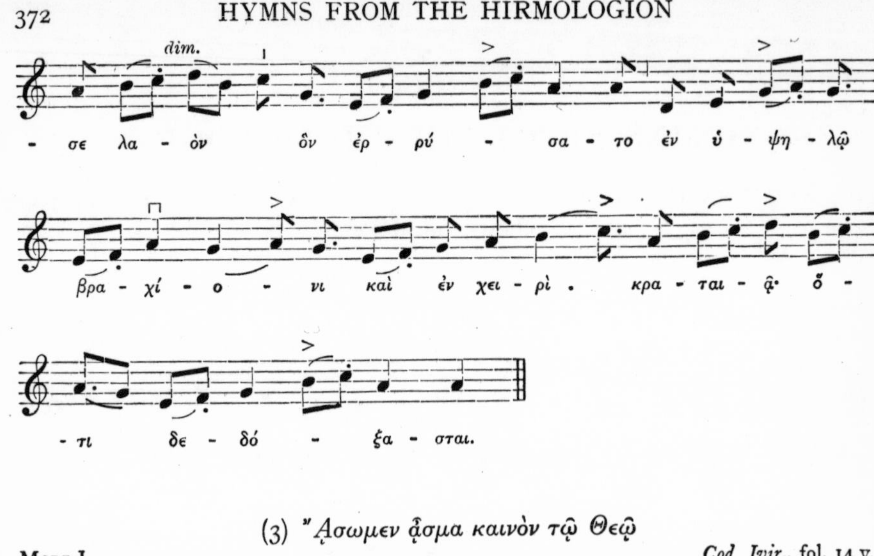
dim.
- σε λα - ὸν ὃν ἐρ - ρύ - σα - το ἐν ὑ - ψη - λῷ
βρα - χί - ο - νι καὶ ἐν χει - ρὶ . κρα - ται - ᾷ· ὅ -
- τι δε - δό - ξα - σται.

(3) Ἄσωμεν ᾆσμα καινὸν τῷ Θεῷ

Mode I — *Cod. Ivir.*, fol. 14 v.

Ἄ - σω - μεν ᾆ - σμα και - νὸν . . τῷ Θε - ῷ τῷ ἐκ δου - λεί - ας

Φα - ρα - ὼ λυ - τρω - σα - με - νῳ . . τοὺς υἱ - οὺς . . Ἰσ - ρα - ὴλ

καὶ ἐν ἐ - ρή - μῳ τού - τους δι - α - θρέ - ψαν - τι·

ὅ - τι ἐν - δό - ξως δε - δό - ξα - σται.

(4) Ἄσωμεν ᾠδὴν τῷ Θεῷ

Mode I — *Cod. Ivir.*, fol. 17 r.

Ἄ - σω - μεν ᾠ - δὴν τῷ Θε - ῷ τῷ μό - νῳ νι - κη - τῇ τοῦ

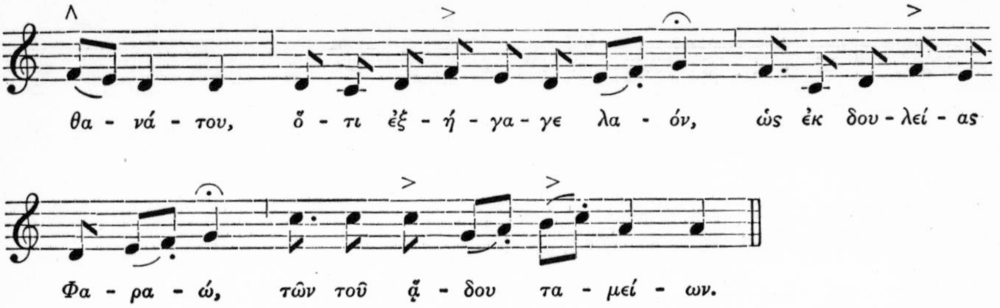

θα - νά - του, ὅ - τι ἐξ - ή - γα - γε λα - όν, ὡς ἐκ δου - λεί - as
Φα - ρα - ώ, τῶν τοῦ ᾅ - δου τα - μεί - ων.

(5) Ἄσωμεν τῷ Κυρίῳ τῷ ἐν θαλάσσῃ

MODE II *Cod. Ivir.*, fol. 27 r.

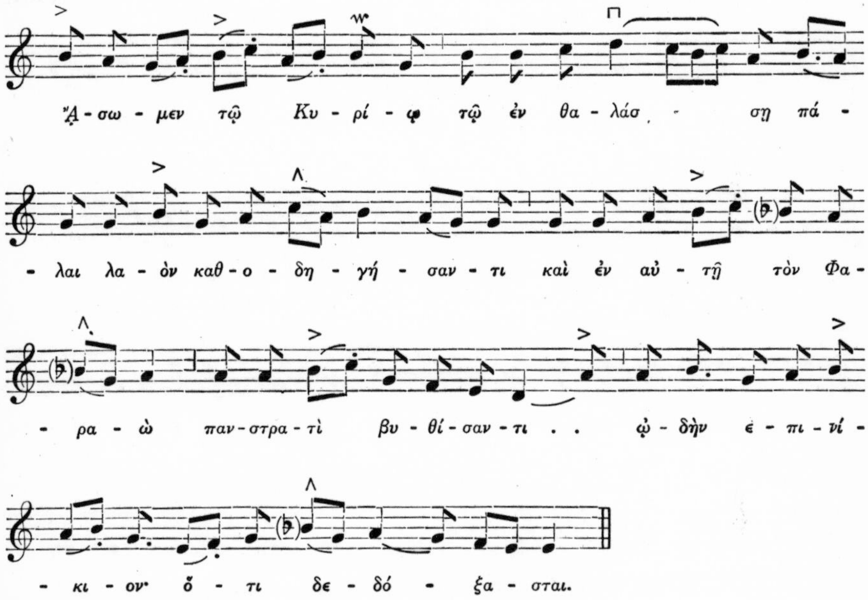

Ἄ - σω - μεν τῷ Κυ - ρί - ῳ τῷ ἐν θα - λάσ - ση πά -
- λαι λα - ὸν καθ - ο - δη - γή - σαν - τι καὶ ἐν αὐ - τῇ τὸν Φα -
- ρα - ὼ παν - στρα - τὶ βυ - θί - σαν - τι . . ᾠ - δὴν ἐ - πι - νί -
- κι - ον· ὅ - τι δε - δό - ξα - σται.

(6) Ἄσωμεν τῷ Κυρίῳ ᾆσμα καινόν

MODE II *Cod. Ivir.*, fol. 29 v.

Ἄ - σω - μεν τῷ Κυ - ρί - ῳ ᾆ - σμα και - νόν, ὅ - τι πα -
- ρα - δό - ξως τὸν Ἰσ - ρα - ὴλ δι - έ - σω - σε δου - λεί - as

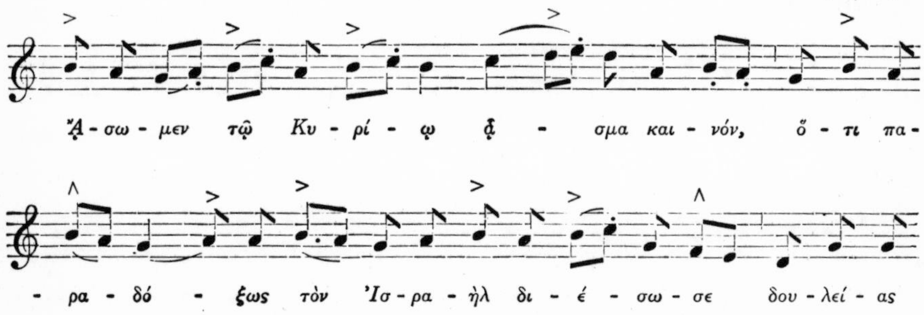

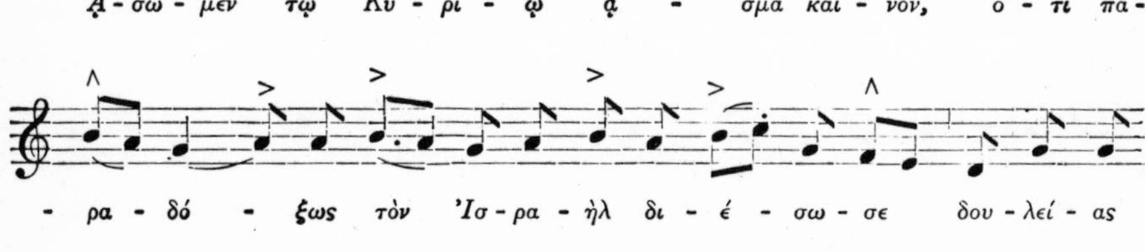

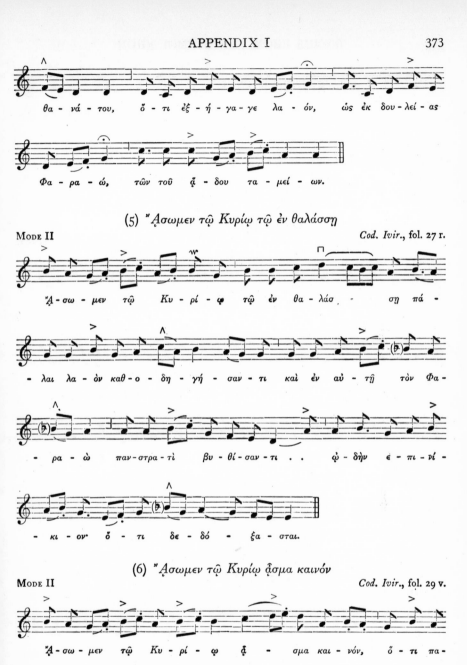

λυ - τρω - σά - με - νος καὶ τυ - ραν - νοῦν - τας ἐ - χθροὺς ἐ - κά -

- λυ - ψε θά - λασ - σα.

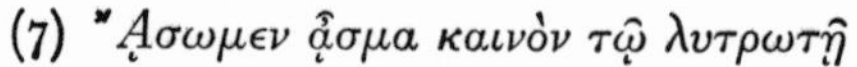

(7) Ἄσωμεν ᾆσμα καινὸν τῷ λυτρωτῇ

Mode III — *Cod. Ivir.*, fol. 50 r.

dim.
Ἄ - σω - μεν ᾆ - σμα και - νὸν τῷ λυ - τρω - τῇ καὶ Θε - ῷ

ἡ - μῶν οἱ δι - ὰ σταυ - ροῦ ῥυ - σθέν - τες τοῦ νο - η - τοῦ

Φα - ρα - ώ, καὶ οἰ - κει - ω - θέν - τες τῇ στρα - τι - ᾷ τῶν ἀ - ϋ -

dim.
- λων οὐ - σι - ῶν, ὅ - τι ἐν - δό - ξως δε - δό - ξα - σται.

(8) Ἄσωμεν τῷ Κυρίῳ τῷ ποιήσαντι

Mode III — *Cod. Ivir.*, fol. 54 r.

Ἄ - σω - μεν τῷ Κυ - ρί - ῳ τῷ ποι - ή - σαν - τι θαυ - μα -

dim.
- στὰ τέ - ρα - τα ἐν Ἐ - ρυ - θρᾷ θα - λάσ - σῃ· πόν - τῳ γὰρ ἐ - κά - λυ -

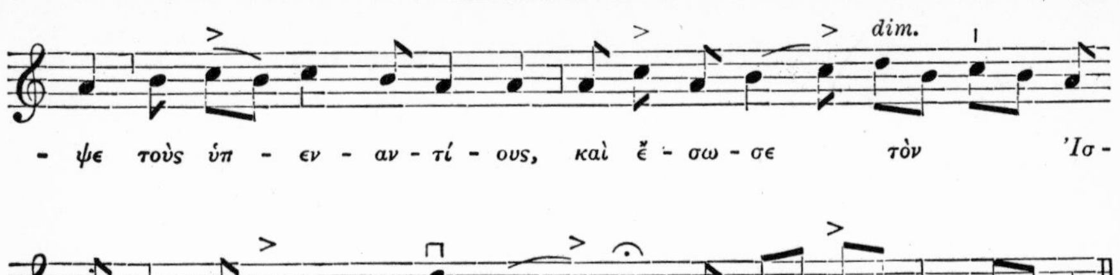
dim.
- ψε τοὺς ὑπ - εν - αν - τί - ους, καὶ ἔ - σω - σε τὸν Ἰσ -

- ρα - ήλ· αὐ - τῷ μό - νῳ ᾄ - σω - μεν, ὅ - τι δε - δό - ξα - σται.

(9) Ἄσομαί σοι, Κύριε, ὁ Θεός μου

Mode IV *Cod. Ivir.*, fol. 69 v.

Ἄ - σο - μαί σοι, Κύ - ρι - ε ὁ Θε - ός μου, ὅ - τι ἐξ - ή - γα - γες λα -

- ὸν δου - λεί - ας Αἰ - γύ - πτου· ἐ - κά - λυ - ψας δὲ ἅρ - μα - τα Φα - ρα -

- ὼ καὶ τὴν δύ - να - μιν.

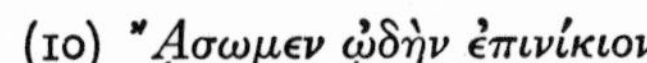

(10) Ἄσωμεν ᾠδὴν ἐπινίκιον

Mode IV *Cod. Ivir.*, fol. 71 v.–72 r.

Ἄ - σω - μεν ᾠ - δὴν ἐ - πι - νί - κι - ον τῷ μό - νῳ Θε - ῷ,

τῷ ποι - ή - σαν - τι πα - ρά - δο - ξα· πά - λαι γὰρ τὸν Φα - ρα -

- ὼ παν-στρα - τὶ ἐν θα - λάσ - σῃ ἐ - βύ - θι - σεν.

(11) Ἄσωμεν τῷ Κυρίῳ τῷ ποιήσαντι
Mode I Plagal
Cod. Ivir., fol. 87 r.
Ἄ - σω - μεν τῷ Κυ - ρί - ῳ τῷ ποι - ή - σαν - τι θαυ - μα -
dim.
- στὰ τέ - ρα - τα ἐν ' - ρυ - θρᾷ θα - λάσ - σῃ ᾠ - δὴν ἐ - πι - νί -
- κι - ον, ὅ - τι δε - δό - ξα - σται.
(12) Ἄσωμεν τῷ Κυρίῳ τῷ τὸν λαόν
Mode II Plagal
Cod. Ivir., fol. 105 v.
dim.
Ἄ - σω - μεν τῷ Κυ - ρί - ῳ τῷ τὸν λα - ὸν δου - λεί - ας Αἰ - γύ -
- πτου ἀπ - αλ - λά - ξαν - τι, καὶ Φα - ρα - ὼ βυ - θί - σαν - τι.
(13) Ἄσωμεν τῷ Κυρίῳ, ἐνδόξως γάρ
Mode III Plagal (Barys)
Cod. Ivir., fol. 117 r.
Ἄ - σω - μεν τῷ Κυ - ρί - ῳ, ἐν - δό - ξως γὰρ δε - δό - ξα - σται· ὅ -
- τι δι - έ - σω - σε λα - ὸν χει - ρὸς Φα - ρα - ω - νί - τι - δος.

(14) Ἄσωμεν τῷ Κυρίῳ πάντες λαοί
Mode IV Plagal
Cod. Ivir., fol. 136 r.
Ἄ - σω - μεν τῷ Κυ - ρί - ῳ πάν - τες λα - οί, τῷ ἐν θα - λάσ -
- σῃ Ἐ - ρυ - θρᾷ τὸν Φα - ρα - ὼ βυ - θί - σαν - τι, ἐ - πι - νί -
- κι - ον ᾠ - δὴν ᾄ - δον - τες, ὅ - τι δε - δό - ξα - σται.
(15) Τὸν Φαραὼ σὺν ἅρμασιν
Mode I
Cod. Ivir., fol. 17 v.
Τὸν Φα - ρα - ὼ σὺν ἅρ - μα - σιν ἐν τῇ θα λάσ - σῃ Χρι - στὸς κατ -
- ε - πόν - τι - σε καὶ δι - ή - γα - γε λα - ὸν ὑ - μνοῦν - τα καὶ
λέ - γον - τα· ᾄ - σω - μεν τῷ Κυ - ρί - ῳ, ἐν - δό - ξως γὰρ
δε - δό - ξα - σται.

(16) Ἐξάρχει πάλαι

Mode I
Cod. Ivir., fol. 20 r.
Ἐξ - άρ - χει πά - λαι νε - α - νί - δων ᾄ - δου - σα Μα - ρι -
- ὰμ ἡ . . προ - φῆ - τις ᾆ - σμα και - νὸν τῷ ἐν θα - λάσ - σῃ Ἐ -
- ρυ - θρᾷ δι - α - γα - γόν - τι λα - όν· ἐξ - άρ - χει δὲ
νῦν τῶν ἀπ' αἰ - ῶ - νος . κτι - σμά - των . . ᾄ - δου - σα και -
- νό - τε - ρον τῷ τὴν ἁ - γνὴν Θε - ό - παι - δα ἐξ ἀ - γό -
- νου καὶ στεί - ρας προ - α - γα - γόν - τι γα - στρός.
(17) Ἐπὶ τὴν ἄβυσσον
Mode II
Cod. Ivir., fol. 38 r.
Ἐ - πὶ τὴν ἄ - βυσ - σον μο - λῶν ὁ Ἰσ - ρα - η - λί - της λα -
- ὸς ᾠ - δὴν ἀν - έ - μελ - πε τῷ ἐν χει - ρὶ κρα -

- ται - ᾆ δυ - να - τῶς συν - τρί - ψαν - τι πο - λέ - μους Φα - ρα -

- ὼ τοῦ τυ - ράν - νου. Ἄ - σω - μεν τῷ . . Κυ - ρί - ῳ ἐν - δό -

- ξως γὰρ δε - δό - ξα - σται.

(18) *Θαυμάσια τὰ ἔργα σου, Κύριε*

MODE IV PLAGAL — *Cod. Ivir.*, fol. 143 v.

Θαυ - μά - σι - α τὰ ἔρ - γα σου, Κύ - ρι - ε, καὶ ἡ ψυ - χή

μου γι - νώ - σκει σφό - δρα· ἐ - κά - λυ - ψας γὰρ Φα - ρα - ὼ καὶ

τὴν δύ - να - μιν αὐ - τοῦ εἰς θά - λασ - σαν Ἐ - ρυ - θρὰν καὶ ἐ -

- πο - δή - γη - σας λα - ὸν . . . . . . ὕ - μνον σοι βο - ῶν - τα.

(19) Τῷ ἐν νεφέλῃ

MODE I PLAGAL — *Cod. Ivir.*, fol. 92 r.

Τῷ ἐν νε - φέ - λῃ φω - τει - νῇ τὸν Ἰσ - ρα - ὴλ ὁ - δη - γή - σαν -

- τι ᾠ - δὴν ἐ - πι - νί - κι - ον λα - οὶ πάν - τες ᾄ - σω - μεν.

B. THE SECOND ODE: EXAMPLES OF THE EIGHT MODES

Nativity Kanon

Χριστὸς γεννᾶται. Kosmas of Crete

MODE I — *Cod. Ivir.*, fol. 6 v.; *Hirmol.*, p. 6.

Πρό - σε - χε, . . οὐ - ρα - νέ, καὶ λα - λή - σω· ὅ - τι ὁ

Λό - γος τοῦ Πα - τρὸς . . ἐ - κὼν κα - τα - βέ - βη - κεν ἐ -

- πὶ τῆς γῆς κλί - νας οὐ - ρα - νούς, καὶ γέ - γο - νεν ἄν - θρω -

- πος, ἵ - να τὸν ἄν - θρω - πον σώ - σῃ ὡς φιλ - άν - θρω - πος.

Nativity Kanon

Ἄσωμεν τῷ Κυρίῳ ᾆσμα καινόν. John Damascene

MODE II *Cod. Ivir.*, fol. 30 r.; *Hirmol.*, p. 41

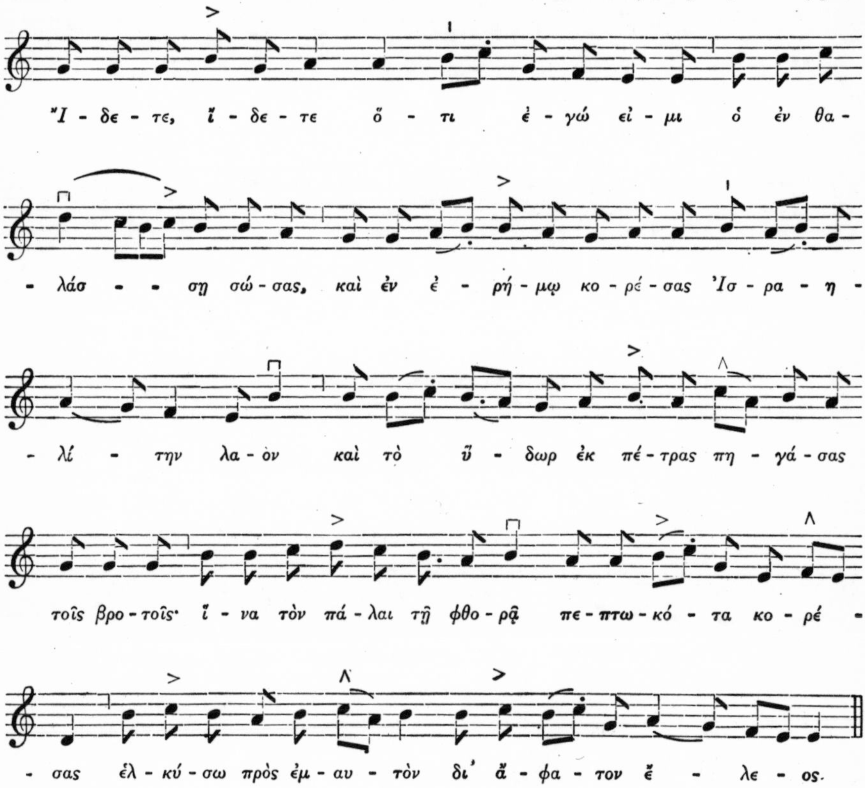

Ἴ - δε - τε, ἴ - δε - τε ὅ - τι ἐ - γώ εἰ - μι ὁ ἐν θα -
- λάσ - - ση σώ - σας, καὶ ἐν ἐ - ρή - μῳ κο - ρέ - σας Ἰσ - ρα - η -
- λί - την λα - ὸν καὶ τὸ ὕ - δωρ ἐκ πέ - τρας πη - γά - σας
τοῖς βρο - τοῖς· ἵ - να τὸν πά - λαι τῇ φθο - ρᾷ πε - πτω - κό - τα κο - ρέ -
- σας ἑλ - κύ - σω πρὸς ἐμ - αυ - τὸν δι' ἄ - φα - τον ἔ - λε - ος.

Kanon for the Feast of the Purification of the B.V.M.

Βραχίονι ὑψηλῷ. Andrew of Crete

MODE III *Cod. Ivir.*, fol. 49 r.; *Hirmol.*, p. 73

Ὡς ὄμ - βρος ἐπ' ἄ - γρω - στιν, καὶ ὡσ - εὶ νι - φε - τὸς ἐ -
- πὶ χόρ - τον κα - τα - βή - τω ἐ - πὶ γῆς τὰ ῥή - μα - τά μου.

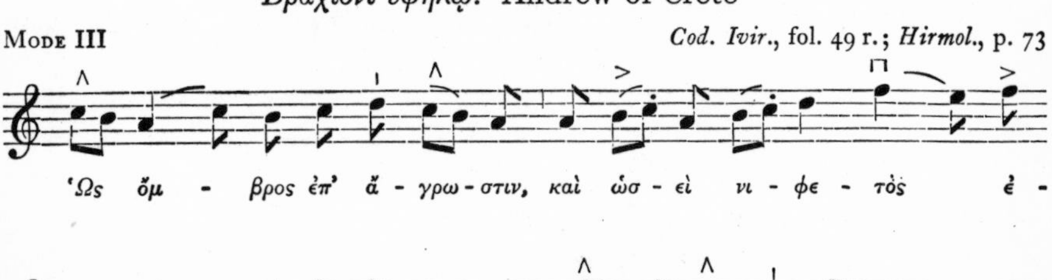

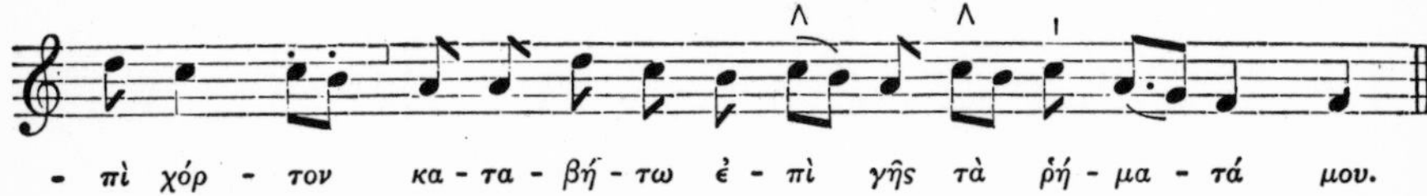

Τὸ ᾆσμα τὸ νοητόν. Andrew of Crete.

MODE IV *Cod. Ivir.*, fol. 76 r.; *Hirmol.*, p. 108

Ἴ - δε - τε, ἴ - δε - τε ὅ - τι ἐ - γώ εἰ - μι Θε - ός, ὁ ἐν ἐ -

- ρή - μῳ φυ - γά - δα πά - λαι λα - ὸν κο - ρέ - σας τῆς τοῦ μάν - να

τρο - φῆς, καὶ ἀ - να - γα - γὼν αὐ - τοὺς εἰς ὄ - ρος ἅ - γι - άσ - μα -

- τος, τῇ ἐξ - ου - σί - ᾳ καὶ τῇ ἰ - σχύ - ι τῇ ἐ - μῇ.

Ἄσωμεν τῷ Σωτῆρι τῶν ὅλων. Andrew of Crete

MODE I PLAGAL *Cod. Ivir.*, fol. 90 r.; *Hirmol.*, p. 138

Ἀ - λη - θι - νὰ τὰ ἔρ - γα Κυ - ρί - ου τοῦ Θε - οῦ ἡ - μῶν, καὶ

πᾶ - σαι αἱ ὁ - δοὶ αὐ - τοῦ κρί - σεις.

Kanon for Maundy Thursday

Τμηθείσῃ τμᾶται. Kosmas of Crete.

MODE II PLAGAL *Cod. Ivir.*, fol. 101 v.; *Hirmol.*, p. 162

Ὥσ - περ ὄμ - βρος ἐπ' ἄ - γρω - στιν, Χρι - στέ, καὶ ὡσ - εὶ νι - φε -

- τός . . . . ἡ γλυ - κεῖ - α γέ - γο - νε φω - νὴ τοῖς μα - θη -

- ταῖς . . σου ἐν τῇ νι - πτῆ - ρι τοῦ θεί - ου βα - πτί - σμα - τος, τὴν

χά - ριν προ - εμ - φαί - νου - σα, καὶ τα - πει - νώ - σε - ως τύ - πον

ἡ - μῖν προ - ϋ - πο - γρά - φου - σα, ἱ - ε - ρουρ - γεῖν σοι τὰ θεῖ -

- α ὡς Θε - ῷ ἀ - λη - θεῖ.

Τῷ ὑποβρύχιον ποιήσαντι. Anon.

MODE III PLAGAL (BARYS) *Cod. Ivir.*, fol. 121 v.; *Hirmol.*, p. 212

Πρόσ - ε - χε, οὐ - ρα - νέ, καὶ λα - λή - σω, καὶ γῆ, ἐν - ω -

dim.
- τί - ζου τὰ ῥή - μα - τά μου· ὅ - τι ὄ - νο - μα Κυ - ρί - ου ἐ -

- κά - λε - σα· δι - ὰ τοῦ - το δῶ - μεν αὐ - τῷ με - γα - λω - σύ - νην.

Τῷ θαυμαστὰ τέρατα ποιήσαντι. Andrew of Crete

MODE IV PLAGAL *Cod. Ivir.*, fol. 137 r.; *Hirmol.*, p. 227

Με - γα - λω - σύ - νην δῶ - μεν καὶ δό - ξαν τῷ σαρ - κω - θέν - τι

Θε - ῷ εἰς σω - τη - ρί - αν ἡ - μῶν.

APPENDIX II

HYMNS FROM THE STICHERARION

3 October

Feast of S. Denys the Areopagite

MODE IV *Cod. Dal.*, fol. 30 r.

Τῆς οὐ - ρα - νί - ου γνώ - σε - ως ἀ - θε - ώ - ρη - τον βυ - θὸν, σὲ
κα - λέ - σο - - μεν, λαμ - πρό - τα - τε μάρ - τυς τοῦ Χρι - στοῦ· ὡς
γὰρ ὁ - πλί - την καὶ στερ - ρὸν ὑ - πέρ - μα - χον τῆς ἐκ - κλη - σί -
- ας . . . ἀ - νυ - μνοῦ - μέν σε, σο - φέ· πυ - ρὶ γὰρ ἐλ - λαμ - φθεὶς τῷ
ἁ - γνο - τά - τῳ, ἠ - ξι - ώ - θης ἅ - μα ταῖς ἄ - νω στρα -
- το - λο - γί - αις τὸ φω - τει - νὸν πε - ρι - βό - λαι - ον ἐν - δύ -
- σα - σθαι Χρι - στόν, καὶ λαμ - πρυν - θῆ - ναι τῇ αἴ - γλῃ τοῦ Πνεύ -

- μα - τος τὸν νοῦν, . . Δι - ο - νύ - σι - - - ε· δι - ὸ
σοῦ . . . . . . τὴν παγ - κόσ - μι - ον μνή - μην παν - η - γυ - ρί - ζον - τες,
πι - στῶς δο - ξά - ζο - μεν τὸν δο - ξά - σαν - τά σε Κύ - ρι - ον.

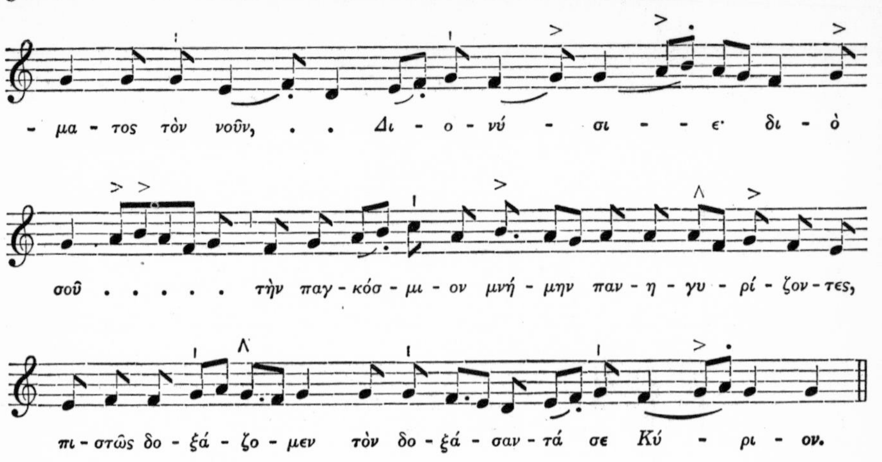

24 December

Cod. Dal., fol. 90 r.

Mode IV Plagal — Sophronius, Patriarch of Jerusalem

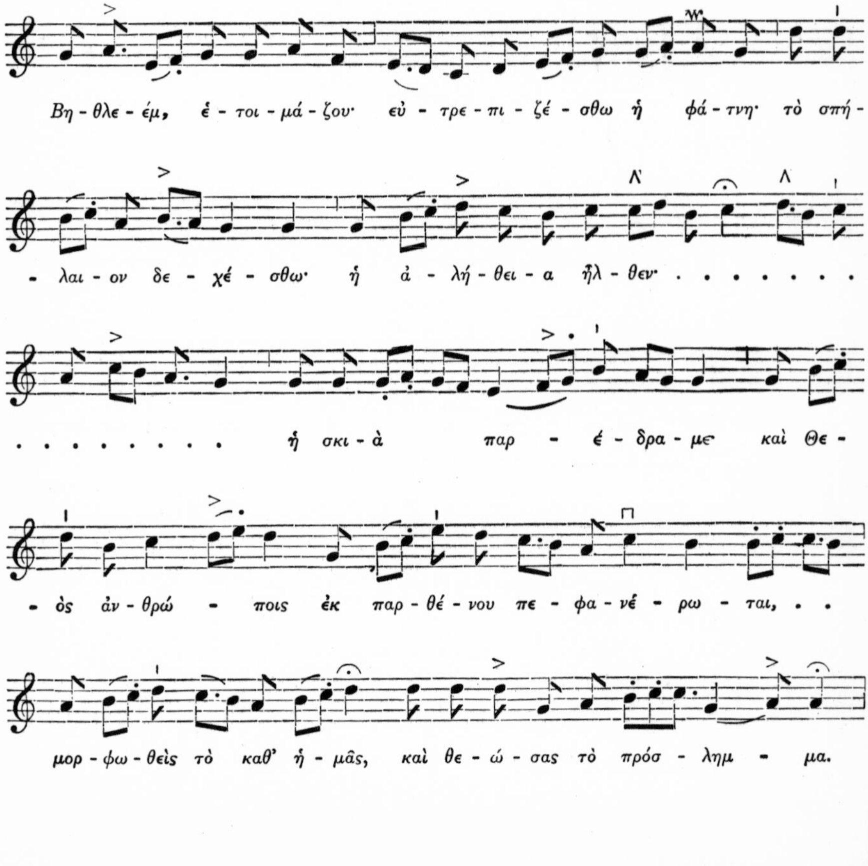

Βη - θλε - έμ, ἑ - τοι - μά - ζου· εὐ - τρε - πι - ζέ - σθω ἡ φά - τνη· τὸ σπή -
- λαι - ον δε - χέ - σθω· ἡ ἀ - λή - θει - α ἦλ - θεν· . . . .
. . . . ἡ σκι - ὰ παρ - έ - δρα - με καὶ Θε -
- ὸς ἀν - θρώ - ποις ἐκ παρ - θέ - νου πε - φα - νέ - ρω - ται, . .
μορ - φω - θεὶς τὸ καθ' ἡ - μᾶς, καὶ θε - ώ - σας τὸ πρόσ - λημ - μα.

acc.
Δι - ὸ . . . . Ἀ - δὰμ ἀ - να - νε - οῦ - ται σὺν τῇ Εὔ - ᾳ,

acc.
κρά - ζον - τες· Ἐ - πὶ γῆς . . . . . εὐ - δο - κί - α ἐπ - ε -

φά - νη, σῶ - σαι τὸ γέ - νος ἡ - μῶν.

MODE IV PLAGAL

Τά - δε λέ - γει Ἰ - ω - σὴφ πρὸς τὴν παρ - θέ - νον· Μα - ρί -

- α, τί τὸ δρᾶ - μα τοῦ - το . . . .

ὃ ἐν σοὶ τε - θέ - α - μαι; . . ἀ - πο - ρῶ . . καὶ ἐξ - ί -

- στα - μαι, καὶ τὸν νοῦν κα - τα - πλήτ - το - μαι. Λά - θρᾳ

τοί - νυν ἀπ' ἐ - μοῦ γε - νοῦ ἐν τά - χει, Μα - ρί - α.

τί τὸ δρᾶ - μα τοῦ - το . . . .
ὃ . ἐν σοὶ τε - θέ - α - μαι; ἀν - τὶ τι - μῆς αἰ - σχύ - νην, ἀντ' εὐ -
- φρο - σύ - νης τὴν λύ - πην, ... ἀν - τὶ τοῦ ἐπ - αι - νεῖ -
- σθαι τὸν ψό - γον μοι προσ - ή - γα - γες. Οὐκ - έ - τι φέ - ρω λοι - πὸν
τὸ ὄ - νει - δος ἀν - θρώ - πων· ὑ - πὸ γὰρ ἱ - ε - ρέ - ων
ἐκ τοῦ να - οῦ ὡς ἄ - μεμ - πτον Κυ - ρί - ου σε παρ - έ - λα - βον· καὶ
τί . . . . τὸ ὁ - ρώ - με - νον;
Mode III
Νῦν προ - φη - τι - κὴ πρόρ - ρη - σις πλη - ρω - θῆ - ναι ἐπ - εί - γε -
- ται μυ - στι - κῶς ἡ φά - σκου - σα· Καὶ σύ, Βη - θλε - έμ, γῆ Ἰ -

- ού - δα, οὐ - δα - μῶς ὑπ - άρ - χεις ἐ - λα - χί - στη ἐν τοῖς ἡ -
- γε - μό - σι προ - ευ - τρε - πί - ζου - σα τὸ σπή - λαι - ον· ἐκ σοῦ
γάρ μοι ἐξ - ε - λεύ - σε - ται ἡ - γού - με - νος . τῶν ἐ - θνῶν
δι - ὰ σαρ - κός, ἐκ παρ - θέ - νου κό - ρης Χρι - στὸς ὁ Θε - ός,
ὃς . . . . ποι - μα - νεῖ τὸν λα - ὸν αὐ - τοῦ, τὸν νέ - ον
Ἰ - σρα - ήλ. Δῶ - μεν αὐ - τῷ ἅ - παν - τες με - γα - λω - σύ - νην.

Mode II *Cod. Dal.*, fol. 92r.

Ὅ - τε Ἰ - ω - σὴφ, παρ - θέ - νε, λύ - πῃ ἐ - τι - τρώ - σκε - το,
πρὸς Βη - θλε - ὲμ ἀπ - αί - ρων, ἐ - βό - ας πρὸς αὐ - τόν· Τί ὁ -
- ρῶν με ἔγ - κυ - ον στυγ - νά - ζεις καὶ τα - ράτ - τε - σαι . . . ἀ - -

- - - - - - γνο - - ῶν . . . . . ἄ - λως τὸ ἐ - μοὶ
φρι - κτὸν μυ - στή - ρι - ον; Λοι - πὸν . . . . . ἀ - πό - θου φό - βον ἅ -
- παν - τα . . . . τὸ πα -
dim. acc.
- ρά - δο - ξον ἐν - νο - ῶν· Θε - ὸς κάτ - ει - σι γὰρ . . . .
ἐ - πὶ τῆς γῆς δι' ἔ - λε - ον, ἐν τῇ μή - τρᾳ μου νῦν, ...
καὶ σάρ - κα προσ - ε - λά - βε - το· ὅν - περ τι - κτό - - με - νον
ὄ - ψει ὡς ηὐ - δό - κη - σε· καὶ τῆς χα - ρᾶς πλη - σθεὶς . . . . .
. . . . προσ - κυ - νή - σεις ὡς κτί - στην σου·
ὃν ἄγ - γε - λοι ὑ - μνοῦ - - - σιν ἀ - παύ - στως καὶ δο - ξά - ζου -

-σι . . . . σὺν Πα - τρὶ . . . .

. . . . καὶ Ἁ - γί - ῳ Πνεύ - μα - τι.

25 December

Mode II Plagal — *Cod. Dal.*, fol. 98v.

Δό - - ξα ἐν ὑ - ψί - στοις Θε - ῷ, καὶ ἐ - πὶ γῆς

εἰ - ρή - νη. Σή - - με - ρον δέ - χε - ται ἡ Βη - θλε - ὲμ . . .

. . . . τὸν καθ - ή - με - νον δι - ὰ παν - τὸς σὺν Πα - τρί. Σή - -

- με - ρον ἄγ - γε - λοι τὸ βρέ - φος τὸ τεχ - θὲν θε - ο - πρε - πῶς δο - ξο -

- λο - γοῦ - σι. Δό - - - ξα ἐν ὑ - ψί - στοις Θε - ῷ, καὶ

ἐ - πὶ γῆς εἰ - ρή - νη, ἐν ἀν - θρώ - ποις εὐ - δο - κί - α.

25 December
Mode I Plagal
Cod. Dal., fol. 91v.
Δεῦ - - - - - - - - - - - - - τε . .
. . . . χρι - στο - φό - ροι λα - οί, κατ -
dim.
- ί - δω - μεν θαῦ - μα πᾶ - σαν ἔν - νοι - αν ἐκ - πλῆτ-τον καὶ συν -
dim.
- έ - χον καὶ εὐ - σε - βῶς ἀν - υ - μνοῦν-τες πί - στει προσ - κυ - νή -
- - σω - μεν. Σή - με - - - - ρον . . . .
. . . . . πρὸς τὴν Βη - θλε - ὲμ ἐγ - κυ - μο - νοῦ - σα κό - ρη πα -
- ρα - γί - νε - ται τοῦ γεν - νῆ - σαι τὸν Κύ - ρι - ον· χο - ροὶ δὲ
ἀγ - γέ - λων προ - τρέ - χου - σι. Καὶ ταῦτα βλέ - - - πων

. . . . . . ἐ - βό - α Ἰ - ω - σὴφ ὁ μνή - - -
- στωρ· . . . . Τί . . τὸ ἐν σοὶ . . ξέ - νον μυ - στή - ρι -
- ον, παρ - θέ - νε; . . . . καὶ πῶς μέλ - λεις λο - χεῦ - σαι ἡ
ἀ - πει - ρό - - - - - - ζυ - γος . . δά - μα - λις;
Δεῦ - - - - - - - - - - - - - -
- τε . . . . χρι - στο - φό - ροι λα - οί, . .
dim.
κατ - ί - δω - μεν τί ἐ - βου - λεύ - σα - το Ἰ - ού - δας ὁ προ -
acc.
- δό - της σὺν ἱ - ε - ρεῦ - σι ἀ - νό - μοις . . . . . κα - τὰ

Good Friday

MODE I PLAGAL *Cod. Vatop.* 1492, fol. 200r.; *Cod. Dal.*, fol. 248v. (version faulty)

τοῦ Σω - τῆ - - ρος ἡ - μῶν. Σή με - - - ρον . . . .
. . . . ἔ - νο - χον θα - νά - του τὸν ἀ -
θά - να - τον Λό - γον πε - ποί - η - καν, ... καὶ Πι - λά - τῳ προ -
- δώ - σαν - τες . . . ἐν τό - πῳ Κρα - νί - ου ἐ - σταύ - ρω - σαν.
Καὶ ταῦ - τα πά - - - σχων . . . . ἐ - βό - α
ὁ Σω - τὴρ ἡ - μῶν . . . λέ - - - γων· . . . .
dim.
Ἄ - - φες αὐ - τοῖς, . . Πά - τερ, τὴν ἁ - μαρ - τί - αν ταύ -
- την, ... ὅ - πως γνῶ - σι τὰ ἔ - θνη τὴν ἐκ νε -
- κρῶν . . . . μου ἀ - - - - νά - στα - σιν.

Wednesday in Holy Week

Cod. Dal., fol. 232v.
KASIA

acc.
Κύ - ρι - ε, ἡ ἐν πολ - λαῖς ἁ - μαρ - τί - αις πε - ρι - πε - σοῦ -
- σα γυ - νὴ τὴν σὴν . . . . . αἰ - σθο - μέ - νη Θε - ό - τη -
- τα, μυ - ρο - φό - ρου ἀ - να - λα - βοῦ - σα τά - ξιν, ὀ - δυ -
- ρο - μέ - νη μύ - ρον σοι πρὸ τοῦ ἐν - τα - φι - α - σμοῦ κο - μί - ζει·
Οἴ - μοι· . . λέ - γου - σα, ὅ - τι νύξ με συν - έ - χει οἶ -
- στρος ἀ - κο - λα - σί - ας, ζο - φώ - δης τε . . . . καὶ ἀ - σέ - λη -
- νος ἔ - ρως τῆς ἁ - μαρ - τί - ας· δέ - ξαι μου . . τὰς πη -
- γὰς τῶν δὰ - κρύ - ων, ὁ νε - φέ - λαις . . στη - μο - νί - ζων τῆς

θα - λάσ - σης τὸ ὕ - δωρ· κάμ - φθη - τί μοι πρὸς τοὺς στε - να - γμοὺς τῆς καρ -

- δί - ας, ὁ κλί - νας τοὺς οὐ - ρα - νοὺς . . . . . τῇ ἀ - φρά - στῳ

σου κε - νώ - σει· κα - τα - φι - λή - σω . . τοὺς ἀ - χράν -

- τους σου πό - δας, ἀ - πο - σμή - ξω . . τού - τους δὲ πά - λιν

τοῖς τῆς κε - φα - λῆς μου βο - στρύ - χοις· ὧν ἐν τῷ Πα - ρα - δεί - σῳ

Εὔ - α τὸν δει - λι - νὸν . . . . . κρό - τον τοῖς ὠ - σὶν ἠ -

- χη - θεῖ - σα . . τῷ φό - βῳ ἐ - κρύ - βη· ἁ - μαρ - τι - ῶν μου τὰ

πλή - θη . . . . . . καὶ κρι - μά - των σου ἀ - βύσ - σους τίς ἐξ -

- ι - χνι - ά - σει, ψυ - χο - σῶ - στα, Σω - τήρ μου; Μή με .

τὴν . . . σὴν δού - λην παρ - ί - δῃς . . . ὁ ἀ - μέ - τρη -
- τον ἔ - χων τὸ ἔ - λε - ος.
Good Friday
Mode II Plagal
Cod. Vatop. 1499, fol. 300v.
Ὦ . . . . πῶς . . . . ἡ πα - ρά -
- νο - μος συν - α - γω - γὴ τὸν βα - σι - λέ - α τῆς κτί - σε -
- ως . . κατ - ε - δί - κα - σεν θα - νά - τῳ, μὴ αἰ - δε - σθεῖ -
- σα τὰς εὐ - ερ - γε - σί - ας, ἃς ἀ - να - μι - μνή - σκων
προ - η - σφα - λί - ζε - το λέ - γων πρὸς αὐ - τούς· Λα - - - -
- ός . . . . . . μου, . . τί . . ἐ - ποί - η - σα ὑ - -
acc.
- μῖν; . . . . οὐ θαυ - μά - των ἐ -

- νέ - πλη - σα τὴν ᾿Ι - ου - δαί - αν; . . . . . . οὐ νε - -

- κροὺς . . . . ἐξ - α - νέ - στη - σα μό - νῳ τῷ λό - γῳ; οὐ πᾶ -

- σαν μα - λα - κί - αν ἐ - θε - ρά - πευ - σα καὶ νό - σον;

τί . . . . οὖν . . . . μοι . . . ἀν -

- τα - πο - δί - δο - τε; εἰς τί ἀ - μνη - μο - νεῖ - τέ μου; ἀν - τὶ τῶν

ἰ - α - μά - των πλη - γάς μοι ἐ - πι - θέν - τες, ἀν - τὶ ζω - ῆς

νε - κροῦν-τες, κρε - μῶν - τες ἐ - πὶ ξύ - λου ὡς κα - κοῦρ - -

- γον τὸν εὐ - ερ - γέ - την, ὡς πα - ρά - νο - - μον

τὸν νο - μο - δό - την, ὡς κα - τά - κρι - τον τὸν πάν - των Βα -

- σι - λέ - α. Μα - κρό - θυ - με Κύ - ρι - ε, δό - ξα σοι.

Maundy Thursday

Cod. Dal., fol. 233v.

Ἰ - ού - δας ὁ δοῦ - λος καὶ δό - λι - ος, ὁ μα - θη -

- τὴς καὶ ἐ - πί - βου - λος, ὁ φί - λος καὶ δι - ά - βο - λος, ...

ἐκ τῶν ἔρ - γων ἀπ - ε - φάν - θη· ἠ - κο - λού - θει γὰρ

acc.
τῷ δι - δασ - κά - λῳ, καὶ καθ' ἑ - αυ - τὸν . . . . ἐ - με -

· λέ - τη - σε τὴν . . προ - δο - σί - αν· ἔ - λε - γεν ἐν ἑ -

- αυ - τῷ· Πα - ρα - δώ - σω αὐ - τὸν . . καὶ κερ - δή - σω τὰ

συν - αχ - θέν - τα χρή - μα - τα· . . . . ἐ - πε - ζή - τει

δὲ . . . . καὶ τὸ μύ - ρον πρα - θῆ -

- ναι, καὶ τὸν Ἰ - η - - - σοῦν . . . . . . δό - λῳ κρα -

- τη - θῆ - ναι· ἀ - πέ - δω - κεν ἀσ - πασ - μόν, παρ - έ - δω -

- κεν τὸν Χρι - στόν· καὶ ὡς πρό - βα - τον ἐ - πὶ σφα -

acc.
- γήν . . . . οὕ - τως ἠ - κο - λού - θει ὁ μό - νος εὔ -

- σπλαγ - χνος καὶ φιλ - άν - θρω - πος.

APPENDIX III

MELISMATIC CHANT

Nativity Kontakion

25 December

Mode III
Cod. Ashburnham.
Romanos, fol. 75 v.
(1) Ἡ παρ-θέ - - - - - - - -
νος σή - - - με - ρο - - - - - - - - ν·
(2) τὸν ὑ - πε - - ρού - σι - ον τί - - - - - - -
- - - - - - - - κτει·
(3) καὶ ἡ γῆ . . . . τὸ σπή - -
- - - - - - - - λαι - ο - - - - - - ν
(4) τῷ ἀ - προ - - σί - τῳ προ-σά - - - - - - - - -

γει. . . πλ.ά (5) Ἄγ
γε - - λοι . . . . με - τὰ ποι - μέ
νω - ν (6) δο - ξο -
λο - - - - γοῦ
σι - - - ν·
α ν α ν (7) μα
γοι . . . . δὲ . . . . με - τὰ ἀ - στη

- - - - - - - - - - - - - - - ρο - -
- s (8) ὁ - - δευ - - πο - - - - ροῦ - - - - -
fol. 76 v.
- - - - - - - - - - - - - - - - - -
- - - - - - - - - - - - - - - - - -
- - σι - - ν α ν α ν (ες) (9) δι' ἡ - μᾶ - - - - -
- - - - - - - - - - s γὰ - - - ρ ἐ - γεν - νή -
- - - - - - θη (10) παι-δί - - - - - - - - - -
- - - - - ο - - - ν νέ - ον· ὁ πρὸ . . αἰ - ώ -
- νω - ν θε - - ός. α ν ε ε α ν ε ε ε s: Γ

Kontakion in honour of Symeon Stylites

1 September

fol. 45 r.
μι - λος τῶν ἀγ - γέ - - - - λων γέ - γο - νας,
C
(6) ὅ - - - - - - - - - - - - - σι - ε . . . πλ.β′
D
(7) σὺν αὐ - τοῖ - - s Χρι-στῷ . . . . . . τῷ θε - ῷ .
. . . . β′· ;,
E
(8) πρεσ-βεύ - - - ων ἀ - παύ - - - στως ὑ - πὲρ
πάν - - - - - - - - των ἡ - - μῶ - - -
- - - - - - - - - - - - ν.

Oikos

fol. 45 v.
(1) Τοῦ Συ - με - ὼ - ν τὸν ἄ - - - -
- - μεμ - πτο - ν βί - - - - - - - - -
fol. 46 r.
- - ο - ν β̈ (2) ποί - α γλῶσ-σα ἀν - -
- θρώ - - - - - - - - - - - - - -
- πων πλ.α′ (3) αὐ - ταρ - κέ - - - σει πο -
- - τέ (4) πρὸς ἔ - - - παι -
- νον ἐξ - η - - γή - - - - - - - - -
- - - - - - - - - - - - - - - - - -

- - - σα - σθαι; πλ. β̈ (5) ὅ - - μως ὑ -
- μνή - - - σω θε - - οῦ
σο - φί- - - - - - , - - - - - - - -
- - - - - - - - - - - ᾳ· (6) τὰ
τοῦ ἥ - ρω - ος ἆ - - -
- - θλα, (7) καὶ τοὺς ἀ - γῶ -
fol. 46 v.
- - νας τοῦ ἐν τῇ γῇ ὡς φω -
- στῆ - ρος φα - νέ - ν - το - s· πλ. β̈ (8) τοῖς
πᾶ - - - - - - - σι βρο - τοῖ -

Refrain by choir:

[(14) πρεσβεύων ἀπαύστως ὑπὲρ πάντων ἡμῶν].

Magnificat. Luke i. 46–8

βλε-ψεν ἐ-πὶ τὴ - - ν τα-πεί-νω - - σι - - - -

- - ν [τῆς δούλης αὐτοῦ].

APPENDIX IV

TABLE OF INTONATION FORMULAE AND INCIPITS OF APPENDED STICHERA

From Cod. Vindobon. phil. gr. 194, fols. 9–11

The folio numbers on the right side of the music examples refer to those of the Sticherarium Codex Dalassenos, *M.M.B. Facsimilia*, vol. i.

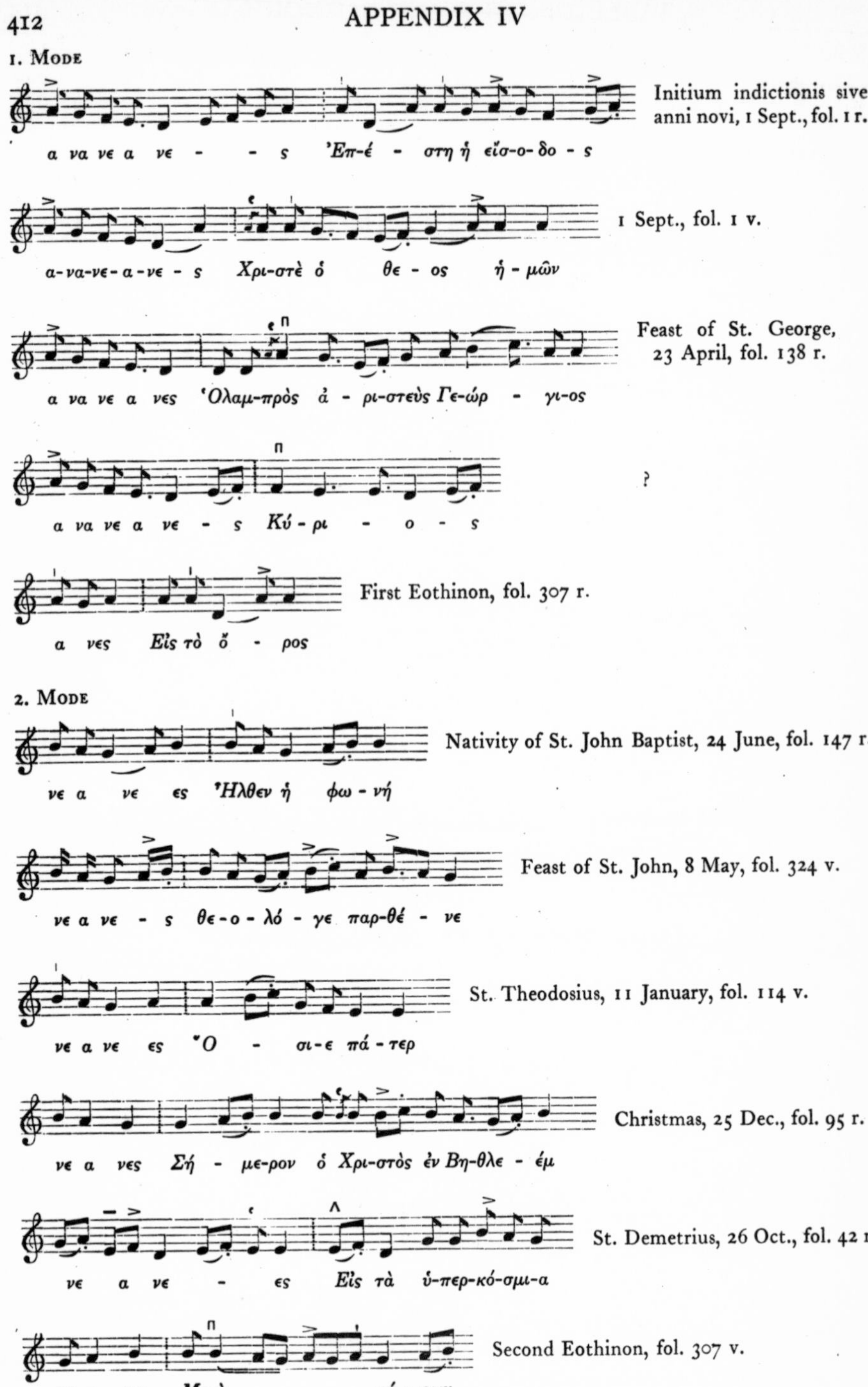
1. Mode
α να νε α νε - - ς Ἐπ-έ - στη ἡ εἴσ-ο-δο - ς
Initium indictionis sive anni novi, 1 Sept., fol. 1 r.
α-να-νε-α-νε - ς Χρι-στὲ ὁ θε - ος ἡ - μῶν
1 Sept., fol. 1 v.
α να νε α νες Ὀλαμ-πρὸς ἀ - ρι-στεὺς Γε-ώρ - γι-ος
Feast of St. George, 23 April, fol. 138 r.
α να νε α νε - ς Κύ - ρι - ο - ς
?
α νες Εἰς τὸ ὄ - ρος
First Eothinon, fol. 307 r.
2. Mode
νε α νε ες Ἦλθεν ἡ φω - νή
Nativity of St. John Baptist, 24 June, fol. 147 r.
νε α νε - ς θε-ο-λό - γε παρ-θέ - νε
Feast of St. John, 8 May, fol. 324 v.
νε α νε ες Ὅ - σι-ε πά - τερ
St. Theodosius, 11 January, fol. 114 v.
νε α νες Σή - με-ρον ὁ Χρι-στὸς ἐν Βη-θλε - έμ
Christmas, 25 Dec., fol. 95 r.
νε α νε - ες Εἰς τὰ ὑ-περ-κό-σμι-α
St. Demetrius, 26 Oct., fol. 42 r.
νε α νες Μετὰ μύ - ρων
Second Eothinon, fol. 307 v.

3. Mode
α νε ε ε α νε ε ε ες· Χρι-στὲ ὁ θε - ὸς ἡ - μῶν
Exaltation of the Holy Cross, 14 Sept., fol. 16 r.
α νε ε ε α νε ε ε ες· Ὅ - σι - ε Ἀν - τώ - νι - ε
St. Antony, 17 Jan., fol. 117 v.
α νε ε α νε ε ε ε - s. Φο - βε-ρὸν τὸ ἐμ-πε - σεῖν
Palm Sunday, evening, fol. 227 v.
α νε ε α νε ε ε s· Τῆς Μα-γδα-λή - νης Μα - ρί - ας
Third Eothinon fol. 307 v.
να να νε ε ε ες· Νῦν εἰς ση - μεῖ - ον
Whit Sunday, fol. 272 r.
4. Mode
α α γι α α α· Δεῦ - τε πάν-τες οἱ πι - στοί
All Saints, fol. 275 v.
α α γι α α· Ὄρ-θρος ἦν βα-θύς
Fourth Eothinon, fol. 308 r.
α γι α· Τὸν κα-τὰ τῶν Μα - κα - βαί - ων
De sanctis Machabaeis martyribus, 1 August, fol. 167 v.
α γι α· Τὸ πνεῦμα τὸ ἅ - γι-ον
Whit Sunday, fol. 273 r.
α γι α· Σή-με-ρον χα-ρᾶς εὐ - αγ - γέ - λι-αι
Feast of the Annunciation, 25 March, fol. 136 v.

1. pl. Mode

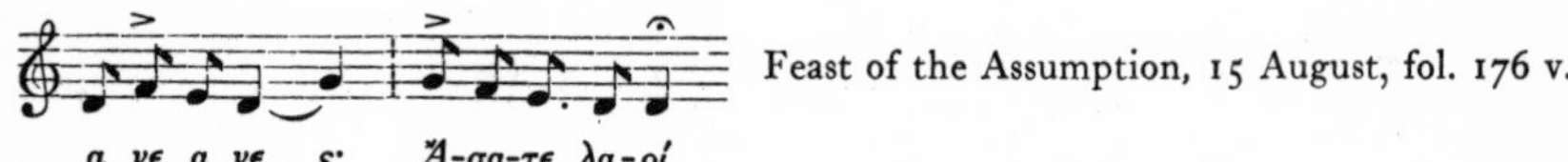

2. pl. Mode

BARYS

(3. PL. MODE)

α α νες· Ἰ - δοὺ σκο - τί-α καὶ πρω - ί

Seventh Eothinon, fol. 309 v.

α α νες· Ἐ- τα - ράτ - τε - το . . Ἡ - ρώ - δης

Vigil of Christmas, fol. 92 r

α α νες· Δα-υι-τι-κὴν προ - φη - τί-αν ἐκ - πλη-ρῶν

Stich. Anatolikon for Saturday, fol. 290 v.

α α α νες· Εἰς τὸ ὄ - ρος τῶν ἐ-λαί-ων

Feast of the Ascension, fol. 269 v.

α α νες Θάμ-βος ἦν κατ - ι - δεῖν

Good Friday, fol. 249 v.

4. PL. MODE

νε α γι ε Φα - νε - ρῶν

Eleventh Eothinon, fol. 311 r.

νε α γι ε ε Πι-στού-με-νος

15 August, fol. 178 r.

νε α γι ε Σή-με-ρον [ἡ κτί - σις φω-τί - ζε - ται]

Epiphany, fol. 112 v.

νε α γι ε να να Δό-ξα Χσοι ριστὲ Σω-τήρ

Stich. Anatol. for Saturday, fol. 292 v.

νε α γι ε Παν-το-κρά-τορ Κύ-ρι - ε

Dominica Publicani et Pharisaei, fol. 186 r.

APPENDIX V

TABLES OF FORMULAE OF THE HIRMI OF THE FIRST MODE

INITIA, MEDIAE, AND FINALES

From Cod. Saba 599 and Cod Iviron 470

A

(1)
Cod. Sab
Σοῦ ἡ τρο - παι - οῦ - χος δε - ξι - ά
(2)
Θε - ο - πρε - πῶς ἐν ἰ - σχύ - ϊ δε - δό - ξα - σται
(3)
Ἄ - σω - μεν λα - οὶ
(4)
προ - θύ - μως δεῦ - τε γη - γε - νεῖς, τῇ καρ - δί - ᾳ
(5)
Τῷ δι - α - βι - βά - σαν - τι
(6)
Κα - τα - βή - τω ὡς δρό - σος
(7)
Ὁ μό - νος εἰ - δὼς τῆς τῶν βρο - τῶν,
(8)
Δεῦ - τε πό - μα πί - ω - μεν και - νόν, . .
(9)
Στε - ρέ - ω - σόν μου τὸν νοῦν
(10)
Ῥάβ - δος ἐκ τῆς ῥί - ζης Ἰ - εσ - σαὶ

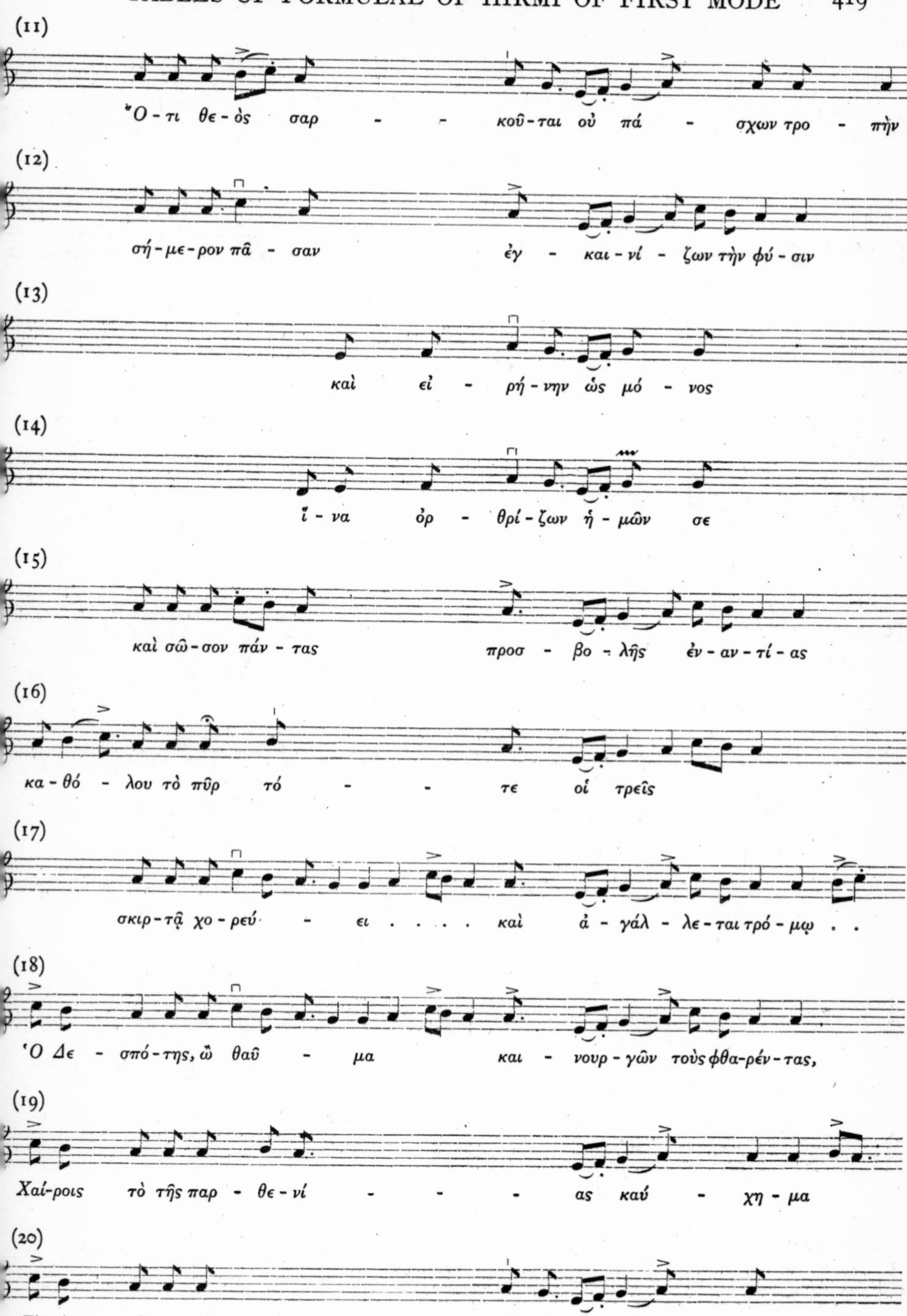
(11)
Ὅ - τι θε - ὸς σαρ - - κοῦ - ται οὐ πά - σχων τρο - πὴν
(12)
σή - με - ρον πᾶ - σαν ἐγ - και - νί - ζων τὴν φύ - σιν
(13)
καὶ εἰ - ρή - νην ὡς μό - νος
(14)
ἵ - να ὀρ - θρί - ζων ἡ - μῶν σε
(15)
καὶ σῶ - σον πάν - τας προσ - βο - λῆς ἐν - αν - τί - ας
(16)
κα - θό - λου τὸ πῦρ τό - - τε οἱ τρεῖς
(17)
σκιρ - τᾷ χο - ρεύ - ει . . . . . καὶ ἀ - γάλ - λε - ται τρό - μῳ . .
(18)
Ὁ Δε - σπό - της, ὢ θαῦ - μα και - νουρ - γῶν τοὺς φθα-ρέν - τας,
(19)
Χαί-ροις τὸ τῆς παρ - θε - νί - - - ας καύ - χη - μα
(20)
Σὲ τὴν οὐ - ρα - νῶν ὑ - ψη - λο - τέ - ραν

B
Cod. Saba
(1)
ὁ - δοὶ βυ-θοῦ και-νουρ-γή - σα - σα.
(2)
ἐ-πι-νί - κι - ον ᾆ-σμα Χρι-στῷ . . τῷ Θε-ῷ
(3)
τῷ θαυ - μα - στῷ Σω - τῆ - ρι, ὅ - τι δε - δό - ξα - σται
(4)
ἐ - πι - νί - κι - ον, ὅ - τι δε - δό - ξα - σται
(5)
τὸν σταυ - ρόν σου τὴν ὑ - γρὰν τῇ ῥάβ - δῳ τε - μὼν
(6)
ἀν - υ - μνή - σα - τε, λα - οί, ὅ - τι δε - δό - ξα - σται.
(7)
βρα - χί - ο - νι ὑ - ψη - λῷ ὅ - τι δε - δό - ξα - σται.
(8)
τῇ λυ - τρω - τῇ χει - ρί σου ἀ - να - μέλ - πον - τι.
(9)
ᾄ - σω - μεν ὅ - τι δε - δό - ξα - σται.
(10)
ἐν ἀ-γαλ-λι-ά - σει· οἱ πι - στοὶ ὅ - τι δε - δό - ξα - σται.

(11)
ἐν - το - λῶν στή - ρι - ζόν με Δέ - σπο - τα.
(12)
ἵ - να ὑ - μνῶ τὴν σὴν ἀ - γα - θό - τη - τα.
(13)
ἐν Κυ - ρί - ῳ Θε - ῷ στε - ρε - ού - με - νος.
(14)
δό - ξα τῇ δυ - νά - μει σου, Κύ - ρι - ε.
(15)
καὶ γὰρ ἐ - πλή - σθη ἡ γῆ
(16)
δό - ξα τῇ δυ - νά - μει σου.
(17)
καὶ ἡ σε - λή - νη ἔ - στη ἐν τῇ τά . . ξει αὐ - τῆς
(18)
καὶ με - τὰ βό - λου ἐ - δό - ξα - σά . . σε σω - τήρ.
(19)
Ἀβ - βα - κοὺμ προ - θε - ω - ρή - σας, Χρι - στέ . . .
(20)
δό - ξα τῇ δυ - νά - μει σου.
(21)
φα - ει - νὸν ἀ - να - τεί - λας ἡ - μῖν.

C
(1)
Cod. Saba
ἐκ θα - νά - του καὶ φθο - ρᾶς ἐ - λευ - θε - ρώ - σαν - τι.
(2)
ἐν - δό - - ξως, ὅ - τι δε - δό - ξα - σται.
(3)
- τε Πα - τρὶ καὶ βρο - τοῖς δο - ξά - ζο - μεν.
(4)
Ἄ - σω - μεν τῷ Κυ - ρί - ῳ ᾆ - σμα και - νὸν . .
(5)
οὐ - ρα - νέ, καὶ λα - λή - σω καὶ ἀν - υ - μνή - σω Χρι - στὸν
(6)
Ὁ ἱ - ε - ρὸς . . Ἀβ - βα - κοὺμ
(7)
Τῆς σῆς αἰ - νέ - σε - ως.
(8)
με - λῳ - δοὺς τῇ βά - σει τῆς πί - στε - ως.
(9)
σω - μα - τω - θεὶς . . ἀν - έ - τει - λας ἥ - - λι - ος.
(10)
φιλ - άν-θρω - πε Χρι - στέ, ὁ Θε - ὸς ἡ - μῶν.

D

(1)
Cod. Saba
Ἀ - να - - στά - σε - ως ἡ - μέ - ρα λαμ - πρυν - θῶ - μεν λα - οί . .
(2)
Ὁ θει - ό - τα - τος προ - ε - τύ - πω - σε πά - - λαι Μωυ - σῆς . .
(3)
ἡ - μᾶς δι - ε - βί - βα - σεν ἐ - πι - νί - κι - ον ᾆ . . . δον - τας.
(4)
Χρι - στὸς γεν - νᾶ - ται δο - ξά - σα - τε
(5)
πα - ρα - δό - ξως τοὺς υἱ - οὺς . . . . Ἰσ - ρα - ὴλ . . .
(6)
Στε - ρέ - ω - σόν . . με, Χρι - στὲ
(7)
ὅ - τι ἀν - έ - στη Χρι - στὸς ὡς παν - το - δύ - - να - μος.
(8)
Τὸ θεῖ - ον καὶ ἄρ - ρη - τον κάλ - - λος
(9)
Θε - ὸς ὢν εἰ - ρή - νης πα - τὴρ . . . οἰ - κτιρ - μῶν . .

E
(1)
Cod. Iviron
Ὠ - δὴν ἐ - πι - νί - κι - ον ᾄ - σω - μεν πάν - τες,
(2)
Ἴ - δε - τε, ἴ - δε - τε ὅ.- τι αὐ - τὸς ἐ - γώ εἰ - μι,
(3)
ὁ δου - λω - θέν - τα τὸν λα - - - ὸν τοῦ Ἰσραήλ,
(4)
Λί - θον ὃν ἀπ - ε - δο - κί - μα - σαν οἱ οἰ - κο - δο - μοῦν - τες,
(5)
Τὸν προ - φή - την Ἰ - ω - νᾶν ἐκ - μι - μού - με - νος βο - ῶ· . .
(6)
τὴν ζω - ήν μου ἀ - γα - θέ, ἐ - λευ - θέ - ρωσον φθορᾶς,
(7)
ταῖς τρι - κυ - μί - αις κατ - αν - τλού - με - νος τῶν πα - θῶν κλυ - δω - νί - ζο - μαι
(8)
. . . . τού - τους, ὑ - μνεῖ - τε . . Κύ - ρι - ον, . . .
(9)
Χρι - στὸς . . . ὁ Θε - ὸς ἡ - μᾶς δι - ε - βί - βα - σεν
(10)
εἰ - ρή - νην παρ - ε - χό - - με - νον, ἀπ - έ - στει - λας ἡ - μῖν. . . .

F

(1) *Cod. Iviron*

καὶ σώ-σαν - τι τὸν Ἰσ - ρα - ήλ, ὅ - τι δε - δό - ξα - σται.

(2)

ἣν ἐξ ἐ - θνῶν ἐξ - η - γο - ρά - σα - το.

(3)

Εὐ - λο - γη - τὸς ὁ Θε - ὸς ὁ τῶν πα - τέ - ρων ἡ - μῶν.

(4)

ἅ - γι - ος γὰρ πλὴν σοῦ φιλ-άν - θρω - πε·

(5)

ἐκ φθο - ρᾶς τὴν ζω - ήν μου, Κύ - ρι - ε.

(6)

ὁ Θε - ὸς ὃν ἀν - υ - μνοῦν - τες με - γα - λύ - νο - μεν.

(7)

- τε Πα - τρὶ καὶ βρο - τοῖς δο - ξά - ζο - μεν·

(8)

τοῦ ἀ - εὶ . . . με - γα - λύ - νειν σοί.

(9)

ἐξ - ῆλ - θε λα - ῶν εἰς ἀ - νά-πλα - σιν Λό - γος.

G

Media and finalis

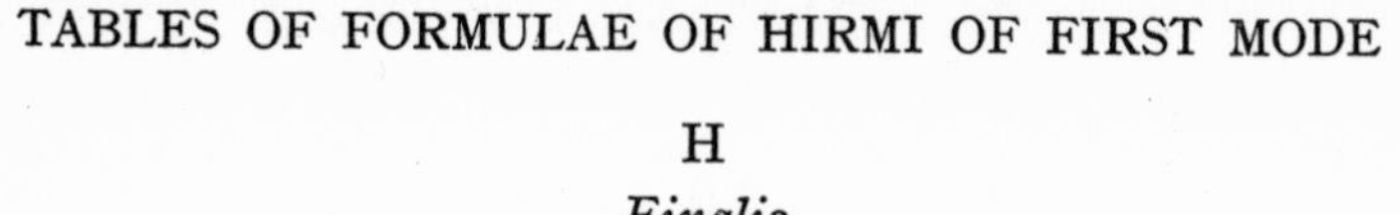

H

Finalis

(11) *Cod. Iviron*

ᾠ - δὴν ἐ - πι - νί - κι - ον, ὅ - τι δε - δό - ξα - σται.

(12)

ὁ Θε - ὸς ὃν ἀν - υ - μνοῦν-τες με-γα - λύ - νω - μεν.

(13)

οὐκ ἔ-στιν ἅ - γι - - - - ος πλὴν σοῦ, φιλ - άν - θρω - πε.

(14)

ὅ - τι τὸ ὄ - νο - - - - μα Κυ - ρί - ου ἐ - κά - λε - σα.

(15)

καὶ ἀν - υ - μνή - σω τὸν ἐκ παρ - - θέ - νου σαρ-κω - θέν - τα Θε - ὸν . . ἡ - μῶν.

(16)

καὶ ἐν σοὶ ἐ - - - στε - ρε - ώ - θη ἡ καρ - δί - α μου.

(17)

δό - ξα τῇ δυ - νά - μει σου, Κύ - ρι - ε.

(18)

θε - ο - τό - κε Μα - ρί - α, με - γα - λύ - νω - μεν.

(19)

καὶ συμ - φώ - νως ἐν αἰ - νέ - σει με - γα - λύ - νω - μεν.

(20)

καὶ ταύ - την στε - ρέ - ω - σον ὡς παν - το - δύ - να - μος.

(21)

ἀν - ά - γα - - γε ἐκ φθο - ρᾶς τὴν ζω - ὴν ἡ - μῶν.

BIBLIOGRAPHY

THE following list of books and articles is intended to provide an introduction to the study of Byzantine musical palaeography, to the method of transcribing, and to Byzantine hymnography. Special reference is made to books on Greek and Byzantine palaeography which contain facsimiles of the ecphonetic and musical notation.

In addition a list is given of manuscripts which have been used for the study of the various phases of Byzantine musical notation. Photographic copies of all these manuscripts are in the hands of the present author. For most of these I have to thank the Royal Danish Academy of Science and Letters; I owe the rest to the courtesy of the National Libraries of Paris, Athens, and Vienna and to the library of Grottaferrata.

I. BYZANTINE HISTORY AND CIVILIZATION

BARDY, G., *La Question des langues dans l'Église ancienne*, vol. i. Paris, 1948.

BAYNES, N. H., *The Byzantine Empire*. The Home University Library, vol. cxviii, London, 1925.

—— *Byzantine Studies and other Essays*. London, 1955.

BRÉHIER, L., *L'Église et l'Orient au moyen âge. Les Croisades*. 6me éd., Paris, 1928.

—— *La Civilisation byzantine*. Le Monde byzantin, vol. iii. Paris, 1950.

BURY, J. B., *A History of the Eastern Roman Empire* (A.D. *802–867*). London, 1912.

COTTAS, V., *Le Théâtre à Byzance*. Paris, 1931.

DALTON, O., *East Christian Art*. Oxford, 1925.

DEMUS, O., *Byzantine Mosaic Decoration*. London, 1948.

DE WALD, E. T., *The Illustrations in the MSS. of the Septuagint*, vol. iii, *Psalms and Odes*. Princeton, Part 1, 1941; Part 2, 1942.

DIEHL, C., *Histoire de l'empire byzantin*. Paris, 1919.

—— *Byzance: grandeur et décadence*. Paris, 1919.

—— *Manuel de l'art byzantin*. 2 vols., 2nd ed., Paris, 1925–6.

—— and MARÇAIS, G., *Le Monde oriental de 395 à 1081*. 2nd ed., Paris, 1944.

—— GUILLAND, R., OECONOMOS, L., and GROUSSET, R., *L'Europe orientale de 1018 à 1453*. Paris, 1945.

DVORNIK, F., *Les Slaves, Byzance et Rome*. Paris, 1926.

EVERY, G., *The Byzantine Patriarchate 451–1204*. London, 1947.

GAY, J., *L'Italie méridionale et l'empire byzantin*. Paris, 1904.

GRABAR, A., *Byzantine Painting*. Geneva, 1953.

GROUSSET, R., *L'Empire du Levant*. Paris, 1946.

HUSSEY, J. M., *Church and Learning in the Byzantine Empire 867–1185*. Oxford, 1937.

—— *The Byzantine World*. Hutchinson's University Library, London, 1957.

KRUMBACHER, K., *Geschichte der byzantinischen Literatur*. 2nd ed., Munich, 1897.

LA PIANA, G., *Le Rappresentazioni sacre nella letteratura bizantina dalle origini al sec. X*. Grottaferrata, 1912.

LA PIANA, G., 'The Byzantine Theater', *Speculum*, xi (1936), 171–211.

OSTROGORSKI, G., *History of the Byzantine State*. Translated by J. M. Hussey, Oxford, 1956.

PARGOIRE, J., *L'Église byzantine de 527 à 847*. Paris, 1905.

PUECH, A., *Histoire de la littérature grecque chrétienne depuis les origines jusqu'à la fin du IVe siècle*. 3 vols., Paris, 1930.

RAMBAUD, A., *L'Empire grec au Xe siècle*. Paris, 1870.

—— *Études sur l'histoire byzantine*. Paris, 1912.

RUNCIMAN, S., *The Emperor Romanus Lecapenus and his Reign*. Cambridge, 1929.

—— *A History of the first Bulgarian Empire*. London, 1930.

—— *Byzantine Civilization*. London, 1932.

—— *A History of the Crusades*. 3 vols., Cambridge, 1951–4.

SATHAS, K., *Ἱστορικὸν δοκίμιον περὶ τοῦ θεάτρου καὶ τῆς μουσικῆς τῶν Βυζαντινῶν*. Venice, 1878.

TALBOT, RICE, D., *Byzantine Art*. Oxford, 1935.

VASILIEV, A. A., *History of the Byzantine Empire*. 2nd ed., 2 vols., Wisconsin, 1958.

VOGT, A., *Le Théâtre à Byzance et dans l'empire du IVe au XIIIe siècle. I, Le Théâtre profane*. Bordeaux, 1932. (Offprint from *Revue des questions historiques*, lix (1931), 257–96.)

WEITZMANN, K., *Illustrations in Roll and Codex*. Princeton, 1947.

II. LITURGY

ALLATIUS, L., *De libris et rebus ecclesiasticis Graecorum dissertationes et observationes variae*. Paris, 1646.

Apostolos (*Ἀπόστολος*). Rome, 1882.

ASSEMANI, J. A., *Codex liturgicus ecclesiae universalis in XV libros distributus*. 13 vols., Rome, 1749–66. Reprint Paris–Leipzig, 1902.

ATTIÉ, A., *La Divine Liturgie de St Jean Chrysostome*. Harissa (Lebanon), 1926.

BAUMSTARK, A., *Die Messe im Morgenland. Sammlung Kösel*. Munich, 1906.

—— *Festbrevier und Kirchenjahr der syrischen Jakobiten*. Paderborn, 1910.

—— 'Das Alter der Peregrinatio Aetheriae', *O.C.*, N.S. i (1911), 32–76.

—— 'Das Typikon der Patmos-Handschrift 266 und die altkonstantinopolitanische Gottesdienstordnung', *J.L.* vi (1923), 98–111.

—— 'Denkmäler d. Entstehungsgeschichte des byzantinischen Ritus', *O.C.*, 3e Série, ii (1927), 1–32.

—— *Liturgie comparée*. Prieuré d'Amay, 1939.

BORGIA, N., '*Ὡρολόγιον*, Diurno delle chiese di rito bizantino', *O.C.* xvi. 153–254. Rome, 1929.

BRIGHTMAN, F. E., *Liturgies Eastern and Western* [, vol. i]: *Eastern Liturgies*. Oxford, 1896.

BROU, DOM L., 'Les Chants en langue grecque dans les liturgies latines', *Sacris Erudiri*, i (1948), 165–80; iv (1952), 226–38.

CABROL, F., *Les Origines liturgiques*. Paris, 1906.

CLUGNET, L., *Dictionnaire grec-français des noms liturgiques*. Paris, 1895.

CONYBEARE, F. C., *Rituale Armenorum*. Oxford, 1905.

COUTURIER, A., *Cours de liturgie grecque-melkite.* 3 vols., Jerusalem, 1912, 1914, 1930.

DANIEL, H. A., *Codex liturgicus ecclesiae universae in epitomen redactus.* 4 vols., Leipzig, 1853.

DELEHAYE, H., *Propylaeum ad Acta Sanctorum Novembris. Synaxarium Ecclesiae Constantinopolitanae.* Brussels, 1902 (reprint 1954).

—— 'Deux Typica byzantins de l'époque des Paléologues', *Académie R. de Belgique, Mémoires*, 2me série, tome xiii. Brussels, 1921.

DMITRIEVSKI, *Opisanie liturgicheskikh rukopisei*, vol. i, *Τυπικά.* Kiev, 1895; vol. ii, *Εὐχολόγια.* Kiev, 1901; vol. iii, *Τυπικά.* Leningrad, 1917.

DUCHESNE, L., *Origines du culte chrétien.* 5me éd., Paris, 1923. English translation: *Christian Worship, its Origin and Evolution.* London, 1931.

EUSTRATIADES, S., *Ἡ Θεοτόκος ἐν τῇ ὑμνογραφίᾳ.* Paris, 1930.

—— *Θεοτοκάριον.* Paris, 1931.

—— *Εἱρμολόγιον.* Chennevières-sur-Marne, 1932.

FORTESCUE, A., *The Orthodox Church.* London, 1911.

GLAUE, P., *Die Vorlesung heiliger Schriften im Gottesdienst*, vol. i. Leipzig, 1907.

GOAR, J., *Εὐχολόγιον sive Rituale Graecorum.* Paris, 1647; 2nd ed., Venice, 1730.

GOUSSEN, H., 'Über georgische Drucke und Handschriften die Festordnung u. den Heiligenkalender des altchristlichen Jerusalems betreffend', *Liturgie und Kunst*, Band iv (1923), 3–47.

HARNACK, A., 'Über den Ursprung des Lektorates'. *Texte u. Untersuchungen*, ii. 5. Leipzig, 1886.

Heirmologion (*Εἱρμολόγιον*). Cf. Eustratiades.

HÖEG, C., and ZUNTZ, G., 'Remarks on the Prophetologion', *Quantulacumque: Studies presented to Kirsopp Lake*, pp. 189–226. London, 1937.

Horologion (*Ὡρολόγιον*). Rome, 1937.

JANIN, R., *Les Églises orientales et les rites orientaux.* Paris, 1926.

KLUGE, T., and BAUMSTARK, A., 'Quadragesima und Karwoche Jerusalems im siebten Jahrhundert', *O.C.*, N.S. v (1915), 201–33.

LANGFORD-JAMES, R. LL., *A Dictionary of the Eastern Orthodox Church.* London, 1923.

MAXIMILIAN OF SAXONY, PRINCE, *Praelectiones de liturgiis orientalibus.* 2 vols., Freiburg i. Br., 1908–13.

MEESTER, P. DE, 'Liturgies grecques', in *D.A.C.L.*, vol. vi, cols. 1591–1662.

—— *Officio dell' Inno Acatisto* [Greek-Italian]. Rome, 1903.

—— 'L'Inno acatisto', *Bessarione*, Ser. II, vols. vi and vii (1904).

Menaia (*Μηναῖα τοῦ ὅλου ἐνιαυτοῦ*). 6 vols., Rome, 1888–1902.

MERCENNIER, F., and PARIS, F., *La Prière des Églises de rite byzantin.* Prieuré d'Amay, vol. i, 1937; vol. ii. 1, 1939; ii. 2, 1948.

NEALE, J. M., *A History of the Holy Eastern Church.* Part I, General Introduction. 2 vols., London, 1850.

NILLES, N., *Kalendarium Manuale.* 2 vols., Innsbruck, 1896–7.

OESTERLEY, W. O. E., *The Jewish Background of the Christian Liturgy.* Oxford, 1925.

Papadopoulos-Kerameus, A., *Ἀνάλεκτα Ἱεροσολυμιτικῆς σταχυολογίας*, vol. ii. St. Petersburg, 1894.

Pentekostarion. Rome, 1883.

Peradze, G., and Baumstark, A., 'Die Weihnachtsfeier Jerusalems im siebten Jahrhundert', *O.C.*, Serie III, vol. i, pp. 310–18.

Pétré, H., *Éthérie, Journal de voyage*, Sources chrétiennes. Paris, 1948.

Pitra, J.-B., *Juris ecclesiastici graeci historia et monumenta*. Paris, 1868.

Raes, A., *Introductio in Liturgiam Orientalem*. Rome, 1947.

Rahlfs, A., 'Die alttestamentlichen Lektionen der griechischen Kirche', *Nachrichten d. kgl. Gesellschaft der Wissenschaften zu Göttingen, Philol.-Hist. Kl.*, 1916.

Salaville, S., *An Introduction to the Study of Eastern Liturgies*. London, 1938.

Schermann, T., 'Ägyptische Abendmahlsliturgien d. ersten Jahrtausends.' *Studien zur Geschichte u. Kultur des Abendlandes*, vi, fasc. 1/2. Paderborn, 1912.

—— 'Die allgemeine Kirchenordnung, frühchristliche Liturgien u. kirchliche Überlieferung', 3 vols., ibid., 3. Ergänzungsband, vol. i, 1914; vol. ii, 1915; vol. iii, 1916.

Schneider, H., 'Die biblischen Oden', *Biblica*, xxx (1949), 28–65, 239–72, 433–52, 479–500.

Swainson, C. A., *The Greek Liturgies chiefly from Original Authorities*. Cambridge, 1884.

Thibaut, J.-B., *La Liturgie romaine*. Paris, 1924.

—— *Ordre des Offices de la Semaine Sainte à Jérusalem du IVe au Xe siècle*. Paris, 1926.

Trempelas, P. N., *Αἱ τρεῖς Λειτουργίαι κατὰ τοὺς ἐν Ἀθήναις κώδικας*. Athens, 1935.

—— *Μικρὸν Εὐχολόγιον*, Athens, vol. i, 1950; vol. ii, 1955.

Triodion. Rome, 1879.

First printed editions of the Byzantine books for the Holy Service: *Psalter*, Venice, 1485; *Horologion*, Venice, 1509; *Oktoechos*, Rome, 1520; *Parakletike*, Venice, 1522; *Triodion*, Venice, 1522; *The Divine Liturgies*, Venice, 1526; *Euchologion*, Venice, 1526; *Apostolos*, Venice, 1542; *Pentekostarion*, Venice, 1544; *Typikon*, Venice, 1545; *Menaia*, Venice, 1548; *Evangeliarion*, Venice, 1550; *Hirmologion*, Venice, 1568; *Anthologion*, Venice, 1587.

In the middle of the nineteenth century B. Koutloumousianus prepared a revised edition of the liturgical books, which was published partly at Venice, partly at Constantinople. Recently a new edition of the liturgical books has been produced at Athens, published by M. Saliveros.

The most convenient edition of the liturgical books for the use of scholars is that published by the 'Propaganda' in Rome: *Εὐχολόγιον μέγα*, 1873; *Ὡρολόγιον τὸ μέγα περιέχον τὴν πρέπουσαν αὐτῷ ἀκολουθίαν*, 1876; *Τριῴδιον κατανυκτικὸν περιέχον ἅπασαν τὴν ἀνήκουσαν αὐτῷ ἀκολουθίαν τῆς ἁγίας καὶ μεγάλης Τεσσαρακοστῆς*, 1879; *Πεντηκοστάριον χαρμόσυνον τὴν ἀπὸ τοῦ Πάσχα μέχρι τῆς τῶν ἁγίων πάντων κυριακῆς ἀνήκουσαν αὐτῷ ἀκολουθίαν περιέχον, ἐπὶ τέλους δὲ καὶ τὰ ἑωθινὰ εὐαγγέλια τὰ ἐν τῷ ὄρθρῳ ἑκάστης τῶν ἐν τῷ μεταξὺ τούτων ἑορτῶν ἀναγιγνωσκόμενα*, 1889; *Παρακλητικὴ ἤτοι Ὀκτώηχος ἡ μεγάλη περιέχουσα πᾶσαν τὴν ἀνήκουσαν αὐτῇ ἀκολουθίαν μετὰ τῶν ἐν τῷ τέλει συνηθῶν προσθηκῶν*, 1885; *Μηναῖα τοῦ ὅλου ἐνιαυτοῦ*, 6 vols., 1888–1901.

A critical edition of the *Lectionaria* was started in 1939 under the editorship of C. Höeg and S. Lake as a supplement to the *M.M.B.*: vol. i, *Prophetologium*, fasc. i, *Lectiones Nativitatis et Epiphaniae*; fasc. ii, *Lectiones hebd. primae et secundae quadrag.*; fasc. iii, *Lectiones hebd. 3ae et 4ae quadr.*; ed. C. Höeg and G. Zuntz, *M.M.B.*, Copenhagen, 1939–52.

III. HYMNOGRAPHY

AUBRY, P., *Le Rhythme tonique dans la poésie liturgique et dans le chant des Églises chrétiennes au moyen âge.* Paris, 1903.

BAUMSTARK, A., *Die christlichen Literaturen des Ostens. Sammlung Göschen.* 2 vols., Leipzig, 1911.

—— 'Psalmenvortrag und Kirchendichtung des Orients', *Gottesminne*, vii (1912), 290–305, 413–32, 540–58, 887–902.

—— 'Hymns (Greek, Christian)' in Hastings's *Encycl. of Rel. and Ethics*, vol. vii.

—— *Geschichte der syrischen Literatur.* Bonn, 1922.

BONNER, C., 'The Homily on the Passion by Melito Bishop of Sardis', *Studies and Documents*, ed. by K. and S. Lake, vol. xii. London, 1940.

BOUVY, É., *Poètes et Mélodes. Étude sur les origines du rhythme tonique dans l'hymnographie de l'Église grecque.* Nîmes, 1886.

CAMMELLI, G., 'L'Inno per la Natività di Romano il Melode', *Studi Bizantini*, pp. 43–58. Rome, 1925.

—— *Romano il Melode: Inni.* Florence, 1930.

CANTARELLI, R., *Poeti bizantini.* 2 vols., Milan, 1948.

CARPENTER, M., 'The Origin and Influence of the Christmas Kontakion of Romanos', in *Harvard Studies in Classical Philology*, 1930, pp. 190–1.

—— *Romanos and the Mystery Play of the East.* University of Missouri Studies, xi. 3. 1936.

CHRIST, W., 'Über die Bedeutung von Hirmos, Troparion und Kanon in der griechischen Poesie des Mittelalters'. *Sb.B.A.* 1870, ii. 76 sqq.

—— and PARANIKAS, M., *Anthologia graeca carminum christianorum.* Leipzig, 1871.

DEL GRANDE, C., *L'Inno acatisto in onore della Madre di Dio*, Florence, 1948.

ÉMEREAU, C., *Saint Éphrem le Syrien.* Paris, 1919.

—— 'Hymnographi byzantini', *E.O.* 1922–6.

—— 'Acathisti auctor', *E.O.* xxi (1922), 259–63.

GASSISI, S., 'Innografi italo-greci. Poesie di S. Nilo juniore e di Paolo monaco, abati di Grottaferrata', *O.C.* v (1905), 26–81.

GRIMME, H., 'Der Strophenbau in den Gedichten Ephraems des Syrers', *Collect. Friburg.* ii. Fribourg, 1893.

HANDSCHIN, J., 'Das Zeremonienwerk Kaiser Konstantins und die sangbare Dichtung', *Rektoratsprogramm d. Universitat Basel für 1940 u. 41.*

HUGLO, DOM M., 'L'Ancienne Version latine de l'hymne acathiste', *Muséon*, tome lxiv (1951), 27–61.

JACOBI, L., 'Zur Geschichte des griechischen Kirchenliedes', *Zeitschrift für Kirchengeschichte*, herausgeg. von Th. Brieger, v (1882), 177–250.

KIRCHHOFF, K., *Simeon, Licht vom Licht. Hymnen.* Hellerau, 1930; 2nd ed., 1951.

KIRCHHOFF, K., *Die Ostkirche betet. Hymnen aus den Tagzeiten der byzantinischen Kirche.* 4 vols., Hellerau, 1934–7.
—— *Osterjubel der Ostkirche.* 2 vols., Münster, 1940.
KRUMBACHER, K., 'Kasia', *Sb.B.A.* 1897, pp. 305–70.
—— 'Studien zu Romanos', ibid., 1898, ii. 69–269.
—— 'Umarbeitungen bei Romanos', ibid., 1899, pp. 1–156.
—— 'Romanos und Kyriakos', ibid., 1901, pp. 693–765.
—— 'Die Akrostichis in der griechischen Kirchenpoesie', ibid., 1903, pp. 561–691.
—— 'Miszellen zu Romanos', *Abh.B.A.* 1907, vol. xxiv. 3, pp. 1–138.
KRYPIAKIEWICZ, P. F., 'De Hymni Acathisti auctore', *B.Z.* xviii (1909), 357–82.
MAAS, P., 'Das Kontakion', *B.Z.* xix (1910), 285–306.
—— *Frühbyzantinische Kirchenpoesie.* Kleine Texte für Theologie und Philologie, nos. 52–3, Bonn, 1910.
—— 'Das Weihnachtslied des Romanos', *B.Z.* xxiv (1923–4), 1–13.
MEYER, W. (SPEYER), 'Anfang und Ursprung der lateinischen und griechischen rhythmischen Dichtung', *Abh.B.A.* 1884, vol. xvii. 2, pp. 267–450.
—— 'Pitra, Mone und die byzantinische Strophik', *Sb.B.A.* 1896, pp. 49–66.
MIONI, E., *Romano il Melode.* Turin, 1937.
MONE, F. J., *Lateinische Hymnen des Mittelalters.* 3 vols., Freiburg, 1853–5.
NEALE, J. M., *Hymns of the Eastern Church.* 2nd ed., London, 1863.
PAPADOPOULOS-KERAMEUS, A., '*Ὁ Ἀκάθιστος ὕμνος, οἱ Ῥῶς καὶ ὁ Πατριάρχης Φώτιος*', *Βιβλιοθήκη Μαρασλῆ*, vol. ccxiv. Athens, 1903.
PITRA, J.-B., *L'Hymnographie de l'Église grecque.* Rome, 1867.
—— *Analecta sacra spicilegio Solesmensi parata*, vol. i. Paris, 1876.
STEVENSON, E., 'Du rhythme dans l'hymnographie de l'église grecque', *Revue des questions historiques*, xi (1876), 482–543.
THÉARVIC, M., 'Photius et l'Acathiste', *E.O.* vii (1904–5), 293–300.
TREMPELAS, P. N., *'Εκλογὴ ἑλληνικῆς ὀρθοδόξου ὑμνογραφίας.* Athens, 1949.
WELLESZ, E., 'Melito's Homily on the Passion: An Investigation into the Sources of Byzantine Hymnography', *J.T.S.* xliv (1943), 41–52.
WESSELY, C., 'Les plus anciens monuments du Christianisme écrits sur papyrus'. *Patrologia Orientalis*, Paris, tome iv (1906), pp. 99–210.
WEYH, W., 'Die Akrostichis in d. byzant. Kanonesdichtung', *B.Z.* xvii (1908), pp. 1–69.

IV. EARLY CHRISTIAN AND BYZANTINE MUSIC

ABERT, H., *Die Lehre vom Ethos in der griechischen Musik.* Leipzig, 1899.
—— *Die Musikanschauung des Mittelalters und ihre Grundlagen.* Leipzig, 1905.
—— 'Ein neuentdeckter frühchristlicher Hymnus mit antiken Musiknoten', *Z.M.W.* iv (1921–2), 524–9.
—— 'Das älteste Denkmal der christlichen Kirchenmusik', *Die Antike*, ii (1926), 282–90.
AUDA, A., *Les Modes et les tons de la musique.* Bruxelles, 1931.
BERTHELOT, M., and RUELLE, C. E., *Collection des anciens alchimistes grecs.* 3 vols. Paris, 1887–8.

BOURGAULT-DUCOUDRAY, L. A., *Études sur la musique ecclésiastique grecque.* Mission musicale en Grèce et en Orient, janvier–mai 1875. Paris, 1877.

CHRYSANTHOS OF MADYTOS, *Θεωρητικὸν μέγα τῆς μουσικῆς*. Trieste, 1832.

DÉVAI, G., 'The Musical Study of Cucuzeles in a Manuscript of Debrecen', *Acta Antiqua Academiae Scientiarum Hungaricae*, tom. iii, fasc. 1–2. Budapest, 1955.

DI SALVO, B., 'La Trascrizione della notazione paleobizantina.' (1) *Bolletino della Badia greca di Grottaferrata*, iv (1950), 114–30; (2) ibid., v (1951), 92–110; (3) ibid., pp. 220–35.

—— 'Qualche appunto sulla chironomia nella musica bizantina', *Orientalia christiana periodica*, xxiii (1957), 192–201.

FLEISCHER, O., *Die spätgriechische Notenschrift. Neumenstudien*, iii. Berlin, 1904.

GAISSER, H., *Le Système musical de l'église grecque d'après la tradition.* Rome, 1901.

—— 'Les "Heirmoi" de Pâques dans l'Office grec', *Étude rythmique et musicale. O.C.* iii (1903). Offprint Rome, 1905.

—— 'L'Origine du "tonus peregrinus" ', in *Documents, mémoires et vœux du Congrès intern. d'histoire de la musique*, pp. 93–100. Paris, 1901.

—— 'L'Origine et la vraie nature du mode dit "chromatique oriental" ', ibid., pp. 93–100.

—— 'Die Antiphon "Nativitas tua" und ihr griechisches Vorbild', *Riemann Festschrift*, pp. 154–66. Leipzig, 1909.

GASTOUÉ, A., *Les Origines du chant romain. L'Antiphonaire grégorien.* Paris, 1907.

—— *Introduction à la paléographie musicale byzantine. Catalogue des MSS. de musique byzantine.* Paris, 1907.

—— 'La Tradition ancienne dans le chant byzantin', *T.S.G.*, vol. v, 1899.

—— 'L'Origine du "Tonus Peregrinus" ', ibid., vol. vii, 1901.

—— 'Note sur les chants de l'Église grecque', ibid., vol. viii, 1902.

—— 'Über die 8 "Töne", die authentischen und die plagalen', *Kirchenmusikalisches Jahrbuch*, Bd. xxv (1930), pp. 25–30.

—— 'L'Importance musicale, liturgique et philologique du MS. Hagiopolite', *B.* 1930.

GÉROLD, TH., *Les Pères de l'Église et la musique.* Paris, 1931.

GOMBOSI, O., 'Studien zur Tonartenlehre des frühen Mittelalters', *A.M.*, vols. x–xi (1928–9).

HÖEG, C., *La Notation ekphonétique. M.M.B. Subsidia*, i. 2. Copenhagen, 1935.

—— 'La Théorie de la musique byzantine', *R.É.G.* xxxv (1922), 321–34.

—— *Musik og Digtning i Byzantinsk Kristendom.* Copenhagen, 1955.

—— 'Introduction' to, and 'Index Canonum' of *Hirmologium Athoum, M.M.B. Ser. Facsimilia.* ii. Copenhagen, 1938, pp. 5–28.

—— 'Introduction' to *Contacarium Ashburnhamense*, ibid. iv. Copenhagen, 1956, pp. 5–47.

—— 'The Oldest Slavonic Tradition of Byzantine Music', *Proceedings of the British Academy*, London, 1953, pp. 37–66, 4 Plates.

—— 'Les Rapports de la musique chrétienne et de la musique de l'antiquité classique', *B.*, t. xxv–xxvii (1955–7), fasc. 2, Brussels, 1958, pp. 383–412.

HUNT, A. S., 'A Christian Hymn with Musical Notation', in *Oxyrhynchus Papyri*, Part xv, no. 1786, with a transcript of the music by H. Stuart Jones.

IDELSOHN, A. Z., *Jewish Music in its Historical Development*. New York, 1929 (reprinted 1944).

—— 'Die Maqamen der arabischen Musik', *S.I.M.* xv (1913–14), 1–63.

—— 'Parallelen zwischen gregorianischen und hebräisch-orientalischen Gesangsweisen', *Z.M.W.* iv (1922), 515–24.

—— 'Der Kirchengesang der Jakobiten', *Archiv für Musikwissenschaft*, iv (1922).

JEANNIN, J., 'Le Chant syrien', *Journal asiatique*, 1912, pp. 295–363 and 389–448.

—— and PUYADE, J., 'L'Octoëchos syrien', *O.C.*, N.S. iii (1913), 82–104, 277–98.

—— PUYADE, J., and LASSALLE, A. CH., *Mélodies liturgiques syriennes et chaldéennes*. 2 vols., 1924.

LAILY, P.-A., 'Analyse du Codex de musique grecque no. 19, Bibliothèque Vaticane (fonds Borgia)', *Publications musicales byzantines, Séminaire Sainte-Anne, Jérusalem*. Harissa, 1949.

MERLIER, M., *Études de musique byzantine. Le premier mode et son plagal*. Paris, 1935.

PALIKAROVA VERDEIL, MME R., *La Musique byzantine chez les Bulgares et les Russes (du IXe au XIVe siècle)*. *M.M.B. Subsidia*, vol. iii. Copenhagen, 1953.

PAPADOPOULOS, G., *Συμβολαὶ εἰς τὴν ἱστορίαν τῆς παρ' ἡμῖν ἐκκλησιαστικῆς μουσικῆς*. Athens, 1890.

—— *Ἱστορικὴ ἐπισκόπησις τῆς Βυζαντινῆς ἐκκλησιαστικῆς μουσικῆς*. Athens, 1904.

PAPADOPOULOS-KERAMEUS, A., '*Βυζαντινῆς ἐκκλησιαστικῆς μουσικῆς ἐγχειρίδια*,' *B.Z.* iv (1899), 111–21.

PARISOT, J., *Rapport sur une mission scientifique en Turquie d'Asie*. Paris, 1899.

—— *Rapport sur une mission scientifique en Turquie et Syrie*. Paris, 1902.

—— 'Essai sur le chant liturgique des Églises orientales', *R.O.C.* 1898, pp. 221–32.

—— 'Les Huit Modes du chant syrien', *T.S.G.* 1901, pp. 259 sqq.

PETRESCO, J. D., *Les Idiomèles et le canon de l'Office de Noël*. Paris, 1932.

POIRÉE, E., 'Chant des sept voyelles', *Documents du Congrès intern. d'histoire de la musique*. Paris, 1901, pp. 28–38.

PSACHOS, K. A., '*Η παρασημαντικὴ τῆς Βυζαντινῆς μουσικῆς*. Athens, 1917.

QUASTEN, J., 'Musik und Gesang in den Kulten der heidnischen Antike und christlichen Frühzeit', *Liturgiegeschichtliche Quellen und Forschungen*, Heft 25. Münster, 1930.

REBOURS, J.-B., *Traité de psaltique. Théorie et pratique du chant dans l'Église grecque*. Paris, 1906.

—— 'Quelques manuscrits de musique byzantine', *R.O.C.* 1904–5.

REESE, G., *Music in the Middle Ages*, ch. iii, pp. 57–91, and Bibliography. London, 1941.

REINACH, TH., *La Musique grecque*. Paris, 1926.

REINACH, TH., 'Une Ligne de musique byzantine', *Revue archéologique*, 1911.

—— 'Un Ancêtre de la musique de l'Église', *R.M.* iii. 8–25.

RIEMANN, H., *Die byzantinische Notenschrift im 10. bis 15. Jahrhundert.* Leipzig, 1909.

—— *Studien zur byzantinischen Musik.* Byzantinische Notenschrift, Neue Folge, Leipzig, 1915.

—— 'Die Martyrien der byzantinischen liturgischen Notation', *Sb.B.A.*, 1882.

—— 'Die Metrophonie der Papadiken', *S.I.M.* ix (1907–8), 1–31.

RUELLE, C. E., 'Le Chant gnostico-magique des sept voyelles grecques', *Documents du Congrès int. d'hist. de la musique*, Paris, 1901, pp. 15–27.

—— 'Le Chant des sept voyelles grecques d'après Démétrius et le papyrus de Leyde', *R.É.G.* ii (1889), 38–44.

SIMONETTI, M., 'Studi sull' innologia popolare cristiana dei primi secoli', *Atti d. Accad. Naz. dei Lincei, Memorie*, Ser. VIII, vol. iv, fasc. 6. Rome, 1952.

STRUNK, O., 'The Tonal System of Byzantine Music', *The Musical Quarterly*, xxviii (1942), 190–204.

—— 'Intonations and Signatures of the Byzantine Modes', ibid. xxxi (1945), 339–55.

—— 'St. Gregory Nazianzus and the Proper hymns for Easter', *Late Classical and Medieval Studies.* Princeton, 1955.

—— 'The Notation of the Chartres fragment', *Annales Musicologiques*, tome iii, Paris, 1955, pp. 7–37.

—— 'The Byzantine Office at Hagia Sophia', *Dumbarton Oaks Papers*, IX and X, Cambridge (Mass.), 1956, pp. 175–202.

TARDO, L., *L'Antica melurgia bizantina.* Grottaferrata, 1938.

—— 'La Musica bizantina e i codici di melurgia della Biblioteca di Grottaferrata', *Accademie e Bibl. d'Italia.* Rome, 1931.

—— 'I codici melurgici della Vaticana e il contributo alla musica bizantina del monachismo greco della Magna Grecia', *Archivio stor. per la Calabria e la Lucania*, i (1931), 1–24.

—— *'Η Βυζαντινὴ μουσική.* Athens, 1933.

—— *Hirmologium Cryptense E γ II*, Facs. ed., *M.M.B.*, vol. iii, ed. L. T., Rome, 1950; *Index Hirmorum*, 1951.

THIBAUT, J.-B., *Origine byzantine de la notation neumatique de l'Église latine.* Paris, 1907.

—— *Monuments de la notation ekphonétique et hagiopolite de l'Église grecque.* St-Pétersbourg, 1913.

—— *Le Panégyrique de l'Immaculée dans les chants hymnographiques de la liturgie grecque.* Paris, 1909.

—— 'La Notation de Saint Jean Damascène ou Hagiopolite', *Izvestija russk. archeol. Instituta Konstantinop.* iii. 138–79. Sofia, 1898.

—— 'La Musique byzantine et le chant liturgique des Grecs modernes', *E.O.* ii (1898), 353–68.

—— 'Étude de musique byzantine. Le chant ekphonétique', *B.Z.* viii (1899), 122–47.

THIBAUT, J.-B., 'La Notation de Saint Jean Damascène', *Vizant. Vremmenik*, vi, 1–12. St-Pétersbourg, 1899.

—— 'La Musique byzantine', *T.S.G.* 1898.

—— 'Les Traités de musique byzantine', *B.Z.* ix (1900), 479–82.

—— 'Étude de musique byzantine. La notation de Koukouzélès', *Izvest. russk. archeol. Instit. Konst.* vi (1900), 361–90; Sofia 1900.

—— 'Assimilation des "Echoi" byzantins et des modes latins avec les anciens tropes grecs', *Documents du Congrès intern. d'hist. de la musique*, Paris, 1901, pp. 77–85.

—— 'Les Notations byzantines', ibid., pp. 86–92.

—— 'Les Orgues à Byzance', *Revue d'hist. et de critique music.* i (1901), 17 sqq.

—— 'Les Notations byzantines', ibid., pp. 102 sqq.

—— 'Le Système tonal de l'Église grecque', ibid. ii (1902), 43 sqq.

—— 'La Musique byzantine chez les Slaves', *T.S.G.* x (1904), 157–62.

—— 'La Musique byzantine', ibid. xiv, 1908.

TIBY, O., *La Musica bizantina. Teoria e storia.* Milan, 1938.

TILLYARD, H. J. W., *Byzantine Music and Hymnography.* London, 1923.

—— *Handbook of the Middle Byzantine Notation, M.M.B. Subsidia*, vol. i, fasc. i. Copenhagen, 1935.

—— *The Hymns of the Sticherarium for November, M.M.B. Transcripta*, vol. ii. Copenhagen, 1938.

—— *The Hymns of the Octoechus*; Part I, *M.M.B.*, vol. iii, 1940; Part II, vol. v, 1952.

—— *Twenty Canons from the Trinity Hirmologium, M.M.B.*, Amer. Ser. 2. Copenhagen, 1952.

—— *The Hymns of the Hirmologium*, Part III. 2, transcribed by Aglaïa Ayoutanti; revised and annotated by H. J. W. Tillyard, *M.M.B. Transcripta*, vol. viii. Copenhagen, 1956.

—— 'Greek Church Music', *The Musical Antiquary*, ii (1911), 80–98, 154–80.

—— 'Studies in Byzantine Music', ibid. iv. 202–22.

—— 'A Musical Study of the Hymns of Casia', *B.Z.* xx (1911), 420–85.

—— 'The Acclamation of Emperors in Byzantine Ritual', *A.B.S.* xviii (1911–12), 239–60.

—— 'Zur Entzifferung der byzantinischen Neumen', *Zeitschrift d. Int: Musikgesellschaft*, xv (1913), 32 sqq.

—— 'Fragment of a Byzantine Musical Handbook in the Monastery of Laura on Mt. Athos', *A.B.S.* xix (1912–13), 95–117.

—— 'Rhythm in Byzantine Music', ibid. xxi (1914–16), 125–47.

—— 'The Problem of Byzantine Neumes', *American Journal of Archaeology*, 1916, pp. 62 sqq.

—— 'The Modes in Byzantine Music', *A.B.S.* xxii (1916–18), 133–56.

—— 'Some Byzantine Musical MSS. at Cambridge', ibid. xxiii (1918–19), 194–204.

—— 'The Problem of Byzantine Neumes', *J.H.S.* xli (1921), 29–49.

—— 'Signatures and Cadences of the Byzantine Modes', *A.B.S.* xxvi (1923–5), 78–87.

TILLYARD, H. J. W., 'The Canon for Easter with Music from a Byzantine Hirmologus', *Laudate*, i (1923), 61–71.

—— 'The Stenographic Theory of Byzantine Music', *L.* ii (1924), 216–25; iii (1925), 28–32; and *B.Z.* xxv (1925), 333–8.

—— 'Byzantine Musical Notation—A Reply', *B.Z.* xxiv (1923–4), 320–8.

—— 'Some New Specimens of Byzantine Music', *A.B.S.* xxvii (1925–6), 151–72.

—— 'A Byzantine Musical Handbook at Milan', *J.H.S.* xlvi (1926), 219–22.

—— 'A Canon by Saint Cosmas', *B.Z.* xxviii (1928), 25–37.

—— 'The Stichera Anastasima in Byzantine Hymnody', ibid. xxxi (1931), 13–20.

—— 'The Morning Hymns of the Emperor Leo', *A.B.S.*, Part i, vol. xxx, pp. 86–108; ibid., Part ii, vol. xxxi, pp. 115–47.

—— 'Early Byzantine Neumes', *L.* viii (1930), 204–16.

—— 'Byzantine Music at the End of the Middle Ages', *L.* xi (1933), 141–51.

—— 'Early Byzantine Neumes: A New Principle of Decipherment', *L.* xiv (1936), 183–7.

—— 'Byzantine Neumes: The Coislin Notation', *B.Z.* xxxvii (1937), 345–58.

—— 'Monumenta Musicae Byzantinae: A Reply', *The Music Review*, iii (1942), 103–14.

—— 'The Stages of Early Byzantine Notation', *B.Z.* 1952, pp. 29–42.

—— 'Gegenwärtiger Stand der byzantinischen Musikforschung', *Die Musikforschung*, vii (1954), 142–9.

—— 'Recent Byzantine Studies', *Music & Letters*, xxxv (1954), 31–5.

—— 'Byzantine Music about A.D. 1100', *The Musical Quarterly*, xxxix (1953), 223–31.

—— 'The Byzantine Modes in the Twelfth Century', *A.B.S.* xlviii (1953), 182–90.

WACHSMANN, K., *Untersuchungen zum vorgregorianischen Gesang*. Regensburg, 1935.

WELLESZ, E., *Aufgaben und Probleme auf dem Gebiete der byzantinischen und orientalischen Kirchenmusik. Liturgiegeschichtliche Forschungen*, Heft 6. Münster i. W., 1923.

—— *Byzantinische Musik*. Breslau, 1927. (*Música Bizantina*, Barcelona, 1930, transl. by R. Gerhard.)

—— *Trésor de musique byzantine*. Paris, 1934.

—— *Die Hymnen des Sticherarium für September. M.M.B. Transcripta*, vol. i. Copenhagen, 1936.

—— *Eastern Elements in Western Chant. M.M.B.*, Amer. Ser., vol. i, 1947.

—— 'The Akathistos Hymn', introduced and transcribed. *M.M.B. Transcripta*, vol. ix. Copenhagen, 1957.

—— 'Fragen und Aufgaben musikalischer Orientforschung', *Oesterreich. Monatsschrift für den Orient*, 1914, pp. 332–4; 1915, pp. 88–90.

—— 'Byzantinische Musik', ibid., 1915, pp. 197–201.

—— 'Der Ursprung des altchristlichen Kirchengesanges', ibid., 1915, pp. 302–5.

—— 'Die Kirchenmusik im byzantinischen Reich', *O.C.*, N.S. vi (1916), 91–125.

WELLESZ, E., 'Die Erforschung des byzantinischen Hymnengesanges', *Zeitschrift für die oesterreich. Gymnasien*, 1917, pp. 6–38.

—— 'Die Entzifferung der byzant. Notenschrift', *O.C.*, N.S. vii (1918), 97–118.

—— 'Probleme der musikalischen Orientforschung', *Jahrbuch der Musikbibliothek Peters*, 1917, pp. 1–18.

—— 'Die Rhythmik der byzantinischen Neumen', *Z.M.W.* ii (1920), 617–38; iii. (1921), 321–36.

—— 'Beiträge zur byzantinischen Kirchenmusik', ibid. iii. 482–502.

—— 'Some Exotic Elements of Plainsong', *Music and Letters*, iv (1923), 275–81.

—— 'Byzantinische Musik', in G. Adler's *Handbuch der Musikgeschichte*, vol. i, 2nd ed., Berlin, 1929, pp. 126–36.

—— 'Die byzantinischen Lektionszeichen', *Z.M.W.* xi (1929), 513–34.

—— 'Ein griechisches Evangelium der Wiener Nationalbibliothek mit ekphonetischen Lesezeichen', *Kirchenmusikalisches Jahrbuch*, xxv (1930), 9–24.

—— 'Das Problem der byzantinischen Notationen und ihrer Entzifferung', *B.*, 1930, pp. 556–70.

—— 'Studien zur Palaeographie der byzantinischen Musik. i. Die prosodischen und die ekphonetischen Zeichen', *Z.M.W.* xii (1929–30), 385–97.

—— 'Die Epochen der byzantinischen Notenschrift', *O.C.* 1932, pp. 277–88.

—— 'Byzantine Music', *Proceedings of the Mus. Association*, 1932–3, pp. 1–22.

—— 'Studien zur byzantinischen Musik', *Z.M.W.* xvi (1934), 213–28, 414–22.

—— 'Über Rhythmus und Vortrag der byzantinischen Melodien (Eine musikpalaeographische Studie)', *B.Z.* xxxiii (1933), 33–66.

—— 'Der Stand der Forschung auf dem Gebiete der byzantinischen Kirchenmusik', *B.* xi (1936), 729–37.

—— 'The Earliest Example of Christian Hymnody', *The Classical Quarterly*, xxxix (1945), 34–45.

—— 'Words and Music in Byzantine Liturgy', *The Musical Quarterly*, xxxiii (1947), 297–310.

—— 'Kontakion and Kanon', *Atti del Congresso Internaz. di Musica Sacra*, Rome, 1952, pp. 131–3.

—— 'Early Byzantine Neumes', *The Musical Quarterly*, 1952, pp. 68–79.

—— 'Epilegomena zu den "Eastern Elements in Western Chant"', *Die Musikforschung*, v (1952), 131–7.

—— 'Notes on the Alleluia', *Kongressbericht d. Intern. Ges. für Musikwissenschaft*, Utrecht, 1952, pp. 423–7.

—— 'Das Prooemium des Akathistos', ibid. vi (1953), 193–206.

—— 'Early Christian Music', *N.O.H.M.*, ii (Oxford, 1954), 1–13.

—— 'Music of the Eastern Churches', ibid., pp. 14–52.

—— 'Byzantine Music and its Place in the Liturgy', *The Royal Musical Association*. London, 1954.

—— 'The "Akathistos". A Study in Byzantine Hymnography', *Dumbarton Oaks Papers*, ix and x, Cambridge (Mass.), 1956, pp. 141–74.

—— 'Byzantinische Musik.' *Das Musikwerk*. Eine Beispielsammlung zur Musikgeschichte. Cologne, 1959.

PALAEOGRAPHY

ALLEN, T. W., *Notes on Abbreviations in Greek Manuscripts*. Oxford, 1889.

AMPHILOCHIOS, *Paleografičeskoje opisanie grečeskich rukopisej IX i X věka*. Moscow, 1879.

BENEŠEVIČ, V., *Monumenta Sinaitica Archaeologica et Palaeographica*, fasc. 2. S.-Pétersbourg, 1912.

BICK, J., *Die Schreiber der Wiener griechischen Handschriften*. Vienna, 1920.

CERETELI, F. G., and SOBOLEVSKI, S., *Exempla codicum Graecorum litteris minusculis scriptorum annorumque notis instructorum*. Vol. i, *Codices Mosquenses*. Moscow, 1911; vol. ii, *Codices Petropolitani*. Moscow, 1913.

FRANCHI DE' CAVALIERI, P., and LIETZMANN, I., *Specimina codicum Graecorum*. Bonn, 1910.

GARDTHAUSEN, V., *Griechische Palaeographie*. 2 vols., 2nd ed., Leipzig, 1911 and 1913.

—— 'Beiträge zur Palaeographie. i. Zur ältesten Minuskelschrift. iii. Die jüngere Unciale. v. Zur griechischen Minuskel in Unteritalien. vi. Zur Notenschrift der griechischen Kirche', *Sitzungsberichte der sächsischen Akademie der Wissenschaften*, 1877–80.

GRAUX, C., and MARTIN, M. A., *Facsimilés des manuscrits grecs d'Espagne*. Paris, 1891.

HANSCHKE, P., *De accentuum graecorum nominibus*. Bonn, 1914.

HUNGER, H., 'Codices Vindobonenses Graeci', *Biblos-Schriften*, Bd. 4. Vienna, 1953.

—— 'Studien zur griechischen Paläographie', ibid., Bd. 5. Vienna, 1954.

LAKE, K. and S., *Dated Greek Minuscule Manuscripts*, fasc. i–x.

LAUM, M., *Das alexandrinische Akzentuationssystem*. Paderborn, 1928.

LEHMANN, O., *Die tachygraphischen Abkürzungen der griechischen Handschriften*. Leipzig, 1880.

LOWE, E. A., 'An Unknown Latin Psalter on Mount Sinai', *Scriptorium*, ix (1955), 177–99.

MONTFAUCON, B. DE, *Palaeographia Graeca*. Paris, 1708.

Monumenta Musicae Byzantinae, Series I, Facsimilia, vols. i–iv.

OMONT, H., *Facsimilés des plus anciens manuscrits grecs en onciale et en minuscule du IVe au XIIe siècle*. Paris, 1892.

—— *Facsimilés des manuscrits grecs datés de la Bibliothèque Nationale du IXe au XIVe siècle*. Paris, 1890.

—— *Facsimilés des manuscrits grecs du XVe et XVIe siècle*. Paris, 1887.

PALAEOGRAPHICAL SOCIETY. *Facsimiles of Manuscripts and Inscriptions*, edited by E. A. Bond and E. M. Thompson, London, 1873–94 (2nd series): New Palaeogr. Soc., London, 1892 sqq.

SABAS, *Specimina palaeographica codicum graecorum et slavonicorum bibliothecae Mosquensis Synodalis saec. vi–xvii*. Moscow, 1863.

STEFFENS, F., *Proben aus griechischen Handschriften und Urkunden*. Trier, 1912.

THOMPSON, E. M., *Introduction to Greek and Latin Palaeography*. Oxford, 1912.

WATTENBACH, W., *Schrifttafeln zur Geschichte der griechischen Schrift*. Berlin, 1876–7.

—— *Scripturae graecae specimina*. Berlin, 1883.

CATALOGUES OF LITURGICAL MSS. WITH MUSICAL NOTATION

CLARK, K. W., Checklist of Manuscripts in St. Catherine's Monastery, Mount Sinai. Library of Congress. Photoduplication Service. Washington, D.C., 1952.

—— Checklist of Manuscripts in the Libraries of the Greek and Armenian Patriarchats in Jerusalem, ibid., 1953.

DEVREESSE, R., 'Les Manuscrits grecs de l'Italie Méridionale', *Studi e Testi*, clxxxiii. Rome, 1955.

GASTOUÉ, A., *Catalogue des manuscrits de Musique byzantine*. Publications de la Société Internationale de Musique, Section de Paris. Paris, 1907.

RICHARD, M., *Répertoire des bibliothèques et des ms. grecs*. Paris, 1948.

ROCCHI, A., 'Codices Cryptenses seu Abbatiae Cryptae Ferratae' in *Tusculano, digesti et illustrati*. Rome, 1884.

SAKKELION, I. and A., *Κατάλογος τῶν χειρογράφων τῆς ἐθνικῆς βιβλιοθήκης τῆς Ἑλλάδος*, Athens, 1892, ch. vi: *Ἐκκλησιαστικὴ Μουσική*, pp. 158–75.

TARDO, DOM L., 'I codici melurgici della Vaticana e il contributo alla musica bizantina del monachismo greco della Magna Grecia.' *Archivio storico per la Calabria e la Lucania*, i. 225–39. Rome, 1931.

—— 'La Musica bizantina e i codici di melurgia della Biblioteca di Grottaferrata', *Rivista d. Accademie e Biblioteche*, vol. iv. 15 pp. Rome, 1931.

TIBY, O., 'I Codici musicali italo-greci di Messina', ibid., vol. xi, 14 pp. Rome, 1937.

Since the revision of the final proofs some important works have been published which I was unable to utilize: Eric Werner's *The Sacred Bridge* on the interdependence of liturgy and music in synagogue and church during the first millennium (London–New York 1959) has already become an indispensable textbook. In the Introduction to his transcriptions of the 'Hymns of the Pentecostarium', *M.M.B.*, *Transcripta* vii (1960), H. J. W. Tillyard deals extensively with Early Byzantine notation and makes a valuable contribution to the deciphering of that phase of notation. Studies on the Akathistos have been carried forward by G. G. Meersseman in his 'Der Hymnos Akathistos im Abendland', *Spicilegium Friburgense*, 2 (1958), and 3 (1960), and by G. Marzi in 'Melodia e Nomos nella musica bizantina', *Studi di Filologia classica*, viii (Bologna, 1960).

LIST OF HYMNOGRAPHERS FROM THE FIFTH TO THE FIFTEENTH CENTURIES

THE following list contains the names of the best-known hymnographers which are found in the Tropologia, Typika, and other liturgical books. In many cases the dates of birth and death are not known, so that only the century in which they lived can be given, and even this is not always certain. To give only one example: the reform ascribed to Koukouzeles is placed at the beginning of the twelfth century by Papadopoulos, in the middle of the thirteenth by Thibaut, and in the fourteenth by Krumbacher. The difficulty is increased by the fact that there are three musicians, Gregory, Joasaph, and John, who all have the surname Koukouzeles. The present list is based on Papadopoulos's *Συμβολαὶ εἰς τὴν ἱστορίαν τῆς παρ' ἡμῖν ἐκκλησιαστικῆς μουσικῆς*, Gastoué's *Catalogue des MSS. de musique byzantine*, Krumbacher's *Geschichte der byzantinischen Literatur*, and Tillyard's *Byzantine Music and Hymnography*. Lists of the musicians (*μελουργοί*) of the school of Koukouzeles and of the Neo-Greek school can be found in Gastoué's *Catalogue* and Thibaut's *Monuments*.

Anatolius, Bishop of Thessalonike	saec. IX
Anatolius, Patriarch of Constantinople	†458
Anatolius the Younger of Constantinople	saec. VIII
Andrew of Crete	saec. VII
Andrew Pyrrhus	saec. IX(?)
Arsenius of Grottaferrata	saec. XI(?)
Arsenius of the Studion	saec. IX
Athanasius the Younger, Patriarch of Alexandria	saec. XIII
Bartholomew, Abbot of Grottaferrata	†*c.* 1040
Basil Pegoriotes the Younger, Bishop of Caesarea	912–59
Byzantius, *vide* Leo Byzantius	
Clement, Abbot of the Studion	saec. IX
Constantine Porphyrogennetus	917–59
Cosmas, *vide* Kosmas	
Cucuzeles, *vide* Koukouzeles	
Cyprian of the Studion	saec. IX
Elias Syncellus	saec. VIII
Elias Theotokariographus, Bishop of Crete	saec. VIII
Ephraim of Karia	saecc. VII–VIII(?)
Gabriel Hieromonachus	saec. IX
George, Bishop of Amastris	*fl. c.* 870
George, Bishop of Nicomedia	saec. IX
George Skylitzes	*fl.* saec. XI
Germanus of Constantinople, Bishop of Cyzicus	645–740

Germanus of Grottaferrata . . . . . saec. XI
Germanus of Constantinople . . . . . †1240
Giobascus Vlachus . . . . *fl.* saec. XIII
Gregory Koukouzeles, *vide* Koukouzeles
Gregory Nazianzen . . . . . . †389
Gregory Sinaïtes . . . . †1310

Ignatius, Patriarch of Constantinople . . . †870
Isidorus Vouchiras, Patriarch of Constantinople . . †1349

Jacob of Edessa . . . . †710
Joasaph Koukouzeles, *vide* Koukouzeles
John Damascene . . . . *c.* 675–*c.* 749
John Glykys . . . . saec. XIV
John Kaminiates . . . . †904
John Koukoumas . . . . (?)
John Koukouzeles, *vide* Koukouzeles
John Mauropus, Bishop of Euchaita . . . †1060
John Vatatzes . . . . †1222
John Zonaras . . . . saec. XI
Joseph of Sicily, 'Xenos', 'the Hymnographer' . . †883
Joseph Studites . . . . †833
Justinian, Emperor . . . . . . *reg.* 527–65

Kasia (Ikasia, Kassiane) . . . . . . saec. IX
Kosmas of Jerusalem . . . . . . saec. VIII
Koukouzeles, Gregory . . . . . . (?)
Koukouzeles, Joasaph, the Younger, Domesticus of the Vatopedi . . . . saecc. XIV–XV
Koukouzeles, John Papadopoulos, Magister . . saec. XIV
Kyriakus . . . . saecc. V–VI

Leo 'Byzantius' . . . . saec. VII(?)
Leo Magister . . . . *fl.* saec. XI
Leo VI 'the Wise' . . . . *reg.* 886–917

Mark 'the Monk' . . . . saecc. XIV–XV
Methodius . . . . †312
Methodius Homologetes . . . . . . †846
Metrophanes, Bishop of Smyrna . . . . †*c.* 910
Michael Ananeotes . . . . †830

Nicolaus, Abbot of the Studion . . . . . †868
Nikephorus Blemmydes 1198–1272
Nikephorus Ethikos . . . . . . saec. X
Nikephorus, Patriarch of Constantinople . . . †806
Niketas Serron . . . . †1075
Nilus the Younger . . . . *c.* 910–1005

Panaretus Patzadas	saec. X
Petrus of the Studion	saec. IX
Photius, Patriarch of Constantinople	†891
Romanus	saecc. V–VI
Sergius of Jerusalem	*fl.* saec. IX
Sophronius of Damascus, Patriarch of Jerusalem	†638
Stephanus Sabbaïtes	saec. VIII
Symeon Metaphrastes	*c.* saec. X
Symeon Studites	*fl.* 840
Synesius of Cyrene	*c.* 375–430
Tarasius, Patriarch of Constantinople	†784
Thecla, the Nun	saec. IX
Theodore I Lascaris, Emperor of Nicaea	*reg.* 1204–22
Theodore 'Graptos'	†838
Theodore of the Studion	759–826
Theodosius of Syracuse	saec. IX
Theoktistus Studites	saec. IX
Theophanes Studites	759–*c.* 842
Theophanus 'Graptos'	†*c.* 850
Theophilus Autokrator	*reg.* 829–42
Theosteriktus 'the Monk'	saec. IX
Xenus Koronis, Protopsaltes of Saint Sophia	*fl.* saecc. XIV–XV

LIST OF HYMNS

TROPARIA, HIRMI, KONTAKIA

Only those quoted in full in the text are given. Reference to the Odes is made by the first line of the first stanza. M indicates that the music is given.

CHRONOLOGICAL SURVEY

330 May 11.	Inauguration of 'New Rome' by the Emperor Constantine I.
c. 330–79.	St. Basil the Great. The foundation of Greek monasticism.
4th–5th centuries.	The first period of Syrian hymnography: Ephrem.
5th century.	The beginnings of Byzantine hymnography: Auxentius.
527–65.	Justinian I.
5th–7th centuries.	Development of Byzantine hymnography: the Kontakion. Anastasius, Kyriakus, and Romanus.
635–7.	The conquest of Syria by the Arabs.
637.	The fall of Jerusalem.
7th–8th centuries.	The third period of Byzantine hymnography: the Kanon. Andrew of Crete, John Damascene, Kosmas of Jerusalem.
717–40.	Leo III the Isaurian.
726.	Outbreak of the Iconoclast controversy. Decree against Image-worship.
740–75.	Constantine V. Intensification of the Iconoclast movement.
780.	Death of Leo IV. His widow Irene regent 780–90, 792–7.
787.	Condemnation of Iconoclasm by the Seventh Oecumenical Council at Nicaea.
797–802.	Irene Empress.
8th century.	Syrian and South Italian hymnography.
9th–10th centuries.	The Studion monastery in Constantinople becomes the centre of Byzantine hymnography. Theodore, Joseph, Theophanes.
9th–12th centuries.	Early Byzantine notation.
843.	Council of Constantinople. End of the Iconoclast controversy.
867–1057.	The Macedonian Dynasty.
912–59.	Constantine VII Porphyrogennetus.
1081–1204.	The Comnenian Dynasty.
11th century.	End of hymnography in the East. Continuation in Sicily and southern Italy up to the 12th century.
12th–15th centuries.	Middle Byzantine (Round) notation.
1204–61.	Latin Empire.
1261–1453.	The Palaeologan Dynasty.
1453, May 30.	The fall of Constantinople.
15th–19th centuries.	Late Byzantine (Koukouzelian) notation. 'Kalophonic' chant.
1821.	Reform of musical notation by Chrysanthos of Madytos.

INDEX

(*Compiled by* Miss V. M. Elliott)

PRINTED IN GREAT BRITAIN
AT THE UNIVERSITY PRESS, OXFORD
BY VIVIAN RIDLER
PRINTER TO THE UNIVERSITY

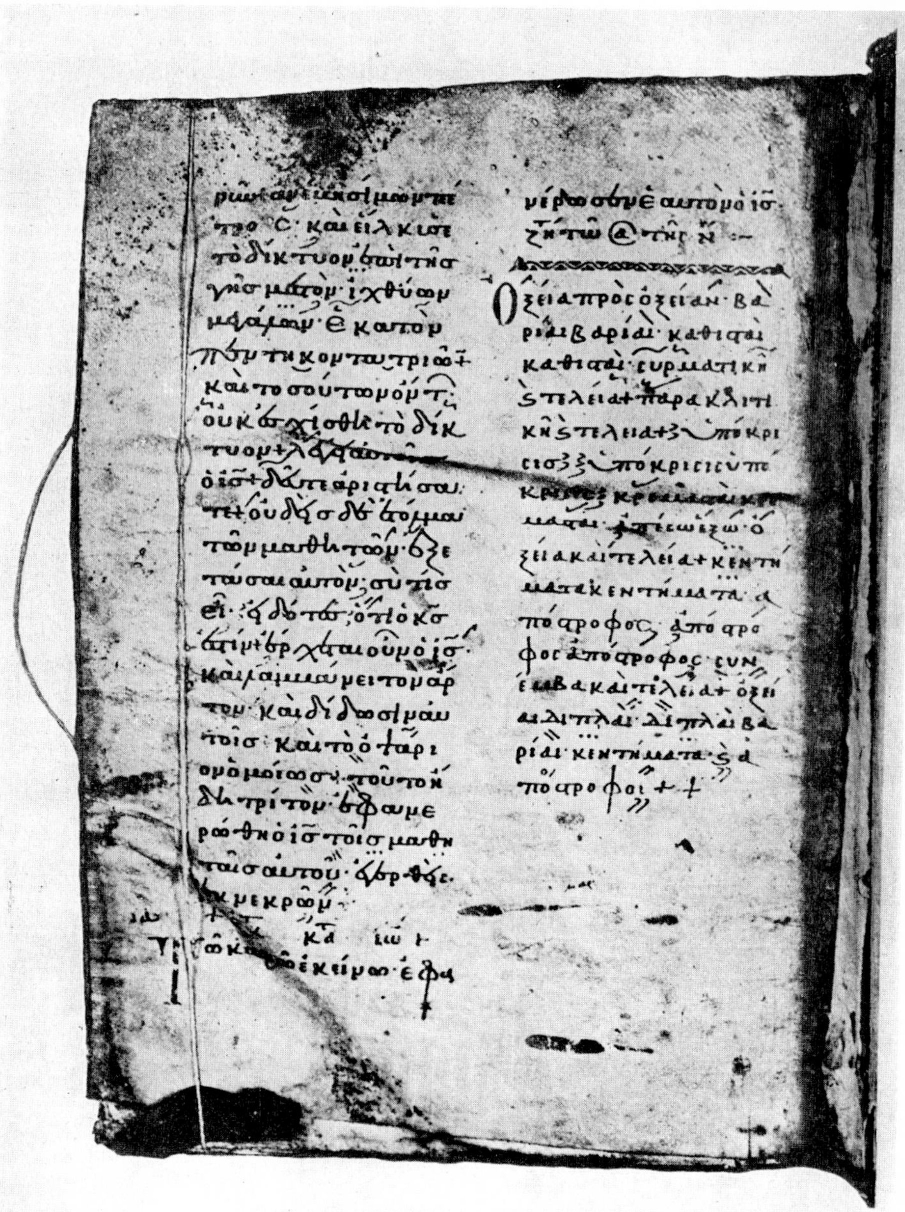

LIST OF EKPHONETIC SIGNS

Cod. Leimon. 38, fol. 318 r., saec. xi/xii

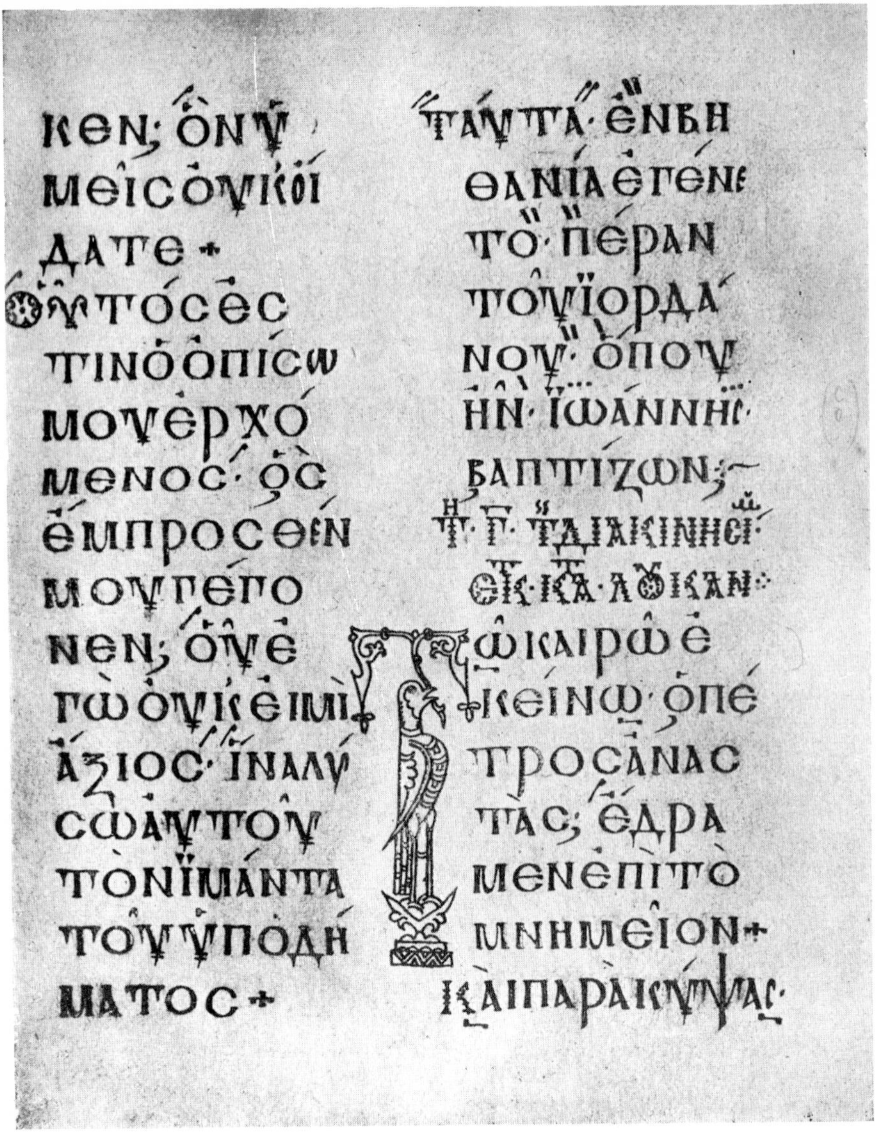

ΚΕΝ· ΟΝΥ
ΜΕΙϹΟΥΚΟΙ
ΔΑΤΕ·
ΟΥΤΟϹΕϹ
ΤΙΝΟΟΠΙϹΩ
ΜΟΥΕΡΧΟ
ΜΕΝΟϹ· ΟϹ
ΕΜΠΡΟϹΘΕΝ
ΜΟΥΓΕΓΟ
ΝΕΝ· ΟΥΕ
ΓΩΟΥΚΕΙΜΙ
ΑΞΙΟϹ· ΙΝΑΛΥ
ϹΩΑΥΤΟΥ
ΤΟΝΙΜΑΝΤΑ
ΤΟΥΥΠΟΔΗ
ΜΑΤΟϹ·

ΤΑΥΤΑ· ΕΝΒΗ
ΘΑΝΙΑΕΓΕΝΕ
ΤΟ· ΠΕΡΑΝ
ΤΟΥΙΟΡΔΑ
ΝΟΥ· ΟΠΟΥ
ΗΝ· ΙΩΑΝΝΗϹ
ΒΑΠΤΙΖΩΝ·
Τ Γ· ΤΔΙΑΚΙΝΗϹΙ·
ΕΚ ΚΑ· ΛΟΥΚΑΝ·
ΤΩΚΑΙΡΩΕ
ΚΕΙΝΩ· ΟΠΕ
ΤΡΟϹΑΝΑϹ
ΤΑϹ· ΕΔΡΑ
ΜΕΝΕΠΙΤΟ
ΜΝΗΜΕΙΟΝ·
ΚΑΙΠΑΡΑΚΥΨΑϹ

EKPHONETIC NOTATION

Cod. Sinait. 204, saec. x

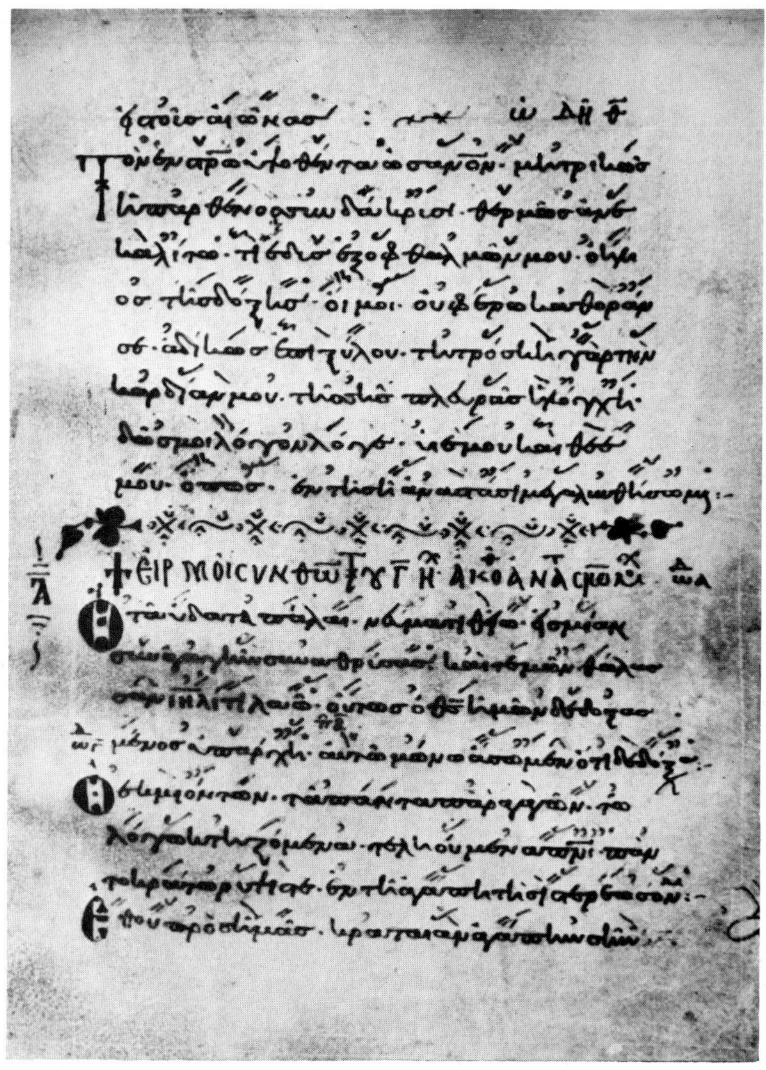

EARLY BYZANTINE NOTATION

Hirmologium Athoum

Codex Laurae 152 (formerly B32). End of the Hirmi of Mode II and beginning of Mode III

PLATE IV

EARLY BYZANTINE NOTATION

Cod. Patriarch. Hierosolym., Saba 83, fol. 48 r., saec. ix/x

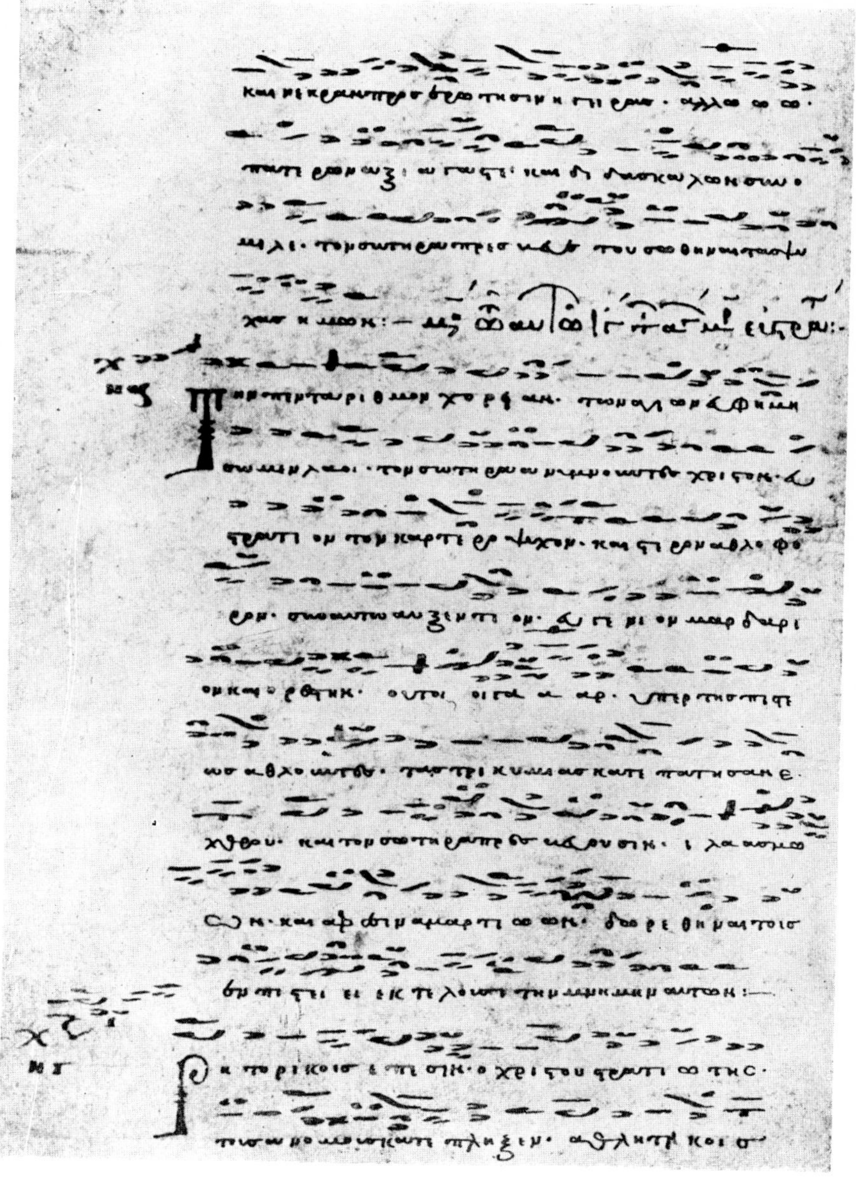

MIDDLE BYZANTINE NOTATION

Cod. Vindobon. theol. gr. 181, fol. 78 v., A.D. 1221

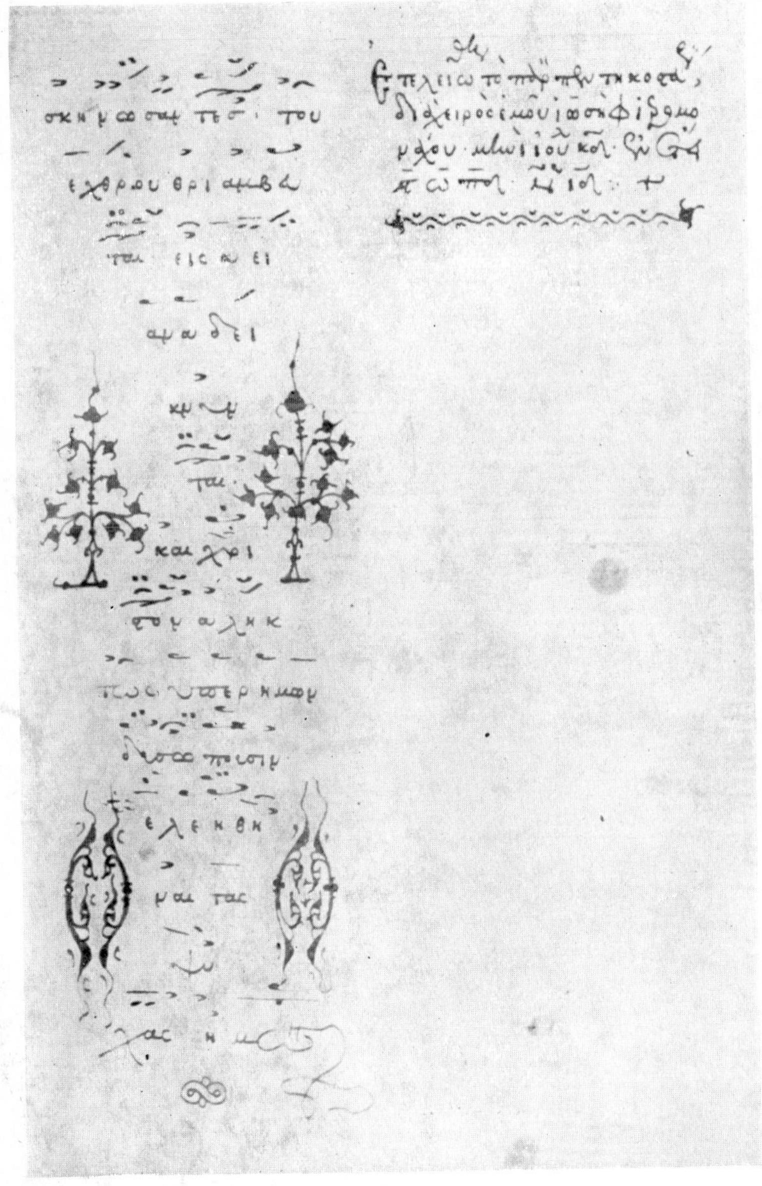

LATE MIDDLE BYZANTINE NOTATION

Cod. Koutloumoussi 3380, foll. 292 v.–293 r., A.D. 1376. Pentekostarion, finished by Joseph Hieromonachos, on 24 July 1376

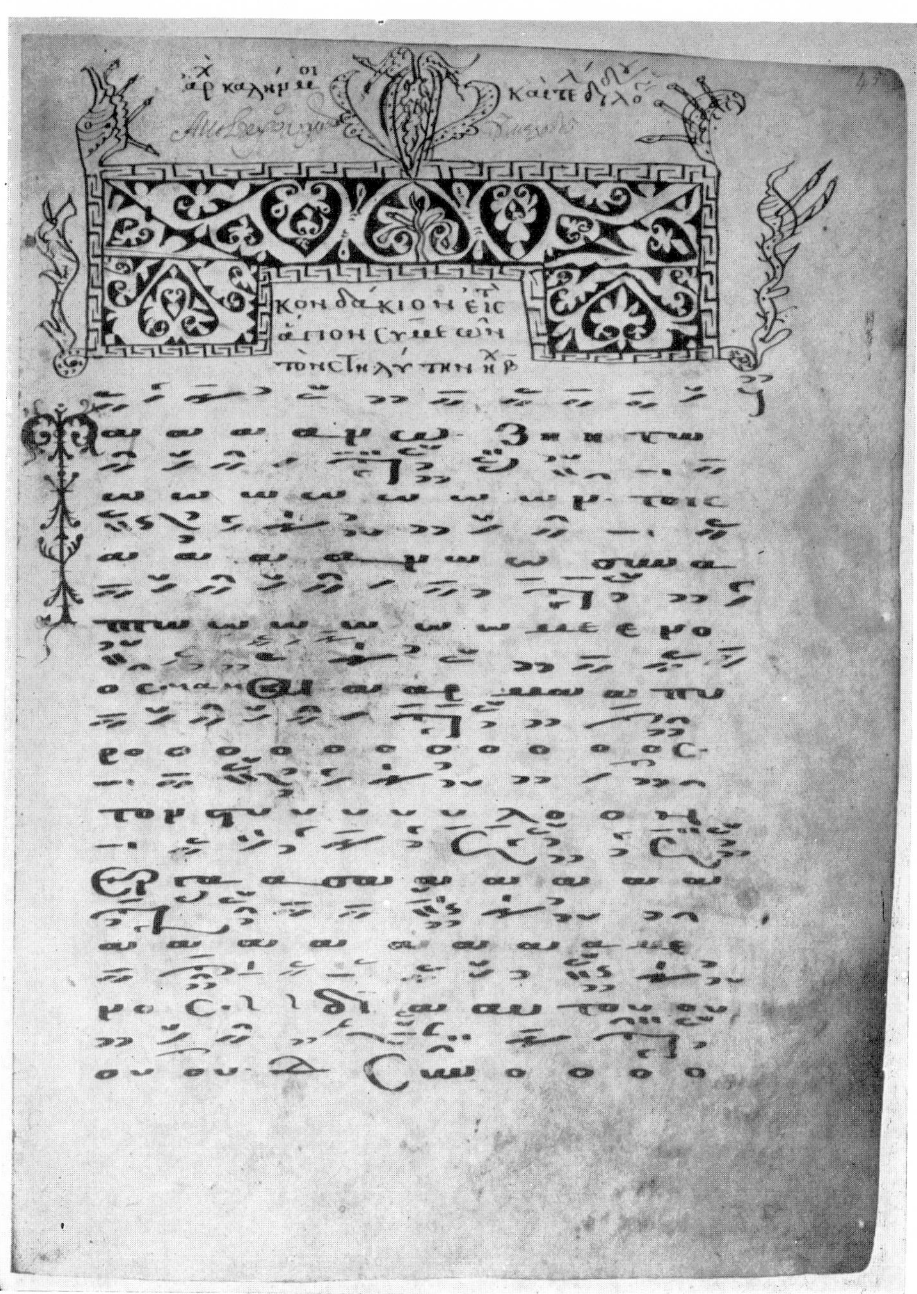

From *Monumenta Musicae Byzantinae*, IV, edited by Carsten Høeg (E. Munksgaard, Copenhagen, 1956)

LATE BYZANTINE NOTATION

Cod. Ashburnham. L. 64, fol. 45 r., A.D. 1289